Hellenic Studies 39

ILIAD 10
AND
THE POETICS OF AMBUSH

Recent Titles in the Hellenic Studies Series

The New Sappho on Old Age
Textual and Philosophical Issues

Hippota Nestor

Homer the Classic

Recapturing a Homeric Legacy
Images and Insights from the Venetus A Manuscript of the Iliad

Fragments of Sappho
A Commentary

Genos Dikanikon
Amateur and Professional Speech in the Courtrooms of Classical Athens

The Politics of Ethnicity and the Crisis of the Peloponnesian League

Zeus in the Odyssey

Practitioners of the Divine
Greek Priests and Religious Officials from Homer to Heliodorus

The Oral Palimpsest
Exploring Intertextuality in the Homeric Epics

Sappho in the Making
The Early Reception

C. P. Cavafy, The Canon
The Original One Hundred and Fifty-Four Poems

The Feast of Poetry
Sacrifice and Performance in Aristophanic Comedy

King of Sacrifice
Ritual and Royal Authority in the Iliad

Concordia Discors
Eros and Dialogue in Classical Athenian Literature

Paradise Earned
The Bacchic-Orphic Gold Lamellae of Crete

Plato's Symposium
Issues in Interpretation and Reception

The Epic City
Urbanism, Utopia, and the Garden in Ancient Greece and Rome

Ritual and Performativity
The Chorus in Old Comedy

Weaving Truth
Essays on Language and the Female in Greek Thought

http://chs.harvard.edu/chs/publications

ILIAD 10
AND
THE POETICS OF AMBUSH

A MULTITEXT EDITION
WITH ESSAYS AND COMMENTARY

CASEY DUÉ AND *MARY EBBOTT*

CENTER FOR HELLENIC STUDIES
Trustees for Harvard University
Washington, D.C.
Distributed by Harvard University Press
Cambridge, Massachusetts, and London, England
2010

Iliad 10 and the Poetics of Ambush
  by Casey Dué and Mary Ebbott
Copyright © 2010 Center for Hellenic Studies, Trustees for Harvard University
All Rights Reserved.
Published by Center for Hellenic Studies, Trustees for Harvard University,
  Washington, D.C.
Distributed by Harvard University Press, Cambridge, Massachusetts, and London,
  England
Production: Ivy Livingston
Cover design and illustration: Joni Godlove
Printed in Ann Arbor, MI, by Edwards Brothers, Inc.

Second corrected printing, 2011.

LIBRARY OF CONGRESS CATALOGING-IN-PUBLICATION DATA
  Dué, Casey, 1974–
  Iliad 10 and the poetics of ambush : a multitext edition with essays and
  commentary / by Casey Dué and Mary Ebbott.
      p. cm. — (Hellenic Studies Series ; 39)
  Includes bibliographical references and index.
  ISBN 978-0-674-03559-1 (alk. paper)
  1. Homer. Iliad. Book 10. 2. Epic poetry, Greek--History and criticism. 3. Trojan
  War--Literature and the war. 4. Epic poetry, Greek. 5. Trojan War--Poetry. I.
  Ebbott, Mary. II. Homer. Iliad. Book 10. III. Title. IV. Series.
  PA4037.D79 2010
  883'.01--dc22

                                                              2010023639

Contents

Acknowledgments vii

A Note on the Aims of this Volume ix

I. Essays   1

    1. Interpreting *Iliad* 10 3

    2. The Poetics of Ambush 31

    3. Tradition and Reception: Rhesos, Dolon, and the Doloneia 89

    4. *Iliad* 10: A Multitextual Approach 153

II. Texts   167

    1. *Iliad* p609 169

    2. *Iliad* p425 175

    3. *Iliad* p46 187

    4. Venetus A: *Marcianus Graecus Z.* 454 (= 822) 193

Plates   223

III. Commentary   229

Bibliography 383

Image Credits 401

Index of Sources 403

General Index 417

Acknowledgments

WE GRATEFULLY ACKNOWLEDGE the support provided by a National Endowment for the Humanities Collaborative Research grant, which funded in large part the research and writing of this book. Any views, findings, conclusions, or recommendations expressed in this publication do not necessarily reflect those of the National Endowment for the Humanities. We are also profoundly grateful for the support of several individuals who contributed to the project in various ways. Carolyn Higbie read through a large portion of the text and offered numerous suggestions for improvement, as did Francesca Behr, David Elmer, and Rick Newton. Alexander Loney and Bart Huelsenbeck contributed their editions of the papyri included in Part II. Christopher W. Blackwell and D. Neel Smith are the architects of the Homer Multitext (HMT) project, in connection with which this book was conceived and developed. Their genius makes possible all aspects of the HMT and the digital publication of this book as part of the HMT. Under their guidance, moreover, a wonderful group of undergraduate and graduate student researchers at four different institutions assisted in the creation of the digital texts used for this volume. The Center for Hellenic Studies (CHS) sponsors and publishes the Homer Multitext, and it was as directors of a CHS summer seminar that we first became inspired to write a commentary on *Iliad* 10. Two years later we offered the seminar again and began the project in earnest. We thank the students of those seminars for their collegial exchange of ideas on the topics discussed in this volume. We learned a great deal from both groups, which included Meghan Barry, Robert Brewer, William Duffy, Katie Lamberto, Alexander Loney, Suzanne Lye, Jack Mitchell, Andrew Porter, Sean Signore, Jeremy Thompson, and Vincent Tomasso. The same is true for audiences at the CAMWS annual meetings in Gainesville and Cincinnati, where we presented early versions of some of this work. We thank Noel Spencer and Ryan Hackney for their excellent proofreading. We offer our special thanks to Jill Robbins for her beautiful line drawings and for overseeing production of the entire volume. Her knowing eye for both Greek art and book design has been our great fortune. We have had the special privilege of participating for the past several years in an *Iliad* translation group with Douglas Frame, Leonard Muellner, and Gregory Nagy. These group meetings have given us the chance to regularly think through ideas and wrestle with questions, and often simply to appreciate Homeric poetry, with three of the premier Homeric scholars of our time. Of course, none of these people is to blame for any remaining mistakes or errors in interpretation in this book, but we are deeply grateful for the expertise and insight they have shared with us. Finally, we would like to thank each other. When we applied for the NEH grant, we promoted this kind of sustained collaboration as a way to produce more thoughtful and thorough scholarship in a timely manner; what we discovered in the process was also how much pleasure collaboration brought to our work.

A Note on the Aims of This Volume

WITH THIS VOLUME OF TEXTS, essays, and commentaries we seek to place *Iliad* 10 in its historical and oral traditional contexts. We argue throughout that a better understanding of the oral tradition in which our *Iliad* developed allows us not only to better understand *Iliad* 10 but also the *Iliad* as a whole and indeed the entire corpus of poetry that has been labeled "Homeric" at different times and places. Currently, few commentaries on the *Iliad* take an oralist approach to Homeric poetry. The standard reference works occasionally refer to the work of Milman Parry and Albert Lord but do not apply their arguments systematically. Beginning students of Homer who wish to understand the *Iliad* and *Odyssey* as oral poetry have only limited guidance available.[1] We are hoping to fill this gap by offering a commentary that makes extensive use of the work of Parry and Lord and clearly situates it within the history of Homeric scholarship. It is our hope as well to offer students of Homer an introduction to the transmission of the Homeric poems in all of its complexity. For this reason we have included multiple historical witnesses to the text of *Iliad* 10, including three fragmentary papyri and the tenth-century CE Venetus A manuscript of the *Iliad*, together with separate text commentaries. Last, but

---

[1]   The many scholarly articles and monographs written from a Parry-Lord perspective are too numerous to list here. But these are not readily apparent to students, who typically rely on a few standard reference works unless directed otherwise. Companion volumes, such as the *New Companion to Homer* (Powell and Morris 1997), the *Cambridge Companion to Homer* (Fowler 2004), or the *Blackwell Companion to Ancient Epic* (Foley 2005), generally have several very valuable and instructive articles, aimed at advanced undergraduates and graduate students, which illuminate the Homeric poems and which are ultimately grounded in the work of Parry and Lord. These are often combined, however, with other articles that take very different approaches to the concepts of authorship, composition, and transmission. As result, students are not given a consistent demonstration of Parry-Lord methodology throughout the volume. Foley 2002 provides an excellent introduction to approaches to oral poetry in general.

not least, we seek to offer a new reading of *Iliad* 10, one that we feel advances previous work done on this controversial book. Our intended audience therefore includes undergraduates, graduate students, and scholars of Homeric epic, and in the commentaries and essays that follow we hope that all audiences will find something of value, although some comments will be of more immediate value to some audiences and others to others.

Our general commentary is based on the text of the Venetus A and is unconventional in some aspects: it is designed to be an interpretive commentary. In creating a commentary on this book, we wanted to employ the well-established scholarly format for a new purpose—to examine the oral traditional nature of *Iliad* 10 line-by-line. Our choices about what to comment on, and how extensively, have been driven by our goals of exploring the oral poetics of the book in general and the poetics of ambush in particular. Anyone who has consulted a commentary on an ancient Greek text has likely had the experience of looking for a comment on a particular word or phrase and finding no comment there. We have had that experience ourselves, and we have no doubt that it will happen for readers of our commentary as well. Certainly we have not attempted to explain every distinctive feature of Homeric morphology and syntax that appears in this book. But we are also fully aware that ours is not the only commentary on *Iliad* 10, and we have written our commentary not to replace all others, but to explicate particular aspects of the language. Many of the comments therefore focus on particular lines, phrases, and words that relate closely to the ambush theme, or that have seemed particularly troublesome to commentators who approach the book as either a written composition or as "un-Homeric" in some way (or that have been previously explained with such an approach). Because of our desire to examine the oral traditional nature of the whole, however, some comments are not specific to ambush, but rather are meant to illustrate important aspects of our overall approach: how formulas and themes operate in the poetry, how Parry and Lord's work explains certain features of the language, how a traditional audience might understand a particular phrase or reference (and how we can reconstruct that understanding), or how particular lines are revealing in terms of the textual tradition, including what information the scholia offer.

Our approach not only affects what we choose to address but also the degree to which we go into detail. Some of the notes are quite extensive, in effect short articles that range widely in the epics or that deeply engage previous scholarship, while others are briefer and/or more basic, to the point of defining what to many of our scholarly colleagues will be obvious. As uneven as this may seem at first glance, we are attempting to reach our multiple audiences without assuming that what seems basic and obvious to us is so for every reader. As we discuss in the essay on our multitextual approach, too often Homeric scholarship relies on conventions that obfuscate rather than illuminate, and we would rather err in going too far in the other direction, for it has been our goal throughout to make the material as accessible as possible.

Throughout the volume the translations of Greek and Latin texts are our own, except where noted. We have attempted to make our translations as literal as possible.

PART ONE

ESSAYS

1

Interpreting *Iliad* 10

Assumptions, Methodology, and the Place of the Doloneia within the History of Homeric Scholarship

IN THIS ESSAY we propose to give a brief overview of how previous scholars have evaluated *Iliad* 10 and to situate their work and ours within the history of Homeric scholarship. It is our hope that this discussion will allow our readers to better understand the assumptions and methodologies that underlie our interpretations, and to see how our approach differs from those of previous commentaries (most notably those of Walter Leaf 1900 and J. B. Hainsworth 1993). In the commentary in this volume we will not engage point by point the work of these previous scholars, nor such important monographs as those of Shewan 1911 and Danek 1988. Instead we will take the opportunity to explain here where our approaches intersect and where they diverge. *Iliad* 10's status as the epic's most doubted book (with *Iliad* 2 as a close rival), the book least likely to be judged "Homeric," and the one most frequently avoided among contemporary scholars, makes it particularly revealing of some of the central disagreements and developments in Homeric scholarship over the last two centuries.[1] This essay is not, however, simply an exercise in rehashing older views and disputes, for what this overview reveals is how deeply entrenched certain ideas and approaches are in Homeric scholarship, even if they go by different names at different times. Judgments about *Iliad* 10 have become similarly entrenched, and our goal in reviewing them is to move beyond what are essentially Analyst or Unitarian positions in order to pose new questions about this poetry.

---

[1] A recent article that discusses the history of scholarly objections to *Iliad* 8 (Cook 2009a) is similarly illuminating.

The Homeric Question

In 1795, nearly two centuries of speculation about the nature and genius of Homeric poetry came to a head when Friedrich August Wolf published his *Prolegomena ad Homerum*. Wolf argued that the Homeric poems had been transmitted by rhapsodes in an oral tradition that had corrupted the texts irreparably over time. For this reason, the true and genuine text of Homer could never be recovered. Although many of the claims made by Wolf had been maintained by others before him, Wolf's *Prolegomena* led to an intensification of the debates of the eighteenth century that gave rise to the so-called Homeric Question, which would dominate scholarly discussions of Homer in the nineteenth century.[2] The "question" (in reality, many interrelated questions) became increasingly concerned with authorship. Did the *Iliad* and *Odyssey* have the same author? If so, when did he live? If not, how did the poems come to be in the form that we now have them? Fierce opposition arose between scholars who believed in Homer, a single genius and creator of the two foundational epics of Western literature, and those who saw the Homeric texts as the products of potentially many poets composing over many generations. These Unitarians on the one hand (as exemplified by Scott 1921) and Analysts on the other (as exemplified by Wilamowitz-Moellendorff 1884 and 1916), armed with all of the tools of philology, scrutinized the poems and produced learned readings in defense of variations on these two positions. Analysts further debated among themselves about the age and authenticity of various portions of the poems, even as they searched for the oldest and "most Homeric" segments.[3]

Expanding on Wolf's *Prolegomena*, Gottfried Hermann argued that there was a historical kernel of the *Iliad* composed by Homer, and the fame of this poem led to its expansion by other poets over time (see

---

[2] For more on the views of scholars prior to Wolf, see the introduction to the English translation of Wolf (edited by Grafton, Most, and Zetzel [1985]) as well as Simonsuuri 1979 and Dué 2006b. For an overview of the history of the Homeric Question see Turner 1997. Heiden 2009 reviews a recent reconsideration of the history of the Homeric Question by Luigi Ferreri.

[3] For more detailed accounts of the Homeric Question and the Analyst and Unitarian approaches to the text see the introduction by Adam Parry to the collected works of his father Milman Parry (1971 = MHV) as well that of Frank Turner in the *New Companion to Homer* (1997). Much of the most disparaging language used of *Iliad* 10 has its origins in the work of Analyst scholars. Turner 1997:137 cites Wilamowitz-Moellendorff's assessment of the *Iliad* as "a miserable piece of patchwork" and August Fick's "The present *Odyssey* is a crime against human intelligence." For more on the Unitarian approach, see our discussion of Shewan 1911, below.

Hermann 1832 and 1840). Much of what Wolf himself had said already pointed in this direction. But Wolf's relatively brief remarks also paved the way for a competing theory. The renowned philologist Richard Bentley had asserted long before Wolf that Homeric poetry originally consisted of loosely connected songs that were gathered together in an epic poem under the direction of the Athenian tyrant Peisistratos, 500 years after they were composed (see Bentley 1713:18). Inspired by Wolf, Karl Lachmann published influential papers that sought to prove that our *Iliad* consists of eighteen individual "lays" that were stitched together in the time of Peisistratos (Lachmann 1847). This view, which was built on Wolf's arguments about the loosely connected nature of Homeric poetry in its earliest phases (see e.g. Wolf 1795/1985:137 [chapter 33]), was the starting point for a century's worth of debate among Analyst scholars about the number and relative chronology of the individual lays.

In the case of *Iliad* 10, the search for individual songs brought together to make up our *Iliad* seems to find support in one scholion. It was in the wake Villoison's publication of the Venetus A and B manuscripts with their scholia that Wolf wrote his influential *Prolegomena*.[4] It is not in these manuscripts, however, but in that known as the Townley (T) that the Analysts could find the type of evidence they sought for *Iliad* 10. At the beginning of Book 10 in that manuscript, the first scholion reads: φασὶ τὴν ῥαψῳδίαν ὑφ' Ὁμήρου ἰδίᾳ τετάχθαι καὶ μὴ εἶναι μέρος τῆς Ἰλιάδος, ὑπὸ δὲ Πεισιστράτου τετάχθαι εἰς τὴν ποίησιν ("They say that this epic composition was arranged separately by Homer and not to be part of the *Iliad*, but it was arranged into that poem by Peisistratos").[5] This note indeed seems to support the idea of a separate lay, but the evidence cannot be attributed to any particular source. More recent scholars also cite the scholion as evidence that *Iliad* 10 is not genuine in some way, but in so doing they seem to ignore that the scholion does posit "Homer" as the composer, suggesting that

---

[4]   Although Villoison had argued that the scholia in these manuscripts helped to stabilize the text of the *Iliad* and allow us to get closer to the "original," Wolf argued that the scholia and the multiple readings they offered destabilized the text and rendered the recovery of Homer's own words impossible; see Nagy 2004:4–5. The importance of the scholia for our approach to understanding the poetry will be apparent in our commentary.

[5]   A similar comment is also present in the commentaries of Eustathius. His version reads: Φασὶ δὲ οἱ παλαιοὶ τὴν ῥαψῳδίαν ταύτην ὑφ' Ὁμήρου ἰδίᾳ τετάχθαι καὶ μὴ ἐγκαταλεγῆναι τοῖς μέρεσι τῆς Ἰλιάδος, ὑπὸ δὲ Πεισιστράτου τετάχθαι εἰς τὴν ποίησιν ("The ancients say that this epic composition was arranged separately by Homer and not counted among the parts of the *Iliad*, but it was arranged into that poem by Peisistratos," *Commentarii ad Homeri Iliadem* III, p. 2).

it is traditional. In fact, the comment is evidence neither that *Iliad* 10 is "un-Homeric" nor that it is by a later author who fit his composition to the *Iliad*, as some would have it.[6]

The work of the Analyst critics, and their debates with Unitarian critics who defended the unity of the epic, was the state of Homeric scholarship when, in the last decades of the nineteenth century, the archaeological work of Heinrich Schliemann uncovered the previously unknown Bronze Age civilization of the Mycenaean Greeks. Whereas in earlier centuries Homeric poetry had been linked to eighteenth-century notions of "folk poetry" (see Dué 2006b), the poems now came to be associated with the palatial structures and rich tombs uncovered by Schliemann. Physical objects, certain kinds of weapons and armor, architecture, and art mentioned in the poems were now seen to be the everyday artifacts of a real world ruled by kings not unlike those who fight in the *Iliad*. Walter Leaf, who published *A Companion to the Iliad for English Readers* in 1892 and a second edition of his two-volume commentary on the *Iliad* in 1900–1902, argued that our *Iliad* consists of series of both older songs, which were composed in the Mycenaean Bronze Age and handed down without much change for many centuries, and newer songs, all of which were gathered together into their final form under the direction of Peisistratos (Leaf 1900:xvi–xxi). The kernel of the poem, Leaf maintained, was the wrath of Achilles, and various other epic material, four centuries in the making, was made to fit around this central core.[7]

Leaf, working within the Analyst tradition of scholarship, sought in his commentary to the *Iliad* to separate the earlier and later strata of the poem (not unlike an archaeologist), and thereby explain aspects of the work that seemed to him incongruous or inelegant. Although Leaf understood the various songs of the *Iliad* to be orally composed and transmitted (Leaf 1900:xvi), his commentary connects the songs to individual authors, some of whom he judges to be more skilled than others. As a result, Leaf feels free in his commentary to criticize the style of particular poets. *Iliad* 10 receives much of Leaf's harshest criticism. Arguing that *Iliad* 10 (like *Iliad* 9) "can never have

---

[6] See further below on the theory of Danek 1988, which is favored by Hainsworth 1993.

[7] Lang 1995 offers an example of a more recent argument for an evolution of the song that explains what seem to be inconsistencies. In her argument, the song started as a linear telling of the Trojan War. Once it became a song about Achilles' wrath, parts of the earlier tradition were arranged to fit it. For example, the so-called "viewing from the walls" by Helen and Priam seems to belong more naturally to the beginning of the war than its tenth year, according to Lang, but this scene was then fitted to the "restart" of the fighting after Achilles' withdrawal.

existed independent of the Μῆνις [the song of Achilles' wrath]" (Leaf 1900:423), he summarizes the place of the book in the epic tradition this way: "Everything points, in fact, to as late a date as this [the second half of the seventh century BCE] for the composition of the book. It must, however, have been composed before the *Iliad* had reached its present form, for it cannot have been meant to follow on I [*Iliad* 9]. It is rather another case of a parallel rival to that book, coupled with it only in the final literary redaction" (Leaf 1900:424). Leaf's audience would have been well aware of the universal condemnation of the book, and of the perceived problems that Leaf alludes to here. *Iliad* 9 takes up too much of the night, it has been argued, to allow for another episode. The reference to Achilles at 10.106–107, Leaf suggests, also seems out of place immediately after the failed embassy. Rhesos and the capture of his horses are not mentioned anywhere else in the epic, much as the embassy to Achilles goes unmentioned in places where it seems logical (to us) to do so.

In his brief introduction to *Iliad* 10, Leaf gives, in addition to these structural objections, three primary reasons for believing the book to be a late composition. He says that it has a "mannered style" that is at odds with the "harmony and symmetrical repose of the Epic style," and he finds the length of preparations that begin the book out of proportion with the length of the narration of the night mission itself (Leaf 1900:423–424). He next offers linguistic evidence, consisting of unusual word forms and other forms that come from later stages of the Greek language. And, finally, he cites "pseudo-archaisms," words that he argues are deliberately used by the poet to create the illusion of antiquity. Such objections have, as we will see, been countered by the work of later scholars. Though much of the introduction is devoted to these three points, they may not have been what influenced Leaf's thinking the most, however. Leaf's introduction to the book in fact begins with a quotation of the scholia we have just examined, which seems to reveal that already in antiquity *Iliad* 10 was thought at least by some to be a separate composition. He adds: "These noteworthy words ... correspond too closely with the probabilities of the case to allow us to treat them as a mere empty guess." For Leaf, the scholion seems to confirm a generally understood feeling about the book—one that does not need extensive argumentation.[8]

---

8   Cf. Shewan 1911:14: "All the critics, a few Unitarians excepted, are satisfied that it is late ... So sure are they that they do not trouble to give reasons, unless perhaps that its language is peculiar, or that it is 'stuffed with oddities.' They rely on common consent."

Individual notes in his commentary make clear Leaf's hostility to the book, and some of these are discussed in our commentary below. At the risk of taking Leaf's words out of context, we will simply highlight here some of the words Leaf uses to describe the poetry: "inappropriateness" (10.1), "so confused as to be practically unintelligible" (10.5), "turgid and tasteless" (10.5), "strange" (10.7), "unsuitable" (10.8), "burlesque" (10.84). That Leaf is applying his own aesthetic criteria to the poetry is evident, and such criticism would not be considered a valid scholarly methodology today. But we must ask to what degree an anachronistic aesthetic has influenced the more seemingly scientific arguments made in Leaf's introduction and elsewhere in his notes. More recent scholars do not, for the most part, indulge in Leaf's insulting language,[9] but many have similar visceral reactions to the book, and it seems clear that these "gut-level" judgments have had a major influence on critical work on the book. Hainsworth's 1993 commentary (discussed below) offers this conclusion on the status of the book within our *Iliad*: "Taken separately ... these points are of little weight; taken together they make up a body of evidence that the majority of critics have found persuasive, if not conclusive" (Hainsworth 1993:154). Much like Leaf's, Hainsworth's reasons for objecting to the book seem based on an intuitive response, not a carefully articulated argument based on an understanding of oral poetics. Less restrained is Michael Nagler, who calls *Iliad* 10 "a disaster stylistically, because of its folkloristic departures from normalcy; heroically, because of the disgraceful conduct exhibited by Odysseus and Diomedes; thematically, because it takes place in the dead of night; and structurally, because it leads to an Achaean victory" (Nagler 1974:136). The tradition of Leaf's condemnation of *Iliad* 10, which is in many ways emblematic of nineteenth-century Analyst criticism, has lived on among many scholars, even those whose approaches and schools of thought differ substantially from Leaf's.

A decade after Leaf's commentary, Alexander Shewan devoted an entire monograph to a spirited defense of *Iliad* 10 (Shewan 1911). In it, he assesses the reception of the book in his own day this way: "There is hardly a textbook of Greek literature or handbook to Homer

---

9   Note, however, such critical judgments of Hainsworth's as "crudely simplistic" and "cheap victory" (Hainsworth 1993:154). Fenik also expresses his low opinion of the Doloneia: "A marked inferiority in technique here cannot possibly be interpreted away, even with the best of will. There is no good reason for the patrol, it performs no function whatever, it brings no change or development in the situation" (Fenik 1964:40).

but regards it with disfavour, tempered only occasionally by a word of tolerant pity or faint praise ... The Doloneia now lies buried below a cairn heaped up to keep its unclean spirit out of the Homeric world, and every passer by adds a boulder or a pebble" (Shewan 1911:viii). He quotes, for example, R. M. Henry, who calls it "by common consent one of the most worthless books of the *Iliad* from a poetical point of view" (Henry 1905:192).

Shewan follows William Gladstone in taking scholars to task for "precipitate application of the canons of modern prose" to a work of ancient poetry (Shewan 1911:3). He treats every objection raised and systematically uncovers the flaws and biases of these arguments, exploring the book's vocabulary, usage, versification, *hapax legomena*, and "pseudo-archaisms," to name just a few subjects extensively discussed.[10] Shewan engages directly virtually all of the leading scholars of his day, with the result that his arguments are best understood in relation to late-nineteenth-century scholarship. On the charge of late "Odyssean" language, for example, Shewan shows that previous studies relied on the highly questionable schematizations of Analyst critics as to which parts of the *Iliad* are earlier and later. Few scholars would accept such schemas in the wake of Parry and Lord (see below), but Shewan in many ways anticipates Parry and Lord by arguing that all of extant Homeric poetry should be treated as a single system. He counters K. Orzulik (1883), who alleges that *Iliad* 10 is Odyssean (and therefore, by the logic of the time, late), this way:

> In effect he asks us to look on words or phrases which do not occur in that ancient and select piece of Homeric poetry as more or less tainted. But that is unreasonable. The *Ur-Ilias* is not a thesaurus of the epic language. The Lay of the Wrath is, even in its dimensions as assigned by the most liberal of the upholders of the kernel theory, of but small compass. If the *Ur-Ilias* be made long enough, we shall have no difficulty in vindicating the Doloneia.
>
> Shewan 1911:29

---

[10] Chantraine (1937) has also examined such features in the textual tradition of *Iliad* 10. He focuses on variation in the textual record, especially instances where one variation is linguistically later than another and editors must choose between them. His conclusion is that these variations could have coexisted for a long time as the poetry was performed by rhapsodes, making an editor's choice between them necessarily arbitrary.

Shewan goes on to make two crucial points here: that we should judge Homer by Homer, and that we should understand that the poet is drawing on a variety of older traditional material, some of which is no doubt older than others (1911:34). He asserts that no one can show *Iliad* 10 to be more "Odyssean" than any other book. Even if one could, we have to acknowledge that Odysseus is one of the main characters in the book, and this can explain what affinities there are, if any.

Shewan questions (as do we) whether something that seems to us unusual is necessarily late (1911:49–50): "What is wanted, but never supplied, is proof that the word or form was unknown in, say, the 10th century B.C." Might some of the unusual features of this book belong to a very old tradition? After all, our "database" for evaluating traditional epic language is limited by what little has survived. Our view is that *Iliad* 10 exemplifies the theme of ambush, which is thematically associated with nighttime action, a theme that is uncommon in the surviving epics but would probably not seem unusual if more epic survived. Shewan, too, suggests this explanation (Shewan 1911:55): "The author had for once to narrate the events of a night anxiety, with much watching and waking, ending in a scouting expedition. One result was that he had to describe dress and accoutrements appropriate to the situation ... Words may be rare to us; we cannot say they were really rare." *Iliad* 10 is our only extended example of a night raid in extant epic poetry. It is an unusual theme from our perspective, but that does not mean it is "late" or "un-Homeric." [11] The traditional theme of ambush at night almost certainly long predates our *Iliad*.

As valuable as Shewan's energetic and exhaustive argumentation is, it is entirely, as we have already seen, the product of its own time. That time is nearly a century before our own, and it predates the paradigm-shifting discoveries of Parry and Lord later in the twentieth century. Much of Shewan's defense of *Iliad* 10 is a reaction to the excesses of Analyst scholarship in its most extreme applications. Most problematic, however, is that Shewan's defense (like Unitarian criticism more generally) is founded on an application of a modern literary aesthetic not unlike that which he criticizes in others. Shewan's overarching thesis is that *Iliad* 10 is, like the rest of Homeric poetry, the work of a single poetic genius: "'Wherever there is poetry there is a poet.' For an *Iliad* or an *Odyssey* the genius of the poet is needed, to select, to blend, to transform and re-create. That, with the evidence which the poems themselves present of transcendent creative power, is the great argument

---

[11] See also Thornton 1984:168 on this point.

for the existence of Homer" (Shewan 1911:xviii). Although Shewan is far more willing to see *Iliad* 10 and the rest of the *Iliad* and *Odyssey* as part of a single system, he is adamant that the uniformity he finds is the work of a single poet. And as Shewan makes clear in his opening pages, the primary reason to accept *Iliad* 10 as part of the *Iliad* is because it is, according to him, good poetry (see e.g. Shewan 1911:6, 10).

Shewan calls the thesis that *Iliad* is a "traditional book which [in the words of Gilbert Murray] 'grew as its people grew' ... not merely improbable, but even unthinkable" (Shewan 1911:xix). Indeed, such a thesis was unthinkable for those scholars of the early twentieth century who perceived the poetry of the *Iliad* to be layered but also uniform, traditional but also dynamic and creative—the work, it seemed to them, of a master poet who was responsible for the sophisticated design and emotionally affective content of our *Iliad*. It was in the 1930s, when Milman Parry and his assistant Albert Lord went to Yugoslavia to study the oral epic tradition that then still flourished there, that the Homeric poems began to be understood as not only traditional but *oral*—that is, as products of performance rather than composition through the technology of writing.[12] Of course, scholars before Parry and Lord had proposed that the *Iliad* and *Odyssey* were composed orally, but never before had the system by which such poetry could be composed been demonstrated, nor were the implications of the creative process truly explored. In two expeditions to the former Yugoslavia in 1933–1935, Parry and Lord collected 12,544 songs, stories, and conversations from 169 singers of the South Slavic epic song tradition. Their unsurpassed, original fieldwork has been matched only by the work of Albert Lord himself, who took additional trips in the 1950s and 1960s. No two of the songs collected are exactly alike, nor do any two of the singers have exactly the same repertoire. These singers composed extremely long epic poems *in performance*. In order to do this they drew on a vast storehouse of traditional themes and phrases that worked within the meter or rhythm of the poetry. That is to say, they created and used what are called formulas to build each verse as they went along, instead of employing static, individual words or words memorized in a fixed order. Just as formulas are the building blocks of a line in performance, themes are the larger components that make up songs. The poets recorded by Parry and Lord moved from one theme to

---

[12] On the work of Parry and Lord, its implications, and its legacy in Homeric scholarship, see also Foley 1997 and 2005b and the introduction by Mitchell and Nagy to the (2000) second edition of Lord 1960.

another as they sang; themes would have been connected in the oral poet's mind and his plan for the song from their habitual association in the tradition.[13] This performance method results in each song being a new composition, which is the reason why no two songs that Parry and Lord recorded were ever exactly the same. Parry and Lord applied this fieldwork to the Homeric poems by analogy, and they were able to show how the workings of the South Slavic system reveal a great deal about how the *Iliad* and *Odyssey* were composed.

The work of Parry and Lord and the scholars who have built on their efforts suggests that in its earliest stages of development there was a great deal of fluidity in the Greek oral epic tradition. Countless variations on the story of the Trojan War and the episodes within it, the anger of Achilles, the returns of the heroes, and any number of traditional tales, are known to have been current in different times and different places in antiquity, and were likely sung by countless poets whose names are now lost to us. At the same time, because Greek oral epic poetry was traditional in content already in ancient times, any given audience on any given occasion of performance knew the story and the characters already. There would have been nothing about the story, the language, the rhythm of the song, or the characters that was new for that audience. A poet in a traditional song culture like that of the ancient Greeks could compose poetry in performance using techniques, plots, characters, and language that he had inherited from many previous generations of singers. The material and techniques were traditional, but each performance was a new composition—a recomposition, in and for performance. We assert that the very fact that the *Iliad* and *Odyssey* are "oral traditional" often allows even deeper and more complex levels of meaning than may be found in poetry that is composed in a literate, text-based culture.

How do Parry and Lord's fieldwork and the resulting thesis that the *Iliad* was composed within an oral traditional system affect our understanding of *Iliad* 10? In our essay "The Poetics of Ambush" and in the commentary, we explore answers to this question in detail. For now, let us simply show how this approach takes a fundamentally different starting point in attempting to answer these questions and explicate the poetics of this book. Rather than begin with the question of authorship or authenticity, a Parry-Lord approach seeks to understand how *Iliad* 10 relates to the larger system of oral composition-in-performance

---

[13] On composition by theme in the South Slavic and Homeric oral traditions, see also Powell 1977 and Friedrich 2002.

in which these epics were composed. Because of certain duplications in the plots of Books 9 and 10 of the *Iliad*, as well as the time elapsed during the course of the night during which these events take place, it has been argued that *Iliad* 10 is a clumsy forgery (by someone other than "Homer") meant to replace *Iliad* 9. (Note, however, that *Iliad* 9 was suspected throughout the nineteenth century of not being composed by "Homer.") Instead of relying on such an unsatisfactory avoidance of the problems noted by scholars, a Parry-Lord approach might be as follows. First, we could make an analogy with the South Slavic tradition, where Parry and Lord documented that the most accomplished singers could expand their songs indefinitely by adding episodes paratactically, as the mood of the audience or occasion required. The events of the night in question highlight the effects of Achilles' wrath and withdrawal, which constitute the central theme of the poem. It is in keeping with the poetics of an oral tradition to add additional episodes to this particular night.[14] Second, *Iliad* 10 is the only surviving example of an extended narrative about a night raid in Homeric poetry, even though we know there were many such episodes in the larger epic tradition.[15] In this commentary we argue that the night raid is a traditional theme, with its own traditional language, subthemes, conventions, and poetics, but nonetheless part of the same system of oral poetry to which the entire *Iliad* belongs. Finally, as Albert Lord himself suggested (Lord 1960/2000:194), *Iliad* 10 may be a legitimate multiform of *Iliad* 9, both books orally composed within the same traditional poetic system and therefore both equally "Homeric."

Recent Homeric Scholarship and our Approach to *Iliad* 10

The work of Parry and Lord revolutionized Homeric studies. Although it took several decades for the implications of Parry's arguments to be fully appreciated, and Lord did not publish his trailblazing *Singer of Tales* until 1960, the terms of Homeric debate have since fundamentally changed. The past seventy-five years of scholarship has sought to better understand the composition of our poems in light of Parry's

---

[14] This concept is very different from the ideas of Leaf that we noted above. He conceived of the two books as "rivals" of one another that were only thrown together in some final text-based redaction. With paratactic addition, episodes such as we see in *Iliad* 9 and 10 could have been sung in sequence by the same singer for the same audience on the same occasion.

[15] These are discussed below in our essay entitled "The Poetics of Ambush." See also Kullmann 1960:86 and Fenik 1964:12–13.

and, later, Lord's work, and even those who are hostile to Parry's methodology must ground their arguments in an entirely new framework. Before Parry went to Yugoslavia, many scholars believed that the *Iliad* and *Odyssey* had been orally composed, but they did not understand how the compositional process worked, and, as a result, they applied inappropriate methods of scholarly criticism or relied on assumptions that can seem comical now. For example, in the 1880s August Fick proposed that the *Iliad* was composed in Aeolic Greek and later translated by Ionic singers into their own dialect, and he even went so far as to produce editions of the *Iliad* (1886) and *Odyssey* (1883) with the Aeolic dialect restored wherever possible. Parry's fieldwork by contrast provided a living example in which to observe how a poetic diction might evolve as its "vocabulary" of formulaic language passed from singer to singer and from one generation of singers to the next, thereby rendering the previous century's body of scholarly inquiry into the question essentially obsolete.

Not all of the implications of this fieldwork, as articulated by Parry himself before his death and later by Lord, have been fully embraced, however, and much scholarship has been devoted to refining Parry's initial findings about the economy of Homeric diction and the nature of the Homeric formula.[16] There is strong resistance among those who feel that Parry's work somehow minimizes the artistry of the poems or that the principles he outlined restrict the creativity of poets composing in this medium.[17] Thus even those who accept Parry's findings often seek to amend significant aspects of his arguments. We may be considered more "fundamentalist" in our acceptance of Parry and Lord's work than most scholars.[18] Though we would argue against the notion of an "orthodoxy" in their work, or ours, we do nevertheless feel that the scope of Parry's and Lord's insights has been ignored, misread or misrepresented, or dismissed too quickly.[19] Some (though certainly not all) efforts to revise Parry and Lord are built on

[16] On these concepts see Lord 1960/2000:30–67, Nagler 1967, Hainsworth 1968, Clark 1994, Edwards 1997, and Russo 1997 with further bibliography *ad loc.*

[17] Cf. Edwards 1997: "I shall discuss the progress made in certain specific areas, beginning with the realization of the problems Parry's discoveries caused for appreciating Homer's creative genius" (261). Such a formulation does not take into account Lord's emphasis on the creativity of the oral poet, a creativity that operates within the tradition, not apart from or in opposition to it (see e.g. Lord 1960/2000:13, 29).

[18] The phrase "dogmatic fundamentalism of the Parry-Lord orthodoxy" was applied to Dué 2002 by Evans 2003.

[19] See the recent review by Beck (2008) for a concise discussion of the debate over Parry's work especially in terms of the creativity of the oral poet. Friedrich responds at *BMCR* 2009.02.29.

a misunderstanding of the principles they documented in their field-work and a lack of awareness of, or at least appreciation for, the kind of meaning made possible by an oral poetic tradition. That is not to say, however, that our approach and interpretations have not also greatly benefited from the work of scholars who have sought to better understand such essential concepts as the Homeric formula and the complex relationship between orality and literacy in ancient Greece. There is, however, a significant difference between scholarship that expands the central insights of Parry and Lord's work, even while modifying certain notions or definitions, and scholarship that sets out to "prove" Parry (more often than Lord) "wrong" in order to conclude, usually with no further justification, that Homer wrote, or somehow "broke free" of the oral tradition of these epics.

Indeed, there persists a strong contingent of scholars who prefer to see a single genius at a fixed point in time behind the *Iliad* and *Odyssey* as we now have them. This individual poet is sometimes conceived of as literate, and at other times imagined as dictating the poems to another literate person.[20] It is an understandable preference, given our own literate culture's conceptions of authorship and artistic genius. As Casey Dué (2006b) has pointed out, Parry himself seems to have begun his research with an interest in primitive genius. His first study of Homeric style, his 1928 doctoral thesis, begins with a quote about originality and primitive literature from Ernest Renan: "Comment saisir la physionomie et l'originalité des littératures primitives, si on ne pénètre la vie morale et intime de la nation, si on ne se place au point même de l'humanité qu'elle occupa, afin de voir et de sentir comme elle, si on ne la regarde vivre, ou plûtot si on ne vit un instant avec elle?"[21] Yet, even in spite of this expressed desire to understand poetry in the context of its culture, both Parry and Lord, at least at the very beginning of their careers, seem

---

[20] M. L. West is the most recent and most prominent scholar to maintain that Homer was literate. For a summary and critique of the various dictation theories see Nagy 1996b:30–35. One of the most significant problems is that the dating of this literate poet (or his literate recorder) in these arguments is to the time when alphabetic writing was a new technology for the ancient Greeks. The ancient Greeks themselves imagined Homer as an individual (named Homer), but recently scholars have shown that the ancient biographical information about the figure of Homer conforms to known patterns of Greek folklore, mythology, and poetics, and has no basis in any reliable information preserved from the lifetime of such a man. From the earliest references to Homer in antiquity this figure is already a mystery and a source of controversy, laid claim to by many groups, revered by all, but belonging to none. See Graziosi 2002. For a comparable attribution of an oral tradition to a single preeminent singer, see Foley 1998.

[21] Parry 1928:1, quoting Renan 1890:292. See Lord 1948:34.

to have believed in a Homer, whose Yugoslav counterpart each thought they had found in Ćor Huso and Avdo Međedović, respectively.

Since those early publications, however, our understanding of oral traditions has evolved considerably, thanks not least to Lord, who undertook additional fieldwork and continued publishing until his death in 1991 (and whose book *The Singer Resumes the Tale* was published posthumously in 1995). A generation of scholars, moreover, has embraced Parry's initial theories and their subsequent development by Lord. For every scholar who persists in attributing what is "good" about Homeric poetry to the creativity of a poetic genius, there is another scholar who approaches Homeric poetry as a system of interconnected poetic and cultural associations whose significance can often be uncovered with careful study of the poetry that has survived. These scholars do not deny that composers of epic poetry in the tradition that created our *Iliad* and *Odyssey* had creative power, nor do they rule out the possibility that one such composer could have risen to prominence. But in searching for meaning in Homeric poetry these scholars have focused on the way that the poetics of an oral tradition operate differently from those of a predominantly literate culture. In short, the absence of the intentionality of a master poet does not mean that there is not beauty, artistry, or a sophisticated structure in the poetry; it only means that they are achieved differently—and therefore must be interpreted and appreciated differently.

Some of Lord's fundamental insights about how meaning is achieved and therefore must be understood have led to greater understanding of creativity and meaning in oral traditional poetry, as exemplified by the work of John Miles Foley, Richard Martin, and Gregory Nagy, among many others. In Lord's discussion of the training of the singer, he observes that the singers learn the language of oral performance of poetry holistically, as a child learns a language. Thought, meter, and language are not separate in the process of composing-in-performance (Lord 1960/2000:31–36). Foley, who has continued the comparative work with the South Slavic oral tradition that Parry and Lord began (see e.g. Foley 1999:37–111), has built on this idea to arrive at his general dictum that "oral poetry works like language, only more so" (Foley 2002:127–128). As in language generally, Foley argues following Lord, the poet's thought, not meter, is the driving force of expression. One way in which oral poetry is "more so," Foley has shown, is that the compositional units that singers think and compose in are not individual words, but phrases, lines, and even combinations of multiple lines that have a meaning greater than the sum of the individual words.

Both the singer and the audience who are within the tradition have easy access to this greater meaning because of their familiarity with the conventions of this language. Those of us outside the tradition (as all of us reading Homeric epic are) must reconstruct the traditional meaning as far as possible. Another way in which oral poetry is like language but more so, according to Foley, is through the added dimensions of performance (tone, gestures, pauses, etc.), which for Homeric poetry we do not have the opportunity to experience firsthand.

The special kind of meaning that Foley identifies and the way that singers use it and audiences experience it he calls "immanent art" (Foley 1991, see also Foley 1999 and 2002:109–124). When Lord briefly addresses the question of meaning in formulaic epithets, which those wanting to prove Parry wrong often choose as their target, he reiterates Parry's definition of the "essential meaning" of the noun-epithet formula, but then adds the following idea of a traditionally intuitive meaning embedded in the formula:

> Nevertheless, the tradition, what we might term the intuitions of singers as a group and as individuals who are preserving the inherited stories from the past—the tradition cannot be said to ignore the epithet, to consider it as mere decoration or even to consider it as mere metrical convenience. The tradition feels a sense of meaning in the epithet, and thus a special meaning is imparted to the noun and to the formula ... I would prefer to call it the traditionally intuitive meaning.
>
> Lord 1960/2000:66

Foley's concept of immanent art and his applications of that concept systematically expand and enhance Lord's own intuitive understanding of the deep meaning that resides in traditional language.[22] In Foley's own words, an approach based in immanent art "seeks to understand the idiomatic implications" of the multiform formulas,

---

[22] We may compare as well the work of Christos Tsagalis, who writes of the formula this way (Tsagalis 2008:xx): "The formula is not an external characteristic of epic language but a *symbiotic* feature operating on multiple levels and guiding us into a labyrinthine path of associations and interconnections. Formulaic diction is a mechanism whose surviving traces in Homeric epic cannot be attributed to recognized traditions but to a *diachronically diffused set of relations* going back to Indo-European strata. The reconstruction of this framework helps us to explore the deep structure of the epics by looking beyond the elliptical shape into which originally complex imagery has been crystallized during the process of shaping epic song." See also Graziosi and Haubold 2005 on the "resonance" of Homeric diction.

scenes, and themes in an oral tradition "as indexes of a more-than-literal meaning, as special signs that point toward encoded traditional meanings. It aims beyond a nuts-and-bolts grammar and toward a working fluency in the language of oral poetry" (Foley 2002:109). In this way, Foley claims, we can see the artistry of the poet within his use of the traditional language.

In our analysis of *Iliad* 10, these useful concepts provide an important foundation for our interpretation of both small and large units of composition and meaning. We can argue that a certain formula has a particular resonance within the theme of ambush, for example, or that we see a flexibility of the traditional arming scene that allows the poet to adapt it for a night mission. As Foley has shown, we need not reject Parry's ideas of the usefulness of formulas for composition-in-performance (they are certainly so) simply because he did not also address the artistic possibilities inherent in them. Foley's focus on the creation of meaning does not, as other scholarship has attempted to do, overturn the work of Parry and Lord, but rather uses their comparative fieldwork and their analysis of Homeric epic by analogy to construct the very kind of appropriate criticism and appreciation of Homeric language that Parry called for so many years ago.[23]

Richard Martin's work extends the concepts of orality, traditionality, and performance in terms of understanding genres of both speech and poetry. He has taken the notion of expansion in oral composition-in-performance that Parry and Lord observed in action with the Serbian singers as a means of explaining the monumental size and rhetoric of the Homeric epics, and has extended the comparative work of Parry and Lord to include traditional poetry from African, Irish, and other cultures. He has also explored how epic incorporates and represents various other genres or subgenres, and how Homeric epic reflects its own performance medium. Some of the genres or traditional themes Martin has identified and explored, such as the cattle raid, are directly relevant to the connections we see between themes operating within the night missions of *Iliad* 10. But underlying this particular application

---

[23] Parry MHV 2 (= 1928:1–2), at the very beginning of his work "The Traditional Epithet in Homer," asserts the same kind of need for understanding how meaning is implicitly created through this traditional language: "The task, therefore, of one who lives in another age and wants to appreciate that work correctly, consists in precisely rediscovering the varied information and the complexities of ideas which the author assumed to be the natural property of his audience." Similarly, Parry argues that by understanding how the language of oral traditional poetry operates in practice "we are compelled to create an aesthetics of traditional style" (MHV 21 = Parry 1928:25–26).

of Martin's work are the conceptual advances he has made in terms of understanding the play of genres within epic.

The work of Gregory Nagy, under whose direction we each wrote our dissertations, has informed and influenced ours to a considerable extent, one that is impossible to quantify. The range of his work and the numerous ways in which he has broadened the understanding of Homeric poetry are also difficult to summarize. His research includes comparative linguistics and the Indo-European background to the poetry, the religious concept of the hero and how it informs the epics, the performance of Homeric epic in antiquity, the textual tradition, the reception of Homeric poetry in other genres, synchronic and diachronic approaches to the epics, and the structure of mythical narratives (see Nagy 1974, 1979, 1990a, 1990b, 1996a, 1996b, 2002, 2003, 2004, 2009). Although our interpretation of individual lines within the commentary as well as our overall approach will reveal the influence of Nagy's work, we will highlight here just two important overarching ideas that have deeply affected what we want to achieve in this volume. The first is how the natural multiformity of composition-in-performance, articulated by Lord in terms of what he observed in the performances of the Serbian singers,[24] is reflected in the textual transmission of the Homeric epics. Nagy has asserted the importance of the scholia for understanding this aspect of the transmission. Our own explication of the text of *Iliad* 10, as introduced in the essay "*Iliad* 10: A Multitextual Approach" and the textual commentaries that accompany the four texts included in this volume, also understands multiforms within the textual record in terms of possible variations produced in performance that are equally possible and valid within the tradition.

The second key idea of Nagy's that we would like to highlight here is a related one: the epic tradition evolved over time, and therefore we are required to take a diachronic perspective. In his evolutionary model, Nagy identifies five stages of evolution, which move from relatively most fluid to relatively most rigid over several centuries (for the most recent articulation of the model, see Nagy 2004:27). The implications of this model are many and significant. It fundamentally rejects

---

[24] For example, Lord 1960/2000: "To the superficial observer, changes in oral tradition may seem chaotic and arbitrary. In reality this is not so. It cannot be said that 'anything goes.' Nor are these changes due in the ordinary sense to failure of memory of a fixed text, first, of course, because there is no fixed text, second, because there is no concept among singers of memorization as we know it, and third, because at a number of points in any song there are forces leading in several directions, any one of which the singer may take" (120).

the model which posits that an oral tradition came to an abrupt halt sometime in the eighth century BCE when the new technology of writing was used to record the monumental epics of a single singer, who was able to transcend the limits of said tradition, which he effectively ended, and whose works we (for the most part) have in our textual sources dating only from the tenth century CE onwards. In replacing that outdated and untenable model, Nagy's evolutionary model offers a better framework for understanding how an oral tradition and the technology of writing coexist and influence one another for a long time before writing becomes dominant. Under this model, the hypothesis that *Iliad* 10 was later inserted (interpolated) into a text that had been composed otherwise by a single author and was fixed at some earlier point becomes highly unlikely, if not impossible. Indeed, through the work of Parry, Lord, Foley, Martin, Nagy, and others, we recognize that this is simply not the way oral traditional poetry operates. Therefore, we have the opportunity to consider *Iliad* 10 within the tradition and to try to understand it in oral poetic and evolutionary terms, rather than mistakenly applying a false notion about the "text" of the *Iliad* to it. We will return to these points again later.

We must note, however, that this significant body of scholarship is not well represented in the standard commentaries on Homer, most notably the Cambridge commentary edited by Geoffrey Kirk. Although the scholars who have contributed to that commentary are some of the world's preeminent Homerists of the last few decades, and the learning represented therein should not be minimized, we feel strongly that the picture they create of the oral poetic background of the *Iliad* is inaccurate. The individual editors have all explored the nature of oral poetry in depth in their various publications,[25] but they apply it in ways that we find highly problematic. Each of these scholars in varying degrees merges our modern notion of authorship with Lord's picture of an illiterate, orally composing bard. Rather than explore how meaning might be conveyed differently in an oral composition process, these scholars seem to prize the individual contribution of a single singer over the system as a whole. None denies of course that many previous generations of singers contributed to the traditional material with which their Homer works, but none is willing to let go of the genius of the individual master-poet, whom they credit with crafting the *Iliad* as we now know

---

[25] See especially Kirk 1962 and 1976, Janko 1982, and Hainsworth 1968. M. W. Edwards has published many articles emphasizing the possibility of and mechanisms for individual creativity in an oral traditional medium. See e.g. Edwards 1966, 1980, 1997, and 2005.

it. As a result, the criticism that they offer is not very different from what one might find for a modern author. If a passage seems particularly beautiful or bad or unusual, they look to the author's intention for the evaluation of that passage.

In a 1970 publication, J. B. Hainsworth (one of the Cambridge editors) engaged directly the question of whether a new kind of criticism is necessary for oral poetry.[26] It is worth examining this essay in some detail, since Hainsworth is the author of the latest and currently most influential commentary on *Iliad* 10 (Hainsworth 1993). He begins by noting that conventional literary criticism for Homeric poetry is anachronistic and inadequate:

> Some of these judgments are no more than the stock responses of their age to epic poetry. The critic regards the poems from his own point of view; he discovers what he expects to find; and he passes a judgment that illuminates the workings of his own mind but sheds nothing but darkness upon Homer's.
>
> Hainsworth 1970:90

Hainsworth's use of the name Homer here to imply an individual's mind, akin to the critic's, is significant. Few scholars have studied the oral aspects of Homeric poetry and the work of Parry and Lord in as much depth as Hainsworth, but he is insistent in his assignation of the *Iliad* to an author named Homer. The rest of the essay then is devoted to trying to determine in what ways we may detect Homer's particular poetic skills. Hainsworth suggests that we understand our *Iliad* as a performance, and approach it as we might a dramatic performance. Thus there are two levels to consider: the poem itself, and the performance of it. He asserts that the *Iliad* is a particularly good performance, with few lapses. But is it also a good poem, and by what standards may we judge it? Hainsworth concludes that it is indeed a good poem, and he looks to what the poem says about itself and its own purpose in trying to determine how it is good. To this approach we have no objection. But once again the problem of authorship presents itself. Hainsworth seems to be determined to define, not just what is good about Homeric poetry, but what is good about *Homer*:

---

[26] The question has been asked and answered (usually negatively) by many. See e.g. Austin 1975 (passim), Kirk 1976:201–217, and Edwards 1997. Cf. Richardson 1978, reviewing Kirk 1976: "It is refreshing to find Homer once again restored to the company of his peers (Virgil and Milton in fact) after a generation in which he consorted chiefly with guslars."

Contamination or transfer of plots might be a stroke of genius and imagination ... They are the means whereby Homer has extended his poems to their monumental length, an important piece of artistry, for a poet *who could not transcend his tradition* in this way could only lengthen his poem by over-ornamentation of its original episodes.

Hainsworth 1970:96, emphasis ours

Even though elsewhere in the essay Hainsworth quotes Parry as saying that "[t]he fame of a singer comes not from quitting the tradition but from putting it to the best use,"[27] he assumes that a composer fully immersed in the tradition cannot compose poetry of the sophisticated, complex quality of our *Iliad*. He must "transcend his tradition."[28] And so, although he admits that conventional literary approaches are inadequate, Hainsworth concludes that Homer is a special case "unlike typical oral poetry" and "amenable to the canons of orthodox criticism":

The art of the episodes certainly resembles that of oral epic in other lands, and we should be prudent at this level to consider carefully the assumptions of our criticism. But the greater architecture of the poems appears to be unlike typical oral poetry. It is more like drama, and therefore more amenable to the canons of orthodox criticism. For all the proliferation of comparative studies Homer remains a very special case.

Hainsworth 1970:98

It seems to us that Hainsworth, no less than the scholars of previous eras that he criticizes, has failed to transcend his own age in his finding that Homer is a "special case," an oral poet who can be an author (in the modern sense of that word). The Homer who composes orally but who can for the most part be treated as a modern literary figure is perhaps the most prevalent of paradigms in which current Homeric

---

[27] Hainsworth 1970:91 quoting Parry 1932:14.

[28] Lord points out that such a goal implies a writing poet: "His manner of composition differs from that used by a writer in that the oral poet makes no conscious effort to break the traditional phrases and incidents" (1960/2000:5). Later, in response to Cedric Whitman's conception of a "Homer" who saw the benefit of writing his song down, Lord asserts: "The trouble with Whitman's 'creative artist' is that, in spite of the fact that he is said to compose entirely as an oral poet, he is not in the tradition; he is not an oral *traditional* poet. *And oral poets who are not traditional do not exist*" (1960/2000:155; original emphasis).

scholarship operates, and this assumption is central to the most recent approaches to *Iliad* 10. Hainsworth's 1993 commentary on *Iliad* 10 is grounded in the assumption that *Iliad* 10 is oral traditional poetry, but has been composed by someone other than "Homer," a poet who is by implication throughout not nearly as skilled as our Homer (see especially Hainsworth 1993:151–155). As we noted earlier, even while admitting that most arguments offered by earlier scholars against the book have proven flawed, Hainsworth asserts that points that seem of little weight unto themselves add up to only one conclusion—namely, that the book was not originally part of the *Iliad* and was composed and adapted to the *Iliad* by a later poet.[29]

Hainsworth is in this respect following the basic arguments of Georg Danek, whose 1988 monograph *Studien zur Dolonie* is the most recent extended treatment of *Iliad* 10 before our own. Danek's monograph is not unlike Shewan's in many respects. It offers a spirited defense of *Iliad* 10 as an orally composed, traditional piece of poetry. But rather than emphasize its shared features with Homeric poetry as Shewan does, Danek emphasizes the book's unusual features. Like Shewan, Danek argues that the Doloneia is good poetry composed by a good poet, but for Danek that poet is not Homer. He is instead a poet working in the same tradition, somewhat later than the composer of the *Iliad*. This poet strives for a personal style that is lively. He makes clever use of convention, deliberately alludes to the *Iliad*, tries to introduce colloquial words, attempts to make scenes more visually stimulating, and intentionally varies formulaic language.

Danek, like many scholars following Parry and Lord, seeks to reconcile our understanding of the *Iliad* as traditional, orally composed poetry with the long-held feeling that *Iliad* 10 is somehow different. Like Shewan's, his rigorous analysis of individual passages reveals that the language and style are not as different as has long been assumed, but it is different enough in his eyes to assert different authorship. The fieldwork of Parry and Lord, however, is at odds with Danek's hypothesis. Danek assumes that his poet of the Doloneia could both be traditional and seek to create a personal style. But poets in a traditional process like that which Parry and Lord describe do not seek to innovate. Parry asserted that such a poet "would not think of trying to express ideas outside the traditional field of thought of the poetry" and

---

[29] See Hainsworth 1993:154. A similar argument was made by Klingner 1940, who appreciates the differences a night setting requires, but who uses those differences to argue against its place in the *Iliad*.

"make[s] his verses easily by means of a diction which time has proved to be the best."[30] An example of an approach that seeks in the poetics of oral poetry a deeper appreciation of how *Iliad* 10 is thematically consistent with the *Iliad* as a whole is found in Dan Petegorsky's 1982 doctoral dissertation. Petegorsky argues that a search for "texts" and assumptions about "lateness" should be set aside, and we should rather investigate why a poet might evoke a theme that seems—to us, with our frame of reference—"Odyssean." In contrast to Danek's conclusion, Petegorsky argues that the different thematic feel to the Doloneia, rather than exposing its inauthenticity or non-Homeric authorship, instead defines the *Iliad*'s place within the epic tradition.[31]

Following Parry and Lord, we have taken an approach different from that of previous scholars to understanding the unusual content of *Iliad* 10 and indeed the poetics of the *Iliad* as a whole, and our approach differs significantly from some of the latest scholarly work on the book. We have seen that a combination of insistence on an individual author and distaste for the poetry of *Iliad* 10 has led to the conjecture that it was composed by an entirely different author. Martin West's 1998–2000 Teubner *Iliad*, an edition that is quickly becoming the standard text of the poem for most scholars and translators and will likely influence our understanding of Homeric poetry for decades to come, brackets *Iliad* 10 in its entirety as an interpolation that does not belong in the poem. West's Homer, however, is not the orally composing bard of Danek or Hainsworth. His Homer is described on the first page of his introduction to the Teubner text this way : "Ilias materiam continet iamdiu per ora

---

[30]   Parry 1932:7–8 (= MHV 330). See also note 28, above, for Lord on the necessary traditionality of the poet.

[31]   Petegorsky 1982:175–254. Similarly, Thornton (1984:164–169) gives in an appendix a brief "defense" of *Iliad* 10 in which she argues ways it can be seen as integrated into the *Iliad* as a whole. Another notable exception to the general condemnation of *Iliad* 10 and/or speculation about separate authorship in the twentieth century can be found in the work of Stanley 1993: "For their part, Unitarian students of the overall design of the poem, including Sheppard [1922:83] and Whitman [1958:283–284], have rejected the *Doloneia* as an interlude at best. We shall see, on the contrary, that it is indispensable to the larger pattern of Books 8–17, no less than to the entire twenty-four-book structure, and is thus essential to the discourse of our *Iliad*" (1993:119). But Stanley's concluding remarks about the book reveal an essentially negative view of the actions of Odysseus and Diomedes in *Iliad* 10: "their achievement, now and later, is based not on heroic honor but on clever exploitation; and its rewards are merely a surplus of things, not tokens of glory" (1993:128). In "The Poetics of Ambush" and in the commentary below we make precisely the opposite argument, namely, that *mētis* and *biē* are complementary paths to achieving glory and distinction (*kleos* and *kudos*) in Homeric epic and that both are prized as being characteristic of the "best" of the Achaeans.

cantorum diffusam, formam autem contextumque qualem nos novimus tum primum attinuit, cum conscripta est; quod ut fieret, unius munus fuit maximi poeta" ("The *Iliad* contains material diffused through the mouths of singers for a long time, but the form and construction that we now know was first attained when it was written down. In order for this to happen, it had to be the work of one, very great poet"). West acknowledges the oral tradition that furnished material on which the *Iliad* was based, but then says that *our Iliad* took its form when it was first written down. This was the work of a *maximus poeta*, a genius, who could write. That the poet was also the writer is made clear as West continues: "per multos annos, credo, elaboravit et, quae primum strictius composuit, deinceps novis episodiis insertis mirifice auxit ac dilatavit" ("Throughout many years, I believe, he labored over it, and what he had at first put together concisely, he later wonderfully expanded and extended it by inserting new episodes"). It would seem that we have entered a new millennium without gaining new ground when it comes to the Doloneia or our appreciation of oral poetics.

In the following essay, "The Poetics of Ambush," we present in great detail our exposition of the traditional theme of ambush as expressed in *Iliad* 10, but as also seen in several other places within the ancient Greek epic tradition. For now we situate our work within current Homeric scholarship by highlighting our methodological debts to the work of Parry, Lord, and those who have carried on and expanded their insights. Our starting assumptions are that this episode is as traditional as any other part of the epic and that it is our task to understand it within that tradition. The commentary serves to demonstrate that an oral-traditional approach not only illuminates certain portions of the epic, but also succeeds on a sustained, line-by-line analysis of an entire book.

In terms of our approach, the question of authorship is a futile one. When we use the name "Homer," we mean it not as an individual author, the master-poet, but rather as a convenient name for the *Iliad* and *Odyssey* traditions.[32] Similarly, when we use the term "Homeric," we mean belonging to that tradition. We need then to further define what we mean by "tradition." As John Foley has noted (1999:xii), "tradition" is a wide-ranging concept that is not easy to define, and it does indeed encompass several interrelated concepts. One defining aspect of "tradition" is the notion of "handing down," and one of our

---

[32] See Nagy 1996b:20–22 on the dangers of implying such an individual when one uses "Homer" as the subject of a verb.

basic assumptions is that there was a "handing down" of epic songs in ancient Greek culture for many centuries, starting in the second millennium BCE. This process of "handing down" reveals how closely the epic tradition is related to epic language. We have discussed how the fieldwork of Parry and Lord provided a systematic explication of how this language works in performance, allowing the singer to rapidly compose as he performs. It is also this language that allows the songs, an important conduit of cultural memory, to be learned and recomposed in performance by the next generation of singers. So when we speak of "traditional language" we mean the formulaic phrases and themes that make up the singers' repertoire within this culture over time. Tradition, in the sense of handing down the language of songs composed in performance, is both conservative and dynamic.[33] There is a cultural premium placed on singing the song the same way every time, just as the singer learned it, but, because each performance recomposes the song anew, the singer may create, from his experience with the traditional language, new phrases.[34] If a new phrase is found to be good and useful by other singers, it can become traditional in the sense that it will be used by these other singers. But, as Parry and Lord's fieldwork has shown, the singer is not consciously attempting to create something new.[35] Because, as we have just seen, several scholars

[33] Foley makes note of these aspects in his definition of tradition as "a dynamic, multivalent body of meaning that preserves much that a group has invented and transmitted but which also includes as necessary, defining features both an inherent indeterminacy and a predisposition to various kinds of changes or modifications. I assume, in short, a living and vital entity with synchronic and diachronic aspects that over time and space will experience (and partially constitute) a unified variety of receptions" (Foley 1995:xii).

[34] As we note several times in this book, Lord describes the language of epic singing as operating the way language itself does (Lord 1960/2000:35–36). Thus the opportunity for change is ever present. He also emphasizes the creative opportunities for the poet: "It is sometimes difficult for us to realize that the man who is sitting before us singing an epic song is not a mere carrier of the tradition but a creative artist making the tradition" (Lord 1960/2000:13). Likewise, Nagy notes: "Moreover, I recognize that tradition is not just an inherited system: as with language itself, tradition comes to life in the here-and-now of real people in real situations" (Nagy 1996b:15). See also Lord 1960/2000:36–43 for his argument that the singer's creation of phrases by analogy with others he has learned is the basis for his artistry.

[35] As Lord puts it: "In order to avoid any misunderstanding, we must hasten to assert that in speaking of 'creating' phrases in performance we do not intend to convey the idea that the singer *seeks originality* or fineness of expression. He seeks expression of the idea under stress of performance. Expression is his business, not originality, which, indeed, is a concept quite foreign to him and one that he would avoid, if he understood it. To say that the *opportunity* for originality and for finding the 'poetically' fine phrase exists does *not* mean that the *desire* for originality also exists" (Lord 1960/2000:44–45, original emphasis).

have insisted that the language of *Iliad* 10 is idiosyncratic (whether in a good way or bad way, because the composer either wanted to create something new or was a hack), our investigations into the traditional nature of the language of *Iliad* 10 is intended to explore and explain the ways in which it is like the rest of the system of epic language as exemplified by the *Iliad* and *Odyssey*.

One other crucial aspect of "tradition" still to discuss is the song's reception by the audience. The singer uses the language of tradition, not simply because it is necessary for the composition of the song, but because that language conveys meaning to his audience.[36] As Foley describes this process: "Either explicitly or implicitly oral poets are constantly establishing and reestablishing the authority of their words and 'words' by reaffirming their ties to an ongoing way of speaking, to an expressive mode larger than any one individual … It creates a frame of reference within which the poet will operate and identifies for the audience what well-marked path to follow" (Foley 2002:91). Because the songs are handed down from generation to generation, their subject matter and language are already familiar to the audience, opening up the possibility for greater and special meaning, what Foley calls "traditional referentiality." Tradition, then, also means this larger frame of reference for any one instance of a formula or theme. When we speak of a "traditional audience," we mean members of the culture within which the song was handed down and recomposed in performance. In this aspect of tradition, too, there is variability and both synchronic and diachronic aspects.[37] But when we invoke a traditional audience,

---

[36] Parry describes the goal of anyone who wants to truly understand traditional poetry as recovering what the audience would know implicitly (MHV 2; see above, note 23). Foley succinctly states: "Tradition comprises the body of implications summoned by performance and shared between performer and audience" (Foley 2002:130).

[37] As Dué 2002 notes: "This traditional audience is not a precisely definable entity if we think of each performance as a new composition, and, depending on the time, place, and occasion of performance, the definition of 'tradition' changes. What is 'tradition' in Lesbos in, say, 600 B.C. might be unfamiliar if not obscure in Chios in 550 B.C." (2n5). On the traditional audience, see also Lord 1960/2000:148–157 and Martin 1993:227–228 and 238. On traditional referentiality, see also Danek 2002:5–6, building on the work of Foley: "a story, though presented in one individual performance, is nonetheless only understandable as a metonymy within a larger context. Thus, the version of the performed song evokes pars pro toto the entire background of its tradition, doing so on three levels: (1) On the level of language through the usage of traditional poetic diction and through formulaic phrases. (2) On the level of (the smallest units of) content through the usage of traditional motifs and type-scenes. (3) On the level of song structure through the usage of traditional patterns of plot." Kelly 2007 is a commentary on *Iliad* 8 that seeks to explicate the traditional referentiality of that book. In many ways then Kelly's approach overlaps with our own. See, however,

we do so in an attempt to capture the way that meaning in this larger frame is created between singer and audience. We, as outsiders to the culture, must recover this dynamic as best we can using the evidence that remains.

The approach we have taken intersects in some ways with the aims of Neo-Analyst scholars, such as Jonathan Burgess, who seek to show that in an oral tradition it is possible for a poet composing an epic like the *Iliad* to make use of the themes and structures of other traditional poems in ways that would be meaningful for an audience.[38] Like Burgess, we understand *Iliad* 10 to have been composed and performed within a long oral tradition of such poetry, and we argue that it is an example of a very ancient theme, the *lokhos* (see "The Poetics of Ambush"). For us, the theme of *lokhos*, with its traditional structure and diction, long predates our received text of the *Iliad*. So too do the narrative traditions about Rhesos predate our *Iliad* (see Fenik 1964 and our essay "Tradition and Reception," below). Neo-Analysts have not typically applied their theoretical framework to *Iliad* 10 for the reasons already discussed in this essay. The Doloneia is usually thought to be a late composition, not an early one.

Our goal then is to better explicate the poetics of *Iliad* 10 and in turn to better understand the Homeric oral tradition as a whole. We have chosen this book because we feel it is the least understood of all the forty-eight books that comprise our *Iliad* and *Odyssey* and because it is almost universally denounced as "un-Homeric." We do not seek to replace Hainsworth's thorough 1993 commentary on the book, but rather to add to it and offer an alternative explanation/approach to many passages. Like Hainsworth, we understand *Iliad* 10 to be oral traditional poetry. But the results of our investigations are often very different from Hainsworth's. Rather than look to the intention or skill of a particular composer in order to explain the poetry, we attempt to ground our readings in the meanings made possible by an oral tradition. In de-emphasizing authorship we do not deny the possibility that some form of authorship, in terms of the poet as a creative artist

---

Cook 2009b for some of the limitations of Kelly's methodology. Unlike Kelly, we have not restricted ourselves to the *Iliad* in trying to recover the poetics of ambush that underlie *Iliad* 10.

[38] See especially Burgess 2006 and, for an overview of the approach, Finkelberg 2003. Danek, whose 1988 book we have discussed above, also takes a Neo-Analytical approach to the Homeric poems (see e.g. Danek 1998 and 2002). For a model for our contention, explored further below in "The Poetics of Ambush," that *Iliad* 10 may interact with or allude to similar episodes in the Epic Cycle, we can look to Burgess 2001. For interactions between the *Iliad* and *Odyssey* see Nagy 1979 and Edwards 1985.

composing in performance, could exist in this oral tradition. But when the search for Homer's genius is abandoned, many more illuminating possibilities often present themselves.

What is at stake in taking this approach is a better understanding of the language, structure, evolution, and cultural meaning of the epics. Our arguments confront deeply entrenched ideas about the Doloneia. The condemnation of *Iliad* 10 is so extensive that even a relatively recent book devoted to the theme of ambush, written from an avowedly oralist perspective, does not discuss *Iliad* 10, our most extensive example of ambush in surviving Greek epic.[39] Ignoring or only barely acknowledging *Iliad* 10 is a strategy employed by many scholars, who likely feel they must ignore it so as not to incur the charge of making arguments about Homer based on an "interpolated," "un-Homeric," or otherwise problematic text. Nevertheless, we feel that there is an entirely different way of treating this book. Rather than dismiss it as "un-Homeric" or pass over it in silence, we propose to show that *Iliad* 10 offers us unique insight into such important topics as the process of composition-in-performance, the traditional themes of Archaic Greek epic, the nature of the hero, and the creativity and artistry of the oral traditional language.

With this volume, we hope to make a contribution, through the application of Parry and Lord's work on oral poetry, to the scholarship on *Iliad* 10 and on the *Iliad* as a whole. Like all scholars, we are operating under assumptions that may in time prove flawed, and we assume that we will be linked in the history of scholarship with a group of Homerists who began publishing in the late twentieth century, many of whom are the associates and former students of Gregory Nagy, who was himself a student and associate of Albert Lord. We would be proud to be so linked. But, by making our assumptions plain at the outset, we want to recognize and affirm what this approach offers in terms of understanding the poetry in its own cultural contexts, as well as to acknowledge the gaps in our knowledge and evidence. We hope to attract those readers who are willing to consider our arguments with an open mind. There will be some who on principle will reject our findings, but we hope that the majority of our readers, regardless of their Homeric affiliations, will find in our approach a way forward.

---

[39] See Edwards 1985. Edwards included a short appendix on *Iliad* 10 in his 1981 dissertation, but it does not appear in his 1985 monograph, where *Iliad* 10 is mentioned only in passing.

2

The Poetics of Ambush

T HE PHRASE "POETICS OF AMBUSH" encapsulates our approach and our goals for this volume, so let us begin here by defining what we mean by it. When we speak of "poetics" we mean that we are proposing a theory of the structure and functioning of the traditional language within which *Iliad* 10, as well as several other episodes within the epic tradition, was created and therefore must also be understood and interpreted. Similar to the way Todorov has defined poetics in general, our poetics takes the epic tradition as its object of study, but also seeks the laws governing its discourse within the epic tradition itself.[1] Todorov has further explained: "Interpretation both precedes and follows poetics: the notions of poetics are produced according to the necessities of concrete analysis, which in its turn may advance only by using the instruments elaborated by doctrine" (1981:7–8). In our case, we will use the episodes of ambush (more on our use of that term in a moment) to define the poetics involved, and once we have proposed those definitions, we can assess how they function in various episodes. Because our evidence of the traditional language is necessarily limited by what has survived (indeed, *Iliad* 10 is our most extensive surviving ambush episode), the alternation between poetics and interpretation that Todorov describes is a short cycle back and forth. Nevertheless, a knowledge of the system—that is, a poetics—is necessary for a complete understanding of these episodes and a proper interpretation of them.

Defining and applying "poetics" in this way is also true to the nature of the oral tradition as a systematic and traditional language

---

[1] Todorov 1981: "Poetics ... aims at a knowledge of the general laws that preside over the birth of each work ... [and] it seeks these laws within literature itself. Poetics is an approach therefore at once 'abstract' and 'internal'... The goal of this study is no longer to articulate a paraphrase, a descriptive résumé of the concrete work, but to propose a theory of the structure and function of literary discourse, a theory that affords a list of literary possibilities, so that existing literary works appear as achieved particular cases" (6–7).

(as defined in Parry and Lord's work), and we are indeed concerned here with an oral-traditional poetics. That is, since poetics is a theory of *how* meaning is created, our poetics of ambush seeks to explain how the traditional language creates meaning in an oral composition-in-performance for a traditional audience. Within the system that Parry and Lord articulated, we define ambush as a *theme*, a "group of ideas regularly used in telling a tale in the formulaic style of traditional song" (Lord 1960/2000:68). By defining ambush as a theme, we examine how the theme is involved in both how the singer composes the song (which is how Lord explores the definition and structure of the theme) and how the audience understands it. In this way "theme" is in some ways like "genre" when genre is defined as something like "a set of norms and expectations that structure our reading of texts, allowing us to organize sense making according to conventional patterns, and to perceive variations in the use of convention."[2] In terms of Homeric epic specifically, Foley has argued similarly that a theme "cues idiomatic meaning and participates in the reception as well as the composition of Homeric poetry" (1999:169). The theme, then, will have certain features that define and identify it as such, and in turn it will shape the audience's expectations of what will happen and how to understand it.

When we use the word "ambush" in the phrase "poetics of ambush," we mean it as a convenient name for a theme that encompasses many types of activities. Ambush is one of the most prominent of these activities, which is why we have chosen it to stand for the whole, but the theme also includes spying missions, raids on enemy camps, cattle rustling, and other types of epic warfare that happen at night. Action at night is a key characteristic of the ambush theme, and we may also recognize an ambush by several other telling characteristics. The heroes wear animal skins, crouch in hidden positions, sometimes in marshy or woody locations near a road, endure discomfort as they lie in wait, and use planning and intelligence to overcome a foe that they might otherwise not be able to. The term *lokhos* 'ambush' and related words are, of course, significant, but they may not always be explicit. We will discuss in greater detail each of these markers of the ambush theme, as well as

---

[2] Brooks 1981:xv–xvi. Compare also Todorov 1990:18, where he states that genres "function as 'horizons of expectation' for readers and 'models of writing' for authors." Since we are dealing with oral poetics, we would replace "readers" with "audience," "writing" with "composing," and "authors" with "singers" in this formulation. Of course, when we compare theme to genre, we are still speaking of a subgenre of epic, with which it is not contradictory.

how these different kinds of activities may be considered sub-themes that are traditionally linked with one another.

The Traditionality of Ambush Episodes

Although *Iliad* 10 has been portrayed by some scholars as an anomaly, allusions to night raids, episodes of ambush, spying missions, and other forms of "irregular warfare" are, in fact, frequent in the ancient Greek epic tradition.[3] In this essay we will have occasion to discuss the exploits of Tydeus, the wooden horse and the sack of Troy, the attack on the suitors in the *Odyssey*, and episodes thought to have been part of the Epic Cycle, such as the ambush of Troilos by Achilles and the stealing of the Palladion by Odysseus and Diomedes. These last two narratives are generally met with suspicion and often with outright condemnation by modern scholars who denigrate them as un-Homeric and even un-heroic. Indeed, scholars have used the ambush techniques employed in these episodes as evidence of the un-Homeric and un-heroic nature of the Epic Cycle. Malcolm Davies, for example, summarizes two of these incidents as follows:

> Next in Proclus' summary comes Achilles' murder of Troilus ... His death at Achilles' hands becomes a very popular motif in later literature and art, but it is variously represented. Sometimes he is depicted as killed in ambush or slaughtered at the altar of Apollo; sometimes his killing is associated with Achilles' sighting of Polyxena, with whom Achilles falls in love; sometimes Achilles himself is given homosexual feelings for Troilus. All and any of which are quite incompatible with the heroic world as constructed by Homer.

> After this ... Odysseus, with Diomedes' aid, carried off the Palladium from Troy. Here too Odysseus' collaboration with a colleague has Homeric precedent ... but this episode is more profoundly unHomeric in several ways.[4]

As we have seen in our essay "Interpreting *Iliad* 10: Assumptions, Methodology, and the Place of the Doloneia within the History of Homeric Scholarship," *Iliad* 10, too, has met with vehement resistance and has

---

[3] For the concept of irregular warfare as pertains to the Trojan War and its representation in the *Iliad* (as well as attestations of its use in the Bronze Age Mediterranean) see Strauss 2006:140.

[4] Davies 1989:47 and 66.

been categorized as "un-Homeric."[5] In that essay and in this volume as a whole we do not deny the unusual character of the Doloneia, but we seek to propose an alternative to the usual explanations and solutions offered with respect to *Iliad* 10. We argue that *Iliad* 10 gives us our best look at an alternative type of warfare poetics, namely, the poetics of ambush. Using comparative evidence as well as what we know of the Epic Cycle and the epic tradition as a whole, we hope to show that such warfare was not construed as un-heroic and should not be viewed as un-Homeric in some way (however "Homer" is conceived); ambush is in fact a traditional theme (as defined by Albert Lord), the *lokhos*, with its own traditional language, sub-themes, conventions, and poetics.[6] As we will see below, *polemos* (what we frequently refer to as 'conventional battle') is also a theme, and the two are not entirely antithetical to one another. The best heroes star in both kinds of warfare. Some overlap of diction is therefore inevitable, but we will argue that *polemos* and *lokhos* each represent a distinct narrative theme that is recognizably different and compositionally independent from the other. The mechanics of the transition from one theme to the other in this very *polemos*-centered epic are explored below.

Polemos and *Lokhos*

Ambush warfare and the night raid in the epic tradition are linked by their use of cunning or trickery (*mētis*) and endurance of prolonged hardship, as opposed to the outright brute force (*biē*) and face-to-face fighting of the battlefield. As Anthony Edwards notes in his overview of the subject: "The λόχος, or ambush, is a stratagem employing a small number of picked men and relying upon planning and dissimulation rather than speed and force."[7] We propose to treat the reconnaissance mission, the night raid, and the ambush, all encompassed by the Doloneia, as partaking of this larger theme. Many of the best known night episodes in the epic tradition, such as the stealing of the Palladion, are best understood within the poetics of ambush, which,

---

[5]   See e.g. Buchan 2004: "the actions of the Doloneia itself are quintessentially unheroic and therefore not to be publically articulated. There is nothing heroic about the deliberate lying to Dolon to gain information or about the manner in which Diomedes enjoys the killing of the unarmed, sleeping Thracians" (119–120).

[6]   See Lord 1960/2000:68–98.

[7]   Edwards 1985:18. See the commentary on 10.316 for Dolon's epithet ποδώκης 'swift-footed' as perhaps an important quality for spying missions; Dolon's swiftness is overcome, however, by Odysseus' strategy when Odysseus and Diomedes ambush him.

as we have noted, encompasses several different forms of irregular or guerilla warfare. Likewise, most of the attested ambushes in the epic tradition occur at night. We discuss below how such episodes are linked thematically within the system of Homeric oral traditional poetry so that any one can easily suggest, and modulate into, another.

Anthony Edwards has treated most comprehensively the theme of the ambush in the *Iliad* and the *Odyssey*. In his 1985 study of the character of Achilles in the *Odyssey*, Edwards explores the character of Odysseus as a type associated with ambush warfare, in contrast to Achilles, who exemplifies, in his argument, the invincible spearman in conventional battle.[8] In the course of this study, Edwards demonstrates that ambush warfare is not "unheroic" in any sense of that word, though he argues that the *Iliad* and *Odyssey* do conceive of the ambush within different ethical frameworks. A key passage is *Iliad* 1.225–228, in which Achilles attacks Agamemnon for his lack of courage, noting that he has never once had the endurance (τέτληκας) to go on ambush missions with the "best of the Achaeans":

> οἰνοβαρές, κυνὸς ὄμματ' ἔχων, κραδίην δ' ἐλάφοιο,
> οὔτέ ποτ' ἐς πόλεμον ἅμα λαῷ θωρηχθῆναι
> οὔτε λόχον δ' ἰέναι σὺν ἀριστήεσσιν Ἀχαιῶν
> τέτληκας θυμῷ· τὸ δέ τοι κὴρ εἴδεται εἶναι.

> *Iliad* 1.225–228

> You drunkard, with a dog's eyes and a deer's heart,
> whenever it comes to arming yourself for war with the rest
> of the warriors
> or going on an ambush with the best of the Achaeans,
> you don't have the heart for it. That looks like death to you.

Edwards uses this brief passage to explore a number of oppositions, which he goes on to treat in detail. These oppositions include:

> *Polemos* 'conventional battle' and *lokhos* 'ambush'
> *Biē* 'force' and *mētis* 'cunning'
> Achilles and Odysseus
> *Iliad* and *Odyssey*

---

[8] Edwards notes that Achilles' chief epithets have to do with swiftness, signifying "the irresistible onset and inescapable pursuit of the ἄριστος Ἀχαιῶν," but also the swiftness of his impending death (see Edwards 1985:16). Whereas the Achilles-type hero is ὠκύμωρος 'swift to die', the cunning of the ambush-type hero allows him to escape death at various points.

Edwards makes the case that the *Odyssey* is unique in its privileging of ambush warfare over the traditional *polemos* and that the poem consistently associates this type of warfare with the traditional character of Odysseus. In the *Iliad*, *polemos* and *lokhos* are frequently cited as alternative forms of warfare. Edwards argues that the *lokhos* is a valid form of warfare in the *Iliad*, but it is often characterized as the resort of the weak against a *promakhos anēr*.

But we cannot take this schema too far. Even in the *Iliad* Achilles can be the hero of ambush. In *Iliad* 21, we learn that Achilles captured the Trojan Lykaon at night, in what is presumably a night raid with unmistakable suggestions of ambush:

> ἔνθ' υἷι Πριάμοιο συνήντετο Δαρδανίδαο
> ἐκ ποταμοῦ φεύγοντι Λυκάονι, τόν ῥά ποτ' αὐτὸς
> ἦγε λαβὼν ἐκ πατρὸς ἀλωῆς οὐκ ἐθέλοντα
> ἐννύχιος προμολών· ὃ δ' ἐρινεὸν ὀξέϊ χαλκῷ
> τάμνε νέους ὄρπηκας, ἵν' ἅρματος ἄντυγες εἶεν·
> τῷ δ' ἄρ' ἀνώϊστον κακὸν ἤλυθε δῖος Ἀχιλλεύς.
>
> *Iliad* 21.34–39

> There Achilles encountered the son of Dardanian Priam,
> Lykaon, as he was fleeing out of the river, whom once he
>   himself
> had led away after he captured him, unwilling as he was,
>   from his father's orchard,
> attacking him at night. Lykaon was cutting a wild fig tree
>   with sharp bronze,
> cutting new branches to be rails of a chariot.
> For him, an unexpected evil came, radiant Achilles.

Whatever distinctions may exist between the *Iliad* and the *Odyssey*, an exclusive denigration or privileging of ambush warfare is not among them. The theme of ambush, like its heroes, is much more complex and adaptable than that.

Diomedes in the *polemos* and in the *lokhos*

Like Achilles, Diomedes is a versatile hero who plays a starring role in both the *lokhos* and the *polemos*. Because Diomedes is the leader of the night raid in *Iliad* 10, it is fitting to explore his character in some depth. An Iliadic hero of the first rank, he is first mentioned in the Catalogue of Ships as the bringer of eighty ships, and like Menelaos he is known for his battle cry (*Iliad* 2.563; see our commentary on 10.283 for more on this epithet). Until he is injured, Diomedes is the best offensive warrior of the Achaeans during Achilles' absence.[9] In *Iliad* 4, Agamemnon rebukes Diomedes, asserting that he does not measure up to his father Tydeus, who was one of the Seven Against Thebes and who died in that unsuccessful assault. Diomedes holds his tongue, but Sthenelos counters the rebuke by citing their role in the successful expedition of the Epigonoi against Thebes (*Iliad* 4.404–410). Diomedes' take on the exchange reveals much about his character:

> τὸν δ' ἄρ' ὑπόδρα ἰδὼν προσέφη κρατερὸς Διομήδης·
> τέττα, σιωπῇ ἧσο, ἐμῷ δ' ἐπιπείθεο μύθῳ·
> οὐ γὰρ ἐγὼ νεμεσῶ Ἀγαμέμνονι ποιμένι λαῶν
> ὀτρύνοντι μάχεσθαι ἐϋκνήμιδας Ἀχαιούς·
> 415 τούτῳ μὲν γὰρ κῦδος ἅμ' ἕψεται εἴ κεν Ἀχαιοὶ
> Τρῶας δῃώσωσιν ἕλωσί τε Ἴλιον ἱρήν,
> τούτῳ δ' αὖ μέγα πένθος Ἀχαιῶν δῃωθέντων.
> ἀλλ' ἄγε δὴ καὶ νῶϊ μεδώμεθα θούριδος ἀλκῆς.
> 420 ἦ ῥα καὶ ἐξ ὀχέων σὺν τεύχεσιν ἆλτο χαμᾶζε·
> δεινὸν δ' ἔβραχε χαλκὸς ἐπὶ στήθεσσιν ἄνακτος
> ὀρνυμένου· ὑπό κεν ταλασίφρονά περ δέος εἷλεν.

Iliad 4.411–421

Then powerful Diomedes gave him a fierce look and
    addressed him:
"Keep quiet and be persuaded to obey my words.
For I do not feel indignation toward Agamemnon who shep-
    herds the warriors
for urging on the well-greaved Achaeans to fight.
415 Radiant glory will accompany this man if the Achaeans
cut down the Trojans and take holy Ilion,
and he will have great sorrow if the Achaeans are cut down.
But come, let's remember our fury and battle resolve."
He spoke and leapt to the ground from his chariot together
    with his armor.

[9] See Benardete 1968 for his argument that Diomedes' *aristeia* is definitive for the overall plot and themes of the *Iliad*, because it is during his *aristeia* that both *kleos* and mortality come into focus and become the compelling forces of the war. Higbie 1995:87–101 uses Diomedes as a standard for her investigation into names and naming type-scenes and notes that he "may appear in the greatest number of long battle scenes of anyone in the *Iliad*" (92). Schnapp-Gourbeillon 1981:95–131 examines the character of Diomedes both in his *aristeia* in *Iliad* 5 and in *Iliad* 10.

420 And the bronze on his chest clanged so terribly as the lord
      Diomedes
    rose up, fear would have taken hold of even a man with an
      especially enduring heart.

This scene is our first extended presentation of Diomedes in the *Iliad*.
We see him eager to distinguish himself in the front line of battle, and
he is depicted as a terrifying warrior in full battle gear.

But it is in *Iliad* 5 that Diomedes makes his mark, during his famous
aristeia, in the course of which he challenges Apollo himself and wounds
Aphrodite and Ares:

Αἰνείᾳ δ' ἐπόρουσε βοὴν ἀγαθὸς Διομήδης,
γιγνώσκων ὅ οἱ αὐτὸς ὑπείρεχε χεῖρας Ἀπόλλων·
ἀλλ' ὅ γ' ἄρ' οὐδὲ θεὸν μέγαν ἅζετο, ἵετο δ' αἰεὶ
435 Αἰνείαν κτεῖναι καὶ ἀπὸ κλυτὰ τεύχεα δῦσαι.
τρὶς μὲν ἔπειτ' ἐπόρουσε κατακτάμεναι μενεαίνων,
τρὶς δέ οἱ ἐστυφέλιξε φαεινὴν ἀσπίδ' Ἀπόλλων·
ἀλλ' ὅτε δὴ τὸ τέταρτον ἐπέσσυτο δαίμονι ἶσος,[10]
δεινὰ δ' ὁμοκλήσας προσέφη ἑκάεργος Ἀπόλλων·
440 φράζεο Τυδεΐδη καὶ χάζεο, μηδὲ θεοῖσιν
ἶσ' ἔθελε φρονέειν, ἐπεὶ οὔ ποτε φῦλον ὁμοῖον
ἀθανάτων τε θεῶν χαμαὶ ἐρχομένων τ' ἀνθρώπων.

Iliad 5.432–442

Diomedes well-known for his battle-cry sprang upon
      Aeneas,
    though he knew that Apollo himself held him in his arms.
    But he had no holy fear of the great god, but he kept going
435 for Aeneas, trying to kill him and strip him of his famous
      armor.
    Three times he sprang upon him, raging to kill him,
    and three times Apollo struck hard his shining shield.
    But when he rushed at him like a divine force for a fourth
      time,
    calling on him in terrifying voice Apollo who works from
      afar addressed him:

---

[10] See Nagy 1979:143–144 on what it means to be δαίμονι ἶσος in the *Iliad* and how the
phrase situates Diomedes here as a ritual antagonist to Apollo, and therefore also like
Achilles.

440 "Take thought, son of Tydeus, and withdraw, and with the
gods
don't wish to think on equal terms, since not ever can our
kinds be the same,
the immortal gods and the people who walk on earth."

The language here of three charges followed by a potential fourth is similar to that used for Patroklos during his *aristeia* (compare *Iliad* 16.702–711 and 16.784–793), where Apollo, unseen, does indeed strike the first blow in a series that will result in Patroklos' death. The prolonged and supernatural nature of Diomedes' *aristeia* marks him as one of the foremost warriors in the *polemos*. The way that Diomedes is introduced at the start of his *aristeia* likewise characterizes him as a *promakhos anēr*:

ἔνθ' αὖ Τυδεΐδῃ Διομήδεϊ Παλλὰς Ἀθήνη
δῶκε μένος καὶ θάρσος, ἵν' ἔκδηλος μετὰ πᾶσιν
Ἀργείοισι γένοιτο ἰδὲ κλέος ἐσθλὸν ἄροιτο·
δαῖέ οἱ ἐκ κόρυθός τε καὶ ἀσπίδος ἀκάματον πῦρ
5   ἀστέρ' ὀπωρινῷ ἐναλίγκιον, ὅς τε μάλιστα
λαμπρὸν παμφαίνῃσι λελουμένος ὠκεανοῖο·
τοῖόν οἱ πῦρ δαῖεν ἀπὸ κρατός τε καὶ ὤμων,
ὦρσε δέ μιν κατὰ μέσσον ὅθι πλεῖστοι κλονέοντο.

Iliad 5.1–8

But now to Diomedes, son of Tydeus, Pallas Athena
gave both power and boldness, so that standing out among
all
the Argives he would win true fame.
From his helmet and shield she ignited an untiring fire,
5   like an autumn star that shines most of all,
shines brightly having just bathed in the Okeanos.
That was how she ignited the fire from his head and
shoulders,
and she stirred him toward the middle, where most of the
men were rushing to battle.

Just as Diomedes is connected to Patroklos by way of traditional language in the previous passage, he is here similarly connected to Achilles, who is compared to a similar star while on the battlefield (*Iliad* 22.26–32).

There is another parallel to Achilles in this passage. Diomedes does not have an extended arming scene before his *aristeia* in our *Iliad*. With the exception of the description of the dressing of Diomedes and Odysseus for the night raid in *Iliad* 10, there are only four of these extended arming scenes for heroes in the *Iliad*: those of Paris (3.328–338), Agamemnon (11.15–55), Patroklos (16.130–154), and Achilles (19.364–424). Yet this description, with its emphasis on Diomedes' helmet and shield, functions not unlike an arming scene, and the imagery of fire and star parallel the arming scene of Achilles:

αὐτὰρ ἔπειτα σάκος μέγα τε στιβαρόν τε
εἵλετο, τοῦ δ᾽ ἀπάνευθε σέλας γένετ᾽ ἠΰτε μήνης.
ὡς δ᾽ ὅτ᾽ ἂν ἐκ πόντοιο σέλας ναύτῃσι φανήῃ
καιομένοιο πυρός, τό τε καίεται ὑψόθ᾽ ὄρεσφι
σταθμῷ ἐν οἰοπόλῳ· τοὺς δ᾽ οὐκ ἐθέλοντας ἄελλαι
πόντον ἐπ᾽ ἰχθυόεντα φίλων ἀπάνευθε φέρουσιν·
ὣς ἀπ᾽ Ἀχιλλῆος σάκεος σέλας αἰθέρ᾽ ἵκανε.

Iliad 19.373–379

And then the shield, great and massive,
Achilles took, and from it there was a far-reaching gleam, as
    from the moon.
As when out in the middle of the sea a gleam appears to
    sailors
from a burning fire, and it burns high in the mountains
at a shepherds' station, and the sailors, against their will, by
    gusts of winds
are carried over the sea swarming with fish, far away from
    their loved ones,
so did the gleam from the shield of Achilles reach all the
    way up to the aether.

Fire and star images seem to be imagery of salvation, in addition to making the hero conspicuous among other heroes for his *aristeia*.[11] Diomedes becomes a savior for the Greeks in Achilles' absence, but his star quickly burns out; when Achilles reenters battle in *Iliad* 19, the Greeks are once again in desperate need of him.

Diomedes plays a starring role in one other major episode of the *Iliad*, also a time of extreme need due to Achilles' refusal to reenter

---

[11] See Nagy 1979:338–341.

battle, and that is of course *Iliad* 10, the Doloneia.[12] Here he is paired with Odysseus in a night ambush, a kind of warfare that requires a different set of skills than the conventional *polemos*. As noted above, the Doloneia has long troubled scholars, who find the actions of Odysseus and Diomedes in that night raid to be un-Homeric and even un-heroic. But if we look at the Greek epic tradition as a whole, taking into account what we know of the Epic Cycle, we find that Diomedes traditionally excelled at the kind of ambush warfare depicted in *Iliad* 10.

In the *Cypria*, Diomedes and Odysseus drown Palamedes, ambushing him while he is fishing:

Παλαμήδην δὲ ἀποπνιγῆναι προελθόντα ἐπὶ ἰχθύων θήραν, Διομήδην δὲ τὸν ἀποκτείναντα εἶναι καὶ ᾽Οδυσσέα ἐπιλεξάμενος ἐν ἔπεσιν οἶδα τοῖς Κυπρίοις.

Cypria testimonium 30 [Bernabé] = Pausanias 10.31.2

Palamedes was drowned when he went out to catch fish. Diomedes was the killer and also Odysseus, as I know from reading the epic poem the *Cypria*.

Malcom Davies is scornful of such a portrayal of these heroes. "The collaboration of Odysseus and Diomedes is Iliadic, but further from Homeric values one could hardly go than this tale of cowardly and treacherous murder [...] of a fellow Greek."[13] We need not focus here on the question of whether or not the Doloneia and the actions attributed to Diomedes in the Epic Cycle are "Homeric," a term which is loaded with multiple assumptions about the epics and their composition. For the moment it is enough to recognize that these actions do seem to be an important part of the epic tradition. Diomedes is a stellar fighter in the *polemos*, but he is equally good at the *lokhos*.

The sack of Troy is itself the ultimate night ambush, and Diomedes is involved in several nighttime escapades leading up to and during the sack of Troy. In testimonium 34 [Bernabé] of the *Cypria*, a lesser-known version of Polyxena's story has her being wounded by Odysseus and Diomedes during the sack:

ὑπὸ Νεοπτολέμου φασὶν αὐτὴν (sc. Πολυξένην) σφαγιασθῆναι Εὐριπίδης καὶ Ἴβυκος. ὁ δὲ τὰ Κυπριακὰ ποιήσας φησίν

---

[12] See Rabel 1991 and the general commentary on *Iliad* 10.85.
[13] Davies 1989:48.

ὑπὸ Ὀδυσσέως καὶ Διομήδους ἐν τῆι τῆς πόλεως ἁλώσει τραυματισθεῖσαν ἀπολέσθαι.

Scholia to Euripides Hecuba 41

Euripides and Ibycus say that Polyxena's throat was cut by Neoptolemos. But the composer of the *Cypria* says that she died after being wounded by Odysseus and Diomedes in the capture of the city.

In the epic now known as the *Little Iliad,* according to the summary of it by Proklos, Odysseus is instrumental in the ambush and capture of Helenos, the prophetic son of Priam, and it is Diomedes, according to Proklos, who brings back Philoctetes (whose presence was required, according to the prophecy of Helenos, for the successful capture of Troy) from Lemnos:[14]

μετὰ ταῦτα Ὀδυσσεὺς λοχήσας Ἕλενον λαμβάνει, καὶ χρήσαντος περὶ τῆς ἁλώσεως τούτου Διομήδης ἐκ Λήμνου Φιλοκτήτην ἀνάγει.

After this Odysseus captures Helenos in an ambush, and as a result of Helenos' prophecy about the city's conquest Diomedes brings Philoctetes back from Lemnos.

Also narrated in the *Little Iliad,* according to Proklos, was the theft of the Palladion, which survives in several variant versions in which Diomedes or Odysseus or both try to get sole possession of it, each betraying the other.[15] The Palladion is of course yet another item that had been foretold to be required for the successful capture of Troy.

In all of these episodes Diomedes is linked, as he is in the Doloneia, with Odysseus, the hero most closely identified with ambush warfare. Odysseus is the hero who blinds the Cyclops by ambush, and, as Edwards has shown, his attack on the suitors is structured like an ambush is many ways. We have noted as well that the sack of Troy is an ambush, of which Odysseus is the mastermind. Indeed, the *mētis* that governs ambush warfare is Odysseus' signature trait.[16] But it should not be

---

[14] See Davies 1989:63.

[15] Davies 1989: "In other words, like the detail of Palamedes' death in the Cypria, another unHomeric story of cowardice, treachery and deceit" (67).

[16] On Odysseus' *mētis,* see Detienne and Vernant 1974/1978:18–19, Haft 1990, and the commentary below. On the *mētis*-related epithets of Kronos and Zeus, both of whom use an ambush style of attack to overthrow their fathers, see further below. On *mētis* in general, see especially Detienne and Vernant 1974/1978: "it implies a complex but

forgotten that Odysseus has his fair share of conventional fighting. The *Odyssey* ends with Odysseus about to engage the families of the suitors in battle, and Laertes rejoicing that he will have a contest for *aretē* with his son and grandson. When Demodokos sings about the fall of Troy in *Odyssey* 8, Odysseus is the hero "raging like Ares" (8.518) through the streets of Troy. In *Iliad* 4.354–355, Odysseus angrily responds to the rebuke of Agamemnon by asserting that he "mixes with the champions of the Trojans" (προμάχοισι μιγέντα / Τρώων).[17] In *Iliad* 11, Odysseus and Diomedes together stave off a rout of the Greek forces before they both are wounded.[18]

Homeric heroes and the *lokhos*

Similarly, Achilles should not be pigeonholed as solely the hero of *biē*, for he, too, is an ambusher. In *Iliad* 9, Achilles points out how much effort he has devoted to fighting the war, describing it this way:

> ὡς δ' ὄρνις ἀπτῆσι νεοσσοῖσι προφέρῃσι
> μάστακ' ἐπεί κε λάβῃσι, κακῶς δ' ἄρα οἱ πέλει αὐτῇ,
> ὣς καὶ ἐγὼ πολλὰς μὲν ἀΰπνους νύκτας ἴαυον,
> ἤματα δ' αἱματόεντα διέπρησσον πολεμίζων
> ἀνδράσι μαρνάμενος ὀάρων ἕνεκα σφετεράων.
>
> *Iliad* 9.323–327

> Like a bird that brings food to her fledgling young
> in her bill, whenever she finds any, even if she herself fares
>   poorly,
> so I passed many sleepless nights,
> and spent many bloody days in battle,
> contending with men for the sake of their wives.

The days spent in bloody battle are an obvious part of Achilles' contribution to the war effort, but just how has Achilles spent those sleepless nights? The scholia in the Townley manuscript (*ad* 21.37) suggest that

---

very coherent body of mental attitudes and intellectual behaviour which combine flair, wisdom, forethought, subtlety of mind, deception, resourcefulness, vigilance, opportunism, various skills, and experience acquired over the years. It is applied to situations which are transient, shifting, disconcerting, and ambiguous, situations which do not lend themselves to precise measurement, exact calculation, or rigorous logic" (1991:3–4).

[17] On this passage see Cook 2009a:145.

[18] For Odysseus as a spearman, see also Edwards 1985:39n42 with additional citations *ad loc.*

it is in ambush: ἐννύχιος: εἶπε γὰρ "πολλὰς μὲν ἀΰπνους νύκτας ἴαυον" ("At night: For he said 'I passed many sleepless nights"). The Trojan youth Lykaon was one of the unfortunate warriors that Achilles came upon *ennukhios* 'at night' (*Iliad* 21.37) in ambush. It is in fact a comment on the word *ennukhios* in the passage about Lykaon at *Iliad* 21.37 that leads the scholiast to quote the passage in *Iliad* 9.[19]

Another youth ambushed by Achilles according to the tradition is Troilos.[20] The ambush and death of Troilos was narrated in the *Cypria*, according to the summary of Proklos, and appears frequently in vase paintings. A tradition that the death of Troilos was required for the capture of Troy seems to be as early as the Archaic period.[21] Of the four scenes in the story, perhaps the most commonly depicted is Achilles crouching behind a fountain house as Polyxena, Troilos' sister, draws water from the fountain (see Plate 1).[22] In the surviving examples, next to Achilles there is usually a tree, which, along with his crouching position, very likely serves to signify that Achilles is hiding in ambush. Unlike the capture of Lykaon, however, this ambush does not seem to have been conceived of by ancient artists as occurring at night. Achilles is generally depicted with his war helmet on, carrying his shield and long spear. He does not have any special clothing or gear. Instead, his posture and position make clear what kind of warfare is being undertaken.[23] Odysseus and Diomedes, by contrast, are depicted without helmets during the theft of the Palladion and in Doloneia scenes, or, in the case of later South Italian vases, with traveling caps and clothes.[24] On an Archaic black-figure vase in the Getty Museum that shows Diomedes killing Rhesos (Plate 2), a contrast is made between the helmet and shields that appear suspended (as though hung up on the

---

[19] On the scholion quoted here see Gantz 1993:603.

[20] See Apollodorus *The Library Epitome* 3.32 with additional citations in the edition of Frazer (1921) *ad loc.*

[21] On the Troilos episode in literature and art, see especially the comprehensive treatment and bibliography in Kossatz-Deissmann 1981, as well as d'Agostino 1987, Robertson 1990, and Scaife 1995.

[22] The other three episodes are the fleeing of Troilos (usually on horseback) and Polyxena (on foot), the killing of Troilos, and the battle over his corpse.

[23] The iconography of this scene may have been influenced by or have developed in conjunction with another style of ambush warfare that occurs in daytime battle. Further below, we discuss the way that archers fight in battle; they crouch behind the shields of their comrades or other objects. In vase painting, archers are depicted in very much the same position as Achilles is in the Troilos scenes.

[24] See Lissarrague 1980, Williams 1986, and Boardman and Vafopoulou-Richardson 1986. For more on the Doloneia scenes on Greek vases, see "Tradition and Reception" below.

wall) and the unarmed men being killed by the likewise unhelmeted Diomedes.[25]

The Achilles of our *Iliad* is clearly a *promakhos anēr*, but the epic tradition as a whole knew Achilles as an ambusher. The scholion in the Venetus A manuscript at *Iliad* 22.188 records that even such a seemingly canonical confrontation as that between Hektor and Achilles at the climax of the *Iliad* could be narrated as an ambush:

> σημειῶδες ὅτι μόνος Ὅμηρός φησι μονομαχῆσαι τὸν Ἕκτορα,
> οἱ δὲ λοιποὶ πάντες ἐνεδρευθῆναι ὑπὸ Ἀχιλλέως.

It is significant that only Homer says that he fought Hektor in man-to-man combat. All the rest say that he was ambushed by Achilles.

It is far from clear what the scholiast means by "the rest" (οἱ δὲ λοιποὶ) here—we were not able to find a similar comment anywhere else in the scholia—but the implications of the comment are easily grasped: in some versions, Achilles took Hektor down by ambush.

It becomes less surprising that the best warriors in conventional battle are also frequently seen as the best in ambush warfare when we consider that both the *Iliad* and the *Odyssey* associate ambush warfare with exceptional courage and endurance. In *Iliad* 13, Meriones makes his claim to be one who fights "among the first" (13.270), which conventionally signifies the bravery of a warrior in conventional battle. In response, Idomeneus praises Meriones for his courage and abilities as a warrior who is excellent at ambush:

> οὐδὲ γὰρ οὐδ' ἐμέ φημι λελασμένον ἔμμεναι ἀλκῆς,
> 270 ἀλλὰ μετὰ πρώτοισι μάχην ἀνὰ κυδιάνειραν
> ἵσταμαι, ὁππότε νεῖκος ὀρώρηται πολέμοιο.
> ἄλλον πού τινα μᾶλλον Ἀχαιῶν χαλκοχιτώνων
> λήθω μαρνάμενος, σὲ δὲ ἴδμεναι αὐτὸν ὀΐω.
> τὸν δ' αὖτ' Ἰδομενεὺς Κρητῶν ἀγὸς ἀντίον ηὔδα·
> 275 οἶδ' ἀρετὴν οἷός ἐσσι· τί σε χρὴ ταῦτα λέγεσθαι;
> εἰ γὰρ νῦν παρὰ νηυσὶ λεγοίμεθα πάντες ἄριστοι
> ἐς λόχον, ἔνθα μάλιστ' ἀρετὴ διαείδεται ἀνδρῶν,
> ἔνθ' ὅ τε δειλὸς ἀνὴρ ὅς τ' ἄλκιμος ἐξεφαάνθη·
> τοῦ μὲν γάρ τε κακοῦ τρέπεται χρὼς ἄλλυδις ἄλλῃ,
> 280 οὐδέ οἱ ἀτρέμας ἧσθαι ἐρητύετ' ἐν φρεσὶ θυμός,
> ἀλλὰ μετοκλάζει καὶ ἐπ' ἀμφοτέρους πόδας ἵζει,

---

[25] Getty Museum 96.A.E.1 (550–540 BCE).

ἐν δέ τέ οἱ κραδίη μεγάλα στέρνοισι πατάσσει
κῆρας ὀϊομένῳ, πάταγος δέ τε γίγνετ' ὀδόντων·
τοῦ δ' ἀγαθοῦ οὔτ' ἄρ τρέπεται χρὼς οὔτέ τι λίην
285 ταρβεῖ, ἐπειδὰν πρῶτον ἐσίζηται λόχον ἀνδρῶν,
ἀρᾶται δὲ τάχιστα μιγήμεναι ἐν δαῒ λυγρῇ·
οὐδέ κεν ἔνθα τεόν γε μένος καὶ χεῖρας ὄνοιτο.

Iliad 13.269–287

"And I claim that I have not at all forgotten my battle
resolve,
270 but rather in the front lines throughout the battle that
confers radiant glory
I stand my ground, whenever the strife of war has arisen.
Some other of the bronze-wearing Achaeans may have
overlooked my fighting, but I think that you yourself know it."
Then Idomeneus the leader of the Cretans spoke back to him:
275 "I know your merit, what sort of man you are—why do you
need to say these things?
For if now beside the ships all of the best men [*aristos*] were
being chosen
for an ambush—the place where the merit of men most
shines through,
where the coward and the resolute man are revealed
(for the skin of the inferior man turns a different color at
every turn
280 and he can't restrain the spirit in his body and keep from
trembling
but he keeps shifting his weight and he sits on both feet
and the heart in his chest beats loudly
as he thinks about doom, and his teeth chatter,
whereas the skin of a brave man does not change nor is he
at all
285 frightened, when he first sits in an ambush of men,
but he prays to mix in mournful combat as soon as
possible)—
there one could not reproach your mighty hands."

In this exchange, there is no opposition or contradiction between
Meriones' claim and Idomeneus' praise: instead, *polemos* and *lokhos* are
complementary, and the two characterizations show that Meriones is a
complete warrior who excels at both. In addition, here we see ambush

described as "the place where the merit of men most shines through, where the coward and the resolute man are revealed" (*Iliad* 13.277–278). We can see that it involves crouching and staying still for long periods of time, time when lesser men are overcome by their fears. Ambush requires a particular kind of courage, different from that required to fight in front in conventional battle, and one that reveals *aretē* most of all. Thus, rather than being "lesser" or based in "cowardice" as some modern commentators would have it, Idomeneus' words portray ambush as type of warfare only for the *anēr alkimos* (*Iliad* 13.278).

In the *Odyssey*, ambush is described in similar terms in several key places. In *Odyssey* 4, Menelaos praises Odysseus' bravery and endurance inside the wooden horse, which is termed a *lokhos*:[26] οἷον καὶ τόδ᾽ ἔρεξε καὶ ἔτλη καρτερὸς ἀνὴρ/ἵππῳ ἔνι ξεστῷ ("What a thing he accomplished and endured, the powerful man, inside the wooden horse," *Odyssey* 4.271–272). Menelaos goes on to tell how Odysseus restrained the men who wanted to respond to Helen's voice as she mimicked their wives, thereby saving all the Achaeans. In *Odyssey* 11, Odysseus praises Achilles' son Neoptolemos' exploits in battle and his demeanor during this same ambush, making Achilles proud:[27]

> ‘αὐτὰρ ὅτ᾽ εἰς ἵππον κατεβαίνομεν, ὃν κάμ᾽ Ἐπειός,
> Ἀργείων οἱ ἄριστοι, ἐμοὶ δ᾽ ἐπὶ πάντ᾽ ἐτέταλτο,
> 525 ἠμὲν ἀνακλῖναι πυκινὸν λόχον ἠδ᾽ ἐπιθεῖναι,
> ἔνθ᾽ ἄλλοι Δαναῶν ἡγήτορες ἠδὲ μέδοντες
> δάκρυά τ᾽ ὠμόργνυντο, τρέμον θ᾽ ὑπὸ γυῖα ἑκάστου·
> κεῖνον δ᾽ οὔ ποτε πάμπαν ἐγὼν ἴδον ὀφθαλμοῖσιν
> οὔτ᾽ ὠχρήσαντα χρόα κάλλιμον οὔτε παρειῶν
> 530 δάκρυ᾽ ὀμορξάμενον· ὁ δέ με μάλα πόλλ᾽ ἱκέτευεν
> ἱππόθεν ἐξέμεναι, ξίφεος δ᾽ ἐπεμαίετο κώπην
> καὶ δόρυ χαλκοβαρές, κακὰ δὲ Τρώεσσι μενοίνα.
> [...]
> 538 ὣς ἐφάμην, ψυχὴ δὲ ποδώκεος Αἰακίδαο
> φοίτα μακρὰ βιβᾶσα κατ᾽ ἀσφοδελὸν λειμῶνα,
> γηθοσύνη, ὅ οἱ υἱὸν ἔφην ἀριδείκετον εἶναι.

Odyssey 11.523–532, 538–540

---

[26] The wooden horse is called a *lokhos* at *Odyssey* 4.277, 8.515, 11.525.

[27] Verse 11.525 is bracketed by some scholars because the scholia say that Aristarchus did not know it. Many scholars, however, have defended the verse, which is attested in all the manuscripts. The language is similar to that of *Iliad* 5.751. See Edwards 1985:31n30.

Then when we went down into the horse that Epeios toiled
    to make
with the best [*aristos*] of the Argives, and it was laid entirely
    upon me
525   to open the door to our close-packed [*pukinos*] ambush or
    close it,
there other rulers and leaders of the Danaans
wiped away tears and their limbs trembled underneath
    them.
I never the whole time saw with my eyes
his fair skin turn pale or him from his cheeks
530   wiping tears. Instead he especially begged me
to let him go out of the horse, and he kept feeling for the
    handle of his sword
and his spear heavy with bronze, and plotted evil for the
    Trojans.
[...]
538   So I spoke, and the soul of the swift-footed Achilles
went, taking long strides through the meadow of asphodel,
rejoicing, because I had said that his son had particularly
    distinguished himself.

In this passage, as in other descriptions of ambush, we find that it
was the "best" men who were chosen for the ambush of Troy.[28] Still,
even among these best men there exists a great deal of fear during the
"waiting period" before the surprise attack of an ambush. Neoptolemos
distinguishes himself by not showing any of the physical manifestations of fear, just as Meriones is credited with doing in *Iliad* 13.

The purpose of this discussion so far has been simply to explore
the complexity of the Greek warrior hero and to suggest that modern
notions of "heroic" behavior have colored our approaches to Homeric
epic. The *lokhos* warfare of *Iliad* 10 does not seem so anomalous when we
consider the Archaic epic tradition as a whole and what both the *Iliad*
and the *Odyssey* have to say about ambush. By approaching Homeric
poetry as a system, of which the *Iliad* and *Odyssey* happen to be the only
two surviving examples, we can look for traditional narrative patterns
that explain what may seem unusual from a modern literary perspective. It is possible to reconstruct a great deal of the system we have lost

[28] See also *Iliad* 1.227, 6.188, 13.276; *Odyssey* 4.278, 8.512, 14.218, 15.28. On the motif of
selecting picked men, cf. Edwards 1985:21 and 22 and see further below in "Ambush
as a Narrative Pattern."

by carefully studying allusions to and summaries and quotations of the lost epics of the Epic Cycle. This more inclusive approach to Homeric poetry is what we adopt in this commentary, in which we hope to show that the figures of Diomedes and Odysseus behave in an entirely traditional manner in *Iliad* 10. If even Achilles can be a master of the *lokhos*, then it should not surprise us that a hero as versatile as Diomedes in the literary and mythological tradition has done his fair share of both kinds of fighting. And while the affinities between *Iliad* 10, the *Odyssey*, and even the Epic Cycle have been noticed before, it is our hope that we can move past using those affinities to make claims about the book's late or non-Homeric authorship, and instead focus on how the poetics of the book add to our understanding of the poetics of the *Iliad* and the nature of the Homeric hero.

The Theme of Ambush

Let us turn now more directly to *Iliad* 10. Anthony Edwards, whose 1985 work treats the topic of ambush most directly, does not discuss this book except by a passing reference, where he notes that the narrative of this night raid is structured as an ambush.[29] Indeed, if we were to try to place this book of the *Iliad* within the oppositions that Edwards traces, we would have to put it squarely on the side of the *lokhos/mētis/* Odysseus/*Odyssey*. Edwards therefore, perhaps strategically, avoids any extensive discussion of *Iliad* 10 in this study, since his interest is in showing how the *Iliad* and the *Odyssey* treat the theme of the ambush differently and, more specifically, have a different ethical view of this kind of warfare. And yet, *Iliad* 10 as an example of a glorious Iliadic ambush does not completely discredit Edwards's arguments, with some modifications. The different treatments of ambush are distinctions not between the *Iliad* and *Odyssey* per se, but between two overarching thematic clusters or megathemes, of which the *Iliad* and the *Odyssey* (in many of its episodes) are each the best (and in fact only) surviving representatives.[30] Either tradition can allude to or make use

---

[29] Edwards 1985:38. Edwards's 1981 doctoral dissertation includes a two-page appendix on *Iliad* 10.

[30] Edwards seems inclined in this direction in the one place that he addresses *Iliad* 10 in his 1985 work, though he does not develop the idea further: "Fenik has shown that at one stage in the development of the *Iliad*, the *Doloneia* ... was in fact an attempt to assassinate Hector as a response to his devastating victory during the preceding day. Following in the wake of the *Presbeia* and Achilles' refusal to return to battle, this *Doloneia* would have been an attempt to achieve by δόλος what otherwise required the βίη of Achilles. Although our *Iliad* may itself exhibit no overt awareness of this tradition ... still the episode preserves an instance of open rivalry between Odysseus

of the narrative patterns of the other, and when one does, the narrative will necessarily take on a distinctly different flavor.[31] In the history of Homeric scholarship *Iliad* 10 has often been asserted to be "Odyssean," and that charge has been used to maintain a variety of theories about the book (including that it is a "late" composition). In the model that we propose, *Iliad* 10 need only be viewed as related to the *Odyssey* in that it shares the theme of ambush and has Odysseus as a central character.[32] In other words, *Iliad* 10 and the *Odyssey* are similar in terms of language because they partake of the same theme, and theme and language are inseparable. Further below, we will also examine how they both partake of themes related to a journey, making the overlap of thematic language and details even greater.

We can start to examine the poetics of the ambush theme as illustrated in one aspect of *Iliad* 10 that has often stood out: the elaborate attention paid to the dressing of each hero, and the unusual clothing that they put on.[33] Two different types of description and characterization comprise the first half of the book. First, Agamemnon, Menelaos, Nestor, Odysseus, and Diomedes are each described as dressing as they set out into the night. Agamemnon and Diomedes each wear a lion skin, Menelaos wears a leopard skin, and Nestor wears a *khiton* and *khlaina*. Each takes a weapon (*egkhos* or *doru*), with the exception

---

and Achilles over the ambush and the spearfight" (39–40). Here he is suggesting that the traditions behind the two characters embody the difference and rivalry between ambush and conventional battlefield warfare. See also Edwards's 1981 dissertation, where he discusses even more directly the *Iliad* and *Odyssey* as co-evolving oral traditions.

[31] Petegorsky 1982:176 makes this point as well: "If an episode or a passage in the *Iliad* strikes us as 'Odyssean' in character, we should take this as an indication not that the passage in question has as its source a passage in the *Odyssey* and is therefore 'late', but rather that at this point in the poem, the poet is, for whatever reason, employing themes that evoke what we recognize as an Odyssean frame as opposed to an Iliadic one."

[32] We may compare Martin's (2000:60–61) similar formulation about the affinities between Nestor's tale of a cattle raid undertaken in his youth in *Iliad* 11 and the *Odyssey*: "It is the occurrence of this theme, and not any alleged 'late' compositional traits, that accounts for the similarity between Nestor's tale and the *Odyssey* at the level of diction. The appearance of a number of words only here in the *Iliad*, but with parallels in the *Odyssey*, does not mean that an 'Odyssey-Poet' composed Nestor's speech." On the cattle raid as an epic theme and its affinities with ambush, see also below.

[33] See e.g. the commentaries of Leaf 1900 and Hainsworth 1993 *ad loc.* Hainsworth comments that "the lion skin of 23 (cf. 177) betrays this Book's taste for exotic detail." Leaf takes the animal skins to be pseudo-archaisms meant to mark them as "hero[es] of the very olden times."

of Odysseus, who grabs only a shield. Second, Nestor and Diomedes are described in the state in which they are found by the others, with the result that each is characterized as a vigilant warrior. The elderly Nestor is found to be sleeping on a soft bed (εὐνῇ ἔνι μαλακῇ), but his battle weapons and gear are directly beside him, ready to be put on at a moment's notice (*Iliad* 10.74–79). Diomedes, on the other hand, "[t]hey found outside of his shelter together with his armor, and around him his companions slept, and they had their shields under their heads. Their spears were planted with the spearheads up, and far and wide the bronze was shining, like the lightning of father Zeus. But the hero slept, and under him was spread the skin of a wild ox, and under his head was spread a shining tapestry" (*Iliad* 10.150–156). Diomedes is so ready for battle that he is not even inside his tent. He and his men are found sleeping outside with their armor, ready for battle.

At almost the midpoint of the book, just as Diomedes and Odysseus head out on their expedition, a lengthy description of the arming of Odysseus and Diomedes takes place:

ὣς εἰπόνθ' ὅπλοισιν ἔνι δεινοῖσιν ἐδύτην.
255 Τυδεΐδη μὲν δῶκε μενεπτόλεμος Θρασυμήδης
φάσγανον ἄμφηκες· τὸ δ' ἐὸν παρὰ νηῒ λέλειπτο·
καὶ σάκος· ἀμφὶ δέ οἱ κυνέην κεφαλῆφιν ἔθηκε
ταυρείην, ἄφαλόν τε καὶ ἄλλοφον, ἥ τε καταῖτυξ
κέκληται, ῥύεται δὲ κάρη θαλερῶν αἰζηῶν.
260 Μηριόνης δ' Ὀδυσῆϊ δίδου βιὸν ἠδὲ φαρέτρην
καὶ ξίφος, ἀμφὶ δέ οἱ κυνέην κεφαλῆφιν ἔθηκε
ῥινοῦ ποιητήν· πολέσιν δ' ἔντοσθεν ἱμᾶσιν
ἐντέτατο στερεῶς· ἔκτοσθε δὲ λευκοὶ ὀδόντες
ἀργιόδοντος ὑὸς θαμέες ἔχον ἔνθα καὶ ἔνθα
265 εὖ καὶ ἐπισταμένως· μέσσῃ δ' ἐνὶ πῖλος ἀρήρει.
τήν ῥά ποτ' ἐξ Ἐλεῶνος Ἀμύντορος Ὀρμενίδαο
ἐξέλετ' Αὐτόλυκος πυκινὸν δόμον ἀντιτορήσας,
Σκάνδειαν δ' ἄρα δῶκε Κυθηρίῳ Ἀμφιδάμαντι·
Ἀμφιδάμας δὲ Μόλῳ δῶκε ξεινήϊον εἶναι,
270 αὐτὰρ ὃ Μηριόνῃ δῶκεν ᾧ παιδὶ φορῆναι·
δὴ τότ' Ὀδυσσῆος πύκασεν κάρη ἀμφιτεθεῖσα.
τὼ δ' ἐπεὶ οὖν ὅπλοισιν ἔνι δεινοῖσιν ἐδύτην,
βάν ῥ' ἴεναι, λιπέτην δὲ κατ' αὐτόθι πάντας ἀρίστους.

Iliad 10.254–273

So the two spoke and they put on the terrible implements of
   war.
255   To the son of Tydeus Thrasymedes who stands his ground in
         battle gave
   a two-edged sword—for he [Diomedes] had left his at the
         ship—
   and a shield. And on his head he placed a leather cap
   of bull's hide, without a plume or a boss, the kind which is
         called
   a skull-cap, and it protects the head of flourishing, vigorous
         young men.
260   Meriones gave to Odysseus a bow and a quiver
   and a sword, and he placed on his head a leather cap
   made of hide. On the inside many leather straps
   were stretched tight, and on the outside white tusks
   from a white-tusked boar were arrayed one after another,
265   well and skillfully. And in the middle there was a layer of felt
         fastened to it.
   This helmet from Amyntor of Eleon, the descendant of
         Ormenos,
   Autolykos took, breaking into his closely fitted [*pukinos*]
         house,
   and he [Autolykos] gave it to Amphidamas of Kythera to
         take to Skandeia.
   Amphidamas gave it to Molos as a guest gift,
270   and he gave it to his son Meriones to carry.
   Then it surrounded and closely covered the head of Odysseus.
   So when the two had put on the terrible implements of war,
   they set out to go, and the two of them left there in that
         place all the best [*aristos*] men.

The armor that they wear is in many ways atypical. Most distinctive is what they wear on their heads. Diomedes and Odysseus wear leather skull-caps (κυνέην ... ταυρείην ... ἥ τε καταῖτυξ κέκληται—the word καταῖτυξ is used only here in extant Greek literature), and the history of Odysseus' headgear is elaborately described: Odysseus' own maternal grandfather Autolykos stole it and gave it away as a gift to Amphidamas, who likewise gave it as a gift to Molos, who then gave it to the Cretan Meriones, who now gives it to Odysseus along with the other weapons Odysseus will carry, a bow and quiver and sword (see the next section for more on the bow and quiver).

Meriones must give Odysseus all of this gear because when Odysseus left his tent, unlike the other heroes who dressed in skins and cloaks and took their weapons, he took only his shield.[34] The history of the helmet as a gift indicates that such an object may have prestige as well as utility.[35] Its prestige reflects on "the best men," who wear such equipment for these dangerous and important missions. That it was originally stolen by the thief extraordinaire Autolykos seems related to the stealth that it affords the wearer, which makes it even more fitting for Odysseus, who is very much like his grandfather, as we know from *Odyssey* 19.395–412.

Diomedes, too, is given a sword as well as a shield by Thrasymedes because he left his own back at the ships (*Iliad* 10.255–257). Thus the leaders of the guard lend their equipment to the leaders of the ambush. These details suggest thematic possibilities: the night meeting itself is hastily arranged, so the leaders who were awoken have dressed both in a hurry and for a meeting, not a mission, while the guards are fully armed for their post.[36] Nighttime activities, as we will explore further below, are associated with confusion and haste in general. Odysseus' story about a night ambush in *Odyssey* 14 includes one ambusher leaving behind his cloak and another dropping his so that he can run faster.[37] These details serve their own particular purpose in Odysseus' telling of the story (see our commentary on *Iliad* 10.53 and 10.149), but they may also signal traditional associations within the theme of ambush.

---

[34] See Haft 1984:295–299 for the resemblances between Meriones and the persona Odysseus creates for himself in the Cretan lies of the *Odyssey*. In addition to the sharing of armor here, she also notes that "both heroes excel in ambush" (298).

[35] Higbie 1995:195–203 discusses the "geneaology of objects," such as this helmet, and also horses and armor, and concludes that "the Homeric world treasured possessions as much for their ancestry as for their intrinsic value" (1995:203). She notes that even though it is here borrowed, the boar's tusk helmet becomes a distinctive attribute of Odysseus in later Greek art (1995:202–203).

[36] Wathelet 1989:219–220 sees a different possible significance to the borrowing of armor. Since Diomedes and Odysseus are wearing the equipment of others, he argues, they are in disguise. Wathelet then connects this disguise to initiation rituals, which he says are also connected to the night. His arguments are an intriguing connection to another aspect of ambush we explore below: its connection especially to young men.

[37] See Muellner 1976:96–97, especially n43, for his arguments on how these stories create cross-references, and how the ambush theme affects the use of εὔχομαι in the *Odyssey* passage. Block 1985:6 also sees this tale as a reworking of the Doloneia. Newton 1998:144–147 sees parallels between this story and another Iliadic episode that starts at night: the test of the army in *Iliad* 2, in which Odysseus throws off his cloaks as he starts to run.

In a well-known 1958 article, James Armstrong argues that formulaic arming scenes are employed at climactic moments in the poem with great effect. He analyzes in detail four major arming scenes of the *Iliad*, namely, those of Paris in *Iliad* 3, Agamemnon in *Iliad* 11, Patroklos in *Iliad* 16, and Achilles in *Iliad* 19, arguing that formulaic language in these passages is manipulated for various poetic purposes, and that each scene resonates with what came before, so that there is a cumulative effect over the course of the poem.[38] Characterization through detail within formulaic themes and language and the resonance that Armstrong identifies, however, need not be literary. Instead, we can understand these scenes, following Albert Lord (1960/2000:89–91), as orally composed variations on the same theme.[39] The structure, as Lord points out, is consistent in all of these examples of the theme. The hero starts by putting on his greaves, then his breastplate, then a sword, a shield, a helmet, and finally a spear or two. But these are elaborated with further details, and this expansion of the theme indicates something about both the warrior who is arming and the moment in the battle for which he is arming. Conversely, Lord notes that the arming of a warrior can and does happen in one line, such as Menelaos at *Iliad* 3.339, showing a compression of the theme.

Similar to the expanded arming scene of Paris and the subsequent, compressed version of Menelaos in *Iliad* 3, we see that after the series of dressing scenes and the arming scene of Diomedes and Odysseus in *Iliad* 10, Dolon has a more compressed version, only three lines long (*Iliad* 10.333–335). He, too, dresses for his mission in attire that seems unusual, but which is appropriate for a nocturnal spying mission. He actually wears his animal pelt, that of a wolf, as he goes, and also has a skin cap, specified as made from the hide of a marten. He takes two weapons with him, a bow and a spear. That all three of these spies take weapons with them reflects, of course, the dangerous nature of their missions, but it also reveals that spying missions often become ambushes, a phenomenon we will address in greater detail below.

In the night raid/ambush tradition, it seems that the dressing and arming of heroes have a poetic purpose similar to the expanded arming

---

[38]   See *Iliad* 3.328–338, 11.15–55, 16.130–154, and 19.364–424. Armstrong's larger point is that this is the work of an orally composing master poet who makes use of the oral traditional system of formulaic language in ways that we might call "literary." Our own analysis of the dressing/arming scenes in *Iliad* 10 develops and understands Armstrong's insights in a different way. On the function and importance of descriptions of armor/arming scenes for the conferral of *kleos,* see also Morris 1992:4–19.

[39]   See also Lord 1991:89–93.

scenes of conventional battle. Like these scenes, they contribute both to suspense, by increasing the audience's anticipation of the coming ambush or raid, and to characterization, as the details of each dressing or arming passage reveal important aspects of the hero's character as a fighter. Using arming scenes from Slavic epic as a comparison, Lord argues that there could also be a ritual aspect to the expanded or 'ornamental' arming scene: in the *Iliad* that ritual aspect "is probably one of dedication to the task and saving the hero's people, even of sacrifice. Each of these men is about to set out upon a mission of deep significance, and the 'ornamental' theme is a signal and mark, both 'ritualistic' and artistic, of the role of the hero" (Lord 1960/2000:91). Although Lord does not include the arming scene of *Iliad* 10 in his discussion, it shares in this thematic significance. Odysseus and Diomedes, too, are arming for a special mission, and the details of what they wear, as we have just seen, are also a signal that they are taking on a particular role: at night the task is ambush, and that is what our heroes dress for.

Another "special" arming scene likewise reveals how this theme can take on characteristics specific to the context and to the warrior who is arming.[40] In *Iliad* 5, Athena responds to Ares' aid to Hektor and the Trojans by going into battle to help the Achaeans. Athena arms herself in an extended description (*Iliad* 5.733–747), which includes very special equipment specific to Athena herself: the war tunic of Zeus and his aegis, a helmet that not only includes the *phaloi* that Agamemnon's helmet has (*Iliad* 5.743 = 11.41) and that the leather caps at night lack (*aphalon, Iliad* 10.257), but is also fitted with the fighting men of a hundred cities (*Iliad* 5.744).[41] Such details make the theme divine, as it describes a kind of armor that no mortal could have.[42] Yet this sequence is recognizably the same theme and uses the same formulas when appropriate, such as when her spear is βριθὺ μέγα στιβαρόν ("heavy, big, sturdy," *Iliad* 5.746) just as Achilles' is (*Iliad* 19.388). Thus we see how the composition of the theme works: the singer has a basic struc-

---

[40] Armstrong 1958:342n11 notes this arming scene only in the footnote, and excludes it from his discussion as too unusual for his argument. That he is unable to accommodate this scene, which structurally has much in common with the four he does discuss, perhaps indicates that his argument is too limited.

[41] When Athena wants to return to battle in *Iliad* 8, she arms again (*Iliad* 8.384–391). The scene there shows how the compression or expansion of a theme works: several details are not included in the second description, but the structure remains. We can also compare Athena's dressing/arming scene in *Odyssey* 1.96–101.

[42] Fenik 1968:73–74 also recognizes this scene as a typical arming scene but "on a divine level."

ture and vocabulary that can be adapted to individual contexts.[43] Just as Agamemnon's armor is more elaborate in some details and Achilles' arming scene adds details such as how he tries it out because it is new to him, the details of the arming or dressing theme for a night mission share in the thematic structure, but the equipment is different because it is appropriate to the context. The fact that Athena takes off her *peplos* (*Iliad* 5.734–735) before arming for battle demonstrates her transition from one realm to another: she is the goddess of weaving and she made the *peplos* herself, but she is also a goddess of war, and the change in what she wears signals a change in her activity. The dressing scenes that begin *Iliad* 10 show the heroes wearing animal skins, which are not part of their usual daytime attire, and similarly signal a different milieu, where different kinds of missions will be suggested and undertaken.

We can add one final dressing scene, one that occurs at night, as a comparison. Rick Newton (1998) has compared the way Eumaios dresses for his nightwatch over the swine to the traditional arming scene, noting that the verb ὁπλίζετο 'armed himself' (*Odyssey* 14.526) is used to describe his action and that the sequence of items follows that of the traditional theme as seen in the *Iliad*.[44] Newton notes that there are two marked differences in this sequence, again appropriate to the context: Eumaios puts on a cloak in place of a shield and a goat-skin in place of a helmet. Building on Newton's insights, we can note that both the cloak and the goat-skin are appropriate, not only to Eumaios' mission of guarding the swine, but also to the night, since we have seen both cloaks and animal skins as significant elements in the night dressing scenes in *Iliad* 10. The fact that Eumaios' dressing scene occurs just after the disguised Odysseus has told him his story about an ambush at Troy (*Odyssey* 14.462–506) also makes the thematic connections evident.

Thus the dressing and arming scenes in *Iliad* 10 are consistent with a theme seen elsewhere in the epic. But even more importantly, they serve to signal that the poet is moving into a different poetic register. The poet transitions by way of such scenes from one larger theme to another, and the alternative style of clothing is emblematic of not only this alternative mode of fighting but also an alternative poetics. The dressing scenes are our point of entry into this alternate, nighttime poetic world, in which heroes wear animal skins and leather caps, employ cunning rather than meet the enemy face-to-face, and do

---

[43] Lord 1991:91 makes a similar point when he compares *Iliad* 3.338, from the arming scene of Paris, and *Iliad* 16.139, from the arming scene of Patroklos: "the basic lines in each case have been adapted to the hero of the moment, Paris or Patroclus."

[44] Newton 1998:149–150. See *Odyssey* 14.528–531.

things that they might not in broad daylight. Please see the commentary in Part Three on these lines for more ways in which specific details of the clothing described in this passage are best understood within the poetics of ambush.

Weapons of ambush

In addition to the animal skins and leather caps that signal a nighttime ambush theme, there is an additional detail to be noted in these arming scenes in *Iliad* 10 that is not present in the arming scenes that occur before conventional battle: both Odysseus and Dolon take a bow (*Iliad* 10.260 for Odysseus; *Iliad* 10.333 for Dolon). Why would this weapon appear only in the night arming scenes? Applying a practical approach to that question, McLeod (1988) demonstrates that the bow is known to be a particularly effective weapon in the dark of night. Working from both the information provided in *Iliad* scholia and comparative military sources, McLeod explains that an archer in the darkness has an advantage in shooting targets lit by campfires or torches (McLeod 1988:121–123). He then extends his argument to suggest that skilled archers may also be able to find targets in the dark by aiming at sound, and concludes that "the possibility remains that archers could be effective even in total darkness" (McLeod 1988:123–124).

The utility of a bow in the dark helps to explain why the arming scene includes the weapon only at night. It may even underlie the compressed simile of Apollo coming "like night" (*Iliad* 1.47) when he descends from Olympos to shoot arrows of plague at the Achaeans. And there are further thematic associations between archery and ambush. Odysseus, who excels at the ambush, is also a preeminent archer, as he himself boasts to the Phaeacians (*Odyssey* 8.215–222). Odysseus claims there that "Philoktetes alone surpassed me with the bow in the district of Troy, when we Achaeans used the bow" (*Odyssey* 8.219–220). But our *Iliad* does not present Odysseus as an archer in conventional battle at Troy, and the *Odyssey* stipulates that Odysseus left his bow at home when he went to war (*Odyssey* 21.38–41). That bow, and Odysseus' ability to wield it as no one else in Ithaka can, will be the key to his triumph over the suitors in what Edwards has identified as the most extended ambush theme in our Homeric epics.[45] That Odysseus equips himself with a bow here, then, is an indication that we should expect his skills as an ambusher to be at the forefront in the episode that is about to

---

[45] See Edwards 1985:22–23 and 36–37. See also the section below, "The ambush as a narrative pattern."

unfold. Since he does not have his own bow, Odysseus borrows that of Meriones, who has it with him on guard duty (again attesting to its usefulness at night), and who, as we see elsewhere, is both a good archer (*Iliad* 13.650–652, 23.859–883) and a good ambusher (*Iliad* 13.274–291).

In Meriones and Odysseus, then, we have two examples of warriors in the *Iliad* whom we know to be good archers, but who usually, if not always, fight as spearmen in conventional battle, and whom we additionally know to be good ambushers. When we look at the archers who fight regularly with the bow during daytime battle, we can see that a thematic overlap exists between archery and ambush in terms of hidden positions and unexpected attacks. Paris is explicitly said to be in an ambush position when he wounds Diomedes with his arrow (ἐκ λόχου, *Iliad* 11.379). He has used the column on the grave-mound of Ilos as a place of concealment (*Iliad* 11.371–372).[46] The archer, like the ambusher, waits while hidden to effect a surprise attack. Diomedes is in the process of stripping the corpse of Agastrophos and obviously does not see Paris before he shoots. There is a difference in sequence between ambush with a spear or sword and the kind of ambush Paris achieves with his bow during conventional battle: usually, after ambushers have waited for their victims, they spring out of their hiding place to attack; by contrast Paris shoots and hits his victim, and *then* springs out from his hiding place to boast of his success (ἐκ λόχου ἀμπήδησε καὶ εὐχόμενος ἔπος ηὔδα, *Iliad* 11.379).[47] Diomedes had been wounded earlier by another arrow, one shot by Pandaros, and when Diomedes prays to Athena that she grant him the opportunity to kill Pandaros, he describes him as the one "who hit me first," (ὅς μ' ἔβαλε φθάμενος, *Iliad* 5.119). Although it is difficult to convey in English, the participle φθάμενος here expresses the notion that Pandaros hit Diomedes while Diomedes was unaware that he was a target; in other words, Pandaros got the jump on him and therefore got the better of him.[48]

---

[46] This grave-mound, a manmade (ἀνδροκμήτῳ, *Iliad* 11.372) landmark on the Trojan plain, also figures in other night raid/ambush episodes: it is where Hektor holds the council before sending Dolon out as a spy (*Iliad* 10.415), and Priam has just passed it when Hermes comes to meet him as he moves toward the Achaean camp (*Iliad* 24.349). See Hainsworth 1993:243 (*ad* 11.166) for the tomb's place in the geography of Troy.

[47] See Muellner 1976:90–92 for his discussion of the anomalous use of εὔχομαι in this line—those differences may be another indication that we are dealing with unconventional warfare in this case.

[48] Van Wees 1988:5 states that this sequence is a very common one: "Usually, as far as one can tell, the victim is unaware of any immediate threat when he is hit by a spear or arrow." Building on this observation, Farron 2003:178–179 argues that, because warriors are more often than not unaware that they are under attack, "attacking

Pandaros' more famous shot at Menelaos provides another picture of archery as a surprise attack from a hidden position—in other words, a picture of how archery is like ambush. After Athena, disguised as Laodokos, persuades Pandaros that he would win *kudos* and the thanks of all the Trojans were he to kill Menelaos (*Iliad* 4.92–104), Pandaros takes out his bow, an action that prompts the story of how he acquired the bow. Pandaros, in fact, ambushed and killed the goat whose horn he then used to make the bow. Pandaros was "waiting in a hiding place" (δεδεγμένος ἐν προδοκῇσι, *Iliad* 4.107), and only when the goat walked over the rock did Pandaros shoot him. The impending shot at Menelaos is, of course, equally unsuspected because of the current cease-fire enforced by the oaths taken by both sides before the duel between Menelaos and Paris. Yet to make it even more unsuspected, Pandaros hides behind the shields of his comrades while he strings the bow:

καὶ τὸ μὲν εὖ κατέθηκε τανυσσάμενος ποτὶ γαίη
ἀγκλίνας· πρόσθεν δὲ σάκεα σχέθον ἐσθλοὶ ἑταῖροι
μὴ πρὶν ἀναΐξειαν ἀρήϊοι υἷες Ἀχαιῶν
πρὶν βλῆσθαι Μενέλαον ἀρήϊον Ἀτρέος υἱόν.

Iliad 4.112–115

And stringing it he placed it well down near the ground,
angling it, and his good comrades held their shields in front,
lest the Ares-like sons of the Achaeans rush him
before he hit Menelaos, the Ares-like son of Atreus.

When no hiding place (such as that Paris found behind the grave of Ilos or Pandaros had while hunting the goat) is available on the battle-field, one is created for the archer by the shields of his comrades. This position we also see depicted in vase painting: the archer crouching, angling his bow upwards, behind his comrades and their shields (see e.g. Louvre E 635 and Boston 01.8074, which has a "close-up" within its tondo of an archer partially hidden behind a shield, in Plates 3 and 4). The images of Achilles attacking Troilos discussed above show Achilles in much the same position (see Plate 1b). This overlap in the iconography of archery and ambush finds an analogue in the passage from the *Iliad* we have been discussing: Athena is reported to choose Pandaros in particular for this attack (*Iliad* 4.88), and we suggest that she does so

---

someone unawares is normal and acceptable," but that attitudes such as those expressed by Hektor at *Iliad* 7.235–242 and Diomedes here offer a perspective that finds it less than courageous.

not because his moral character would make him more willing to break the truce, but rather because an archer (and Pandaros is an excellent archer; see *Iliad* 2.827) is perfectly suited to an ambush enacted on an open plain in broad daylight.[49]

How an archer fights behind the shield of a comrade is most fully developed in the remarkable description of how Teucer shoots his arrows while he is protected by the shield of his brother Ajax (*Iliad* 8.266–272).[50] The description once again illustrates that archers fight from hidden positions even during conventional battle, and the subsequent list of Teucer's kills shows that it is a successful method (*Iliad* 8.273–277). The way the two brothers fight together is also presented as a strategy they often employ, and their cooperative style provides one more link to ambush tactics. As we will see in further detail below, ambushes are frequently organized with two leaders, and at times consist of just two men, as we have in *Iliad* 10. Once Diomedes and Odysseus pair up for the night raid, dual verbs are frequently used to describe their actions, expressing a tight coordination between them. Ajax and Teucer present another kind of alternative fighting method involving pairs, and another example of how such alternative fighting, rather than being untraditional, may be quite an old element within the epic tradition.[51]

Another shared feature of archery and ambush lies in how each has been understood and interpreted in modern scholarship: that is, both archery and ambush have been thought to be negatively portrayed in the Homeric epics. Steven Farron has challenged the general consensus about archery, stating that, "In fact, there is no evidence in the *Iliad* that military archery was ineffectual or lower class" (2003:169). He points out that insults of archers come not from the narrator but in the words of men like Diomedes who have just been wounded by these archers (which demonstrates that they are indeed effective). Farron also highlights the passages in which Teucer's success with the bow in

---

49 Van Erp Taalman Kip (2000:390–392) also argues, in the context of the involvement of the gods rather than anything to do with ambush, that Athena looks for Pandaros not because of his moral failings, as other commentators understand it, but because she needs an archer.

50 See Edgeworth 1985 for his argument that the fighting method of Ajax and Teucer seems very old and that together they make up the perfect Mycenean warrior. See Ebbott 2003:39–44 for an explanation of how the simile here that Teucer returns behind Ajax's shield like a child hiding behind his mother relates to Teucer's illegitimacy.

51 See Page 1959:235–238, Edgeworth and Mayrhofer 1987, Nagy 1997, and Ebbott 2003:41–44 for arguments that the dual *Aiante* originally meant Ajax and Teucer rather than Ajax and Ajax. See also our commentary on 10.53.

battle is praised or desired by his comrades (2003:171–175). In the end, he allows that "military archery did have enough negative connotations for Homer to use them when he wanted to denigrate a character, nation, or action," by which he means either Paris in particular or the Trojans collectively (2003:184). This conclusion, however, seems to fall back into the same problem that Farron identified earlier of evaluating the statements of characters as if they reflect general attitudes. As we have already begun to see in scholarly reactions to episodes of ambush, both in the Homeric epics and the Epic Cycle, such assumptions are often based on the interpreter's own notions of what is "heroic" or "honorable" and are not entirely based in what the epics themselves have to say. The controversial scene featuring a debate about archery in Euripides' *Herakles* (140–235) reveals just how complex and even conflicting the ancient attitudes can be.[52]

Yet Farron does suggest that the archery of Pandaros and Paris, as well as the onslaught of unnamed masses of Trojan archers, is presented as changing the course of battle in a way that spear-fighting does not (2003:174–178). Similarly, ambush missions achieve what conventional battle cannot. As we see in episodes in the Epic Cycle, night raids such as the stealing of the Palladion and, of course, the ambush by the wooden horse, are the methods by which the Achaeans ultimately win the war. In the *Odyssey*, Odysseus uses ambush to overcome the superior numbers of the suitors. The night raid of *Iliad* 10 has been criticized for its ineffectiveness, but such a characterization ignores the reactions of the Achaeans themselves, who rejoice in the victory (*Iliad* 10.540–542, 10.565–566).[53]

Although we have seen that bows can be an especially effective weapon at night, and that there are shared thematic concepts between archery and ambush, the bows that Dolon and Odysseus take on their respective missions are not in fact used as weapons in this episode. That is, we do not see the bow in action at night here. Diomedes uses his spear to stop Dolon in his tracks (*Iliad* 10.369–375), and he uses his sword to kill the Thracians (*Iliad* 10.482–484, 10.489), but Dolon never uses any of his weapons, and Odysseus uses his bow only to whip the horses (*Iliad* 10.500, 10.516). Any expectations raised by the inclusion of the bows in the arming scenes are, in the end, confounded by how this episode turns out, yet the confounding of expectations may itself be

---

[52] See George 1994 for a detailed study of this debate within Euripides' *Herakles*.

[53] Petegorsky 1982:188–189, 191, 200–212 argues that the Doloneia is exceptional within the *Iliad* in showing the effectiveness of *mētis*. In so doing it returns the narrative to the Achaean reliance on the strength of Achilles to save them.

a feature of spying mission and ambush episodes. Another possibility is that the bow, like the special caps and other gear worn by Odysseus and Diomedes in *Iliad* 10, is a narrative signal so closely associated with ambush warfare that a poet would naturally include it as part of a spy's equipment, whether or not it is ever actually used in the episode.

Sensory and spatial aspects of the night

One practical reason behind some of the differences in clothing and armor we find in *Iliad* 10 has to do with another nexus within the poetics of ambush, namely, the effect that the darkness of night has on the sense of sight. In the dark, the sense of sight is, of course, diminished, and the difficulty of moving through the darkness is emphasized in this book, as are the dangers attendant on the inability to see clearly. The corollary to this difficulty in seeing at night is the need for ambushers or spies to move undetected, to remain unseen. As we see in *Iliad* 10 when Nestor and Agamemnon arrive at Diomedes' encampment, metal such as bronze can shine even in the dark:

> ἔγχεα δέ σφιν
> ὄρθ' ἐπὶ σαυρωτῆρος ἐλήλατο, τῆλε δὲ χαλκὸς
> λάμφ' ὥς τε στεροπὴ πατρὸς Διός·

> *Iliad* 10.152–154

> Their spears
> were planted with the spearheads up, and far and wide the bronze
> was shining, like the lightning of father Zeus.

Whatever light is available at night, from the moon or from watch- or campfires, will be reflected by the metal armor used in daytime fighting, making metal a liability on ambush or spying missions. (For how that particular liability becomes decisive in the night raid episode in *Aeneid* 9, see our discussion of it in our essay, "Tradition and Reception.") These thematic elements of sight and stealth in the dark are one reason for leather helmets or other gear that seem unusual at first glance but are actually appropriate to maneuvers in the dark.

With the proper equipment, a dark night is generally an asset to an ambusher. Darkness enables hiding, the surprise nature of the attack, and a successful escape afterwards. We see all of these benefits in the compressed story of an ambush that Odysseus tells within one of his Cretan tales (*Odyssey* 13.259–270). There we see that the dark night (νὺξ δὲ μάλα δνοφερὴ κάτεχ' οὐρανόν, *Odyssey* 13.269) allows him to strike his victim, Orsilokhos, after lying in wait for him near the road with a comrade (ἐγγὺς ὁδοῖο λοχησάμενος σὺν ἑταίρῳ, *Odyssey* 13.268). After the murder darkness also helps him to escape from Crete unseen (*Odyssey* 13.269–270). Although darkness may require advance planning to navigate its difficulties, it gives the ambusher a definite advantage.

Because sight is limited at night, hearing becomes a more important sense. But what one hears, especially in the dark, is less certain and more in need of interpretation. Visual and auditory perception are highlighted from the beginning of *Iliad* 10, as Agamemnon sees the numerous campfires of the Trojans on the plain and hears their music and the din of their activity (*Iliad* 10.11–13). As we discuss in our commentary on those lines, the description of these sights and sounds and Agamemnon's reaction to them reveal that we are seeing and hearing from his point of view. In other words, Agamemnon's distress focalizes the sights and sounds from the Trojan camp, and his reaction forefronts his own interpretation, namely, that his perceptions mean trouble for the Achaeans.

Similarly, when the Achaean leaders arrive at the guards' post, it is the sounds that the guards hear in the night that are given prominence in the description of their vigilance. Nestor and the others find, to their relief, that the guards have not fallen asleep (a concern expressed by Agamemnon at *Iliad* 10.97–99); rather, they are sitting awake with their weapons (*Iliad* 10.180–182). The guards are then compared to watchdogs, specifically to watchdogs who are keeping a "hard watch" (δυσωρήσωνται) after they hear some undefined beast moving through the woods on a mountain. The dogs raise a commotion, and they can have no sleep that night. The Achaean night watch is in the same position, the simile makes clear: sleep is lost to them, and they keep turning toward the plain whenever they hear something from the Trojan camp (*Iliad* 10.183–189). Multiple comparisons within one simile, such as the choice between a lion or wolf, are not unusual in Homeric similes, but within the action of this simile the unspecified beast (is it a lion? a wolf?) highlights the uncertainty of the watchers, in that they do not even know exactly what they are guarding against.[54] We can imagine that the Achaean guards have a similar reaction to the noises they hear: Are the Trojans attacking? Or are they just moving about (ἰόντων, *Iliad* 10.189)? Both inside and outside of the simile, the noises in the

---

[54] The two possible nocturnal predators are also reflected in the lion's skin worn by Diomedes (*Iliad* 10.177–178) and the wolf's skin worn by Dolon (*Iliad* 10.334).

night are more ominous because of the inability to see what is actually happening. Though they turn toward the noise in both cases as if to see, the guards and the guard dogs must rely on their hearing to prepare for a possible attack.

Later, the need to interpret sounds correctly becomes a key element in the capture of Dolon. Odysseus shows off his ambush skills and *mētis* when he and Diomedes first embark on their mission. Just as Diomedes hoped his partner would (*Iliad* 10.224–226), Odysseus is the first to perceive Dolon, and uses his intelligence in planning their strategy. Odysseus suggests that they get ahead of Dolon on the plain so that they can rush and seize him, and if Dolon outruns them he will still be cut off from Troy (*Iliad* 10.344–348). So they let Dolon pass them and run after him from behind, at which point hearing and seeing come into play. Dolon hears their footsteps and perceives that those footsteps are behind him. Then we are told how he interprets the noise and its location:

> τὼ μὲν ἐπιδραμέτην, ὅδ' ἄρ' ἔστη δοῦπον ἀκούσας.
> ἔλπετο γὰρ κατὰ θυμὸν ἀποστρέψοντας ἑταίρους
> ἐκ Τρώων ἰέναι πάλιν Ἕκτορος ὀτρύναντος.
> ἀλλ' ὅτε δή ῥ' ἄπεσαν δουρηνεκὲς ἢ καὶ ἔλασσον,
> γνῶ ῥ' ἄνδρας δηΐους, λαιψηρὰ δὲ γούνατ' ἐνώμα
> φευγέμεναι· τοὶ δ' αἶψα διώκειν ὡρμήθησαν.
>
> *Iliad* 10.354–359

> The two ran after him, and he came to a stop having heard
>   the noise.
> For he [Dolon] thought in his heart that it was his comrades
>   coming to turn him back,
> his comrades from the Trojans, with Hektor summoning
>   him to come back.
> But when they were a spear's throw away or even less,
> he recognized that they were enemy men, and he moved his
>   nimble knees
> to flee. But they immediately started to pursue.

Dolon's assumption, based on the sound of someone running up behind him, that is, from the same direction he has come, is that they must be his comrades, also coming from the Trojan camp. He assumes they have come to deliver a message to abort the mission. Odysseus' strategy cuts Dolon off from an escape route and has the added benefit of hindering

Dolon's ability to interpret the sound of their approach correctly. Only once Diomedes and Odysseus are much closer can Dolon see that they are not his comrades at all, and he realizes his appraisal was wrong. Dolon is a swift runner (*Iliad* 10.316), but the fact that he stops when he hears the footsteps gives Diomedes and Odysseus an advantage in capturing him.

Recognizing that vision is limited at night, the Achaeans take measures to prevent missing someone or something in the dark. As Agamemnon and Menelaos make their plans to gather the other leaders, Menelaos asks Agamemnon where he should meet him (*Iliad* 10.62–63). Agamemnon tells him to wait with the guards so that they do not somehow miss each other (*Iliad* 10.65).[55] Similarly, when Odysseus places the spoils from Dolon on a tamarisk bush, he makes a sign, a *sēma*, so that they will not miss it (*Iliad* 10.466–468, here the verb is λανθάνω).[56] Agamemnon also instructs Menelaos to "call out" wherever he goes as he awakens the leaders for the meeting (φθέγγεο δ' ᾗ κεν ἴῃσθα, *Iliad* 10.67). Calling out will give warning of Menelaos' approach, since in the dark it is easier to be heard than seen. Wondering who is approaching, Nestor says much the same to Agamemnon himself—he obviously cannot see him clearly—and he tells him to call out and not to approach silently (φθέγγεο, μηδ' ἀκέων ἐπ' ἔμ' ἔρχεο, *Iliad* 10.85). We can compare this to the other gathering of leaders that happens earlier in the night, in *Iliad* 9. There, Agamemnon instructs his herald to summon each man by name to the assembly, but not to shout (κλήδην εἰς ἀγορὴν κικλήσκειν ἄνδρα ἕκαστον, / μὴ δὲ βοᾶν, *Iliad* 9.11–12), perhaps so that the nearby enemy not overhear them. Within the confines of the encampment, then, sound is used to avoid confusion, and words and voices are meant to identify friends. Such a use of sound is something that Dolon does not consider when he assumes those behind him to be Trojan comrades.

A historical example of the confusion that can happen when fighting at night, even with calling out a verbal signal such as a pass-word, is offered by Thucydides' account of the Athenian night attack on Epipolae, near Syracuse (Thucydides 7.43–44). After initial success in their attack, the Athenians pushed on until they were in turn routed

---

[55] See the commentary on this line for more on the verb ἁβροτάξομεν 'to miss, to fail to see.'

[56] Other examples of λανθάνω at night show that it is all too easy to go unseen in the dark: for example, the successful eluding of guards by Phoinix (*Iliad* 9.474–477); Priam eluding the guards of the Achaean camp (*Iliad* 24.566, 24.681); and Odysseus ambushing Orsilokhos and getting away unseen (*Odyssey* 13.270).

by the Boeotians. Since some Athenians were still advancing as their comrades started retreating, it was difficult, Thucydides tells us, to tell friend from foe. Even the use of the password did not help, since everyone asked for it at once, and the enemy could discern it and use it to their advantage.[57] Thucydides emphasizes just how difficult it is to fight at night (as well as to get an accurate account of it afterwards) with a question: "in a night battle, how would anyone know anything clearly?" (ἐν δὲ νυκτομαχίᾳ ... πῶς ἄν τις σαφῶς τι ᾔδει; Thucydides 7.44). He reports that there was a moon on the night in question, but that the moonlight only allows one to see the form of a body—not enough to trust in the recognition of those on one's own side (Thucydides 7.44).

We have already seen that some of these same concerns and problems are present in the night episode in *Iliad* 10 and that careful planning is necessary to avoid the kind of confusion the Athenians suffered at Epipolae. In addition to the precautions taken because of limited sight and the possibility for confusion related to sound, we see a great deal of attention paid to spatial orientation in this episode. Odysseus asks for details about not only the night watch (*Iliad* 10.408) but also the arrangements of the Trojan camp (*Iliad* 10.424–425). Dolon provides these details (*Iliad* 10.428–431) before directing Odysseus and Diomedes to the Thracians, who are "farthest apart from the others" (*Iliad* 10.434), a factor that seems to make them a better target for an ambush. This detailed information is necessary because of the difficulties of moving, as well as fighting, in the dark. Below we will discuss how ambush is structured like a journey, both a going there and a returning home, and such information is necessary to successfully complete that journey, to navigate a terrain that might even be familiar in daylight, but which presents new dangers on this night in particular. When Diomedes and Odysseus ambush the Thracians, confusion is further averted by planning: Odysseus and Diomedes divide the tasks to be done (*Iliad* 10.480–481). When Odysseus has finished freeing the horses, he signals to Diomedes with a single sound (*Iliad* 10.502): his whistle balances the need for quiet as part of stealth with the inability to signal with a gesture or some other means that relies on sight.

Once we realize how the dark of night affects the strategies and actions of these kinds of missions, and therefore the language used

---

[57] The use of a password at night and its discovery by the enemy are also key elements in the portrayal of a night attack in the tragedy *Rhesos*: see Euripides *Rhesos* 521–522, 572–573, 687–688.

to express them, we can better understand certain figures of speech that would otherwise seem problematic. We find one such figure of speech in a line that has long bothered Homeric scholars, the climactic moment when Diomedes kills Rhesos. Here is how the verses read in the Venetus A text:

ἀλλ' ὅτε δὴ βασιλῆα κιχήσατο Τυδέος υἱός,
τὸν τρισκαιδέκατον μελιηδέα θυμὸν ἀπηύρα
ἀσθμαίνοντα· κακὸν γὰρ ὄναρ κεφαλῆφιν ἐπέστη
τὴν νύκτ' Οἰνείδαο πάϊς διὰ μῆτιν Ἀθήνης.

Iliad 10.494–497

But when the son of Tydeus reached the king,
from him the thirteenth he took away the honey-sweet life
[*thumos*]
as he gasped for breath. For a bad dream stood at his head
that night, the descendent of Oineus [Diomedes], through
the scheme [*mētis*] of Athena.

In the Venetus A manuscript, there is an *obelos* next to 10.497, and the corresponding scholion indicates that it is athetized "because it is paltry even in its composition [*sunthesis*: its connection to the previous line], and because it means but does not say that Diomedes stands by Rhesos like a dream, and because 'through the scheme of Athena' is vexing, for it was rather through the report of Dolon" (ἀθετεῖται, ὅτι καὶ τῇ συνθέσει εὐτελές· καὶ μὴ ῥηθέντος δὲ νοεῖται ὅτι ὡς ὄναρ ἐφίσταται τῷ Ῥήσῳ ὁ Διομήδης, καὶ τὸ <διὰ μῆτιν Ἀθήνης> λυπεῖ· μᾶλλον γὰρ διὰ τὴν Δόλωνος ἀπαγγελίαν). The intermarginal A scholion on the line notes that this line was not in the editions of either Zenodotus or Aristophanes.

Bernard Fenik has examined the perceived anomalies in these lines, which have caused modern scholars, as well, to challenge both the inclusion of 10.497 in our text and the meaning of the line; they have done so not only for the reasons stated in the A scholia, but also because of the accusative τὴν νύκτ(α) (Fenik 1964:44–54). Fenik adduces parallel uses of the accusative to mean 'time when' rather than 'extent of time' in Homeric epic, and as a result he dismisses that element as a reason for excluding the line. Instead, Fenik argues that the bad dream is an older element within the tradition about Rhesos that is being referred to in a compressed way here, and, similarly, that the *mētis* of Athena is part of a tradition that is not explained or explored in full in this version.

Thus, following Fenik, one way to understand the difficulties here is to recognize a broader tradition about Rhesos, one that encompasses the other versions we see reported in the scholia and in other ancient authors.[58] As we have seen in other places, the compression that makes certain things opaque for us would have been more easily understood by a traditional audience who would readily know the stories alluded to. But there may be a particular reason for the abrupt equation between the bad dream and Diomedes here, and that is the surprise element of the ambush in the dark. The scholion notes that the line means Diomedes is like a bad dream, but does not explicitly say so—that is, we do not have a word such as ὡς to indicate that a comparison is being made. Instead, we, or the audience, hear first about the bad dream standing at Rhesos' head, as dreams do in Homeric epic, but then the dream comes into focus and is embodied as Diomedes.

We can compare the similar action in the dark that takes place when Achilles first captures Lykaon, a passage that we examined above in our discussion of Achilles as an ambusher. This description of a nighttime attack also uses an apposition, this time between Achilles and what his presence means for Lykaon—an unexpected evil:

ἔνθ᾽ υἷι Πριάμοιο συνήντετο Δαρδανίδαο
ἐκ ποταμοῦ φεύγοντι Λυκάονι, τόν ῥά ποτ᾽ αὐτὸς
ἦγε λαβὼν ἐκ πατρὸς ἀλωῆς οὐκ ἐθέλοντα
ἐννύχιος προμολών· ὃ δ᾽ ἐρινεὸν ὀξέϊ χαλκῷ
τάμνε νέους ὄρπηκας, ἵν᾽ ἅρματος ἄντυγες εἶεν·
τῷ δ᾽ ἄρ᾽ ἀνώϊστον κακὸν ἤλυθε δῖος Ἀχιλλεύς.

Iliad 21.34–39

There Achilles encountered the son of Dardanian Priam,
Lykaon, as he was fleeing out of the river, whom once he
    himself
had led away after he captured him, unwilling as he was,
    from his father's orchard,
attacking him at night. Lykaon was cutting a wild fig tree
    with sharp bronze,
cutting new branches to be rails of a chariot.
For him, an unexpected evil came, radiant Achilles.

---

[58] See "Tradition and Reception" for more on the Rhesos tradition as a whole, and our disagreements with Fenik there.

Unlooked-for evil comes to Lykaon and suddenly, coming out of the darkness, that evil *is* Achilles. The abrupt appearance of the metaphor is an aural experience similar to the eyes finally focusing in the dark, such as when Dolon finally discerns that the men running toward him are his enemies, but only after it is too late to escape. The appositions in *Iliad* 21 and *Iliad* 10, the unlooked-for evil that suddenly appears and the bad dream that comes true, emphasize the unexpected and unseen nature of the attacks. The mental picture created is especially frightening: the emergence of the enemy from the previously empty darkness. The performance language for episodes including attacks at night, we suggest, may have developed a special use of language, this abrupt, almost jarring apposition, to recreate verbally what happens within the story visually as the enemy comes into the focus of his victim.

The ambush as a narrative pattern

Just as night raid and ambush narratives are marked by their own thematically appropriate arming scenes, so too do these narratives have a traditional structure attested in various levels of complexity, compression, and expansion. Anthony Edwards has argued that the second half of the *Odyssey* leading up to the slaughter of the suitors is our most expanded example of the ambush narrative pattern, featuring all three of the standard elements he identifies as belonging to an ambush: planning, concealment, and surprise attack.[59] Another way to think about the structure of the ambush theme is that it is composed of several smaller themes.[60] These sub-themes are associated with the larger theme, but in performance a singer may choose to include them or not, or to expand or compress any one sub-theme.[61] When we examine specific uses of the ambush theme in what survives of the Greek oral epic tradition, then, we should not be surprised if all of the elements or sub-themes we identify as being associated with the ambush theme are not present in each instance. Conversely, as we shall discuss below, the presence of several of these sub-themes will indicate that the ambush theme is operative even if the word λόχος is

[59] See Edwards 1985:22–23 and 36–37.
[60] Lord 1960/2000:71 describes the use of smaller themes to compose a larger theme this way: "Although he [= the singer] thinks of the theme as a unit, it can be broken down into smaller parts: the receipt of a letter, the summoning of a council, and so forth. Yet these are subsidiary to the larger theme."
[61] Using the example of the theme of a hero arming for battle, a sub-theme of ambush that we discussed in detail above, Lord observes that "the poet has a choice of using a short form of these themes (or of omitting them entirely) or of elaborating them" (Lord 1960/2000:88).

not explicitly used to describe it. The sub-themes that constitute an ambush include: (1) selecting the best men as leaders and/or partici- pants; (2) preparing and arming for the ambush; (3) choosing a location for the ambush; (4) the ambushers concealing themselves and enduring discomfort while they wait; (5) the surprise attack; (6) returning home.

The decision to undertake a spying mission or an ambush is often born of a situation of desperation, or the need to defeat an enemy who was not or cannot be beaten in conventional battle.[62] In *Iliad* 10, Agamemnon and the other Achaeans fear complete destruction and that the Trojans may even attack at night (*Iliad* 10.43–45 and 10.100– 101). In other variations on the theme, a single hero has defeated many challengers or overcome other means to kill him, so an ambush is used to exact revenge or as a last-resort attempt on his life: examples include Tydeus (*Iliad* 4.385–398) and Bellerophon (*Iliad* 6.187–190). The besieged city on the Shield of Achilles sends out men on an ambush (*Iliad* 18.513–522). And of course, the Achaeans find no way to take Troy other than to use the ambush of the wooden horse.

In the planning phase, the bravest men (*aristoi*) volunteer and/ or are chosen to go on the mission, and the right location is chosen. Often the ambush consists of two men or a small group of men led by two leaders. This is the case with the slaughter of the suitors (led by Odysseus and Telemakhos in *Odyssey* 22) and the ambush of Tydeus (led by Maion and Polyphontes in *Iliad* 4.394–395). On the Shield of Achilles, the two leaders are Athena and Ares (*Iliad* 18.516). In one Cretan lie (*Odyssey* 13.256–286) Odysseus claims he is in exile for killing Idomeneus' son Orsilokhos in an ambush, and the thematic pull of two ambushers is so strong that he ambushes Orsilokhos with a nameless companion (λοχησάμενος σὺν ἑταίρῳ, *Odyssey* 13.268). In Odysseus' tale of an ambush at Troy, told to Eumaios in *Odyssey* 14, the presence of the speaker as a third leader tacked on to the initial two, Menelaos and Odysseus (τοῖσι δ' ἅμα τρίτος ἦρχον ἐγών, *Odyssey* 14.471), might be an intentional clue as to the true nature of the storyteller's identity.[63] In any case, in *Iliad* 10, the selection process is narrated in full, and it includes many details as to who is selected and why. In addition, the importance that the two work as a team is highlighted in two ways in *Iliad* 10. First, Diomedes specifically requests a partner, explaining

---

[62] We can compare an example from outside Homeric epic: Herakles ambushes the Aktorione Molione when he cannot defeat them on the battlefield (Pindar *Olympian* 10.26–34; Apollodorus 2.7.2).

[63] See the commentary below *ad* 10.53 and 10.149. Haft 1984, Reece 1994, Newton 1998, and Marks 2003 all interpret this story from different perspectives.

how much better it is for two men to work together on such a mission (*Iliad* 10.220–226). Second, once the mission begins, the dual is used frequently to refer to Diomedes and Odysseus working together.

Other instances of ambush, however, include only the number of the best and bravest to be chosen. In *Odyssey* 4.663–672, Antinoos says he needs a fast ship and twenty men for the ambush of Telemakhos.[64] In *Odyssey* 4.531–532, Proteus reports that Aigisthos likewise chose twenty of the best men in the district for the ambush of Agamemnon (κρινάμενος κατὰ δῆμον ἐείκοσι φῶτας ἀρίστους εἷσε λόχον).[65] We hear in the *Iliad* that fifty men are sent to ambush Tydeus (*Iliad* 4.392–393). In other instances, the emphasis is given to the best men without a specific number: for example, against Bellerophon are sent the best men chosen from broad Lycia (κρίνας ἐκ Λυκίης εὐρείης φῶτας ἀρίστους, *Iliad* 6.188–189), but a precise number is not included. Similarly, in one of his Cretan lies, Odysseus describes how as a leader of ambush, he would choose the best men (ὁπότε κρίνοιμι λόχονδε ἄνδρας ἀριστῆας, *Odyssey* 14.217–218).

Along with the selection of men, there must also be a plan or a plot for an ambush, and for this element the thematic vocabulary often includes βουλή and/or δόλος. We see the need for a plan, βουλή, in *Iliad* 10 from the beginning of the night episode (*Iliad* 10.5).[66] Similarly, Proteus asks Menelaos, who has just successfully ambushed him, who among the gods told him the plans so that Menelaos could take him, unwilling as he was, in ambush (τίς νύ τοι, Ἀτρέος υἱέ, θεῶν συμφράσσατο βουλάς, / ὄφρα μ' ἕλοις ἀέκοντα λοχησάμενος, *Odyssey* 4.462–463). The presence of the word δόλος can give an ambush-like feel to an episode not otherwise identified as such (for example, Hephaistos trapping Ares and Aphrodite in his bed; see the use of δόλος in this song at *Odyssey* 8.276, 8.282, and 8.317). Confining our examination of the word only to those episodes which are explicitly called or structured as an ambush, however, we see δόλος used to describe the ambush with the Trojan horse (*Odyssey* 8.494), the ambush of Bellerophon (*Iliad* 6.187), the ambush of Proteus by Menelaos (*Odyssey* 4.437 and 4.453), the ambush on the Shield of Achilles (*Iliad* 18.526),

---

[64] See also *Odyssey* 4.778, where Antinoos chooses the twenty best men, ἐκρίνατ' ἐείκοσι φῶτας ἀρίστους, and Athena's warning to Telemakhos that the best of the suitors are setting the ambush at *Odyssey* 15.28.

[65] The location chosen for the ambush of Agamemnon, a feast, does not seem to have been a good one, since we are told that none of the twenty men chosen survived the ambush.

[66] See the full discussion in the commentary at 10.1ff. and 10.43–44, in conjunction with the discussion of the ambush-theme adjective *pukinos* at 10.5–9.

the death of Agamemnon (*Odyssey* 3.325, 4.92, and 11.439), the suitors' attempted ambush of Telemakhos as predicted by Eurykleia (*Odyssey* 2.368), and the death of the suitors at the hands of Telemakhos (*Odyssey* 1.296) and Odysseus (*Odyssey* 11.120). The preeminent hero of ambush, Odysseus, is known for his skills at deception and trickery, and so is often associated with the word δόλος. He even introduces himself to the Phaeacians as Odysseus, son of Laertes, who is known to mortals for all sorts of tricks (πᾶσι δόλοισιν, *Odyssey* 9.19).[67]

In *Iliad* 10, the planning of the mission and selection of men is followed by an arming scene. If other night raid episodes from the Epic Cycle survived, we might have more examples of such scenes. As it is, only one other ambush in the Homeric epics, Menelaos' ambush of Proteus, shows particular preparations of dress. The preparation for the disguise and concealment is narrated here in some detail. Menelaos tells Telemakhos about how he was delayed in Egypt and could only find out how to get home by ambushing the sea god Proteus (*Odyssey* 4.351–480): the ambush is suggested by the goddess Eidothea (τόν γ' εἴ πως σὺ δύναιο <u>λοχησάμενος</u> λελαβέσθαι, *Odyssey* 4.388), who also does the planning and makes preparations for it. She suggests ambushing Proteus in his sleep, as he lies among the seals, and orders Menelaos to choose his three best men: as we have seen, it is always the best (*aristoi*) who go on ambushes (*Odyssey* 4.403–409). To enable the four men to hide while they wait for the arrival of Proteus and for the moment he falls asleep, Eidothea provides them with four seal hides recently

---

[67] See also *Iliad* 3.202, 4.339, 11.430, and 23.725; *Odyssey* 3.122, 13.292–293, and 19.212. *Dolos* is also used to refer to the ambush (at night) of Ouranos by Gaia and Kronos in *Theogony* 174–175: εἶσε δέ μιν κρύψασα λόχῳ· ἐνέθηκε δὲ χερσὶν / ἅρπην καρχαρόδοντα· δόλον δ' ὑπεθήκατο πάντα ("[Gaia] hid him and sat him down in an ambush. She put a sickle with jagged teeth in his hands and revealed the whole trick"). It is because of this trick that Kronos receives the epithet ἀγκυλομήτης (*Theogony* 18 and 137; *Iliad* 2.205, 2.319, 4.49, 4.75, 9.37, 11.450, 16.431, 18.293; *Odyssey* 21.415). Likewise Zeus is called μητίετα when he is born (*Theogony* 456). He will in turn ambush Kronos, again with the help of Gaia, in *Theogony* 494–496: Γαίης ἐννεσίῃσι πολυφραδέεσσι δολωθεὶς / ὃν γόνον ἄψ ἀνέηκε μέγας Κρόνος ἀγκυλομήτης / νικηθεὶς τέχνῃσι βίηφί τε παιδὸς ἑοῖο ("Tricked by the eloquent suggestions of Gaia, great Kronos who is crooked and crafty sent back up his offspring, conquered by the skill and force of his son"; see also *Theogony* 471). For Zeus' traditional epithet μητίετα, see *Iliad* 1.175, 1.508, 2.197, 2.324, 6.198, 7.478, 8.170, 9.377, 10.104, etc.; *Odyssey* 14.243, 16.298, 20.102. The seizure of Persephone in the *Homeric Hymn to Demeter* seems to be similarly structured as an ambush. Gaia is said to grow the flowers that Persephone is picking when she is taken "by a plot" (δόλον, 8). Later Persephone says the she was taken "through the shrewd [*pukinos*] *mētis* of the son of Kronos" (Κρονίδεω πυκινὴν διὰ μῆτιν, 415). For the adjective *pukinos* and its associations with ambush, see the general commentary below on 10.5–9.

skinned for the plot (δόλος) she has arranged (*Odyssey* 4.435–437). They will hide beneath these animal skins, a parallel to those skins featured in the dressing scenes in *Iliad* 10. Although these preparations differ from those of the arming scene we have in *Iliad* 10, the two scenes do share ambushers who dress or equip themselves specifically for stealth.

Following the selection of men, the drafting of plans, and the arming or equipping of the ambushers, comes the selection of a location, also chosen with a view to stealth, since the ambushers will need to wait there undetected in order to take their victim(s) by surprise. Edwards notes that in the *Odyssey* great care is given to setting up the house properly for Odysseus' and Telemakhos' slaughter of the suitors. On the Shield of Achilles in *Iliad* 18, men from the city at war choose a place that is "suitable for ambush" (εἶκε λοχῆσαι, *Iliad* 18.520), at a watering place on a river. In the Cretan lie that Odysseus tells to Athena in *Odyssey* 13, Odysseus says that he ambushed his victim near a road during the dark of night: the darkness provided the necessary stealth, for no one saw him kill Orsilokhos (13.268–270). This description is very similar to the place where Odysseus and Diomedes ambush Dolon, for there, too, they move off the road to wait until he passes (*Iliad* 10.344–350). For their attempt at ambushing Telemakhos, the suitors choose a rocky island in the channel between Ithaka and Samos, where ships can be hidden (*Odyssey* 4.842–847). Intriguingly, the suitors are called "Achaeans" as they wait in ambush: the phrasing τῇ τόν γε μένον λοχόωντες Ἀχαιοί ("in that place the Achaeans waited for him in ambush") suggests a formula that could be used within any ambush theme after the location has been chosen. In his Cretan lie of *Odyssey* 14, Odysseus describes their hidden position in the ambush before Troy:

> ἡμεῖς μὲν περὶ ἄστυ κατὰ ῥωπήϊα πυκνά,
> ἂν δόνακας καὶ ἕλος, ὑπὸ τεύχεσι πεπτηῶτες
> κείμεθα, νὺξ δ' ἄρ' ἐπῆλθε κακὴ βορέαο πεσόντος,
> πηγυλίς·

> *Odyssey* 14.473–476

> We got down under the dense [*pukinos*] shrubs that were
>   around the city,
> in the reeds and the marsh, and crouching beneath our
>   armor
> we lay there, while an evil night came over us as the North
>   wind fell,
> and it was icy cold.

A marshy or forested area provides good hiding places, and in ambush scenes in vase painting, we often see the location portrayed with plants of some kind (see Plate 1b).[68] The wooden horse is no doubt the most famous location for an ambush in the epic tradition. In the commentary below (on *Iliad* 10.5–9) we discuss how the place of ambush has poetic affinities with an animal's lair in the traditional diction. The place of ambush and the animal's lair, like the cunning that characterizes ambush, are modified by the adjective *pukinos* 'close packed' (i.e. with elements that come one right after another). Conceptually, the place of ambush and the cunning required to orchestrate an ambush are closely linked, such that the wooden horse is referred to as a *pukinon lokhon* (*Odyssey* 11.525) in what is surely a semantically loaded phrase.

Once the location is selected, the chosen men conceal themselves. As in the example from *Odyssey* 14 cited above, the period of concealment is marked by its hardship, which includes cold, lack of sleep, and the discomfort of a crouching position.[69] It is also known for the fear that accompanies the men as they wait for the right moment to attack. As we have noted already, in *Odyssey* 4 Menelaos describes the way that the Achaean heroes were tormented by Helen and had to be restrained from exiting the horse too soon. In the *Odyssey* 11 passage discussed above, we learn that it was Odysseus' task to choose the moment to open up the wooden horse. The brave man does not let his fear show during this period of time, as we have seen in the descriptions of ambush in *Odyssey* 11 and *Iliad* 13 above. In one of Odysseus' Cretan lies, he says that when he went on an ambush his audacious spirit never looked toward death, but that he was the very first to spring out and attack the enemy (οὔ ποτέ μοι θάνατον προτιόσσετο θυμὸς ἀγήνωρ,/ ἀλλὰ πολὺ πρώτιστος ἐπάλμενος ἔγχεϊ ἔλεσκον / ἀνδρῶν δυσμενέων ὅ τέ μοι εἴξειε πόδεσσι, *Odyssey* 14.219–221).

Menelaos' description of his ambush of Proteus also highlights the discomfort involved. Once Eidothea has prepared the seal skins for Menelaos and his chosen best men, she sits them down and covers them with the seal skin, and Menelaos says this would have been a most dreadful ambush because of the endurance it would have required:

---

[68] Again, if we compare the ambush of the Aktorione Molione by Herakles, we see that he waited for them in a λόχμη 'thicket' (Pindar *Olympian* 10.30). The boar that scars Odysseus similarly lies hidden in a dense thicket before charging: ἐν λόχμῃ πυκινῇ κατέκειτο μέγας σῦς, *Odyssey* 19.439).

[69] On the hardship that characterizes ambush, see also Edwards 1985:22 and the commentary below on 10.248. In the story in *Odyssey* 14, surprisingly, most of the men do seem to go to sleep; Odysseus says he could not because he was too cold.

ἔνθα κεν αἰνότατος λόχος ἔπλετο· τεῖρε γὰρ αἰνῶς
φωκάων ἁλιοτρεφέων ὀλοώτατος ὀδμή·
τίς γάρ κ' εἰναλίῳ παρὰ κήτεϊ κοιμηθείη;

Odyssey 4.441–443

Then it would have been a most dreadful ambush. For
dreadfully it was wearing us out,
that most deadly smell of the sea-raised seals.
For who would go to bed next to a monster of the sea?

Eidothea comes to their rescue again by placing ambrosia under their noses so that they can endure their wait there, hidden under the seal skins, and indeed Menelaos relates how they wait all morning with an enduring spirit (πᾶσαν δ' ἠοίην μένομεν τετληότι θυμῷ, *Odyssey* 4.447). Because Proteus sleeps during the day, this ambush on a sleeping target takes place in daylight instead of the dark, but the concealment and need for endurance remains. The language of endurance, as it does here, often includes some form of the verb τλάω, which is fitting since ambush requires both endurance and daring to overcome fear and accomplish the mission. Odysseus, the champion of ambush, has not one but three distinctive epithets that can relate to this quality of endurance: πολύτλας, ταλασίφρονος, and τλήμων.

The waiting and endurance, the fear and discomfort, are all in service of the surprise attack itself. Leaving their hiding place, the ambushers make some sort of quick movement. Sometimes the movement is expressed as springing or leaping, as when Odysseus describes how he would leap out first in ambush (ἐπάλμενος, *Odyssey* 14.220) or when Odysseus leaps onto the threshold with his bow to begin the slaughter of the suitors (ἆλτο δ' ἐπὶ μέγαν οὐδὸν ἔχων βιόν, *Odyssey* 22.2).[70] In other cases, the movement is described as running or rushing at the victims, as when Menelaos and his men rush at Proteus (ἡμεῖς δὲ ἰάχοντες ἐπεσσύμεθ', *Odyssey* 4.454) or the ambushers run at the shepherds on the Shield (οἳ μὲν τὰ προϊδόντες ἐπέδραμον, *Iliad* 18.527). In the case of the ambush from the Trojan horse, the ambushers pour out, giving a picture of all of them moving quickly together (ἱππόθεν ἐκχύμενοι, *Odyssey* 8.515). Similarly, when Odysseus and Diomedes ambush Dolon in *Iliad* 10, Odysseus plans for them to conceal themselves off of the road until Dolon passes, and then rush at him (ἐπαΐξαντες,

---

[70] Compare also how Paris springs from his place of ambush after he shoots Diomedes (ἐκ λόχου ἀμπήδησε, *Iliad* 11.372).

Iliad 10.345 and ἐπαΐσσων, 10.348). When they do make their move, they run after Dolon (τὼ μὲν ἐπεδραμέτην, *Iliad* 10.354).

Many factors contribute to the surprise nature of the attack. Night is, of course, often the time when ambush occurs, as we see in the examples of the suitors' attempt to ambush Telemakhos (*Odyssey* 16.365–370) and the ambushes Odysseus describes in his Cretan lies (*Odyssey* 13.259–272, νύξ at 13.269 and *Odyssey* 14.468–503, νύξ at 14.475). The darkness adds to both the concealment prior to the attack and the surprise, since the victims do not see the attackers clearly until it is too late, which is precisely what happens to Dolon (*Iliad* 10.354–359). Similarly, when Achilles ambushes Lykaon at night, Lykaon does not see him in time to escape (*Iliad* 21.34–39). The fact that Lykaon is out cutting branches for chariot rails at night seems to be a consequence of the siege of Troy, making his foray outside of the city another example of a dangerous night mission. When his father Priam makes his own nighttime journey outside the city and into the Achaean camp, his appearance in Achilles' shelter produces great surprise for Achilles and his companions (*Iliad* 24.483–484).

In a nocturnal attack, part of the element of surprise may be that the victims, such as Rhesos and the Thracians in *Iliad* 10, the Trojans when the Achaeans emerge from the Trojan horse, or Proteus in *Odyssey* 4, are sleeping.[71] A sleeping victim may be the most unsuspecting, but in other examples the victims are similarly unprepared for a fight because of their involvement in some peaceful activity. Agamemnon is attending a feast that Aigisthos has arranged as the place of ambush (*Odyssey* 4.535 and 11.410). On the Shield of Achilles, the ambushers attack herdsmen who are said to be delighting in their pipes (οἳ δὲ τάχα προγένοντο, δύω δ' ἅμ' ἕποντο νομῆες / τερπόμενοι σύριγξι· δόλον δ' οὔ τι προνόησαν, *Iliad* 18.526–527). Such an attack on herders may give us clues as to other ambushes that are narrated only in compressed form. For example, Andromache relates that Achilles killed all seven of her brothers while they were tending their cattle and sheep (*Iliad* 6.421–424). Since they, like the herdsmen on the Shield, seem not to have been on the lookout for treachery, we may infer that Andromache's brothers are among the victims of Achilles as an ambusher.[72]

---

[71] As we noted above, Menelaos' attack on the sleeping victim happens during the day, due to Proteus' own sleeping habits. Below we will also add Polyphemos to the list of sleeping ambush victims when we discuss how the Cyclops episode in *Odyssey* 9 is structured as an ambush without ever being called one.

[72] When Achilles and Aeneas face off in *Iliad* 20, Achilles recalls that Aeneas was tending cattle the previous time that Achilles attacked him (though at the moment of attack

In ambushes, the number of attackers and attacked is usually unequal, but the numerical advantage can be on either side and does not ensure success. As we have seen above, Tydeus and Bellerophon are each attacked by many, but each succeeds in killing all of them (or all but one intentionally left alive). On the other hand, the number of suitors matches that of Telemakhos and his crew when they plan to ambush him, but they also fail. Odysseus, Telemakhos, and their loyal servants successfully ambush the larger number of suitors; the Achaeans in the wooden horse successfully ambush the larger number of Trojans; and Odysseus and Diomedes successfully ambush a larger number of Thracians. In the ambush of Agamemnon, no one is left alive, except Aigisthos for the time being (*Odyssey* 4.536–537). The planning and skill of the ambushers seem to be much more important factors than numbers. But whether one is the attacker or the attacked, an ambush can be an occasion for renown if he survives. When Nestor proposes the spying mission in *Iliad* 10, he declares that the spy, if he gets back successfully, will have *kleos* as well as offerings from his comrades (*Iliad* 10.211–217). When Tydeus successfully kills his ambushers, he is said to have accomplished *mermera erga*, the same phrase used for Hektor's deeds in conventional battle.[73]

The success or failure of a surprise attack is expressed in terms of returning home, and it is through this concept that ambush shares thematic language and details with the theme of the journey, especially the *nostos*, the journey of homecoming. For spying missions or ambushes seem to be conceived of as having the same overall structure of a journey, and the two themes share the particular spatial structure of going out and, more importantly, coming home. If spies do not return, they cannot share the crucial information they were sent to obtain. Because of the stealth involved, if the warriors on an ambush die, their loved ones may not know where they died or be able to recover their bodies. We see this concern expressed similarly in connection with deaths that happen during a journey. For example, Telemakhos says that if his father had died at Troy, he would have had a proper burial and the *kleos* of a warrior, but since he apparently died

---

Aeneas was separated from the cattle, 20.187–190). This episode was narrated in the *Cypria*, according to the summary of Proklos, where it is characterized as a cattle raid (on which see further below). The reference here suggests that the episode is yet another instance of Achilles as a lone ambusher.

[73] See the commentary on 10.47–48, 10.289, and 10.524 for more on this phrase in an ambush context.

before reaching home, he is without *kleos* (*Odyssey* 1.234–243).[74] In *Iliad* 10, we see the other Achaeans anxiously awaiting the homecoming of Diomedes and Odysseus, indicating both the necessity of the return and the danger involved in such missions (*Iliad* 10.536–539). When they do arrive, they are greeted in the same language used elsewhere in the epics for welcoming those who have just completed a journey (*Iliad* 10.542; see our commentary on this line). In contrast, the narrator says, just as Dolon leaves the Trojan camp, that he will not bring the information back to Hektor that he is being sent to gather; since he will not come back, we know immediately that his mission will not be a success (*Iliad* 10.336–337; see also the commentary on these lines).

The similarities between homecoming journeys and ambush-themed missions are revealed in several places. When Priam is about to set out on a nighttime infiltration into the enemy camp in *Iliad* 24, Hecuba asks him to pray to Zeus for his arrival back home (τῇ σπεῖσον Διὶ πατρί, καὶ εὔχεο <u>οἴκαδ' ἱκέσθαι</u> / ἄψ ἐκ δυσμενέων ἀνδρῶν, *Iliad* 24.287–288). And in another sort of collocation of these themes, Menelaos has to successfully ambush Proteus in order to realize his homecoming (τόν γ' εἴ πως σὺ δύναιο <u>λοχησάμενος</u> λελαβέσθαι, / ὅς κέν τοι εἴπῃσιν ὁδὸν καὶ μέτρα κελεύθου / <u>νόστον</u> θ', ὡς ἐπὶ πόντον ἐλεύσεαι ἰχθυόεντα, *Odyssey* 4.388–390).

The failure of an ambush, even in very compressed versions of ambush narratives, is expressed in terms of a failed return home. For example, in the ambush of Tydeus by fifty Thebans, we hear that "he killed them all, and released only one to return home" (πάντας ἔπεφν', ἕνα δ' οἶον ἵει <u>οἶκον δὲ νέεσθαι</u>, *Iliad* 4.397). Similarly, in the failed attempt to ambush Bellerophon, the ambushers never return home (κρίνας ἐκ Λυκίης εὐρείης φῶτας ἀρίστους / εἷσε λόχον· τοὶ δ' <u>οὔ τι πάλιν οἶκον δὲ νέοντο</u> / πάντας γὰρ κατέπεφνεν ἀμύμων Βελλεροφόντης, *Iliad* 6.188–190).[75]

So, when Diomedes is looking for a partner for the nocturnal spying mission in *Iliad* 10, he chooses Odysseus for the qualities that make him a good ambusher, especially his ability to get home:

---

[74] Compare *Odyssey* 14.365–372, and see discussion in the commentary at 10.211–212.

[75] By contrast, two verbs meaning to 'return (home)' are used in the *Iliad* only in a *polemos* context: ἀπονέομαι and ἀπονοστέω have the marked meaning of a return to Troy for the Trojans (ἀπονέομαι at *Iliad* 3.313, 12.73, 14.46, 20.212, 21.561, 24.330; ἀπονοστέω at *Iliad* 8.499, 12.115) and either a return from Troy to their homes or a return to their ships for the Achaeans (ἀπονέομαι at *Iliad* 2.113, 2.288, 5.716, 9.20, 15.295, 15.305, 16.252, 17.415; ἀπονοστέω at *Iliad* 1.60, 17.406).

τοῖς δ' αὖτις μετέειπε βοὴν ἀγαθὸς Διομήδης·
εἰ μὲν δὴ ἕταρόν γε κελεύετέ μ' αὐτὸν ἑλέσθαι,
πῶς ἂν ἔπειτ' Ὀδυσῆος ἐγὼ θείοιο λαθοίμην,
οὗ περὶ μὲν πρόφρων κραδίη καὶ θυμὸς ἀγήνωρ
ἐν πάντεσσι πόνοισι, φιλεῖ δέ ἑ Παλλὰς Ἀθήνη.
τούτου γ' ἑσπομένοιο καὶ ἐκ πυρὸς αἰθομένοιο
ἄμφω νοστήσαιμεν, ἐπεὶ περίοιδε νοῆσαι.

Iliad 10.241–247

Among them in turn Diomedes well-known for his battle-
cry spoke,
"If you are ordering me to choose a companion myself,
how could I overlook god-like Odysseus,
whose heart and audacious spirit are especially ready
for every kind of labor [*ponos*], and Pallas Athena loves him?
With him accompanying me even from burning fire
we could return home [*nostos*], since he is an expert at
devising [*noos*]."

In the commentary on these lines, we discuss further how the qualities of the willing heart and audacious spirit are appropriate to ambush, but here we will emphasize that Diomedes says that Odysseus could get them home even from a blazing fire. And on an ambush, as on a journey, getting home is a crucial aspect of the mission. Athena, the goddess who loves both Odysseus and Diomedes, tells Diomedes during the ambush to remember his homecoming (νόστου δὴ μνῆσαι μεγαθύμου Τυδέος υἱὲ, *Iliad* 10.509, see also the commentary on this line). Only that way can the mission be a success.

Once we recognize that the theme of ambush overlaps with that of the journey, sharing both formulaic language (since formulas work in service of theme) and structure, certain aspects of *Iliad* 10 are more easily understood. The meal and especially the bath that end the episode are often found in the context of a journey with similar language, and they have been seen as out of place here or too "Odyssean" (see commentary on 10.566–579). As we have seen with other aspects of the language in *Iliad* 10, it is Odyssean not because it is late or non-Iliadic or non-Homeric, but because it shares in the same themes as the *Odyssey*, including both ambush and journey. In the next section we will discuss how spying missions, ambushes, and night raids are thematically related, but all of these resemble journeys because they all seem to be conceived very generally as narratives of "going there and getting back."

Thematic Connections between Spying Missions, Cattle Raids, and Ambush

As we mentioned above, we are treating as part of the theme of ambush other similarly structured episodes, such as night raids and spying missions. There seems to be considerable thematic overlap between such episodes. We propose that each particular episode is best understood within the framework of a larger ambush theme that encompasses them all. Albert Lord describes the working of what he calls the "habitual association of themes" in the composition of oral poetry. He notes that such associations need not be linear, that theme 'b' always follows theme 'a', and that this is due to "a strong force that keeps certain themes together. It is deeply embedded in the tradition" (Lord 1960/2000:97–98). Lord later picks up this point in his discussion of the song as a whole in an oral tradition: "At the end of the previous chapter we saw that some themes have a tendency to cling together, held by a kind of tension, and to form recurrent patterns of groups of themes. They adhere to one another so tenaciously that their use transcends the boundaries of any one song or of any group of songs" (Lord 1960/2000:112). It is this strongly felt connection between the associated themes of ambush, night raids, spying missions, and other types of guerilla or alternative warfare that allows any one of these sub-themes to call up another within the structure of a song. That is, we see in these various episodes, as scattered as they may be in what has survived of the epic tradition outside of *Iliad* 10, a recurrent pattern of groups of themes, all of which we are referring to as ambush.

The example we adduce, a song within the song of the *Odyssey*, demonstrates how any of these themes can lead to another. Helen tells Telemakhos and their assembled guests a story about Odysseus infiltrating the city of Troy as a spy. She sets the story up as an epic performance, a performance parallel to those of Demodokos in the court of the Phaeacians or Phemios in Ithaka. She notes that this will be entertainment (μύθοις τέρπεσθε, *Odyssey* 4.239) as part of the feast (and, of course, she has distributed the *nēpenthes* drug to ensure it can be entertainment rather than a cause for grieving, *Odyssey* 4.220–239). Like the epic narrator, she makes a disclaimer that she is unable to tell all of what Odysseus did,[76] but the disclaimer already leads us into the ambush theme:

---

[76] Compare e.g. *Iliad* 12.176 for an example of the narrator saying that it is difficult to tell all of what happened in the battle at the Achaean wall.

πάντα μὲν οὐκ ἂν ἐγὼ μυθήσομαι οὐδ' ὀνομήνω,
ὅσσοι Ὀδυσσῆος <u>ταλασίφρονός</u> εἰσιν ἄεθλοι·
ἀλλ' οἷον τόδ' ἔρεξε καὶ <u>ἔτλη</u> καρτερὸς ἀνὴρ
δήμῳ ἔνι Τρώων, ὅθι πάσχετε πήματ' Ἀχαιοί.

Odyssey 4.240–243

I could not perform nor name everything,
how many ordeals there were for Odysseus *with his enduring
   heart*
But [I will tell] the following example which that powerful
   man did and *endured/dared*
in the district of the Trojans, where you Achaeans were
   suffering pains.

The language of endurance and daring that Helen uses to introduce the
tale alerts her audience and us to the theme she will be performing: a
theme of ambush, naturally starring a hero of ambush, Odysseus.

But as the tale begins it involves a spying mission. The element
of disguise—Odysseus dresses in rags and makes himself look beaten
and like a beggar of no account (*Odyssey* 4.244-249)—also appears in
the larger theme of the ambush of the suitors in the *Odyssey*. Entering
the enemy city or camp is described twice here (ἀνδρῶν δυσμενέων
κατέδυ πόλιν εὐρυάγυιαν, *Odyssey* 4.246 and τῷ ἴκελος κατέδυ Τρώων
πόλιν, *Odyssey* 4.249), using formulaic language that connects this
spying mission to night episodes such as those in *Iliad* 10 (e.g. ἀνδρῶν
δυσμενέων δῦναι στρατὸν ἐγγὺς ἐόντων / Τρώων, *Iliad* 10.220-221,
εἰ γὰρ δὴ μέματον Τρώων καταδῦναι ὅμιλον, *Iliad* 10.433 and ὅππως
τοῦσδ' ἵππους λάβετον καταδύντες ὅμιλον / Τρώων, *Iliad* 10.545-
546). The craftiness associated with ambush is also apparent in this
episode. Helen relates that, although she recognizes Odysseus, he
evades her questioning with his cunning (ὁ δὲ κερδοσύνῃ ἀλέεινεν,
Odyssey 4.251). The importance of *nostos* and *noos* that we have seen to
be shared between ambush and journey themes also appears here, as
Helen swears not to reveal Odysseus until he returns safely to the ship,
and then he details the whole *noos* of the Achaeans to Helen (*Odyssey*
4.252-256). And finally, the successful spying mission (Odysseus brings
back much "intelligence": ἦλθε μετ' Ἀργείους, κατὰ δὲ φρόνιν ἤγαγε
πολλήν, *Odyssey* 4.258) does become an ambush when Odysseus kills
many men before he leaves Troy (πολλοὺς δὲ Τρώων κτείνας ταναήκεϊ
χαλκῷ, *Odyssey* 4.257). We also see the importance of the return here.
Only upon return can Odysseus share the information he has learned

with the Achaeans and then, of course, go on subsequent missions inside Troy, including stealing the Palladion and hiding within the wooden horse, as Menelaos' story (a performance directly responding to Helen's) goes on to relate (*Odyssey* 4.265–289).

As we can see from this compressed example in Helen's narration of one of Odysseus' exploits, the language of spying missions and that of ambush episodes have much in common. As Lord noted about closely associated themes, one easily leads to the other. In Proklos' summary of the *Little Iliad*, we see a similar episode briefly described: "Odysseus, disfiguring himself, goes into Ilion as a spy. He is recognized by Helen; jointly, they plan the capture of the city. Odysseus kills some Trojans and returns to the ships." Whether we should consider this the same episode that Helen relates or not (one key difference being the detail that Helen is helping Odysseus to plot the destruction of Troy, rather than just learning of their plans), this summary reveals that an expanded version of such a mission existed.

Even without a full version, connections emerge from recurrences of these themes across the Homeric texts and the Epic Cycle. The *Little Iliad* as a whole includes several such ambush episodes: Odysseus ambushes Helenos, Diomedes and Odysseus steal the Palladion from Troy, and the wooden horse is built and filled with the warriors who will ambush all of Troy. Thus the whole song seems to be a series of ambush themes, connected one to another and culminating in the greatest ambush at Troy, for it is by ambush warfare that the city is at long last sacked. In *Iliad* 10, we see a spying mission theme double to become two spying missions, which then turns into an ambush of one spy by the other two, prompting a night raid that includes an ambush of sleeping victims. Even *Odyssey* 4 seems to be built on themes of ambush: not only do the two aforementioned stories about Odysseus have to do with ambush, but the visit with Menelaos also includes the story of his ambush of Proteus, from whom he learns of Aigisthos' ambush of Agamemnon. The book then ends with the suitors' plan to ambush Telemakhos. Thus, as in *Iliad* 10 or the *Little Iliad*, these connected themes build on one another to create the larger song.

A final epic theme that seems closely connected to the theme of ambush is that of the cattle raid, or, as a variation, horse or even sheep rustling. Tales of stealing horses have an obvious parallel in the taking of Rhesos' horses in the Doloneia. In addition, Nestor's cattle raiding tale in *Iliad* 11, our best example from Homeric epic, takes place at night (the cattle raids described at *Iliad* 11.669–684 begin a long chain of events in Nestor's story).[77] We have noted Richard Martin's discussion of how Nestor draws on a different but nevertheless traditional type of epic tradition when he tells his tale.[78] Like the surviving episodes of ambush, stories involving cattle raids and horse thieving are alluded to in a very compressed manner in the Homeric epics. In a reference to a tradition perhaps related to the one referred to in Nestor's reminiscence, in *Odyssey* 15.226–240, where the background of Theoklymenos is recounted, we hear that his ancestor Melampous rustled cattle on behalf of Neleus, Nestor's father, for the sake of Neleus' daughter.[79] Such a detail is intriguing in the context of the *Odyssey*, and must reflect a deep tradition of these kinds of stories.

We can find another example of a compressed raiding story, this time with horses and sheep, within the story of how Odysseus obtained his bow as a guest-gift from Iphitos. The two meet in Messene on their individual journeys to retrieve lost livestock: some men had stolen sheep from Ithaka and Iphitos had lost his horses, who were then stolen by Herakles. They meet at the house of a man named Ortilokhos, whose name means something like "inciter of ambush" (*Odyssey* 21.13–38). Again, because the story is so compressed, we have only these tantalizing traces of a possibly larger story, but those traces are nevertheless suggestive that ambush and cattle raids are, like spying missions and ambushes, themes that could easily be connected in the mind of a singer.[80]

When we look at the wider epic tradition, we find still other episodes of cattle raids. According to Proklos' summary, in the *Cypria*, Kastor and Polydeukes are on a cattle raid when Kastor is killed (the episode is also told in Pindar *Nemean* 10.55–90, where the cattle are briefly mentioned). In the same epic, Achilles drives off the cattle of Aeneas, an episode that seems to have been told just before the episodes

---

[77] See also Tsagalis 2008:153–187 for the connection between the dark of night and the destruction of cattle, as encapsulated in the formula νυκτὸς ἀμολγῷ. For a modern fictional parallel to this nighttime cattle raid, compare Larry McMurtry's *Lonesome Dove* (1985).

[78] Martin 2000. See above, note 32.

[79] See Reece 1994:162–166 for his arguments that the figure of Theoklymenos is a substitute for Odysseus himself in an alternate, older tradition in which Telemakhos travels to Crete and meets up with his father, who returns with him disguised as a seer. Whether or not that version of the story existed, what we are arguing here is that this particular element of Theoklymenos' story seems to belong to an old tradition.

[80] Crissy 1997:43–45, 53 draws parallels between Herakles killing Iphitos in this compressed narrative and Odysseus killing the suitors (in an ambush) with this same bow.

of his ambushes of Troilos and Lykaon.[81] If we also include the Homeric Hymns, Sarah Iles Johnston (2002) has recently shown that such a cattle raid tradition is in fact the central theme of the *Homeric Hymn to Hermes*, whose diction resembles that of *Iliad* 10 in many places.[82] Hermes in fact steals Apollo's cattle on the *evening* of his birthday, again showing an association between this theme and nighttime (*Homeric Hymn to Hermes* 68–78). His talent for thieving and trickery (the hymn calls him cunning, a cattle driver, and a watcher by night, among other epithets, *Homeric Hymn to Hermes* 13–15) naturally associates him with both types of story (ambush and cattle raid), with the result that the traditional diction associated with this god spans both themes.[83] Finally, as we will note in the following section, Hermes does appear in the other episode in the *Iliad* of crossing into enemy territory, when Priam makes his "night raid" into the Achaean encampment in *Iliad* 24.

The Ambush Theme in Other Episodes

Familiarity with the traditional structure of ambush allows us to see that what we are calling the poetics of ambush can also enhance our understanding of episodes that might not be deemed ambushes by strict definition. Nowhere is the blinding of the Cyclops called a *lokhos*, but with Odysseus as its mastermind we should not be surprised that the episode exhibits many of the traditional features of ambush. In *Odyssey* 9, Odysseus and his ships enter the harbor of the island opposite the land of the Cyclopes under the cover of darkness. There is a thick mist and no moon (9.143–145). The night here is described as νύκτα δι' ὀρφναίην. This formula, which emphasizes night's darkness, is found elsewhere in Homer only in *Iliad* 10—and it is also found in the *Homeric Hymn to Hermes*. In the commentary below (on 10.41), we argue that this formula is closely linked to the theme of ambush.

Odysseus leaves most of his men on the island and from there takes only his own ship over to the land of the Cyclopes. When they arrive he chooses the twelve best of his men from his ship to accompany him in his quest to meet the Cyclops (κρίνας ἑτάρων δυοκαίδεκ' ἀρίστους, *Odyssey* 9.195). We have seen that the selection of the "best" men is a traditional component of ambush. This motif recurs once the men are

---

[81] Cf. *Iliad* 20.187–190 and above, p. 76n72. The reference to this raid in *Iliad* 20 is highly suggestive of ambush, and provides another example of the overlap between these two themes.

[82] See further in our commentary on 10.41, 10.267, and 10.466.

[83] In visual depictions of the Doloneia, Hermes is sometimes included: see Lissarrague 1980:18.

imprisoned inside the Cyclops' cave. Odysseus has the men draw lots to see who will join him in the blinding, and he says that the lots fell to those he himself would have chosen (τοὺς ἄν κε καὶ ἤθελον αὐτὸς ἑλέσθαι, *Odyssey* 9.334). Prior to the drawing of lots Odysseus tells us that he came up with a plan: ἥδε δέ μοι κατὰ θυμὸν ἀρίστη φαίνετο βουλή (*Odyssey* 9.318). This verse is the same (with the substitution of οἱ for μοι) as *Iliad* 10.17, describing Agamemnon's nighttime deliberations.

It almost goes without saying that the situation Odysseus has gotten himself into in this episode requires *mētis* to overcome the *biē* (*Odyssey* 9.476) of Polyphemos. First, there is the *mētis* of getting the Cyclops drunk. Next, the blinding itself is compared by way of a simile to the craft of a blacksmith. A second level of *mētis* is required to get out of the cave once Polyphemos is blinded. Odysseus tells us that he "schemed and schemed" (in the translation of Samuel Butler— the Greek is βούλευον at *Odyssey* 9.420 with δόλος and μῆτις at *Odyssey* 9.422: πάντας δὲ δόλους καὶ μῆτιν ὕφαινον), and finally came up with another *boulē* at *Odyssey* 9.424 (using the sheep as a disguise), for which the formula ἥδε δέ μοι κατὰ θυμὸν ἀρίστη φαίνετο βουλή is used once again. The importance of *mētis* is highlighted in the most famous lines of the episode, the pun that so perfectly captures Odysseus' heroic identity: "Surely *mē tis* (or, *mētis*) is killing you by trickery or by *biē*?" to which Polyphemos has been tricked into replying: "No one is killing me by trickery or by *biē*" (*Odyssey* 9.406–408).

Finally, the Cyclops episode is characterized by two other important features of ambush warfare, namely, the use of disguise/concealment and the endurance of hardship over a long period of time, usually during the night. In the commentary below, we explore the possibility that the many traditional epithets for Odysseus built on the root *tla-* evoke his ability to endure the hardships of ambush warfare (see commentary on 10.248). So, too, in this episode does Odysseus display such endurance. Once Polyphemos is blinded, Odysseus hangs on to the belly of a ram (for that is how he and his men conceal themselves) and waits for the Cyclops to open up the cave in the morning (*Odyssey* 9.435): ἐχόμην τετληότι θυμῷ ("I held on with an enduring heart"). He cannot go to sleep and he cannot let go, he can only endure and lament the men he has lost (στενάχοντες, *Odyssey* 9.436). The living ram as a covering or disguise is a twist on the animal skins worn at night in the ambush theme.[84]

---

[84] That the trick with the ram and sheep is akin to animal skins was suggested by Block 1985:3, who compares it to the seal skins under which Menelaos and his men

Many of the elements of this episode and the traditional phrases and verses used in its telling have parallels in the other adventures Odysseus relates in *Odyssey* 9–12, with the result that we can see ambush themes underlying many of these episodes. That *Iliad* 10 likewise makes use of the poetics of ambush does not make the book "Odyssean" in the various potentially misleading ways that scholars over the past two centuries have used that term. *Iliad* 10 and the adventures of Odysseus do not resemble each other because they have the same individual author or because they were composed at the same late date. Rather, they are both manifestations of the overarching theme of alternative warfare, which is fueled primarily by *mētis*, the characteristic most associated with the traditional character of Odysseus.

Are there any other episodes in the *Iliad* that make use of the poetics or traditional structure of ambush in this way? To a certain extent it is likely that all narration of action or warfare that occurs during the night could be shown to share certain elements of diction, formulas, and narrative patterns, as we will see, for example, when we consider the openings of Books 2, 9, and 10 in the commentary below. But we have found ourselves returning to one episode in the *Iliad* again and again in our commentary: the expedition of Priam to the tent of Achilles in *Iliad* 24 (see especially on 10.1ff., 10.41, 10.267, 10.285, and 10.384). We get a glimpse of the theme of the night raid as early as *Iliad* 24.24, where we learn that the gods, distressed by Achilles' desecration of Hektor's corpse, "kept urging the sharp-sighted slayer of Argos [Hermes] to steal the body." Zeus dismisses the idea as impractical, but Hermes nevertheless plays a vital role in the ensuing mission, since he is the one who accompanies Priam through the Achaean camp. In the commentary below (see 10.267), we suggest that Hermes, who has close ties with and is a helper to Odysseus in the *Odyssey*, has a special affinity for ambush warfare. There are significant overlaps in formulaic diction between various ambush narratives, *Iliad* 10, and the *Homeric Hymn to Hermes*.[85] But other gods are also said to accompany heroes on ambush. The best example is on the shield of Achilles, where Athena and Ares together lead the ambush party from the city at war (*Iliad* 18.516). In *Iliad* 10, Odysseus and Diomedes each pray to Athena and ask her to accompany them on their mission, and she is there both

---

hide. Block does not connect it with ambush. We have seen that Menelaos' ambush of Proteus is called exactly that, and both hiding places/tricks are related to the ambush theme in terms of the thematic signals of animal skins and the enduring of discomfort.

[85] See also above on cattle raiding as an epic theme closely associated with ambush.

to breathe *menos* into Diomedes and to warn him to leave before it is too late (*Iliad* 10.482, 507–512). Athena explicitly promises her help to Odysseus when he ambushes the suitors, reassuring Odysseus that, with her help, he could overcome many more men single-handedly (*Odyssey* 20.44–53). Given the arguments we have made about the Cyclops episode in *Odyssey* 9, these verses now stand out: καὶ τις θεὸς ἡγεμόνευε / νύκτα δι' ὀρφναίην ("A god led the way through the dark night," *Odyssey* 9.142–143). It seems likely and fitting that, like *Odyssey* 9, *Iliad* 24 makes use of some of the traditional narrative patterns of ambush warfare. Priam has to sneak through the enemy camp in the dark of night on a highly dangerous mission. If more of the Epic Cycle had survived, we would most likely find that the various nighttime exploits of Diomedes and Odysseus, including their infiltration of the city of Troy, shared many elements with *Iliad* 24. Ultimately, *Iliad* 24 focuses on an episode in which the face-to-face assault of the *polemos* is set aside, and an alternative strategy, stealth followed by supplication, is adopted. Ambush is itself an alternative means of achieving warfare objectives, but it is nevertheless a traditional theme, one invoked in several places in the *Iliad* and *Odyssey* as we have them and, from what we can tell from the surviving evidence, one that was prevalent in the larger ancient Greek epic tradition.

3

Tradition and Reception
Rhesos, Dolon, and the Doloneia

IN THIS ESSAY, we pair two concepts for investigation: the tradition-ality of the characters of Rhesos and Dolon and the reception of these characters and the story of the Doloneia in later works. Both concepts involve exploring what we know about these characters, the story of the Doloneia, and ambush in general from outside of *Iliad* 10. We start by looking at what we can discern about the characters of Rhesos, first, and then Dolon as part of a larger tradition, within which the songs and mythic stories that comprise our *Iliad* were performed and handed down.[1] The characters of Rhesos and Dolon appear in the *Iliad* only in the tenth book, and this fact has led to questions about the place of each in the oral tradition. These questions both stem from and contribute to the dispute over the authorship and traditionality of the book and its place within our *Iliad*. We propose to move beyond these questions by using the evidence that survives to understand their traditionality in new ways.

In the section on reception we will investigate how the theme and poetics of ambush, as exemplified by the Doloneia, have been received and reworked in subsequent literature. We focus on the tragedy *Rhesos* and on Virgil's *Aeneid*, two works whose reception of the Homeric Doloneia is extensive and which therefore offer the opportunity for deeper exploration. Our objective in these explorations is to examine how the features of the ambush theme as we have seen them in *Iliad* 10 are evoked in these works, whose engagement with the story of the Doloneia is wide-ranging, and to consider what more that engagement can tell us about the poetics of ambush. We will see that both of these investigations, into the past and the "future" of the Doloneia, open

---

[1] For more on what we mean by "tradition" see our essay above, "Interpreting *Iliad* 10."

up new paths for understanding *Iliad* 10. Considering this additional evidence is a necessary step toward understanding the tradition on its own terms.

Rhesos

In his 1964 work, *Iliad X and the Rhesus: The Myth*, Bernard Fenik examined in detail the evidence for a traditional myth of Rhesos. We will begin our discussion from his arguments. Fenik has persuasively shown that there is a tradition of some kind behind the figure of Rhesos, an argument not always accepted in the past.[2] Three important medieval manuscripts of the *Iliad*, the Venetus A (Marcianus Graecus Z. 454 [= 822]), the Venetus B (Marcianus Graecus Z. 453 [= 821]), and the Townley ("T," British Museum, Burney 86), preserve in their scholia accounts of what Fenik calls the Rhesos story. In these versions, Rhesos seems to have an expanded role, compared to the one we see in *Iliad* 10. In one version, Rhesos fights one day at Troy and causes so much damage to the Achaeans that Diomedes and Odysseus are sent on a nocturnal mission to assassinate him. In another, there is an oracle that if Rhesos and his horses drink from the Skamandros, he will become invincible. In both of these versions, then, Rhesos seems to have a more detailed role and to pose an explicitly greater danger to the Achaeans than he does in *Iliad* 10.

Fenik argues that the versions contained in the scholia "are clearly alternative accounts to the *Iliad* story, and not minor variants of a single, basic tale" (Fenik 1964:6). He adds further that both alternatives "seem clearly designed for a situation *different from that in which K [= Iliad 10] is imbedded.* Or, correspondingly, the K version is clearly fitted to the *Iliad*, no matter how uncomfortably it sits in its present surroundings" (Fenik 1964:7, original emphasis).[3] Fenik then defines his central question as being whether these versions were "post-Homeric" or whether the author of *Iliad* 10 (whom he takes to be someone other than "the *Iliad* poet") knew of them in some form (Fenik 1964:7–8). If that poet did know them, does our knowledge of these other versions help to solve difficulties in the interpretation of *Iliad* 10? Comparing the story of Rhesos in these other versions to narratives about other Trojan allies

---

[2] See Leaf 1915:3 for his argument that Rhesos is an invented character, with neither locality nor legend: "The natural conclusion is that the Rhesos of the *Doloneia* is a purely literary creation of the moment, devoid of local or legendary background."

[3] We will discuss further below this latter question of how well the *Iliad* 10 version of Rhesos' story fits within the *Iliad* as a whole.

like Penthesilea, Memnon, and Eurypylos, Fenik argues that the story pattern belongs to the Cyclic epic tradition and that Rhesos' appearance at Troy more appropriately belongs after the events of the *Iliad*. The Cyclic Rhesos story could very well be quite old, and certainly older than the *Iliad* as we know it (Fenik 1964:8–16).

Our approach finds many points of agreement with Fenik's. He argues in terms of an oral poetics and an oral tradition at work in all of these versions, and he assumes an early tradition out of which the *Iliad* developed. But we also have important points of divergence from his arguments, since Fenik views *Iliad* 10 both as the work of an individual, even idiosyncratic, author (whom he calls only "the K poet") and as a "later insert" (Fenik 1964:16). These assumptions then set up his entire argument, namely, that this particular *author* knew the other versions but was specifically shaping his story to fit within the *Iliad* (as we know it). In the end, then, his assumptions are revealed to be literary at the core. As sympathetic as we are to some of Fenik's arguments, and as much as we are building on his understanding of the Rhesos tradition, we must also define a separate set of assumptions and a different conclusion about the relationship between these multiple versions as well as the place of *Iliad* 10 within the Iliadic tradition.

Fenik begins his examination of the Rhesos story with the scholia, and we, too, want to examine them in detail for the valuable information they provide. For the Townley scholia, we depend on the edition of Maass (1887), but for the Venetus A and Venetus B, we are able to directly access the scholia on the images of the manuscript published as part of the Homer Multitext Project (http://www.homermultitext. org). In each manuscript, the comment that we will discuss here is keyed to *Iliad* 10.435, the first line in which Rhesos' name appears. At this point Dolon tells Diomedes and Odysseus about the arrival of Rhesos and especially about his armor and horses. Here is the scholion from each manuscript:

Venetus A: Ῥῆσος γένει μὲν ἦν Θρᾷξ, υἱὸς δὲ Στρυμόνος τοῦ αὐτόθι ποταμοῦ καὶ Εὐτέρπης μιᾶς τῶν Μουσῶν. διάφορος δὲ τῶν καθ᾽ αὑτὸν γενόμενος ἐν πολεμικοῖς ἔργοις ἐπῆλθε τοῖς Ἕλλησιν, ὅπως Τρωσὶ συμμαχήσῃ, καὶ συμβαλὼν πολλοὺς τῶν Ἑλλήνων ἀπέκτεινεν. δείσασα δὲ Ἥρα περὶ τῶν Ἑλλήνων Ἀθηνᾶν ἐπὶ τὴν τούτου διαφθορὰν πέμπει. κατελθοῦσα δὲ ἡ θεὸς Ὀδυσσέα τε καὶ Διομήδη ἐπὶ τὴν κατασκοπὴν ἐποίησε προελθεῖν. ἐπιστάντες δὲ ἐκεῖνοι κοιμωμένῳ Ῥήσῳ αὐτόν τε καὶ τοὺς ἑταίρους αὐτοῦ κτείνουσιν, ὡς ἱστορεῖ Πίνδαρος. ἔνιοι δὲ λέγουσι νυκτὸς παραγεγονέναι τὸν Ῥῆσον εἰς τὴν Τροίαν, καὶ πρὶν γεύσασθαι αὐτὸν τοῦ ὕδατος καὶ οἱ ἵπποι αὐτοῦ τοῦ Σκαμάνδρου πίουσιν καὶ τῆς αὐτόθι νομῆς, ἀκαταμάχητος ἔσται εἰς τὸ παντελές.

[at the bottom of the folio] ὅσοι ἐκ Μουσῶν τίκτονται. Ὀρφεὺς ἐκ Καλλιόπης ἢ Κλειοῦς, Λίνος Τερψιχόρης ἢ ὥς τινες Εὐτέρπης, Ῥῆσος Τερψιχόρης ἢ Εὐτέρπης Θρᾷξ, Θαλείας Παλαίφατος, Ἐρατοῦς Θάμυρις ὁ Θρᾷξ, Μελπομένης καὶ Ἀχελῴου Σειρῆνες, Πολυμνίας Τριπτόλεμος.

Rhesos by birth was Thracian, and the son of Strymon the river there and of Euterpe, one of the Muses. Being excellent among his own people in the deeds of war, he went against the Greeks, to act as an ally to the Trojans, and joining battle he killed many of the Greeks. Hera, fearful for the Greeks, sends Athena for the purpose of this man's destruction. Coming down, the goddess made both Odysseus and Diomedes go forth on a spying mission. Those men, standing over the sleeping Rhesos, kill both him and his comrades, as Pindar gives the story. But some say that Rhesos arrived at Troy during the night, and before he tasted the water and his horses drink from the Skamandros and the pasture there, he will be utterly unconquerable.[4]

The following number are born from Muses: Orpheus from Kalliope or Kleio, Linos from Terpsikhore or, as some say, Euterpe, Thracian Rhesos from Terpsikhore or Euterpe, Palaiphatos from Thaleia, Thamyris the Thracian from Erato, the Sirens from Melpomene and Akheloos, Triptolemos from Polymnia.

Venetus B: Ῥῆσος Στρυμόνος τοῦ ποταμοῦ Θράκης καὶ Εὐτέρπης τῆς Μούσης υἱός. ἱστορεῖ δὲ Πίνδαρος ὅτι καὶ μίαν ἡμέραν πολεμήσας πρὸς Ἕλληνας, μέγιστα αὐτοῖς ἀνεδείξατο κακά. κατὰ δὲ θείαν πρόνοιαν νυκτὸς αὐτὸν Διομήδης ἀναιρεῖ.

Rhesos is the son of Strymon the river in Thrace and Euterpe the Muse. Pindar gives the story that having fought in battle

---

4   This translation reflects what actually appears in the text of the scholia, a text that others have found in need of correction because of the syntax problems in this last sentence. See below for further discussion.

for even one day against the Greeks, he demonstrated the greatest evils for them. And by divine forethought Diomedes kills him at night.

Townley: Ῥῆσος Στρυμόνος τοῦ ποταμοῦ τῆς Θρᾴκης υἱὸς καὶ Εὐτέρπης Μούσης. ἱστορεῖ δὲ Πίνδαρος ὅτι καὶ μίαν ἡμέραν πολεμήσας πρὸς Ἕλληνας μέγιστα αὐτοῖς ἐνεδείξατο κακά, κατὰ δὲ πρόνοιαν Ἥρας καὶ Ἀθηνᾶς ἀναστάντες οἱ περὶ Διομήδεα ἀναιροῦσιν αὐτόν.

Rhesos is the son of Strymon the river of Thrace and Euterpe, a Muse. Pindar gives the story that having fought in battle for even one day against the Greeks he proved to be the greatest evils for them, and having been roused by the forethought of Hera and Athena, those around Diomedes kill him.

Fenik identifies two basic narrative patterns in what the scholia report (Fenik 1964:5–6). The first is what he calls the "Pindar version," since the scholia attribute it to Pindar: namely, that Rhesos fought in battle for one day and was so successful that the gods (Hera, and/or Athena, or "divine forethought") prompted the Achaeans (Diomedes in particular, perhaps with Odysseus) to kill him. This version appears in one form or another in all three scholia. The second narrative pattern, which Fenik calls the "oracle version," appears only in the Venetus A scholion, and there in somewhat abbreviated form: in Dindorf's edition, which Fenik uses, Dindorf supplied from Eustathius' commentary on 10.435 the additional words τῆς χώρας φονευθῆναι· χρησμὸς γὰρ ἐδέδοτο αὐτῷ, φασίν, ὅτι εἰ αὐτὸς γεύσεται τοῦ ὕδατος after ὕδατος in the A scholia, so that it reads "But some say that Rhesos arrived at Troy during the night, and was killed before he tasted the water of the area. For an *oracle* had been given to him, they say, that if he tasted the water and his horses drank from the Skamandros and the pasture there, he will be utterly unconquerable." Let us note, then, that the word "oracle" itself is not in this scholion in the Venetus A, but also acknowledge that this version of the story seems to be one that Virgil knew and used (see *Aeneid* 1.469–473: we will return to this passage in the Reception section below). Although there do seem to be two basic narrative patterns referred to here, we note that there are also differences within these summaries of the so-called "Pindar version." As often happens within Greek mythology, so also in this case there is multiplicity and multiformity both on the level of narrative pattern and on the level of narrative detail. The version of Rhesos' story in *Iliad*

10, therefore, need not be a direct "reworking" of one or both of these versions, but may have its own tradition. We will consider still further additional details about the multiplicity of possible traditions about Rhesos below, but for the moment we will continue our discussion of the implications of these scholia for our understanding of the story of Rhesos within *Iliad* 10.

As we have noted, Fenik argues that each of these other versions is impossible within the narrative of the *Iliad*, that Dolon is absent from and extraneous to these other versions, and also that they follow narrative patterns commonly seen in the Epic Cycle or other traditional stories (Fenik 1964:6–12). Fenik concludes that the so-called "K Poet" has tried to fit the story of Rhesos, which belongs elsewhere in the story of the Trojan War, into the *Iliad*, with poor results (Fenik 1964:40–63). That the seeming multiplicity of the Rhesos tradition might inform the composition of *Iliad* 10 has also been suggested in a different way by Gaunt, who proposes that there may have been two versions within the epic tradition that an oral poet could sing: one in which Odysseus endeavors to kill some prominent warrior on the Trojan side, taking Diomedes with him, and the other in which Diomedes volunteers to go on a spying mission and chooses Odysseus as his companion (Gaunt 1971:195–196). Gaunt adds that Dolon may have been common to both versions—in fact, Dolon seems to act as the link that allows the shift from one of these versions to the other in the course of *Iliad* 10 in Gaunt's reconstruction. His conclusion is based on a particular understanding of oral poetry, in which the poet introduces the murder of Rhesos into the reconnaissance narrative because it "offers more of the immediate excitement which the audience is looking for" (Gaunt 1971:198). Such a view of oral composition-in-performance, however, neglects Lord's affirmation of the observable planning by the singer: "In all these instances one sees also that the singer always has the end of the theme in his mind. He knows where he is going. As in the adding of one line to another, so in the adding of one element in a theme to another, the singer can stop and fondly dwell upon any single item without losing a sense of the whole ... The singer's mind is orderly" (Lord 1960/2000:92).

Thus the individual interpretations of both Fenik and Gaunt (both of which do take oral tradition into account) attempt to explain perceived problems with the way Rhesos' death is portrayed in *Iliad* 10 through some idea that one or more traditions about Rhesos may have existed before the composition of *Iliad* 10. Both also assert that there has been some conflation, combination, or adaptation of this tradition in the Iliadic version, as evidenced by the differences between *Iliad* 10 and the versions reported by the scholia or within different parts of *Iliad* 10 itself. Our approach to the Rhesos tradition, grounded in the well-established evidence about oral composition-in-performance and oral traditions, will start from an assumption that there is no individual author of *Iliad* 10, whether the same or different from the author of the *Iliad* as a whole. Making an assumption that there is an individual author, as Fenik does, results only in implications that this author was either incompetent or overly ambitious in trying to adapt this story to the *Iliad* when it does not belong there (Fenik 1964:7, 62–63). We also will look at the interaction between the singer and audience in a way different from Gaunt, whose conclusions imply a "primitive" nature to oral composition-in-performance. As John Foley has shown in several publications, this interaction between performer and audience creates not primitive simplicity and narrative deficiencies, but rather greater meaning and complexity in narrative. We need also to be careful in attributing our aesthetic or ethical reactions to the ancient audience. Starting from these assumptions, then, we can reconsider the place of the ambush of Rhesos within the epic tradition as a whole and within the *Iliad* in particular.

As we seek to understand what the scholia can tell us about the Rhesos tradition, let us also examine what all these versions have in common. All three list the parentage of Rhesos as the river Strymon and the Muse Euterpe (the additional scholion on the Venetus A, however, adds the possibility that his mother is instead the muse Terpsikhore, and we see this same pair of alternates in the list with Linos).[5] All three versions of the "Pindar" story are clear in making Diomedes responsible for his death, and this seems to be implied in the abbreviated "oracle" version as well (if we assume that what is not different carries over from one reported version to the next). In the Venetus A and B scholia, we are also given clear indications that Rhesos was killed at night (κοιμωμένῳ Ῥήσῳ in the "Pindar" version and νυκτός for the "oracle version" in the Venetus A and νυκτός in the Venetus B). The Townley scholia is not as clear in this regard, but the participle ἀναστάντες may indicate that Hera and Athena rouse the Achaeans *from sleep* (compare *Iliad* 10.32, 10.55, 10.176, 10.179, 24.689), suggesting that they attack at night.

---

[5] Apollodorus 1.3.4 lists Strymon as Rhesos' father and Euterpe as his mother, but adds that "some say" his mother was Kalliope. Note that in the *Iliad* Rhesos' father is identified as Eioneus (*Iliad* 10.435).

The consistent inclusion of his parentage places Rhesos within a larger mythical context (one that, we will see below, has local implications). That Diomedes is featured as his killer or co-killer in each of these versions suggests not only that Rhesos has a solid position within the tradition of the Trojan War, but also that the timing of his arrival might indeed traditionally belong to that period when Achilles has withdrawn and Diomedes is the offensive star for the Achaeans, as he is beginning in our *Iliad* 5.[6] Most significantly, however, Rhesos' death is associated in these versions with the night, placing it firmly in an ambush context. Killing him while he is asleep, as the Venetus A scholion describes it, is most obviously an ambush, but even the minimal time indicator "at night" evokes the associations between any kind of night mission and ambush, *lokhos* instead of *polemos*. We should also note that the "Pindar version" in the Venetus A connects the death of Rhesos with a spying mission (τὴν κατασκοπήν), yet another indication of an ambush context (we have discussed the connection between spying missions and ambushes in "The Poetics of Ambush," above). Thus the death of Rhesos by ambush is a key part of his tradition, and the narrative in *Iliad* 10 is traditional in this way.

Recognizing the ambush context of the Rhesos narrative then allows us to reconsider possible parallels with or connections to other traditional narratives, such as the narratives focused on omens or oracles and those of the "late-coming allies" that Fenik identifies. In the larger tradition about the Trojan War, there are several incidents driven by particular prophesies of one sort or another, and many also relate to the goal of defeating Troy. The "oracle version" of Rhesos' story appears, as we have seen, only in truncated form in the Venetus A scholia, but it does share in this pattern. Several of these oracle driven incidents, however, also involve ambush, either to get the prophecy or as a result of it. For example, in the *Little Iliad*, according to Proklos' summary of it, while on a spying mission, Odysseus ambushes the Trojan prophet Helenos, who then reveals that in order to capture Troy the Achaeans must retrieve Philoktetes and also enlist Neoptolemos in the war. The elements of spying mission, ambush, prophecy, and the conditions that must be met for an Achaean victory are all present in this example. The "oracle version" of Rhesos' story contains all of these elements as well, if we draw the conclusion that an invincible

---

[6] Alternately, the fact that Diomedes and Odysseus are the killers of this great threat could indicate that Rhesos arrives as an ally only after Achilles' death. But, as Fenik notes, that possibility still varies from the pattern of the late-arriving allies that are killed by Achilles or by Neoptolemos (Fenik 1964:8–10).

ally of the Trojans (had he and his horses eaten and drunk there) would prevent the destruction of Troy. We can also compare Menelaos' ambush of Proteus, as he relates it in the *Odyssey* (4.384–480), to receive the prophecy that will help him return home (the ultimate goal in that epic).

In both the ambush of Helenos and the ambush of Proteus, the ambush precedes the specifics of the prophecy, although in both of these cases also getting the information from the prophet is the object of the ambush—that is, the existence of an important prophecy is known and motivates the ambush of the prophet. In the case of the oracle associated with Rhesos, we would have to assume that the Achaeans know the details of the oracle and plan the ambush in order to prevent the condition from being fulfilled. In that order of events, the episode more closely resembles the theft of the Palladion, where the Achaeans are told that they must steal the cult statue before they can conquer Troy: in that case, too, a prophecy motivates the ambush narrative. But thematic elements and connections, as Lord has shown and as we have discussed in "The Poetics of Ambush" with attention to this theme in particular, need not always come in the same order to be the same theme.[7] Therefore, the ambush in the "oracle version" of the Rhesos tradition can be seen to fit this traditional ambush theme.

Now let us consider the possible connections between ambush and the other narrative pattern found in the scholia's descriptions, the one Fenik calls the "late-coming ally." Exemplified by Penthesilea, Memnon, or Eurypylos, this theme is focused on daytime battle, in which the ally has an *aristeia*, and culminates in a one-on-one duel in which Achilles or Neoptolemos defeats the ally (Fenik 1964:8–9). Rhesos does not fit this pattern, Fenik points out, in that he is not killed by Achilles or Neoptolemos, and (more importantly for our discussion) "he is killed at night and not in the course of his *aristeia*" (Fenik 1964:10). Even in what little the scholia tell us about the Rhesos tradition, that he inflicts huge damages in an *aristeia* that consists of one day of fighting, all indications point to the killing of Rhesos at night, by ambush. Fenik sees this significant difference from the "late-coming ally" pattern as proof that a so-called "K poet" altered the pattern so as to fit the story of Rhesos into the *Iliad*. We, however, view the ambush at night as a consistent part of the Rhesos tradition, and argue that it is indicative a different narrative pattern.

---

7   See Lord 1960/2000:81–82, 94, 97.

The need to kill Rhesos by ambush after his *aristeia* (since presumably he could not be killed during it) fits within the ambush theme precisely because ambush is a strategy used when *polemos* tactics fail. This version of Rhesos' story is credited by the scholia to Pindar, and we can compare a similar situation narrated in Pindar's *Olympian* 10. There Pindar tells a compressed story in which Herakles slays Kteatos and Eurytos, otherwise known as the Aktorione Molione, by ambush at Kleonai, since they had earlier defeated his army (*Olympian* 10.26–34).[8] Even this brief description includes typical ambush elements: Herakles waits in a wooded area and slays them on the road.[9] Apollodorus (2.7.2) gives us the further details that Herakles had made a truce with them because he was ill, but they attacked his army and killed many while Herakles retreated. He then ambushes them on their way to the Isthmian games. The key sequence is that Herakles ambushes them because earlier he could not defeat them in a standing battle. Within the tradition of the Trojan War, the primary example of this kind of ambush is the use of the wooden horse to ambush and defeat the Trojans when ten years of *polemos* alone could not.

All of these thematic connections between ambush and the versions of Rhesos' story recorded by the scholia suggest that the ambush of Rhesos in *Iliad* 10 is traditional: that is, his death by ambush, and not just the figure of Rhesos himself, is traditional. For all the differences we might notice in the attested versions of the story, in every one of them Rhesos is killed in an ambush by Diomedes and perhaps also Odysseus. For Fenik, the differences also highlight what he sees as a lack of proper motivation for killing Rhesos (Fenik 1964:7, 40–41). In his argument, the oracle or an *aristeia* results in a better-defined need for an ambush specifically directed at Rhesos.[10] There are two (somewhat related) ways we may think about this question further, however. The first is to reconsider whether the ambush is improperly or insufficiently motivated. We disagree with Fenik's assertion that the Achaeans have no need to feel fearful on this night, as they would have had to feel in the other versions of the story (Fenik 1964:61). *Iliad* 10 as we have it

---

8 We are grateful to Douglas Frame for this reference. See Frame 2009:111–113 for his discussion of this passage in relation to the Iliadic stories about Nestor and the Aktorione Molione.

9 See our essay above, "The Poetics of Ambush" for how these elements belong to the ambush theme.

10 Davies 2005:30 ascribes the lack of a reference to the oracle about Rhesos, and therefore, in his argument, also a lack of sufficient motivation, to the *Iliad*'s screening out of "folk-tale motifs," among which he counts "the conditional oracle or prophecy." Davies also thinks that *Iliad* 10 is a "later insertion" that shares this trait with the *Iliad*.

establishes and repeatedly emphasizes the dire situation in which the Achaeans find themselves. In particular the fear they feel is caused and reinforced by the Trojans' presence near their camp and is elevated by *not knowing* what the Trojans are planning. This fear keeps Agamemnon from sleeping (*Iliad* 10.3–4, 11–16), prompts Menelaos to first suggest a spying mission (*Iliad* 10.37–41), and creates a great "need" for the Achaeans (*Iliad* 10.43, 85, 118, 142, 172).[11] When the poetry itself articulates these motivations, how can we say that they do not exist?

Even if there is clear motivation for the spying mission, is that also motivation for the ambush of Rhesos? Perhaps, from a compositional point of view—ambush occurs frequently along with a spying mission.[12] But we should also not discount the possibility that the information that Dolon gives Odysseus and Diomedes about Rhesos (*Iliad* 10.433–441) provides further motivation—even if it is not the motivation that we would like to see. In Homeric epic, warriors on the battlefield often stop to strip armor instead of fighting on, or they go off after horses (Hektor for example goes after Achilles' horses once he has killed Patroklos, *Iliad* 16.862–867, 17.75–76). Therefore, hearing about Rhesos' horses and armor may provide some motivation for Odysseus and Diomedes. Add to that the details of a newly arrived ally (who will be fresh for fighting in the morning) in an unprotected camp, and the possibility for an ambush seems both ripe for the taking and valuable for the Achaean "need" on this night.

We have been arguing so far that just what *Iliad* 10 makes explicit might provide us with an internally coherent motivation for the ambush of Rhesos. We can now add a second approach, one grounded in oral poetics, and consider the ways in which a traditional audience might have understood the ambush of Rhesos. A great deal of scholarship has shown that audiences within an oral tradition bring to their reception of any one performance their experience in hearing all other performances within the tradition. John Foley has argued, based on comparative fieldwork in oral traditional poetry, that the interaction between singer and audience can take advantage of this knowledge on the audience's part, so that even individual formulas and lines imply

---

[11] See Rabel 1991 on "the theme of need" in *Iliad* 9–11.

[12] Indeed, the capture of Dolon is itself an ambush, already shifting the theme. As we have discussed in "The Poetics of Ambush," spying missions often result in an ambush—that is, the two themes are closely linked. So, in terms of the thematic composition of this episode, the one element is enough to suggest the other, and since the ambush of Rhesos is a traditional story, it is easily linked to the spying mission.

the entire sequence of the theme or song to come.[13] In an analogous way, Laura Slatkin, among others, has shown how the larger mythical tradition about characters (in Slatkin's case, Thetis) informs their portrayal within the Homeric epics and how the compressed allusions to these wider narratives can create greater, more complex meaning.[14] In these interrelated ways, then, on both the level of the language and that of the myth, the knowledge and experience a traditional audience brings to an individual performance of a traditional song expands its meaning beyond the explicit. It is incumbent upon us, in turn, to try to reconstruct this larger meaning as much as we can—in Foley's words, to become "fluent" in the language of Homeric poetry.[15]

By giving us a glimpse into the larger mythic tradition about Rhesos, the scholia can aid us in our reconstruction of what a traditional audience might bring to their reception of *Iliad* 10. If an audience knows about one or both of these other versions that the scholia relate, they might implicitly understand the significance of the killing of Rhesos, even if it is never explicitly stated.[16] Such an interplay between the implicit and explicit sets up an interesting dynamic for the audience, who would understand what the ambush means for the Achaeans' long-term victory in the war. In this way, the motivation is not supplied by the *aristeia* or the oracle on the surface of the narrative, but from the audience's perspective the importance of the mission still exists. Perhaps there are also compressed allusions to these other versions, similar to what Slatkin sees in the Iliadic portrait of Thetis, that would call to mind for the audience the threat that Rhesos poses to the Achaeans. When Dolon makes special mention of Rhesos and his horses and armor, which above we argued could be considered motivation enough for Diomedes and Odysseus, does it also evoke for the audience the oracle about Rhesos becoming invincible if he and his horses

---

[13] See, for example, Foley 2002:109–124, especially 118: "What this single decasyllable *implies* idiomatically dwarfs what it seems to say explicitly" (emphasis in original).

[14] Slatkin 1991. See also Edwards 1985, Dué 2002, and Marks 2003 for other investigations of characters within the larger epic tradition.

[15] Foley 2002:120–121. Doing so then prevents anachronistic or inappropriate readings: "By concentrating on the implied meaning of their 'words,' we can avoid some of the pitfalls inherent in a merely textual reading and at least partially understand their registers on their own terms" (Foley 2002:120).

[16] Petegorsky 1982:210–211 understands the motivation for killing Rhesos in much this same way. He argues that, as Fenik has shown, the audience would likely have been familiar with another version of Rhesos' story, and that Diomedes and Odysseus thus "kill a hero who, in a different context, poses the same kind of threat to the Achaeans that Hector does after Book Eight and Achilles' rejection of the embassy" (211).

drink from the Skamandros and eat at Troy? We discussed above the parallel ambush and prophecy story concerning Helenos; now let us emphasize that he was a *captive* of Diomedes and Odysseus when he made his prophecies about Philoktetes and Neoptolemos. Does Dolon's effusive detail in answering Odysseus' questions about the allies, even if it is an attempt to save his life, recall for the audience a situation in which captives give information crucial to the overall Achaean victory, thus also evoking the traditional threat that Rhesos poses?

The information given by Dolon is highlighted again just before the ambush of Rhesos, as Odysseus says to Diomedes:

οὗτός τοι Διόμηδες ἀνήρ, οὗτοι δέ τοι ἵπποι,
οὓς νῶϊν πίφραυσκε Δόλων ὃν ἐπέφνομεν ἡμεῖς.
ἀλλ᾽ ἄγε δὴ πρόφερε κρατερὸν μένος· οὐδέ τί σε χρὴ
ἑστάμεναι μέλεον σὺν τεύχεσιν, ἀλλὰ λύ᾽ ἵππους·
ἠὲ σύ γ᾽ ἄνδρας ἔναιρε, μελήσουσιν δ᾽ ἐμοὶ ἵπποι.

Iliad 10.477–481

"This, Diomedes, is the man, and these are the horses,
whom Dolon (the man we killed) signaled to us two.
Come on, bring on overpowering violence [*menos*]. You must
      not
just stand there in your armor, but release the horses.
Or else you kill the men, and I'll take care of the horses."

In these lines we again have an emphasis on Rhesos, the man (and then also his men), the horses, and the armor. These words and their collocation may once again evoke for a traditional audience the importance of killing Rhesos, either before he fulfills the conditions of the oracle, or (in this case) *before* any possible *aristeia*.

We have now seen that there are other ways to understand the motivation for the ambush of Rhesos within *Iliad* 10. There is an internal logic within the episode, a compositional logic to the connected themes of spying and ambush, and a traditional logic for the audience as to why killing Rhesos is an important victory for the Achaeans. Let us turn now to reconsider Fenik's argument that the Rhesos story does not belong in the *Iliad* and sits "uncomfortably" there as a later addition (Fenik 1964:7, see also 62). If we again start from our assumption that we are not looking for the "authorship" of *Iliad* 10, we can once more come to conclusions that uncover a different relationship between *Iliad* 10 and the epic as a whole from the one Fenik suggests. We will then also consider yet another possible tradition for Rhesos and discuss how competing traditions coexist.

As we have pointed out in our essay "Interpreting *Iliad* 10: Assumptions, Methodology, and the Place of the Doloneia within the History of Homeric Scholarship," many of the objections to *Iliad* 10 overall are based on the aesthetic judgment of the individual critic. The argument is often made that the spying mission and ambush of Rhesos do not belong in the *Iliad* and are patently "separate" because they have no result and are never referred to again in the subsequent events in the *Iliad*. It is true that there is no direct reference to the events of this episode in later episodes, and that the captured horses of Rhesos are not mentioned again, unlike, for example, the captured horses of Aeneas, which are used by Diomedes in the chariot race for Patroklos' funeral games (*Iliad* 23.290–292).[17] Such an argument situates the Doloneia outside of the *Iliad* structurally. An additional criticism, that it is "Odyssean" in nature, objects to it thematically and, in some articulations, chronologically.[18] Although we can and do reject such assertions purely from an understanding of the oral traditional nature of the epics, we can also answer such objections by examining the role *Iliad* 10 does play in the epic as a whole.

Dan Petegorsky has argued that instead of misapplying conceptions about authorship, relationships between "texts," or the idea of "lateness" with respect to the Doloneia, and instead of seeking a strictly structural significance for the Doloneia, we should focus on the Doloneia's thematic importance within the *Iliad*.[19] His examination of the presence and function of the Doloneia in the *Iliad*, he asserts, shows "how important the episode is in contributing to the thematic coherence of the poem as a whole" (Petegorsky 1982:177). The Doloneia, Petegorsky persuasively argues, far from being "separate" or divorced from the rest of the *Iliad*, serves the epic's overall momentum, as it builds towards Achilles' return as the only way to overcome Hektor. His discussion is complex and compelling, especially as concerns the role of *mētis* in the *Iliad*, but we will have to summarize it here only with respect to the Doloneia and Rhesos. In the previous episode on this night, the embassy to Achilles, Achilles has refused to return to battle to face the threat Hektor poses and, noting the wall that the Achaeans have built, has advised them that the wall will not hold Hektor back

---

[17] See, however, the argument of Thornton (1984:165–167) for indirect references or allusions to the events of *Iliad* 10 in other parts of the *Iliad*.

[18] See Petegorsky 1982:176, 201–202, 209.

[19] Petegorsky 1982:175–254.

(*Iliad* 9.346–355). Later, Achilles says that the Achaean leaders will need to come up with a "better *mētis*," μῆτιν ἀμείνω (*Iliad* 9.421–426). This challenge, Petegorsky argues, evokes a theme of *mētis*, or, looking at it thematically, his challenge "demands that they make use of essentially Odyssean skills in an Iliadic context" (Petegorsky 1982:177–178). Unlike all the other plans that the Achaeans attempt in Achilles' absence, however, this one does succeed—but not in turning back Hektor. Instead, its success actually highlights that the only way to succeed against Hektor is through Achilles' strength, which is the programmatic message of the *Iliad*, with its focus on Achilles. The Doloneia does, however, remind us that Troy itself will eventually be taken by *mētis*. In effect, the Doloneia exposes the limited role of *mētis* within the *Iliad* through thematic contrast. Nestor's words about Achilles and Hektor at *Iliad* 10.103–107, the offer of *kleos* for the spying mission that is tied to a *nostos* (*Iliad* 10.211–213, see our commentary on these lines), and even the references to the superiority of the horses of Achilles at *Iliad* 10.401–404 and (more obliquely, as Petegorsky argues) at *Iliad* 10.555–557 all serve to emphasize the necessity of Achilles' strength for effecting the death of Hektor and, consequently, the taking of Troy.[20]

To sum up, Petegorsky argues that Achilles' challenge to the Achaeans in *Iliad* 9, to find a better *mētis* to save the ships, evokes a particular kind of episode, an Odyssean one, in which Odysseus is the star, *mētis* prevails, and *nostos* is achieved. Recalling the arguments we have made that intersect with Petegorsky's examination of these thematic elements, we would rephrase the thematic evocation he reveals—namely, that Achilles' challenge evokes an ambush theme. We can build on Petegorsky's arguments by saying that the plan and ambush in *Iliad* 10 show how *mētis* succeeds when the force used in the *polemos* does not. Or, with the ambush of Rhesos understood in its larger tradition, we may extend Petegorsky's reasoning and return to our point above that the ambush reveals how *mētis* overcomes an enemy who cannot otherwise be beaten in the *polemos*. In the Iliadic tradition, Hektor can be overcome in the *polemos*—by Achilles only. So, although Rhesos is explicitly only an indirect threat and is a greater

---

[20] Petegorsky 1982:209–211 refutes Fenik's assertion that the Doloneia cannot portray the night mission as an assassination attempt against Hektor, showing that it is not the attempt that the *Iliad* excludes, but rather the success of such an attempt, since Achilles must be the killer of Hektor. Fenik (1964:20) also makes the (rather baseless) argument that an assassination attempt would be an unacceptable portrayal of Odysseus and Diomedes (whereas a "negative" portrayal of Odysseus and Diomedes is consistent in the *Rhesos*). Fenik here seems to ascribe his own understanding of ambush as "negative" to an epic tradition that includes many such episodes.

threat implicitly, his ambush nevertheless reveals the important role of *mētis* and ambush in the overall epic tradition about Troy and the general suppression of that importance in the *Iliad*. That general suppression may also account for the dearth of direct references to the events of the Doloneia in the subsequent books of the *Iliad*.

The Rhesos tradition, then, has a very particular place in the Iliadic tradition. The question raised by Achilles as to whether *mētis* will serve the "need" of the Achaeans on this night is answered in a particular way, which allows an Achaean success while at the same time maintaining the greater need for Achilles' return. We can add to Petegorsky's arguments about the thematic importance of the Doloneia for the *Iliad* as a whole one more consideration about the Rhesos tradition: namely, his tradition may have had local significance as well.

There are traces in other ancient works of the Rhesos tradition that might expand our understanding of that tradition even further. A fragment of Hipponax (fr. 72 West), the poet of the sixth century BCE, includes Rhesos being stripped of his arms, chariot, and horses, but perhaps indicates his origins from a different place.[21] Parthenios, in the first century BCE, citing the earlier or contemporary source Asclepiades the Myrlean, relates a romance involving Rhesos before he leaves for Troy (Parthenios *Romances* 36, in Martini's 1902 edition). There are two especially intriguing details in this story: one, that Diomedes kills Rhesos while fighting, rather than in ambush; the other, that the romance is with a woman named Arganthone who likes to hunt, and Rhesos courts her by hunting with her. The first detail is interesting in that it contradicts the epic (and Pindaric) tradition that Rhesos was killed in ambush and locates his death during his *aristeia*, more analogous to the other late-coming allies we discussed above. That this particular genre follows a different narrative pattern may show a generic preference: compare the stories about Achilles falling in love with Penthesilea as he kills her. Falling during an *aristeia* may be a common feature of romance stories centered on Trojan heroes.

The second detail, about hunting, leads us to the latest reference to the Rhesos tradition we will examine, that in Philostratos' *Heroikos*, which also features a hunting Rhesos. In this brief passage, which we quote in full, we see that there is a local version, involving both song and the kind of cult worship that includes sacrifices to the hero, epiphanies of the hero, and the hero's help in maintaining the prosperity of the community:

---

[21] Shewan 1911:15.

You should also know something about the Thracian Rhesos. Rhesos, whom Diomedes killed at Troy, is said to inhabit Rhodope, where they celebrate many of his wonders in song. They say that he breeds horses, serves as a soldier, and hunts wild beasts. A sign that the hero is hunting is that wild boars, deer, and all the wild beasts on the mountain come to the altar of Rhesos by twos or threes to be sacrificed unbound and to offer themselves to the sacrificial knife. This same hero is also said to keep the mountains free of pestilence. Rhodope is extremely populous, and many villages surround the sanctuary. For this reason I think even Diomedes will cry out in defense of his fellow soldiers. If we believe this Thracian still exists (whom Diomedes killed as one who had done nothing famous at Troy nor displayed there anything worthy of mention other than his white horses) and we make sacrifices to him while traveling through Rhodope and Thrace, then we would dishonor those who have performed divine and brilliant works, believing the fame surrounding them fabulous tales and idle boasting.

Heroikos 17.3–6 (trans. Maclean and Aitken)

Although the Vinedresser earlier tells the Phoenician that passion for the Homeric epics means that some worthy men are not remembered at all (*Heroikos* 14.2), in the passage about Rhesos, he seems to uphold the Homeric version of Rhesos' story (and a particular understanding of it) over a local cult tradition in which Rhesos is a hunter as well as a soldier, and in which he has done things that the Rhodopians sing about (ᾅδουσιν, *Heroikos* 17.3). This passage not only suggests that such local traditions about Rhesos existed but also reveals the tensions that can exist between Homeric versions and local versions. As Gregory Nagy has argued, the Homeric epics are Panhellenic in nature and thus screen out local details and variations.[22] The resulting tensions between the Panhellenic epics and these local versions can create the same kinds of tensions within the epics themselves that we see in the passage from Philostratos. Thus, as the Iliadic tradition incorporates Rhesos into its own Panhellenic version, focused on Achilles and Hektor as the chief rivals, and shapes his narrative to its own thematic agenda, we can understand any remaining peculiarities not as evidence of a different author unsuccessfully attempting

---

[22] Nagy 1996b:39–42, 52–54, 124–125.

to insert his work into that of another, but as the natural tensions between coexisting, and even competing, versions of songs within an oral tradition.

In this brief examination of the Rhesos tradition beyond the *Iliad* and those versions reported in the *Iliad* scholia, we are not arguing that all of these versions were part of the epic tradition or influenced the Homeric portrayal of Rhesos. We argue, rather, that the wider tradition helps us understand the version that has been shaped by the epic tradition. In the case of Rhesos, we have seen a multiform tradition that seems to have connections to local cult activities, but that on the Panhellenic level is consistently associated with an ambush theme. As we turn to consider Dolon, we will be dealing with fewer sources for our evidence, and so we will have to use additional methods to uncover and understand his traditionality.

Dolon

We do not have the same external evidence for a Dolon tradition that we have for the Rhesos tradition. As many note, Dolon appears only in *Iliad* 10 and the *Rhesos* in our extant Archaic and Classical Greek literary sources, although he is pictured on early vase paintings as well. The vase paintings will be important later in our consideration of Dolon's possible traditionality. But a careful examination of what we are told about Dolon in the *Iliad* can also yield information about how to understand his role within the Iliadic tradition.

In *Iliad* 10, Dolon is introduced in four lines before he starts to speak and accepts Hektor's challenge to go on the spying mission:

> ἦν δέ τις ἐν Τρώεσσι Δόλων Εὐμήδεος υἱὸς
> κήρυκος θείοιο πολύχρυσος πολύχαλκος,
> ὃς δή τοι εἶδος μὲν ἔην κακός, ἀλλὰ ποδώκης·
> αὐτὰρ ὃ μοῦνος ἔην μετὰ πέντε κασιγνήτῃσιν.
> ὅς ῥα τότε Τρωσίν τε καὶ Ἕκτορι μῦθον ἔειπεν·

Iliad 10.314–318

There was among the Trojans someone named Dolon, son of
Eumedes.
Eumedes was a divine herald, and Dolon had much gold and
much bronze.
He was not good-looking, but he was swift-footed.
And he was the only son among five sisters.

> It was he who at that point spoke words [*muthos*] to the
> Trojans and Hektor.

We learn this much about Dolon before he speaks and goes off on his mission never to return (as we hear at *Iliad* 10.336–337: see also our commentary on these lines). If we look for more information on Dolon's background in the scholia on these lines found in the same three manuscripts that we examined in connection with Rhesos, we see that they do not provide any information beyond what is in the text itself. This is in contrast to what we saw with Rhesos, above: in that case, the scholia articulated other known versions of his story. The scholia dealing with Dolon comment on the attributes ascribed to Dolon here in the text and the presentation of Dolon generally within the *Iliad*.

When external evidence is not present to suggest the traditionality of a character outside of our *Iliad*, the suggestion is sometimes made that the character was "invented" for the episode in which they appear.[23] This concept of "invention" is rooted in a particular understanding of the composition of the epic. In this understanding, the monumental poet Homer (or, in this case often "the Doloneia poet," who is considered separate from, later than, and inferior to the monumental poet Homer) takes traditional material as his basis, but composes an independent, monumental poem as he "breaks free" from the constraints of the tradition.[24] The invention of characters is necessary in order for this individual poet to fill out the structure he has created for the *Iliad* as he molds the tradition to his own literary purposes. We hope it is

---

[23] Hainsworth's commentary on 10.314 glosses Dolon's name as "Sneaky" and says it "is an obviously invented name, created for this episode and alien to the primary forms of the Rhesos-saga" (1993:186). Hainsworth cites Fenik's arguments that Dolon does not appear in the non-Iliadic versions of the Rhesos story as represented in the scholia and that he is "unnecessary" to it (Fenik 1964:17). Fenik himself says that he does "not mean to imply that the K poet necessarily invented Dolon, although he may well have done so" (Fenik 1964:18n3). See, however, Dué 2002: "The attribution of 'invention' to an epic poet working within a traditional system or a vase-painter representing traditional narrative is a very problematic concept" (31). And conjecturing that a character is "invented" because his name seems appropriate neglects the fact that many of the names of traditional epic characters are meaningful within their traditional narratives: see, for example, Nagy 1979:69–83 on Achilles' name; Wathelet 1989:216–218 on the names of Diomedes, Odysseus, Dolon, and Eumedes; and Higbie 1995 on heroes' names in general.

[24] On the inherent flaws in any combination of "Homer + verb," see Nagy 1996b:20–22. The particular combination "Homer invented" is connected with a common misconception of Homer as a master poet who has somehow "broken free" of the oral tradition. See Nagy 1996b:26–27.

clear by now that we reject such an understanding of the composition of the epic. As Lord so eloquently put it about his conception of Homer: "He is not a split personality with half of his understanding and technique in the tradition and the other half in a parnassus of literate methods. No, he is not even 'immersed' in the tradition. He *is* the tradition" (1960/2000:147).[25] With this empirically-based recognition of how oral poets operate within and indeed embody the tradition they sing, we must also reject the notion of inventing a character as a creation outside of the tradition. If we speak of the invention of a character like Dolon, who appears in both epic poetry and the visual arts, we are dealing with two different kinds of innovation. For the invention of a character involves not only a radical addition to the system of traditional epic composition and song (both in terms of narrative content and diction), but also the creation of the myth around which the system of composition is built.[26]

Several characters in the *Iliad* have supposedly been invented, including Euphorbos, Briseis, and even Patroklos.[27] Casey Dué has argued with reference to Briseis, however, that because innovation within an oral, traditional poetic system happens only over a long period of time, we must seek a new model for understanding the roles of minor characters within our *Iliad*:

> It cannot be claimed therefore that Briseis or any character
> is the "invention" of any one poet, even though traditional

---

[25] Similarly, see Lord 1960/2000: "It is sometimes difficult for us to realize that the man who is sitting before us singing an epic song is not a mere carrier of the tradition but a creative artist making the tradition" (13) and *"oral poets who are not traditional do not exist"* (155, original emphasis).

[26] For a refutation of the arguments of those who speak of the invention of myth (e.g. Willcock 1964 and 1977), see Nagy 1992 and 1996b:113–146. Nagy argues from the perspective of social anthropology that for the ancient Greek poets "creativity is a matter of applying, to the present occasion, myths that already exist" (Nagy 1992:312). Lowell Edmunds also speaks of the application of traditional stories or myths to the present occasion: "A story, or myth, is therefore, in retrospect, a set of variants on a fundamental pattern, while, on the occasion of any retelling, the present, individualist version is the authoritative one. Myth occurs, one could say, at the juncture of performance with tradition" (Edmunds 1997:420). Edmunds's definition of myth is in accord with the process of composition-in-performance of oral traditional poetry. We may compare Nagler's (1974:26) words on Homeric diction: "all is traditional on the generative level, all original on the level of performance." On the application of mutually contradictory variations of the same myth on different occasions within the same poem, see Edmunds 1997:421–422.

[27] On Patroklos as an invented character, see Howald 1924:11–12 as well as Dihle 1970:159–160 and bibliography *ad loc.* More recent discussions include Allan 2005 and Burgess 1997 and 2005. For Euphorbos, see Nickel 2002 and Allan 2005.

tales can be shown (by an outsider to that tradition) to change over time. If we are to appreciate the *Iliad* and *Odyssey* as oral traditional poetry, a different model must account for Briseis' and other minor characters' brief appearances. Such a model presents itself in the poetic technique of compression and expansion ... In the more fluid stages of the evolution of the *Iliad*, it is possible that multiple variations on expanded narratives about Briseis coexisted. Briseis had not only a history, but possibly many histories. In less fluid stages of a poem there are fewer variations, but variation continues to occur on the level of expansion and compression. I argue that Briseis' seemingly minor role in the *Iliad*, like that of many other characters, is a compression of at least one variation on her story.

Dué 2002:87

Using this approach to consider the introduction of Dolon in our text, we can understand the details given there to point to possible alternative or expanded versions. The details about Dolon's family seem to place him within a traditional context: he appears not out of nowhere, but has a father, the herald Eumedes, and five sisters. As the scholiasts point out, other details introduced here, such as Dolon's swiftness and his wealth, do indeed come into play when he is captured: even though he is swift, Odysseus outsmarts him so that his swiftness does not allow him to escape (*Iliad* 10.341–377), and Dolon says, quite formulaically, that his father will gladly pay much ransom to get him back alive (*Iliad* 10.378–381). But the four-line introduction has resonance beyond its immediate context: this compressed version can point to a wider tradition about Dolon himself, as well as show how Dolon fits into traditional story patterns.[28]

---

[28] Dué 2002:8n24 similarly discusses the character of Briseis in terms of her syntagmatic and paradigmatic significance within the *Iliad*: "the *paradigmatic* aspects of the figure of Briseis are connected to the experiences ... that unite her with the other women of the *Iliad* and *Odyssey* (and women in general). The *syntagmatic* aspect of her character is the extent to which she has her own narrative that is independent of other women and the way they are portrayed in epic. The terms paradigmatic and syntagmatic derive ultimately from linguistics, and are pictured as operating on respectively vertical and horizontal axes of selection and combination. To put it another way (following Jakobson) the term syntagmatic is used of metonymic relationships (that is relationships where meaning is determined by connection), whereas the term paradigmatic refers to metaphorical relationships (where meaning is determined by substitution)." We can apply this same formulation to Dolon.

We should recognize first that the introduction of Dolon is composed formulaically in a way that is similar to other introductions of characters entering Homeric narratives for the first time. Four other characters are introduced with the same formula that we find at *Iliad* 10.314: ἦν δέ τις ἐν Τρώεσσι Δόλων Εὐμήδεος υἱός. In what follows, we will examine these introductions, and then see what kinds of inferences we can draw from each one and from the group collectively.

The first instance of the formula we will examine occurs at *Iliad* 5.9-10 and introduces Dares, whose sons are about to face Diomedes on the battlefield:

> ἦν δέ τις ἐν Τρώεσσι Δάρης ἀφνειὸς ἀμύμων
> ἱρεὺς Ἡφαίστοιο· δύω δέ οἱ υἱέες ἤστην
> Φηγεὺς Ἰδαῖός τε μάχης εὖ εἰδότε πάσης.
> τώ οἱ ἀποκρινθέντε ἐναντίω ὁρμηθήτην·

Iliad 5.9–12

> There was among the Trojans someone named Dares, a
>   wealthy man, faultless,
> a priest of Hephaistos; he had two sons,
> Phegeus and Idaios, both of whom knew well every kind of
>   battle.
> Emerging from the throng the two of them faced Diomedes
>   and rushed at him.

Structurally, the first line and a half are very similar to *Iliad* 10.314–315: each line begins ἦν δέ τις ἐν Τρώεσσι, completed by the man's name and epithets. Such similarities suggest that this phrasing would have indeed been useful and good for a poet in performance. The similarity continues in the next line, which describes his occupation as divinely sanctioned and notes his wealth.[29] Dares' son Phegeus becomes Diomedes' first victim, and Idaios escapes with his life only because Hephaistos rescues him, covering him in darkness so that, we are told, Dares would not lose both sons. Diomedes then drives off their horses (*Iliad* 5.12–26).[30]

---

[29] See our commentary on 10.314–315 for more on the unnecessary enjambment in these lines.

[30] See Thornton 1984:68–69, who argues that this rescue of a potential victim of Diomedes is a 'sign-post' directing the audience to the later important rescue of Aeneas by Aphrodite (the 'goal' in Thornton's terms). See also Thornton 1984:80–82 for her brief discussion of the expansion of Diomedes' *aristeia* through the doubling of motifs.

Another instance of the formula introduces Eukhenor, at *Iliad* 13.663–664, followed by a longer description of his life story. Eukhenor is not a man among the Trojans, as we have seen in the first two examples, but an Achaean fighter with a very specific backstory:

ἦν δέ τις Εὐχήνωρ Πολυΐδου μάντιος υἱὸς
ἀφνειός τ' ἀγαθός τε Κορινθόθι οἰκία ναίων,
665 ὅς ῥ' εὖ εἰδὼς κῆρ' ὀλοὴν ἐπὶ νηὸς ἔβαινε·
πολλάκι γάρ οἱ ἔειπε γέρων ἀγαθὸς Πολύϊδος
νούσῳ ὑπ' ἀργαλέῃ φθίσθαι οἷς ἐν μεγάροισιν,
ἢ μετ' Ἀχαιῶν νηυσὶν ὑπὸ Τρώεσσι δαμῆναι·
τώ ῥ' ἅμα τ' ἀργαλέην θωὴν ἀλέεινεν Ἀχαιῶν
670 νοῦσόν τε στυγερήν, ἵνα μὴ πάθοι ἄλγεα θυμῷ.
τὸν βάλ' ὑπὸ γναθμοῖο καὶ οὔατος· ὦκα δὲ θυμὸς
ᾤχετ' ἀπὸ μελέων, στυγερὸς δ' ἄρα μιν σκότος εἷλεν.

Iliad 13.663–672

There was someone named Eukhenor, a son of the seer
    Polyidos,
both wealthy and valiant, dwelling and making his home in
    Corinth.
Fully aware of his destructive doom he boarded the ship.
For often the valiant old man Polyidos told him
that he would perish from a painful disease in his own halls
or would be subdued at the hands of the Trojans near the
    ships of the Achaeans.
Thus he avoided at the same time both the painful penalty
    of the Achaeans
and the hateful disease, so that he would not experience
    suffering in his heart.
Him Paris hit under the jaw and through the ear. Swiftly his
    life
left from his limbs, and the hateful darkness took him.

Eukhenor has also been understood as a character whose "purpose is to remind the audience that Achilles will die at Troy at the hands of Paris after having made a similar choice."[31] Nickel (2002), for example, explores the idea that Eukhenor is a 'doublet' of Achilles. Fenik earlier

---

[31] Nickel 2002:226. Nickel does not state that Eukhenor is invented using that term. But the idea that Eukhenor has a particular purpose in Achilles' story having only to do with Achilles himself is typical of the "invention" concept.

proposed this idea, but says that, for all of the resemblance between Eukhenor's choice and Achilles', Eukhenor's story also resembles other traditional story patterns.[32] Fenik argues that when Eukhenor is considered within the epic as a whole: "All the other details of his life and death—his wealth, the circumstances of his death, the action of Paris with his bow—are fully typical with the *Iliad* itself without reference to Achilles."[33] From our understanding of how oral traditional poetry operates, what Fenik calls "fully typical" we would call "fully traditional."

As many commentators have pointed out, as Eukhenor's story is told, he is also in the process of being killed, and therefore he plays no further direct role in the action. Yet Eukhenor and his story appear to be traditional, and if we consider possible local variations or expansions, such as those Dué examines for Briseis—variations that would have been screened out as the *Iliad* became a Panhellenic epic—we can imagine that Eukhenor might have had an epic of his own sung at Corinth about his choice to go to war. The compressed reference to the Achaean leaders coming to collect him for war (implied by the "penalty" he avoids) is reminiscent of Epic Cycle tales about heroes such as Achilles and Odysseus. Another sign of his traditionality can be found in the scholion on the line that introduces Eukhenor (*Iliad* 13.663) in the Townley manuscript of the *Iliad*. There, the scholiast notes that Pherekydes provides a genealogy for Eukhenor.[34] This genealogy extends back five generations on his father's side, and three on his mother's side. His mother, Pherekydes says, was Eurydameia, the daughter of Phyleus, the son of Augeus. This background not only places Eukhenor within a wider tradition that includes Herakles, but also means that he has an uncle, Meges, also fighting at Troy. According to this same scholion, Eukhenor and his brother, Kleitos, fought with the Epigonoi in their successful assault on Thebes. All of this adds up to a great deal of material for a song within an oral tradition.

[32] Fenik 1968:148–149. Fenik does, however, believe that characters can be "invented" and given a biography modeled on a general pattern: he makes such an argument in his discussion of minor Trojan characters who are introduced just before they are killed (Fenik 1968:151–152).

[33] Fenik 1968:149. Later, Fenik reasserts that Eukhenor is a doublet of Achilles (Fenik 1968:152).

[34] The scholion from the Townley manuscript in Maass' edition reads: ἦν δέ τις Εὐχήνωρ Πολυΐδου· Φερεκύδης οὕτω γενεαλογεῖ· "ἀπὸ Μελάμποδος Μάντιον, οὗ Κλεῖτον, οὗ Κοίρανον, οὗ Πολύϊδον·" εἶτα "Πολύϊδος" φησί "γαμεῖ Εὐρυδάμειαν τὴν Φυλέως τοῦ Αὐγέου· τῷ δὲ γίνεται Εὐχήνωρ καὶ Κλεῖτος, οἳ Θήβας εἷλον σὺν τοῖς Ἐπιγόνοις· ἔπειτα ἐς Τροίην ἔρχονται σὺν Ἀγαμέμνονι, καὶ θνήσκει Εὐχήνωρ ὑπὸ Ἀλεξάνδρου."

Similar to Eukhenor, Podes, the son of Eetion, is introduced as he is killed, in his case by Menelaos, who is protecting the body of Patroklos (*Iliad* 17.575–580). In many manuscripts and in modern editions, we do not see the same ἦν δέ τις introductory formula at *Iliad* 15.575, but it does appear in at least three manuscripts, according to Allen's edition, including the Genavensis. If we acknowledge this recorded multiform as a performance variant[35] and thus include Podes in this category, we see again a compressed life story: Podes was wealthy and valiant, and Hektor honored him most of all as comrade, friend, and guest at banquets. As a brother of Andromache, we might expect him, as well, to have a traditional story that could be expanded in other versions. The fact that Andromache says that Achilles killed all seven of her brothers on the same day (*Iliad* 6.421–424) may in fact point us to differing and competing versions of these stories.[36]

Finally, the suitor Ktesippos is introduced with this formula at *Odyssey* 20.287. Ktesippos memorably throws an ox foot at Odysseus, provoking Odysseus' famously sardonic smile. Just before making that throw, immediately preceding his first speech in our *Odyssey*, Ktesippos is introduced as follows:

ἦν δέ τις ἐν μνηστῆρσιν ἀνὴρ ἀθεμίστια εἰδώς,
Κτήσιππος δ' ὄνομ' ἔσκε, Σάμη δ' ἐνὶ οἰκία ναῖεν·
ὃς δή τοι κτεάτεσσι πεποιθὼς πατρὸς ἑοῖο
μνάσκετ' Ὀδυσσῆος δὴν οἰχομένοιο δάμαρτα.
ὃς ῥα τότε μνηστῆρσιν ὑπερφιάλοισι μετηύδα·

Odyssey 20.287–291

There was someone among the suitors who knew
    lawlessness,
his name was Ktesippos, and he dwelt and made his home in
    Same.
This man, trusting in the property of his father,
wooed the wife of Odysseus, who was gone for a long time.
It was he who at that point spoke among the overweening
    suitors.

Structurally, this introduction has even more in common with that of Dolon, since it is also made just before the character speaks for the first

---

[35] See our following essay "*Iliad* 10: A Multitextual Approach" for more on the terms multiform and performance variant.

[36] See p. 76 for our argument that Achilles ambushed the brothers of Andromache.

time. In both cases we have the ἦν δέ τις ἐν formulaic beginning (cf. *Iliad* 10.314), four lines of description, and then a speech introduction that uses the formulaic line beginning ὅς ῥα τότε (cf. *Iliad* 10.318). We have fewer biographical details here, however: simply his hometown and the fact that his father was wealthy.

Looking at all five examples, we can see that Dolon is introduced in a formulaic way, and that each man introduced in this way has specific details provided that may be expanded into a longer story. Eukhenor, of course, is the example in which the pattern is easiest to see because something of an expansion is already present in this version. But the details that follow in the brief appearance of the sons of Dares point to the possibility of a larger story as well, as Hephaistos saves Idaios so that Dares will not be totally bereft (*Iliad* 5.22–24). Other Trojans so rescued, such as Paris and Aeneas, have connections to larger stories beyond the *Iliad*.

Details that evoke possible expanded versions are common to introductions like Dolon's. Another common thread is that each man is introduced at a transition point. The introduction of Dares and his sons marks the beginning of Diomedes' expansive *aristeia*. Ktesippos is introduced at the first meal of the day on which the suitors will be slaughtered: although Telemakhos has asserted control over the suitors in their treatment of the stranger, Ktesippos will begin the abuse again, marking the beginning of the end for the suitors—as is further indicated by Odysseus' smile (*Odyssey* 20.257–303). The introduction and subsequent death of Eukhenor mark a swinging of momentum from the Achaeans back to the Trojans, as Eukhenor's death is followed by a shift in focus to Hektor and his renewed charge (*Iliad* 13.674–688). Similarly, the death of Podes happens as the focus shifts from Menelaos and the fight over Patroklos' body back to Hektor in battle and Apollo's arrival in disguise to guide him (*Iliad* 17.582–590).

Dolon's introduction comes at a point where the focus of the narrative has just shifted from the Achaean camp to that of the Trojans. But the doubling of the spying mission theme (that is, Dolon's introduction occurs when Hektor proposes a mission parallel to the one Nestor proposes for Diomedes and Odysseus) marks another kind of transition as well, since it will transform the spying mission into an ambush (see our essay "The Poetics of Ambush" on how these themes are related and one can be transformed into the other). Within the larger structure of the song, then, such introductions of characters come at moments when a longer important episode is starting and/or a series is coming to an end before a new focus begins. This is only indirectly associated with the traditionality of the characters so introduced themselves, but it helps us to see that such introductions are not spur of the moment "inventions" but rather part of a larger pattern within the structure of songs.

A third point of commonality is that deaths follow these introductions, immediately for Eukhenor and Podes and later that same day for Ktesippos (*Odyssey* 22.285–291). In Dares' case, the death of his son immediately follows. Dolon will also die the same night, and as he leaves the camp the narrator says as much. Within his discussion of Eukhenor, Fenik adduces examples of Trojan victims such as Iphiton, Satnios, and Simoeisios, who are introduced as they are killed, and argues that these biographies "are all composed according to a single mould with the purpose of achieving a distinct kind of pathos" (Fenik 1968:152).[37] Fenik focuses on the mention of each man's mother in these cases. We instead address cases in which fathers are mentioned. For example, in the case of Dares we have the direct reference to his grief (*Iliad* 5.24) and an implied reference in the story of Eukhenor, since it is his father who informs him of the choice he faces in how he will die (*Iliad* 13.666–668). In the case of Podes, his father Eetion is already dead, but his close relationship with Hektor transfers the grief theme to Hektor himself, who feels grief (*akhos*) when told of Podes' death (*Iliad* 17.591). As unsympathetic as we might find Ktesippos, we know from the reactions of the suitors' families in general in *Odyssey* 24 that they, too, grieve their loss. And, similarly, we discuss in the commentary on 10.314–317 the ways in which Dolon's introduction, especially the details that he is his father's only son and that he has five sisters, may connect to lament traditions and evoke sympathy.

From these comparisons of Dolon's introduction to other, similarly introduced men, we can see how even brief biographies have a traditionality at least within the Homeric tradition, if not one like that of Rhesos, which seems to reach outside of it. We can therefore postulate a traditionality for Dolon thus far. The next step is to contextualize that character's story within traditional story patterns (see Dué 2002:87–88). Seeing the parallels between Dolon's introduction and those of Dares' sons, Eukhenor, Podes, and Ktesippos is one way to do so. Understanding a lament tradition to be compressed into the intro-

---

[37] Similarly, Janko's commentary on *Iliad* 13.660–672 characterizes the introduction ἦν δέ τις as "wealthy but doomed characters" (1992:128). Fenik also says that some of these characters may be invented.

duction of characters who are going to die is another.[38] Scholars have also attempted to understand Dolon's story in terms of story patterns beyond Homeric poetry, and even beyond epic.

Gernet, starting from the more elaborate description in the tragedy *Rhesos* of Dolon's wolf skin as a disguise, not merely a garment, suggests connections between Dolon's story and the Arcadian cult of Zeus Lykaios and the myth of Lykaon, who was transformed into a wolf (Gernet 1936:190–193). Gernet understands an initiation ritual involving the wearing of a wolf skin to be alluded to here, a ritual in which the initiate is separated from human society for a fixed period of time while he lives as a "wolf" (Gernet 1936:193).[39] Emphasizing the nighttime setting of the Doloneia and investigating the story patterns of nocturnal exploits, Gernet again finds the tragedy more instructive. In that version Dolon is not simply going on a spying mission; he intends to return with Odysseus' head. The "hunt for heads" pattern, then, includes Dolon losing his own in *Iliad* 10.[40] Gernet explores possible associations with the wolf as an outlaw figure, as seen in other cultures with initiation ceremonies that involve masks and wolf figures, and between wolves and death, demons, or revenants (Gernet 1936:200–208). All of these possible connections serve Gernet's working hypothesis that there is a religious and ritual background to Dolon's wolf skin in the *Iliad* and in the *Rhesos*.

Davidson, building on the work of Gernet and Fenik, also surveys myths and initiation rituals involving wolves, tricksters, and horse swapping. She argues that *Iliad* 10 exemplifies epic's incorporation of other traditions, concluding: "If one accepts Fenik's suggestion that the Rhesus myth of the play *Rhesus* is pre-Iliadic, then I suggest that the Dolon myth is also that old ... Many of the details that seem hazy in Book X can be clarified if we look at such other traditions" (Davidson 1979:66). More recently, Wathelet (1989) has also explored possible religious undertones to the Doloneia. He argues that Rhesos, with his magnificent horses and chariot, could be associated with a cult of a Sun god, and that Dolon has affinities with the god Hermes (1989:218–219, 226–231). This story, in Wathelet's analysis, also has the structure of an initiation ritual. Schnapp-Gourbeillon (1981:95–131), however, has questioned this ritual reading of Dolon's wolf skin, arguing that it must be read in connection with the animal skins the Achaeans wear earlier in *Iliad* 10.

---

[38] For this approach, see Tsagalis 2004:179–192 and the commentary below on 10.314–317.

[39] Wathelet 1989:220 also understands a rite of passage underlying Dolon's wolf skin.

[40] Gernet 1936:196–197. Cf. *Rhesos* 219–223 and our discussion of the tragedy below.

While Davidson and Wathelet focus on cult and ritual in determining the traditionality or pre-Iliadic existence of Dolon, Malcolm Davies, who does not cite Gernet directly, frames his arguments in terms of folktales and their quest narratives. He proposes that Dolon is the "ambivalent helper" figure in such quest stories, and that his wolf skin is suggestive of the metamorphosis or disguise such figures often take (Davies 2005:31–32). Another folktale motif that Davies explores is that this helper is often a doublet of the adversary. In exploring what Dolon and Rhesos have in common, Davies comes to a similar proposal to that of Gernet, asking "whether Dolon and Rhesus, like Nereus and Geryon, share an original status as death-demons," especially considering their associations with night (Davies 2005:32). These types of story patterns or cult associations offer a different type of traditionality, and suggest that there is something old, perhaps even Indo-European, about nighttime missions and figures like Dolon, at least, if not this particular character.

So far, then, we have seen possible ways of thinking about Dolon as a traditional figure within the Homeric epic tradition, within myth or folklore, and within cult and ritual. All these possibilities remain uncertain without further evidence. But, as we noted at the beginning of this examination of Dolon, he also appears in vase painting, which gives us yet another perspective on his individual tradition. François Lissarrague (1980) also takes the narratives of Dolon in *Iliad* 10 and the tragedy *Rhesos* as a starting point in his examination of eight different vase paintings from the sixth to fourth centuries BCE that depict Dolon, sometimes explicitly labeling the figure by name, other times identifying him by the wolf skin and/or as one man captured by two others (see Plate 5). On the earliest (590–575 BCE) of these vases, a Corinthian cup, Dolon is nude and, since he is placed under the handle of the vase, he is also somewhat removed from what looks to be a conventional battle scene in the central part of the painting.[41] Considering this

---

[41] Although he does not believe Dolon to be a traditional character, Friis Johansen (1967:74–75) asserts that this early sixth-century BCE Corinthian cup "makes it reasonable to assume that the Doloneia was known in Corinth as part of the *Iliad* at the beginning of the sixth century." Snodgrass concludes: "We should take this as a sign that the Doloneia, before it became the tenth book of the *Iliad*, had both literary and non-literary antecedents" (1998:121). Elsewhere Snodgrass notes his own reluctance to acknowledge that Doloneia scenes are among the earliest and most common of the "Iliadic" scenes on vases (1998:131). Lowenstam (1992:184) comments on this phenomenon, specifically as it relates to the Doloneia in art: "It is curious that some of the passages in the Homeric poems which the Analysts confidently determined to be 'late' are those for which we have the earliest artistic evidence." Ahlberg-Cornell

image, Lissarrague cautions that we should not try to fit text to image or image to text, for they "speak two different languages": "Texte et image parlent deux langages différents, utilisent deux codes différents, et constituent deux univers plus parallèls que complémentaires" (Lissarrague 1980:14). Our approach to the visual images is similar: the visual artists follow the conventions of their medium and are not dependent on particular texts.[42] When we investigate the question of Dolon's tradition we must take both into account.[43]

Lissarrague contrasts the positioning of Dolon on the periphery of this early image with his positioning in the Attic vase paintings in which he is front and center, depicted between Diomedes and Odysseus (Lissarrague 1980:17–19). In these images, dated from 510–460 BCE, there are certain motifs that Lissarrague identifies as common to the three vases he presents: the composition of the figures (with Dolon in the middle), use of animal disguise, vegetal decoration, the armament of the heroes, and the gestures and postures. These visual signifiers have much in common with what we have identified in our "Poetics of Ambush" essay above as signals that indicate a particular poetic register within a particular theme. Just as we discussed there in connection with the dressing scenes in which the heroes put on animal skins in *Iliad* 10, Lissarrague emphasizes the wearing of skins as a putting on of a certain identity (Lissarrague 1980:19–20). The vegetation in the background, he argues, is part of Dolon's camouflage as he moves through the night, and it shares features with scenes of Achilles ambushing Troilos. Lissarrague wants to understand the vegetation as generally associated with "an animal and savage world" (1980:21). We would argue instead that the plants indicate an ambush setting in both cases.

In "The Poetics of Ambush," we argued for the thematic as well as visual associations between archery and ambush, and Lissarrague also notes this association in passing (Lissarrague 1980:22). But he argues

---

(1992) does not include the Doloneia in her otherwise comprehensive survey of epic scenes in early Greek art.

[42] For more on how to understand the relationship between visual images and the Homeric epics as oral-traditional poetry, see Lowenstam 1992, 1997, and 2008. Lowenstam (1992:188) points out that "vases furnish not only our earliest alternative versions of some Homeric stories but sometimes also our first view of stories known to the tradition and Epic Cycle although not utilized or delineated in the versions of the *Iliad* and *Odyssey* that we possess." Thus these vase paintings can indicate a wider tradition about Dolon and can tell us something about that wider tradition, perhaps especially through individual details in the depictions of him.

[43] See also Dué 2002:27–36 on the question of the relationship between art and epic, and what that relationship means for understanding traditionality.

that some weapons are associated with the hunt, others with combat, and that, whichever Dolon has, Diomedes and Odysseus have the other (Lissarrague 1980:22–24).[44] Explaining how gestures and postures indicate that Dolon has fallen into a trap, and that his death will follow (1980:24–26), Lissarrague concludes that these elements all "tendent à présenter une vision cohérente du mythe tournée vers la domaine de la chasse, réversible et ambiguë, où sont mises en avant les puissances et les limites de la ruse" (Lissarrague 1980:26). Although Lissarrague associates the imagery with hunting and reads into it the idea that the hunter becomes the hunted, we instead would argue that the painters here have their own "language" of representing ambush, and that ambush has the same kind of ambiguity or reversal that Lissarague describes built into its theme. Dolon therefore has a parallel existence in the visual artistic tradition, which in some ways resembles what we have in our texts, but in other ways does not. If one concedes (as we assert) that the images are not dependent on the texts, these images provide evidence of a separate tradition for Dolon that reaches back at least into the early sixth century BCE.

In this investigation into the traditionality of Dolon, we have combined an examination of his introduction in *Iliad* 10, as it fits into patterns seen in the *Iliad* and *Odyssey*, with a brief discussion of the vase paintings, the best external evidence we have for Dolon's traditionality. We have particularly focused on the early vases that Lissarrague analyzes because they offer us the strongest evidence of narratives about Dolon that may be independent of the *Iliad*.[45] We will simply note here that the artistic depictions of Dolon and the Doloneia continue for centuries (see Williams 1986). As we will see in the following section on reception, the Doloneia remained a subject that artists, both painters and poets, continued to find worthy of portrayal and interpretation.

Reception: The Doloneia and the Theme of Ambush in the *Rhesos* and the *Aeneid*

When we look to the reception of the Doloneia in later works of poetry, we see that Ovid, for example, expected his readers to be well acquainted

---

[44] "Ainsi dans tous les cas que nous connaissons Ulysse et Diomède s'opposent à Dolon par l'habillement et les armes, et dans une certaine mesure leurs rôles peuvent s'inverser" (Lissarrague 1980:24).

[45] Lowenstam 1997 discusses the question of what vase paintings, especially those that have differences from the Homeric epics as we know them, can tell us about the dating of the *Iliad* and *Odyssey*.

with the story. In the *Ars Amatoria* (2.123–144) Ovid offers Odysseus as an example of someone whom the ladies (and even goddesses) love, not because he is good looking, but because he is eloquent. In illustration of this point, Ovid portrays Calypso as asking Odysseus again and again to tell her about the fall of Troy, and as they walk along the beach, Calypso requests specifically that he tell her about the death of Rhesos. Her request, however, is phrased in a learned allusion (*illic quoque pulchra Calypso / Exigit Odrysii fata cruenta ducis*, *Ars Amatoria* 2.129–130); Rhesos' name is not used until *Ars Amatoria* 2.137. In his story, Odysseus includes the death of Dolon, as well as that of Rhesos and his horses, as he draws the two camps in the sand to illustrate the story.[46] This brief passage offers the allusion in a playful manner, typical of Ovid, but for our purposes we note simply that Ovid represents the episode as one that both Calypso and Ovid's own audience would want to hear. Ovid uses the Doloneia also in *Heroides* 1.37–46. In this letter from Penelope to Odysseus, who is not yet home, she informs him that she has heard from Telemakhos, who heard from Nestor, how Odysseus, helped only by one man, killed Rhesos and Dolon and infiltrated the Thracian camp at night: in other words, she has heard the Doloneia. In both of these poems, Odysseus is in the middle of his "odyssey"—within the story, his own epic is not yet complete. Yet, out of all the stories of Odysseus at Troy that could be used in these situations, it is perhaps the prestige of an Iliadic episode that has motivated the choice of the Doloneia.

These brief examples from Ovid are a hint that there was a lively interest in the Doloneia in his time, and that Ovid saw it as a story ripe with intertextual possibilities. Because of the history of doubts about the authorship of *Iliad* 10, which we survey in our essay "Interpreting *Iliad* 10," references or allusions to the Doloneia are also often discussed strictly in terms of authenticity.[47] In our discussion of the reception

---

[46] We have to leave aside here the intertextuality between Ovid and Virgil (e.g. in the phrases *tentoria Rhesi*, *Ars Amatoria* 2.137, cf. *Aeneid* 1.469, and *somno proditus*, *Heroides* 1.40, cf. *Aeneid* 1.470), and also between these two poems of Ovid, as *Heroides* 1 also has a Trojan veteran draw the Trojan plain, this time with wine, as he tells his story (compare *Ars Amatoria* 2.131–138 and *Heroides* 1.31–36).

[47] For one example, in a brief remark within a discussion of Ovid's use of myth, Graf uses his own assumptions about the "inauthenticity" of *Iliad* 10 to interpret *Heroides* 1. Graf says that Ovid uses a "wealth of Homeric details" to seem authentic, but that referring to the Doloneia was a clever way to distance his text from Homer's (Graf 2002:112 and 112n26). The simpler conclusion, it seems to us, would be that the poem includes Odysseus' exploits in the Doloneia as part of the knowledge of the *Iliad* that Penelope displays in her letter. Because Graf does not accept *Iliad* 10 as "Homeric," he has to find another explanation for why Ovid would include it. Similarly, editors

of the Doloneia, however, we will not pursue that particular line of inquiry. Since we hope we have convincingly argued for the traditionality of *Iliad* 10, we instead want to focus on the reception of the theme of ambush. In the works we will examine, then, we will consider how the characters of Rhesos or Dolon are presented, but our focus will be on whether and how the poetics of ambush that we have identified are received and construed. We will show how these works highlight what we have seen as the traditional theme, either through their use of the same elements, or through a reworking of these poetics. Because of our focus, we have not attempted to be exhaustive and find every subsequent reference to the Doloneia. Rather, we have concentrated here on major works that have well-known associations with *Iliad* 10: the Athenian tragedy *Rhesos* and Virgil's *Aeneid*.

The *Rhesos*

Before we examine in detail the ways in which this Athenian tragedy engages the poetics of ambush, we first acknowledge that questions have been raised about its authorship as well. It is firmly attributed to Euripides in the manuscript tradition, yet a significant portion of the scholarship on this drama focuses on arguments over that attribution.[48] Arguing for or against Euripidean authorship is not our purpose

---

starting with Bentley have bracketed at least some of the lines of the Doloneia passage in *Heroides* 1.39–46 as an interpolation. Knox bases his bracketing of *Heroides* 1.39–40 on the repetition of *dolo* at the ends of lines 1.40 and 1.42, saying that it is "rhetorically emphatic but without point" (Knox 1995:97). On the contrary, we would argue that the close association between ambush and *dolus* 'guile' provides the point of the repetition. See "The Poetics of Ambush" for our discussion of the association of the Greek equivalent δόλος with ambush.

[48] Rolfe 1893 reviewed the debate over the tragedy's authorship during the nineteenth century. About the great degree of disagreement over authorship and date he states: "Almost without exception they have begun with a preconceived theory of the authorship for the play, and have supported their theory without regard to any other possibility" (Rolfe 1893:65). The debate seems to have continued in a similar manner in the twentieth and twenty-first centuries. Porter 1929:ix notes that the question of authenticity has dominated interest in the tragedy and that judgments either way are based on personal assessments of the play's artistic merits. After an extended discussion of the evidence (1929:xxx–liv), he suggests that Euripides planned the play and it was completed and produced by his son. Grube 1961:439, 447 argues that the *Rhesos* is genuine and perhaps an early play of Euripides. Ritchie 1964 also argues for Euripidean authorship and notes that more recent arguments against it have added to earlier judgments based on aesthetics by examining "vocabulary, style and technique" (Ritchie 1964:vii). In Fraenkel's 1965 review of Ritchie, he argues against Euripidean authorship, and that conclusion seems to be gaining acceptance, as discussed by Fantuzzi (2006a) in his review of François Jouan's 2004 edition of the

here. Rather, what matters for our discussion is that the *Rhesos* is part of the same song culture in which *Iliad* 10 was produced. Regardless of authorship, the *Rhesos* has always been understood as an Athenian tragedy, produced in either the fifth or fourth century BCE, and we also have sure evidence that the *Iliad*, including *Iliad* 10, was known in Athens at that time. In other words, the audience for the tragedy was also an audience for the epic.[49] And, indeed, that *Iliad* 10 has influenced the *Rhesos* is commonly argued in the scholarship on the *Rhesos*.[50] We will also not be arguing for or against the dramatic merits of the play, but we will rather focus exclusively on how the *Rhesos* presents the theme of ambush.

---

play. Fantuzzi (2005:272) also argues that Fraenkel's review "has helped to establish a kind of suspension of judgment on the problem of authenticity, which had absorbed nearly all of the scholarly attention devoted to this tragedy over the last two centuries. However, there is general scholarly agreement that if this tragedy is not by Euripides, then it has to be dated to the fourth century." Poe 2004 examines issues of stagecraft and concludes that what he sees as breaches of norms in the *Rhesos* are "evidence of an author who, despite his considerable literary knowledge, was not completely familiar with the fifth century theater or with conventions of tragic structure and the limitations that these imposed" (2004:32). For further conclusions in favor of Euripides' authorship, see Lattimore 1958:2–5, Devereux 1976:259, 310–311, and Burnett 1985:50–51. For other arguments against Euripides as author, see Björck 1957, Kitto 1977, and Bryce 1990–1991.

[49] Goward 1999:4 makes a similar argument about the tragic audience: "The fifth-century audience who heard the four-yearly competitive recital of the Homeric poems at the Great Panathenaic festival were the same people who watched the dramatic competition in the theater of Dionysus." The ancient literary testimony for performance at the Panathenaia is Plato, *Ion* and the dialogue *Hipparkhos*, also attributed to Plato. Davison 1958 is a seminal study on the form of the festival. He discusses the musical contests and suggests that competitions of performing Homeric epic date back well into the sixth century BCE (Davison 1958:36–41). Neils 1992b provides a detailed description of the Panathenaic festival and Shapiro's article in the same volume outlines the performance of Homeric epic during the festival (Shapiro 1992:72–75). See especially Nagy 1996a and Nagy 2002 for more on the performance of Homeric poetry at the Panathenaic festival.

[50] For example, Fenik argues that Dolon's presence in the play is at least partly attributable to the influence of the *Iliad* (Fenik 1964:17). Kitto (1977:334) argues that the poet took the "Homeric Doloneia as his main 'source'" but then tried to make the story different. Zuntz argues that the play's inclusion in the "schoolbook" editions of Euripides' plays, and therefore its survival, is attributable to its use of an Iliadic episode as its plot (Zuntz 1965:255–256). Bond 1996 examines Homeric "echoes" in the *Rhesos* and argues that the *Rhesos* "seems to presuppose a knowledge of specific Iliadic details" (Bond 1996:266) and that "we must remember that the powerful influence of epic on the audience's reception as well as the visual aspect of the drama must have enhanced the experience" (Bond 1996:272). Fantuzzi 2005 explores intertextuality between the *Rhesos* and the *Iliad* and Fantuzzi 2006b argues that the *Rhesos* is a "continuation" of *Iliad* 10.

Story and tradition in the *Rhesos*

We have seen already above in the section on Rhesos that Bernard Fenik has used the eponymous tragedy as evidence of a Rhesos tradition that is different from the Homeric Doloneia. But, as we also saw in that discussion, when multiple traditions exist there can be a tension between them that underlies the presentation of one version. Such tensions are detectable in the *Rhesos* in its awareness of *Iliad* 10. The *Rhesos* presents the story of this night raid and ambush from the Trojan point of view, and it seems to set itself up as a parallel or alternative to the *Iliad* 10 account in its opening details.[51] Hektor is asleep onstage as the play opens (*Rhesos* 1–10), while in the *Iliad* we hear that he is awake and has not let the Trojans sleep (*Iliad* 10.299–301). *Iliad* 10 also opens with Agamemnon awake as the rest of the Achaeans sleep (*Iliad* 10.1–4). The report of the Chorus that there is activity in the Achaean camp parallels Agamemnon's glances at the Trojan camp (*Iliad* 10.11–13), as well as the description of the Achaean guards on the night watch looking toward the Trojans and hearing their movements (*Iliad* 10.180–189). The dialogue between Hektor and Aeneas about how to respond (*Rhesos* 87–148) is similar in structure, although not in content, to that between Agamemnon and Menelaos (*Iliad* 10.36–72). We see that, after some disagreement, their conclusion is to let the allies continue to sleep, while Agamemnon and Menelaos, cooperative throughout, resolve to wake the Achaean leaders.

As these examples demonstrate, there is at play in the *Rhesos* an engagement with the same narrative pattern we at the beginning of *Iliad* 10. In these several ways, the *Rhesos* follows a similar structure to *Iliad* 10, while key details are different.[52] The tragedy may be purposefully evoking the epic version, but reworking it from the Trojan side. Additionally, the sequence of events seen in both works suggests that there may be a traditional pattern to the beginning of these night episodes (or at least this one in particular), and these two extended treatments of such episodes display that traditional pattern, consisting of an opening focus on the leader of the forces, fear or concern about the enemy's activities, consultation with another leader, and formulation of an initial plan. We need not make too stark a distinction

---

[51] It is, of course, necessary for the events to be presented from the Trojan point of view, since they are the ones who suffer the tragic loss of Rhesos. In other words, the play also presents these events as a success for the Achaeans.

[52] Fantuzzi (2006b:149–152), taking a very different approach, calls the beginning of the play "intertextual misdirection," as it uses familiar elements from *Iliad* 10 and shifts the perspective.

between these two possibilities: the Rhesos myth and the several ambush episodes within the tradition of the Trojan War, as well as the ambush theme's specific expression in *Iliad* 10 as a larger whole, could have influenced the composition of the *Rhesos*.

Another way in which the drama can be seen to engage particular aspects of this larger theme and its expression in *Iliad* 10, again with a resulting tension, is through a kind of metacommentary on aspects of the Doloneia. What we mean by "metacommentary" is that the dialogue of the tragedy explicitly comments on aspects of the story and the ambush theme that are traditional to the epic or otherwise implicit in it. Such commentary dominates the brief scene in which Dolon appears, starting with the way that Dolon is introduced. Hektor asks for a volunteer for the spying mission, and Dolon stands up to say he is willing to do it (*Rhesos* 149–157). We have no narrator, as we do in the epic (a factor we will encounter again below, when we look at the messenger-speeches in the play), to introduce Dolon. Dolon himself speaks in the first person, and so Hektor's response must include his name. But Hektor's response delays Dolon's name until the second line, commenting on him first: "You are surely rightly named and city-loving, Dolon" (ἐπώνυμος μὲν κάρτα καὶ φιλόπτολις / Δόλων, *Rhesos* 158–159).[53] That Dolon is "rightly named" must be a play on the fact that his name sounds like δόλος 'trick' (see further in the commentary on 10.447). As we discussed in our essay "The Poetics of Ambush," the concept of trickiness and the word δόλος itself are associated with the ambush theme, including spying missions. Hektor's response hints at those associations as it draws attention to Dolon's name.

Those associations are made more explicit, and the metacommentary is taken even further, when Dolon describes what he will wear for his mission. He says that his equipment will be fitting for his task and for stealthy movement (πρέπουσαν ἔργῳ κλωπικοῖς τε βήμασιν, *Rhesos* 205). He then elaborates further on how the wolf skin will disguise his movements and confuse the enemy, and that this ploy is his δόλος (*Rhesos* 208–215). We have seen that wearing animal skins is a signal of a night episode in the epic, but in the tragedy a detailed explanation of how and why an animal skin might be worn on a night mission is given. It is as if the tragedy feels the need to answer an implicit question about why animal skins are worn at night or why Dolon traditionally wore a wolf skin in particular.

---

[53] We are using Diggle's 1994 edition of the *Rhesos*.

Just before Dolon's departure, the Chorus emphasizes his return: they say they hope Hermes sends Dolon there and back again (ἐκεῖσε καὶ πάλιν, *Rhesos* 216). We have seen in the epic theme that a crucial part of a spying or ambush mission is the successful return, and, in one example, Hermes plays a direct role (Priam's mission into enemy territory at night, and his successful return, in *Iliad* 24). Dolon's response reflects the significance of the homecoming, and also shows the thematic connection between spying missions and ambushes, when he adds his desire to murder Odysseus or Diomedes to his original reconnaissance mission, before he arrives home (ἥξω πρὸς οἴκους, *Rhesos* 219–223). His wishful thinking reverses the way in which a spying mission actually becomes an ambush both here and in *Iliad* 10. Thus this brief scene with Dolon presents several elements of the traditional narrative pattern of the ambush theme, some of which are commented on to explain their presence. These explanations, however, do not necessarily reflect the meaning we see within the epic theme. Instead, the tragedy seems to put an almost practical or realistic spin on these traditional elements.

Such a metacommentary can also be seen in the portrayal of Rhesos. The theme of a "late-arriving ally" for the Trojans seems to be a traditional one, as Fenik identifies.[54] But the tragedy, although it places Rhesos' arrival, as the *Iliad* does, during a night when Achilles has withdrawn and the Trojans have the upper hand, seems to pose a question as to why an ally would arrive so late in the war. When the messenger has informed Hektor that Rhesos and his army have arrived, Hektor responds that because the Trojans are now winning they will find many more allies willing to help, but he does not want their help since they were not there when the Trojans were struggling (*Rhesos* 319–326). His words put a political spin on what in the epic tradition is a narrative pattern. When Rhesos arrives, Hektor immediately rebukes him for arriving so late and refutes several potential excuses (*Rhesos* 396–421). Rhesos admits that he is late in coming and gives a long explanation of factors that had detained him (*Rhesos* 422–443).[55] This *agōn* scene between Hektor and Rhesos thus makes the traditional narrative of the late-arriving ally an object of considerable scrutiny in the play.

---

[54] Fenik 1964:8–10, citing also Kullmann 1960.

[55] Fantuzzi (2006b:153–155) also discusses what he describes as a challenge to Rhesos' participation in the war. He compares this to the other Rhesos traditions found in the scholia and his Iliadic portrayal.

As their argument continues, it becomes a question of who will be the savior of Troy. Rhesos ends his response by claiming that his arrival is still at the right time (ἐν καιρῷ δ' ὅμως, *Rhesos* 443), since Hektor has made no progress in defeating the Achaeans. In this way, the situation of the two leaders facing and arguing with one another creates a dramatic tension out of what in the epic tradition would be a tension between episodes or versions. The Iliadic version offers Hektor as the only rival for Achilles, but Rhesos wants to face him here (*Rhesos* 491). In the *Rhesos*, Rhesos boasts that all he needs is one day to finish what Hektor has taken ten years to start (*Rhesos* 443–453). Through his own speech, Rhesos alludes to and even combines the alternate traditions, both that of an overpowering one-day *aristeia* (which, as we have seen above, in some versions prompts the night ambush), and that of gaining invincibility once he and his horses eat and drink at Troy.

In the *Iliad* we do not have any opportunity to see what Rhesos is like as a character—he is asleep and then dead the only time he appears. In the *Rhesos*, his character is presented as overconfident in his abilities to win the war in a single day of fighting, but his tragic mistake is related to ambush in particular. When Rhesos learns that Achilles is no longer fighting, he asks who is the next best of the Achaeans. Hektor names Ajax and Diomedes, and then describes Odysseus and his ambush exploits at length, including his theft of the Palladion and his spying mission into Troy (*Rhesos* 497–509).[56] In his reply Rhesos rejects ambush:

> οὐδεὶς ἀνὴρ εὔψυχος ἀξιοῖ λάθρα
> κτεῖναι τὸν ἐχθρόν, ἀλλ' ἰὼν κατὰ στόμα.

> *Rhesos* 510–511

> No one who is a courageous man would think it right by
>   stealth
> to kill his enemy, but rather goes face-to-face.

He goes on to claim that he will kill Odysseus the ambusher and schemer (*Rhesos* 512–517). In other words, Rhesos claims that courage is found only in the *polemos*, whereas the Homeric epics, as we have seen, ascribe courage to ambush; indeed, they tell us that it is precisely

---

56 Hektor's concluding statement about Odysseus is that in him "we wrestle with an astounding evil" (κακῷ δὲ μερμέρῳ παλαίομεν, *Rhesos* 509). See the commentary on 10.289 and 10.524 for the phrase *mermera erga* in an ambush context.

in ambush that a warrior's excellence especially shines forth.[57] In this drama, though, Rhesos' rejection sets up the tragic irony that this courageous warrior will be killed by the very man he asserted he would kill, and in the way that he claims courageous men do not fight.

His particular blindness in this matter is compounded by the fact that the other leaders on both sides are on guard against such attacks. One of Hektor's first questions upon being awoken is if there is some sort of ambush in the night (μῶν τις λόχος ἐκ νυκτῶν, *Rhesos* 16–17).[58] Aeneas advises undertaking a spying mission before engaging in an all-out battle at night because he suspects a trick (δόλον, *Rhesos* 128) on the part of the Achaeans (*Rhesos* 123–130). The Chorus worries that Dolon has been caught in an ambush (κρυπτὸν λόχον, *Rhesos* 560). When Odysseus and Diomedes do not find Hektor sleeping where Dolon told them they would find him, Odysseus wonders if an ambush has been set up (μῶν λόχος βέβηκέ ποι;, *Rhesos* 577). Even Paris comes to find Hektor to tell him that an enemy has infiltrated the camp (*Rhesos* 644–645). Rhesos' denigration of ambush tactics seems to expose him as misguided more than it expresses any firm criticism of the strategy.

Ambush, then, may be the way in which the author of the *Rhesos* attempts to make the death of the central character a tragic event.[59] Although modern scholars have questioned the tone of the play, [60] the lament of Rhesos' mother at the end of the play (*Rhesos* 906–949) suggests that there is, at least, a sense of loss and grief. The ways in which the drama uses, confronts, and reinterprets the epic poetics of

---

[57] See our essay "The Poetics of Ambush" and especially *Iliad* 13.277. Compare Turnus' rejection of ambush tactics, discussed below.

[58] Diggle brackets these lines in his edition. In the manuscripts, some have δόλος in place of λόχος. See above and "The Poetics of Ambush" for the associations between these words.

[59] Fantuzzi 2006b, arguing from a different approach, also sees the use of *dolos* as integral to the attempt to create a tragedy, which he argues is a genre especially concerned with *doloi*: "Both the *Rhesus*' staging of the anxiety about the enemies' *doloi* and of the generalized misunderstanding of reality, and the formal, minimalistic *dolos* of the misleading intertextuality make clear to the audience just how far the Doloneia of the *Rhesus* is from being a mere dramatization of the Doloneia of *Iliad* 10. It also underscores just how cleverly the author selected the only section of the *Iliad* concerned with the *doloi* of an ambush and a treacherous raid as an homage to the poetics of tragedy, a genre that privileged actions involving *doloi* and atmospheres of misunderstanding or lack of knowledge of reality" (152).

[60] Björck 1957:17 argues that "the plot of the Rhesus is no more a tragedy than two gangsters waylaying the first suitable victim to come their way." Kitto 1977:335–337, 344–346 asks whether the play was meant to be a parody or burlesque. Burnett 1985 argues for a comic or absurd tone to the tragedy, but she also considers *Iliad* 10 a "rogue's comedy" (1985:15).

ambush, both answering and generating tensions between this version and other versions of the myth of Rhesos, results in a creative use of the story and tradition, and at the same time interrogates the very same poetics.

Drama in the dark

Another aspect of the Homeric poetics of ambush prominently explored in the tragedy *Rhesos*, one that is appropriate to its genre and conditions of performance, is the effect darkness has on the characters' senses and movement.[61] Just as the darkness in the night episodes affects the clothing and armor worn by the warriors and the planning and strategy of both meeting and mission in Homeric epic,[62] the tragedy also calls attention to the limitations and special requirements of the dark. There are many examples of the effects of darkness in the play, but we will cite just a few having to do with identifying others in the dark, and then consider in more detail how action in the dark affects the play's two messenger-speeches.

When Hektor is awoken at the beginning of the *Rhesos*, he cannot immediately recognize the chorus/night guard, and he asks whether it is a friend speaking.[63] This reaction is similar to Nestor's when he is awoken in the epic (*Iliad* 10.80–85). The idea that the darkness confuses, and especially obscures the difference between friend and enemy, is also present elsewhere in *Iliad* 10. As we observed above, for example, Dolon stops after he hears men behind him and assumes they must be Trojans, only to recognize, too late, that he is wrong. As we will see below, Rhesos' charioteer twice assumes that the men who infiltrate their camp are allies, even though he also assumes they are there to steal from the Thracians.

The need to be able to tell the difference between friend and foe is repeatedly emphasized in the use of a password (ξύνθημα/σύνθημα or σῆμα) in the Trojan camp. A password is meant to be an auditory way to tell friend from enemy precisely because it is difficult to see

---

61 Walton 2000, in an important study focused on performance rather than provenance, examines the setting of the tragedy at night and speculates on how the actors would indicate the action as taking place in the dark. Björck 1957:10 notes the quantity and variety of words meaning "night" or "darkness" in the play.

62 See the section "Sensory and spatial aspects of the night" in our essay "The Poetics of Ambush."

63 Walton 2000:141–142 discusses how these opening lines establish for the audience that the characters are dealing with darkness, and speculates on how this effect might have been reinforced by gestures and stage movements.

in the dark.[64] That the password is "Phoibos" is meaningful, not only because of Apollo's favoritism toward the Trojans, but also because it then "illuminates" this crucial difference. In the central part of the drama, Hektor tells Rhesos the password (*Rhesos* 520–521). We learn that Diomedes and Odysseus have ambushed Dolon when we hear that they learned the password from him (*Rhesos* 573), and Odysseus uses the password as a trick to get away from the Trojan guards (*Rhesos* 687–689). These examples show how limited vision complicates the identification of friend or foe, a problem that is further explored in the messenger-speeches.

The two messenger-speeches reveal an especially creative exploration of what action in the dark means for the performance conventions of tragedy. The first is delivered by a shepherd, who reports to Hektor the arrival of Rhesos (*Rhesos* 284–316); the second is delivered by Rhesos' charioteer, who reports that Rhesos has been killed (*Rhesos* 756–803). The messenger role is that of a narrator above all, and the messenger-speech is a narration within drama, one that reports events that happen offstage and are not witnessed directly by the audience.[65] But what kind of narrator is the messenger? Epic employs an all-seeing narrator in the poet's own persona, and it is the characters who are affected by the darkness of night. Tragedy must use characters to narrate events, and, as characters, they are mostly limited to their own experience. Since the messenger is a character within drama, we might expect his ability to see, and thus his ability to tell what he sees, to be affected by darkness in ways similar to the characters of epic.[66] In

---

[64] See our essay "The Poetics of Ambush" for the historical use of a password in a night battle during the Peloponnesian War.

[65] See Bremer 1976, de Jong 1991, and Barrett 2002 on the function of tragic messengers. Bremer 1976 outlines reasons why narration is a formal technique of Greek tragedy. De Jong 1991:30–103 treats in detail the messenger as narrator and as focalizer. She emphasizes that the messenger-speech is a first-person narrative, as opposed to an omniscient one, and that the messenger focalizes the events through his own experience of them, a type of narrator she terms "I-as-witness" (see de Jong 1991:60 for the term). Barbara Goward's book on narrative technique in Greek tragedy argues for broadening the category of messenger-speeches to "message narratives" to include even more examples of narration of what has happened away from the audience's eyes, since such narration is integral to the genre (1999:18–19, 26–27).

[66] De Jong has argued that the messenger, not only relates events as he saw them, but also includes his own emotional reactions: "The messenger's addressees are made to see the events exactly as he saw them, hence to share his experience of growing understanding, agitation and see-sawing emotions, from happiness to dismay, from joy to fear, from apprehension to exhilaration" (1991:38). Barrett, on the other hand, characterizes a typical tragic messenger (from all three tragedians) as an eye-witness (and therefore part of the action), but also a detached narrator with special

the *Rhesos*, as we have already seen, the effects of the darkness place a special emphasis on senses other than vision, especially hearing, and this emphasis is prominent in the messenger-speeches as well. But the charioteer's messenger-speech takes the need for additional interpretation to the point where it grants the interpretive role to the audience, who can interpret the sights that the charioteer himself cannot.

Tragic messengers are normally "eyewitnesses," but if the messengers themselves cannot see, what do they report instead? The first messenger-speech in the *Rhesos*, delivered to Hektor by a shepherd announcing the arrival of Rhesos and the Thracian army on Mount Ida (*Rhesos* 264–317), shows that the usual eyewitness function is changed under nocturnal circumstances. To Hektor's question about their route, the shepherd's answer, which begins his extended narrative, signals the need for interpreting information that is gathered in the dark: "I do not know exactly, but I can at least guess" (οὐκ οἶδ' ἀκριβῶς· εἰκάσαι γε μὴν πάρα, *Rhesos* 284). As he continues his account, he mentions that it was the noise (πολλῇ ἠχῇ, *Rhesos* 290) the army made that first drew his and his fellow shepherds' attention and caused them to fear (φόβον, *Rhesos* 287; θάμβει ἐκπλαγέντες, *Rhesos* 291). For, as he explains, they interpreted these noises as an attack by the enemy Argives (*Rhesos* 292–293). But it was another sound—the non-Greek language of the intruders—that convinced them otherwise (*Rhesos* 294–295). Thus the sounds they hear in the dark are the first sources of information: unfamiliar sounds cause fear, and their first guess at what such sounds might mean is wrong.[67] In a typical messenger-speech, de Jong has observed, sounds usually have a minimal importance, especially compared with sights.[68] But in this case, sounds take on a new prominence. It is only after the shepherd has questioned 'who goes there' and has gathered enough information from listening that he sees Rhesos before him (καὶ παντ' ἀκούσας ὧν ἐφιέμην μαθεῖν / ἔστην· ὁρῶ δὲ Ῥῆσον, *Rhesos* 300–301). (The horses and gold armor of Rhesos then seem to "light up" the dark night, although the noise the army makes is still prominent, *Rhesos*

---

knowledge, who has an authority similar to that of an epic narrator (Barrett 2002:xvi–xvii, 168–169). Barrett makes an exception, however, of the charioteer's messenger-speech in the *Rhesos*, and we will argue below that the darkness, a significant part of the ambush theme, changes the kind of messenger-speech the charioteer can deliver.

[67] We also see a similar fright (*phobos*) when Diomedes and Odysseus come onstage (walking carefully, they say, since they cannot see well) and hear noises that they cannot identify immediately (*Rhesos* 565–571).

[68] De Jong 1991:145. She does not include the messenger-speeches from the *Rhesos* in her study. Walton 2000:143–144 points out that hearing is emphasized over seeing also when Diomedes and Odysseus are onstage.

303–308.) These details from the shepherd's report show that vision is not the sole or even the most prominent means by which he gathers information in the dark. Because he cannot see what is happening (in this case, at first), interpretation of other sensory input is necessary—though it is not necessarily reliable.

The report of Rhesos' death given by his charioteer further reveals the elements of night and ambush (appropriately, since he is reporting an ambush). Here, too, we find an emphasis on multiple senses due to the limitations of sight. In this case, what the charioteer does perceive by sight he interprets incorrectly. He begins his extended narrative about what has happened offstage with a brief description of how the Thracians set up an unguarded camp, since they had been assured that the Trojans were guarding the whole area, and fell asleep (*Rhesos* 762–769). We saw above the portrayal of Rhesos as the only leader who does not guard against ambush; here the charioteer, in particular, but also the encampment as a whole are shown to be completely unprepared for an ambush.

The "eyewitness" function of the tragic messenger becomes more evident in the next part of the charioteer's description: he says that he awoke again to feed the horses and saw two men wandering around the camp, who retreated as he started to move toward them (*Rhesos* 770–775). This part of his account sets up the expectation that the charioteer will be awake to witness the attack on the camp, while also revealing his mindset: he explains that he thought the men he saw were allies (συμμάχων, *Rhesos* 777) coming to steal from them (which is presumably why he did not ask them for the password). Although he witnesses this intrusion, he nonetheless says that after he warned them to leave he thought nothing further of it and went back to sleep (*Rhesos* 776–779). The unmet expectation that the charioteer will be able to report what he saw in a conscious state, coupled with his exposed inability to interpret correctly the threat to the camp, leads to his description of his ensuing nightmare and subsequent actions (*Rhesos* 779–803):

> ηὗδον δ' ἀπελθὼν αὖθις ἐς κοίτην πάλιν.
> 780 καί μοι καθ' ὕπνον δόξα τις παρίσταται·
> ἵππους γὰρ ἃς ἔθρεψα κἀδιφρηλάτουν
> Ῥήσωι παρεστὼς εἶδον, ὡς ὄναρ δοκῶν,
> λύκους ἐπεμβεβῶτας ἑδραίαν ῥάχιν·
> θείνοντε δ' οὐρᾷ πωλικῆς ῥινοῦ τρίχα
> 785 ἤλαυνον, αἱ δ' ἔρρεγκον ἐξ ἀρτηριῶν

θυμὸν πνέουσαι κἀνεχαίτιζον φόβῳ.
ἐγὼ δ' ἀμύνων θῆρας ἐξεγείρομαι
πώλοισιν· ἔννυχος γὰρ ἐξώρμα φόβος.
κλύω δ' ἐπάρας κρᾶτα μυχθισμὸν νεκρῶν·
790 θερμὸς δὲ κρουνὸς δεσπότου παρὰ σφαγῆς
βάλλει με δυσθνῄσκοντος αἵματος νέου.
ὀρθὸς δ' ἀνᾴσσω χειρὶ σὺν κενῇ δορός·
καί μ' ἔγχος αὐγάζοντα καὶ θηρώμενον
παίει παραστὰς νεῖραν ἐς πλευρὰν ξίφει
795 ἀνὴρ ἀκμάζων· φασγάνου γὰρ ᾐσθόμην
πληγῆς, βαθεῖαν ἄλοκα τραύματος λαβών.
πίπτω δὲ πρηνής· οἱ δ' ὄχημα πωλικὸν
λαβόντες ἵππων ἵεσαν φυγῇ πόδα.
ἆ ἆ·
ὀδύνη με τείρει κοὐκέτ' ὀρθοῦμαι τάλας.
800 καὶ ξυμφορὰν μὲν οἶδ' ὁρῶν, τρόπῳ δ' ὅτῳ
τεθνᾶσιν οἱ θανόντες οὐκ ἔχω φράσαι
οὐδ' ἐξ ὁποίας χειρός. εἰκάσαι δέ μοι
πάρεστι λυπρὰ πρὸς φίλων πεπονθέναι.

I was sleeping having gone back to bed again.
780 And some apparition is standing next to me in my slumber.
For the mares which I cared for and used to drive
standing next to Rhesos, I saw, I seemed to see in my dream,
wolves treading on their backs, where a rider sits.
The two of them striking with their tails the hair of the
        horse's hide
785 drove them on, but the horses were snorting from their
        nostrils,
breathing their life's breath and rearing back in fear.
And I woke up to ward off the beasts from
the horses; for the frightening nightmare had roused me
        ready for action.
I lifted up my head and heard the gasping of dying men.
790 A warm spurt from the slaughter of my master
hit me, a spurt of the dying man's fresh blood.
I darted up with my hand empty of a spear.
While I was trying to see clearly and hunting around for a
        spear,
someone standing near strikes me with a sword in my lower
        ribs—

795   it was some man in his prime. For I perceived the blow
of the sword, taking a deep gash of a wound.
I fell on my face, and they took the chariot
and horses and hurled their feet in flight.
Ah, ah.
Sharp pain wears me down, and wretch that I am I can no
      longer stand upright.
800   I know this calamity seeing it, but in what way
the dead have died I am not able to tell,
not by what sort of hand. But it seems likely to me
that we have suffered the present sad events at the hands of
      our friends.

In what he reports in this section, the charioteer's powers of interpretation seem to be most successful when based on information gathered from senses such as hearing and touch: he can report that it is blood that touches him and men who gasp, and he can discern the youth of the man who struck him (assuming it is Diomedes who did so).

Yet in this speech he describes his dream in terms of what he saw, as would be expected in a messenger-speech: he saw (εἶδον, *Rhesos* 782) the horses that he tends and drives and the wolves jumping upon the horses' backs and driving them off. The attack on the horses in the dream, which he terms a nightmare (ἔννυχος φόβος, *Rhesos* 788), awakens their faithful keeper ready to defend them. His failures of seeing and interpretation happen, not in the dream, but while the charioteer is awake. The first time he wakes up, he says, he sees (λεύσσω, *Rhesos* 773) two men in the camp through the dense darkness (πυκνῆς δι' ὄρφνης, *Rhesos* 774),[69] but we know that he incorrectly interprets them as *allies* coming to steal from the camp. From what little he does see he also miscalculates the possible threat they pose (*Rhesos* 777–778). When he wakes after his nightmare, he cannot see well enough to find a weapon to defend himself and his comrades (*Rhesos* 793). Although he then claims to know from seeing (οἶδ' ὁρῶν) the calamity that has occurred, his knowledge is admittedly limited since he cannot say how it happened or who did it (*Rhesos* 800–803). Any seeing he does, therefore, is restricted to the result, not the actions that produced the result.[70] Even his description of the perpetrators escaping with the

---

[69] See our commentary on *Iliad* 10.5–9 for the ambush associations of πυκινός/πυκνός and also on 10.41 for the epic formula νύκτα δι' ὀρφναίην.

[70] As Barrett 2002 asserts: "It is true that he reports *that* Rhesos died, but he does not know *how* he died" (183).

horses results from an inference of what happened—he is flat on his face as they run off (*Rhesos* 797). And his interpretation is once again misguided: he suspects *philoi* as the perpetrators (*Rhesos* 803). The only true seeing he reports, then, is his dream, an internal sight that is itself qualified as "dreamlike seeing" (ὡς ὄναρ δοκῶν, *Rhesos* 782).

That the charioteer's nightmare evokes and perhaps even reworks the bad dream (κακὸν ὄναρ) of *Iliad* 10.496 is a point that has been made before.[71] If we consider the compressed image of the bad dream in the epic and the more elaborate nightmare in the tragedy in terms of performance, however, the tragedy needs a character to see the dream so that the audience can experience it, too.[72] For the ancient audience listening to the performance, seeing the nightmare also involves interpreting it correctly. They have seen Odysseus and Diomedes onstage, and Odysseus may even have been wearing the wolf skin that they stripped from Dolon's corpse after killing him, making him look like a wolf, perhaps especially "in the dark."[73] Just as the epic audience makes mental connections between Diomedes and the lion in the simile at *Iliad* 10.485–488, as Diomedes kills the Thracians, here the tragic audience can make the mental connection between the wolves in the nightmare and the Achaeans, and know who has killed Rhesos and taken the horses.

---

[71] See Fenik 1964:51–52, Paduano 1973:27, and Barrett 2002:181.

[72] Leaf 1900 *ad* 10.497, Messer 1918:97, Fenik 1964:52, Burnett 1985:34, and Barrett 2002:181 have all made the point that the dream is transferred to the charioteer specifically because this is tragedy and it needs to be reported. Messer 1918:56–59 includes a good discussion of the differences between these genres. The consequences of that transference, however, are interpreted differently within these arguments. We do not necessarily agree with Burnett and Barrett that the transference somehow diminishes the character of Rhesos. Our point is that the dream is what the charioteer is an eyewitness to, and, by describing it, he lets the audience in on the dream as well. Poe 2004:24 notes that the messenger-speech "is a narrative that is intended primarily for the ears of the audience."

[73] In both the *Iliad* and the *Rhesos*, Dolon dresses in a wolf skin before setting out for the Achaean camp (*Iliad* 10.334 and *Rhesos* 208–213). In the *Rhesos* Dolon speaks elaborately about his wolf skin as a disguise appropriate to his stealthy mission, one that will confuse the perception of the enemy, since they will think that a real wolf has been in their camp (*Rhesos* 205–215). Unlike the *Iliad*, in which Diomedes and Odysseus explicitly leave behind the spoils they took from Dolon with the intention of picking them up after they return (*Iliad* 10.458–468), in the *Rhesos* Odysseus mentions onstage that they are carrying the equipment (τάδε σκυλεύματ') they stripped from Dolon's corpse (*Rhesos* 591–593). Ritchie 1964:76 also speculates about whether Odysseus wears the wolf skin onstage in his discussion of the wolves in the charioteer's dream. Paduano 1973:28 objects to Ritchie's "ultrarealistic" explanation of why the charioteer dreams of wolves in particular as attacking the horses. Devereux 1976:276–278 follows Ritchie and elaborates further on the idea that the dream wolf is Odysseus. Burnett 1985:40–41 and Bond 1996:260 both argue that Odysseus comes onstage in Dolon's wolf skin.

The charioteer's inability to name Diomedes and Odysseus as the killers and thieves does more than create a dramatic tension for Hektor's arrival: it gives the *audience* the role of omniscient narrator. The symbolism in the dream, the only "vision" that the charioteer can report as a reliable eyewitness, is such that the audience can interpret it better than the dreamer himself. And the dream, once decoded, is an accurate report of the theft of the horses. Thus another generic convention comes into play, for such superior knowledge on the part of the tragic audience is a common feature of tragedy.[74] Still, the dream imparts this knowledge in a particular way, by describing an unreal vision that the audience can interpret as they might any other messenger report describing offstage events. As they replicate the vision in their own minds, they make the same kinds of interpretations that they would for Homeric similes. Sights in the dark are not straightforward—they require interpretation—and the *Rhesos* plays with the witnessing conventions of the messenger-speech when that messenger is unable to see events in the dark. The audience members have not literally *seen* them either, yet through the report of the dream and their interpretive abilities they are able to formulate a complete understanding of the offstage events.

In the epic, we see in several places how the darkness affects the characters: what they see or do not see, how they interpret those sights, the prominence of hearing, the need for careful planning so as not to miss people or objects in the dark, and the usefulness of darkness for achieving an ambush mission. In the tragedy, since characters are also narrators, the darkness affects the very conventions of that narration in messenger-speeches, changing what it means to be an eyewitness, while still conveying to the audience the information it needs—if interpreted correctly—about what has happened offstage. The poetics of ambush are thus far-reaching within the tragedy, expressed even in these seeming anomalies in generic conventions.

Virgil's *Aeneid*

Similar to the way in which we restricted the scope of our examination of the reception of the Doloneia in the *Rhesos*, we will also be focusing on a rather limited idea of reception in Virgil's *Aeneid*. Virgil's reception of Homeric epic, as well as the larger tradition about the Trojan War, is significant and extensive, and a thorough consideration of all of

---

[74] As often happens in Greek tragedy, the characters only learn for sure what really happened through a divinity, in this case the Muse (*Rhesos* 938–940).

its poetic implications is beyond our scope here. In addition, Virgilian scholars have considered the points of comparison between the Doloneia and the night episode in *Aeneid* 9 and drawn various conclusions about how the episode, and the way it responds to the Doloneia, is important to the themes and program of the *Aeneid* as a whole.[75] Our goal here is not to provide an interpretation of the *Aeneid*, however, but rather to explore how Virgil's reception of the Doloneia contributes to our understanding of the poetics of ambush. Like scholars before us, our interpretation of Virgil's reception is influenced by our own understanding of the Doloneia. As just one example of this kind of influence, we can see in the scholarship that, if one has a negative opinion of Dolon in the *Iliad*, references or allusions to him in the *Aeneid* will also seem negative, and interpretation will proceed from that assumption. But, instead of engaging here in a point-by-point agreement with or refutation of these assumptions and interpretations, we have tried in this volume to make our own assumptions clear and acknowledge that of course they color our interpretations in this case as well. In this discussion there are three passages we want to examine: the stories of Rhesos and Dolon, mentioned separately, and, of course, the night episode in *Aeneid* 9, with Nisus and Euryalus as an ambushing pair.

Rhesos in Carthage

The reference to Rhesos comes in the first book of the *Aeneid*, as Aeneas stares in wonder at the pictures on the temple of Juno in Carthage (*Aeneid* 1.453–493).[76] As he looks, a series of scenes depicting events from the Trojan War is described.[77] Events that appear to correspond to our *Iliad* include the rout of the Achaeans by the Trojans (*Aeneid* 1.467), Achilles turning the Trojans back (*Aeneid* 1.468), the ambush of Rhesos (*Aeneid* 1.469–474), the supplication of Athena by the Trojan women (*Aeneid* 1.479–482), Achilles dragging Hektor's corpse and Priam's ransom of it (*Aeneid* 1.483–487), and, perhaps, the picture of Aeneas himself among the Achaean champions (*Aeneid* 1.488).[78] The others we might term "Cyclic" episodes: Achilles killing Troilos (*Aeneid* 1.475–478), also told

---

[75] For examples, see Duckworth 1967, Lennox 1977, Grandsen 1984:100–119, Pavlock 1985, Hardie 1994, Fowler 2000, Casali 2004.

[76] For more on these pictures, see Williams 1960, Stanley 1965, Thomas 1983, Clay 1988, Lowenstam 1993, Putnam 1998, and Casali 2004:347–348.

[77] Lowenstam 1993:38n4 details how different scholars have divided the series into different numbers, ranging from four to nine, of discrete scenes or pictures.

[78] Clay 1988:202, 204, and 204n28 instead reads Aeneas as being in the same picture with Memnon.

in the *Cypria*; the presence of Memnon (*Aeneid* 1.489); and the fighting of Penthesilea and the Amazons (*Aeneid* 1.490–493), both also told in the *Aithiopis*. Since we are interested in particular in the reference to Rhesos, let us look at that one in detail first, and then consider how it fits into the series. Depending on how the divisions between scenes are made, this is either the second or third picture described:[79]

> Nec procul hinc Rhesi niveis tentoria velis
> 470 agnoscit lacrimans, primo quae prodita somno
> Tydides multa vastabat caede cruentus,
> ardentisque avertit equos in castra prius quam
> pabula gustassent Troiae Xanthumque bibissent.
>
> *Aeneid* 1.469–474

> Not far from here the tents of Rhesus with their snow-white
>   cloths
> he recognized, weeping, [the tents] which, betrayed by the
>   first sleep,
> the blood-stained son of Tydeus destroyed with abundant
>   slaughter,
> and he turned the dazzling horses into his camp, before
> they had tasted the pastures of Troy and had drunk the
>   Xanthus.

In this encapsulation of the story of Rhesos at Troy, we see a compression of detail as well as narrative in a metonymic series of connections that the viewer/reader must make. In the *Iliad*, it is Rhesos' horses that are described as "whiter than snow" (λευκότεροι χιόνος, *Iliad* 10.437). Here that color is transferred to the tents of his encampment,[80] and the tents in turn stand for Rhesos and the Thracians—*quae prodita* (*Aeneid* 1.470) grammatically agrees with the *tentoria* (*Aeneid* 1.471)—but we know that the men themselves were betrayed by sleep and destroyed in the slaughter Diomedes committed. This compression relies on a reader who knows the story as well as Aeneas does to understand all that the picture represents.

We can notice next that only Diomedes is named as killer and taker of the horses. Does the absence of Odysseus again reflect the

---

[79] The text we have used for the *Aeneid* is Mynors 1969, unless otherwise noted.

[80] Putnam 1998:249 argues that color is an important element in this picture, with a contrast both between the whiteness of the tents and the darkness of the night, and also between the white of the tents and the blood-red of the slaughter.

compression of the story? Perhaps, and we should also remember that in the Greek epic tradition different versions of ambush episodes could feature one or the other for both of these heroes.[81] But there may also be other reasons to single out Diomedes. Odysseus will be featured prominently in Aeneas' telling of the fall of Troy (see e.g. *Aeneid* 2.7, 2.44, 2.90, 2.122, 2.164, 2.261, 2.762), and even in his tale of his wanderings (see e.g. *Aeneid* 3.273 and 3.613–654); there may be a desire to postpone mentioning his name, leaving it for Aeneas' own version of the sack of Troy by ambush. It has been noted before that Achilles dominates the pictures here: even in the non-Iliadic pictures he has a role, whether named or unnamed.[82] Diomedes can be a substitute for Achilles, which may help to motivate his name here, while Odysseus will instead loom over Aeneas' story of the fall of Troy and his wanderings in Books 2 and 3.[83] Papaioannou agrees that Diomedes is associated with Achilles here, and also argues that the *Aeneid* often pairs Aeneas and Diomedes, in anticipation of the embassy to Diomedes by the Italians (Papaioannou 2000:198–200).[84] Thus the association of Aeneas and Diomedes, because of their battle in *Iliad* 5 and the prominence of Diomedes in the second half of this epic (where ambush is also conspicuous), may likewise be a reason to focus on his role in the ambush here.

In the final two lines, a particular version of the Rhesos story is revealed. The placement of the scene ("not far," *Aeneid* 1.469, from the scenes of the Trojans routing the Achaeans and Achilles turning the Trojans back) as well as the details we have looked at thus far give it,

---

[81] See our commentary on 10.243.

[82] Clay 1988:204 recounts the several depictions of Achilles within the series. Lowenstam 1993:48 also emphasizes his prominence, and Putnam 1998:256 argues that Achilles' "overriding presence" is a key to understanding Aeneas' reactions to the pictures.

[83] Putnam 1998:257 notes that Diomedes is indirectly present in the scene of the Trojan women supplicating Athena, and so Achilles is present, explicitly or implicitly, in all the pictures except those that involve Diomedes or the one involving Aeneas himself. Although we read the picture of Aeneas differently from the way Putnam does (he calls it "post-Iliadic" [1998:254], while in our view it could also possibly show Aeneas in battle with Diomedes or Achilles), his point nevertheless supports the idea of Diomedes as an Achilles substitute in these pictures, just as he can be in the *Iliad* itself. In his reading, Putnam does make interesting connections with Aeneas as an Achilles substitute, and later as a Diomedes, too (1998:267).

[84] Papaioannou recognizes the ambush context of both the Rhesos picture and that of Troilos, but her argument that Virgil has left Odysseus out of the scene in order to emphasize Diomedes' warrior status misrepresents the basic sequence of events in *Iliad* 10. The spying mission is not Odysseus' idea and he is not the one who chooses to take Diomedes with him, as she states (Papaioannou 2000:199). Fletcher 2006:227–231 also emphasizes the pairing of Aeneas and Diomedes in *Aeneid* 1 and further argues that Virgil separates Diomedes and Odysseus as part of his "rewriting" of the character of Diomedes (2006:233).

as we noted, an Iliadic feel. When we hear that the horses have not yet eaten or drunk at Troy (*Aeneid* 1.472–473), however, we recognize an allusion to the version in which an oracle predicted Rhesos' invincibility if his horses did indeed do so. Thus we do not have a simply Iliadic reference here: instead, the description makes us first think of *Iliad* 10, but then adds this key detail from an alternate version, one, as we saw above, that is more explicit about the danger Rhesos presents to the Achaeans, and therefore the hope he embodies for the Trojans. This meaning of the final line is yet another compression, then, and the reader/viewer must have knowledge of the story to grasp its full importance.

A similar mixing of Iliadic and non-Iliadic details has also been noted in the scene depicting Hektor (*Aeneid* 1.483–487). In that description we are directed to think of the death, dragging, and ransom of Hektor in *Iliad* 22 and 24. Yet the specific details, such as dragging his body around the walls of Troy, rather than the tomb of Patroklos, and the "selling" of his body for gold (*Aeneid* 1.483–484), recall other versions of this same story.[85] This mixing suggests that Virgil is not relying on any one source or even one version in the Rhesos picture either, but rather creating his own out of the multiform tradition he has inherited.[86] Defining a version of this episode for inclusion within Aeneas' story (and Aeneas is presented as the audience for the story of Rhesos, as we hear his reaction to it in the middle of its description) then paves the way for Aeneas' (and Virgil's) own definitive narrative of the fall of Troy in *Aeneid* 2.[87] For us, Virgil's is the best and most extensive surviving version of the fall of Troy, but if we can imagine how many other versions were circulating during Virgil's lifetime, we can see how Virgil might have needed to assert his version in Aeneas' narrative. Creating a particular version that alludes to several others may have been a way to do that.

---

[85] See Williams 1960:150, Stanley 1965:270–273, Kopff 1981:930, and Putnam 1998:253 for the possible sources to which Virgil may be alluding.

[86] Kopff 1981:944 similarly argues that in *Aeneid* 2, "as elsewhere, Virgil follows the main traditions, inserts variants, and invents as he needs, in order to create the effects he is seeking." Later, he concludes "it was not enough to suggest an alternative to only one Greek author, no matter how great, but instead to the whole Trojan tradition" (Kopff 1981:944).

[87] Putnam also argues for several connections between these pictures and Aeneas' narrative of the fall of Troy. About this picture in particular he says: "The linkage from the horses of Rhesus and death of Troilus to the wooden horse is strongly forged. The talismans of Troy's downfall help conjoin ekphrasis and narrative into one continuous tale of defeat" (Putnam 1998:263).

The affinity between these pictures and Aeneas' narrative of the sack of Troy indicates that ambush is a key theme, since both the death of Rhesos and the story Aeneas tells are indeed ambush narratives. With that connection in mind, the story of Rhesos can be read as being paired with the picture of the ambush of Troilos by Achilles (*Aeneid* 1.474–478) as well.[88] As several scholars have noted, both of these episodes involve particular portents related to the fall of Troy: the oracle about Rhesos included here and a prophecy that connected the fates of Troilos and Troy.[89] Putnam goes further in arguing that the next scene, the supplication of Athena by the Trojan women, evokes the theft of the Palladion, and that the use of the variation of dragging Hektor around the walls calls to mind the breach that will be the downfall of the city (Putnam 1998:260). In this line of reasoning, all of these scenes are associated with the eventual defeat of Troy,[90] but we should also note that they are all associated with ambush. The eventual fall of Troy that underlies these four episodes, which Aeneas will narrate in full in *Aeneid* 2, arrives through a series of ambushes, beginning with that of Rhesos.[91]

Scholars have also argued that these pictures have long-range connections within the *Aeneid* to events in the second, or Iliadic, half of the poem. Stanley asserts that the order of the pictures, which does not follow the order of events at Troy themselves (as we can see just from the placement of the Rhesos and Troilos pictures), instead follows the events they correspond to in the *Aeneid* 7–12: "the panels provide clues *in sequence* to what lies ahead, though the roles of Greek and Trojan,

---

[88] Williams 1960:145–148 persuasively argues that this is indeed an ambush of Troilos, and not, as some scholars had suggested, a version in which Troilos faced Achilles in battle. The picture of Troilos is said to be in "another part" (*parte alia, Aeneid* 1.474), and so its spatial relationship to the picture of Rhesos is difficult to envision precisely. Thomas 1983:180n17 assumes that the pictures are arranged simply in a line, so this picture just follows that of Rhesos.

[89] Williams 1960:149 notes a prophecy that said that if Troilos reached the age of twenty Troy would not fall. See also Kopff 1981:938–939 and Putnam 1998:259.

[90] Williams 1960:149 also argues that the pictures of Rhesos, Troilos, the Trojan women, and Hektor are "a portrayal of the *fata Troiana*."

[91] In addition to these examples of ambush, there may be others. Clay 1988:205 connects the picture of Rhesos, a man slain in his sleep at night, with the ekphrasis on Pallas' belt, which depicts the murder of the sons of Aegyptus on their wedding night (*Aeneid* 10.497–499). That event, too, might be thought of as an ambush. Kopff 1981:943 argues that Camilla is "slain only by ambush, not in a regular fight." Camilla's focus on the gold armor of Chloreus (*Aeneid* 11.768–777) could perhaps be an elaboration of a similar theme seen in the gold armor of Rhesos as Dolon describes it (*Iliad* 10.438–441). Also, she is killed by an arrow, and we have seen in "The Poetics of Ambush" that there is a thematic connection between archery and ambush in the Homeric epics.

the besieger and besieged, will be reversed in the war between Trojan and Latin" (Stanley 1965:274, original emphasis). The picture of Rhesos is in the position it is in here, according to Stanley's analysis, because it prefigures the night episode in *Aeneid* 9, which we will examine in detail below. Stanley's insight has been accepted and further explored in subsequent studies.[92] Lowenstam, for example, has drawn parallels in both theme and diction between the description of the Rhesos picture on the temple walls and the night raid of Nisus and Euryalus (Lowenstam 1993:38–39, 43–45). With this presaging nature of the pictures as well as Stanley's point about the reversal of roles in mind, we can then consider that Aeneas' reaction to the picture of Rhesos also shares in the foreshadowing. We have seen that this description alludes to the fall of Troy, especially with the inclusion of the oracle, and so Aeneas' tears as he recognizes the scene (*agnoscit lacrimans*, *Aeneid* 1.470) are first and foremost related to that interpretation of the picture.[93] But, if the picture indeed also points ahead to the night raid of Nisus and Euryalus, then Aeneas' grief may also be proleptic, as the reversal of Diomedes' success in this picture is found in the Trojan ambushers' ultimate failure.[94]

Thus this compressed depiction of the ambush of Rhesos begins and implicates a series of ambushes: that of Troilos, most immediately; the sack of Troy, which Aeneas will narrate in *Aeneid* 2, in the nearer term; and then the extended night episode of Nisus and Euryalus in *Aeneid* 9. What seems at first simply an allusion to the Trojan past is instead part of a larger pattern at work in the poem as a whole. It also indicates that Virgil was working within a wider epic tradition, one that encompassed other versions of the story of Rhesos. The death of

---

[92] Clay 1988:203–204. Putnam 1998:265 connects Diomedes' killing of Rhesos in his sleep to the ambush of Troy at night with the wooden horse and to *Aeneid* 9. The ambush of Troilos is connected, not to another ambush episode, but rather to deaths of young warriors at the hands of those more experienced, including Pallas, Lausus, and even Turnus. Stanley 1965:275 argues for Lausus; Kopff 1981:938–939, 943 for Pallas, Lausus, and Camilla (the last he argues is an ambush); Clay 1988:204 and 204n26 and Lowenstam 1993:39–40 for Pallas and Lausus; Putnam 1998:265–266 for Pallas and Lausus, but especially Turnus as Aeneas takes the role of Achilles.

[93] Fletcher 2006:230 argues that his tears are additionally an allusion to Diomedes' capture of Aeneas' own horses at Troy.

[94] Casali 2004:348 sees a different connection between the two, arguing that Aeneas is a "resisting reader," who interprets the death of Rhesos from a Trojan rather than a Greek point of view; his reaction parallels the way in which readers of the *Aeneid* may react to the slaughter committed by Nisus and Euryalus (rather than the failure and death of the ambushers themselves) as another occasion for tears.

Rhesos, which many have seen as a marginal event within the *Iliad*, takes on a symbolic importance within the *Aeneid*.

Action at night in *Aeneid* 9

Virgil's own night episode in *Aeneid* 9 reveals his deep understanding of the Homeric poetics of ambush, reflecting these poetics while reworking them for Virgil's own poetic purposes. The night mission undertaken by Nisus and Euryalus shares common elements with both *Iliad* 9 and *Iliad* 10. It recalls at times the mission of Dolon as well as that of Diomedes and Odysseus,[95] and even includes an incident that was avoided by the careful planning of the ambushers in the Homeric tradition. Much of the scholarship on this episode acknowledges its reception of the Doloneia, and some scholars also argue for the Euripidean *Rhesos* and other literary models as influences.[96] This scholarship often focuses on understanding the meaning of the episode for the *Aeneid* as a whole, and seeks to interpret Virgil's portrayal of the ambushers. Our purpose here, however, is simply to investigate how the theme of ambush is developed.

In the scholarship on *Aeneid* 9, we encounter objections or controversies similar to those made for *Iliad* 10 about its place in the epic and its portrayal of characters.[97] One argument even proposes that *Aeneid* 9 seems so out of place because Virgil knew that *Iliad* 10 did not belong in the *Iliad* and was alluding to the so-called "Homeric exegetical tradition" about the episode.[98] As we hope is clear by now, in our approach any seeming strangeness of these episodes is a result not of different authorship or the interpolation of one work into another, but of the difference in theme. And since we have already made the case for the significance of ambush in the first half of the *Aeneid*, we argue that

---

[95] See Casali 2004:324–327 with bibliography on this use of both as models for Nisus and Euryalus. Our interpretations differ from some of Casali's concerning the character of Dolon and the Trojans in *Iliad* 10. See also Hardie 1994 on the relationship of this episode to *Iliad* 10.

[96] Pavlock 1985 and Fowler 2000 both include the *Rhesos* as an influence. Casali 2004 expands his examination further to other plays of Euripides, as well as the poetry of Ennius and Lucretius. Kopff 1981:937 suggests that the episode of the theft of the Palladion in the *Little Iliad* may also have been an influence.

[97] For the latter, see both "Interpreting *Iliad* 10" and "The Poetics of Ambush" above.

[98] Casali 2004:321–323. In another argument, however, Casali asserts that "Virgil's interest in the Doloneia is not limited to the new elaboration of Book 9, but ... it frames the whole poem" (2004:324). See also Fowler 2000:91 for a critical approach that treats the Nisus and Euryalus episode as "a unit" based on an idea that *Iliad* 10 is a "separable part of the epic." Duckworth 1967:129–130 reviews and rejects older views that assert that the night episode is self-contained, or even separately composed.

instead of the night episode being deliberately out of place in this epic, it engages the poetics of ambush in this different thematic register, even as it reworks those same poetics. The way in which ambush is evoked earlier in *Aeneid* 9, before the Nisus and Euryalus episode, also argues against its separation from the rest of the epic, or even from the rest of the book. We will start by looking at these earlier instances at the beginning of the book. Then, when we examine the Nisus and Euryalus episode, we will focus on aspects of it that have received less attention in recent scholarship, but which are intimately bound to the theme of ambush.

Even before night falls and Nisus conceives the plan for a mission to get a message to Aeneas, the beginning of *Aeneid* 9 signals the coming night adventure. The second simile of the book compares Turnus as he attacks the Trojan fort by day to a wolf trying to get into a sheep pen at night (*Aeneid* 9.59–66).[99] This wolf is an ambusher (*lupus insidiatus*, *Aeneid* 9.59) who works in the middle of the night (*nocte super media*, *Aeneid* 9.61). As we have seen in the Homeric poetics of ambush, here also the hardship of such an attack is emphasized, as the wolf endures wind and rain (*ventos perpessus et imbris*, *Aeneid* 9.60) and his continuing hunger wears him out (*collecta fatigat edendi ex longo rabies*, *Aeneid* 9.63–64). The fact that he has been hungry for a long time also suggests that his situation is desperate, another characteristic of ambush episodes. Although the focus of the simile is on the wolf's rage as he tries to attack (and so also Turnus' rage), the "absent" prey (*in absentis*, *Aeneid* 9.63) and the wolf's "jaws dry of blood" (*siccae sanguine fauces*, *Aeneid* 9.64) suggest that this ambush will not be successful. The failure of ambush is a recurring feature in the episodes in the second half of the *Aeneid*, as we will continue to see—failure that stands in contrast to the successful ambush by Diomedes and Odysseus in *Iliad* 10 and in so many other episodes in the wider tradition of the Trojan War. In other words, the failure of the wolf within the simile seems to have longer-range implications than Turnus' failure to get the Trojans to fight outside their walls at this moment.

Turnus himself, however, disavows ambush tactics soon after this simile. Even though on this day he cannot provoke the Trojans into a battle, he tells his men that he will be able to defeat them far more easily than the Greeks did: he does not need a thousand ships, or ten

---

[99] Virgil uses other wolf similes in night battles (*Aeneid* 2.355–360) or ambush situations, as when Arruns kills Camilla (*Aeneid* 11.809–815). See our commentary on 10.485 for more on similes describing lions that attack flocks at night in the *Iliad*.

years, or ambush tactics to do so (*Aeneid* 9.148–155). He specifically mentions two famous ambush episodes from the Epic Cycle, the theft of the Palladion and the wooden horse:

> tenebras et inertia furta
> Palladii caesis summae custodibus arcis
> ne timeant, nec equi caeca condemur in aluo:
> luce palam certum est igni circumdare muros.

Aeneid 9.150–153

> Let them not fear darkness and the unskilled theft
> of the Palladion after the guards of the highest citadel have
>   been slaughtered,
> nor that we will be laid up in the blind belly of a horse:
> in daylight, openly, we are resolved to surround their walls
>   with fire.

Pairing these two ambush episodes indicates that they are both part of the tradition that Virgil knew about the Trojan War—as is already apparent when Aeneas mentions them in his narration of the end of the war in *Aeneid* 2 (the theft of the Palladion at *Aeneid* 2.162–170 and the men emerging from the wooden horse at *Aeneid* 2.250–267). When we compare *Aeneid* 9.151 with *Aeneid* 2.166, we see that Turnus here describes the theft of the Palladion and the ambush of its guards in almost exactly the same way Aeneas had, with only a change in the grammatical case of '*Palladium*'. Whether or not Virgil is imitating the formulaic language of oral epic in this repetition, the effect of it is that Turnus, not only knows the story, he knows it the way Aeneas tells it.[100] Turnus' scorn for such actions, however, is a different reaction from Aeneas' anger and horror in describing them, revealing that there are multiple ways of interpreting these same events.

After his speech, Turnus allows his men to retire for the night. Although, or perhaps even because, Turnus renounced such strategies, the Trojans, of course, will use them on this very night. The *Aeneid* presents this war in several ways as "another" Trojan War: at times the Trojans are in the same position as they were in that war, but at other

---

[100] *Aeneid* 9.151 is bracketed as an interpolation in Hardie's (1994) edition of the text. We have built our argument on the text as received in the manuscripts, which universally contain the line. Mynors's edition of this line reads *Palladii caesis late custodibus arcis*. If we read '*late*' rather than '*summae*' (both readings have good manuscript support) the echo is less noticeable, but does not entirely change our point.

times they are in the position of the Greeks. In terms of the plan for a night reconnaissance mission, they are very much like the Achaeans in *Iliad* 10: trapped by an aggressive army, desperate, and without their best warrior. It is this kind of situation that suggests something as bold as a night mission.

When Nisus first mentions his idea for a mission to Euryalus, he says he wants to do something great (*aliquid ... magnum*, *Aeneid* 9.186) that will bring him a reputation (*fama*, *Aeneid* 9.195). Both here and when he makes his proposal to the Trojan leaders, the mission he proposes is to deliver a message to Aeneas about the dire situation of the Trojan encampment (see *Aeneid* 9.195-196, 9.236-245). In *Iliad* 10 reconnaissance missions (both Diomedes and Odysseus and also Dolon start off on spying missions) are similarly associated with glory (*kleos*, *Iliad* 10.212; *kudos*, *Iliad* 10.307) as well as material rewards.[101] As we have seen, these missions are closely associated with ambush in Homeric epic, and missions of stealth (such as the theft of the Palladion just mentioned by Turnus) often become ambushes as well. Virgil's night mission undergoes just such a transformation when Nisus spies the sleeping enemy (*Aeneid* 9.316-323); the influence of the epic tradition is certainly felt in this transformation. For Nisus and Euryalus, just as for Diomedes and Odysseus, the sleeping, unprotected enemy is too easy a target to resist.[102] Hints that the mission will become an ambush begin already in Nisus' repeated thoughts prior to leaving: he thinks about how the enemy encamped outside are not only sleeping but drunk (*Aeneid* 9.189-190 and 9.236-237). He calls his proposal "ambush" (*insidiis*, *Aeneid* 9.237) that will include "huge slaughter" (*ingenti caede*, *Aeneid* 9.242). Pinpointing when the transformation occurs is not important, however; what is significant for us is that it echoes the poetics of ambush from the Greek epic tradition.

Before Nisus and Euryalus leave on their mission, there is a brief arming scene (*Aeneid* 9.303-307). Even though Nisus and Euryalus were just on guard duty, and therefore presumably armed, there is a communal aspect to this scene, with leaders giving weapons to the pair.

---

[101] The glory promised to Nisus and Euryalus in the famous apostrophe at *Aeneid* 9.446-449 is perhaps the most contentious point of interpretation of this episode. To participate in this argument is beyond our scope here. We will simply note that the promise of glory is an intertextual moment with *Iliad* 10.

[102] So Lennox 1977:336, who argues that the ambush is not part of the original plan but rather "it is a chance which Nisus cannot pass by, a chance, not a premeditated idea." Duckworth 1967:131-132, however, argues that getting a message to Aeneas is a pretext for the slaughter that Nisus desires to achieve all along.

A group contribution of armor is also present in the Achaean arming scene in *Iliad* 10, when the armed guards give equipment to Diomedes and Odysseus.[103] Further Homeric influences on this arming scene can be detected in the lion skin given to Nisus (*Aeneid* 9.306). Dressing in animal skins is a key to the register of night missions (see "The Poetics of Ambush"), and both Agamemnon and Diomedes similarly dress in a lion skin (*Iliad* 10.23–24 and 10.177–178). The *Iliad* is not explicit about whether Diomedes wears this skin while on the mission, as it is about Dolon in his wolf skin, but the *Aeneid* alludes to both Diomedes' dress at night and the Iliadic similes that compare him to a lion (*Iliad* 10.297 and 10.485–486). Likewise Nisus, who is given the lion skin specifically for the mission, is compared to a lion as he kills the Rutulians in the skin of one (*Aeneid* 9.339–341).[104]

A strategically important aspect of the equipment worn by Diomedes and Odysseus is that their headgear is made for stealth: it has no plumes or bosses and is made of leather and tusks, not metal.[105] Euryalus will become visible to his eventual captors because he puts on a crested helmet (*galeam … cristis decoram*, *Aeneid* 9.365) that shines as it reflects the moonlight (*Aeneid* 9.372–374).[106] The spies on both sides in the *Iliad* understand the importance of special dress for night missions and equip themselves accordingly. Dolon is unlucky, not conspicuous, when he is seen by Odysseus. It is Euryalus' inexperience, however, that proves fatal when he puts on the shiny helmet.

In another contrast, the teamwork that we have seen to be important for Diomedes and Odysseus' success seems to break down between this pair of ambushers in the *Aeneid*. Like Odysseus (*Iliad* 10.479–481), Nisus divides the tasks to be done in the ambush (*Aeneid* 9.321–323), but Euryalus goes beyond the task of standing guard, and does not immediately heed Nisus' command that they should leave (*Aeneid* 9.355–356). In the details of fighting and killing in this episode, we also see further

---

[103] See *Iliad* 10.254–272 and our commentary on these lines. The legacy of objects, such as the legacy of the helmet that Meriones gives Odysseus at *Iliad* 10.260–271, is, however, transferred to the spoils here—namely, the belt of Rhamnes that Euryalus strips from him (*Aeneid* 9.359–364).

[104] See Lowenstam 1993:45 for the verbal echoes he sees between this scene and the picture of Rhesos in *Aeneid* 1. See also Pavlock 1985:214–215 on this simile.

[105] See our commentary on *Iliad* 10.254–272 and 10.257 in particular.

[106] In the arming scene, we hear that Aletes "exchanged" helmets with Nisus (*galeam fidus permutat Aletes*, *Aeneid* 9.307). Because it does not seem that during the mission Nisus is wearing a metal helmet, as *galea* means in *Aeneid* 9.365 and 9.373, perhaps we should understand that the exchange was Nisus' metal helmet for some non-metal headgear that Aletes was wearing, one more appropriate for Nisus' mission.

affinities with *Iliad* 10 and the poetics of ambush. Both Odysseus and Dolon take bows with them, and, although Nisus uses spears instead of arrows, his success in killing Sulmo and Tagus, two of Euryalus' captors (*Aeneid* 9.411–419), nevertheless demonstrates the advantages of shooting from an unseen position, which is the very advantage that a bow gives at night.[107] Also, we see the decapitation of victims happen on both sides: more famously, the heads of Nisus and Euryalus are displayed to the Trojans the next morning (*Aeneid* 9.465–467), but the Trojans too cut off the head of Remus during their ambush (*Aeneid* 9.332–333). As morally troubling or aesthetically displeasing as we may find these acts, we nevertheless should recognize the connection to the decapitation of Dolon (*Iliad* 10.455–457) and see how such an act can be part of the ambush theme.

The unhappy end of Nisus and Euryalus brings us back to a central way in which Virgil has reworked the poetics of the Doloneia. The mission here, as was suggested in the simile of the ambushing wolf near the beginning of *Aeneid* 9, results in failure. The contrast is evident if we are thinking of Nisus and Euryalus as Diomedes and Odysseus, who make the all-important return safe and sound. When we compare this pair with Dolon, we see that there is a repetition of Trojan failure in these night forays.[108] Achaean ambush is successful over and over, not only in *Iliad* 10 (as we have already seen in the picture of Rhesos on the temple), but also in the sack of Troy that Aeneas relates in *Aeneid* 2.[109] But unlike the one-sided success of ambush in the Trojan War, failure of ambush tactics occurs on both sides in this war. Turnus sets an ambush (in the daytime) for Aeneas and his men at a narrow pass (*Aeneid* 11.511–516; 522–531). He leaves his place of ambush, however, when Camilla's death is reported to him, and just misses his chance to inflict damage on Aeneas and his troops. Night falls soon after and delays any chance of battle between Aeneas and Turnus (*Aeneid* 11.896–915). Although Turnus himself contradicts his earlier rejection of ambush by his actions, the epic as a whole stays true to his words—unlike the Trojan War, this war will not be determined by ambush.

---

[107] See the section "Weapons of ambush" in our essay "The Poetics of Ambush" and our commentary on *Iliad* 10.260 and 10.333.

[108] Casali 2004:330 makes the interesting point that "The Doloneia in *Aeneid* 9 is an intertextual repetition, but in the narrative world of the poem it is also a real repetition of the past."

[109] In that narrative of the sack of Troy, we note that the Trojans use ambush tactics of their own. They put on the armor of the Achaeans they have killed and succeed initially, but the ambush later fails when they are attacked by other Trojans in the darkness and confusion (*Aeneid* 2.386–412).

Dolon's son in Italy

Turnus' failed ambush in *Aeneid* 11 brings us to the final passage we want to examine. Almost a bookend to the reference to Rhesos in *Aeneid* 1, there is in *Aeneid* 12 a short passage about the death of Dolon's son Eumedes while fighting for the Trojans in Italy, which also recapitulates Dolon's story in *Iliad* 10 (*Aeneid* 12.346–361). We did not hear in the *Iliad* that Dolon had a son, so what is he doing here? Eumedes is the first "personalized" victim of Turnus after Aeneas leaves the battlefield with an injury. The absence of Aeneas once again may evoke an ambush situation, but in this battlefield meeting, the ambush happens only in the backstory:

> Parte alia media Eumedes in proelia fertur,
> antiqui proles bello praeclara Dolonis,
> nomine avum referens, animo manibusque parentem,
> qui quondam, castra ut Danaum speculator adiret,
> 350   ausus Pelidae pretium sibi poscere currus;
> illum Tydides alio pro talibus ausis
> adfecit pretio nec equis aspirat Achilli.
> Hunc procul ut campo Turnus prospexit aperto,
> ante levi iaculo longum per inane secutus
> 355   sistit equos biiugis et curru desilit atque
> semianimi lapsoque supervenit, et pede collo
> impresso dextrae mucronem extorquet et alto
> fulgentem tingit iugulo atque haec insuper addit:
> 'en agros et, quam bello, Troiane, petisti,
> 360   Hesperiam metire iacens: haec praemia, qui me
> ferro ausi temptare, ferunt, sic moenia condunt.'

Aeneid 12.346–361

> In another part, Eumedes rushes into the middle of battle,
> the splendid-in-war offspring of old Dolon,
> reproducing his grandfather with his name and his father
>   with his spirit and hands,
> his father who once, when he went as a spy on the Danaan
>   camp,
> 350   dared to ask as his price the chariot of Peleus' son.
> The son of Tydeus, in return for such great daring, bestowed
>   on him

another price, and he [Dolon] no longer aspires to the
    horses of Achilles.
When Turnus spotted this man from afar in the open field,
    having pursued him first through the long space with his
       light javelin,
355 he brings his yoked horses to a stop and jumps down from
    his chariot and
    overtakes him, fallen and half-alive, and with a foot pressed
       on his neck
    he twists out the pointed sword from Eumedes' right hand
       and deep
    in his throat he thrusts it as it shines and he adds these
       things over him:
    "Behold the fields and the Hesperia you sought, Trojan, with
       war;
360 lying there, measure them out: these rewards those who
    dare to try me with a sword get, this way do they found city
       walls."

Eumedes' introduction at this point in the narrative only to be killed and boasted over by Turnus a few lines later is strongly reminiscent of the introductions of such characters in the *Iliad* that we have explored above, including Dolon himself. In the Iliadic passages, the warrior's life history and lineage are narrated just before that warrior dies, far from his home and family. In this way the introduction takes the place of a lament for the fallen warrior. Here, however, the only story given is that of Eumedes' father Dolon. We cannot be sure that Virgil did not know a son of Dolon from the epic tradition. Whether he did, or whether he "invented" one for this passage, it does not seem to be the pathos of Eumedes' death that is the focus here, but rather Dolon himself. So, as Virgil evokes a typical feature of Homeric epic, he also changes its form from a traditional allusion to a specifically intertextual reference. The highly textual nature of this reference is disclosed by the adjective modifying Dolon: *antiquus*. Dolon is not 'ancient' within the story—he is the same generation as Aeneas himself. He is only ancient from a point of view outside the story, like the *Iliad* in comparison with the *Aeneid*.

    This intertextuality continues even after the story of Dolon is recounted. For Eumedes is not only like his father in his hands and spirit, he dies in a similar fashion. Though Eumedes' own death is not portrayed as an ambush, Dolon also has a spear thrown at him from afar, is then overtaken on foot, and is finally killed with a sword to his throat (*Iliad* 10.372-377, 10.455-456).[110] There is a verbal connection in this passage as well. The death of both father and son is attributed to their "daring": Dolon is daring in his asking for the horses of Peleus as a price (*pretium*) for his spying mission, and he is instead rewarded with death for his daring (*ausus ... ausis*, which frame the lines, *Aeneid* 12.350-351), while Turnus' vaunt over Eumedes similarly says death is the reward (*praemia*) granted to those who dare (*ausi*) to try him in battle (*Aeneid* 12.360-361).[111] In the Greek epic tradition, daring is portrayed as a necessary quality for such night missions and thus as uniformly positive—even for Dolon's daring to enter the enemy camp.[112] Virgil complicates that conception of daring in multiple ways here: by ascribing it first to Dolon's particular aspirations for a reward, and then to the Trojans' aspirations for a new city in Italy. Turnus offers Eumedes just enough ground for his grave, ground that is directly compared to the city walls that the Trojans hope to found (*Aeneid* 12.359-360).[113] Virgil has not allowed ambush to be a determining factor in this war, but in this final allusion to the Doloneia, ambush is nevertheless implicated in a problematic way in the Trojans' hopes and goals for this war.

The evocation of Dolon in this final book of the *Aeneid* is deliberate, and it suggests that the Doloneia should be understood as a thread that has been woven through the entire tapestry of the *Aeneid*.[114] When

[110] Fletcher 2006:252-256 also argues that Turnus is in several ways assimilated to Diomedes in *Aeneid* 12, including in this passage. Francesca Behr, in personal communication, suggests that this description of Eumedes' death also foreshadows the way Turnus himself dies, making the Doloneia allusion even more potent within *Aeneid* 12.

[111] The phrase *pro talibus ausis* is also used in other ambush contexts: at *Aeneid* 2.535, during the sack of Troy, in Priam's words about Neoptolemos killing Polites in front of him, and also, in some manuscripts, at *Aeneid* 9.252, where Aletes' words characterize Nisus' proposal for the night mission this way. In other manuscripts (and in Mynors' edition) the phrase used instead is *pro laudibus istis*, suggesting that daring can be positive as well as negative. We thank Francesca Behr for these references.

[112] See, for example, *Iliad* 10.205, 10.231, 10.244, 10.248, 10.307, and 10.319, and our commentary on these lines.

[113] Williams 1973 *ad* 12.359-360 notes the similarity of Turnus' vaunt here to what Turnus says when he thinks he is pursuing a fleeing Aeneas (really the phantom Juno created) at *Aeneid* 10.649-650, making the connection to the founding of the city even stronger. In his "economic" reading of this passage, Coffee 2009:62 connects the language of price and reward here with *misthos* in *Iliad* 10.304, arguing that it receives greater emphasis here. He further argues that Turnus' taunt characterizes the Trojan cause as one simply of mercenary gain.

[114] For one further example, Smith 2005:153-157 argues that Aeneas' rejection of Magus' supplication on the battlefield and the way he kills him recall the death of Dolon in *Iliad* 10.

we look at the reception of the Doloneia in the *Rhesos* and the *Aeneid* through the lens of the poetics of ambush, we get a very different impression from that offered by the oft-repeated idea that "even in antiquity" the authenticity of the Doloneia was doubted. Instead, we find that the theme of ambush (best represented for us in *Iliad* 10, but, as we have seen, a fairly common theme in the larger Greek epic tradition) is one that is alluded to, interrogated, and reworked for various poetic purposes. There is no evident preconception in these works that the Doloneia is un-Iliadic. Instead of imposing a modern scholarly prejudice on them, we suggest that more fruitful approaches to understanding the relationship between these texts will make the question of "authenticity" neither their starting assumption nor the object of investigation. As we hope we have shown in our brief treatments of these works, our knowledge and appreciation of the theme and poetics of ambush is deepened and enhanced by investigating its reception. The *Rhesos* and the *Aeneid* allow us to perceive how the poetics of ambush were understood and developed even further in antiquity, with the result that we can better appreciate how the theme of ambush operates in Homeric epic. At the same time, as we have only begun to point out here, we can better understand the *Rhesos* and the *Aeneid* once we have an appreciation for the poetics of ambush.

4

Iliad 10

A Multitextual Approach

T HIS VOLUME TAKES A MULTITEXTUAL APPROACH in its presentation of
the transmitted texts of *Iliad* 10. We want to avoid presenting a
critical text that obscures the multiformity of the oral tradition or is
misleading about the historical realities about the textual transmission. For that reason we have chosen to include four separate witnesses
that illustrate the text of part or all of *Iliad* 10 at various points in its
textual history: the second-century BCE papyrus 609, the third-century
CE papyrus 425, the sixth-century CE papyrus 46, and the tenth-century
CE Venetus A manuscript of the *Iliad* (*Marcianus Graecus* Z. 454 [= 822]).
A brief description of each document precedes our presentation of its
text, and a commentary on the text is provided on following pages.
The commentary is indeed what makes this a *critical* edition of these
texts, but critical in a way different from what is usually indicated by
the term. We are not judging which text is right or wrong (see below
for more on our practices of textual criticism); instead, we attempt to
critically assess what these witnesses contain in terms of the textual
tradition and the oral tradition that preceded it. In the commentary we
point out textual multiformity in these witnesses, and explain both how
they agree with or differ from other witnesses and what some of the
implications of the differences may be. Although these commentaries
on the texts are not as exhaustive as a full *apparatus criticus* covering
every witness to the text of *Iliad* 10 would be, by focusing more closely
on these select witnesses we can explore the differences between texts
in greater detail than can be done in an apparatus.

By presenting the texts in this manner we are adhering to the
goals of the Homer Multitext (http://www.homermultitext.org), a
digital project of which we are editors. The Homer Multitext views
the full historical reality of the Homeric textual tradition as it evolved

from the pre-Classical era to the medieval. It is an edition of Homer that is digital and web-based. Unlike the standard format of printed editions, which intend to offer a reconstruction of an original text as it supposedly existed at the time and place of its origin, the Homer Multitext offers the tools for discovering, viewing, and understanding a variety of texts as they existed in a variety of times and places. We feel that this approach is necessary, and methodologically superior, when dealing with an oral tradition like that in which our *Iliad* and *Odyssey* were composed. As we explain in more detail below, the texts included in this print edition are a small but significant sample of the witnesses to *Iliad* 10. The selected texts were produced at different time periods and illustrate the multiformity that we describe in this essay. The Venetus A is the oldest and best complete manuscript of the *Iliad* and, moreover, is rich in the marginal commentary called scholia. Our readers, if they are so inclined, can also consult this manuscript for themselves, by means of high-resolution digital images available freely online (http://www.homermultitext.org). Thus these texts, presented in such a way that the reader can see exactly what each one records, will, we hope, provide a window onto the tradition in a way distinct from the usual layout of a text of the *Iliad*.

In the digital Homer Multitext, a far greater number of texts will be available for comparison than we are able to present here. In what follows we explain how a multitextual approach differs from conventional textual criticism and why we have adopted it for our edition of *Iliad* 10.

Textual Criticism of Oral Poetry

The received practice of textual criticism, in this case as applied to ancient Greek texts, has the goal of recovering the original composition of the author.[1] To create a critical edition, a modern editor assembles a text by collating the various written witnesses to an ancient Greek text, understanding their relationship with each other, knowing the kinds and likelihoods of mistakes that can occur when texts are copied by hand, and, in the case of poetry, applying the rules and exceptions of the meter as well as grammar. The final published work will then represent what she or he thinks are the author's own words (or as close to them as possible). An editor may follow one manuscript almost exclusively or pick and choose between different manuscripts to compile what seems truest to the original. The editor also places in

---

[1]   See Reynolds and Wilson 1991.

the *apparatus criticus* what she or he judges to be significant variants recorded in the witnesses. The reader must rely on the editor for the completeness of the apparatus in reporting variants. For a text that was composed and originally published in writing, this goal of recovering the original text and these practices for achieving it are valuable and productive, even if the author's original composition may never be fully achieved because of the state of the evidence.

Because the *Iliad* and *Odyssey* were not composed in writing, however, this editorial system cannot be applied in the same way. Our versions of these epics result from a long oral tradition in which they were created, performed, and re-performed, all without the technology of writing. In the earliest phases of this tradition, the *Iliad* and *Odyssey* would never have been performed exactly the same way twice. In other words, in a tradition in which the composition occurs during the course of performance, there is no one "author's original composition" to attempt to recover. The fundamental difference in the composition and history of this poetry, then, means that we must adjust the assumptions in our understanding of the variations in the written record. What does it mean when we see variations, which still fit the meter and language of the poetry, in the witnesses to the texts? These kinds of variations are of a kind different from those that are more clearly scribal errors. Instead of "mistakes" to be corrected or choices that must be weighed and evaluated, as an editor would do in the case of a text composed in writing, we assert that these variations are testaments to the system of language that underlies the composition-in-performance of the oral tradition.

The *Iliad* and *Odyssey* as oral poetry

As we have already noted elsewhere in this volume (see "Interpreting *Iliad* 10"), we have learned from the comparative fieldwork of Milman Parry and Albert Lord that the Homeric epics were composed in performance during a long oral tradition that preceded any written version.[2] In this tradition, the singer did not memorize a static text prior to performance, but would compose the song as he sang it. How is this possible, especially for a song such as the *Iliad*? As Parry and Lord were able to illustrate comparatively by way of the South Slavic tradition, the composition depends on a traditional system that can best be understood as a specialized language with its own specialized grammar and

---

[2] See Parry 1971, Lord 1960/2000, Lord 1991, and Lord 1995; see also Nagy 1996a and Nagy 2002.

vocabulary. We refer to this specialized language as "formulaic," using Parry's terminology. This traditional language is most familiar to us in name-epithet combinations (e.g. "swift-footed Achilles"), but, as scholarship over the past seventy-five years has shown, the whole epic is composed using this formulaic system. A singer trained in this system of language and in the traditional stories, as Parry and Lord themselves observed in action, can then rapidly compose while performing (Lord 1960/2000).

One of the most important revelations of the fieldwork of Parry and Lord is that every time the song is performed in an oral composition-in-performance tradition, it is composed anew. The singers themselves do not strive to innovate, but they nevertheless compose a new song each time (Dué 2002:83–89). The mood of the audience or occasion of performance are just two factors that can influence the length of a song or a singer's choices between competing, but still traditional, elements of plot. The term "variant," as employed by textual critics when evaluating witnesses to a text, is not appropriate for such a compositional process. Lord has explained the difference this way: "the word *multiform* is more accurate than 'variant,' because it does not give preference or precedence to any one word or set of words to express an idea; instead it acknowledges that the idea may exist in several forms" (Lord 1995:23). Our textual criticism of Homeric epic, then, needs to distinguish what may genuinely be copying mistakes from what are performance multiforms: that is, what variations we see are very likely to be part of the system and the tradition in which these epics were composed (Dué 2001a).

Once we begin to think about the variations as parts of the system rather than as mistakes or corruptions, textual criticism of the Homeric texts can then address fresh questions. Some of the variations we see in the written record, for example, reveal the flexibility of this system. Where different written versions record different words, but each phrase or line is metrically and contextually sound, we must not necessarily consider one "correct" or "composed by Homer" and the other a "mistake" or an "interpolation." Rather, each could represent a different performance possibility, a choice that the singer could have made, and would have been making rapidly without reference to a set text (in any sense of that word). John Foley has used the term "oral-derived poetry" to describe the *Iliad* and *Odyssey* because we no longer have direct access to the performance tradition and, instead, must rely exclusively on texts, which themselves are at a remove of many years from any particular performance (Foley 1995:60–98, 137–143). In terms of interpreting the poetry, however, Foley argues that we are still required to understand its "traditional idiom": "Poems composed in a particular register must be received in the same register, to the extent that such fidelity is possible over gaps of space, time, and culture" (Foley 2002:132). We believe that a new kind of textual criticism is necessary because of Homeric epic's special register of performance, and that this new criticism should help to recover, rather than obscure, what is natural and particular to that register. By means of this criticism, then, considering and properly understanding the multiforms that remain in the textual record will help us to receive the poems in their own register.

Representing multiformity

It is difficult to indicate the parity of these multiforms in a standard critical edition on the printed page. In most editions, one version of the text must be chosen for the text on the upper portion of the page, and the other recorded variations must be placed in an apparatus below, often in smaller text, a placement that necessarily gives the impression that these variations are incorrect or at least less important. The abbreviations required by the format of a typical apparatus further obscure what each witness actually contains, and the abbreviated format provides little explanation of why any of the variations is indeed significant. Within a digital medium, however, the Homer Multitext will be able to show where such variations occur, indicate clearly which witnesses record them, and allow users to see them in an arrangement that more intuitively distinguishes them as performance multiforms. Thus a digital edition—one that can more readily present parallel texts—enables a more comprehensive understanding of these epics.

For this printed edition, we are, like standard editions of the past, restricted to the physical page. Nevertheless, we have sought to represent the text in a more historically valid way by including the complete surviving texts of a number of witnesses from a broad time span. We hope, moreover, that by providing commentary on these textual witnesses on following pages, we will break free of the model that relegates multiformity to the easily overlooked bottom of the page, with its tiny font and highly abbreviated (and Latin) notational system. We recognize that there are some limitations to the presentation we have adopted. Some comments on the text must be repeated in several places, and we have limited the number of separate texts included in this print edition to four. Still, because this edition encompasses a single book of the *Iliad*, a somewhat modest take on our multitextual approach has been feasible. We have chosen to adopt it, and, by doing so, to encourage new ways of thinking about the text and how it has come down to us.

These four texts, produced at different times over the span of over a thousand years, provide the opportunity to glimpse what the text could look like at different points in time. What we begin to discover from this glimpse is the complexity of the transmission of the *Iliad*. An approach to editing Homer that embraces the multiformity of both the performative and textual phases of the tradition—that is to say, a multitextual approach—can better convey this complexity. The variations that the textual critic of Homer encounters come from many different kinds of sources and many time periods. In his 1931 edition of the *Iliad* Allen includes 188 manuscripts, dating from the tenth century CE on, and the relationship between manuscripts or manuscript families and their descent from earlier exemplars can be only partially reconstructed (Allen 1931). From the scholia that survive in our medieval manuscripts—which include commentary derived from scholarship as old as the second century BCE—we learn of readings attributed to the texts of various cities (some as far away from Greece as Marseilles), texts in the collections of individuals, texts called "common" or "standard," and texts that are "more refined" (Nagy 2004:20). In the literature that survives from Classical Athens, especially the Attic orators and Plato, we find quotations of Homer, some quite extensive, and these texts can vary considerably from the medieval texts of Homer on which we rely for our printed editions (Dué 2001a and Dué 2001b). Some of our earliest witnesses to the text of Homer are the fragmentary papyri that survived in the sands of Egypt from the third century BCE onwards. These texts too are often quite different than their medieval counterparts (Dué 2001a). A multitextual approach can be explicit about these many different channels of transmission, placing each witness in its historical and cultural framework and allowing the reader to understand better the relationships between witnesses, rather than giving the false impression that they are all of the same kind and same time. In the individual introductions to each text that we present in this volume, we make clear the historical context in which these witnesses were produced, and we have ordered them chronologically to give a more immediate impression of the older witnesses that we know only from fragmentary papyri.

From these many types of sources, we find a number of different kinds of multiforms as well. It is easy to find in the textual transmission of the Homeric poems examples of multiforms in which different, but equally formulaic, words and phrases are used (see Dué and Ebbott

2009 for detailed examples of these kinds of multiforms). There are also smaller cases of word change, differences in word division or accent, and other matters of orthography. These differences are important for what they can reveal about the textual tradition and the editorial practices of earlier stages of transmission. As we look at the earliest sources, papyri from the third century BCE or quotations in Classical authors, such as Plato or Aeschines, we also see differences on the level of entire lines of the poetry. There are numerous verses in the papyri that are seemingly intrusive from the standpoint of the medieval transmission. These additional verses, the so-called plus verses, are not present in the majority of the medieval manuscripts of the *Iliad*. Other verses that are canonical in the medieval manuscripts are absent from the papyri—these may be termed minus verses. Composition-in-performance allows for the expansion or compression of the theme or episode that the singer is performing, and these plus and minus verses are evidence of what a performance might have included, the operation of the system underlying the performance, and what the epic tradition included (Dué 2001a).

Fluidity vs. rigidity and a diachronic approach to Homeric poetry

The complexity of the textual transmission of the Homeric epics is only part of the story. As we noted at the beginning of this discussion, we also have to recognize the oral origins of this poetry and reject the notion of an "original" text. To illustrate the intricacies of this aspect of our critical approach, we can make an instructive comparison to the transmission of the works of Shakespeare. As we will see, the comparison helps us to think about the interaction of text and performance, but there will of course be important differences as well. The transmission of Shakespeare's plays is indeed quite complex. Authoritative editions of the plays were not overseen by Shakespeare himself, and the earliest editions seem, in some instances at least, to have been made on the basis of faulty transcripts of actual performances, requiring substantial reconstruction of the text (Greg 1955). The First Folio edition of 1623, which is the most authoritative of the early editions, was put together seven years after Shakespeare's death by two actors in the King's Men, the company for which Shakespeare wrote. The texts of the thirty-six plays included in the edition are of various provenance. Some derive from the heavily annotated copies prepared for prompters; others are based on Shakespeare's own working drafts. It is clear that some plays were revised for subsequent performances during the course of

Shakespeare's lifetime, with the result that there are multiple versions of the same work, all of which are equally Shakespearean. Editors of such Classical authors as Aristophanes and Ovid face similar difficulties.

What the plays of Shakespeare share with the Homeric tradition is that they were created in the context of performance. Individual instances of performance could result in new texts, depending on the occasion of performance, the intervention of actors and/or others involved in the production, or the desire of Shakespeare himself. A transcript created on the basis of a given performance would no doubt vary from transcripts created on other occasions. Such variations can teach us a great deal about the performance traditions of Shakespeare's plays, the creative process, and Shakespeare's working methods. Scholars of recent decades have rightly seen the value in the variation that we find in the textual transmission, and several digital projects have been developed that make the quartos and folios available to an interested public. Of particular note is The Internet Shakespeare Editions (http://internetshakespeare.uvic.ca/index.html), which plans to publish high-resolution photographs of these early editions together with a variety of supplementary information, electronic texts, and fully edited (modern) editions.

But the Shakespeare analogy can only be taken so far. Homeric poetry was not only created *for* performance, it was created *in* performance. In the earliest stages of the tradition, the singer was also the composer, not just the performer. And, as we noted earlier, in these earliest stages of the tradition no song would have ever been sung the same way twice. The content and form of the songs were traditional and the tradition was a highly conservative one, but the compositional process was nonetheless dynamic. As editors of the Homer Multitext, we are not seeking to recover the most authoritative performance, because such a performance does not exist. Rather than screen out variation in the search for the author's own words, we seek out variation for what it can tell us about Homeric composition-in-performance and the evolution of the texts we now recognize as our *Iliad* and *Odyssey*. Those are the kinds of variations we highlight in these texts.

Perhaps unexpectedly, a much more modern text provides us with a different and interesting analogy. The Homer Multitext faces some of the same questions, problems, and demands as those laid out by Loranger in editing William Burroughs's *Naked Lunch* (Loranger 1999). Loranger points out that there is no *one* definitive version of *Naked Lunch*, that none of the changes to the narrative "can be considered accidental variants ... [or] deliberate authorial revisions" (Loranger

1999:#2). The narrative underwent an evolution (#1), and its assembly has its own mythology, as she terms it (#6–7). She begins and ends by looking for a *reliable* edition, and argues that such an edition would have to allow readers to move, in any order, between the different textual elements, fragments, and even images, such as the drawings Burroughs produced for the U. S. edition (#1, 24). We are in no way looking to create a "postmodern" Homer, but what we know about oral composition-in-performance, in which each time the song is sung it is composed anew, requires a similar attention to the song's evolution as much as we can trace it and to the creation or application of tools for allowing the reader to explore and understand that evolution.

By taking an evolutionary view of the Homeric epics, we are, of course, talking about an evolution that spans not an author's lifetime, but rather millennia. We see in the witnesses that survive an evolution toward greater, but not complete, agreement among texts. In the reverse view, moving further back in time, we see greater variation at earlier stages of transmission. Questions of how much variation is natural to the Homeric tradition and how much variation can be recovered are complicated ones to answer because they are tied to the uncertainty surrounding the figure of Homer (if he ever existed) and questions related to authorship.[3] It was at one time fashionable in Homeric Studies to apply statistics to the Homeric corpus.[4] Scholars attempted to use mathematical methods to find which parts of the Homeric diction could be deemed "formulaic" and which parts innovations on the part of a master poet, imagined as Homer. Parry, for example, by way of demonstration analyzed the first fifteen verses of the *Iliad* and found them to be over ninety percent "formulaic" (Parry 1930 in Parry 1971:301–304). Later, Albert Lord analyzed the same passage, and, although his definition of the individual formulas involved differed slightly from Parry's, the results were roughly the same (Lord 1960:142–144). The fundamental problems with this kind

---

[3] See Nagy 1996b and Dué 2006a.

[4] In addition to the examples discussed here, two others should be noted. In 1924, T. W. Allen analyzed variations in early papyrus texts to come up with percentage degrees of difference from the medieval texts of Homer (Allen 1924). In 1982, Richard Janko published a statistical analysis of the dialects and other language features in Homer, Hesiod, and the Homeric Hymns and used them to argue (among other things) that our *Iliad* was composed and fixed in the eighth century BCE (Janko 1982). The studies of both Allen and Janko are marred by their small sample size, which limits the strength of any inferences that can be drawn from analysis of the data. Allen himself admitted as much, noting that "many of the figures are meaningless" (Allen 1924:300).

of analysis are twofold, as Lord himself already pointed out in 1960. First and foremost, it is based on incomplete data. Only two of the large number of Archaic Greek epics that we know were current in antiquity have survived to the current day. If more of the Epic Cycle (as these other epics are commonly called) had survived, we would have a much larger amount of material to work with. Because of the relatively small amount of comparison material, our understanding of the nature of the formula and the composition process is imperfect. Second, if the tradition in which the Greek poets were working is as Parry and Lord described, then *every* verse should be formulaic, and there is much to suggest that this is true of Homeric poetry (Lord 1960:47 and 147).[5]

For Shakespeare, multiformity—that is to say, the existence of multiple versions of the same text—is an unintended accident of transmission. For most of the plays, there is only one version that Shakespeare himself would have considered definitive, even if he would have acknowledged other drafts he produced, and even though we no doubt consider those drafts worth saving and studying today. For Homeric epic, the relative uniformity of the medieval manuscripts is the accident of transmission, and multiformity is the natural result of the process by which they were created. Many hundreds of the relatively uniform medieval texts of Homer survive, whereas no complete text of Homer survives on papyrus and only certain passages are quoted in Classical authors. In a 2001 publication, Dué (2001a) examined in detail a Homeric quotation from the orator Aeschines, together with some Ptolemaic papyri. Dué found that the kinds of variation presented in those sources are formulaic and traditional: there are extra verses, alternative verses, and variation within lines, but the nature of the variations is such that they are equally as "Homeric" as those that survived in our medieval transmission. This kind of variation, which is primarily on the level of formula and fluctuation in the number of verses, would not interest all readers of Homer, but it is what is to be expected in a relatively late stage of the transmission, at a point when the poems had largely been fixed. For even as early as

---

[5] Ahuvia Kahane (1997) has written an excellent overview of the potential rewards and pitfalls of "quantifying epic": "A quantitative approach therefore enables us to learn about a *non-textual* or rather a *hyper-textual* version of Homer. This version is perhaps better known simply as *the epic tradition* (which, of course, is assumed to be larger and more fluid than our extant *Iliad* and *Odyssey*)" (1997:333, original emphasis). We share Kahane's conception of a larger, more fluid epic tradition within which the *Iliad* and *Odyssey* were composed, and this is perhaps the most basic of the assumptions on which we have built our reconstruction of the poetics of ambush.

the Classical period—whence the earliest textual evidence survives—the Homeric poems seem to have had a cohesiveness and unity that borders on the adjective "fixed."

Before we attempt to go even further back in time, and consider a far more fluid state of the epic poetry, it might be helpful here to consider the evolutionary model for the development of the Homeric poems that has been proposed by Gregory Nagy. Nagy (2004:27) traces the evolution of the poems in five stages, moving from "most fluid" to "most rigid":

> In response to the challenge posed by Lord's concept of multi-formity, the evolutionary model presents an alternative to the numerous attempts at reconstructing an "original" text of Homer. In terms of this model, I envisage five periods of progressively less fluidity, more rigidity:
>
> (1) a relatively most fluid period, with no written texts, extending from the early second millennium into the middle of the eighth century in the first millennium BCE.
>
> (2) a more formative or "Panhellenic" period, still with no written texts, from the middle of the eighth century to the middle of the sixth BCE.
>
> (3) a definitive period, centralized in Athens, with potential texts in the sense of *transcripts*, at any or several points from the middle of the sixth century to the later part of the fourth BCE; this period starts with the reform of Homeric performance traditions in Athens during the régime of the Peisistratidai.
>
> (4) a standardizing period, with texts in the sense of transcripts or even *scripts*, from the later part of the fourth century to the middle of the second BCE; this period starts with the reform of Homeric performance traditions in Athens during the régime of Demetrius of Phalerum, which lasted from 317 to 307 BCE.
>
> (5) a relatively most rigid period, with texts as *scripture*, from the middle of the second century onward; this period starts with the completion of Aristarchus' editorial work on the Homeric texts, not long after 150 BCE or so, which is a date that also marks the general disappearance of the so-called "eccentric" papyri.

When we discuss the relative multiformity of the Classical and Ptolemaic eras, we are speaking of periods (3) and (4) in Nagy's scheme, the "definitive" period and "standardizing" period, respectively. We can also compare Nagy's suggestion of the possibility of "transcripts" at this time to our discussion of the multiformity that we find in the textual transmission of Shakespeare, where we noted the influence of transcripts on the early printed editions of the plays.

Can a multitextual approach to the Homeric epics tell us anything about Nagy's periods (1) and (2), the "most fluid" and "formative" phases of our *Iliad* and *Odyssey*? This is our hope, that by making available the historical witnesses to the texts of these poems, as they circulated in antiquity and the medieval period, we can allow users of the Homer Multitext to understand with even more precision than we do now the workings of the traditional system within which our poems were created, as well as the interpretive possibilities that are opened up when the system is viewed diachronically.

The most fluid and formative phases of Homeric poetry are only accessible to us through careful study of what survived to later periods, and in this sense some of our discussions of the multiforms must remain somewhat speculative. Our knowledge of other oral traditions, studied by anthropologists working while these traditions were/are still flourishing, is another important resource that can help us go further back, as we consider the kinds of meaning that are conveyed and preserved by performance–generated texts.[6] The difficulties inherent in this enterprise should not deter us from the work, however; that the answers revealed by a Multitext may at times make us uncomfortable because of our own notions about Homer should not keep us from raising these questions.

It has frequently been asserted that the multiformity of the Homeric tradition is not interesting, and that the few variations we do find are banal and inconsequential. From our perspective, this assertion is simply untrue.[7] It seems that the expectation or desire would be for a recorded variation that would dramatically change the story—Achilles goes home! Odysseus dies at sea! Variation of such magnitude can and does appear on the level of myth, but the idea that the manuscripts, coming as late in the tradition as they do, would have as much multiformity as earlier stages of the textual tradition, not to mention

---

[6]   See Foley 1991, Foley 1995, Foley 1999.
[7]   See especially Dué 2001a.

the full oral tradition itself, is both misinformed and misleading. What is interesting about the multiforms that are recorded in our textual sources—and let us emphasize again that the further back in time the source goes, the greater the multiformity we see—is that they serve both as a window onto the underlying system of oral poetry and as crucial evidence for the textual tradition itself. The multiforms go to the heart of the Homeric Question. It would be intellectually dishonest and scientifically invalid, moreover, to try to show how "multiform" our text of Homer is with percentages, charts, and graphs—though, as we have pointed out, such attempts have been made. It is more intellectually honest to assert that every verse in Homeric poetry is at least potentially a multiform, and to explore the implications of that potential whenever we analyze the text for its poetic possibilities. The commentaries herein attempt to do just that. On a larger scale, the Homer Multitext seeks to give users many of the tools they need to confront and explore the poetics of a multiform epic tradition. The present printed edition is more modest in its aims, but it nevertheless seeks to understand the controversial *Iliad* 10 as the product of a dynamic oral system of poetry that evolved through time, and throughout this edition we resist any efforts to pin its composition down to one time, place, or singer.

The Texts

Please note that, in the commentary below, we follow the manuscript sigla devised by T. W. Allen, whose 1931 *editio maior* contains a comprehensive list and description of all the manuscripts and papyri known to him at that time. We have supplemented Allen's sigla with additional papyrus numbers, particularly those that are not yet published, but which are included by Martin West in his 1998–2000 edition of the *Iliad*. West's edition does not contain a comprehensive list of medieval manuscripts, but instead relies on twenty manuscripts that he has determined to be the oldest and most important. In general, the lack of a universally agreed upon standard reference system for medieval manuscripts and papyri has been a major problem in Homeric studies in recent decades. The Mertens-Pack project (http://www2.ulg.ac.be/ facphl/services/cedopal/indexanglais.htm) is working to correct this situation in terms of the papyri, but, with so many competing systems out there, there is clearly a need for a universal registry that can reconcile these systems and provide a standard point of reference, a registry of canonical identifiers. The Center for Hellenic Studies is sponsoring such a project, which is under the direction of Christopher W. Blackwell and D. Neel Smith (see http://chs75.harvard.edu/first1kyears/). But at this point we must still work with these competing systems as best we can, and try to make our work understandable within their frameworks. Although not all of the manuscripts below are cited in the commentary, for the convenience of those who may be using West's edition, we offer the following equivalency chart:

Allen A = West A (*Marcianus Gr. Z.* 454 [= 822])*

Allen B = West B (*Marcianus Gr. Z.* 453 [= 821])*

Allen C = West C (*Laurentianus* 32.3)

Allen D = West D (*Laurentianus* 32.15)

Allen E3 = West E (*Escorialensis* Y.I.1 [291])*

Allen E4 = West F (*Escorialensis* Ω.I.12 [509])*

Allen Ge = West G (*Genavensis* 44)*

Allen Vi5 = West H (*Vindobonensis* 117)

Allen M1 = West M (*Ambrosianus Gr.* A 181 sup. [74])

Allen U4 = West N (*Marcianus Gr. Z.* 458 [= 841])*

Allen O8 = West O (*Oxon. Bodl.* New College 298)

Allen P11 = West P (*Paris. Gr.* 2766)

Allen O5 = West R (*Oxon. Bodl. Auct.* T.2.7))

Allen T = West T (*Lond. Bibl. Brit.* Burney 86)

Allen V1 = West V (*Vaticanus Gr.* 26)

Allen V16 = West W (*Vaticanus Gr.* 1319)

[West X (*Sinaeticus*), which is in fragments, is not included in Allen]

[West Y (*Paris. suppl. gr.* 663), which is in fragments, is not included in Allen]

Allen Ve1 = West Z (*Rom. Bibl. Nat. Gr.* 6 + *Matrit.* 4626)

* Digital images of these manuscripts are (or soon will be) freely available on-line at: http://www.homermultitext.org

PART TWO

TEXTS

Iliad p609

(Mertens-Pack 864.1; P. Mich. 6972)

Text based on the edition of Alexander Loney, after the edition of A. Edwards (1984)[1]

THIS PAPYRUS ROLL dates to the second century BCE and is a palimpsest, meaning that the papyrus had been written on and erased before these verses were written on it. The earliest of the texts of *Iliad* 10 presented in this volume, it is also the most "multiform" from the standpoint of the medieval tradition, as exemplified by the Venetus A. It belongs to the papyrus collection of the University of Michigan (P. Mich 6972); a digital photograph of the papyrus is available online through the Advanced Papyrological Information System (http://www.columbia.edu/cu/lweb/projects/digital/apis/). This papyrus was published by A. Edwards (1984).

The papyrus has two columns, containing 10.421–434 and 10.445–460. It exhibits both horizontal multiformity on the level of individual words and whole lines, and also vertical multiformity, with a so-called "plus verse" between 10.432 and 10.434. Many of these multiforms are not supported by any other extant manuscript or witness, and yet the variations themselves are demonstrably formulaic and, therefore, "Homeric." The antiquity of this papyrus fragment and the attestation of these particular multiforms elsewhere in Homeric epic should give these variations weight; we resist approaches that dismiss them (or similar multiformity) in the early Homeric papyri as "eccentric."[2]

Note: The spaces between letters should be taken only as an approximation of the gap between visible letters on the papyrus. In

---

[1] Although we have based our text on the (as yet unpublished) XML edition of Loney, any errors of rendering or transcription are our own.

[2] For the term "eccentric" as applied to Ptolemaic Homeric papyri, see especially S. West 1967. For a more extended discussion of the significance of the multiformity presented by the Ptolemaic papyri see Dué 2001a.

order to make comparison between texts easier for the reader, we have added where possible accents and breathings and some editorial marks, such as punctuation and apostrophes to indicate elision. We have not, however, supplied a text for the illegible portions of the papyrus. This is because we do not want to make any assumptions for the reader about what the papyrus contained. Readers interested in seeing a text of the papyrus with supplements should consult the edition of Edwards 1984.

421	γὰρ ἐπιτρωπῶσι φυλάσσειν·
422	ἶδε σχεδὸν εἴαται οὐδὲ γυναῖκες.
423	ἔ τα πολύτλας δῖος Ὀδυσσεύς·
424	εσσι μεμειγμένοι ἱπποδάμοισιν
425	ι νημερτὲς ἔνισπε.
426	λων κατὰ δακρυ γ
427	μάλ' ἀτρεκέως καταλ ξω.
428	αὶ Παίονες ἀγκυλότοξοι
429	ωνεσ δῖοί τε Πελασγοί,
430	ν Λύκιοι Μυσοί τ' ἀγέρωχοι
431	ι αὶ Μήονες ἱπποκορυσταί.
432	εξερέεσθε ἕκαστα;
433	ὁρμᾶται φίλον ἦτορ
433a	δῦναι ι στρατὸν ἐγγύς ων,
434	λυδες, ἔσχατοι ἄλλων·

445	ἤ ῥα κατ' αἶσαν ἔε
446	τὸν δ' ἄρ' ὑπόδρα
447	μὴ δή μοι φύξιν
448	ἐσλά περ ἀγγέλλ
449	ἦμ μὲγ γάρ κέ σε ν
450	ἦ τε καὶ ὕστερον ε
451	ἠὲ διοψόμενος ἤ ἐ
452	ἦν δέ κ' ἐμῆς ὑπὸ χ
453	οὐκέτ' ἔπειτα σὺ πῆ
454	ἦ, καὶ ὃ μέμ μιν ἔμε
455	ἀψάμενος λίσσεσθ
456	φασγάνῳ ἀίξας, ἀπ
457	φθεγγομένου δ' α
458	τοῦ δ' ἀπὸ μὲν κτ
459	καὶ λυκέην καὶ τόξα
460	γ.' Ἀ ναίη ληί

Commentary

10.423 The Venetus A has the formulaic speech introduction line τόνδ' ἀπαμειβόμενος προσέφη πολύμητις 'Οδυσσεύς· This papyrus clearly has πολύτλας δῖος 'Οδυσσεύς at line end and Edwards reconstructs the line as the equally formulaic [τὸν δ' ἠμείβετ'] ἔ[πει]τα πολύτλας δῖος 'Οδυσσεύς. Such multiformity often appears within the textual tradition at this level of formulaic, frequently used lines. See also 10.426 below. Both πολύμητις and πολύτλας are equally traditional and, indeed, distinctive epithets of Odysseus. Each formula also has a connection with ambush poetics (see the general commentary on lines 10.137, 10.148, 10.382 for πολύμητις and 10.248 for πολύτλας). Either is appropriate in this line, and so we need not reject either possibility.

10.425]ι νημερτὲς ἔνισπε Edwards 1984 reads this line as [μο]ι νημερτὲς ἔνισπε. There have been various suggestions for the restoration of the beginning of the line, based on what we find in other witnesses, but the metrical pattern of this text differs from the equivalent phrase we find in the Venetus A (δίειπέ μοι ὄφρα δαείω). Because of this difference, Edwards mentions the possibility that the entire line was different (1984:13 *ad loc.*). We should not assume that we know what was there based on what appears in much later witnesses. The phrasing and placement is similar to what we find at the end of *Iliad* 3.204: ὦ γύναι ἦ μάλα τοῦτο ἔπος νημερτὲς ἔειπες. For the imperative of ἐννέπω, compare also *Odyssey* 4.642, νημερτές μοι ἔνισπε, which is also in a context that leads to plotting an ambush. Finally, as William Duffy has noted, p609's version of the line matches the endings of lines such as *Iliad* 14.470, *Odyssey* 3.101, *Odyssey* 4.314, *Odyssey* 4.331, and *Odyssey* 22.166. δίειπέ μοι ὄφρα δαείω is not attested elsewhere in our *Iliad* or *Odyssey*, and ὄφρα δαείω appears only three times, twice in the *Iliad*.[3]

10.426 λων κατὰ δακρυ[ο]ν The Venetus A reads here τὸν δ' ἠμείβετ' ἔπειτα Δόλων Εὐμήδεος υἱός. Edwards argues for a reconstruction of τὸν δ' ἠμείβετ' ἔπειτα Δόλων κατὰ δάκρυον εἴβων, citing similar formulas in *Odyssey* 11.391 and 24.280, and noting as well that Dolon

---

[3] During a 2007 summer seminar at the Center for Hellenic Studies entitled "The *Iliad* in the 2nd Millennium BCE" William Duffy prepared a commentary on this papyrus under our direction. With his permission we have incorporated his note into our commentary on this text.

is crying in *Iliad* 10.377. Edwards also states that "[t]he substitution of one formula for another, as here, is typical of the eccentric papyri." It is also typical of oral composition in performance, of course, and we have seen that in speech introductions similar kinds of multiforms have been preserved in the textual tradition.

10.427 p609 is in agreement with the main hand of p425 and most manuscripts (with the exception of D, Ge, and T) in reading καταλέξω here instead of ἀγορεύσω. For more on the alternation between these two verbs in our surviving texts, see below on p425 at 10.413.

10.432–434 The papyrus has a so-called plus verse in this sequence. The Venetus A has the following sequence:

432 ἀλλὰ τίη ἐμὲ ταῦτα διεξερέεσθαι ἕκαστα;
433 εἰ γὰρ δὴ μέματον Τρώων καταδῦναι ὅμιλον
434 Θρήϊκες οἳ δ' ἀπάνευθε νεήλυδες ἔσχατοι ἄλλων·

The lines on the papyrus have similar endings to the manuscript's lines 10.432 and 434, although the papyrus seems to have the second person plural indicative form of the verb instead of the infinitive in 432. But on this papyrus there are two lines between these:

433 .... ὁρμᾶται φίλον ἦτορ
433a ...... δῦναι[ ]ι στρατὸν ἐγγὺς [ἐόντ]ων

Edwards 1984 argues that "there can be no doubt that the sense ... is the same as that of K 433." If this is so, we can see here an example of expansion (or, conversely, of compression in the Venetus A version): the singer in performance can expand episodes, scenes, or speeches with more lines if he so chooses. Even a relatively short and simple expansion such as this one seems to be evidence of the performance tradition. The language of these lines is formulaic, and they are just as likely to have been generated by a traditional singer as those found in the majority of witnesses. The phrase φίλον ἦτορ is commonly found at line end, as it is here (though it also appears in other metrical positions as well). Edwards compares the phrasing in the second of these two lines (what we are calling 433a) to *Iliad* 10.221, and argues that the two missing letters after δῦναι were an erased copying mistake. The medievally attested 10.433 (εἰ γὰρ δὴ μέματον Τρώων καταδῦναι ὅμιλον) is also found on papyri 46 and 425, but the verse is not used elsewhere in extant epic.

10.448 ἐσλά The Venetus A manuscript reads ἐσθλά on this line. The two words mean the same thing, but the differences may reflect multiformity at the level of dialect. Buck 1955:77 describes the differences between ἐσθλός, ἔσλος, and ἐσλός as a case of dialectal difference. For more on the dialects within Homeric diction, see the general commentary on 10.18.

10.451 διοψόμενος The Venetus A has the participle διοπτεύσων. Both future participles are used for the same purpose and mean 'to spy'. Both are also *hapax legomena*, so there is no means to choose between them even if we wanted to. Such words, which show up only "once," are an indication of our limited "database" of Homeric poetry (see the general commentary on 10.331 for more on how to understand *hapax legomena* within the tradition). That both of these words, as well as related words like διοπτήρ 'spy' (used in *Iliad* 10.562), happen to show up only in this book is also related to the fact that this is our only surviving extended spying mission in the epic tradition. Spying mission episodes are a part of this epic tradition, though, and so specialized vocabulary was developed as singers composed-in-performance songs about such exploits. Such words are evidence of that performance tradition, rather than evidence of lateness or different authorship.

Iliad p425

(Mertens-Pack 855.1; P. Berol. inv. 11911 + 17038 + 17048 + 21155)

Text based on the edition of Bart Huelsenbeck and Alexander Loney, after the edition of H. Maehler; W. Müller; G. Poethke (1976)[1]

T HE FRAGMENTS of this early-third-century CE papyrus scroll found in Hermoupolis Magna in Egypt reside in the Königlischen Museum, Berlin and were joined and edited most recently by H. Maehler, W. Müller, and G. Poethke (1976).

Preserved on the papyrus are partial verses (often only a few letters) from *Iliad* 10.91, 110–115, 123–144, 150–160, 231–234, 240–253, 254–277, 279–293, 294–316, 320–339, 391–425, 428–465, 469–504, 510–512, 519–530, 535–548, 557–568. Editors of the first edition note affinities with the Venetus A, but there are differences (see e.g. 10.306 and 10.336). Note: The spaces between letters should be taken only as an approximation of the gap between visible letters on the papyrus. We have added where possible accents and breathings and some editorial marks, such as punctuation and apostrophes to indicate elision. We have not, however, supplied a text for the illegible portions of the papyrus. Readers interested in seeing a text of the papyrus with supplements should consult the edition of Maehler, Müller, and Poethke 1976.

91		νος
110	Φ	
111	ε μετοι	
112	καὶ ᾿Ιδομενῆα ἄνακτα.	
113	ἑκαστάτω, οὐδὲ μάλ᾿ ἐγγύς.	

---

[1] Although we have based our text on the (as yet unpublished) XML edition of Huelsenbeck and Loney, any errors of rendering or transcription are our own.

114	ạ καὶ ạἰδοῖον Μενέλαον
115	μεạ

123	ἀλλά μ
124	νῦν δ' ἐ
125	τὸν μὲ
126	ἀλλ' ἴομ
127	ἐν φυλ
128	τὸν δ' ἠ
129	οὕτως
130	Ἀργείω
131	ὣς εἰπ
132	ποσσ
133	ἀμφὶ δ'
134	διπλ
135	εἵλετο δ' ἄλκιμον ἔγχος ἀκαχμένον ὀξέι χαλκῷ
136	ῆ δ' ἰ γ
137	πρῶτ
138	ἐξ ὕπ ạ Νέστ
139	φθε φρέν
140	ἐκ πρ
141	τίφθ'
142	νύκτạ
143	τ γ δ' ἠμείβετ' ἔπειτα Γερήνιος ἱππότα Νέστωρ·
144	διọ
145	
146	
147	
148	
149	
150	εα· τὸν δ'
151	εσιν· ἀ
152	ίδας· ἔγχεα δέ σφιν
153	λạτọ τῆλ
154	ῥọς ός· αὐ
155	ọὸς ἀγρ
156	ς τẹτάν
157	ήνιος ἱ
158	τẹ νẹίκẹ

| 159 | γυχον ὕπ |
| 160 | σμῷ πε |

231	μιλο
232	α.
233	μέμν
234	υμ

240	φαθ᾽τ, ἔδ	
241	ς δ᾽ αὗτις μ	
242	μὲν δὴ ἔτα	μ᾽ α
243	ς ἂν ἔπειθ᾽τ	είοιο
244	έρι μὲν πρ	η αἰ θυμ
245	πάντεσ	δέ ἐ Πα
246	ου γ᾽	υρὸς αἰθ μέγ
247	ἄμφω ν	περείοιδε οῆς
248	τὸν αὖ	ύτλας δ
249	Τυδ ίδη	εαι· μηδ
250	εἰδ ι γάρ	είοις
251	ἀλλ᾽ ἴομεγ·	ὺξ ἄνυται, ἐγ
252	ἄστρα δὲ	ηκε, παρώχω
253	τῶν δύο μ	τη δ᾽ ἔτι μοῖρα λειπ ι.
254	πόγ	ἔν δεινοῖσιν την.
255	δη	μεγεπτόλεμοσ ρασυ ς
256		ς· τὸ δ᾽ ἐὸν παρὰ γ ει
257		νέην κεφαλῆ κ
258		καὶ ἄλλοφον, ἥ τε
259		κάρη θαλε ῶν
260		υ βιὸν ἐ φ
261		ην κ
262		δ᾽ ἔσ
263	ατο στ	ε δ
264	ογτ ς ς θ	
265	ἐπισταμέ	
266	π τ᾽ ἐξ λεῶν	
267	τ᾽ Αὐτ υκο	
268	ρα δ	
269	ἅμα ἐ Μ	

270   ὄ Μ̥   γης
271   ος
272   ὅπ
273   πέ
274   ἦκ
275   ίη·   ῖς̣
276   ς̣ ἄκουσᾳ
277   ᾶτο̣ δ' Ἀ
278
279   έ σ
280   λε' Ἀθή
281   κέσθ
282   ελ̣
283   ο̣ὴν ἀγαθὸς Δι
284   Διὸς τέκος Ἀτ
285   ατρὶ ἄμ'   έι δίῳ
286   ἤει.
287   νας Ἀχαιο ς
288   μείοισι
289   σατο ἔργα
290   ρέστης.
291   με φύλασσε.
292   τωπον
293   εν ἀνήρ
294   ξω χρυσὸν κέρα   ριχεύας.
295   γοι, τῶν δ' ἔκλ   Παλλὰς Ἀθήνη.
296   ο̣ Διὸς κούρῃ
297   λέοντε δύω   α μέλαιναν
298   υας, διά τ' ἔντ̣εα καὶ μέλαν αἷμα.
299   ὲ Τρῶασ ἀγήνορ̶α̶ς̶ ασεν Ἕκτωρ
300   δις κικλήσκετο πάντας ἀρίστους,
301   ἡγήτορε ἠδὲ μέδοντε
302   το   ινὴν ἠρτύνετο βουλήν·
303   τίς κέν μοι τόδε ἔργον ὑποσχόμενος τελέσειεν
304   δώρῳ ἔπι μεγάλῳ· μισθὸς έ οἱ ἄρκιος ἔσται·
305   δώσω γ   όν τε δύ   ύχενας ἵππους,
306   οἵ κεν ἄρ   ἔωσι θοῇ   ηυσὶν Ἀχαιῶν,
307   ὅς τίς κε   η, οἷ τ' αὐτῷ   ος ἄροιτο,
308   γηῶν ὠκ   όρων σχεδὸν ἐλθέμεν ἔκ τε πυθέσθαι,
309   ἠὲ φυλάσσ   ται νῆες θοαὶ ὡς τὸ πάρος περ,
310   ἦ ἤδη χεί   σσιν ὑφ' ἡμ   τέρῃσι δαμέντες

311 φύξιν βου   ουσι μετὰ σφίσιν· οὐδ' ἐθέλουσι
312 νύκτα φ   σέμεναι, καμάτῳ ἀδηκότες αἰνῷ.
313 ὣς ἔφαθ'· οἳ δ'   ρα πάντες ἀκὴν ἐγέν   ντο σιωπῇ.
314 ἦν δέ τι   ρώεσσι Δόλων Εὐμήδεος υἱὸς
315 κήρυκος θείοιο π   ύχρυσος πολύχαλκος,
316 ὃς δή τοι εἶ   ς μὲν ἔ   ν κακός, ἀλλὰ ποδώκης·

320   θαι.
321   ον·
322   λ   ι
323 δωσέμ   να·
324 σοὶ σ δ' ἐ   χ ἅλι   ἀπὸ δόξης·
325 τόφρ   τρατὸν εἶμι   ιαμπερέ   ρ' ἂν ἵκωμαι
326 νῆ' Ἀγ   μεμνονέην, ὅθι που μέλλουσιν ἄριστοι
327 βουλὰς βουλεύειν, ἢ φευγέμεν· ἠὲ μάχεσθαι·
328 ὣς ἔφ   θ', ὃ δ' ἐν χερσὶ σκ   πτρον λάβε καὶ οἱ ὄμοσσεν·
329 ἴστω νῦν Ζεὺς πρῶτος, ἐρίγδουπος πό   ις Ἥρης·
330 μὴ μὲν τοῖς ἵπποισιν ἀνὴρ ἐποχήσ   ται ἄλλος
331 Τρώων· ἀλλὰ σὲ φημὶ διαμπερὲς ἀγλαϊεῖσθαι·
332 ὣς φάτο· καί ῥ' ἐπίορκον ἐᵃπώμοσε, τὸν   ρόθυνεν.
333 αὐτίκα δ' ἀμφ' ὤμοισιν ἐβάλλετο καμπύλα τόξα·
334 ἔσσατο δ' ἔκτ   σθεν ῥῑνὸν πολιοῖο λύκοιο·
335 κρατὶ δ' ἐπὶ κτιδέην κυνέην· ἕλε δ' ὀξὺν ἄκοντα·
336 βῆ δ' ἰέναι προτὶ νῆας ἀπὸ στρατο   δ' ἄρ' ἔμελλεν
337   ὼν ἐκ νηῶν ἂψ Ἕκτορ   θον ἀποίσειν.
338 ἀλ   τε δὴ ῥ' ἵππων   ε καὶ ἀνδρῶν κάλ   ιφ' ὅμῑλον,
339 βῆ   ν' ὁδὸν μεμαώς· τὸν δὲ φ   ἄσατ   προς   τ
340 διογε   ὴς Ὀδυσσεύς, Διομήδεα δὲ προσέειπεν·
341 οὗτός τοι, Διόμηδες, ἀπὸ στρατοῦ ἔρχεται ἀνήρ·
342 οὐκ' οἶδ' εἰ νήεσσιν ἐπίσκοπος ἡμετέρῃσιν·
343 ἦ τινα συλήσων νεκύων κατατεθνειώτων·
344 ἀλλ' ἐῶμέν μιν πρῶτον παρε   ελθεῖν πεδίοιο
345 τυτθόν· ἔπειτα δέ κ' αὐτὸν ἀ   ΐξαντες ἕλοιωμεν
346 καρπαλίμως. εἰ δ' ἄμμε παραφθαίησι πόδεσσιν,
347 αἰεί μιν πρ   τὶ νῆας ἀπὸ στρα   ὄφιν προτιειλεῖν
348 ἔγχει ἐπαΐσσων· μή πως π   τὶ ἄστυ ἀλύξῃ·
349 ὣς ἄρα φωνήσαντε   παρὲξ ὁ   οῦ ἐν νεκύες   ι
350 κλινθήτην· ὃ δ' ἄρ' ὦ   παρέδραμεν ἀφραδίῃⁱσιν.
351 ἀλλ' ὅτε δή ῥ' ἀπέην, ὅσσον τ' ἐ   οὖρα πέλονται
352 ἡμιόνων· αἱ γάρ τε βοῶν προφ   αί εἰσιν
354 τῶ

355 ἔ   κατὰ θυμ   ρέψον
356 ἐκ   έναι, π   τοροσ ότρύγαν
357 ἀλ   πεσα   ηγεκὲς ἢ καὶ ἔλασ
358   δηίου   ψηρ δὲ γούνατ' ἐγ
359 φε   τοὶ δ' αἶψα διώκειν ὁρμήθησαν.
360 ὢ   τε κ   χαρόδο τε δύω κύνε   ε θή
361 ἢ κ μάδ' ἢ λαγῶιο ἐπείγετο   μεγὲ
362 χ   ν ἀν' λήεντα, τε πρ   εμη
363 ὣς τὸν Τυδείδης ἢ   το   ορθος 'Ο
364 λαοῦ ἀποτμήξαν   ν ἐμμ
365 ἀλλ' ὅτε δὴ ἄρ' ἔμελλ   θαι φυλ
366 φεύγων ἐς νῆας, τό   ἔμβ
367 Τυδείδη ἵνα μή τι Ἀχα   λκοχι ώνω
368 φθαίη ἐπευξάμεν   βαλέειν, ὃ δὲ δεύ ερος ἔ
369 δουρὶ δ' ἐπαΐσσω   οσέφη κρατερὸς Διομ
370 ἠὲ μέν', ἠέ σε δουρ   χήσομαι· οὐδέ σέ φημ
371 δηρὸν ἐμῆς ἀπὸ   ρὸς ἀλύξειν αἰπὺν ὄλεθ
372 ἦ ῥ   καὶ ἔγχος ἀφ   ν· ἑκὼν δ' ἡμάρτ νε φ
373 δεξιτερὸν δ' πὲρ   μον ἐΰξου δουρ ς ἀκωκ
374 ἐν γαίη ἐπάγη· ὃ δ' ἄρ' ἔστη τάρβησέ   ε
375 βαμβαίνω   ἄραβος δὲ διὰ στόμα γείνετ' ὀδόν
376 χλωρὸσ ὑπα   δείους· τὼ δ' ἀσθμαίνον ε κιχήτη
377 χειρῶν δ' ἁψάσθην· ὃ δ   ακρύσας ἔπος ηὔ
378 ζωγρεῖτ'· αὐτὰρ ἐγὼν ἐμὲ λύσομαι· ἔστι γὰρ ἔνδ
379 χαλκός τε χρυσός τε πολύκμητός τε σίδηρο
380 τῶν κ' ὔμιν χ ρίσαιτο πατὴρ ἀπερείσια ἄποιν
381 εἴ κεν ἐμὲ ζωὸν πεπύθοιτ' πὶ   υ
382 τὸν   ἀπαμειβόμενος προσέφ   πολ μητι
383 θάρσει, μηδέ τί τοι θάνατος καταθύμιο   ἔστω.
384 ἀλλ' ἄγε μοι τόδε εἰπὲ καὶ ἀτρεκέως κατάλ
385 πῆ δ' οὕτως ἐπὶ νῆας ἀπὸ στρατοῦ ἔρχε ι οἶος
386 νύκτα δι' ἀμβροσίην, ὅτε θ' εὕδουσι ροτοὶ
387 ἦ τινα συλήσων νεκύων κατατεθν ώτων,
388 ἦ σ' Ἕκτωρ προέηκε διασκοπιᾶ θα   α
389 νῆας ἔπι γλαφυράς· ἦ σ' αὐτὸν θυμὸς   κε·
390 τὸν δ' ἡμείβετ' ἔπειτα Δόλων, ὑπὸ δ'   ε υἷα·
391   ἐκ
392   οῦ μ
393   αἰ ἄ
394   οήν
395   σχεδ

396	λάσσοντ ες θοα
397	χείρεσσι ἤμε
398	ν βουλεύ τὰ σφί
399	τα φυλασ εναι, καμάτ
400	δ' ἀπαμ ιβ ενοσ προσέφη πολύμητις Ὀδυσσεύς·
401	γύ τοι μεγάλ δώρων ἐπεμα
402	πων Αἰακίδαο δαΐφρονος· οἳ δ'
403	ράσι γε θνητοῖσι δαμήμενα
404	ω γ' ἢ Ἀχιλλῆϊ, τὸν ἀθανάτη τ
405	γε μοι τόδε εἰπὲ καὶ ἀτρεκέω
406	νῦν δεῦρο κιὼν λίπες Ἕκτορ
407	δέ οἱ ἔντεα κεῖται ἀρήϊα· ποῦ δ
408	ὣς δ' α^{αἰ} τῶν ἄλλων Τρώων φυλακ ε καὶ εὐ
409	ά τε μητιόωσι μ ὰ σφίσιν ἢ άασιν
410	α μένειν παρὰ ν σὶν ἀπόπ γ ἠὲ π
411	ἂψ ἀναχωρήσουσιν, πεὶ δαμάσαν
412	τὸν δ' αὖτε προσέε ε Δόλων Εὐμ δε
413	τοι ἀρ ἐγώ τ ι ταῦτα ἀλ' ἀτρεκέως ἀγορ
414	Ἕκ μὲν μετὰ τ ν, ᾧ βουληφόροι
415	σ βουλεύει θε παρὰ σήματ
416	γ σφιν ἀπὸ φλοίσβου· λακὰς δ' ἃς
417	οὔ τις κεκριμένη ῥ αι στρατὸν οὐ
418	ὅσσαι μὲ ρώων π ρὸς ἐσχάραι, οἵ ν ἀνά
419	οἳ τ^γ ἐγ θασι φυλασσέμεναί τε έλον
420	ἀρ αὖτε πολύκλητοι γ' ἐ ίκου
421	εὕδουσιν, ωσὶν γὰρ ἐπιτροαπέουσι φ άσ
422	οὐ γάρ σφιν παῖδες σχε ὸν εἴαται οὐδὲ υν
423	τὸν δ' ἀπαμειβόμενος προσέφη πο ύμη
424	πῶς γὰρ νῦν, Τρώεσσ μεμιγμένοι ἱπποδά
425	ὕδουσ' ἢ ἀπάνευθε; δίειπέ μοι, ὄφρα δαε
426	ὸν δ' ἡμείβετ' ἔπειτα Δόλων, Εὐμήδεος
427	τοι γὰρ ἐγώ ⚡^καὶ ταῦτα μάλ' ἀτρεκέως ἀγορεύσ ^{καταλέξω}.
428	ρ
429	καὶ Λέλεγε
430	πρὸς Θύμβ
431	καὶ Φρύγε
432	λλὰ τίη μ
433	ἰ γὰρ δὴ μ
434	ρῆϊκες ο πάν
435	Ῥῆσ σ βασι
436	στ υς ἵππου

437	χ ὄνος· θείει̣	
438	υσῷ τε κ	
439	ύσεια π	
440	ν· τὰ μὲν οὔ τι̣	
441	ν φορέειν· ἀλλ'	
442	ν νῦν νηϋ	ν ᾠκυπ
443	α̣ντεσ λίπ	ϊ δεσμ
444	ἔλθ	γ ἐμεῖο,
445	σαν	ἰ οὐκί.
446	ρα ἰδ	ρὸσ Διομ η
447	φ ν γε, Δόλ	ῶ
448	ρ ἀ	ά̣ς·
449	κ̣έ σ̣	ε̣ν·
450	τε̣	
451		ν·
452		
453		
454		
455	ἀψάμενος	
456	φασγάνῳ	
457	φθεγγομέ	
458	τοῦ δ' ἀπὸ μ	
459	καὶ κυνέη	
460	καὶ τά τ^γ Ἀθη	
461	ὑψόσ' ἀνέσ	
462	χαῖρε, θεά,	
463	πάντων ἀ̣	α̣ ις
464	πέμψον ἐ̣	α̣ὶ εὐνάς.
465	ὣς ἄρ' ἐφών	ς̣
466	θῆκεν ἀγ	ἔθηκεν,
467	συμμάρψας	ο̣υς,
468	μὴ λάθ'οι αὖ	α̣ι
469		α καὶ μέλαν αἷμα·
470		ξον ἰόντες·
471		α δέ σφιν
472		ἀ κόσμον
473		πποι·
474		πποι
475		τ̣ο·
476		Διομήδεϊ δεῖξεν·
477		πποι,

478   φνω°μεν ἡμεῖς·
479   ερ   ἔ τί σε χρὴ
480   στάμεν   λεον   τεύχε   ἵππους.
481   ᵉ σύ γ' ἄνδρ   ἔναιρ   λήσουσιν δ' ἐ   οι.
482   ὣς φάτο, τῷ δ' ἔμπνευ   μένος γλαυκ   ήνη·
483   κτεῖνε δ'· ἐπιστροφά   ν· τῶν δὲ σθεᵗᵒγος ὤρνυτ' ἀεικὴς
484   ορι θεινομένων· ἐρ   ίνετο δ' αἴμ   α.
485   δὲ λέων μήλοισι   ηιμάντοι   θὼν,
486   γεσιν ἢ ὄϊεσσι, κακὰ   γέων ἐγ
487   ς μὲν Θρήϊκας ἄ   πώ   ος υἱός,
488   φρα δυώδεκ' ἔπε   πολ   τις δυσσεύς,
489   ν τεινα Τυδείδης   παραστάς,
490   ὸν δ' Ὀδυσεὺς με   οδὸς ἐξερύσασκε,
491   φρονέων κατὰ θ   τριχες ἵπποι
492   διέλθοιεν· μη   υμῷ
493   εκρου̅ⁱς ἐμβαίνοντ   εσσον   ρ ἔτ' αὐτῶν.
494   ἀλλ' ὅτε δὴ βασιλῆα   το Τυδέ   ς υἱός,
495   ὸν τρισκαιδέκατον   θυμὸν ἀπηύρα
496   σθμαίνοντεᵃ κακ ν γὰ   αρ κ   φαλῆφιν ἐπέστηι
497   ἢν νύκτ' Οἰνείδαο πάϊσ δ ἀ μῆτιν Ἀθήνης.
498   ὄφρα δ' ἄρ' ὂ τλήμων Ὀδυσσεὺς λύε μώγυχας ἵππους,
499   σὺν δ' ἤειρεν   μᾶσι καὶ ἐξήλαυνεν   μᵉίλου
500   τόξῳ ἐπιπλήσσων· ἐπε   οὺ μάστιγ   αεινὴν
501   ποικίλου ἐκ δίφροιο νοή   ατο χερσὶν ἑλέσθαι·
502   ῥοίζησεν δ' ἄρα πιφραύσκων Διομήδεϊ δίῳ·
503   αὐτὰρ ὂ μερμήριξε μένων ὄ τεⁱ κύντερον ἔϟᵖδοι·
504   ἢ ὄ γε δίφρον ἑλών, ὅθι τᵖο κα̩ⁱλα τεύχε' ἔκειτο,
505   ῥυμοῦ ἐξερέᵒᵒⁱ ἢ ἐκφέροι ὐ   σ' ἀείρας,
506   ἢ ἔτι τῶν   λεόνων Θρ   γ ἀπὸ θυμὸν ἕλοιτο.
507   ὡς ὃ ταῦθ' ὥρμαινε κατὰ φ   α· τόφρα δ' Ἀθήνη
508   ἐγ'γύθεν ἱσταμένη προσέφη Διομήδεα δῖον·
509   νόστου δὴ μνῆσαι μεγαθύμου Τυδέος υἱὲ
510   ἢας ἔπ
511   μή π
512   ὣς

519   ὸγ
520   ῶρον ἐ ῆμον, ὅ
521   ῥάς τ' ἀσπαίροντας ἐν ἀρ
522   ωξέν τ' ἄρ' ἔπειτα φίλον τ̦'
523   ώων δὲ κλαγγή τε καὶ ἄ
524   νόντων ἄμυδις· θ   α
525   ἄνδρεσ ῥέξαντες ἔβαν   ς ἐπ   ῆας·
526   δ' ὅτε δή ῥ' ἵκανον ὅθι σκοπ ν Ἕκτορ ς ἔκταγ
527   εὑσ μὲν ἔρυκε Διῒ φίλος ὡ   ς ἵππου
528   αμ ζε θορὼν ἔναρα   όωντα
529   θει, ἐπε   πων·
530   ουκ   θην·

535   ῳκ
536   δυ
537   ρ ἐκ
538   ἀλλ' νῶσ δ
539   Ἀργείων οἳ ἄρ
540   οὔ πω πᾶν ε
541   καί ῥ' οἳ μὲν κ
542   δεξιῇ ἠσπά
543   ῶτος δ' ἐ
544   εἴπ' ἄγε μ' ῷ π
545   ὅππωσ τοῦσδ'
546   Τ ων, ἦ τί σφωε
547   αἰνῶς ἀκτίγεσ
548   αἰεὶ μὲν Τ εσ

557   ἴπ
558   ἴπ'π   ήλυ ε

559 Θρη   γακτ᾽ ἀγ
560 ἔκ αν   υς δυ꙰°κ
561 τὸν τρι κ   ϲκοπὸν εἴ   γ
562 τόν   ιοπτῆρα   ατοῦ ἔμμ   ἠμε   οιο
563 Ἕκτω δὲ προέη ε καὶ ἄλλοι Τ   εϲ ἀγα
564 ὡϲ εἰπὼν τάφροιο διήλαϲε μώνυχαϲ ἵππουϲ
565 καν꙼χαλόων· ἅμα δ᾽ ἄλλοι ἴϲαν χαίροντεϲ Ἀχαιοί.
566 οἳ δ᾽ ὅτε   δεω κλιϲί γ εὔτυκτον ἵκοντο·
567 π   τέδη   ἐϋτμ   γ ἱμᾶϲ
568   θ   ποι

Commentary

10.306 οἵ κεν ἄρ[   ] ἔωϲι See also below the textual commentary on Venetus A 10.306. Of the four versions of this verse that survive from antiquity, p425 appears to be in agreement with the version attributed to Aristarchus in the Venetus A scholia. The Venetus A manuscript (A) and the majority of manuscripts read οἵ κεν ἀριϲτεύωϲι θοῆϲ ἐπί νηυϲίν Ἀχαιῶν.

10.336 προτὶ νῆαϲ The manuscripts are divided between this reading and ποτί, but see also below on A, which reads ἐπὶ νῆαϲ here (with the other readings recorded in the margin).

10.341 οὗτόϲ τοι Διόμηδεϲ The papyrus is in agreement with all manuscripts in reading τοι here. The A scholia report here that Aristarchus and "most editions" (αἱ πλείουϲ) read τιϲ (and West, in fact, prints this reading in his 1998 edition). At 10.477, all manuscripts read οὗτόϲ τοι Διόμηδεϲ.

10.372 ἀφ[   ]ν See below the textual commentary on A 10.372.

10.373 ἐϋξου See below the textual commentary on A 10.373.

10.386 νύκτα δι᾽ ἀμβροϲίην, ὅτε θ᾽ εὕδουϲι ροτοὶ[p46 and all manuscripts contain this verse with the variation ὀρφναίην in place of ἀμβροϲίην. The verse is missing entirely in one papyrus (West 1178), and on this basis West brackets it as an interpolation. The variation between ὀρφναίην and ἀμβροϲίην and its significance within the theme of ambush are discussed in the general commentary at 10.41.

10.397–399 See below the textual commentary on A 10.397–399.

10.400 ἀπαμ[ ]ιβ[ ]ενος A and p46 read ἐπιμειδήσας here. See the general commentary on 10.400 for a detailed analysis of the traditional significance of these multiforms of the same formulaic verse.

10.413 ἀγορ[εύσω The A scholia report that Aristarchus had this reading, which is also found in manuscripts D, T, and V16. Most other manuscripts read καταλέξω, which is the verb used by Odysseus in 10.384 and 10.405 in all extant witnesses (though we should note that the verb is not legible in 10.405 on this papyrus). For the phrase ἀτρεκέως ἀγορεύσω, compare *Odyssey* 1.214 and 15.266. For the phrase ἀτρεκέως κατάλεξον/καταλέξω, compare *Odyssey* 1.206, 24.123 and *Iliad* 24.656. (See also 10.427 on this papyrus.) The different shades of meaning in the two verbs seem to be "I will tell you in detail, tell in order" (καταλέξω) or "I will say it aloud, I will relate (the information)" (ἀγορεύσω). Either verb works contextually and metrically in these lines, and so, instead of asking which one is "correct" or "original," we can investigate whether a witness has one consistently rather than the other, or uses both, to better understand how it works within the traditional language and the surrounding formulas.

10.427 αγορευσ[ω^{καταλεξω} Here a corrector (it seems, the scribe himself) has written the alternative reading καταλέξω above αγορευσ[ω on the papyrus. καταλέξω is the reading of p609 and most manuscripts. (For the alternation between the two verbs, see also above on 10.413.) The editors of the 1976 edition note that the scribe seems to have consulted another exemplar or else a ὑπόμνημα after writing the main text and entered corrections and variants in the margins.

10.433–434 p46, p425, and all manuscripts are generally in agreement here, but see p609 above for two entirely different verses in place of what is here 10.433.

10.502 πιφραύσκων See below the textual commentary on Venetus A 10.478 and 10.502. This papyrus is the only witness to read πιφραύσκων with A here.

10.503 κύντερον The papyrus agrees with several manuscripts in having the comparative adjective, but the Venetus A has the superlative κύντατον. See the general commentary on this line.

Iliad p46

(Mertens-Pack 658; P. Cairo Maspero inv. 67172-4 + P. Berol. inv. 10570 + P. Strasb. inv. G 1654 + P. Rein. 2.70)

Text based on the edition of Alexander Loney, after the edition of J.-L. Fournet (1999)[1]

THIS PAPYRUS CODEX from the sixth century CE exists in pieces belonging to four separate collections (the Cairo Museum in Egypt, the Königlischen Museum in Berlin, the Bibliothèque Nationale et Universitaire in Strassbourg, and the Institut de Papyrologie de la Sorbonne in Paris). They were joined together by J.-L. Fournet (1997).

Preserved on the papyrus are partial verses from *Iliad* 1.297–304, 2.494–519, 528–576, 594–614, 631–642, 667–678, 10.372–443, 11.652–683, 689–720, 734–753, and 771–790. We have restricted our presentation of the text and our commentary on the text to the portions from *Iliad* 10. (See Fournet 1999 for a complete text of the papyrus.) The readings of this papyrus agree, for the most part, with those of the Venetus A manuscript, as we would expect from a witness closer in time to it, but there are some variations (see e.g. 10.380, 10.385, and 10.399).

Note: The spaces between letters should be taken only as an approximation of the gap between visible letters on the papyrus. We have added where possible accents and breathings and some editorial marks, such as punctuation and apostrophes to indicate elision, but we have not supplied a text for the illegible portions of the papyrus.

```
372   ἦ α κ   ἔγχος ἀφῆκ   ἑκὼν δ’      νε φωτός·
373   δ ξιτερόνδ’ ὑπ ρ ὦμον εὔξου          κωκὴ
374   ἐγ γαίη¹ ἐπάγη· ὃ δ’ ἄρ’ ἔστη τά
```

---

[1]   Although we have based our text on the (as yet unpublished) XML edition of Loney, any errors of rendering or transcription are our own.

375 βαμβαίνων· ἄραβ ς δὲ διὰ στόμα γίγ

376 χλωρὸς ὑπαὶ δ ίου   τὼ δ' ἀσθμαίνοντ

377 χειρῶν ⲭ'δ' ἀψάσθην· ὃ δὲ δακρύσας ἔπο

378 ζωγρεῖτ', αὐτὰ ἐγὼν ἐμὲ λύσομαι· ἔσ ι

379 χαλκός τε χρυσός τε πολύκμητός τε σί ρ

380 τῶν χ' ὑμῖν χα σαιτο πατὴ   περείσι' ποιγ

381 εἴ κεν ἐμὲ ζωὸν πεπύθοι   πὶ νηυσὶν χαιῶ

382 τὸν δ' ἀπαμειβόμενος προσ   πολύμητ

383 θάρσει, μηδέ τί τ ι θάνατ   αταθ

384 ἀλλ' ἄγε μοι τόδε εἰπὲ κ

385 τίφθ' οὕτως ἐπὶ νῆασ ἀπὸ

386 νύκτα δι' ὀρφ   γ, ὅτε θ' ε

387 ἤ τι   υ   νεκ

388   πιᾶσ

389   ρᾷς;   θυμ

390   ἔπει   πὸ δ

391   σι πα

394   μ

395   σμ

396   τ   αὶ ὡς τὸ

397   σσιν   τέρῃσι δ

398   εὑρισ   ὰ σφίσιν, οὐ

399   μ   μάτω¹ ἀδηκ

400   δ   οσέφη πολύμητ

401   γάλω   ἐπεμαίετο θυ

402   δαο δ   ς· οἳ δ' ἄλεγε

403   ητ   εναι ἠδ' ὀ

404   ι, τ

405   τ

407   γ

408 ὣς δαὶ τῷ   Τρώων φυλακαί τε καὶ εὐν

409   μετὰ σφίσιν, ἦ μεμάασιν

410   ηυσὶν ἀπόπροθεν, ἦε πόλιν δὲ

411   ουσιν, ἐπεὶ δαμάσαντό γ' Ἀχαιούς.

412   ροσέειπε Δόλων Εὐμήδεος υἱός·

413   τοι ταῦτα μάλ' ἀτρεκέως αταλέξω.

414   ρ γ μετὰ τοῖσιν, ὅσοι βουληφόροι εἰσίν,

415 λὰς υλεύει θείου παρὰ σήματι Ἴλου

416 φιν ἀπὸ φλοίσβου υλακὰς δ' ἃ εἴρεαι ἥρως,

417   κριμένη ῥ   αι στρατὸν οὐδὲ φυλᾶσˢει.

418   Τρώων π   ἐσχάραι, οἷσιν ἀνάγκη

419	ρθασι φυ	ἔμεναί τε κέλοντα
420		ολύκλητοι τ' ἐπίκουροι
421		ιτραπέουσι φυλάσσειν·
422	π	δὸν εἴατα δὲ γυναῖκ
423	βόμ	ἔφη Ὀ σ
424	ρώε	μένο
425	άνε	ἔ μ
426	ετ'	ων E
427		τρεκ
429		ῦο
430		οἵ τ
431	ἱ ι	
432	ταῦτα δ	εσθ
433	ματον Τρ	αδῦν
434	δ' ἀπάνε	λυδες
435	φιν Ῥῆσοσ βασ	αις Ἠ
436	καλλίστους ἵππ	ἠδὲ
437	κότεροι χιόνος,	ἀνέμο
438	α δέ οἱ χρυσῶ' τ	ὑρω' εὖ
439	ἐ χ σεια	θαῦμα
440		οἵ
441		άτοισι
442		ασσ ον
443	αὐ νη	

Commentary

10.372 ἦ [ ]α κ[ ] ἔγχος αφηκ[ ] See below the textual commentary on the Venetus A manuscript (A) 10.372.

10.373 δ[ ]ξιτερόνδ' ὑπ[ε]ρ ὦμον εὔξου [   ]κωκὴ p46 is in agreement with p425 and A here, against most manuscripts, which have ἐϋξόου. See below the textual commentary on A 10.373.

10.376 χλωρὸς ὑπαὶ δ[ ]ίου[ ] p46 supports the reading of ὑπαὶ δείους (in p425 and most manuscripts, including A), but there are some recorded variations. See below the textual commentary on A 10.376.

10.380 τῶν χ' ὑμῖν χα[ ]σαιτο p46 read κ' ὔμμιν (as does A) before being corrected to χ' ὑμῖν. Most manuscripts have χ' ὔμμι(ν). ὔμμιν is an Aeolic form (see Chantraine 1988 *GH* I §126–127), and the double *mu* makes the syllable long, which it needs to be here. χ' ὑμῖν is fully

Ionic/Attic, with lengthened upsilon and long final syllable. χ' ὔμμι(ν) combines the rough breathing of Ionic/Attic Greek with the spelling of the Aeolic form. These kinds of variations give us insight into the way that Homeric diction evolved, as Ionic singers took over formulas that had been composed by Aeolic singers. Where possible, the Ionic singers adapted the formulas to their own dialect. See the general commentary on 10.18 and 10.305.

10.385 τίφθ' The text of this papyrus read πῇ δ' before it was corrected. (Compare p425 on this line.) A reads πῇ ᵖᵒᵘ δ'. τίφθ' has some manuscript support (V1). Another variation (recorded as a variation in manuscript C) is ποῖ. Compare the very similar verse at 10.141, where the manuscripts uniformly read τίφθ'. It seems likely that both τίφθ' and πῇ δ' would have felt natural to singers of this verse.

10.386 νύκτα δι' ὀρφ[   ]ν, ὅτε θ' [This verse, which is also found at 10.83 in the manuscripts, is missing in one papyrus (West 1178), and on this basis West brackets it as an interpolation. It is, however, present in p46, p425, and all manuscripts (p425 and some manuscripts read ἀμβροσίην in place of ὀρφναίην). For its significance within the theme of ambush (and the alternation between ἀμβροσίην and ὀρφναίην), see the general commentary below at 10.41.

10.397–399 See below the textual commentary on A 10.397–399.

10.399 ἀδηκ[This is the reading of p46 and most manuscripts. Manuscripts A, B, and E3 have ἀδηκότες. For variation between rough and smooth breathing, see also above on p46, 10.380.

10.413]αταλέξω Most manuscripts read καταλέξω, which is also the verb used by Odysseus at 10.384 and 10.405 in all extant witnesses. But D, T, and V16, as well as p425, read ἀγορεύσω here on 10.413. The A scholia say Aristarchus had ἀγορεύσω. For the distinction in meaning, see above on p425 10.413.

10.423 This line in the papyrus seems to be the same formulaic expression as that found in the Venetus A, but see p609 for a multiform.

10.426 See p609 on this line for a variation; instead of the patronymic epithet Εὐμήδεος υἱός that witness seems to have the formula κατὰ δάκρυον εἴβων.

10.431 Poethke restores this line as [και Φρυγες] ι[ππ]ο̱[μαχοι και Μη]ο̱ν̱ε̱[ς ιπποκορυσται. The epithet ἱππόμαχοι is attested here by ten manuscripts, according to Allen (who also prefers that reading here), and is ascribed to Aristarchus by the A scholia (the T scholia also mentions it). The main text of the Venetus A, however, reads ἱππόδαμοι, a much more commonly used epithet. Poethke's edition of the papyrus shows only the iota and omicron of the word as visible, and his reason for preferring the less common epithet is not evident. Neither possibility need be rejected, however.

10.433–434 p46, p425, and all manuscripts are generally in agreement here, but see p609 above for two entirely different verses in place of what is here 10.433.

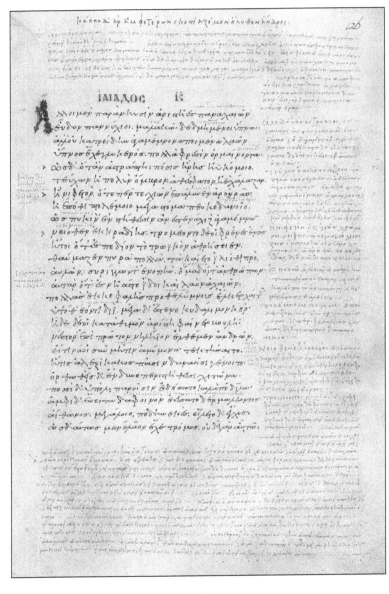

Folio 126 recto of the Venetus A showing the beginning of *Iliad* 10

Venetus A
(Marcianus Graecus Z. 454 [= 822])

M ARCIANUS GR. Z. 454 (= 822) is the earliest extant, complete
manuscript of the *Iliad*, and it is the one on which modern printed
texts are primarily based. (The few medieval manuscripts that predate
it contain commentary and paraphrases or portions of the poem, but
not a complete text.) It was hand copied and assembled by Byzantine
Greek scribes in the tenth century CE, but it is known as the "Venetus
A" because it has been housed at the Biblioteca Nazionale Marciana in
Venice since the sixteenth century. The nearly two hundred manuscripts of the *Iliad* that succeed it are remarkable for the relative
uniformity of their texts, and in this respect they differ considerably
from the ancient witnesses, which show a great deal more variation.
But, although they do not vary in substantial ways from one another, it
is important to understand that the medieval manuscripts of Homeric
epic do not descend from a single exemplar, nor is there a medieval
vulgate for the *Iliad* or *Odyssey*, as is sometimes stated or (more often)
assumed without justification. It is clear that a substantial number of
texts survived the transition from papyrus scrolls to parchment codices
and that there were therefore multiple channels of transmission. What
is not entirely understood is why the versions that survived resemble
each other so closely. It has been postulated that the editorial activities of the scholars associated with the library at Alexandria played a
role in the standardization of the Homeric text. But this theory does
not entirely account for the continued multiformity of the text in the
medieval period.

The Venetus A is invaluable to us for much more than its text of
the *Iliad*, however. This manuscript contains not only the texts of the
poem but also excerpts from the scholarly commentaries of these same
Alexandrian scholars, which are copied into its margins and between

lines of the text itself. These writings, known as scholia, contain notes
on the text that explain points of grammar, usage, definition of words,
interpretation, and disputes about the authenticity of verses and the
correct text. The material contained in these marginal notes derives
from scholarly works that predate the manuscript's construction by
a thousand years or more, and at times preserves variations known at
that time which survive in no other witness. The commentary on the
text below is confined primarily to the readings of the main text of the
Venetus A and reports of alternate readings in the scholia, but see the
general commentary for more on the interpretive questions addressed
in the scholia or raised by the variations we have noted below. We have
made particular note of the places where the text of the Venetus A
either agrees or disagrees with an ancient papyrus witness, verses that
were controversial in antiquity, and places where the medieval manuscript tradition is divided between a number of readings. (For more on
the features and history of this remarkable manuscript, see Dué 2009a.)

1	Ἄλλοι μὲν παρὰ νηυσὶν ἀριστῆες Παναχαιῶν
2	εὗδον παννύχιοι μαλακῷ δεδμημένοι ὕπνῳ·
3	ἀλλ' οὐκ Ἀτρείδην Ἀγαμέμνονα ποιμένα λαῶν
4	ὕπνος ἔχε γλυκερὸς πολλὰ φρεσὶν ὁρμαίνοντα.
5	ὡς δ' ὅτ' ἂν ἀστράπτῃ πόσις Ἥρης ἠϋκόμοιο
6	τεύχων ἢ πολὺν ὄμβρον ἀθέσφατον ἠὲ χάλαζαν
7	ἢ νιφετόν, ὅτε πέρ τε χιὼν ἐπάλυνεν ἀρούρας,
8	ἠέ ποθι πτολέμοιο μέγα στόμα πευκεδανοῖο,
9	ὡς πυκίν' ἐν στήθεσσιν ἀνεστενάχιζ' Ἀγαμέμνων
10	νειόθεν ἐκ κραδίης, τρομέοντο δέ οἱ φρένες ἐντός.
11	ἤτοι ὅτ' ἐς πεδίον τὸ Τρωϊκὸν ἀθρήσειεν,
12	θαύμαζεν πυρὰ πολλὰ τὰ καίετο Ἰλιόθι πρὸ
13	αὐλῶν συρίγγων τ' ἐνοπὴν ὅμαδόν τ' ἀνθρώπων.
14	αὐτὰρ ὅτ' ἐς νῆάς τε ἴδοι καὶ λαὸν Ἀχαιῶν,
15	πολλὰς ἐκ κεφαλῆς προθελύμνους ἕλκετο χαίτας
16	ὑψόθ' ἐόντι Διὶ, μέγα δ' ἔστενε κυδάλιμον κῆρ.
17	ἥδε δέ οἱ κατὰ θυμὸν ἀρίστη φαίνετο βουλὴ
18	Νέστορ' ἐπὶ πρῶτον Νηλήϊον ἐλθέμεν ἀνδρῶν,
19	εἴ τινά οἱ σὺν μῆτιν ἀμύμονα τεκτήναιτο,
20	ἥ τις ἀλεξίκακος πᾶσιν Δαναοῖσι γένοιτο.
21	ὀρθωθεὶς δ' ἔνδυνε περὶ στήθεσσι χιτῶνα,
22	ποσσίδ' ὑπὸ λιπαροῖσιν ἐδήσατο καλὰ πέδιλα,
23	ἀμφὶ δ' ἔπειτα δαφοινὸν ἑέσσατο δέρμα λέοντος
24	αἴθωνος μεγάλοιο ποδηνεκές, εἵλετο δ' ἔγχος.

25 ὡς δ᾽ αὕτως Μενέλαον ἔχε τρόμος· οὐδὲ γὰρ αὐτῷ
26 ὕπνος ἐπὶ βλεφάροισιν ἐφίζανε· μή τι πάθοιεν
27 Ἀργεῖοι, τοὶ δὴ ἕθεν εἵνεκα πουλὺν ἐφ᾽ ὑγρὴν
28 ἤλυθον ἐς Τροίην πόλεμον θρασὺν ὁρμαίνοντες.
29 παρδαλέῃ μὲν πρῶτα μετάφρενον εὐρὺ κάλυψε
30 ποικίλῃ, αὐτὰρ ἐπὶ στεφάνην κεφαλῆφιν ἀείρας
31 θήκατο χαλκείην, δόρυ δ᾽ εἵλετο χειρὶ παχείῃ.
32 βῆ δ᾽ ἴμεν ἀνστήσων ὃν ἀδελφεὸν, ὃς μέγα πάντων
33 Ἀργείων ἤνασσε, θεὸς δ᾽ ὡς τίετο δήμῳ.
34 τὸν δ᾽ εὗρ᾽ ἀμφ᾽ ὤμοισι τιθήμενον ἔντεα καλὰ
35 νηῒ παρὰ πρύμνῃ· τῷ δ᾽ ἀσπάσιος γένετ᾽ ἐλθών.
36 τὸν πρότερος προσέειπε βοὴν ἀγαθὸς Μενέλαος·
37 τίφθ᾽ οὕτως ἠθεῖε κορύσσεαι; ἦ τιν᾽ ἑταίρων
38 ὀτρύνεις Τρώεσσιν ἐπίσκοπον; ἀλλὰ μάλ᾽ αἰνῶς
39 δείδω μὴ οὔ τίς τοι ὑπόσχηται τόδε ἔργον
40 ἄνδρας δυσμενέας σκοπιαζέμεν οἷος ἐπελθὼν
41 νύκτα δι᾽ ἀμβροσίην· μάλα τις θρασυκάρδιος ἔσται ᵉˢᵗᵉιη.
42 τὸν δ᾽ ἀπαμειβόμενος προσέφη κρείων Ἀγαμέμνων·
43 χρεὼ βουλῆς ἐμὲ καὶ σὲ διοτρεφὲς ὦ Μενέλαε
44 κερδαλέης, ἥ τίς κεν ἐρύσσεται ἠδὲ σαώσει
45 Ἀργείους καὶ νῆας, ἐπεὶ Διὸς ἐτράπετο φρήν.
46 Ἑκτορέοις ἄρα μᾶλλον ἐπὶ φρένα θῆχ᾽ ἱεροῖσιν·
47 οὐ γάρ πω ἰδόμην, οὐδ᾽ ἔκλυον αὐδήσαντος
48 ἄνδρ᾽ ἕνα τόσσα δὲ μέρμερ᾽ ἐπ᾽ ἤματι μητίσασθαι,
49 ὅσσ᾽ Ἕκτωρ ἔρρεξε Διῒ φίλος υἷας Ἀχαιῶν
50 αὕτως, οὔτε θεᾶς υἱὸς φίλος οὔτε θεοῖο.
51 ἔργα δ᾽ ἔρεξ᾽ ὅσα φημὶ μελησέμεν Ἀργείοισι
52 δηθά τε καὶ δολιχόν· τόσα γὰρ κακὰ μήσατ᾽ Ἀχαιούς.
53 ἀλλ᾽ ἴθι νῦν Αἴαντα καὶ Ἰδομενῆα κάλεσσον
54 ῥίμφα θέων ἐπὶ νῆας· ἐγὼ δ᾽ ἐπὶ Νέστορα δῖον
55 εἶμι, καὶ ὀτρυνέω ἀνστήμεναι, αἴ κε πίθηται
56 ἐλθεῖν ἐς φυλάκων ἱερὸν τέλος ἠδ᾽ ἐπιτεῖλαι.
57 κείνου γάρ κε μάλιστα πιθοίατο· τοῖο γὰρ υἱὸς
58 σημαίνει φυλάκεσσι καὶ Ἰδομενῆος ὀπάων
59 Μηριόνης· τοῖσιν γὰρ ἐπετράπομέν γε μάλιστα.
60 τὸν δ᾽ ἠμείβετ᾽ ἔπειτα βοὴν ἀγαθὸς Μενέλαος·
61 πῶς γάρ μοι μύθῳ ἐπιτέλλεαι ἠδὲ κελεύεις;
62 αὖθι μένω μετὰ τοῖσι δεδεγμένος εἰσόκεν ἔλθῃς,
63 ἦε θέω μετά σ᾽ αὖτις, ἐπὴν εὖ τοῖς ἐπιτείλω;
64 τὸν δ᾽ αὖτε προσέειπεν ἄναξ ἀνδρῶν Ἀγαμέμνων,
65 αὖθι μένειν, μή πως ἀβροτάξομεν ἀλλήλοισϊν

66   ἐρχομένω· πολλαὶ γὰρ ἀνὰ στρατόν εἰσι κέλευθοι.
67   φθέγγεο δ' ᾗ κεν ἴῃσθα καὶ ἐγρήγορθαι ἄνωχθι
68   πατρόθεν ἐκ γενεῆς ὀνομάζων ἄνδρα ἕκαστον
69   πάντας κυδαίνων· μηδὲ μεγαλίζεο θυμῷ,
70   ἀλλὰ καὶ αὐτοί περ πονεώμεθα· ὧδέ που ἄμμι
71   Ζεὺς ἐπὶ γεινομένοισιν ἵει κακότητα βαρεῖαν.
72   ὡς εἰπὼν ἀπέπεμπεν ἀδελφεὸν εὖ ἐπιτείλας·
73   αὐτὰρ ὁ βῆ ῥ' ἰέναι μετα Νέστορα ποιμένα λαῶν·
74   τὸν δ' εὗρεν παρά τε κλισίῃ καὶ νηῒ μελαίνῃ
75   εὐνῇ ἐνὶ μαλακῇ· παρὰ δ' ἔντεα ποικίλ' ἔκειτο
76   ἀσπὶς καὶ δύο δοῦρε φαεινή τε τρυφάλεια.
77   πὰρ δὲ ζωστὴρ κεῖτο παναίολος, ᾧ ῥ' ὁ γεραιὸς
78   ζώννυθ' ὅτ' ἐς πόλεμον φθισήνορα θωρήσσοιτο
79   λαὸν ἄγων, ἐπεὶ οὐ μὲν ἐπέτραπε γήραϊ λυγρῷ.
80   ὀρθωθεὶς δ' ἄρ' ἐπ' ἀγκῶνος κεφαλὴν ἐπαείρας
81   Ἀτρείδην προσέειπε καὶ ἐξερεείνετο μύθῳ·
82   τίς δ' οὗτος κατὰ νῆας ἀνὰ στρατὸν ἔρχεαι οἶος
83   νύκτα δι' ὀρφναίην, ὅτε θ' εὕδουσι βροτοὶ ἄλλοι,
84   ἠέ τιν' οὐρήων διζήμενος, ἤ τιν' ἑταίρων;
85   φθέγγεο, μὴ δ' ἀκέων ἐπ' ἔμ' ἔρχεο· τίπτε δέ σε χρεώ;
86   τόνδ' ἠμείβετ' ἔπειτα ἄναξ ἀνδρῶν Ἀγαμέμνων·
87   ὦ Νέστορ Νηληϊάδη μέγα κῦδος Ἀχαιῶν
88   γνώσεαι Ἀτρείδην Ἀγαμέμνονα, τὸν περὶ πάντων
89   Ζεὺς ἐνέεικε πόνοισι διαμπερὲς εἰσόκ' ἄϋτμὴ
90   ἐν στήθεσσι μένῃ καί μοι φίλα γούνατ' ὀρώρῃ.
91   πλάζομαι ὧδ' ἐπεὶ οὔ μοι ἐπ' ὄμμασι νήδυμος ὕπνος
92   ἱζάνει, ἀλλὰ μέλει πόλεμος καὶ κήδε' Ἀχαιῶν.
93   αἰνῶς γὰρ Δαναῶν περιδείδια, οὐδέ μοι ἦτορ
94   ἔμπεδον, ἀλλ' ἀλύκτημαι, κραδίη δέ μοι ἔξω
95   στηθέων ἐκθρῴσκει, τρομέει δ' ὑπὸ φαίδιμα γυῖα.
96   ἀλλ' εἴ τι δραίνεις, ἐπεὶ οὐδὲ σέ γ' ὕπνος ἱκάνει,
97   δεῦρ' ἐς τοὺς φύλακας καταβήομεν, ὄφρα ἴδωμεν
98   μὴ τοὶ μὲν καμάτῳ ἀδηκότες ἠδὲ καὶ ὕπνῳ
99   κοιμήσωνται, ἀτὰρ φυλακῆς ἐπὶ πάγχυ λάθωνται.
100 δυσμενέες δ' ἄνδρες σχεδὸν εἵαται· οὐδέ τι ἴδμεν
101 μή πως καὶ διὰ νύκτα μενοινήσωσι μάχεσθαι.
102 τὸν δ' ἠμείβετ' ἔπειτα Γερήνιος ἱππότα Νέστωρ·
103 Ἀτρείδη κύδιστε ἄναξ ἀνδρῶν Ἀγάμεμνον
104 οὔ θην Ἕκτορι πάντα νοήματα μητίετα Ζεὺς
105 ἐκτελέει, ὅσα πού νυν ἐέλπεται· ἀλλά μιν οἴω
106 κήδεσι μοχθήσειν καὶ πλείοσιν, εἴ κεν Ἀχιλλεὺς

107 ἐκ χόλου ἀργαλέοιο μεταστρέψῃ φίλον ἦτορ.
108 σοὶ δὲ μάλ' ἕψομ' ἐγώ· ποτὶ δ' αὖ καὶ ἐγείρομεν ἄλλους
109 ἠμὲν Τυδείδην δουρὶ κλυτὸν ἠδ' Ὀδυσῆα
110 ἠδ' Αἴαντα ταχὺν καὶ Φυλέος ἄλκιμον υἱόν.
111 ἀλλ' εἴ τις καὶ τοῦσδε μετοιχόμενος καλέσειεν
112 ἀντίθεόν τ' Αἴαντα καὶ Ἰδομενῆα ἄνακτα·
113 τῶν γὰρ νῆες ἔασιν ἑκαστάτωι, οὐδὲ μάλ' ἐγγύς.
114 ἀλλὰ φίλον περ ἐόντα καὶ αἰδοῖον Μενέλαον
115 νεικέσω, εἴ πέρ μοι νεμεσήσεαι, οὐδ' ἐπικεύσω
116 ὡς εὕδει, σοὶ δ' οἴῳ ἐπέτρεψεν πονέεσθαι.
117 νῦν ὄφελεν κατὰ πάντας ἀριστῆας πονέεσθαι
118 λισσόμενος· χρειὼ γὰρ ἱκάνεται οὐκέτ' ἀνεκτός.
119 τὸν δ' αὖτε προσέειπεν ἄναξ ἀνδρῶν Ἀγαμέμνων·
120 ὦ γέρον ἄλλοτε μέν σε καὶ αἰτιάασθαι ἄνωγα·
121 πολλάκι γὰρ μεθίει τε καὶ οὐκ ἐθέλει πονέεσθαι
122 οὔτ' ὄκνῳ εἴκων οὔτ' ἀφραδίῃσι νόοιο,
123 ἀλλ' ἐμέ τ' εἰσορόων καὶ ἐμὴν ποτιδέγμενος ὁρμήν.
124 νῦν δ' ἐμέο πρότερος μάλ' ἐπέγρετο καί μοι ἐπέστη·
125 τὸν μὲν ἐγὼ προέηκα καλήμεναι οὓς σὺ μεταλλᾷς.
126 ἀλλ' ἴομεν· κείνους δὲ κιχησόμεθα πρὸ πυλάων
127 ἐν φυλάκεσσ', ἵνα γάρ σφιν ἐπέφραδον ἠγερέεσθαι.
128 τὸν δ' ἠμείβετ' ἔπειτα Γερήνιος ἱππότα Νέστωρ·
129 οὕτως οὔ τίς οἱ νεμεσήσεται οὐδ' ἀπιθήσει
130 Ἀργείων, ὅτε κέν τιν' ἐποτρύνῃ καὶ ἀνώγῃ.
131 ὣς εἰπὼν ἔνδυνε περὶ στήθεσσι χιτῶνα,
132 ποσσὶ δ' ὑπὸ λιπαροῖσιν ἐδήσατο καλὰ πέδιλα,
133 ἀμφὶ δ' ἄρα χλαῖναν περονήσατο φοινικόεσσαν
134 διπλῆν ἐκταδίην, οὔλη δ' ἐπενήνοθε λάχνη.
135 εἵλετο δ' ἄλκιμον ἔγχος ἀκαχμένον ὀξέϊ χαλκῷ,
136 βῆ δ' ἰέναι κατὰ νῆας Ἀχαιῶν χαλκοχιτώνων.
137 πρῶτον ἔπειτ' Ὀδυσῆα Διὶ μῆτιν ἀτάλαντον
138 ἐξ ὕπνου ἀνέγειρε Γερήνιος ἱππότα Νέστωρ
139 φθεγξάμενος· τὸν δ' αἶψα περὶ φρένας ἤλυθ' ἰωή,
140 ἐκ δ' ἦλθε κλισίης καί σφεας πρὸς μῦθον ἔειπε·
141 τίφθ' οὕτως ἐπὶ νῆας ἀνὰ στρατὸν οἶοι ἀλᾶσθε
142 νύκτα δι' ἀμβροσίην, ὅ τι δὴ χρειὼ τόσον ἵκει;
143 τὸν δ' ἠμείβετ' ἔπειτα Γερήνιος ἱππότα Νέστωρ·
144 διογενὲς Λαερτιάδη πολυμήχαν' Ὀδυσσεῦ
145 μὴ νεμέσα· τοῖον γὰρ ἄχος βεβήκεν Ἀχαιούς.
146 ἀλλ' ἕπευ, ὄφρα καὶ ἄλλον ἐγείρομεν ὅν τ' ἐπέοικε
147 βουλὰς βουλεύειν, ἢ φευγέμεν ἠὲ μάχεσθαι.

148 ὡς φάθ', ὁ δὲ κλισίηνδε κιὼν πολύμητις Ὀδυσσεὺς
149 ποικίλον ἀμφ' ὤμοισι σάκος θέτο, βῆ δὲ μετ' αὐτούς.
150 βὰν δ' ἐπὶ Τυδείδην Διομήδεα· τὸν δ' ἐκίχανον
151 ἐκτὸς ἀπὸ κλισίης σὺν τεύχεσιν· ἀμφὶ δ' ἑταῖροι
152 εὗδον, ὑπὸ κρασὶν δ' ἔχον ἀσπίδας· ἔγχεα δέ σφιν
153 ὀρθ' ἐπὶ σαυρωτῆρος ἐλήλατο, τῆλε δὲ χαλκὸς
154 λάμφ'ᵖᵉ ὥς τε στεροπὴ πατρὸς Διός· αὐτὰρ ὅ γ' ἥρως
155 εὗδ', ὑπὸ δ' ἔστρωτο ῥινὸν βοὸς ἀγραύλοιο,
156 αὐτὰρ ὑπὸ κράτεσφι τάπης τετάνυστο φαεινός.
157 τὸν πὰρ στὰς ἀνέγειρε Γερήνιος ἱππότα Νέστωρ,
158 λὰξ ποδὶ κινήσας, ὤτρυνε τε νείκεσέ τ' ἄντην·
159 ὄρσεο Τυδέος υἱέ· τί πάννυχον ὕπνον ἀωτεῖς;
160 οὐκ ἀΐεις ὡς Τρῶες ἐπὶ θρωσμῷ πεδίοιο
161 εἴαται ἄγχι νεῶν, ὀλίγος δ' ἔτι χῶρος ἐρύκει;
162 ὡς φάθ', ὁ δ' ἐξ ὕπνοιο μάλα κραιπνῶς ἀνόρουσε,
163 καί μιν φωνήσας ἔπεα πτερόεντα προσηύδα·
164 σχέτλιός ἐσσι γεραιέ· σὺ μὲν πόνου οὔ ποτε λήγεις.
165 οὔ νυ καὶ ἄλλοι ἔασι νεώτεροι υἷες Ἀχαιῶν
166 οἵ κεν ἔπειτα ἕκαστον ἐγείρειαν βασιλήων
167 πάντη ἐποιχόμενοι; σὺ δ' ἀμήχανός ἐσσι γεραιέ.
168 τὸν δ' αὖτε προσέειπε Γερήνιος ἱππότα Νέστωρ·
169 ναὶ δὴ ταῦτά γε πάντα φίλος κατὰ μοῖραν ἔειπες.
170 εἰσὶν μέν μοι παῖδες ἀμύμονες, εἰσὶ δὲ λαοὶ
171 καὶ πολέες, τῶν κέν τις ἐποιχόμενος καλέσειεν·
172 ἀλλὰ μάλα μεγάλη χρειὼ βεβίηκεν Ἀχαιούς.
173 νῦν γὰρ δὴ πάντεσσιν ἐπὶ ξυροῦ ἵσταται ἀκμῆς
174 ἢ μάλα λυγρὸς ὄλεθρος Ἀχαιοῖς ἠὲ βιῶναι.
175 ἀλλ' ἴθι νῦν Αἴαντα ταχὺν καὶ Φυλέος υἱὸν
176 ἄνστησον· σὺ γὰρ ἐσσι νεώτερος· εἴ μ' ἐλεαίρεις.
177 ὡς φάθ', ὁ δ' ἀμφ' ὤμοισιν ἑέσσατο δέρμα λέοντος
178 αἴθωνος μεγάλοιο ποδηνεκές, εἴλετο δ' ἔγχος.
179 βῆ δ' ἰέναι, τοὺς δ' ἔνθεν ἀναστήσας ἄγεν ἥρως.
180 οἱ δ' ὅτε δὴ φυλάκεσσιν ἐν ἀγρομένοισιν ἔμιχθεν,
181 οὐδὲ μὲν εὕδοντας φυλάκων ἡγήτορας εὗρον,
182 ἀλλ' ἐγρηγορτὶ σὺν τεύχεσιν εἴατο πάντες.
183 ὡς δὲ κύνες περὶ μῆλα δυσωρήσωνται ἐν αὐλῇ
184 θηρὸς ἀκούσαντες κρατερόφρονος, ὥστε καθ' ὕλην
185 ἔρχηται δι' ὄρεσφι· πολὺς δ' ὀρυμαγδὸς ἐπ' αὐτῷ
186 ἀνδρῶν ἠδὲ κυνῶν, ἀπό τέ σφισιν ὕπνος ὄλωλεν·
187 ὡς τῶν νήδυμος ὕπνος ἀπὸ βλεφάροιιν ὀλώλει
188 νύκτα φυλασσομένοισι κακήν· πεδίον δὲ γὰρ αἰεὶ

189 τετράφαθ᾽, ὁππότ᾽ ἐπὶ Τρώων ἀΐοιεν ἰόντων.
190 τοὺς δ᾽ ὁ γέρων γήθησεν ἰδὼν θάρσυνέ τε μύθῳ
192 οὕτω νῦν φίλα τέκνα φυλάσσετε· μηδὲ τιν᾽ ὕπνος
193 αἱρείτω, μὴ χάρμα γενώμεθα δυσμενέεσσιν.
194 ὣς εἰπὼν τάφροιο διέσσυτο· τοὶ δ᾽ ἅμ᾽ ἕποντο
195 Ἀργείων βασιλῆες ὅσοι κεκλήατο βουλήν.
196 τοῖς δ᾽ ἅμα Μηριόνης καὶ Νέστορος ἀγλαὸς υἱὸς
197 ἤϊσαν· αὐτοὶ γὰρ κάλεον συμμητιάασθαι.
198 τάφρον δ᾽ ἐκδιαβάντες ὀρυκτὴν ἑδριόωντο
199 ἐν καθαρῷ, ὅθι δὴ νεκύων διεφαίνετο χῶρος
200 πιπτόντων· ὅθεν αὖτις ἀπετράπετ᾽ ὄβριμος Ἕκτωρ
201 ὀλλὺς Ἀργείους, ὅτε δὴ περὶ νὺξ ἐκάλυψεν.
202 ἔνθα καθεζόμενοι ἔπε᾽ ἀλλήλοισι πίφαυσκον·
203 τοῖσι δὲ μύθων ἦρχε Γερήνιος ἱππότα Νέστωρ·
204 ὦ φίλοι οὐκ ἂν δή τις ἀνὴρ πεπίθοιθ᾽ ἑῷ αὐτοῦ
205 θυμῷ τολμήεντι μετὰ Τρῶας μεγαθύμους
206 ἐλθεῖν, εἴ τινά που δηΐων ἕλοι ἐσχατόωντα,
207 ἤ τινά που καὶ φῆμιν ἐνὶ Τρώεσσι πύθοιτο,
208 ἅσσά τε μητιόωσι μετὰ σφίσιν, ἢ μεμάασιν
209 αὖθι μένειν παρὰ νηυσὶν ἀπόπροθεν, ἦε πόλιν δὲ
210 ἂψ ἀναχωρήσουσιν, ἐπεὶ δαμάσαντό γ᾽ Ἀχαιούς.
211 ταῦτά τε πάντα πύθοιτο, καὶ ἂψ εἰς ἡμέας ἔλθοι
212 ἀσκηθής· μέγα κέν οἱ ὑπουράνιον κλέος εἴη
213 πάντας ἐπ᾽ ἀνθρώπους, καί οἱ δόσις ἔσσεται ἐσθλή·
214 ὅσσοι γὰρ νήεσσιν ἐπικρατέουσιν ἄριστοι
215 τῶν πάντων οἱ ἕκαστος ὄϊν δώσουσι μέλαιναν
216 θῆλυν ὑπόρρηνον· τῇ μὲν κτέρας οὐδὲν ὁμοῖον,
217 αἰεὶ δ᾽ ἐν δαίτῃσι καὶ εἰλαπίνῃσι παρέσται.
218 ὣς ἔφαθ᾽, οἳ δ᾽ ἄρα πάντες ἀκὴν ἐγένοντο σιωπῇ.
219 τοῖσι δὲ καὶ μετέειπε βοὴν ἀγαθὸς Διομήδης·
220 Νέστορ ἔμ᾽ ὀτρύνει κραδίη καὶ θυμὸς ἀγήνωρ
221 ἀνδρῶν δυσμενέων δῦναι στρατὸν ἐγγὺς ἐόντων ^ἐόντα
222 Τρώων· ἀλλ᾽ εἴ τίς μοι ἀνὴρ ἅμ᾽ ἕποιτο καὶ ἄλλος
223 μᾶλλον θαλπωρὴ καὶ θαρσαλεώτερον ἔσται ^ἔστι.
224 σύν τε δύ᾽ ἐρχομένω καί τε πρὸ ὃ τοῦ ἐνόησεν
225 ὅππως κέρδος ἔῃ· μοῦνος δ᾽ εἴ πέρ τε νοήσῃ
226 ἀλλά τέ οἱ βράσσων τε νόος, λεπτὴ δέ τε μῆτις.
227 ὣς ἔφαθ᾽, οἳ δ᾽ ἔθελον Διομήδεϊ πολλοὶ ἕπεσθαι.
228 ἠθελέτην Αἴαντε δύω θεράποντες Ἄρηος,
229 ἤθελε Μηριόνης, μάλα δ᾽ ἤθελε Νέστορος υἱός,
230 ἤθελε δ᾽ Ἀτρείδης δουρὶ κλειτὸς ^κλυτὸς Μενέλαος,

231 ἤθελε δ᾽ ὁ τλήμων Ὀδυσεὺς καταδῦναι ὅμιλον
232 Τρώων· αἰεὶ γάρ οἱ ἐνὶ φρεσὶ θυμὸς ἐτόλμα.
233 τοῖσι δὲ καὶ μετέειπεν ἄναξ ἀνδρῶν Ἀγαμέμνων·
234 Τυδείδη Διόμηδες ἐμῷ κεχαρισμένε θυμῷ
235 τὸν μὲν δὴ ἕταρόν γ᾽ αἱρήσεαι ὅν κ᾽ ἐθέλησθα,
236 φαινομένων τὸν ἄριστον, ἐπεὶ μεμάασί γε πολλοί.
237 μὴ δὲ σύ γ᾽ αἰδόμενος σῇσι φρεσὶ τὸν μὲν ἀρείω
238 καλλείπειν, σὺ δὲ χείρον᾽ ὀπάσσεαι αἰδοῖ εἴκων
239 ἐς γενεὴν ὁρόων, μηδ᾽ εἰ βασιλεύτερός ἐστιν.
240 ὣς ἔφατ᾽, ἔδδεισεν δὲ περὶ ξανθῷ Μενελάῳ.
241 τοῖς δ᾽ αὖτις μετέειπε βοὴν ἀγαθὸς Διομήδης·
242 εἰ μὲν δὴ ἕταρόν γε κελεύετέ μ᾽ αὐτὸν ἑλέσθαι,
243 πῶς ἂν ἔπειτ᾽ Ὀδυσῆος ἐγὼ θείοιο λαθοίμην,
244 οὗ περὶ μὲν πρόφρων κραδίη καὶ θυμὸς ἀγήνωρ
245 ἐν πάντεσσι πόνοισι, φιλεῖ δέ ἑ Παλλὰς Ἀθήνη.
246 τούτου γ᾽ ἑσπομένοιο καὶ ἐκ πυρὸς αἰθομένοιο
247 ἄμφω νοστήσαιμεν, ἐπεὶ περίοιδε νοῆσαι.
248 τόνδ᾽ αὖτε προσέειπε πολύτλας δῖος Ὀδυσσεύς·
249 Τυδείδη μήτ᾽ ἄρ με μάλ᾽ αἴνεε μήτε τί νείκει·
250 εἰδόσι γάρ τοι ταῦτα μετ᾽ Ἀργείοις ἀγορεύεις.
251 ἀλλ᾽ ἴομεν· μάλα γὰρ νὺξ ἄνεται, ἐγγύθι δ᾽ ἠώς,
252 ἄστρα δὲ δὴ προβέβηκε, παρῴχηκεν δὲ πλέω νὺξ
253 τῶν δύο μοιράων, τριτάτη δέ τι μοῖρα λέλειπται.
254 ὣς εἰπόνθ᾽ ὅπλοισιν ἐνὶ δεινοῖσιν ἐδύτην.
255 Τυδείδη μὲν δῶκε μενεπτόλεμος Θρασυμήδης
256 φάσγανον ἄμφηκες· τὸ δ᾽ ἑὸν παρὰ νηῒ λέλειπτο·
257 καὶ σάκος· ἀμφὶ δέ οἱ κυνέην κεφαλῆφιν ἔθηκε
258 ταυρείην, ἄφαλόν τε καὶ ἄλλοφον, ἥ τε καταῖτυξ
259 κέκληται, ῥύεται δὲ κάρη θαλερῶν αἰζηῶν.
260 Μηριόνης δ᾽ Ὀδυσῆϊ δίδου βιὸν ἠδὲ φαρέτρην
261 καὶ ξίφος, ἀμφὶ δέ οἱ κυνέην κεφαλῆφιν ἔθηκε
262 ῥινοῦ ποιητήν· πολέσιν δ᾽ ἔντοσθεν ἱμᾶσιν
263 ἐντέτατο στερεῶς· ἔκτοσθε δὲ λευκοὶ ὀδόντες
264 ἀργιόδοντος ὑὸς θαμέες ἔχον ἔνθα καὶ ἔνθα
265 εὖ καὶ ἐπισταμένως· μέσσῃ δ᾽ ἐνὶ πῖλος ἀρήρει.
266 τήν ῥά ποτ᾽ ἐξ Ἐλεῶνος Ἀμύντορος Ὀρμενίδαο
267 ἐξέλετ᾽ Αὐτόλυκος πυκινὸν δόμον ἀντιτορήσας,
268 Σκάνδειαν δ᾽ ἄρα δῶκε Κυθηρίῳ Ἀμφιδάμαντι·
269 Ἀμφιδάμας δὲ Μόλῳ δῶκε ξεινήϊον εἶναι,
270 αὐτὰρ ὃ Μηριόνῃ δῶκεν ᾧ παιδὶ φορῆναι·
271 δὴ τότ᾽ Ὀδυσσῆος πύκασεν κάρη ἀμφιτεθεῖσα.

272 τὼ δ᾽ ἐπεὶ οὖν ὅπλοισιν ἐνὶ δεινοῖσιν ἐδύτην,
273 βάν ῥ᾽ ἰέναι, λιπέτην δὲ κατ᾽ ^{παρ᾽}αὐτόθι πάντας ἀρίστους.
274 τοῖσι δὲ δεξιὸν ἧκεν ἐρῳδιὸν ἐγγὺς ὁδοῖο
275 Παλλὰς Ἀθηναίη· τοίδ᾽ οὐκ ἴδον ὀφθαλμοῖσι
276 νύκτα δι᾽ ὀρφναίην, ἀλλὰ κλάγξαντος ἄκουσαν.
277 χαῖρε δὲ τῷ ὄρνιθ᾽ Ὀδυσεύς, ἠρᾶτο δ᾽ Ἀθήνῃ·
278 κλῦθί μοι ^{μευ} αἰγιόχοιο Διὸς τέκος, ἥ τέ μοι αἰεὶ
279 ἐν πάντεσσι πόνοισι παρίστασαι, οὐδέ σε λήθω
280 κινύμενος· νῦν αὖτε μάλιστά με φῖλαι Ἀθήνη,
281 δὸς δὲ πάλιν ἐπὶ νῆας ἐϋκλεῖας ἐφικέσθαι
282 ῥέξαντας μέγα ἔργον, ὅ κεν Τρώεσσι μελήσει.
283 Δεύτερος αὖτ᾽ ἠρᾶτο βοὴν ἀγαθὸς Διομήδης·
284 κέκλυθι νῦν καὶ ἐμεῖο Διὸς τέκος Ἀτρυτώνη·
285 σπεῖό μοι ὡς ὅτε πατρὶ ἅμ᾽ ἕσπεο Τυδέϊ δίῳ
286 ἐς Θήβας, ὅτε τε πρὸ Ἀχαιῶν ἄγγελος ᾔει.
287 τούσδ᾽ ἄρ᾽ ἐπ᾽ Ἀσωπῷ λίπε χαλκοχίτωνας Ἀχαιούς,
288 αὐτὰρ ὃ μειλίχιον μῦθον φέρε Καδμείοισι
289 κεῖσ᾽· ἀτὰρ ἂψ ἀπιὼν μάλα μέρμερα μήσατο ἔργα
290 σὺν σοὶ δῖα θεά, ὅτε οἱ πρόφρασσα παρέστης.
291 ὡς νῦν μοι ἐθέλουσα παρίστασο καί με φύλασσε.
292 σοὶ δ᾽ αὖ ἐγὼ ῥέξω βοῦν ἦνιν εὐρυμέτωπον
293 ἀδμήτην, ἣν οὔ πω ὑπὸ ζυγὸν ἤγαγεν ἀνήρ·
294 τήν τοι ἐγὼ ῥέξω χρυσὸν κέρασιν περιχεύας.
295 ὡς ἔφαν εὐχόμενοι, τῶν δ᾽ ἔκλυε Παλλὰς Ἀθήνη.
296 οἱ δ᾽ ἐπεὶ ἠρήσαντο Διὸς κούρῃ μεγάλοιο,
297 βάν ῥ᾽ ἴμεν ὥς τε λέοντε δύω διὰ νύκτα μέλαιναν
298 ἂμ φόνον, ἂν νέκυας, διά τ᾽ ἔντεα καὶ μέλαν αἷμα.
299 Οὐδὲ μὲν οὐδὲ Τρῶας ἀγήνορας εἴασεν Ἕκτωρ
300 εὕδειν, ἀλλ᾽ ἄμυδις κικλήσκετο πάντας ἀρίστους,
301 ὅσσοι ἔσαν Τρώων ἡγήτορες ἠδὲ μέδοντες·
302 τοὺς ὅ γε συγκαλέσας πυκινὴν ἠρτύνετο βουλήν·
303 τίς κέν μοι τόδε ἔργον ὑποσχόμενος τελέσειεν
304 δώρῳ ἐπὶ μεγάλῳ; μισθὸς δέ οἱ ἄρκιος ἔσται.
305 δώσω γὰρ δίφρόν τε δύω τ᾽ ἐριαύχενας ἵππους
306 οἵ κεν ἀριστεύωσι θοῇς ἐπὶ νηυσὶν Ἀχαιῶν
307 ὅς τίς κεν τλαίη, οἵ τ᾽ αὐτῷ κῦδος ἄροιτο,
308 νηῶν ὠκυπόρων σχεδὸν ἐλθέμεν, ἔκ τε πυθέσθαι
309 ἠὲ φυλάσσονται νῆες θοαὶ ὡς τὸ πάρος περ,
310 ἦ ἤδη χείρεσσιν ὑφ᾽ ἡμετέρῃσι δαμέντες
311 φύξιν βουλεύουσι μετὰ σφίσιν, οὐδ᾽ ἐθέλουσι
312 νύκτα φυλασσέμεναι, καμάτῳ ἀδηκότες αἰνῷ.

313 ὡς ἔφαθ', οἱ δ' ἄρα πάντες ἀκὴν ἐγένοντο σιωπῇ.
314 ἦν δέ τις ἐν Τρώεσσι Δόλων Εὐμήδεος υἱὸς
315 κήρυκος θείοιο πολύχρυσος πολύχαλκος,
316 ὃς δή τοι εἶδος μὲν ἔην κακός, ἀλλὰ ποδώκης·
317 αὐτὰρ ὃ μοῦνος ἔην μετὰ πέντε κασιγνήτῃσιν.
318 ὅς ῥα τότε Τρωσίν τε καὶ Ἕκτορι μῦθον ἔειπεν·
319 Ἕκτορ ἔμ' ὀτρύνει κραδίη καὶ θυμὸς ἀγήνωρ
320 νηῶν ὠκυπόρων σχεδὸν ἐλθέμεν ἔκ τε πυθέσθαι.
321 ἀλλ' ἄγε μοι τὸ σκῆπτρον ἀνάσχεο, καί μοι ὄμοσσον
322 ἠμὲν τοὺς ἵππους τε καὶ ἅρματα ποικίλα χαλκῷ
323 δωσέμεν, οἳ φορέουσιν ἀμύμονα Πηλείωνα,
324 σοὶ δ' ἐγὼ οὐχ ἅλιος σκοπὸς ἔσσομαι οὐδ' ἀπὸ δόξης·
325 τόφρα γὰρ ἐς στρατὸν εἶμι διαμπερὲς ὄφρ' ἂν ἵκωμαι
326 νῆ' Ἀγαμεμνονέην, ὅθι που μέλλουσιν ἄριστοι
327 βουλὰς βουλεύειν ἢ φευγέμεν ἠὲ μάχεσθαι.
328 ὡς φάθ', ὃ δ' ἐν χερσὶ σκῆπτρον λάβε καὶ οἱ ὄμοσσεν·
329 ἴστω νῦν Ζεὺς αὐτὸς ἐρίγδουπος πόσις Ἥρης
330 μὴ μὲν τοῖς ἵπποισιν ἀνὴρ ἐποχήσεται ἄλλος
331 Τρώων, ἀλλὰ σὲ φημὶ διαμπερὲς ἀγλαϊεῖσθαι.
332 ὡς φάτο καί ῥ' ἐπίορκον ἐπώμοσε, τὸν δ' ὀρόθυνεν·
333 αὐτίκα δ' ἀμφ' ὤμοισιν ἐβάλλετο καμπύλα τόξα,
334 ἔσσατο δ' ἔκτοσθεν ῥινὸν πολιοῖο λύκοιο,
335 κρατὶ δ' ἐπὶ κτιδέην κυνέην, ἕλε δ' ὀξὺν ἄκοντα,
336 βῆ δ' ἰέναι ἐπὶ νῆας ἀπὸ στρατοῦ· οὐδ' ἄρ' ἔμελλεν
337 ἐλθὼν ἐκ νηῶν ἄψ Ἕκτορι μῦθον ἀποίσειν.
338 ἀλλ' ὅτε δή ῥ' ἵππων τε καὶ ἀνδρῶν κάλλιφ' ὅμιλον,
339 βῆ ῥ' ἀν' ὁδὸν μεμαώς· τόνδ' ἐφράσατο προσιόντα
340 διογενὴς Ὀδυσσεύς, Διομήδεα δὲ προσέειπεν·
341 οὗτός τοι Διόμηδες ἀπὸ στρατοῦ ἔρχεται ἀνήρ,
342 οὐκ οἶδ' ἢ ᵉⁱ νήεσσιν ἐπίσκοπος ἡμετέρῃσιν,
343 ἦ τινα συλήσων νεκύων κατατεθνειώτων.
344 ἀλλ' ἐῶμέν μιν πρῶτα παρ' ἐξ ἐλθεῖν πεδίοιο
345 τυτθόν· ἔπειτα δέ κ' αὐτὸν ἐπαΐξαντες ἕλοιμεν ᵉˡωμεν
346 καρπαλίμως· εἰ δ' ἄμμε παραφθαίησι πόδεσσιν,
347 αἰεί μιν ποτὶ νῆας ἀπὸ στρατόφιν προτιειλεῖν
348 ἔγχει ἐπαΐσσων, μή πως προτὶ ἄστυ ἀλύξῃ.
349 ὡς ἄρα φωνήσαντε, παρ' ἐξ ὁδοῦ ἐν νεκύεσσι
350 κλινθήτην· ὃ δ' ἄρ' ὦκα παρέδραμεν ἀφραδίῃσι.
351 ἀλλ' ὅτε δή ῥ' ἀπέην ὅσσον τ' ἐπὶ οὖρα πέλονται
352 ἡμιόνων· αἳ γάρ τε βοῶν προφερέστεραί εἰσιν
353 ἑλκέμεναι νειοῖο βαθείης πηκτὸν ἄροτρον·

354 τὼ μὲν ἐπιδραμέτην, ὅδ' ἄρ' ἔστη δοῦπον ἀκούσας.
355 ἔλπετο γὰρ κατὰ θυμὸν ἀποστρέψοντας ἑταίρους
356 ἐκ Τρώων ἰέναι πάλιν Ἕκτορος ὀτρύναντος.
357 ἀλλ' ὅτε δή ῥ' ἄπεσαν δουρηνεκὲς ἢ καὶ ἔλασσον,
358 γνῶ ῥ' ἄνδρας δηΐους, λαιψηρὰ δὲ γούνατ' ἐνώμα
359 φευγέμεναι· τοὶ δ' αἶψα διώκειν ὡρμήθησαν.
360 ὡς δ' ὅτε καρχαρόδοντε δύω κύνε εἰδότε θήρης
361 ἢ κεμάδ' ἠὲ λαγωὸν ἐπείγετον ἐμμενὲς αἰεὶ
362 χῶρον ἀν' ὑλήενθ', ὁ δέ τε προθέῃσι μεμηκώς,
363 ὡς τὸν Τυδεΐδης ἠδ' ὁ πτολίπορθος Ὀδυσσεὺς
364 λαοῦ ἀποτμήξαντε διώκετον ἐμμενὲς αἰεί.
365 ἀλλ' ὅτε δὴ τάχ' ἔμελλε μιγήσεσθαι φυλάκεσσι
366 φεύγων ἐς νῆας, τότε δὴ μένος ἔμβαλ' Ἀθήνη
367 Τυδεΐδῃ, ἵνα μή τις Ἀχαιῶν χαλκοχιτώνων
368 φθαίη ἐπευξάμενος βαλέειν, ὁ δὲ δεύτερος ἔλθῃ.
369 δουρὶ δ' ἐπαΐσσων προσέφη κρατερὸς Διομήδης·
370 ἠὲ μέν' ἠέ σε δουρὶ κιχήσομαι, οὐδέ σέ φημι
371 δηρὸν ἐμῆς ἀπο χειρὸς ἀλύξειν αἰπὺν ὄλεθρον.
372 ἦ ῥα καὶ ἔγχος ἀφῆκεν, ἑκὼν δ' ἡμάρτανε φωτός·
373 δεξιτερὸν δ' ὑπὲρ ὦμον ἐΰξου δουρὸς ἀκωκὴ
374 ἐν γαίῃ ἐπάγη· ὁ δ' ἄρ' ἔστη τάρβησέν τε
375 βαμβαίνων· ἄραβος δὲ διὰ στόμα γίνετ' ὀδόντων·
376 χλωρὸς ὑπαὶ δείους· τὼ δ' ἀσθμαίνοντε κιχήτην,
377 χειρῶν δ' ἀψάσθην· ὁ δὲ δακρύσας ἔπος ηὖδα·
378 ζωγρεῖτ', αὐτὰρ ἐγὼν ἐμὲ λύσομαι· ἔστι γὰρ ἔνδον
379 χαλκός τε χρυσός τε πολύκμητός τε σίδηρος,
380 τῶν κ' ὔμμιν χαρίσαιτο πατὴρ ἀπερείσι' ἄποινα
381 εἴ κεν ἐμὲ ζωὸν πεπύθοιτ' ἐπὶ νηυσὶν Ἀχαιῶν.
382 τὸν δ' ἀπαμειβόμενος προσέφη πολύμητις Ὀδυσσεύς·
383 θάρσει, μηδέ τί τοι θάνατος καταθύμιος ἔστω.
384 ἀλλ' ἄγε μοι τόδε εἰπὲ καὶ ἀτρεκέως κατάλεξον·
385 πῇ ᵖᵒᵘ δ' οὕτως ἐπὶ νῆας ἀπὸ στρατοῦ ἔρχεαι οἶος
386 νύκτα δι' ὀρφναίην, ὅτε θ' εὕδουσι βροτοὶ ἄλλοι
387 ἤ τινα συλήσων νεκύων κατατεθνηώτων;
388 ἦ ς' Ἕκτωρ προέηκε διασκοπιᾶσθαι ἕκαστα
389 νῆας ἐπὶ γλαφυράς; ἦ ς' αὐτὸν θυμὸς ἀνῆκε;
390 τὸν δ' ἠμείβετ' ἔπειτα Δόλων, ὑπὸ δ' ἔτρεμε γυῖα·
391 πολλῇσίν μ' ἄτῃσι παρὲκ νόον ἤγαγεν Ἕκτωρ,
392 ὅς μοι Πηλείωνος ἀγαυοῦ μώνυχας ἵππους
393 δωσέμεναι κατένευσε καὶ ἅρματα ποικίλα χαλκῷ,
394 ἠνώγει δέ μ' ἰόντα θοὴν διὰ νύκτα μέλαιναν

395 ἀνδρῶν δυσμενέων σχεδὸν ἐλθέμεν, ἔκ τε πυθέσθαι
396 ἠὲ φυλάσσονται νῆες θοαὶ ὡς τὸ πάρος περ,
397 ἢ ἤδη χείρεσσιν ὑφ᾽ ἡμετέρῃσι δαμέντες
398 φύξιν βουλεύοιτε μετὰ σφίσιν, οὐδ᾽ ἐθέλοιτε
399 νύκτα φυλασσέμεναι, καμάτῳ ἀδηκότες αἰνῷ.
400 τὸν δ᾽ ἐπιμειδήσας προσέφη πολύμητις Ὀδυσσεύς·
401 ἦ ῥά νύ τοι μεγάλων δώρων ἐπεμαίετο θυμὸς
402 ἵππων Αἰακίδαο δαΐφρονος· οἱ δ᾽ ἀλεγεινοὶ
403 ἀνδράσι γε θνητοῖσι δαμήμεναι ἠδ᾽ ὀχέεσθαι
404 ἄλλῳ γ᾽ ἢ Ἀχιλῆϊ, τὸν ἀθανάτη τέκε μήτηρ.
405 ἀλλ᾽ ἄγε μοι τόδε εἰπὲ καὶ ἀτρεκέως κατάλεξον·
406 ποῦ νῦν δεῦρο κιὼν λίπες Ἕκτορα ποιμένα λαῶν;
407 ποῦ δέ οἱ ἔντεα κεῖται ἀρήϊα, ποῦ δέ οἱ ἵπποι;
408 πῶς δαὶ τῶν ἄλλων Τρώων φυλακαί τε καὶ εὐναί;
409 ἅσσά τε μητιόωσι μετὰ σφίσιν, ἢ μεμάασιν
410 αὖθι μένειν παρὰ νηυσὶν ἀπόπροθεν, ἠὲ πόλινδε
411 ἂψ ἀναχωρήσουσιν, ἐπεὶ δαμάσαντό γ᾽ Ἀχαιούς.
412 τόνδ᾽ αὖτε προσέειπε Δόλων Εὐμήδεος υἱός·
413 τοὶ γὰρ ἐγώ τοι ταῦτα μάλ᾽ ἀτρεκέως καταλέξω.
414 Ἕκτωρ μὲν μετὰ τοῖσιν, ὅσοι βουληφόροι εἰσί,
415 βουλὰς βουλεύει θείου παρὰ σήματι Ἴλου
416 νόσφιν ἀπὸ φλοίσβου· φυλακὰς δ᾽ ἃς εἴρεαι ἥρως
417 οὔ τις κεκριμένη ῥύεται στρατὸν οὐδὲ φυλάσσει.
418 ὅσσαι μὲν ᵞᵃ́ʳ Τρώων πυρὸς ἐσχάραι, οἷσιν ἀνάγκη
419 οἱ δ᾽ ἐγρηγόρθασι φυλασσέμεναί τε κέλονται
420 ἀλλήλοις· ἀτὰρ αὖτε πολύκλητοί τ᾽ ἐπίκουροι
421 εὕδουσιν· Τρωσὶν γὰρ ἐπιτραπέουσι φυλάσσειν·
422 οὐ γάρ σφιν παῖδες σχεδὸν εἵαται οὐδὲ γυναῖκες.
423 τόνδ᾽ ἀπαμειβόμενος προσέφη πολύμητις Ὀδυσσεύς·
424 πῶς γὰρ δὴ Τρώεσσι μεμιγμένοι ἱπποδάμοισιν
425 εὕδουσ᾽ ἢ ἀπάνευθε; δίειπέ μοι ὄφρα δαείω.
426 τὸν δ᾽ ἠμείβετ᾽ ἔπειτα Δόλων Εὐμήδεος υἱός·
427 τοι γὰρ ἐγώ τοι ταῦτα μάλ᾽ ἀτρεκέως καταλέξω.
428 πρὸς μὲν ἁλὸς Κᾶρες καὶ Παίονες ἀγκυλότοξοι
429 καὶ Λέλεγες καὶ Καύκωνες δῖοί τε Πελασγοί,
430 πρὸς Θύμβρης δ᾽ ἔλαχον Λύκιοι Μυσοί τ᾽ ἀγέρωχοι
431 καὶ Φρύγες ἱππόδαμοι καὶ Μῄονες ἱπποκορυσταί.
432 ἀλλὰ τίη ἐμὲ ταῦτα διεξερέεσθαι ἕκαστα;
433 εἰ γὰρ δὴ μέματον Τρώων καταδῦναι ὅμιλον
434 Θρήϊκες οἱ δ᾽ ἀπάνευθε νεήλυδες ἔσχατοι ἄλλων·
435 ἐν δέ σφιν Ῥῆσος βασιλεὺς παῖς Ἠϊονῆος.

436 τοῦ δὴ καλλίστους ἵππους ἴδον ἠδὲ μεγίστους·
437 λευκότεροι χιόνος, θείειν δ' ἀνέμοισιν ὁμοῖοι·
438 ἅρμα δέ οἱ χρυσῷ τε καὶ ἀργύρῳ εὖ ἤσκηται·
439 τεύχεα δὲ χρύσεια πελώρια θαῦμα ἰδέσθαι
440 ἤλυθ' ἔχων· τὰ μὲν οὔ τι κατὰ θνητοῖσιν ἔοικεν
441 ἄνδρεσσιν φορέειν, ἀλλ' ἀθανάτοισι θεοῖσιν.
442 ἀλλ' ἐμὲ μὲν νῦν νηυσὶ πελάσσετον ὠκυπόροισιν,
443 ἠέ με δήσαντες λίπετ' αὐτόθι νηλέϊ δεσμῷ,
444 ὄφρά κεν ἔλθητον καὶ πειρηθῆτον ἐμεῖο
445 ἤ ῥα κατ' αἶσαν ἔειπον ἐν ὑμῖν, ἠὲ καὶ οὐκί.
446 τὸν δ' ἄρ' ὑπόδρα ἰδὼν προσέφη κρατερὸς Διομήδης·
447 μὴ δή μοι φύξίν γε Δόλων ἐμβάλλεο θυμῷ·
448 ἐσθλά περ ἀγγείλας, ἐπεὶ ἵκεο χεῖρας ἐς ἁμάς.
449 εἰ μὲν γάρ κέ σε νῦν ἀπολύσομεν ἠὲ μεθῶμεν,
450 ἤτε καὶ ὕστερον εἶσθα θοὰς ἐπὶ νῆας Ἀχαιῶν
451 ἠὲ διοπτεύσων ἢ ἐναντίβιον πτολεμίξων·
452 εἰ δέ κ' ἐμῇς ὑπὸ χερσὶ δαμεὶς ᵗᵘᵖᵉⁱ_ς ἀπὸ θυμὸν ὀλέσσης,
453 οὐκέτ' ἔπειτα σὺ πῆμά ποτ' ἔσσεαι Ἀργείοισιν.
454 ἦ, καὶ ὁ μέν μιν ἔμελλε γενείου χειρὶ παχείῃ
455 ἁψάμενος λίσσεσθαι, ὁ δ' αὐχένα μέσσον ἔλασσε
456 φασγάνῳ ἀΐξας, ἀπὸ δ' ἄμφω κέρσε τένοντε·
457 φθεγγομένου δ' ἄρα τοῦ γε κάρη κονίῃσιν ἐμίχθη.
458 τοῦ δ' ἀπὸ μὲν κτιδέην κυνέην κεφαλῆφιν ἕλοντο
459 καὶ λυκέην καὶ τόξα παλίντονα καὶ δόρυ μακρόν·
460 καὶ τά γ' Ἀθηναίῃ ληΐτιδι δῖος Ὀδυσσεὺς
461 ὑψόσ' ἀνέσχεθε χειρὶ καὶ εὐχόμενος ἔπος ηὔδα·
462 χαῖρε θεὰ τοῖσδεσσι· σὲ γὰρ πρώτην ἐν Ὀλύμπῳ
463 πάντων ἀθανάτων ἐπιβωσόμεθ'· ἀλλὰ καὶ αὖτις
464 πέμψον ἐπὶ Θρηκῶν ἀνδρῶν ἵππους τε καὶ εὐνάς.
465 ὣς ἄρ' ἐφώνησεν, καὶ ἀπὸ ἕθεν ὑψόσ' ἀείρας
466 θῆκεν ἀνὰ μυρίκην· δέελον δ' ἐπὶ σῆματ' ἔθηκε
467 συμμάρψας δόνακας μυρίκης τ' ἐριθηλέας ὄζους,
468 μὴ λάθοι αὖτις ἰόντε θοὴν διὰ νύκτα μέλαιναν.
469 τὼ δὲ βάτην προτέρω διά τ' ἔντεα καὶ μέλαν αἷμα,
470 αἶψα δ' ἐπὶ Θρηκῶν ἀνδρῶν τέλος ἷξον ἰόντες.
471 οἱ δ' εὗδον καμάτῳ ἀδηκότες, ἔντεα δέ σφιν
472 καλὰ παρ' αὐτοῖσι χθονὶ κέκλιτο εὖ κατὰ κόσμον
473 τριστοιχεί· παρὰ δέ σφιν ἑκάστῳ δίζυγες ἵπποι.
474 Ῥῆσος δ' ἐν μέσῳ εὗδε, παρ' αὐτῷ δ' ὠκέες ἵπποι
475 ἐξ ἐπιδιφριάδος πυμάτης ἱμᾶσι δέδεντο.
476 τὸν δ' Ὀδυσεὺς προπάροιθεν ἰδὼν Διομήδεα δεῖξεν·

477   οὗτός τοι Διόμηδες ἀνήρ, οὗτοι δέ τοι ἵπποι,
478   οὓς νῶϊν πίφραυσκε Δόλων ὃν ἐπέφνομεν ἡμεῖς.
479   ἀλλ' ἄγε δὴ πρόφερε κρατερὸν μένος· οὐδέ τί σε χρὴ
480   ἑστάμεναι μέλεον συν τεύχεσιν, ἀλλὰ λύ' ἵππους·
481   ἠὲ σύ γ' ἄνδρας ἔναιρε, μελήσουσιν δ' ἐμοὶ ἵπποι.
482   ὡς φάτο, τῷ δ' ἔμπνευσε μένος γλαυκῶπις Ἀθήνη,
483   κτεῖνε δ' ἐπιστροφάδην· τῶν δὲ στόνος ὄρνυτ' ἀεικὴς
484   ἄορι θεινομένων, ἐρυθαίνετο δ' αἵματι γαῖα.
485   ὡς δὲ λέων μήλοισιν ἀσημάντοισιν ἐπελθὼν
486   αἴγεσιν ἢ ὀίεσσι κακὰ φρονέων ἐνορούσῃ,
487   ὡς μὲν Θρήϊκας ἄνδρας ἐπῴχετο Τυδέος υἱὸς
488   ὄφρα δυώδεκ' ἔπεφνεν· ἀτὰρ πολύμητις Ὀδυσσεὺς
489   ὅν τινα Τυδείδης ἄορι πλήξειε παραστὰς
490   τὸν δ' Ὀδυσεὺς μετόπισθε λαβὼν ποδὸς ἐξερύσασκε,
491   τὰ φρονέων κατὰ θυμὸν ὅπως καλλίτριχες ἵπποι
492   ῥεῖα διέλθοιεν μὴ δὲ τρομεοίατο θυμῷ
493   νεκροῖς ἀμβαίνοντες· ἀήθεσσον γὰρ ἔτ' αὐτῶν.
494   ἀλλ' ὅτε δὴ βασιλῆα κιχήσατο Τυδέος υἱός,
495   τὸν τρισκαιδέκατον μελιηδέα θυμὸν ἀπηύρα
496   ἀσθμαίνοντα· κακὸν γὰρ ὄναρ κεφαλῆφιν ἐπέστη
497   τὴν νύκτ' Οἰνείδαο πάϊς διὰ μῆτιν Ἀθήνης.
498   τόφρα δ' ἄρ' ὁ τλήμων Ὀδυσεὺς λύε μώνυχας ἵππους,
499   σὺν δ' ἤειρεν ἱμᾶσι καὶ ἐξήλαυνεν ὁμίλου
500   τόξῳ ἐπιπλήσσων, ἐπεὶ οὐ μάστιγα φαεινὴν
501   ποικίλου ἐκ δίφροιο νοήσατο χερσὶν ἑλέσθαι·
502   ῥοίζησεν δ' ἄρα πιφραύσκων Διομήδεϊ δίῳ.
503   αὐτὰρ ὁ μερμήριξε μένων ὅ τι κύντατον ἔρδοι,
504   ἢ ὅ γε δίφρον ἑλών, ὅθι ποικίλα τεύχε' ἔκειτο,
505   ῥυμοῦ ἐξερύοι ἢ ἐκφέροι ὑψός' ἀείρας,
506   ἢ ἔτι τῶν πλεόνων Θρηκῶν ἀπὸ θυμὸν ἕλοιτο.
507   ἕως ὁ ταῦθ' ὥρμαινε κατὰ φρένα, τόφρα δ' Ἀθήνη
508   ἐγγύθεν ἱσταμένη προσέφη Διομήδεα δῖον·
509   νόστου δὴ μνῆσαι μεγαθύμου Τυδέος υἱὲ
510   νῆας ἐπὶ γλαφυράς, μὴ καὶ πεφοβημένος ἔλθῃς,
511   μή πού τις καὶ Τρῶας ἐγείρῃσιν θεὸς ἄλλος.
512   ὡς φάθ', ὁ δὲ ξυνέηκε θεᾶς ὄπα φωνησάσης,
513   καρπαλίμως δ' ἵππων ἐπεβήσετο· κόψε δ' Ὀδυσσεὺς
514   τόξῳ· τοὶ δ' ἐπέτοντο θοὰς ἐπὶ νῆας Ἀχαιῶν.
515   οὐδ' ἀλαοσκοπιὴν εἶχ' ἀργυρότοξος Ἀπόλλων
516   ὡς ἴδ' Ἀθηναίην μετὰ Τυδέος υἱὸν ἔπουσαν·
517   τῇ κοτέων Τρώων κατεδύσετο πουλὺν ὅμιλον,

518 ὦρσεν δὲ Θρηκῶν βουληφόρον Ἱπποκόωντα
519 Ῥήσου ἀνεψιὸν ἐσθλόν· ὁ δ' ἐξ ὕπνου ἀνορούσας
520 ὡς ἴδε χῶρον ἐρῆμον, ὅθ' ἔστασαν ὠκέες ἵπποι,
521 ἄνδράς τ' ἀσπαίροντας ἐν ἀργαλέῃσι φονῇσιν,
522 ὤμωξέν τ' ἀρ' ἔπειτα φίλον τ' ὀνόμηνεν ἑταῖρον.
523 Τρώων δὲ κλαγγή τε καὶ ἄσπετος ὦρτο κυδοιμὸς
524 θυνόντων ἄμυδις· θηεῦντο δὲ μέρμερα ἔργα
525 ὅσς' ἄνδρες ῥέξαντες ἔβαν κοίλας ἐπὶ νῆας.
526 οἱ δ' ὅτε δή ῥ' ἵκανον ὅθι σκοπὸν Ἕκτορος ἔκταν,
527 ἔνθ' Ὀδυσεὺς μὲν ἔρυξε Διῒ φίλος ὠκέας ἵππους,
528 Τυδείδης δὲ χαμᾶζε θορὼν ἔναρα βροτόεντα
529 ἐν χείρεσς' Ὀδυσῆϊ τίθει, ἐπεβήσετο δ' ἵππων·
530 μάστιξεν δ' ἵππους, τὼ δ' οὐκ ἀέκοντε πετέσθην.
532 Νέστωρ δὲ πρῶτος κτύπον ἄϊε φώνησέν τε·
533 ὦ φίλοι Ἀργείων ἡγήτορες ἠδὲ μέδοντες
534 ψεύσομαι, ἦ ἔτυμόν τοι ἐρέω; κέλεται δέ με θυμός.
535 ἵππων μ' ὠκυπόδων ἀμφὶ κτύπος οὔατα βάλλει.
536 αἲ γὰρ δὴ Ὀδυσεύς τε καὶ ὁ κρατερὸς Διομήδης
537 ὧδ' ἄφαρ ἐκ Τρώων ἐλασαίατο μώνυχας ἵππους·
538 ἀλλ' αἰνῶς δείδοικα κατα φρένα μή τι πάθωσι
539 Ἀργείων οἳ ἄριστοι ὑπο Τρώων ὀρυμαγδοῦ.
540 οὔπω πᾶν εἴρητο ἔπος ὅτ' ἄρ ἤλυθον αὐτοί.
541 καί ῥ' οἱ μὲν κατέβησαν ἐπὶ χθόνα, τοὶ δὲ χαρέντες
542 δεξιῇ ἠσπάζοντο ἔπεσσί τε μειλιχίοισι·
543 πρῶτος δ' ἐξερέεινε Γερήνιος ἱππότα Νέστωρ·
544 εἴπ' ἄγε μ' ὦ πολύαιν' Ὀδυσεῦ μέγα κῦδος Ἀχαιῶν
545 ὅππως τοῦσδ' ἵππους λάβετον καταδύντες ὅμιλον
546 Τρώων, ἤ τίς σφωε πόρεν θεὸς ἀντιβολήσας.
547 αἰνῶς ἀκτίνεσσιν ἐοικότες ἠελίοιο.
548 αἰεὶ μὲν Τρώεσς' ἐπιμίσγομαι, οὐδέ τί φημὶ
549 μιμνάζειν παρα νηυσὶ γέρων περ ἐὼν πολεμιστής·
550 ἀλλ' οὔπω τοίους ἵππους ἴδον οὐδ' ἐνόησα.
551 ἀλλά τιν' ὔμμ' ὀίω δόμεναι θεὸν ἀντιάσαντα·
552 ἀμφοτέρω γὰρ σφῶϊ φιλεῖ νεφεληγερέτα Ζεὺς
553 κούρη τ' αἰγιόχοιο Διὸς γλαυκῶπις Ἀθήνη.
554 τὸν δ' ἀπαμειβόμενος προσέφη πολύμητις Ὀδυσσεύς·
555 ὦ Νέστορ Νηλ;ιάδη μέγα κῦδος Ἀχαιῶν
556 ῥεῖα θεός γ' ἐθέλων καὶ ἀμείνονας ἠέ περ οἴδε
557 ἵππους δωρήσαιτ', ἐπεὶ ἦ πολὺ φέρτεροί εἰσιν.
558 ἵπποι δ' οἴδε γεραιὲ νεήλυδες οὓς ἐρεείνεις
559 Θρηΐκιοι· τὸν δέ σφιν ἄνακτ' ἀγαθὸς Διομήδης

560 ἔκτανε, πὰρ δ' ἑτάρους δυοκαίδεκα πάντας ἀρίστους.
561 τὸν τρισκαίδεκατον σκοπὸν εἵλομεν ἐγγύθι νηῶν,
562 τόν ῥα διοπτῆρα στρατοῦ ἔμμεναι ἡμετέροιο
563 Ἕκτωρ τὲ προέηκε καὶ ἄλλοι Τρῶες ἀγαυοί.
564 ὣς εἰπὼν τάφροιο διήλασε μώνυχας ἵππους
565 καγχαλόων· ἅμα δ' ἄλλοι ἴσαν χαίροντες Ἀχαιοί.
566 οἱ δ' ὅτε Τυδείδεω κλισίην εὔτυκτον ἵκοντο,
567 ἵππους μὲν κατέδησαν ἐϋτμήτοισιν ἱμᾶσι
568 φάτνῃ ἐφ' ἱππείῃ, ὅθι περ Διομήδεος ἵπποι
569 ἕστασαν ὠκύποδες μελιηδέα πυρὸν ἔδοντες·
570 νηὶ δ' ἐνὶ πρύμνῃ ἔναρα βροτόεντα Δόλωνος
571 θῆκ' Ὀδυσεύς, ὄφρ' ἱρὸν ἑτοιμασσαίατ' Ἀθήνῃ.
572 αὐτοὶ δ' ἱδρῶ πολλὸν ἀπενίζοντο ^{ἀπονίζοντο} θαλάσσῃ
573 ἐσβάντες κνήμας τε ἰδὲ λόφον ἀμφί τε μηρούς.
574 αὐτὰρ ἐπεί σφιν κῦμα θαλάσσης ἱδρῶ πολλὸν
575 νίψεν ἀπο χρωτὸς καὶ ἀνέψυχθεν φίλον ἦτορ,
576 ἔς ῥ' ἀσαμίνθους βάντες ἐϋξέστας λούσαντο.
577 τὼ δὲ λοεσσαμένω καὶ ἀλειψαμένω λίπ' ἐλαίῳ
578 δείπνῳ ἐφιζανέτην, ἀπὸ δὲ κρητῆρος Ἀθήνῃ
579 πλείου ἀφυσσόμενοι λεῖβον μελιηδέα οἶνον.

Commentary

10.10 τρομέοντο Zenodotus, the first head of the library at Alexandria and a well known Homer scholar, knew of the reading φοβέοντο here, according to the scholia that survive in manuscripts A and T (or "Townley," Burney 86 in the British Museum). The scholia in T seem, however, to derive from a source different from those of A, and so it is notable that both manuscripts mention this multiform. For more on the Alexandrian editors of Homer, see on 10.51–52 in the general commentary in Part Three.

10.46 ἐπὶ φρένα θῆχ' ἱεροῖσιν The scholia in A report that "in some of the commentaries" (ἔν τισι τῶν ὑπομνημάτων) the alternate reading ἐπὶ φρένας εἷχ' ἱεροῖσιν could be found. A first/second-century CE papyrus (288 = Pack³ 853) agrees with the manuscripts.

10.51–52 These lines were athetized by Aristophanes of Byzantium and Aristarchus, two great heads of the library in Ptolemaic Alexandria (second century BCE). The athetesis of these lines is discussed in more detail *ad loc.* in the general commentary in Part Three.

10.53 Αἴαντα Evidence from the Venetus A scholia indicates that Aristarchus may have known a reading Αἴαντε instead of Αἴαντα (which is the reading of papyrus 288 and most manuscripts). See the general commentary in Part Three on this line.

10.54 ἐπὶ νῆας A and most manuscripts have this reading, but the A scholia record that Aristarchus read παρά. In 10.141, A again reads ἐπὶ νῆας, where most manuscripts have κατά (the A scholia at 141 record κατά as an alternate reading). In 10.336, A reads ἐπὶ νῆας where other manuscripts and the scribes of A themselves are divided between ποτὶ and προτὶ (see on p425 and on A 10.336 below). All manuscripts read ἐπὶ νῆας at 10.281.

10.65 ἀβροτάξομεν There are three different spellings of this verb (found only here in our Homeric texts) in the textual tradition: ἀβροτάζομεν, ἀβροτάξομεν, and ἀμβροτάξομεν. See the general commentary *ad loc.* for the possible significance of the variation.

10.84 ἠέ τιν' οὐρήων διζήμενος, ἤ τιν' ἑταίρων This verse was athetized by Aristarchus. The scholion in A explaining the athetesis objects to οὐρήων. It explains that what is meant here is 'one of the guards' and that the word οὖρον, accented like κοῦρον, means 'a guard', but οὐρέα means 'mule' (implied is that the genitive plural is from the latter). A further reason for athetesis is that "the question is inopportune." Although a word meaning 'guards' rather than 'mules' would seem to make more immediate sense here, it is interesting that none of our surviving witnesses appears to have anything other than οὐρήων, and even for Aristarchus or the scholiast, there does not seem to be a witness that he can cite that has the word he thinks it should be.

10.98 ἀδηκότες A and several of the oldest manuscripts have the rough breathing, but the majority have a smooth breathing here. A number of manuscripts report the reading ἀδδηκότες, which lengthens the first syllable (where length is required for meter).

10.141 ἐπὶ νῆας See above on 10.54.

10.142 ἀμβροσίην In A, ὀρφναίην is written in the margin next to νύκτα δι' ἀμβροσίην at this line (see Figure 1), and a thirteenth-century manuscript (Vaticanus Graecus 26, or V1) prints ὀρφναίην here instead of ἀμβροσίην. On the significance of the two adjectives and the variation we find here, see the general commentary in Part Three on 10.41.

Figure 1: Folio 128 verso of the Venetus A, showing an alternate reading for verse 10.142

10.159 ὄρσεο The manuscripts are divided between this reading and ἔγρεο. The scholia indicate that Aristarchus knew both readings. See the general commentary *ad loc.* for the significance of the variation and the attribution to Aristarchus.

10.168 τὸν δ' αὖτε προσέειπε In the margin of A the equally formulaic τὸν δ' ἠμείβετ' ἔπειτα (= 10.143) is recorded as an alternate reading.

10.169 φίλος In the margin of A at this line the alternate reading τέκος (cf. *Iliad* 23.626) is recorded along with φίλος. One of these two readings seems to be attributed to Aristophanes of Byzantium, but it is not entirely clear which.

10.180 ἔμιχθεν In the margin of A next to this line, a scholiast notes that at least one other manuscript has γένοντο here, and we find this reading in a number of manuscripts, including B, C, V1, and V16. We may compare *Iliad* 9.669, which has a similar construction: οἳ δ' ὅτε δὴ κλισίῃσιν ἐν Ἀτρεΐδαο γένοντο. γένοντο is yet another example of an alternate reading that, while lacking a majority of manuscript support, could very well be an authentic reflex of the formulaic system in which the *Iliad* was composed.

10.185 ὀρυμαγδὸς There is a general disagreement about the spelling of this word in the manuscript tradition. Many manuscripts spell the word ὀρυγμαδός, which in this line would be unmetrical. It would also be unmetrical in the most commonly found formula using this word, πολὺς δ' ὀρυμαγδὸς ὀρώρει, which fills the line from the weak caesura in the third foot to the end (*Iliad* 2.810, 4.449, 8.59, 8.63, and *Odyssey* 24.70). The Venetus A consistently spells the word ὀρυμαγδὸς except, interestingly, within the "replacement pages" (those nineteen sheets that replaced lost pages of the original): at *Iliad* 17.424, 17.461, and 17.741 the different and later hand that wrote these lines spells the word ὀρυγμαδός. Here at 10.185 in the Venetus A there is a smudge on the parchment that looks like it may be an erasure of a letter between ὀρυ and μαγδὸς, as if the scribe were hesitating between the two spellings. (A high-resolution image of this spot can be seen at http://www.homermultitext.org.)

10.191 The verse conventionally referred to as 191 (according to the edition of Wolf 1804)— καί σφεας φωνήσας ἔπεα πτερόεντα προσηύδα— is not present in the main text of manuscripts A, D, E4, T, or Ge. It is recorded in the margin of D and included in the main text of most other manuscripts. The verse is a common formula for speech introduction and therefore largely duplicates the purpose of 10.190. In *Iliad* 4.337 and 4.369 we find the same formula used in similar contexts, and in both cases some manuscripts and papyri lack the verse. West 1998 brackets the line in each of these cases. Yet the existence of these three examples suggests that the combination of this line with another speech introduction was, at some phase in the tradition, possible. After *Iliad* 9.224, several manuscripts add a version of this verse (καί μιν φωνήσας ἔπεα πτερόεντα προσηύδα, designated 9.224a). Although the main text of A does not include 9.224a, the A scholia comment explicitly that Aristarchus did not add this verse here, a comment which suggests the verse was known in antiquity. As Dué 2001 has shown, verses that seem repetitive and/or are particularly common were frequently athetized or omitted in Alexandrian editions, which favored shorter texts in keeping with the poetics of the day. (See also the general commentary in Part Three on 10.51–52.) The weak manuscript support for this formulaic verse may well be a reflex of the Alexandrian editorial tradition rather than evidence for interpolation.

10.203 τοῖσι δὲ μύθων ἦρχε In the margin of A next to this line a scholiast notes that at least one other manuscript has τοῖσι δὲ καὶ μετεέιπε here, a common formula for speech introduction (see e.g. *Iliad* 2.336 and 10.219).

10.221 ἐόντων The manuscripts are divided between ἐόντων and ἐόντα. A reads ἐόντων, but the alternate reading is also recorded just above the line. See Figure 2.

10.240 According to the scholia in A, this verse was omitted altogether in the text of Zenodotus (that is to say, it was not present in his text). It was present in the texts of Aristarchus, but he athetized it. See the general commentary *ad loc.* for more on this disputed line.

10.253 Like 10.240, this verse was omitted by the text of Zenodotus, while present but athetized in the texts of Aristarchus and Aristophanes of Byzantium. The textual controversy is alluded to in the *Argonautica* of Apollonius of Rhodes (3.1340–1341): ἦμος δὲ τρίτατον λάχος ἤματος ἀνομένοιο/λείπεται ἐξ ἠοῦς. As Antonios Rengakos has shown, Alexandrian poets like Callimachus and Apollonius of Rhodes displayed their learnedness by alluding to the variant readings of Homer known to them and to the textual problems encountered in the work done by the Alexandrian scholars on the text of Homer. On this very specialized form of allusion, see Rengakos 1993.

Figure 2: Folio 130 recto of the Venetus A, showing two possible readings for verse 10.221

10.281 ἐπὶ νῆας See above on 10.54.

10.291 παρίστασο καί με φύλασσε The scholia in A record that Zenodotus had instead παρίσταο καὶ πόρε κῦδος. The scholia here and in the margins also note that Aristarchus and others also spell παρίστασο without the *sigma*, but only Zenodotus is credited with the change in phrasing following that. με φύλασσε and πόρε κῦδος represent two different interests, both of which are part of the poetics of ambush. με φύλασσε indicates the danger involved, and even the need for teamwork, while πόρε κῦδος relates a desire for the radiant glory to be won by such success. Either phrase, then, is possible and appropriate from the standpoint of these poetics as well as the meter and the necessities of performance. Hainsworth asserts that καὶ πόρε κῦδος "is not a Homeric expression" (1993:184). The expression as such does not appear in our texts other than in the scholia, but both πόρε (*Iliad* 4.219, 16.143, 19.390; *Odyssey* 12.302) and κῦδος (*Iliad* 3.373, 4.145, 18.165) appear in these positions in the line in our texts, so the expression is within the realm of possibility, and we must keep in mind how limited our "database" for Homeric language is.

10.306 οἵ κεν ἀριστεύωσι θοῆς ἐπὶ νηυσίν Ἀχαιῶν The scholia in the A manuscript record three different readings by the three major Alexandrian Homeric scholars, which in turn all differ from this main text. The scholia say that Zenodotus read αὐτοὺς οἳ φορέουσι ἀμύμονα Πηλείωνα; Aristophanes read something slightly different, καλοὺς οἳ φορέουσι ἀμύμονα Πηλείωνα; and Aristarchus read οἵ κεν ἄριστοι ἔωσι θοῆς ἐπί νηυσίν Ἀχαιῶν. See the general commentary *ad loc.* for a more detailed interpretation of how each of these variations might operate within a performance tradition before a traditional audience.

10.318 μῦθον ἔειπεν This is the reading of A, but Allen lists twelve medieval manuscripts that instead read εἶπε παραστὰς (and one more that has that reading in the margin). εἶπε παραστὰς is a formula seen elsewhere in speech introductions in this same metrical position (see e.g. *Iliad* 6.75, 12.60, 12.210, 13.725, 23.155, 23.617), and so we must recognize that either would have been possible in performance and that performance variation is likely the source of this multiform. Such multiformity in our manuscript tradition, moreover, should caution us against making any sort of interpretation about why one formula or the other is used or drawing too fine a distinction among them. That is, whether or not we want to argue that in one performance the emphasis on the public, performative nature of μῦθος was significant, or in another there was significance in making Dolon stand, or stand next to Hektor, we must recognize that either was possible. Privileging one reading at the expense of the other (as one must in a conventionally edited edition) can distort the nature of this oral, traditional poetry and the way it does create meaning with its traditional language.

10.323 ἀμύμονα Πηλείωνα A tiny interior scholion in the A manuscript states: γράφεται καὶ ποδώκεα καὶ ἀμύμονα. That is, a version of this line was known to the scholiast where the epithet is "swift-footed" rather than "faultless." (Compare *Iliad* 8.474, 13.113, 16.281, 18.261, 18.267, 20.27, 20.45, 22.193, 23.35, and 23.793 for the formula ποδώκεα Πηλείωνα.) Because in either case the use of the epithet is what Parry has called "ornamental" (meaning that it is not directly called for by the context), Achilles could be called either here. And indeed, there are several other manuscripts that, according to Allen, transmit the epithet ποδώκεα on this line.

10.332 καί ῥ' ἐπίορκον ἐπώμοσε See the general commentary on this line for how interpretation may have shaped different textual versions of the line.

10.336 ἐπὶ νῆας A reads this (cf. 10.54 and 10.141) where other manuscripts are divided between ποτὶ and προτὶ (see on p425). ποτὶ is recorded as a variant in the margin of A at this line, while the correcting hand has written προτὶ in the far left margin of the page). See Figure 3.

10.338 ἀλλ' ὅτε δή ῥ' ἵππων τε καὶ ἀνδρῶν κάλλιφ' ὅμιλον According to Allen, a few manuscripts read instead ἀλλ' ὅτε δή ῥ' <u>ἕκτορα</u> καὶ ἀνδρῶν κάλλιφ' ὅμιλον, which introduces some metrical problems but makes perfect sense in the context, especially considering Odysseus' pointed question later about where Dolon left Hektor (10.406). Also on this line, the scholia in the Venetus A note that it is marked with a *diplē* "because now 'ὅμιλον' means the number and gathering of the Trojans. In the *Iliad* 'ὅμιλον' more narrowly names battle, and in the *Odyssey* it names a gathering" (ὅτι νῦν μὲν ὅμιλον τὸ πλῆθος καὶ ἄθροισμα τῶν Τρώων λέγει. ἐν μὲν οὖν τῇ Ἰλιάδι πυκνότερον τὴν μάχην ὅμιλον καλεῖ, ἐν Ὀδυσσείᾳ δὲ τὸ ἄθροισμα). In this comment we may be seeing an early concern about the "Odyssean" language in this book. See the essay in this volume, "The Poetics of Ambush" for explanations of the common language between *Iliad* 10 and the *Odyssey*.

Figure 3: Folio 132 verso of the Venetus A, showing three possible readings for verse 10.336

10.349–350 In A and all other manuscripts we find these lines, which describe Diomedes and Odysseus as speaking in the dual, even though only Odysseus actually speaks in our text. The scholia to A and T note however that in the text of Aristophanes of Byzantium and in others (ἐν μέντοι τῇ Ἀριστοφάνους καὶ ἄλλαις ἑτέρως ἐφέρετο) the text was as follows, including one plus verse:

349 ὣς ἔφατ᾽, οὐδ᾽ ἀπίθησε βοὴν ἀγαθὸς Διομήδης.
349a ἐλθόντες δ᾽ ἑκάτερθε παρὲξ ὁδοῦ ἐν νεκύεσσι
350 κλινθήτην

As we discussed above for the plus verse on p609 (see 10.432–434 there), these plus verses can be evidence for the composition-in-performance technique of expansion and thus should be regarded as a true performance multiform. In this case, moreover, the expansion is entirely plausible, since the "expanded" language here is demonstrably formulaic. For this version on 10.349, ὣς ἔφατ᾽, οὐδ᾽ ἀπίθησε βοὴν ἀγαθὸς Διομήδης, compare *Iliad* 2.166, 2.441, 4.68, 5.719, 5.767, 7.43, 8.112, 8.381, 11.195, 12.364, 14.277, 15.78, 15.168, 16.458, 17.246, 17.491, 17.656, 23.895, 24.120, 24.339 and *Odyssey* 5.43 and 22.492 for the same basic formula, with a wide variety of epithet + name formulas filling out the end of the line. Such expanded or compressed versions illustrate the flexibility of the traditional, formulaic language in performance, and either recorded version is equally appropriate.

10.362 μεμηκώς According to Allen, eleven manuscripts have μεμυκώς instead of μεμηκώς. μυκάομαι is a low, groaning sound—it is used for the sounds of cows lowing or bulls bellowing (*Iliad* 18.580, 21.237 in a simile for the sound the Skamandros river makes when ejecting the dead from his waters; *Odyssey* 10.413, 12.395), gates groaning open (*Iliad* 5.749 = 8.393, *Iliad* 12.460), and a shield resounding when hit (*Iliad* 20.260). μηκάομαι seems to be higher pitched, since it is used for the sound of sheep bleating (*Iliad* 4.435, *Odyssey* 9.439). It is used for the sound of various animals when wounded (*Iliad* 16.469, the horse Pedasos = *Odyssey* 10.163, the stag Odysseus kills = *Odyssey* 19.454, the boar Odysseus kills after it has wounded him) and of Irus when injured by Odysseus (*Odyssey* 18.98). Since both are used for animals being injured in an attack (in *Iliad* 18.580, the bull is bellowing as lions attack him), either may seem appropriate here, although we may expect the fawn or hare to have the higher pitched sound. This is a case where either choice may seem equally traditional and possible in the line, but the difference may also be a genuine copying mistake.

In these cases, we have to recognize both possibilities and acknowledge the limitations of the evidence for concluding one way or the other.

10.372 ἦ ῥα καὶ ἔγχος ἀφῆκεν, ἑκὼν δ' ἡμάρτανε φωτός· The lemma of the A scholion on this line appears to confirm that Aristarchus read ἀφῆκεν here, as do p46, p425, other unpublished papyri (1173 and 1174 in West's 1998 edition), and all manuscripts.

10.373 δεξιτερὸν δ' ὑπὲρ ὦμον ἐΰξου δουρὸς ἀκωκὴ p46, p425, and A read this, but most manuscripts have ἐΰξόου, which is unmetrical. The adjective ἐΰξοος is used in many other places in the *Iliad* and *Odyssey*, but it is almost always in the accusative. As here, the accusative version of the formula occupies the space before the bucolic diaeresis (cf. *Iliad* 2.390, 4.105, 11.629, 13.594, 13.706 and *Odyssey* 4.590, 5.237, 8.215, 19.586, 21.92, 21.281, 21.286, 21.326, 21.336, 22.71). There is one other place where we find the form ἐΰξόου, and that is at *Odyssey* 1.128: δουροδόκης ἔντοσθεν ἐΰξόου, ἔνθα περ ἄλλα. There, epic correption allows the –ου to scan short. Thus in 10.373 we may have an instance where the switch of a common formula to another case has resulted in an unmetrical verse, but one that may have felt natural to singers. The phrase ἐΰξου δουρὸς ἀκωκή is analogous to φαεινοῦ δουρὸς ἀκωκή (likewise in final position at *Iliad* 11.253 and *Odyssey* 19.453) and we also find δουρὸς ἀκωκή/η in this position at *Iliad* 16.323, 20.260, and 23.821. Finally, the metrically equivalent phrase δουρὸς ἐρωή/ήν occurs in *Iliad* 15.358, 21.25, and 23.529. As we can see from these examples, the choice between ἐΰξου and ἐΰξόου for a singer would have been intricately connected with the traditional phraseology of this particular verse, and no doubt the choice would have been made unconsciously but differently by different singers, depending on their training and experience with the formulaic diction.

10.376 χλωρὸς ὑπαὶ δείους· τὼ δ' ἀσθμαίνοντε κιχήτην Most manuscripts read ὑπαὶ δείους (as do p46, p425, and most manuscripts, including A), but there are a number of recorded variations, including ὑπ' αἴδους (D) and δδειους (T). See also the general commentary *ad loc.* for the traditional significance of this phrase and its relationship to the theme of ambush.

10.385 πῇ ᵖᵒᵘ δ' The text of papyrus 46 read πῇ δ' before it was corrected to τίφθ'. (See *ad loc.* on p46 and p425.) Another recorded variation (recorded as a variant in manuscript C) is ποῖ.

10.397–399 These lines were athetized by Aristophanes of Byzantium and Aristarchus, according to the A scholia. They are present in fragmentary form p46 and p425. When Dolon relates to his interrogators what Hektor commanded him to do during his spying mission, it is perfectly good oral style for him to use the same formulaic language used in the original command (compare these lines to 10.310–312). We will see again this same phenomenon on 10.409–411, where Odysseus repeats the information Nestor asked them to gather on their spying mission; these lines were also athetized. In this case, the Alexandrian scholars seemed to have an additional objection, which is that Dolon actually changes the person of the verbs in 10.398, as shown in the A text. That is, at 10.311, Hektor says he wants to know what *they* are planning among themselves and whether *they* are willing to keep the night watch, and in the A text, Dolon says to Diomedes and Odysseus that Hektor wants him to find out what *you* are planning and if *you* are willing to keep the night watch. But the pronoun σφίσιν remains in the line, causing a grammatical disagreement. One telling historical sidelight in these scholia is that there seems to be no direct information about Aristarchus' own motivations for athetizing: the scholiast says that in the tetralogy of Nemesion he found a statement saying that it is not possible to find in the commentaries of Aristarchus the reason for placing the *obelos* (the critical sign indicating athetesis) next to these lines. Such comments reveal the long history of scholarly attention to the text and commentary, and that our information about these aspects of the transmission is incomplete, to say the least. See also Chantraine 1937:63–64.

10.409–411 Each of these lines, which are also found at 10.208–210, have an obelos, indicating athetesis, and an asterisk beside them in A. The scholia there tell us that they have been so marked because "they have been unnecessarily transferred here from the speech of Nestor" (ἐκ τῶν τοῦ Νέστορος λόγων μετενηνεγμένοι εἰσὶν οὐ δεόντως). The Alexandrian scholars, including Aristarchus, tended to athetize repeated lines and any verses that seemed unnecessary or repetitive, a practice that reflects the poetic sensibilities of the Alexandrian period. See the general commentary on 10.51–52.

10.413 καταλέξω Reported here and in 10.427, p425 and some manuscripts (D, T, V16) is ἀγορεύσω, which West chooses in this line for his edition. (West prints καταλέξω, however, at 10.427.) The A scholia at 10.413 tell us that καταλέξω was the reading of Aristarchus, but that others had ἀγορεύσω. (There is no corresponding scholion at 10.427 in the A manuscript.) For the distinction between the two verbs, see above on p425 at 10.413.

10.427 καταλέξω See above on p609 at 10.427, p425 at 10.413, and A at 10.413. Manuscripts D, Ge, and T read ἀγορεύσω here (and p425 records it in superscript).

10.463 ἐπιβωσόμεθ᾽ This verb is the reading of the text of the Venetus A manuscript, and it is glossed by an interlinear scholia as "We will call on you for help." The interior scholia include a note that Aristarchus knew ἐπιδωσόμεθα instead, so that it would mean, according to the scholia, "we will honor with gifts." ἐπιδωσόμεθα is the verb in the text of the Venetus B manuscript, as well as several others. See also Chantraine 1937:64.

10.478 πίφραυσκε This is the spelling in A, but most other manuscripts read πίφαυσκε. At 10.502, A and p425 appear to read πιφραύσκων, but there also appears to be a cancellation mark over the *rho* in A. At 10.202, A reads πίφαυσκον.

10.502 πιφραύσκων See also above on A 10.478. Here the *rho* of πιφραύσκων appears to have a cancellation mark above it, which brings A into accord with most manuscripts. p425 appears to read πιφραύσκων.

10.531 The line known as 10.531, which is found in the Laurentianus (D) and several later manuscripts and is written in the margins of E³ and T, is not present in the Venetus A. (So also B, Ge, and a majority of the oldest manuscripts do not have this line.) See the general commentary *ad loc.* for more on how to interpret the presence or absence of this verse within the context of *Iliad* 10.

10.534 ψεύσομαι, ἢ ἔτυμόν τοι ἐρέω; κέλεται δέ με θυμός According to the scholia in the T manuscript, this line was not present in Zenodotus' text. The omission may be because of its similarity to the line found at *Odyssey* 4.140 and the feeling that it belonged there and not here. See the general commentary on this line to understand such repetition from the viewpoint of oral poetics. A includes the particle τοι, which modern editions such as Allen and West omit. The meter requires some exceptions either way: with the particle perhaps there would be synizesis in the final two syllables of ἐρέω to make it work.

10.539 ὀρυμαγδοῦ See above on 10.185 for more on the spelling variations of this word in different manuscripts.

10.570 πρύμνη This is the way A, and all other manuscripts according to Allen, spell this word on this line. But modern editions such as Allen and West instead spell it πρυμνῇ, shifting the accent and thereby making it the adjective rather than the noun. In his edition West credits Bekker with this emendation. But the switch to the adjective seems unnecessary, since we have other cases in which the noun is used in conjunction with νῆυς in the same case (e.g. *Iliad* 7.383: νηῒ πάρα πρύμνῃ Ἀγαμέμνονος "beside the stern of Agamemnon's ship" or, similarly, 10.35 above: νηῒ πάρα πρύμνῃ). To ignore the accentuation in the manuscript and make the change to the adjective is the modern editorial convention not only here but also at e.g. *Iliad* 11.600, 13.333, and 15.348.

PLATES

Plate 1a. White-ground lekythos, attributed to the Athena Painter. Polyxena at the fountain. Paris, Musée du Louvre, F 366.

Plate 1b. Achilles crouches behind a tree.

Plate 2. Black-figure neck-amphora, attributed to the Inscription
Painter: murder of Rhesos by Diomedes. Malibu, The J. Paul Getty
Museum, 96.AE.1.

Plate 3. Black-figure Corinthian krater (known as the Eurytos Vase). Detail: warriors with shields, archer at right. Paris, Musée du Louvre, E 635.

Plate 4. Red-figure cup, attributed to Epiktetos. Drawing of tondo: archer with shield. Boston, Museum of Fine Arts, 01.8074.

Plate 5. Red-figure lekythos: detail, Dolon in wolfskin. Paris, Musée du Louvre, CA 1802.

PART THREE

COMMENTARY

Commentary

10.1ff. The opening lines of this book follow what seems to be a traditional pattern in which a pressing situation causes an inability to sleep, which in turn results in the formulation of a plan of action. We can compare 10.1ff. to the beginnings of Books 2 and 9 for a more complete understanding of the workings and traditional structure of this theme. *Iliad* 2 begins:

> ἄλλοι μέν ῥα θεοί τε καὶ ἀνέρες ἱπποκορυσταὶ
> εὗδον παννύχιοι, Δία δ’ οὐκ ἔχε νήδυμος ὕπνος,
> ἀλλ’ ὅ γε μερμήριζε κατὰ φρένα ὡς Ἀχιλῆα
> τιμήσῃ, ὀλέσῃ δὲ πολέας ἐπὶ νηυσὶν Ἀχαιῶν.
> ἤδε δέ οἱ κατὰ θυμὸν ἀρίστη φαίνετο βουλή ...

Iliad 2.1–5

The rest of the gods and the men who wear horse-hair
    helmets
slept all night long, but deep sleep did not *hold* Zeus.
Instead, he was divided in his mind how Achilles
he would honor, and cause the destruction of many at the
    ships of the Achaeans.
This is the *plan* that seemed best in his heart ...

Iliad 9 similarly starts at night:

> ὣς οἱ μὲν Τρῶες φυλακὰς ἔχον· αὐτὰρ Ἀχαιοὺς
> θεσπεσίη ἔχε φύζα φόβου κρυόεντος ἑταίρη,
> πένθεϊ δ’ ἀτλήτῳ βεβολήατο πάντες ἄριστοι.
> ὡς δ’ ἄνεμοι δύο πόντον ὀρίνετον ἰχθυόεντα
> 5   Βορέης καὶ Ζέφυρος, τώ τε Θρήκηθεν ἄητον
> ἐλθόντ’ ἐξαπίνης· ἄμυδις δέ τε κῦμα κελαινὸν
> κορθύεται, πολλὸν δὲ παρὲξ ἅλα φῦκος ἔχευεν·

ὣς ἐδαΐζετο θυμὸς ἐνὶ στήθεσσιν Ἀχαιῶν.
Ἀτρεΐδης δ' ἄχεϊ μεγάλῳ βεβολημένος ἦτορ
10   φοίτα κηρύκεσσι λιγυφθόγγοισι κελεύων
κλήδην εἰς ἀγορὴν κικλήσκειν ἄνδρα ἕκαστον ...

Iliad 9.1–11

So the Trojans *kept holding* watches. But the Achaeans
were held by awesome panic, the companion of chilling fear,
and all the best men were struck by unendurable sorrow.
As when two winds stir up the sea with all its fish,
5   the North wind and the West wind, which blow from Thrace
coming suddenly, and at the same time a dark wave
towers up, and it pours out much seaweed alongside the sea,
so the heart in the breasts of the Achaeans was torn.
And the son of Atreus, struck in his heart by great sorrow,
10   went about telling the clear-voiced heralds
to call each man by name to assembly ...

The use of ἔχω 'hold' in all three passages suggests that even such a common verb can have a traditional poetic resonance in this context. The simile in 9.4–7 resembles the simile in 10.5–8 (discussed further below), in that both use an example from the natural world to convey a heightened emotional state. Whereas in Books 9 and 10 it is Agamemnon and/or the Achaean warriors who are in turmoil, in Book 2 it is Zeus who cannot sleep, as he turns over in his mind how best to accomplish what he has promised to Thetis in Book 1. (Agamemnon, by contrast, is sleeping soundly in this book, and the Dream sent by Zeus reproaches him for it at *Iliad* 2.23–24.) Zeus' sleeplessness in Book 2 is not elaborated with a simile, but there the emotional state being conveyed is not one of great sorrow and fear, as it is in Books 9 and 10. The sorrow evoked by the similes of 9 and 10 marks in each case the beginning of a change in plan that will lead to a nighttime episode, a sequence that is in keeping with the incendiary power of lament. (For more on the similes' associations with lament, see below. On the power of lament to spur action, see Dué 2006a:47 and bibliography *ad loc.*)

The three passages together give us a sense of both the strongly felt structure and the flexibility of the traditional system in which they were composed. In Books 2 and 10, a single individual cannot sleep. In Book 9, the whole Achaean army remains awake, but once the simile is complete the focus shifts to an individual, Agamemnon, who is of course the same sleepless individual being described in Book 10. The heightened emotional situation in Books 9 and 10 leads to a simile describing that state. If we postulate that Books 9 and 10 are possible multiforms of one another (see above, p. 13), each introducing an alternative narrative that encompasses the same dramatic night, then it is illuminating to note that they begin in much the same way, following a traditional pattern that expresses anxiety or fear and the resultant sleeplessness as a prelude to nighttime action. This pattern seems to be related, though not identical, to descriptions of the cognitive process that leads to a decision being made (characterized by the verb μερμηρίζειν, as in *Iliad* 2.3 and also on 10.503 below, on which see Arend 1933:106–115) and/or a plan being formulated, for which we find the use of the word βουλή at both *Iliad* 2.5 and 10.17. (See also *Iliad* 9.75 and testimonium 1 of the *Cypria* [Bernabé] and below on 10.43–44 and 10.302.) It is instructive to compare the beginning of Book 24, where Achilles, unlike the other Greeks, cannot sleep because of his grief. There, no plan is being formulated, and the scene makes use of virtually none of the formulaic language that we find in 2, 9, and 10. This suggests that, as Lord has argued on the basis of comparative evidence, formulas are closely tied to particular themes (Lord 1960/2000:49). (For further analysis of the relationship between Books 2 and 10, as well as 1 and 9, see Haft 1990 and above, "The Poetics of Ambush").

Although Achilles' sleeplessness in Book 24 does not follow the pattern that we have traced in Books 2, 9, and 10, there is a compressed version of the theme in Book 24, in which Hermes, like Zeus in Book 2, does not sleep as he ponders how to help a mortal. This theme appears after Priam has gone stealthily into the Achaean encampment to supplicate Achilles and ransom Hektor's corpse. After Achilles has agreed both to ransom the corpse and to enforce a cease-fire so that a funeral for Hektor may be held, Priam and his herald go to sleep in the forecourt (*prodomos*) of Achilles' shelter, while Hermes, who escorted Priam to the Achaean encampment, ponders how to get him home safely:

> οἳ μὲν ἄρ' ἐν προδόμῳ δόμου αὐτόθι κοιμήσαντο
> κῆρυξ καὶ Πρίαμος πυκινὰ φρεσὶ μήδε' ἔχοντες,
> 675 αὐτὰρ Ἀχιλλεὺς εὗδε μυχῷ κλισίης ἐϋπήκτου·
> τῷ δὲ Βρισηῒς παρελέξατο καλλιπάρῃος.
> ἄλλοι μέν ῥα θεοί τε καὶ ἀνέρες ἱπποκορυσταὶ
> εὗδον παννύχιοι μαλακῷ δεδμημένοι ὕπνῳ·
> ἀλλ' οὐχ Ἑρμείαν ἐριούνιον ὕπνος ἔμαρπτεν
> 680 ὁρμαίνοντ' ἀνὰ θυμὸν ὅπως Πρίαμον βασιλῆα
> νηῶν ἐκπέμψειε λαθὼν ἱεροὺς πυλαωρούς.

στῆ δ' ἄρ' ὑπὲρ κεφαλῆς καί μιν πρὸς μῦθον ἔειπεν·
ὦ γέρον οὔ νύ τι σοί γε μέλει κακόν, οἷον ἔθ' εὕδεις
ἀνδράσιν ἐν δηΐοισιν, ἐπεί σ' εἴασεν Ἀχιλλεύς.
685 καὶ νῦν μὲν φίλον υἱὸν ἐλύσαο, πολλὰ δ' ἔδωκας·
σεῖο δέ κε ζωοῦ καὶ τρὶς τόσα δοῖεν ἄποινα
παῖδες τοί μετόπισθε λελειμμένοι, αἴ κ' Ἀγαμέμνων
γνώῃ σ' Ἀτρεΐδης, γνώωσι δὲ πάντες Ἀχαιοί.
ὣς ἔφατ', ἔδεισεν δ' ὁ γέρων, κήρυκα δ' ἀνίστη.

Iliad 24.673–689

They there in the forecourt of the home bedded down,
the herald and Priam having schemes one after the other
[pukina] in their minds.
675 But Achilles was sleeping in the inner room of the well-built
tent,
and fine-cheeked Briseis lay next to him.
The rest of the gods and the men who wear horse-hair
helmets [= Iliad 2.1]
slept all night long, overcome by gentle sleep [= Iliad 10.2],
but not Hermes the helper—sleep did not lay hold of him
680 as he pondered in his heart how king Priam
he would send back from the ships without the sacred
guards of the gate noticing.
He stood over his head and addressed words to him:
"Old man, now no evil is a concern to you, seeing how you
sleep
among enemy men, since Achilles allowed you to.
685 And now you have ransomed your dear son, and you have
given much.
But to get you back alive they would give even three times
as much,
those sons of yours whom you left behind, if Agamemnon
the son of Atreus were to recognize you, and all the
Achaeans recognize you."
So he spoke, and the old man was afraid and he got the
herald up.

We find the same traditional language in 24.677–678 as we see in *Iliad* 2.1 and *Iliad* 10.2, respectively. One god or mortal is sleepless while everyone else rests. We do not find the term βουλή here as we do in Books 2 and 10, but we do have the verb ὁρμαίνω at 24.680 to indicate the formulation of a plan. The same verb is used at 10.4, as Agamemnon ponders many things in a state of sleeplessness. The astonishing situation in which this theme appears (that is, Priam sleeping among the enemy and needing to get out without the guards noticing or anyone recognizing him) may also have more in common with the plan that is ultimately formulated here in Book 10, an infiltration of the enemy camp. In other words, Hermes ponders how to achieve the all-important return to one's own camp. Priam's secret expedition to Achilles has much in common with the theme of a spying mission, including the need for stealth, the eluding of guards, and danger in general. If Priam is caught, Hermes tells him, he will need to be ransomed just as he ransomed Hektor from the enemy. We can compare this exchange to Dolon's offer that his father will ransom him, which he makes to Diomedes and Odysseus after they have captured him (see below on 10.378–381). The thematic association between Priam's situation and other nighttime missions for spying or ambush may help us to better understand 24.674, where Priam and his herald are described as "having schemes one after another in their minds." Though it is Hermes who comes up with the plan and ensures their safe homecoming, the words πυκινὰ and μήδεα are so associated with this kind of action (see below on 10.5–9) that Priam and the herald are credited with them even though they go to sleep in the middle of their mission (cf. *Iliad* 24.282 for the use of this same phrase at the beginning of their mission). For a discussion of the poetic implications of other instances of the word *pukinos* in *Iliad* 24 see Lynn-George 1988:230–233 and 240.

10.2 εὖδον In Homeric diction, past tense verbs frequently lack the past tense augment of later Greek. For more on the augment in Homer see on 10.47 below.

10.3 Ἀτρείδην Ἀγαμέμνονα ποιμένα λαῶν The epithet ποιμένα λαῶν 'shepherd of the warriors' is used most often of Agamemnon, to whom it is applied twelve times in the *Iliad* and three times in the *Odyssey*. But the phrase is also used of Nestor (three times in the *Iliad*; three in the *Odyssey*), Menelaos (two times in the *Iliad*; one in the *Odyssey*), and a number of other heroes, including Diomedes, Hektor (see on 10.406), and, in the *Odyssey*, Odysseus. The traditional epithet is the subject of the first of Milman Parry's two doctoral theses published in 1928, theses which would revolutionize Homeric studies (see also above, "Interpreting *Iliad* 10"). Parry's early work on the Homeric poems focuses on the traditional nature of the diction. *L'Épithète traditionelle dans Homère; Essaie* *sur un problème de style homérique* (= *The Traditional Epithet in Homer*) does not propose that the Homeric poems were composed orally, but theorizes that their traditional diction was the result of a system that had developed over a long period of time. Parry demonstrates both the utility of noun-epithet combinations in the composition of hexameter verse and the economy of Homeric diction, which rarely has more than one way of conveying what Parry calls "an essential idea" in the same metrical configuration. The principle of economy is so pervasive that Agamemnon can be called "shepherd of the warriors" even in instances where his leadership is not being stressed. This type of epithet is what Parry calls "ornamental" (MHV 21, 123–127). Since the epithet is applied to multiple heroes, it is also in Parry's terms a generic epithet (MHV 64, 84–95). With respect to generic epithets, Parry says that the quality they express is one associated with heroes in general, rather than a hero in particular, and that the language is traditional and thus has a larger meaning for a traditional audience (MHV 137–138). Albert Lord has expanded on that idea: "The tradition feels a sense of meaning in the epithet, and thus a special meaning is imparted to the noun and to the formula ... I would prefer to call it the traditionally intuitive meaning" (1960/2000:66; see also below on 10.144).

Therefore we need not make a choice between Parry's groundbreaking revelations about the workings of Homeric diction and our appreciation of the beauty of this highly compressed metaphor, which names Agamemnon with reference to his role as the leader of the Achaean forces at Troy. As Parry's student Albert Lord later shows, singers working within an oral composition-in-performance tradition can expand and compress their narratives under the influence of variety of factors. (See especially Lord 1960/2000:99–123.) In Homeric poetry, noun-epithet combinations are the ultimate compression of a hero's story. (See Nagy 1990b: "A distinctive epithet is like a small theme song that conjures up a thought-association with the traditional essence of an epic figure, thing, or concept" [23], as well as Danek 2002:6.) For a traditional audience, these phrases conjure not just the present use but all previous performances, imbuing the language with what John Foley has discussed as "traditional referentiality" and "immanent art" (see especially Foley 1991 and 1999): "'Grey-eyed Athena' and 'wise Penelope' are thus neither brilliant attributions in unrelated situations nor mindless metrical fillers of last resort. Rather they index the characters they name, in all their complexity, not merely in one given situation or even poem but against an enormously larger traditional backdrop" (Foley 1999:18). Similarly, the metaphor of the shepherd is part of a traditional system of expanded associations whose more expanded implications are evoked even in this extremely compressed usage. (See Muellner 1990 and Edwards 1991:48-55.) For more on Parry's work on generic epithets, see our extended discussion of them in connection with the epithet βοὴν ἀγαθός at 10.283.

This particular traditional metaphor of the shepherd juxtaposes, as we so often find in Homeric similes, peaceful pastoral life and war. When the epithet is used of Agamemnon and other heroes, it places them in a category of warriors who are also leaders and rulers. When we consider the poetics of shepherds from traditional Homeric similes, we can see that the metaphor emphasizes their responsibility to the warriors who follow them. Note, as an interesting contrast, that the dream that Zeus sends to Agamemnon in Book 2 tells him that a man who is responsible for the *laoi* and has so many concerns should not sleep all night long (2.24-25), while here that same shepherd of the *laoi* is indeed lying awake and cannot sleep.

By bringing their leadership into focus, this epithet also connects the heroes to other war narratives in which they play the leadership role. We can see why Agamemnon's position as overall leader of the coalition at Troy attracts this particular formula twelve times in the *Iliad*. In the *Odyssey*, a poem that holds Agamemnon up as a negative exemplum for Odysseus throughout its narrative, the formula is only used of Agamemnon three times, and in all three of those cases Agamemnon is being remembered in his role as the leader of Achaean forces at Troy. Used of Diomedes, the epithet likely evoked for an ancient audience his role in the capture of Thebes as one of the *Epigonoi*; when it is used of Nestor, an association is made to the battles of the past that Nestor himself narrates at various points in the poem (see e.g. *Iliad* 11.668ff.). In this way the epithet has both paradigmatic significance, in that it places the hero in the category of leader, and syntagmatic meaning, in that it connects to specific expanded narratives about the hero in the larger epic tradition. (For more on the terms paradigmatic and syntagmatic, see Dué 2002:5-13.)

10.5-9 ὡς δ' ὅτ' ἂν ἀστράπτῃ πόσις Ἥρης ἠϋκόμοιο/.../ὡς πυκίν' ἐν στήθεσσιν ἀνεστενάχιζ' Ἀγαμέμνων This simile has been condemned by previous editors as bad poetry and used as evidence that Book 10 was composed by an inferior poet. In his 1900 commentary, Leaf calls various aspects of the simile "so confused as to be practically unintelligible," "a pointless comparison," "turgid and tasteless," and "an incompetent piece of expression." Much more recently Hainsworth calls it "overstretched, to say the least" and "the first example of much strained thought and language in this book" (Hainsworth 1993 *ad* 10.5–9). In many ways, the response to this simile is emblematic of previous approaches to Book 10 as a whole. The arguments made in the introductory essays of this volume as to why a new approach to Book 10 is necessary are especially applicable here. The prominent position of the simile in this book and its highly compressed structure, which, like so many Homeric similes, defies traditional literary criticism, make it an ideal test case for the approach we have taken in this commentary.

Similes can teach us a great deal about the system in which our *Iliad* was composed. Although similes were once thought to be some of the latest, least traditional passages in the poem, drawn from the poet's real world experiences (see e.g. Shipp 1972:7–144 and 208–222), we now know that this view is incorrect. The similes within epics, like the stories they narrate, have been shown to be traditional and to carry traditional associations that go far beyond the mere words of the similes themselves. (See Notopoulos 1957, Scott 1974, Moulton 1977, Muellner 1990, Martin 1997, and Tsagalis 2008:272–285, as well as Fränkel 1921 and Coffey 1957.) Often in epic we find very compressed similes whose fuller meaning would have been obvious to an audience raised in the tradition. A good example is the description of Hektor at *Iliad* 13.754–755: "He then sped onward, like a snowy mountain, and with a loud cry flew through the ranks of the Trojans and their allies" (ἦ ῥα, καὶ ὁρμήθη ὄρεϊ νιφόεντι ἐοικώς/κεκλήγων, διὰ δὲ Τρώων πέτετ᾽ ἠδ᾽ ἐπικούρων). Mountains and snowstorms have particular associations, some of which are common to our culture, some which are not. For mountains, there is of course the association of height. But what are we to make of the adjective 'snowy'? One possibility is that elsewhere in epic the flashing of armor is compared to the light reflecting off falling snowflakes, an association that would not perhaps come immediately to our minds. (See Janko 1992 *ad* 13.754–755 and *Iliad* 19.357ff.) But Edward Bradley (1967) has explored all references to snow in epic and found that the quality most often associated with it is "incessant movement," a phrase that aptly describes Hektor in *Iliad* 13. So while for us the idea of comparing a quickly striding Hektor to a snowy mountain is almost comical, for an ancient audience the simile, compressed as it is, would no doubt have made perfect sense. It would have been part of a more expanded set of associations with snow and mountains but also more expanded versions of the same simile. So while we have to reconstruct those associations, an ancient audience would have made them effortlessly while listening to the performance. An ancient commentator called the effect of this comparison "savage and fearsome" and something about it must have struck Virgil, who adapts the simile in *Aeneid* 12.699ff.

Combined with the snowy mountain metaphor is another one, that of a bird in attack mode: "with a loud cry he flew through the ranks of the Trojans and their allies." Leonard Muellner has examined this second part of the simile as an example of the way that epic similes and metaphors operate within an expanded system of associations. By comparing this particular instance of bird imagery ("with a loud cry" and "flew") to other bird similes in related contexts, Muellner is able to show that the narrator is drawing on conventional imagery depicting the rapid movements of mustering warriors and their horses—imagery that we can now see pairs well with a comparison to snow. (See Muellner 1990:68n19.)

The traditionality of these similes and metaphors, which are themselves micronarratives within the larger narrative of the poem, allows them to operate in a very different way from similes in the poetry of our literate, text-based culture. For interpreting Homeric similes, we are not restricted to the printed page as we try to elicit the implications of a metaphor—we have the whole of Homeric poetry and even beyond to guide us. If we return now to the simile that opens Book 10, how can we use the corpus of Homeric poetry to understand what significance it might have summoned for an ancient audience?

The idea being conveyed by the simile is the frequency of Agamemnon's expressions of sorrow (ἀναστενάχιζ', 10.9), which are *pukina* (πυκίν', 10.9). The verb ἀναστεναχίζω is related to other verbs of lament. In *Iliad* 23.211, Iris describes Patroklos as "the one whom all the Achaeans are bewailing" (Πάτροκλος, τὸν πάντες ἀναστενάχουσιν Ἀχαιοί; see also *Iliad* 18.315 and 18.355). στενάχω is the verb that describes what Achilles, having just learned of Patroklos' death, is doing when his mother finds him in *Iliad* 18.70, and it is also used for the antiphonal cries of mourners who respond to the solo lamenters at *Iliad* 19.301 and 24.746.

The cries of grief that accompany songs of lamentation are *pukina* because they come thick and fast, one close upon the next. In *Iliad* 18.318, Achilles' expressions of grief (στενάχων) for Patroklos are πυκνά, and, similarly, in *Iliad* 19.312 Achilles is described as grieving in a *pukinos* way (πυκινῶς ἀκαχήμενον). Sorrow in overwhelming abundance can also be thought of as *pukina*. In *Iliad* 16.599, πυκινὸν ἄχος takes hold of the Achaeans when Bathykles is killed. In *Odyssey* 19.516–517, Penelope speaks of the πυκιναὶ [...] μελεδῶναι that torment her as she weeps (ὀδυρομένην, *Odyssey* 19.517). The adjective *pukinos* has a variety of meanings in Homer, all of which are linked by the idea of frequency, density, or closeness. One of the most common contexts for the adjective is in the natural world, where it describes the lairs of animals or places where animals hide. While a connection between natural hiding places for animals and the frequency of one's cries might not seem elegant or logical, the adjective *pukinos* seems to link the two meanings so closely that it is difficult to ascertain which meaning is the primary one in the two extended descriptions of lament mentioned above. If we look at these passages more closely, we find that in both cases the adjective *pukinos* is elaborated upon by way of a simile.

In *Iliad* 18, the frequency of Achilles' cries are compared to the grief of a lion who discovers that his cubs have been killed by a hunter:

αὐτὰρ Ἀχαιοὶ

315 παννύχιοι Πάτροκλον ἀνεστενάχοντο γοῶντες.
τοῖσι δὲ Πηλεΐδης ἁδινοῦ ἐξῆρχε γόοιο
χεῖρας ἐπ' ἀνδροφόνους θέμενος στήθεσσιν ἑταίρου
<u>πυκνὰ</u> μάλα στενάχων ὥς τε λὶς ἠϋγένειος,
ᾧ ῥά θ' ὑπὸ σκύμνους ἐλαφηβόλος ἁρπάσῃ ἀνὴρ
320 <u>ὕλης ἐκ πυκινῆς</u>· ὃ δέ τ' ἄχνυται ὕστερος ἐλθών,
πολλὰ δέ τ' ἄγκε' ἐπῆλθε μετ' ἀνέρος ἴχνι' ἐρευνῶν
εἴ ποθεν ἐξεύροι· μάλα γὰρ δριμὺς χόλος αἱρεῖ·
ὣς ὃ βαρὺ στενάχων μετεφώνεε Μυρμιδόνεσσιν

Iliad 18.314–323

On the other side the Achaeans
315 all night long bewailed Patroklos, lamenting.
And among them the son of Peleus led off the ceaseless
   lamentation,
placing his man-slaying hands on the chest of his companion
with wails *that came thick and fast*, like a well-bearded lion
whose cubs a man who is a deer hunter has snatched away
320 *from the thick woods.* He grieves when he later returns
and he comes to many valleys searching after the tracks of
   the man,
if somewhere he can find him, since piercing fury takes hold
   of him.
So wailing deeply [Achilles] spoke among the Myrmidons.

On a conceptual level the comparison being made is between the grief of Achilles and the lion, but what unites the tenor and vehicle on a verbal level is the word *pukinos*, used in the simile of the woods in which both the hunter and lion lurk.

The association made between these two semantic realms of the same word occurs in the same way in *Odyssey* 19:

> "ξεῖνε, τὸ μέν σ' ἔτι τυτθὸν ἐγὼν εἰρήσομαι αὐτή·
> 510 καὶ γὰρ δὴ κοίτοιο τάχ' ἔσσεται ἡδέος ὥρη,
> ὅν τινά γ' ὕπνος ἕλοι γλυκερός, καὶ κηδόμενόν περ.
> αὐτὰρ ἐμοὶ καὶ πένθος ἀμέτρητον πόρε δαίμων·
> ἤματα μὲν γὰρ τέρπομ' ὀδυρομένη, γοόωσα,
> ἔς τ' ἐμὰ ἔργ' ὁρόωσα καὶ ἀμφιπόλων ἐνὶ οἴκῳ·
> 515 αὐτὰρ ἐπὴν νὺξ ἔλθῃ, ἕλῃσί τε κοῖτος ἅπαντας,
> κεῖμαι ἐνὶ λέκτρῳ, <u>πυκιναὶ δέ μοι ἀμφ' ἀδινὸν κῆρ</u>
> <u>ὀξεῖαι μελεδῶναι ὀδυρομένην ἐρέθουσιν</u>
> ὡς δ' ὅτε Πανδαρέου κούρη, χλωρηῒς ἀηδών,
> καλὸν ἀείδησιν ἔαρος νέον ἱσταμένοιο,
> 520 δενδρέων <u>ἐν πετάλοισι καθεζομένη πυκινοῖσιν</u>,
> ἥ τε θαμὰ τρωπῶσα χέει πολυηχέα φωνήν,
> παῖδ' ὀλοφυρομένη Ἴτυλον φίλον."
>
> *Odyssey* 19.509–522

"Stranger, I for my part would like to speak to you a little
  further.
510 For indeed soon will be the hour for going to bed, a pleasant
  thing,
  at least for anyone whom sweet sleep takes hold of despite
  their cares.
  As for me, a *daimon* has given immeasurable sorrow.
  I spend my days delighting in mourning, lamenting,
  as I look to my tasks and attend to the household.
515 But when night comes, and bedtime takes hold of all,
  I lie in my bed, *while thick and fast in my heart without end*
  sharp sorrows torment me as I weep,
  as when the daughter of Pandareos, the vibrant nightingale,
  sings a beautiful song when spring is newly arrived,
520 *sitting among the thick leaves* of the trees,
  and she pours forth her resounding voice in one song after
  another,
  lamenting her beloved child Itylus."

Once again the frequency of one's sobs and cries are compared by way of a simile to an animal in its haunts—in this case, the nightingale sings from amidst the dense foliage of trees. And much as in the description of Achilles, the point of comparison is the lamentation of Penelope and the sorrowful song of the nightingale, but what links tenor and vehicle verbally is the adjective *pukinos*.

We will return to the idea of the lair momentarily. For the moment though, let us note that here Penelope describes the impossibility of sleep when one is troubled by sorrows, a situation that matches the opening of *Iliad* 10. So too at the beginning of *Iliad* 9, no one is sleeping, including Agamemnon, who is "struck in his heart by great sorrow" (ἄχεϊ μεγάλῳ βεβολημένος ἦτορ, *Iliad* 9.9). He calls an assembly, and when he begins speaking he is crying:

> ἵστατο δάκρυ χέων ὥς τε κρήνη μελάνυδρος
> ἥ τε κατ᾽ αἰγίλιπος πέτρης δνοφερὸν χέει ὕδωρ·
> ὣς ὃ βαρὺ στενάχων ἔπε᾽ Ἀργείοισι μετηύδα

Iliad 9.14–16

> He stood shedding a tear, like a spring whose water flows up
>   from the depths,
> a spring which pours dark water down from a steep rock,
> so wailing deeply he addressed words to the Argives.

This passage recalls the iconic lamenter of Greek myth, Niobe, whose example is invoked by Achilles as he and Priam mourn for fathers and sons in lament-filled *Iliad* 24. Niobe in her grief for her twelve children was transformed into just such a weeping rock. (For more on Niobe as the prototypical lamenting woman in the *Iliad,* see Dué 2002:108–109, and on the metaphor of the spring, see Dué 2006a:160–161.)

We do not find the word *pukinos* in the initial similes of *Iliad* 9, as we saw in *Iliad* 18 and *Odyssey* 19, but these similes share with *Iliad* 10 their use of the diction, metaphors, and imagery of lament in their depiction of the sorrow of the Greeks (especially Agamemnon) and their resultant sleeplessness.[1] An explanation for the absence of the concept in *Iliad* 9, but its presence in *Iliad* 10, we argue, can be found in yet another semantic aspect of *pukinos*—its association with the *lokhos* 'ambush'. The phrase πυκινὸν λόχον is found three times in the *Iliad* and *Odyssey* (*Iliad* 4.392, 24.779; *Odyssey* 11.525). Ambush warfare is

---

[1] We may contrast the similes that describe the anxiety and sorrow of the Greeks at the start of Books 9 and 10 with the one at the end of Book 8 that describes the campfires of the Trojans as they make camp on the plain. The fires are compared to the stars on a windless, clear night (*Iliad* 8.555ff.; see Webster 1958:231–232). Scott (1974:51) notes that similes frequently occur at junctures in the narrative, and that those junctures often correspond with a change in theme, as is the case with the simile under discussion here at 10.5–9.

pukinos because of the cunning involved, and in fact cunning thoughts or schemes are *mēdea pukna* in Homeric epic. In *Iliad* 3, Helen describes Odysseus as the master of this kind cunning: οὗτος δ' αὖ Λαερτιάδης πολύμητις 'Οδυσσεύς ... εἰδὼς παντοίους τε δόλους καὶ μήδεα πυκνά ("That is the son of Laertes Odysseus who is crafty in many ways ... he knows all sorts of tricks and schemes one after the other," *Iliad* 3.200–202). Odysseus, as Helen's description implies, is our ambush hero par excellence. (Like cunning schemes, shrewd counsel is also *pukinos*. See below on 10.43–44.)

Later in *Iliad* 10 the plan that Hektor proposes to the Trojans (namely, to send a spy to the Achaean camp) is called a πυκινὴν ... βουλήν (10.302). (For similar phraseology used in Book 2 of Agamemnon's testing of the troops, see above, pp. 231–235.) As was noted above (see "The Poetics of Ambush"), ambush warfare is characterized by *mētis*, while the *polemos* is characterized by *biē*. For another collocation of *pukinos*, cunning, and ambush, we have the ambush of Bellerophon as it is described in *Iliad* 6:

τῷ δ' ἄρ' ἀνερχομένῳ <u>πυκινὸν δόλον</u> ἄλλον ὕφαινε·
κρίνας ἐκ Λυκίης εὐρείης φῶτας ἀρίστους
εἶσε <u>λόχον</u>· τοὶ δ' οὔ τι πάλιν οἶκον δὲ νέοντο·
πάντας γὰρ κατέπεφνεν ἀμύμων Βελλεροφόντης.

Iliad 6.187–190

But for him as he was going back he wove another *close trick*.
He selected the best men from broad Lycia
and sent them on an *ambush*. These men did not return back
   home:
Faultless Bellerophon slew them all.

One other element seen here (encapsulated in ἄλλον 'another') is that ambush is often used when other means to defeat the enemy have not worked. The king of Lycia has not been able to kill Bellerophon by sending him on various missions or into battle, so he resorts to ambush. A similar sense of desperation drives the plan formed here in *Iliad* 10.

Ambushes are *pukinos* for another reason as well, as we alluded to above: they involve hiding in dark, enclosed spaces, not unlike an animal's lair. In the story of ambush that Odysseus tells Eumaios in *Odyssey* 14, Odysseus and his companions hide in the ῥωπήϊα πυκνά 'dense shrubbery' before the walls of Troy. Here, we return to the similes that elaborate on the grief of Achilles and Penelope. In both of those similes, the word *pukinos* describes the place in which the lamenting creature seeks refuge. In another passage in *Odyssey* 19, the idea of the lair and the place of ambush are directly equated. In the narrative that explains the origins of the scar that Eurykleia recognizes, we find out that on a hunting expedition Odysseus was ambushed by a boar, who rushed forth from a λόχμῃ πυκινῇ and gashed his leg (*Odyssey* 19.439).

Two things remain to be noted. First, it is also likely that ambushes are imagined as *pukinos* because of the density of the men hiding together in a cramped space. The episode of the wooden horse, the *lokhos* (as it is termed at *Odyssey* 4.277 and 8.515) that results in the sack of Troy, involves many men enclosed in a small space. In the ambush of Tydeus narrated at *Iliad* 4.391–398 (called a πυκινὸν λόχον in 4.392), fifty-two men lay in wait for him. Second, a crucial aspect of ambush warfare (which usually happens at night in the cover of darkness) is the necessity of not going to sleep. Staying awake at night in a cramped hiding place surrounded by other men in a closely packed fashion is precisely the kind of endurance ambush requires, and all of these components are encompassed by the adjective *pukinos*.

This exploration of the adjective *pukinos* suggests that the conceptual realms of lament and ambush can be merged in this word. In the simile that describes Agamemnon's grief and sleeplessness, we find that there is no mention of an animal in his lair. Instead, the entire ambush episode that is about to unfold substitutes for such a simile, linked to Agamemnon's sobs by the word *pukinos*. (For more on the traditional referentiality of the word *pukinos*, as used in the phrase *pukinon epos*, see Foley 1991:154–156.)

There are still more parts of the simile that can be unpacked, once we understand the traditional connection between lamentation and ambush and the idea of frequency or closeness that unites them. The frequency of the nightingale's laments in *Odyssey* 19 (they come one right after another) is conveyed by the word θαμά at 19.521. The adjectival form of this word is used of snowflakes (as at *Iliad* 12.278) and, like *pukinos*, of projectiles (arrows, spears, and rocks) thrown in abundance and in quick succession. When Agamemnon's cries are compared to falling snow, the traditional resonance of the simile can be understood by a traditional audience. Both are θαμά. Similarly, in *Iliad* 3.222, Odysseus' persuasive words in the Trojan assembly are compared, in an extremely compressed simile, to snowflakes (νιφάδεσσιν ἐοικότα χειμερίῃσιν). For an audience on the inside of the tradition, this compressed simile would naturally draw on associations between the frequency and denseness of snowflakes and the close-packed nature of Odysseus' *mēdea* (which are called *pukna* twenty lines before).

Possibly related to the metaphor world of snowflakes is the metaphor in *Iliad* 4.274, where the mass of warriors following the two Ajaxes is called a "cloud of foot-soldiers" (νέφος ... πεζῶν). As Mark Edwards notes, the scholia on this line in several manuscripts explain that the metaphor is expressing the "denseness (τὸ πυκνὸν) and frightening aspect of the phalanx" by likening it to "a black and threatening cloud" (τὸ πυκνὸν καὶ καταπληκτικὸν τῆς φάλαγγος μιᾷ λέξει περιέλαβεν εἰκάσας μέλανι καὶ σκυθρωπῷ νέφει). (See Edwards 1991:48; the translation is his.) The lines following *Iliad* 4.274 actually go on to unpack the metaphor by way of a simile:

> 275 ὡς δ' ὅτ' ἀπὸ σκοπιῆς εἶδεν νέφος αἰπόλος ἀνὴρ
> ἐρχόμενον κατὰ πόντον ὑπὸ Ζεφύροιο ἰωῆς·
> τῷ δέ τ' ἄνευθεν ἐόντι μελάντερον ἠΰτε πίσσα
> φαίνετ' ἰὸν κατὰ πόντον, ἄγει δέ τε λαίλαπα πολλήν,
> ῥίγησέν τε ἰδών, ὑπό τε σπέος ἤλασε μῆλα·
> 280 τοῖαι ἅμ' Αἰάντεσσι διοτρεφέων αἰζηῶν
> δήϊον ἐς πόλεμον πυκιναὶ κίνυντο φάλαγγες
> κυάνεαι, σάκεσίν τε καὶ ἔγχεσι πεφρικυῖαι.

> *Iliad* 4.275–282

> 275 As when a goat-herding man sees from a lookout point a
>   cloud
> coming over the sea, driven by the rush of the West wind,
> and to him being at a distance blacker than pitch
> it appears as it comes over the sea, and it brings a great
>   tempest,
> and seeing it he shudders, and drives his flocks into a cave,
> 280 such were the young men nurtured by Zeus who were with
>   the Ajaxes,
> dense phalanxes moving into hostile war,
> dark, bristling with shields and spears.

Here a single word, "cloud," elicits an extended simile that conveys denseness by conjuring the image of a closely packed phalanx. But in what way is a cloud dense? If the simile were not present in our text, and we had only the compressed metaphor of *Iliad* 4.274, we might doubt the scholiast's interpretation. The key must be in the rain portended by the νέφος, which like hail or snow or Agamemnon's sighs—or indeed battle—is *pukinos*. This passage from *Iliad* 4 allows us to see the richness of this tradition, whose metaphors can be so highly compressed yet full of meaning for a traditional audience. So also does the adjective ἀθέσφατον, used to describe hail in 10.6, have traditional associations, in this case with abundance, but used elsewhere in Homer of rain, food, wine, and, most interesting for us, long winter nights (see *Odyssey* 11.373 and 15.392).

Finally, as Hainsworth has pointed out in his discussion of these lines, the phrase "the great jaws of destructive battle" (πτολέμοιο μέγα στόμα πευκεδανοῖο, 10.8) is a perfectly traditional metaphor (we can compare *Iliad* 19.313 and 20.359), but it is "unexpected as an alternative to rain, hail, or snow" (Hainsworth 1993 *ad* 10.8). The adjective πευκεδανός is found nowhere else in the archaic epic that survives, but the image, we submit, is unexpected and strained only for us—not for a traditional audience, for whom long-range connections of the kind we have argued for here are made on a subconscious level. Such connections are only possible within a traditional system, participated in by both performer and audience, in which meaning becomes possible with reference to the tradition. To put it another way, this simile only makes sense if we read it against the backdrop of the tradition in which it was created. It can be highly compressed because every word has resonance that links it to the other uses of that word in the tradition. Such a simile cannot be the work of an idiosyncratic poet trying to manipulate the oral tradition into a new, original style, as Danek, for example, has argued (see Danek 1988 and above, "Interpreting *Iliad* 10"), nor can we agree with Hainsworth that the metaphor we have just cited is "further instance of the pretentious usage of traditional language characteristic of this Book" (Hainsworth 1993 *ad* 10.8). In the system that created the *Iliad* and *Odyssey*—including, we are arguing, *Iliad* 10—the poet does not make use of tradition in an artificial way. When confronted with such a formulation on the part of scholars hostile to *Iliad* 10, it is instructive to consider the words of Albert Lord, who asserts that we must understand the poet to be working "inside an oral tradition of epic song":

> He is not an outsider approaching the tradition with only a superficial grasp of it, using a bit here and a bit there, or trying to present a "flavor" of the traditional, yet ever thinking in terms that are essentially different from it. He is not a split personality with half of his understanding in the tradition and the other half in a parnassus of literate methods. No, he is not even "immersed" in the tradition. He *is* the tradition.

Lord 1960/2000:147

10.10 τρομέοντο Zenodotus, the first head of the library at Alexandria and a well-known Homer scholar, knew of the reading φοβέοντο here, according to the scholia that survive in our medieval manuscripts, but the reading is not attested elsewhere. (The verb τρομέω is likewise used in the middle voice at 10.492. See also *Iliad* 6.151.) Hainsworth (1993 *ad loc.*) notes that Aristarchus, a successor of Zenodotus as head of the library and rival editor of Homer, asserted that "φοβοῦμαι and its cognates signified flight," whereas here φοβέοντο would have the Classical meaning 'fear'. Hainsworth adds the qualification "but that [Aristarchus'] doctrine may not be binding on this Book." Hainsworth's comment reflects his understanding of *Iliad* 10 as likely a later composition than the rest of the *Iliad* (see "Interpreting *Iliad* 10"). We suggest instead that φοβέοντο's lack of manuscript attestation indicates that it was not a particularly old or well-known version of the verse, but this is not necessarily indicative of the lateness of the entire book. A version with φοβέοντο may well have entered the formulaic performance language at a later phase in the Homeric tradition than τρομέοντο, eventually becoming part of the textual tradition known to Zenodotus several centuries later. The third-century CE Stoic philosopher Chrysippus (fragment 906 in the edition of von Arnim 1903) quotes this line with still another variation: περὶ γὰρ δίε νηυσὶν Ἀχαιῶν. This phrase is attested at *Iliad* 9.433 and 13.557 and is in no sense "un-Homeric," though it, like φοβέοντο, is not attested here in the manuscript tradition. These variations highlight the dynamic nature of Homeric diction, which evolved through time and was in a constant state of flux in its early stages. For more on the Alexandrian editors of Homer see on 10.51–52 below.

10.11–13 Agamemnon sees and hears that the Trojans are also awake, and this fact is confirmed later at 10.299–300. These lines convey a nighttime sensory experience: Agamemnon can see the fires, and he marvels at their number, indicating his anxiety at how large the Trojan army seems. The noise he hears reinforces that anxiety. Agamemnon's perception of the playing of music may make the Trojans seem more relaxed—they are not fearful for their destruction, at least in Agamemnon's imagination. (The Trojans are portrayed as noisy in contrast to the silent Achaeans at *Iliad* 3.1–9, 4.429–438, later in Book 10, and elsewhere, so these lines may also reinforce that common characteristic.) Seeing and hearing the Trojan camp from Agamemnon's perspective provides additional insight into the concerns that keep him sleepless. Sensory experiences in the dark call for interpretation in a way that daytime experiences do not: because the sense of sight is limited, the fires are visible, but Agamemnon cannot see any further detail that would let him know what is happening near those fires. Hearing becomes much more important at night, but at this point, what he hears only seems to tell Agamemnon that the Trojans are awake, and perhaps that they are relaxed. These perceptions combine to provide a contrast to the Achaean camp, which is silent now. One motivation for nighttime spying raids, as we will see in more detail below, is that each side is guessing what the other will do, and they send out spies to confirm those guesses.

10.12 πυρὰ πολλὰ τὰ καίετο These fires that Agamemnon wonders at now were ordered by Hektor to be set earlier in the evening (see *Iliad* 8.507–511). In his orders Hektor says that he wants the fires to burn all night long specifically so that he can see if the Achaeans are trying to sail away and thus escape the total destruction he wants to inflict on them. In other words, Hektor, too, is trying to see the enemy in the dark. It is this same motive that prompts Hektor to send a spy (see 10.311), and such details show continuity between the events of the narrative at the end of the day in earlier books and what happens here in Book 10. We also hear in *Iliad* 8.562–565 that the Trojans set a thousand fires, each of which has fifty men and their horses and chariots around it. We can therefore imagine the magnitude of the scene Agamemnon is gazing at here and understand why it inspires his anxiety.

Dan Petegorsky (1982:47ff., 179) argues that there is a connection between these fires and the "atmospheric activity of Zeus alluded to in the simile" at 10.5–9. Both are visible signs, he contends, of "Zeus' hostility towards the Achaeans, concrete tokens of Hector's threat to bring fire against the Achaean camp and ships" (Petegorsky 1982:179). In the interaction between simile and narrative that Petegorsky perceives, we can also add this divine dimension to Agamemnon's fears. That is, the lightening of Zeus not only reflects the storminess of Agamemnon's worried mind, but also represents a further reason for him to indeed be anxious on this night.

10.12 Ἰλιόθι πρὸ In a very early stage of the Greek language, prepositions were adverbs, and their placement is thus far more flexible in Homeric Greek than in Classical Greek. Here πρὸ is strictly adverbial. It is thought that tmesis, the separation of a prepositional prefix from its verb, ceased to be part of the spoken/written language before the Greek of the Linear B tablets (i.e. the thirteenth century BCE) but remained an important part of epic diction because of its deeply ingrained presence in the formulaic system and the flexibility it offered for the creation of new formulas (Horrocks 1997:201). The ending -θι of Ἰλιόθι is locative, a vestige of the Mycenaean Greek case system (attested in Linear B). (On the whole phrase see Chantraine 1988, *GH* I §112.)

10.17 βουλή See on 10.43–44 below.

10.18 ἐλθέμεν is an Aeolic infinitive form (Chantraine 1988, *GH* I §237). Although the language of Homer is primarily Ionic in nature, Aeolic dialect forms make up a considerable percentage of Homeric diction. Before oral composition-in-performance and dialect diffusion were well understood, a considerable amount of scholarly effort was devoted to finding an explanation for the mix of dialects (see MHV 326–327). In the 1880s August Fick ignited Homeric scholarship by proposing that the *Iliad* was composed in Aeolic Greek and later translated by Ionic singers into their own dialect, and he even went so far as to produce editions of the *Iliad* (1886) and *Odyssey* (1883) with the Aeolic dialect restored everywhere possible. Approximately fifty years later Milman Parry theorized that the oral tradition had passed through several distinct historical phases, one of which was an Aeolic phase. He argued that just as singers in the Homeric tradition would have naturally replaced older forms with more current ones, where meter and other strongly felt patterns allowed, but retained them where they did not, so also did Ionic singers, inheriting an Aeolic epic song tradition, replace Aeolic forms everywhere possible, but retained them where the formulas could not easily be adapted in performance. (See especially MHV, and on the theory of an Aeolic phase, see also Palmer 1962, Hoekstra 1965, Janko 1982, and West 1988.) So here the change of ἐλθέμεν to ἐλθεῖν (which is attested at 10.56 and various other places in the *Iliad*) would result in a spondee in the fifth foot (generally avoided in Homer, though not impossible). More recently an alternative theory has been proposed, namely, that Aeolic and Ionic epic traditions coexisted after the end of Bronze Age, but the Aeolic tradition was eventually assimilated into and eclipsed by the Ionic tradition in Asia Minor. (On this complex question see the overview in Horrocks 1997.) In any case, certainly an Aeolic tradition of epic poetry did flourish at one time, as is evidenced by such poems as Sappho 44 (on which see West 1973:191, Nagy 1974:134–39, Horrocks 1997:200, and Dué 2002:59).

10.19 μῆτιν The plan that Agamemnon hopes Nestor will construct is called simply *mētis*. In *Iliad* 9.423, Achilles had in fact advised the

Achaeans to come up with a "better *mētis*" (μῆτιν ἀμείνω), since he was not going to accept Agamemnon's offer. The plan that Nestor devises is to send someone on a nighttime spying expedition. Night raids and ambush warfare are linked in the epic tradition by their use of cunning or trickery (*mētis*) and endurance of prolonged hardship as opposed to the outright brute force (*biē*) of the battlefield (Edwards 1985:18 and above, "The Poetics of Ambush"). Many of the ambushes that are mentioned in epic occur at night: see e.g. *Iliad* 21.34–39 and *Odyssey* 14.468–503. Diomedes will be the hero who volunteers for this particular raid (10.219ff.), and he chooses as his companion Odysseus (10.243), the hero of *mētis*-style warfare. (For more on the relationship between Diomedes and Odysseus, see below on 10.243.)

10.21 ἔνδυνε περὶ στήθεσσι χιτῶνα Here begins the first dressing scene of the book, which, as we have argued above (see "The Poetics of Ambush"), signals to the audience an entry into the narrative world of the night raid/ambush. The animal skins and other unusual items that the heroes put on seem to be special features of this type of story, and serve a practical purpose as well. The skins and leather caps are the equivalent of camouflage, a necessary precaution in warfare of this type. (See also below on κυνέην, 10.257.) We can compare what Agamemnon puts on here to his dressing scene in *Iliad* 2.42–46, where, of course, no night raid will take place:

> ... μαλακὸν δ' ἔνδυνε χιτῶνα
> καλὸν νηγάτεον, περὶ δὲ μέγα βάλλετο φᾶρος·
> ποσσὶ δ' ὑπὸ λιπαροῖσιν ἐδήσατο καλὰ πέδιλα,
> ἀμφὶ δ' ἄρ' ὤμοισιν βάλετο ξίφος ἀργυρόηλον·
> εἵλετο δὲ σκῆπτρον πατρώϊον ἄφθιτον αἰεὶ

Iliad 2.42–46

> He put on a soft *khiton*,
> fine and newly made, and put around himself a great cloak.
> Under his shining feet he fastened fine sandals
> and around his shoulders he placed a silver-studded sword.
> He took up the ancestral scepter which is always unwilting.

In *Iliad* 2, Agamemnon dresses for an assembly; in *Iliad* 10, he dresses for a night raid. Of course, ultimately it will be Diomedes and Odysseus who go on the raid, but this first dressing scene and those that follow set the stage for what is to come, signaling to the audience our entry into the narrative world of the night raid. (See also on 10.254–272.)

In this book, each hero dresses for a night raid, and each hero has his own particular outfit with no doubt its own particular associations in the tradition. (See Reinhardt 1961:247.) Each subsequent dressing scene (there are five) builds our anticipation for the expedition to come. Agamemnon here fittingly puts on the red-gold skin of a large lion, and it seems that, even apart from the resonance of so many lion similes in epic, Agamemnon and Mycenae were especially linked with lions. Several artifacts featuring lions, including the monumental gateway to the citadel, grave steles, seals, and ceremonial daggers, have been excavated at Mycenae. From the Classical period, we can compare the rich lion imagery and metaphors in Aeschylus' *Oresteia* (see e.g. *Agamemnon* 716–736, 821–828, 1223–1226, 1258–1260, *Libation Bearers* 935–938). Nevertheless, other heroes do wear lion skins, including, in this book, Diomedes (10.177), but also, most famously, Herakles, who wears the skin of the Nemean lion obtained during the traditional first of his twelve labors.

10.25 See above at 10.1ff on the use of the verb ἔχε here. Verses 25–31 are a much more compressed version of the theme of the inability to sleep that leads to nighttime action, and they parallel the structure of 10.1–24.

10.29 παρδαλέῃ μὲν πρῶτα μετάφρενον εὐρὺ κάλυψε In this second of the dressing scenes, Menelaos puts on a leopard skin. Outside of Book 10, the only hero who wears an animal skin is Paris, who likewise wears a leopard skin at *Iliad* 3.17 when he makes his challenge to the Achaeans. In that encounter, Menelaos does not wear an animal skin, but it is telling that, in the same passage, Menelaos is compared in a simile to a lion that suddenly finds the body of an animal to eat (*Iliad* 3.23–26). Because of the way that duel comes to an end (Paris is ultimately whisked away to safety by Aphrodite), there is no chance for Menelaos to strip him and take the skin as spoils. Instead, Menelaos' dressing scene here makes him parallel to Paris, Helen's other husband. The two husbands have other common traits as well. As we will see below, Menelaos has a tendency to "give way" (10.121). This tendency is shared by this other younger brother of a leader (it is likewise his brother Hektor who describes Paris as one who gives way, *Iliad* 6.521–523). The connections between the two are a good example of what John Foley calls "traditional referentiality," which is the kind of meaning made possible by tradition for an audience on the inside of that tradition.

We should also note that Paris, our other wearer of leopard skin, has associations with ambush. He fights even in daytime battle as an ambushing archer (in *Iliad* 11 he wounds Diomedes, Machaon, and Eurupylos with his arrows), and, as we have explored above (see pp. 57–61), archery and ambush are conceptually and even visually linked. On the alterity of archer figures, see also Lissarrague 1990:13–34. On attitudes toward archery in the *Iliad*, see also Farron 2003, who disputes Lorimer's (1950:289–305) claim that archery is lower class and ineffective. In several (primarily late) accounts of Achilles' death, Paris ambushes him in the sanctuary of Thymbraion when he comes, unarmed, to arrange his marriage to Polyxena. (See Dictys of Crete 3.2ff, Dares 27, Hyginus 110, and Philostratus *Heroikos* 51.1. with Burgess 1995.) These late sources may preserve a vestige of a tradition about Achilles' death at the hands of Paris by archery and ambush. At the very least, surviving evidence (including what we know of the now lost *Aithiopis*) indicates that in Archaic myth Achilles died after receiving an arrow wound to the ankle (Burgess 1995:225). It may be that Paris' leopard skin is an iconographic sign of his archer status (cf. Naiden 1999: "Like the leopard, archery is crucial yet marginal, inferior yet effective" [200]), and the overlap between the conceptual realms of archery and ambush warfare, which we have explored in detail in "The Poetics of Ambush," might explain why Paris wears a leopard skin even in a non-ambush context.

10.30 ποικίλη The leopard skin is further described as *poikilos*, which in this case has meaning for its physical qualities: the spotted pattern makes it "intricate." But, as we saw with the wide semantic range of *pukinos*, which joins many concepts that might seem quite disparate at first to us, so also in the case of *poikilos* there is another important meaning here. As Detienne and Vernant (1974/1978) have shown, there is an association of this word with *mētis* and with trickery ("la ruse"). In this way, too, the leopard skin in particular shares common associations with ambush. For more on *mētis* and ambush, see above on 10.19 and below on 10.43–44.

10.30–31 αὐτὰρ ἐπὶ στεφάνην κεφαλῆφιν ἀείρας / θήκατο χαλκείην Menelaos wears a helmet that is unsuited to a spying mission or ambush. It is bronze, which, as we hear about the spear points in Diomedes' encampment, shines even through the dark of night (see 10.152–154). Such armament is a liability, therefore, to stealth and to remaining undetected in the dark (see more on 10.257). Diomedes,

Odysseus, and Dolon all wear leather caps to protect their heads on these missions (10.257–259, 10.261–265, 10.335). Although Menelaos is involved in other ambushes within the epic tradition, this subtle detail of his chosen dress here may indicate to a traditional audience that Menelaos is not going to be chosen for this expedition. We may note the anxiety expressed in Agamemnon's words to Diomedes about his choice of partner; the narrator explicitly states that Agamemnon was afraid for his brother Menelaos (see 10.237–240). In the *Odyssey*, however, Menelaos is portrayed as an ambusher: he is inside the Trojan Horse with Diomedes and Odysseus (*Odyssey* 4.280), he is one of the leaders of the night mission Odysseus describes to Eumaios (*Odyssey* 14.470–471), and he successfully ambushes Proteus (*Odyssey* 4.388–463; see above on pp. 72–73 for more on this ambush).

10.32 βῆ δ' ἴμεν This familiar Homeric expression is a good, straightforward example of a formula with a fixed metrical position. There is flexible variation within the formula: it can be expressed in the third-person singular, as here, as well as in the third-person plural (as at 10.297: βάν ῥ' ἴμεν), and it can use either the conjuction δ'(ε) or the particle ῥ'(α). But in the more than thirty uses of all these permutations in the *Iliad* and *Odyssey*, the formula always begins the line, occupying the first foot. Thus this specific way of saying "he/she/they went/left" can be assumed to have been particularly useful at the beginning of the line for the singer as he composed in performance. The formula gains additional flexibility with the use of the later Aeolic infinitive form ἴμεναι (the Aeolic infinitive form ἴμεν is earlier), which extends the phrase into the second foot. We see that version of the formula at least fifteen times. Another version of the formula with the Ionic infinitive form ἰέναι (so either βῆ δ'/ῥ' ἰέναι or βάν δ'/ῥ' ἰέναι) likewise extends into the first syllable of the second foot, and this iteration shows up at least eighteen times in our texts: see examples at 10.136, 10.179, 10.273, and 10.336. The only case in which we see this phrase in a metrical position other than the initial position of the line is when it is part of a longer formula, an example of which we see at 10.73. In this longer formula (which also appears in *Iliad* 20.484 and *Iliad* 21.205), the line begins αὐτὰρ ὁ βῆ ῥ' ἰέναι μετὰ and is completed by a name + epithet formula. This longer formula is used in cases of going after/for a specifically named person, while the various shorter versions can be used in a wide variety of situations of going, but always when the singer starts a new line. Because this formula is used seven times in *Iliad* 10, we can also see that many men are in motion during this night.

10.36 βοὴν ἀγαθὸς Μενέλαος See below on 10.283 for more on this epithet, which is applied in *Iliad* 10 to both Menelaos and Diomedes.

10.37 ἠθεῖε This word cannot be precisely translated into English. Its contexts suggest that it conveys both the affection and respect of younger person for an older one (as of Paris and Hektor in *Iliad* 6.518, Deiphobos and Hektor in *Iliad* 22.229 and 239, and Achilles and Patroklos in *Iliad* 23.94), or of a trusted servant for a respected master (Eumaios and Odysseus in *Odyssey* 14.147).

10.41 νύκτα δι' ἀμβροσίην We find night likewise described in 10.142. Ambrosia, the food of both the gods (see e.g. *Odyssey* 5.93, 5.199, 9.359) and their divine horses, is used by the gods for a variety of other purposes in Homer, including as perfume (*Odyssey* 4.445), as a cosmetic (*Iliad* 14.170), and as a preservative for the corpses of Sarpedon and Patroklos (*Iliad* 16.670 and 16.680, and 19.38). At *Iliad* 1.529, Zeus' hair is described as *ambrosios*, as is sleep at 2.19. In *Iliad* 18.268 and 24.363, night is again ambrosial. There is, as we can see, a wide range of associations for this word.

In 10.83, 10.276, and 10.386, the metrically equivalent phrase νύκτα δι' ὀρφναίην is used in the same position in the line. (See also on 10.142 below and the textual commentaries above on 10.386.) This phrase has a spondee where ἀμβροσίην has a dactyl, but both phrases occupy the same metrical space. νύκτα δι' ὀρφναίην is also found at *Odyssey* 9.143 and the *Homeric Hymn to Hermes* 578. Although it is not impossible to have two metrically equivalent formulas expressing the same essential idea, such duplications are rare in Homer, so we should expect the two adjectives to convey different things. The context of νύκτα δι' ὀρφναίην in *Odyssey* 9 is the ambush-like episode of the Cyclops (see above, "The Poetics of Ambush"), and its use of Hermes (whose nighttime thievery and cunning are celebrated in the *Homeric Hymn*) is likewise suggestive of an association between this word and nighttime escapades. Norman Austin (1975:71–73) sees ὀρφναίη as being particularly evocative of night's darkness, which is of course appropriate for both ambush and thievery. Night is in general ambrosial, according to Austin, because of the welcome rest it brings at the end of the day, but it is particularly so in the *Iliad*: "Night [in the *Iliad*] means the end of a day's fighting. It is relief from weary battle, but, more importantly for the Homeric hero, it means survival through another day." But the night of *Iliad* 10 is marked by anxiety, fear, and a raid on the enemy camp, hence the appropriateness of νύκτα δι' ὀρφναίην. (For alternate views on why night is ambrosial, see Hainsworth 1993 *ad* 10.41 and Heubeck, West, and Hainsworth 1988 *ad* 4.429, 4.445, and 5.93 with bibliography *ad loc.*)

Georg Danek (1988:80) has interpreted the alternation between the formulas νύκτα δι' ἀμβροσίην and νύκτα δι' ὀρφναίην as an intentional variation on the part of the composer of this book. (On Danek's arguments about the composer of *Iliad* 10, see "Interpreting *Iliad* 10.") Danek views the attempt to vary traditional phraseology as a hallmark of this poet's individual style. As we noted above, this approach is problematic from the standpoint of the methodology developed by Parry and Lord in studying oral traditions. It rests on the assumption that a singer within a traditional system would strive to "break free" of that tradition and compose in a new way. Austin's approach is helpful, because it finds two different ways that night can be characterized and shows how context affects the choice of either formula. Throughout his 1975 work, however, Austin himself seeks to counter Parry's demonstration of the economy of Homeric diction, and uses these words as an example of how the poet of the *Iliad* can achieve various literary goals, unconstrained by formulaic diction. But another way to look at it is to say that Austin's account of the different conceptualizations of the night enhances and clarifies Parry's arguments about the economy of Homeric diction, which Parry describes as "free of phrases which, having the same metrical value and expressing the same idea, could replace one another" (MHV 86). There is more than one way to say "night" here, because night is not a monolithic concept. When a poet wants to invoke night with its associations with relief and rest, νύκτα δι' ἀμβροσίην would be easily summoned. The night encompassed by *Iliad* 10, however, is of a different sort, and as a result, the formula νύκτα δι' ὀρφναίην is used three or four times. This interpretation seems strengthened by *Iliad* 24.363, which is identical to 10.83, with the exception of the formula for night:

> τίς δ' οὗτος κατὰ νῆας ἀνὰ στρατὸν ἔρχεαι οἶος
> νύκτα δι' ὀρφναίην, ὅτε θ' εὕδουσι βροτοὶ ἄλλοι,

Iliad 10.82–83

"Who is this that comes down to the ships through the
    encamped mass of warriors all alone
through the dark night, when other mortals are sleeping?"

> πῇ πάτερ ὧδ' ἵππους τε καὶ ἡμιόνους ἰθύνεις
> νύκτα δι' ἀμβροσίην, ὅτε θ' εὕδουσι βροτοὶ ἄλλοι;

Iliad 24.362–363

> "Where, father, are you driving your horses and mules like
>   this
> through the ambrosial night, when the other mortals are
>   sleeping?"

In *Iliad* 24, Priam is attempting to sneak into Achilles' camp during the night undetected; the formula νύκτα δι' ὀρφναίην would seem to be appropriate. (See above on 10.1ff. for more on how Priam's journey has thematic associations with other nighttime missions to the enemy's camp.) But the speaker of these lines is the disguised Hermes, talking to Priam in the form of a young man who should be unaware of Priam's mission. Accordingly, he uses the more innocent-sounding and divine νύκτα δι' ἀμβροσίην. Alternatively, we can interpret the absence of ὀρφναίην as significant within the system that generated the two formulas. As we have seen, the theme of the night raid/ambush attracts its own a subset of formulas, which are not typically found outside of this context in Homer. If Priam's expedition to Achilles, though it takes place at night, is not being characterized as an ambush, night is therefore not dark, but the more generic "ambrosial." (For more on Parry's principle of economy and the attempts that have been made to refute its applicability to the Homeric epics, see the discussion below of Odysseus' smile in 10.400.)

10.43–44 χρεὼ βουλῆς ἐμὲ καὶ σὲ ... κερδαλέης Here again we see a parallel with *Iliad* 9. Compare Nestor's words at 9.74–76: πολλῶν δ' ἀγρομένων τῷ πείσεαι ὅς κεν ἀρίστην/βουλὴν βουλεύσῃ· μάλα δὲ χρεὼ πάντας Ἀχαιοὺς/ἐσθλῆς καὶ πυκινῆς ("When many are gathered you can be persuaded to obey him who counsels the best plan. All of the Achaeans are especially in need of good, close [*pukinos*] counsel"). In 10.17, Agamemnon, after tossing and turning with grief and worry, comes up with a plan (βουλή), a sequence that, as we have seen, parallels the opening of Book 2. He decides that he will go to Nestor and ask *him* to come up with a plan (there called μῆτιν). *Boulē* is used therefore in several places in *Iliad* 2, 9, and 10 to denote a plan of action. As it happens, all three plans are conceived and carried out during the night, and it seems that in these contexts *boulē* is closely associated with *mētis*. (See also 10.302, where Hektor likewise conceives of a πυκινὴν ... βουλήν in a line that matches *Iliad* 2.55 in our texts. According to the testimony that has survived about the *Cypria* [testimonium 1 Bernabé], that epic opened with Zeus in distress about the overpopulation of the earth. It is unfortunately not clear from the context whether Zeus is attempting to sleep or if these thoughts are in fact occurring during the day, but the thoughts that lead to the plan he formulates, called βουλή in line 7 of the surviving fragment, are termed πυκιναῖς πραπίδεσσιν [3].) Here in Book 10 Agamemnon says that their plan must be wily (κερδαλέης); in Book 9 the adjective used is *pukinos* (as at 10.302; see also on 10.5–9 above). In *Odyssey* 13, Athena calls Odysseus "by far the best of all mortals in planning" (βροτῶν ὅχ' ἄριστος ἁπάντων βουλῇ, 13.297–298) and "crafty in intricate ways" (ποικιλομῆτα, 13.293). In *Odyssey* 22.230, Athena tells Odysseus that the city of Troy was taken by his *boulē* (σῇ δ' ἥλω βουλῇ Πριάμου πόλις εὐρυάγυια)—another ambush that according to epic tradition occurred at night. This is how Menelaos describes Odysseus in the wooden horse when he tells Telemakhos the story in *Odyssey* 4:

> ἤδη μὲν πολέων ἐδάην βουλήν τε νόον τε
> ἀνδρῶν ἡρώων, πολλὴν δ' ἐπελήλυθα γαῖαν·
> ἀλλ' οὔ πω τοιοῦτον ἐγὼν ἴδον ὀφθαλμοῖσιν
> οἷον Ὀδυσσῆος ταλασίφρονος ἔσκε φίλον κῆρ.
>
> *Odyssey* 4.267–270

> I have become familiar with the planning and thinking
> of men who are heroes, and I have traveled over much of the
>   earth.
> But I have not yet known with my eyes a man equivalent
> to my friend Odysseus' enduring mind.

The *boulē* of the wooden horse is arguably Odysseus' signature *mētis*, on which see Haft 1990.

10.47 οὐ γάρ πω ἰδόμην, οὐδ' ἔκλυον Note the augment on ἔκλυον. Egbert Bakker (2005) has argued that in Homeric diction the verbal augment has a primarily deictic function, and signifies proximity or immediacy rather than emphasizing a past tense. For this reason we find it used more often in similes and in speeches than in narrative contexts. In speeches, augmented aorists are almost always best translated as perfects (Bakker 2005:116, with further bibliography *ad loc.*). Bakker points out that the use of negating particles like οὔ πω with aorist verbs similarly "effaces the distinctness of any past, making it come into the speaker's present" (Bakker 2005:170). Indeed, our first instance of an augmented aorist in Book 10 is paired with an unaugmented aorist that is preceded by οὔ πω.

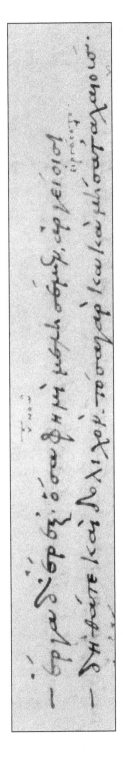

Figure 4: Folio 127 recto of the Venetus A with athetesis marks

10.47–48 οὐ γάρ πω ἰδόμην, οὐδ᾽ ἔκλυον αὐδήσαντος / ἄνδρ᾽ ἕνα τοσσάδε μέρμερ᾽ ἐπ᾽ ἤματι μητίσασθαι See also below at 10.289–290 and 10.524 for more on μέρμερα ἔργα. Agamemnon gives important details as to just what is "astounding" about what Hektor did on the battlefield. He has never seen or even heard tell of one man devising so many astounding deeds in one day. Hektor's deeds on the battlefield are unprecedented in Agamemnon's experience, and are of course the reason why he is sleepless this night. The language even juxtaposes the "one" and "so many": *mermera erga* are accomplished by one man (or two men, as we shall see) who kill many more. In the next day's battle, too, Hektor is reported to be accomplishing *mermera erga* and destroying phalanxes of young men (*Iliad* 11.502–503). On mourning the loss of so many men in one day of battle cf. Aeschylus *Persians* 431–432.

10.51–52 These lines were athetized by Aristophanes of Byzantium and Aristarchus, two great directors of the library in Ptolemaic Alexandria in the second century BCE. Aristarchus was considered the premier editor of Homer in antiquity, and the scholia that survive in our medieval manuscripts of the *Iliad* and *Odyssey* are full of references to him. As Gregory Nagy has demonstrated (see especially Nagy 2004), Aristarchus had available to him at the library of Ptolemaic Alexandria a great number of Homeric texts. Aristarchus' practice was to collate the many texts known to him and to comment on the various readings that he found, often asserting which reading he felt to be the correct one. Unlike a modern editor, however, Aristarchus confined his opinions to his commentary, which was published in its own separate volume. The notes in the commentary were linked to the appropriate passages in the text by means of a system of critical signs. These signs are preserved in the Venetus A manuscript of Homer, and to a lesser extent elsewhere (see Bird 2009). So here, although both Aristarchus and his predecessor Aristophanes did not feel verses 51–52 were composed by Homer, they left them in the text, and indicated their judgment with the sign for athetesis (see Figure 4). The scholia in the margins of the Venetus A tell us that Aristarchus condemned 10.51 because it repeats the content of 10.49, and because δηθά and δολιχόν mean the same thing. There is a tendency among the Alexandrian editors to disapprove of verses that they feel to be repetitive, preferring compression over expansion. This preference for compression is rooted in the poetics of their day (see Dué 2001a), and does not offer us good grounds for condemning the lines. But it is noteworthy that these scholars did not impose their preferences on the text itself, with the result that much more Homeric poetry survives for us today than probably would have otherwise.

10.53 Αἴαντα The Ajax being referred to here is the son of Telamon. (See below on 10.110–113.) Evidence from the Venetus A scholia indicates that Aristarchus may have known a reading Αἴαντε instead of Αἴαντα:

> ὁ μὲν Δίδυμος τὴν Ἀριστάρχειον γραφὴν λέγει "Αἴαντε" δυϊκῶς, ὁ δὲ Τήλεφος λέγει κακῶς εἰρηκέναι τὸν Δίδυμον· οὐ γὰρ ἐπ' ἀμφοτέρους τοὺς Αἴαντας ὁ Μενέλαος πέμπεται.

> Didymus says that the Aristarchean reading is "Αἴαντε" in the dual, but Telephos says that Didymus has misspoken, since Menelaos is not sent to both Ajaxes.

This disagreement in the scholia about Aristarchus' reading may reflect an evolution in the meaning of the dual form Αἴαντε that has been noted by previous scholars. In some early stage of the Greek epic tradition, the dual Αἴαντε referred not to Ajax the son of Telamon and Ajax the son of Oileus as a pair, but rather to Telamonion Ajax and his brother Teucer (whose special fighting style is discussed above at p. 60; see Ebbott 2003:41–43 with references *ad loc.*) The dual form of the name that Aristarchus knew here would be perfectly appropriate in a time when it was understood to refer to Ajax and Teucer. In any case, at 10.228 the two Ajaxes (Αἴαντε δύω) volunteer to go on the spying mission with Diomedes, but it is not clear whether at that point both Ajaxes are volunteering, or whether it is the fighting pair of Ajax and Teucer. It is possible that the dual would have been understood differently by audiences of different periods.

10.53 Ἰδομενῆα κάλεσσον It is significant that Idomeneus figures prominently here among the chief heroes, since he is the speaker of the most explicit description of ambush warfare in Homeric epic. He and Meriones discuss what it takes to succeed in ambush at *Iliad* 13.266–294 (discussed above, pp. 45–47). Idomeneus and Meriones are from Crete, and Odysseus links himself to both Idomeneus and Crete throughout his "Cretan lies" in the second half of the *Odyssey,* including a tale involving the ambush of the son of Idomeneus (*Odyssey* 13.259–275). The alternative warfare of ambush, with its reliance on cunning and dissimulation rather than force, may have been traditionally a Cretan specialty or in some way associated with Cretans. Certainly in the *Odyssey,* mention of Crete functions as a narrative signal for the external audience, and possibly for the internal audience as well, since Odysseus seems to use these stories as a kind of coded message or *ainos* (*Odyssey* 14.508), by which he gauges the recipient's loyalty and character. Crete serves as a cloak for Odysseus' true identity as he carefully and cleverly sets up his return, just as, in war, heroes camouflage themselves for a nighttime spying expedition or ambush. (For more on the concept of the cloak and its connection to Odysseus' *ainos* in *Odyssey* 14, see below at 10.149.)

10.56 ἐλθεῖν ἐς φυλάκων ἱερὸν τέλος ἠδ' ἐπιτεῖλαι A night watch is explicitly set up in *Iliad* 9.80–88, where the guards assemble and take their post armed. There, we hear that the guard consists of seven leaders, each of whom is named, and each leader has a hundred young men with long spears. As we will see later (10.196–197), Meriones and Thrasymedes, named as two of the seven in *Iliad* 9 but given special mention here at 10.57–59, will join the leaders to deliberate about the plan, and, importantly, give Diomedes and Odysseus some of their armor. Back in *Iliad* 9.87, we are told that the guard takes up their post between the ditch and the wall (see further on 10.194). For more on the anxieties about the watch falling asleep, see on 10.98. See Singor 1992:403 for his arguments that the seven leaders of the night watch implies that the Achaean wall has seven gates, and that the adjective *hieros* is used here, as well as for both the gatekeepers of Troy (*Iliad* 24.681) and the walls of Thebes (*Iliad* 4.378), because defensive walls and the life-sustaining protection they provide are "sacred."

10.58–59 Ἰδομενῆος ὀπάων / Μηριόνης The relationship between Idomeneus and Meriones fits into an Indo-European mythical paradigm of the hero and his charioteer. In such relationships, the charioteer often loses his life, thereby saving the life of his more dominant other half. The concept of the *opaōn* is similar to that of the *therapōn* (defined by Gregory Nagy as 'ritual substitute'), which is what Achilles calls Patroklos in *Iliad* 16.244. In that passage, Achilles prays that when Patroklos returns to battle he have the power to fight on his own, instead of as part of the closely linked fighting pair that Achilles and Patroklos normally form. Instead, however, Patroklos dies (at the hands of Apollo, Euphorbus, and Hektor), wearing Achilles' armor and in many ways previewing Achilles' own death, in some traditions at least, at the hands of Paris and Apollo. (On *opaōn* and its application to Meriones, we are indebted to an unpublished paper by Ellen Aitken. On the *therapōn* as a 'ritual substitute' for the hero, as Patroklos functions for Achilles, see Nagy 1979:33 and 292–293. On the relationship between Achilles' and Patroklos' death, see also Burgess 1997.) The night watch seems to be led by younger men in particular, like Meriones here: is there a suggestion that they can better endure the sleeplessness? See further on 10.259 for the association between young men like Meriones and ambush.

10.60 βοὴν ἀγαθὸς See below on 10.283 for more on this epithet.

10.65 ἀβροτάξομεν There are two different spellings of this verb (found only here in our Homeric texts) in the textual tradition: ἀβροτάξομεν and ἀμβροτάξομεν. Sources are nearly evenly divided between them. West (1997: 229) points out that the form ἀμβροτάξομεν "offers the unmetrical sequence – ◡ –, but the difficulty is resolved by going back to an ancient *hamr̥táxomen." We might speculate, then, that the spelling without the *mu* came about because it seemed to solve the metrical difficulty by relying on a plosive + liquid exception to the rule that multiple consonants form a closed syllable (see West 1997: 220–221). In any case, ἀμβροτάξομεν belongs to the categories of older words West identifies that became unmetrical as their form evolved. They were preserved as part of the formulaic language even as these sound-changes occurred in the Greek language as a whole. The antiquity of this word could mean that concern about missing one another in the dark of night is a traditional idea, part of the poetics of night raids or nighttime spying missions.

10.73 αὐτὰρ ὁ βῆ ῥ᾽ ἰέναι μετα See above on 10.32.

10.73 ποιμένα λαῶν See above on 10.3.

10.75 εὐνῇ ἔνι μαλακῇ· παρὰ δ᾽ ἔντεα ποικίλ᾽ ἔκειτο Nestor and Diomedes are described in the state in which they are found sleeping by the others, with the result that each is characterized as a warrior of a particular style. Nestor is an old man and sleeps on a soft bed, but his weapons are right beside him, which implies that he is ready for battle at a moment's notice (see also 10.78–79). The battle gear that lies next to him is not the same as that he puts on to go out in 10.131ff. The shining helmet (10.76) would be inappropriate for a night mission (see below on 10.257). Rather, the armor serves to characterize Nestor as a warrior in his own right and give him distinction. Agamemnon here, as elsewhere in the *Iliad*, looks to Nestor first and foremost for strategy. At *Iliad* 7.325 and 9.84 he is Νέστωρ, οὗ καὶ πρόσθεν ἀρίστη φαίνετο βουλή

("Nestor, whose planning also before was manifestly the best"). Nestor orchestrates most of the events of Book 9, as he does here in Book 10. In Book 11, it is Nestor who sets in motion Patroklos' fatal impersonation of Achilles. On Nestor's role in the *Iliad* and in the larger epic tradition, see Frame 2009.

10.83 ὀρφναίην See on 10.41 above.

10.84 ἠέ τιν' οὐρήων διζήμενος, ἤ τιν' ἑταίρων The idea that someone would be out at night looking for a mule (τιν' οὐρήων) seemed odd to Alexandrian scholars, as it might to us. The A scholia indicates that Aristarchus athetized the line because of that word, suggesting that it should be some form of κοῦρος, to indicate the young men of the guard. Instead of assuming a mistake by the poet (as the scholiast does) or by a scribe, another approach would be to see if there are any traditional associations with mules getting loose at night. There are no examples in surviving Homeric poetry, but there may well have been in the larger tradition. In any case, mules are used in a variety of contexts in the *Iliad*, by both the Trojans and the Achaeans. (See *Iliad* 1.50, 23.111 and 115, 24.716 for οὐρεύς; the word ἡμίονος is also used in this book at 10.352 and throughout the *Iliad* and *Odyssey*.)

10.85 φθέγγεο, μὴ δ' ἀκέων ἐπ' ἔμ' ἔρχεο See "The Poetics of Ambush" on the sensory aspects of the night. In 10.67, Agamemnon told Menelaos to call out (φθέγγεο as here) wherever he went, which in the dark would serve both to wake up his comrades and let them know that he was their fellow Achaean and not an enemy. So here Nestor tells his visitor not to sneak up on him in the dark, but to call out to let him know who he is and why he is there. See also *Iliad* 10.139 and 24.170.

10.85 χρεώ As each hero is roused from sleep the theme of the great need the Achaeans find themselves on this night is emphasized. We saw in 10.43 that Agamemnon speaks to Menelaos of their need for a "plan," *boulē*, just as Nestor does in the opening of *Iliad* 9. Here, Nestor naturally asks what need has caused him to be woken in the middle of the night. In 10.118, he advises Agamemnon to wake up the Greek leaders, citing the "unbearable need" (χρειώ ... ἀνεκτός) that has come upon them. Likewise in 10.142 Odysseus asks what need so great (χρειώ τόσον) has driven Agamemnon and Nestor to wake him. Nestor asks him not to reproach them, since the situation really is that dire: "Such sorrow has come upon the Achaeans" (τοῖον γὰρ ἄχος βεβίηκεν Ἀχαιούς, 10.145). In 10.172, we find χρεώ invoked by Nestor once again, in much the same language as at 10.142: "An especially great need has come upon the Achaeans" (μάλα μεγάλη χρειὼ βεβίηκεν Ἀχαιούς). This theme runs throughout Books 9–11, as Robert Rabel (1991) has demonstrated. Rabel argues that each of these three books has a similar tripartite structure consisting of recognition of need, journey, and return and report.

10.98 καμάτω ἀδηκότες The meaning of ἀδηκότες can be easily gleaned from context, but its derivation is disputed. This formula appears four times in this book (here, 10.312, 10.399, and 10.471), but with the exception of *Odyssey* 12.281 nowhere else in the *Iliad* or *Odyssey*. (See also *Homeric Hymn to Apollo* 460.) Here is another instance of a formula closely tied to the night that has been seen by previous commentators and scholars as evidence of the book's unusual style. We have argued that *Iliad* 10 is essentially our only surviving extended narration of a night raid, and this accident of transmission makes these formulas seem more unusual than would otherwise be the case. If we examine the use of καμάτω ἀδηκότες in this book more closely, we can see why this formula would have been particularly useful for a poet composing a night raid, and for one composing this episode in particular.

We have already observed that the necessity of staying awake is part of the hardship that characterizes ambush warfare. This necessity, as it happens, is likewise an important component of keeping a night watch. Because on this night the Trojans are encamped nearby—which we have seen is a cause of great anxiety for the Achaeans—the importance of the night watch is heightened. It is vital that the Achaean watches not fail in their duty; they must not fall asleep.

In 10.312, Hektor proposes that someone find out if the Achaeans are keeping a proper night watch, or if in fact they are too worn out by the toil of battle to do so (καμάτω ἀδηκότες αἰνῷ). In 10.399, Dolon repeats Hektor's words to Odysseus virtually word for word, as so often happens in Homer when messages and information are relayed. In 10.420–422, Dolon reveals that the allies of the Trojans are not keeping night watches, and are instead leaving security to the Trojans, who have wives and children to protect. And so, in 10.471, we find that Rhesos and his men have done what the Achaeans must not do: they have fallen asleep, overcome by exhaustion (οἱ δ' εὗδον καμάτω ἀδηκότες). In *Odyssey* 12.281, Odysseus attempts to force his men to sail through the night, past the island of the sun god (where Teiresias had foretold disaster). The men refuse, saying that they are too worn out to do so (καμάτω ἀδηκότας ἠδὲ καὶ ὕπνῳ). It seems clear that this formula occurs naturally when the hardship of staying awake is added to the weariness of a day's toil, whether it be a day spent fighting in the *polemos*, or, in the case of the *Odyssey*, a day spent rowing at sea. (Cf. the simile at *Iliad* 7.4–7, which compares the relief that the Trojan soldiers feel when Hektor and Paris return to the battlefield to that experienced by sailors who, when their limbs are giving out from the toil of rowing [καμάτῳ δ' ὑπὸ γυῖα λέλυνται], hope for and receive a favorable wind.) It is not necessary to see these instances in Book 10 as idiosyncratic in their concentration, the work of a particular poet with his own personal and/or Odyssean style, as Danek and Hainsworth have most recently explained them. (See Danek 1988:84–86 and Hainsworth 1993 *ad loc.*) Rather, they are yet another example of the way that formulas and traditional themes go hand in hand.

10.101 μάχεσθαι With the use of this verb 'to fight', we can see that the anxiety is so great among the Achaeans that they fear large-scale attack, and not just a spying mission or an ambush. The fact that they have put seven hundred men on guard duty also reflects their concern that the Trojans will make an all-out assault at night. During the intense battle that occurs the following day, Agamemnon also wonders if the Trojans will stop fighting when night falls (*Iliad* 14.78–79).

10.102 Γερήνιος ἱππότα Νέστωρ See Frame 2009 for an in-depth exploration of the epic tradition about Nestor and how it is encapsulated in the phrase *hippota Nestor*. That Frame could write a work of nearly 800 pages on the implications of this phrase in the epic tradition reveals just how much meaning can be encapsulated in a single epithet. (See also above on 10.3.) Of *gerēnios* Frame writes (2009:600n189):

> In his separate epic traditions Nestor was a young man; only when Nestor was added to the saga of Troy was the figure of the old man created (cf. Cantieni 1942:87). The idea that at Troy Nestor operates among the third generation of heroes during his own lifetime is meant, I think, to establish a sharp divide between the aged Nestor (who is new) and the young Nestor (who is old); a middle-aged Nestor does not exist in epic as far as we know. It was perhaps to distinguish the old hero at Troy from the young hero in Pylos that the *hippóta Néstōr* of ancient Pylian fame became *Gerḗnios hippóta Néstōr* at Troy, if *Gerḗnios*, derived from *géras*, "privilege of the old," simply means "old," as forcefully argued by Bader 1980:55–56: note in particular *Iliad* 4.325, where Nestor, referring to his role as counselor and speaker (i.e. to his Homeric role in essence) says τὸ γὰρ

γέρας ἐστὶ γερόντων, "for that is the privilege of the old"; a full and convincing morphological analysis of the derivation of *Gerēnios* from *géras* has now been offered by Timothy Barnes in an unpublished paper delivered at the 2008 annual meeting of the American Philological Association.

The theory that *gerēnios* relates to the privileges of old age is strengthened by a notice in the Townley scholia to *Iliad* 16.196 that "some" have Γερήνιος ἱππότα Φοίνιξ in place of γέρων ἱππηλάτα Φοίνιξ. (Otherwise, the phrase is used exclusively of Nestor.)

10.103 Ἀτρεΐδη κύδιστε ἄναξ ἀνδρῶν Ἀγάμεμνον On Nestor's address of Agamemnon, see on 10.144 below.

10.104–107 Leaf suggests that these lines "are at least somewhat out of place" because Achilles has just refused to return. This statement follows his argument that it is obvious that *Iliad* 10 "forms no essential part of the story of the *Iliad*" (Leaf 1900:423). Hainsworth (1993, *ad loc.*) similarly remarks, "The open condition, implying the possibility of Akhilleus reentering the fray, is unexpected when such a change of heart has just been ruled out of court. A remote condition ... would certainly be more appropriate." Petegorsky states, "Nestor's reference to Achilles is curious; for it has the effect of conceding to Achilles the role of the hero who will put a stop to Hector, at the very moment when we would expect him to be suggesting an alternative" (1982:203). But, Petegorsky argues, Achilles' refusal has in effect made the situation revert to what it was before the Embassy, and this deference to Achilles as the only way to stop Hektor in fact shows how much the Doloneia takes part in the Iliadic tradition, both thematically and in its narrative momentum towards Achilles' eventual return (1982:177–185). The alternative strategy adopted in *Iliad* 10, one focused on *mētis*, spying, and ambush, will not change the *Iliad*'s traditional course of events, but will highlight through contrast the need for Achilles' strength to save the Achaeans.

10.109 ἠμὲν Τυδείδην δουρὶ κλυτὸν ἠδ' Ὀδυσῆα This line shows that, as we would expect, Diomedes and Odysseus are closely linked in the formulaic diction. For more on Odysseus and Diomedes as a fighting pair, see below on 10.243.

10.110–113 Αἴαντα ταχὺν The swift Ajax is the son of Oileus, as we see also in *Iliad* 14.520–522: Ὀϊλῆος ταχὺς υἱός· οὐ γάρ οἵ τις ὁμοῖος ἐπισπέσθαι ποσὶν ἦεν/ἀνδρῶν τρεσσάντων, ὅτε τε Ζεὺς ἐν φόβον ὄρσῃ ("the swift son of Oileus—there is no one like him for following on foot when men are retreating in flight, whenever Zeus sets a rout in motion"). In 10.112–113, Nestor is referring to Ajax the son of Telamon, whose ships are on the far end of the line (see *Iliad* 11.7–9). In 10.175–176 Nestor tells Diomedes to go wake up the son of Oileus, but the mission itself is not described in our text, nor is the mission of Menelaos to Telamonian Ajax (see above on 10.53).

10.116 πονέεσθαι There is a cluster of three occurrences of this verb: here, in 10.117, and in Agamemnon's response in 10.121. It is also used in 10.70, and the noun from which it is derived, πόνος, appears at 10.89, 10.164, 10.245, and 10.279. These words are also used for the hardships of (daytime) battle, but see our essay "Poetics of Ambush" for a discussion of the associations that "hard labor" has with ambush fighting.

10.121 πολλάκι γὰρ μεθίει Douglas Frame (2009:214–216) demonstrates that "giving way," especially in deference to his brother, is a traditional characteristic of Menelaos. In addition to here, the verb μεθίημι is used of Menelaos in two other places: at *Odyssey* 4.372 and most tellingly at *Iliad* 23.434, where Menelaos gives way to Antilokhos in the chariot race. Frame connects that event in particular with Menelaos' *nostos*, in which he displays hesitancy, lack of incitement, and a lack of *noos*. These same qualities will make him a poor choice for the spying mission: Agamemnon seems to know this, as we see in his fear that Diomedes will choose Menelaos based on status alone (see 10.237–240). As we have noted elsewhere (see 10.31), Menelaos is portrayed as a successful ambusher in the *Odyssey*, but that portrayal seems quite separate from his relationship with his brother, whom, as we have seen earlier on this night, he looks to for direction, even as he is the first to voice the idea of the spying mission.

10.133 χλαῖναν Nestor does not put on an animal skin, but rather an impressive cloak (*khlaina*). For the traditional language of these dressing scenes, compare 10.21–22. See also below on 10.149.

10.136 βῆ δ' ἰέναι See on 10.32.

10.137 Ὀδυσῆα Διὶ μῆτιν ἀτάλαντον This is not the first time that Odysseus' name is mentioned in *Iliad* 10 (see 10.109), but it is the first place that he appears in the narrative, and the first place in our text that he is given a description of any kind. Here and twice in *Iliad* 2, Odysseus is called "the equivalent of Zeus in craft [*mētis*]." Odysseus rivals the gods in this kind of intelligence, by which he engineers alternative warfare and the daring escapes that are his specialty in the *Odyssey*. One of Odysseus' most common epithets in the *Iliad* and *Odyssey*, πολύμητις (as at 10.148), likewise highlights this central aspect of Odysseus' character. Odysseus is the hero who takes down the Cyclops by a carefully orchestrated ambush, and the attack on the suitors is structured like an ambush in many ways. We have noted as well that the sack of Troy is an ambush, of which Odysseus is the mastermind. (For more on *mētis* in the Doloneia, see on 10.19 and "The Poetics of Ambush" above. On Odysseus as the hero of *mētis*, see above on 10.5–9, Haft 1990, and Holmberg 1997:14–15. For Odysseus' epithets in the *Odyssey*, see Austin 1975:25–53.

10.139 φθεγξάμενος· τὸν δ' αἶψα περὶ φρένας ἤλυθ' ἰωή Note the emphasis on the sound of Nestor's voice as he rouses Odysseus from sleep. On the aural aspects of this episode, see above pp. 62–68 and on 10.85.

10.141–142 On the theme of "need," see above on 10.85.

10.142 νύκτα δι' ἀμβροσίην In the Venetus A, the oldest complete medieval manuscript of the *Iliad*, ὀρφναίην is written in the margin next to νύκτα δι' ἀμβροσίην at this line (see Figure 5), and a thirteenth-century manuscript (Vaticanus Graecus 26) prints ὀρφναίην here instead of ἀμβροσίην. On the significance of the two adjectives and the variation we find here, see above on 10.41.

10.144 διογενὲς Λαερτιάδη πολυμήχαν' Ὀδυσσεῦ Nestor, who is the most diplomatic of the heroes in the *Iliad*, addresses Odysseus in connection with both his lineage and with two of his traditional epithets, thereby using an entire hexameter to address him. He does the same with Agamemnon in 10.103 (Ἀτρεΐδη κύδιστε ἄναξ ἀνδρῶν Ἀγάμεμνον), in precisely the way that Agamemnon instructs Menelaos to wake up the heroes in 10.68–69. And as with Agamemnon, Nestor chooses what is perhaps the most honorific of Odysseus' traditional epithets. In the *Iliad*, the epithet διογενὲς 'descended from Zeus' is applied to several heroes, including Patroklos (1.337), Achilles (1.489), Ajax (4.489), and Menelaos (23.294), but in the *Odyssey* it is restricted to Odysseus. πολυμήχανος, on the other hand, is Odysseus' distinctive epithet. It is used of him and him alone, and, with one exception, always in the vocative. That one exception is the signature description of Odysseus by Athena, who in the guise of Mentes tells Telemakhos that his father is on his way home, "since he is a man of many devices (πολυμήχανος, *Odyssey* 1.205)."

Figure 5: Folio 128 verso of the Venetus A, showing an alternate reading for verse 10.142

It is a testament to the economy of Homeric diction that other than the full verse phrase that appears here (and six other places in the *Iliad*, as well as fifteen times in the *Odyssey*) there are only three ways to address Odysseus in the vocative in our *Iliad*, each with a different metrical configuration: ὦ πολύαιν' Ὀδυσεῦ μέγα κῦδος Ἀχαιῶν (9.673, 10.544), ὦ Ὀδυσεῦ πολύαινε (11.430), and [ὦ] Ὀδυσεῦ (9.346, 14.104). This does not mean, however, that the epithets are without semantic weight (see especially the formulation of Lord 1960/2000:66, quoted on 10.3 above). The full verse formula is particularly flexible and can be used or not at a composer's discretion. Its contexts suggest that it conveys formality and respect. In the *Iliad,* the goddess Athena and the heroes Agamemnon, Diomedes, Achilles, and Ajax address Odysseus this way. In the *Odyssey,* Athena, Calypso, and Circe do, as do the shades of Teiresias, Agamemnon, and Achilles.

Diomedes, by contrast, does not get quite the same respect as Agamemnon and Odysseus. In 10.159, Diomedes is addressed as simply "the son of Tydeus." In *Iliad* 9.32–49, Diomedes is the first to speak after Agamemnon's address to the assembled warriors and is sharply critical of him. Nestor praises Diomedes for his abilities as a warrior and for his speaking ability but qualifies the latter: he is the best in counsel for his age group (*Iliad* 9.54). It seems that Diomedes is still too junior in relation to Nestor to get the full honorific address. Three times, however, he is addressed by others with the affectionate full-line formula Τυδεΐδη Διόμηδες ἐμῷ κεχαρισμένε θυμῷ (*Iliad* 5.242, by Sthenelos; *Iliad* 5.826, by Athena; *Iliad* 10.234, by Agamemnon).

10.145 τοῖον γὰρ ἄχος βεβίηκεν Ἀχαιούς See also above on 10.85. The sorrow (*akhos*) that Nestor cites here is of course ultimately the result of the withdrawal of Achilles and its disastrous consequences, and Nestor uses an equivalent phrase when the strife between Agamemnon and Achilles begins (see *Iliad* 1.254; see Nagy 1979:69–72, 94–95 for the equivalence of ἄχος and πένθος in Homeric diction). The Trojans have had a great deal of success in Achilles' absence and are now encamped on the plain. This sorrow is what keeps Agamemnon and Menelaos awake at the opening of this book. Likewise, in *Iliad* 9.9, Agamemnon is "struck in his heart by great sorrow" (ἄχεϊ μεγάλῳ βεβολημένος ἦτορ). Achilles had predicted that Agamemnon would feel sorrow (ἀχνύμενος, *Iliad* 1.241) when the Greeks fell dying. The *akhos* that Achilles experiences when Agamemnon threatens to take and then in fact takes Briseis in *Iliad* 1 initiates his wrath, which in turn leads to the sorrow of the Achaeans. Nagy has argued that there is a "pervasive nexus between ἄχος and Ἀχιλ(λ)εύς" in Homeric diction that is "integrated in the inherited formulaic system and hence deeply rooted in the epic tradition" (Nagy 1979:79). This *akhos* seems to be the root of Achilles' name, which Nagy etymologizes as *Akhí-lāu̯os 'whose host of men is sorrowful [= grieving]'. (See Nagy 1979:69–93 and Nagy 2004:131–137, as well as Palmer 1963:78–79 and Holland 1993.)

10.148 πολύμητις Ὀδυσσεύς On Odysseus' associations with *mētis*, see on 10.5–9 and on 10.137 above. *Polumētis* 'who is crafty in many ways' is one of Odysseus' most commonly used epithets. Other than Odysseus it is only used of Hephaistos (πολυμήτιος, *Iliad* 21.355), who is the god of a different sort of craft. (The English word 'craft', like the Greek *mētis*, encompasses both meanings.) Milman Parry says of this particular epithet: "δῖος and πολύμητις, for the audience, describe the Odysseus of all the epic poems which sang his deeds" (MHV 171). πολύμητις is one of the distinctive epithets of Odysseus, while δῖος is a generic epithet of heroes (see Parry MHV 145 for πολύμητις as a distinctive epithet, and MHV 84 for δῖος as generic). Parry writes:

> Epic lines without epithets would have seemed to them like a heroic character without his traditional attributes. But even now, who among those of us who have any knowledge of the legend has asked why Odysseus should be *crafty* in this or that particular episode? Just so, Homer's listeners demanded epithets and paid them no attention, showing thereby the same lack of exact observation that becomes a habit with the modern reader. And it is this lack of exact observation that explains uses of the epithet which appear to us unmotivated, because we look for their motivations in the lines where they occur, rather than in all the poetry Homer's audience had already heard before they ever heard him sing.
>
> Parry MHV 137–138

As we discussed on 10.3 in connection with the phrase ποιμένα λαῶν, the phrase πολύμητις Ὀδυσσεύς can be used of Odysseus even in situations in which he is not being particularly crafty; the distinctive noun-epithet combination is, to quote the formulation of Nagy once again, "like a small theme song that conjures up a thought-association with the traditional essence of an epic figure" (Nagy 1990b:23). The phrase is not without significance in an ambush context, however, because Odysseus is a pre-eminent ambusher within the tradition as a whole.

Odysseus is called πολύμητις just as he leaves his tent, which marks the beginning of what will become a spying mission/ambush episode that will prominently feature Odysseus' *mētis*. Once that episode is well underway, Odysseus will be again called πολύμητις when he interrogates Dolon (10.382; see also 10.488, where he handles the horses so they are not spooked).

10.149 ποικίλον ἀμφ' ὤμοισι σάκος θέτο Agamemnon and Diomedes each wear a lion skin, Menelaos wears a leopard skin, Nestor wears a *khiton* and *khlaina*, and all take a weapon (*egkhos* or *doru*), but Odysseus takes only a shield and leaves without putting on any outerwear of any kind. This seemingly mundane detail actually serves two significant narrative functions. First and foremost, it sets up the extended arming scene that takes place at the assembly, just before the raid itself (see below on 10.254–272). Odysseus' lack of appropriate gear here means that he will have to borrow armor at the assembly. Second, Odysseus' lack of an animal skin has an intriguing corollary the *Odyssey*, where, in one of his Cretan lies to Eumaios in *Odyssey* 14, Odysseus comes close to revealing his true identity, at least from the perspective of a traditional audience of epic. Odysseus describes how once on a cold night at Troy he went out on an ambush. All the other heroes were dressed for the weather, but he himself had no cloak, and had to come up with a clever scheme to get one from one of his companions on the *lokhos*. Odysseus' Cretan lie may well be playfully alluding to a Doloneia tradition, in which case the story is a coded verbal message (*ainos*) directed at both the internal audience (Eumaios) and the external audience, who will "get" the inside reference. Such a reference is possible if we understand the *Iliad* (including the Doloneia) and *Odyssey* to be co-existing oral traditions, evolving in conjunction with one another. (On the *ainos* as a coded verbal message in *Odyssey* 14, see both Muellner 1976:97 and Nagy 1979:234–237, with further reference *ad loc*.) On the multiple significances of the shield being "intricately patterned" (*poikilos*), see above on 10.30.

10.151 ἐκτὸς ἀπὸ κλισίης σὺν τεύχεσιν Diomedes and his comrades are so ready for battle that they are not even inside their tent. Agamemnon had earlier stated his concern that the Trojans might be planning a night attack (10.100–101), and the preparedness seen here may also reflect the same "state of emergency" that is also prompting the night meeting and spying mission.

10.152–154 ἔγχεα δέ σφιν/ ὀρθ' ἐπὶ σαυρωτῆρος ἐλήλατο, τῆλε δὲ χαλκὸς / λάμφ' ὥς τε στεροπὴ πατρὸς Διὸς Their spears are planted in a kind of palisade, perhaps as a defense while they sleep on this dangerous night, or perhaps so that they are easy to reach in case of attack. The shining of the bronze like lightning is a frequent image in Homeric poetry (see *Iliad* 11.66, which is also an explicit simile, and the metaphorical uses of στεροπή with bronze at *Iliad* 11.83 and 19.363, and *Odyssey* 4.72 and 14.268 = 17.437). In most of those cases, just as here, the gleam of the bronze has a threatening or awe-inspiring quality to it. That the bronze shines this way at night is suggestive in terms of what is visible in the dark.

10.159 ὄρσεο The manuscripts are divided between this reading and ἔγρεο. The scholia indicate that Aristarchus had both readings: ὄρσεο· διχῶς ὁ Ἀρίσταρχος, ἔγρεο καὶ ὄρσεο [A intermarginal scholia]; ἔγρεο· γράφεται καὶ ὄρσεο. διχῶς αἱ Ἀριστάρχου [T interlinear scholia]. This is possible because two separate editions or *ekdoseis* of the text of Homer were attributed to Aristarchus (= αἱ Ἀριστάρχου in the scholia), both of which were known to his student Didymus. From Didymus' scholarly work many of the scholia derive. (On the *ekdoseis* of Aristarchus, see Montanari 1998 and Nagy 2004:85–86. On the sources for the Homeric scholia, see Nagy 2004:3–24 and Blackwell and Dué 2009.)

The sources, both ancient and medieval, are perhaps divided here because both verbs are well attested in the formulaic diction. ἔγρεο occurs here and in two places in the *Odyssey*; ὄρσεο is attested four times in the *Iliad* and once in the *Odyssey*. Clearly, both verbs could be generated by a poet composing in performance. Here is a perfect illustration of the difficulty a modern editor of Homer faces when trying to choose between two or more equally Homeric (= formulaic) variations. We, as the editors of this volume, have for this very reason rejected a traditional text critical approach, and instead have advocated a multi-textual approach that accounts for the multiformity of the Homeric poems at different historical points in their transmission. (See above, "*Iliad* 10: A Multitextual Approach.")

10.159 Τυδέος υἱέ See on 10.144 above. See also Schnapp-Gourbeillon 1981:96–100 for more on Diomedes' patronymic and his youth.

10.159a The third-century CE scholar and poet Diogenes Laertius relates an anecdote (6.53) that features the hexameter line μή τίς τοι εὕδοντι μεταφρένῳ ἐν δόρυ πήξῃ. This verse is probably a literary play on *Iliad* 8.95: μή τίς τοι φεύγοντι μεταφρένῳ ἐν δόρυ πήξῃ. The twelfth-century scholar Eustathius may be in fact thinking of Diogenes and not Homer when he writes (in 519.32) ὁ Νέστωρ τῷ Διομήδῃ κειμένῳ πού φησιν· ἔγρεο, μή τις τοι καθεύδοντι μεταφρένῳ ἐν δόρυ πήξῃ ("Somewhere Nestor says to the sleeping Diomedes, 'Wake up, lest someone pierce you in the back with a spear while you sleep'"; cf. Diogenes Laertius' ἐπέγειραι, ἔφη ...). It is possible that Eustathius had a text of the *Iliad* with this line following 10.159, but the verse is attested nowhere else in our manuscripts.

10.177–178 ἐέσσατο δέρμα λέοντος / αἴθωνος μεγάλοιο ποδηνεκές, εἵλετο δ᾽ ἔγχος Verse 177, after the caesura, and 178 are also used to describe what Agamemnon wears in 10.23–24, which is indicative of their formulaic nature and also suggestive of their use in night raid contexts generally.

10.179 βῆ δ᾽ ἰέναι See on 10.32.

10.180–189 As we discuss in the introductory essay "The Poetics of Ambush," this simile emphasizes the sounds that are made in the dark, as well as describing a scenario of being on the defensive against a nocturnal attack (see above, pp. 63–64).

10.183 δυσωρήσωνται is another *hapax legomenon*, appearing only in *Iliad* 10, but we can understand why it might only appear once in our extant Homeric epics from the simile's interaction with its context. Although in other parts of the poem there are similes describing predatory animals attacking domestic flocks at night, and the retaliation of men and dogs (see e.g. *Iliad* 11.546–557), here the simile is for a particularly "painful" night watch. It is painful both because the young men on guard duty have had an extremely hard day of fighting and because the Trojans are camped out for the first time, closer than ever, during this night. (See also the commentary on 10.331 for more on words that appear only in *Iliad* 10.)

10.194 τάφροιο διέσσυτο The act of crossing the ditch for the meeting conveys a spatial significance to the need the Achaeans feel and the plan they will construct to meet it. In *Iliad* 7, the Achaeans created a new boundary on the landscape by building their wall and ditch. The wall was built in the dark, before the dawn (*Iliad* 7.433). In the subsequent daytime battles, the boundary created by these two elements is of the utmost importance. M. L. West notes that "once they have been built they are frequently mentioned again, in every book from the eighth to the eighteenth, as well as in the twentieth and twenty-fourth" (1969:255). The boundary is mentioned either in order to indicate who is winning at that point or whenever the tide of battle turns. In the battle that takes place on the day before the night of *Iliad* 10, for example, Hektor pens in the Achaeans behind the wall so that the entire space is filled with men and horses (*Iliad* 8.213–216). The Achaeans rally after some inspiration from the gods and cross the ditch on the offensive (*Iliad* 8.253–265), but Hektor forces them back over the ditch as he once again takes the upper hand (*Iliad* 8.340–343). And, of course, the boundary will become even more significant the day after the night of *Iliad* 10, as the Trojans themselves cross it and threaten the ships with fire (the Trojans pass over the ditch and wall at the end of *Iliad* 12). Since the wall and ditch act as a threshold between the camp and the battlefield, one way of understanding the leaders crossing the ditch to hold their meeting is as a shift toward being on the offensive. Only the ditch is mentioned here: Petegorsky (1982:238n13) suggests that the "absence" of the wall presages its breach the next day. (For more on the poetic possibilities and traditional associations offered by the Achaean wall, see Boyd 1995.)

10.199 ἐν καθαρῷ, ὅθι δὴ νεκύων διεφαίνετο χῶρος Another significant feature of the landscape on this night is the number of corpses left on the battlefield. No truce has been allowed this time for the gathering of the dead (compare the truce agreed to at *Iliad* 7.407–411). The Trojan camp is also in a space specifically said to be free of corpses (this same line is also used at *Iliad* 8.491), and a picture of the landscape covered with corpses is repeatedly evoked (10.298, 10.343 = 10.387, 10.469). Such a detail is a reminder of the intense battle of the day before, which is the reason both for the embassy to Achilles and for this meeting, which will result in the spying mission and ambush. It is also a harbinger of the even greater battle that will happen on the next day, adding to the eerie atmosphere of the nighttime landscape.

10.205 θυμῷ τολμήεντι For the importance of a "daring (or enduring) heart" for spying missions or ambush, see below on 10.231, 10.244, and 10.248, as well as "The Poetics of Ambush."

10.206–210 Fenik (1964:41) excoriates these lines, calling the idea that the Trojans might retreat into the city "wholly fatuous," and he uses them to inquire "whether some special grounds, other than general incompetence, were responsible for the K poet's extraordinary failure here." But the assumption that a different, individual author composed these lines leads to the kind of evaluation that Fenik makes. Instead, using approaches based in oral poetics, we can see how these lines do not ignore the situation that the *Iliad* has presented, but rather resonate with what is to come. Diomedes and Odysseus will indeed capture (and kill, ἕλοι can mean both) someone at the edge of the enemy (ἐσχατόωντα): in fact, this can allude to both Dolon, from whom they will get information, and Rhesos, whose army is described as encamped at the edge: ἔσχατοι ἄλλων (10.434). Just so, the Trojans will not consider retreating on this night, though they will the next night (see *Iliad* 18.243–313). Petegorsky (1982:225–230) argues that Nestor's proposal anticipates the later Trojan council scenes, during the next day's fighting, particularly that in *Iliad* 18, in anticipation of Achilles' return.

10.211–212 καὶ ἂψ εἰς ἡμέας ἔλθοι / ἀσκηθὴς When he proposes the spying mission, Nestor includes the crucial completion of the mission: namely, that the spy return to report what he has found out. The return of the spy 'unscathed' connects to the greater theme, and it shares concepts with the theme of the journey. One concern with any of these nighttime or secret operations, such as spying missions or ambushes, is that, if those who undertake them do not return, their comrades may never know what happened to them. Whether, how, and by whom a spy has been killed cannot be verified, and it is such knowledge that allows a warrior to be buried and honored after death. This lack of knowledge provides a strong contrast to daytime battle, in which one comrade will see another fall, and will subsequently go to protect his corpse or to attack his killer in retaliation. That sequence in battle is a pattern we see again and again in the *Iliad*. The same contrast between a death in open battle (bringing honor) and a death that occurs on a journey (resulting in an inability to bury and honor the person lost because of a lack of knowledge as well as the lack of the corpse) is expressed by loved ones of Odysseus in the *Odyssey*. The sentiment is first expressed by Telemakhos:

> νῦν δ' ἑτέρως ἐβόλοντο θεοὶ κακὰ μητιόωντες,
> 235 οἳ κεῖνον μὲν ἄϊστον ἐποίησαν περὶ πάντων
> ἀνθρώπων, ἐπεὶ οὔ κε θανόντι περ ὧδ' ἀκαχοίμην,
> εἰ μετὰ οἷσ' ἑτάροισι δάμη Τρώων ἐνὶ δήμῳ,
> ἠὲ φίλων ἐν χερσίν, ἐπεὶ πόλεμον τολύπευσε.
> τῷ κέν οἱ τύμβον μὲν ἐποίησαν Παναχαιοί,
> 240 ἠδέ κε καὶ ᾧ παιδὶ μέγα κλέος ἤρατ' ὀπίσσω.

νῦν δέ μιν ἀκλειῶς Ἅρπυιαι ἀνηρέψαντο·
οἴχετ᾽ ἄϊστος ἄπυστος, ἐμοὶ δ᾽ ὀδύνας τε γόους τε
κάλλιπεν·

Odyssey 1.234–243

But now the gods have willed it otherwise, devising evils,
235 who have made that man [Odysseus] unseen beyond all
mortals, since I would not grieve this way at his death
if among his comrades he was subdued in the district of the
Trojans
or in the hands of his friends, when he had finished war.
All the Achaeans would have made a burial mound for him,
240 and he would have won great fame [*kleos*] even for his child
in the future.
But now the Arpuiai whirlwinds have snatched him up
without fame [*kleos*].
He is gone, unseen, unheard of. And for me pain and laments
he left behind.

Later (*Odyssey* 14.365–372), Eumaios says something very similar in
response to the disguised Odysseus' story about the fate of Odysseus.
He, too, contrasts the unknown circumstances of Odysseus' presumed
death at sea with a death in battle, after which a man's comrades can
bury him. A known death in battle brings *kleos*, which, having as its root
meaning 'something heard' (see Nagy 1979:16, §2n3), is contrasted in
Telemakhos' words not only with an "unglorious" death (*Odyssey* 1.241)
but also with Odysseus himself, who is "unseen" and "unheard of"
(*Odyssey* 1.242). In *Iliad* 10, in the same line as ἀσκηθής (10.212), Nestor
promises *kleos* to the man who undertakes this mission, but the return
is necessary for that *kleos* to come about. For if a man were to go out
on a nighttime spying mission, or an ambush, and not come back, he,
too, would be unseen, unheard of, and could not be buried or honored
properly.

So the need to complete the mission, the need for a return, is one
way that a spying mission resembles a journey in epic diction. Coming
back unscathed, ἀσκηθής, is used elsewhere in Homeric epic of a return
home or of some other completion of a journey. It is used prominently
in *Odyssey* 5 of the need to have both Telemakhos (*Odyssey* 5.26) and
Odysseus (*Odyssey* 5.144, 5.168) return to their fatherland (πατρίδα
γαῖαν). At the very beginning of the story of his wanderings, Odysseus
says that he would have returned home unscathed if the sea currents

had not prevented him from making his way to Ithaka (*Odyssey* 9.79–81). Thus arriving unscathed seems especially associated with sailing journeys, as Odysseus also uses it in one of his Cretan lies, in this case for an easy sailing from Crete to Egypt (*Odyssey* 14.255; cf. Solon fr. 19 [West], who says that Kypris sent him home unscathed [*askēthēs*] in a fast ship for a good homecoming [*nostos*] to his own land). In one additional case in the *Odyssey*, Odysseus tells Achilles that Neoptolemos was very successful in battle and ambush (see pp. 47–48), and later adds that he was never hurt in the fighting—he was ἀσκηθής, never touched by a weapon. Although the context has referred to both battle and ambush, the word actually describes Neoptolemos as he boards his ship for the journey home, again displaying the connection between sailing journeys and *nostos*. The "Odyssean" language that many scholars have noted in Book 10, and have even cited as proof of its non-Iliadic nature, may be a thematic result, not only of the greater prominence of ambush in the *Odyssey*, but also of this thematic overlap between spying missions or ambushes and journeys, especially journeys home and those over the sea.

In the *Iliad*, ἀσκηθής is used in one other context, and that is, in fact, daytime battle. As Achilles prays to Zeus that Patroklos will be successful in saving the Achaeans and their ships from the Trojan onslaught, he asks as well that Patroklos then return unscathed to him at the swift ships: ἀσκηθής μοι ἔπειτα θοὰς ἐπὶ νῆας ἵκοιτο (*Iliad* 16.247). Patroklos is not going on an ambush here, and there is no concern that what happens to him will be unknown. Instead, the fact that he is going as Achilles' substitute must also be a special kind of departure for battle, and the desire for the substitute to come back unscathed evokes this same word (see Nagy 1979:292–295 for Patroklos as a ritual substitute for Achilles in this battle). Zeus' reaction is to grant the first part of Achilles' prayer, but not the safe return: σόον δ᾽ ἀνένευσε μάχης ἐξαπονέεσθαι (*Iliad* 16.252). Petegorsky (1982:220–221) argues that these two uses of ἀσκηθής in the *Iliad* highlight the isolation of Patroklos going into battle without Achilles, in contrast to the pairing of Diomedes and Odysseus.

10.212–213 κλέος 'glory in song' and δόσις 'gift' are not incompatible rewards in Homeric epic. Throughout the *Iliad* material prizes are a physical manifestation of a warrior's place in the song tradition and are a major sources of contention among heroes. In *Iliad* 1, when Agamemnon threatens to take Achilles' prize (γέρας), the woman Briseis, Achilles says that he does not intend to continue fighting ἄτιμος ('without honor', *Iliad* 1.171). As Casey Dué has noted, the dispute over prize women in *Iliad* 1 is actually about τιμή (*Iliad* 1.161, 1.174, 1.412, 1.503–510). This word is generally translated as 'honor', but it conveys specifically the honor heroes receive after death in cult and song as immortalized heroes (Dué 2002:45; see also Nagy 1979:118). In *Iliad* 9, Achilles, struggling with his mortality, rejects the gifts of Agamemnon and at the same time rejects the glorious death he will have in battle (*Iliad* 9.410–416). So too do the competitions for the prizes at the funeral games for Patroklos in *Iliad* 23 have far greater significance than their material value. In *Iliad* 23.700–737, Ajax and Odysseus compete in wrestling, foreshadowing their competition for the arms of Achilles after his death and for the title of "best of the Achaeans." In *Iliad* 23, neither can decisively defeat the other, and eventually Achilles calls the contest a draw, pronouncing that the victory (along with two equal prizes) belongs to both. (The individual contests have been analyzed by various scholars. See e.g. Douglas Frame's analysis of the chariot race in Frame 2009:131–172 and further bibliography *ad loc.*) In *Iliad* 24, Achilles accepts a ransom for Hektor's body, even though he knows that he too will soon be dead. He asks Patroklos not to be angry with him for accepting it, and says that they will share it equally (*Iliad* 24.589–595).

When we understand that prizes are inextricably linked with *kleos* in this tradition, we can better understand episodes in which heroes act in ways that we might call "selfish," episodes which are often incompatible with modern notions of heroism (see e.g. Stanford 1965 *ad Odyssey* 9.229). The *Little Iliad*, according to Proklos, narrated the theft of the Palladion, a story that survives in several variant versions in which Diomedes or Odysseus or both try to get sole possession of it, betraying the other (see Gantz 1993:643–644). Likewise, Rick Newton (2008 and 2009) has discussed the way that Odysseus seeks gifts at the expense of his comrades throughout his adventures. Newton suggests that, in the *Odyssey*, guest-gifts function like a *geras* does in the *Iliad*: guest-gifts, whatever their intrinsic material value, are tokens of honor and prestige for their recipient (cf. *Odyssey* 5.29–42 and 11.355–361). Odysseus' heroic pursuit of guest-gifts generates delays in his homecoming and is instrumental in causing the death of his comrades along the way. See also Newton 2005, especially p. 141: "[In] Odyssean hospitality ... the acquisition of property ... enhances the honor and status of the hero ... But that heroic hospitality, like successful warfare in the *Iliad*, comes at a price, and a high one ... Odysseus will reach Ithaca late and alone." An analogy can be made between the Iliadic deaths of countless Achaeans due to Achilles' wrath over his stripped *geras* and the loss of Odysseus' entire fleet and crew during his *Odyssey nostos*.

Note also that Nestor says there is *kleos* for undertaking a spying mission, making it parallel to fighting in battle. Nestor promises the sheep and a share at a banquet (see Nagy 1979:118–141 for connections between hero cult and portions at feasts), but the horses of Rhesos also become the reward and a visible sign of the success Diomedes and Odysseus achieve.

10.219 βοὴν ἀγαθὸς See below on 10.283 for more on this epithet.

10.220 ἔμ' ὀτρύνει κραδίη καὶ θυμὸς ἀγήνωρ In a simile in *Iliad* 12, when Sarpedon is about to make his attack on the Achaean wall, we see a lion on ambush (*Iliad* 12.299–308). The lion is hungry, but it is nevertheless his audacious heart that bids him to attack the flocks and go to their densely packed enclosure (κέλεται δέ ἑ θυμὸς ἀγήνωρ / μήλων πειρήσοντα καὶ ἐς πυκινὸν δόμον ἐλθεῖν, *Iliad* 12.300–301). He is desperate enough that he will make his attack even though the flocks are guarded by dogs and men. The formula θυμὸς ἀγήνωρ thus is used to indicate the motivation to undertake a particularly risky endeavor, and it seems to be used frequently, though not exclusively, for nighttime or ambush situations. Here, the nocturnal nature of the lion's attack is not explicit, but is implied by the animals being in their pen and by the use of the adjective *pukinos* for that pen (see above on 10.5–9 for more on the associations between *pukinos* and ambush). Other examples of ambush contexts in which we see the formula θυμὸς ἀγήνωρ include the suitors' plan to ambush Telemakhos (*Odyssey* 4.658), Odysseus preparing the wine-skin before he meets Polyphemos (*Odyssey* 9.213), and the ambushes Odysseus describes in one of his Cretan lies (*Odyssey* 14.217–219). See below on 10.244 for more on the qualities of κραδίη καὶ θυμὸς ἀγήνωρ and their association with nighttime spying missions and ambush. See also below on 10.297 for more on similes involving lions at night.

10.222 On the significance of the verb ἕπομαι, which is also used of gods who "accompany" heroes, see on 10.285.

10.224–226 Anthony Edwards (1985:22) identifies two leaders as a common feature of the Homeric ambush, and so Diomedes' request for a partner may already indicate that the spying mission that Nestor proposed will become an ambush. Robert Rabel (1991, see esp. 288–291) sees an emphasis in *Iliad* 10 on cooperation among heroes in order to achieve success that contrasts strongly with Achilles' choice to "go it alone" in *Iliad* 9. In Diomedes' description of the ideal night raid team, νόος and νοέω are cited three times in three lines, together with μῆτις (cf. *Iliad* 23.590). It is no surprise, therefore, that he chooses Odysseus. For Odysseus' association with *mētis* and *noos*, see on 10.137 and 10.247, respectively.

10.227–231   We can compare this list with the list of those willing to duel with Hektor (after Nestor's rebuke) in *Iliad* 7.162–168. These lists comprise a kind of subtheme that occurs in these types of "selection" situations but also in situations in which the Achaeans "regroup" to fight back (e.g. *Iliad* 8.261–266, after Diomedes leads the charge). This subtheme seems related both to the idea of volunteering for dangerous assignments, and, in the larger scheme, to the contention among the heroes for who is the "best"—for more on which, see below on 10.236.

10.228   Αἴαντε As discussed above on 10.53, at one time this dual referred to the fighting team of Ajax and Teucer, which would be a most appropriate meaning here. The dual, then, could mean not that Ajax son of Telamon and Ajax son of Oileus each individually volunteered (no other two warriors are listed as volunteering this way), but rather that Ajax and Teucer volunteered as a team. This interpretation is strengthened by the fact that two-horse chariot teams are described in the dual (as at 10.530–531), as are Diomedes and Odysseus when they are working as a unit, as we will see. (See below on 10.243.) Likewise, when Diomedes makes his case for taking a partner on the expedition (10.222–226), he uses the dual to describe the advantages of such a pair. The Aktorione-Molione, the possibly conjoined twins who fought Nestor in his youth (*Iliad* 11.709–752 and 23.638–642), are, of course, yet another pair of warriors who are described in the dual. The dual thus seems to be a traditional way of referring to a closely linked fighting team.

If the dual in this line is referring to Ajax and Teucer, then there is no mention of Ajax the son Oileus volunteering. We can speculate that in some performances of *Iliad* 10, especially those composed at a time when the dual was understood to refer to Ajax and Teucer, this dual meant that fighting team, although in our version Ajax son of Oileus is specifically named as someone to gather for the meeting at 10.110. It is worth noting that in *Iliad* 7.164, when the two Ajaxes are included among the heroes who volunteer to fight Hektor one-on-one, the form attested there is the plural, not the dual.

10.231 ὁ τλήμων Ὀδυσεὺς On this epithet, Milman Parry offers the following:

> The epithet τλήμων, found twice in the *Iliad*, presents a partic-
> ular interest because it never occurs in the *Odyssey*, despite
> the greater importance of the role played by Odysseus in the
> latter poem. One might be tempted to see in it a word original
> with the poet of the *Iliad* or of the Doloneia, only the meaning
> of the epithet rules out such a conclusion. Like πολύτλας,
> τλήμων could never have been invented for the *Iliad*. It is an
> epithet whose origin is in some poem describing the wander-
> ings of Odysseus, and which eventually came, like πολύτλας,
> to be applied to him under all circumstances. For in the *Iliad*
> Odysseus has not yet suffered more than other heroes. So we
> have here a formula indubitably deriving from the tradition
> and yet never used by the poet (or poets) of the *Odyssey*. Ought
> we to infer that the author of the *Odyssey* knew this formula
> but never had occasion to make use of it? It could be pointed
> out in support of this conclusion that the other words of these
> two lines are often found in the same position [citing 10.231
> and 10.498, on which, see below]. It is also true that in the
> *Odyssey* Odysseus never has occasion to manage horses or to
> enter the throng of battle. But all this remains uncertain.
>
> MHV 82

For more on the significance of this epithet, see below on 10.248, where we connect Odysseus' epithets from τλάω with the endurance and daring required for ambush. Here, we see both semantic fields of the word at work: ὁ τλήμων Ὀδυσεὺς is followed in the very next line by the phrase: αἰεὶ γὰρ οἱ ἐνὶ φρεσὶ θυμὸς ἐτόλμα ("For the spirit [*thumos*] in his heart [*phrēn*] was always daring"); on the *thumos* as the moti-vator in risky undertakings, see also on 10.220 above). If we connect Odysseus' epithet to the theme of ambush, we need not state with Parry that it could never have been invented for the *Iliad*, or assert that it is more appropriate for the *Odyssey* (Hainsworth 1993 *ad loc.*). Rather, it is appropriate in an ambush context, wherever that theme is invoked. On the significance of the definite article here, see Haft 1990:46–48 (with further bibliography *ad loc.*), who notes that although ὁ + epithet phrases are relatively rare in Homer, ὁ τλήμων Ὀδυσεὺς is one of four such phrases applied to Odysseus in the *Iliad* and *Odyssey*, and should be understood as demonstrative (i.e. "that [well-known] enduring Odysseus"). See also on 10.363.

10.234 Τυδεΐδη Διόμηδες ἐμῷ κεχαρισμένε θυμῷ For commentary on this full line formula of address, see on 10.144 above.

10.236 τὸν ἄριστον Agamemnon tells Diomedes to choose the "best" man. The question of who is the "best of the Achaeans" is a theme that runs throughout the *Iliad*, as Gregory Nagy has shown. In the catalogue of ships (*Iliad* 2.761), the narrator asks the Muses who was the best (*aristos*) of the Achaeans, and answers that it was Ajax, so long as Achilles had *mēnis* (2.768–769). But as Nagy points out, the claim to being best of the Achaeans is a disputed and divided one in the *Iliad*, precisely because the acknowledged best, Achilles, has withdrawn. The *Odyssey* tradition is not divided, however. There, Odysseus is the unquestioned best (Nagy 1979:26–35 and passim). So too in the Doloneia tradition is Odysseus the "best," and here he is so in part because of his association with *nostos* 'return, homecoming', as Diomedes states explicitly (see below on 10.243).

An interesting correlation to this competition to be the "best" in epic is that ambushes feature the "best" men. (See also Edwards 1985:18–24.) There are several examples of the best men going on ambush in Homeric epic. Achilles states that Agamemnon does not go on ambush with the best (σύν ἀριστήεσσιν, *Iliad* 1.227). Idomeneus' description of ambush involves a gathering of the best (ἄριστοι, *Iliad* 13.276). Those in the Wooden Horse are the best (*Odyssey* 4.272, 8.512–513, 11.523–524), and the best men are selected for ambushes of Bellerophon (*Iliad* 6.188), Proteus (*Odyssey* 4.409), and Agamemnon (*Odyssey* 4.530–531). Even in a Cretan lie, Odysseus says that he used to choose the best men for ambush (*Odyssey* 14.217–218). We can also see that the best are involved in ambush warfare because both Odysseus and Achilles participate in nighttime ambushes (see "The Poetics of Ambush").

10.237–240 The narrator makes clear that Agamemnon is referring to his brother Menelaos when he advises Diomedes not to choose his partner based on social status. See above on 10.30–31 and 10.121 for how Menelaos is portrayed as not the best choice. It is, however, an unexpected argument coming from Agamemnon, who depends on social status for his authority, as we see in his dispute with Achilles in *Iliad* 1 (see also Wilson 2002 for her argument that Agamemnon relies on this kind of status). It is also Agamemnon who insists on his status as kinglier (βασιλεύτερός, 10.239) in Book 9 (160), arguing that Achilles should yield to him for that reason. (Although Odysseus leaves that argument out when he delivers Agamemnon's offer to Achilles, Achilles seems to know it anyway, as he says in his response that Agamemnon should give his daughter in marriage to someone who is kinglier than he [*Iliad* 9.392].) This word thus provides a telling thematic contrast to the embassy, and perhaps is an indication that the two nighttime missions are performance alternatives of each other. We should also note that, in ambush, being the "best" is defined strictly in terms of the skills needed to be successful, and not in terms of social standing. The question of how to define the "best" that underlies the conflict between Agamemnon and Achilles is made explicitly moot for this spying mission.

10.240 This verse was omitted altogether in the text of Zenodotus (that is to say, it was not present in his text). It was present in the texts of Aristarchus, but he athetized it. The A scholia on these lines say that it was athetized because it is redundant (περισσός), tacked on (παρέλκων), and not in keeping with Homer's *dianoia*, all of which are common reasons given in the scholia for athetesis. As noted above (see on 10.51–52), Alexandrian editors frequently drew on their own sense of what is appropriate and poetic to determine the authenticity of verses, and athetized those they felt were not in keeping with those standards. It was the practice of Aristarchus, however, to leave verses that were well attested in the texts available to him in his text, and to indicate by way of the athetesis mark his objection to them. Zenodotus' text seems to have been considerably shorter than that of Aristarchus. We may compare 10.253, which received treatment similar to 10.240. It was omitted in the text of Zenodotus, and present but athetized in the texts of Aristarchus and Aristophanes of Byzantium. Martin West (2001a) has speculated that Zenodotus' shorter text derives from an Ionian rhapsodic performance tradition, as opposed to the Athenian tradition on which the other Alexandrian editors seem to have relied.

10.241 βοὴν ἀγαθὸς See below on 10.283 for more on this epithet.

10.243 πῶς ἂν ἔπειτ᾽ Ὀδυσῆος ἐγὼ θείοιο λαθοίμην Diomedes chooses Odysseus to go with him on the expedition, and that choice is marked in the formulaic language by a shift to the dual from 10.254 onwards, where the two heroes are understood to be a closely linked pair. (See also above on the dual Αἴαντε at 10.53 and 10.228.) The ensuing events of this book have long troubled scholars, who find the actions of

Odysseus and Diomedes during this night raid to be un-Homeric and even un-heroic. (See "The Poetics of Ambush.") But if we look at the Greek epic tradition as a whole, taking into account what we know of the now lost poems of the Epic Cycle, we find that Diomedes and Odysseus traditionally excel at the kind of ambush warfare depicted in *Iliad* 10. Diomedes is a stellar fighter in the *polemos*, but he is equally good at the *lokhos*. The sack of Troy is the ultimate night ambush, and both Odysseus and Diomedes are involved in several nighttime escapades leading up to and during its fall, including the following.

In testimonium 34 [Bernabé] of the *Cypria*, a lesser-known version of Polyxena's story has her being wounded by Odysseus and Diomedes during the sack.

> ὑπὸ Νεοπτολέμου φασὶν αὐτὴν (sc. Πολυξένην) σφαγιασθῆναι Εὐριπίδης καὶ Ἴβυκος. ὁ δὲ τὰ Κυπριακὰ ποιήσας φησίν ὑπὸ Ὀδυσσέως καὶ Διομήδους ἐν τῆι τῆς πόλεως ἁλώσει τραυματισθεῖσαν ἀπολέσθαι.

> Scholia to Euripides, *Hecuba* 41

> Euripides and Ibycus say that Polyxena's throat was cut by Neoptolemos. But the composer of the *Cypria* says that she died after being wounded by Odysseus and Diomedes in the capture of the city.

In the *Little Iliad*, Odysseus seems to have been connected to the ambush and capture of Helenos, the prophetic son of Priam, and it is Diomedes, according to Proklos, who brings back Philoktetes from Lemnos. (Cf. Sophocles' *Philoktetes*, where Odysseus is the one who goes to get him.) Philoktetes' presence is required, according to Helenos, for the successful capture of Troy:

> μετὰ ταῦτα Ὀδυσσεὺς λοχήσας Ἕλενον λαμβάνει, καὶ χρήσαντος περὶ τῆς ἁλώσεως τούτου Διομήδης ἐκ Λήμνου Φιλοκτήτην ἀνάγει.

> *Little Iliad*, from the summary of Proklos

> After this Odysseus captures Helenos in an ambush, and as a result of Helenos' prophecy about the city's conquest Diomedes brings Philoktetes back from Lemnos.

Also narrated in the *Little Iliad*, according to Proklos, was the theft of the Palladion, which survives in several variant versions in which Diomedes or Odysseus or both try to get sole possession of it, betraying the other. The Palladion is yet another item that had been foretold to be required for the successful capture of Troy. In these ambush style episodes we find Odysseus and Diomedes frequently working as a team, though sometimes they split up the work or act on their own. As the episode with the Palladion suggests, the advantages of working as a team do not cancel out the desire on the part of each hero to obtain great glory for himself.

Still another attested collaborative ambush by Odysseus and Diomedes is the killing of Palamedes. In *Cypria* testimonium 30 [Bernabé], Diomedes and Odysseus drown Palamedes, ambushing him while he is fishing:

> Παλαμήδην δὲ ἀποπνιγῆναι προελθόντα ἐπὶ ἰχθύων θήραν,
> Διομήδην δὲ τὸν ἀποκτείναντα εἶναι καὶ Ὀδυσσέα ἐπιλεξάμενος
> ἐν ἔπεσιν οἶδα τοῖς Κυπρίοις.

Pausanias 10.31.2

> Palamedes was drowned when he went out to catch fish. Diomedes was the killer and also Odysseus, as I know from reading it in the epic poem the *Cypria*.

In all of these episodes Diomedes is linked, as in the Doloneia, with Odysseus. Indeed, Odysseus has long been understood to be the hero of *mētis*. (See on 10.137 and 10.148 above.) But it should not be forgotten that, like Diomedes, Odysseus has his fair share of traditional fighting. The *Odyssey* ends with Odysseus about to engage the families of the suitors in battle, and with Laertes rejoicing that he will have a contest for *aretē* with his son and grandson (*Odyssey* 24.515). When Demodokos sings about the fall of Troy in *Odyssey* 8, Odysseus is the hero raging "like Ares" through the streets of Troy (*Odyssey* 8.515). In *Iliad* 11.310–319, Odysseus and Diomedes together stave off a rout of the Greek forces before both are wounded. Recent scholarship has focused on the oppositions set up between *mētis* and *biē* in Homeric poetry (see e.g. Nagy 1979:45–48), but as Donna Wilson (2005) has recently pointed out, the two concepts are also complementary in many respects.

10.243   This verse is also used at *Odyssey* 1.65 (and compare how the phrasing of *Odyssey* 1.66 is similar to that of 10.244). There, it is Zeus speaking in response to Athena, saying that he could not overlook Odysseus. Since *Iliad* 10, like the *Odyssey*, features Odysseus in a prominent role, the formula seems to be useful and good for introducing Odysseus in a starring role.

10.244 πρόφρων κραδίη καὶ θυμὸς ἀγήνωρ At both 10.220 above and 10.319 below, the formula ἔμ' ὀτρύνει κραδίη καὶ θυμὸς ἀγήνωρ ("my heart and audacious spirit rouse me") is used when Diomedes and Dolon, respectively, respond to the call for a spying mission. Here, Diomedes says that he is choosing Odysseus as his partner in the mission because his heart and audacious spirit are ready and eager for all kinds of labors; these personal qualities of courage and boldness are what impel men to go on nighttime or spying missions or on ambushes. We can compare the opposite in Achilles' denunciation of Agamemnon in *Iliad* 1.225–228, when he says that Agamemnon has the heart (κραδίη) of a deer and never arms himself for war or goes on an ambush with the best of the Achaeans, enduring it in his spirit (θυμός). It is clear that there is a deep-rooted association between these qualities and the daring feats of these types of missions. See also on 10.231 and 10.248.

10.245 φιλεῖ δέ ἑ Παλλὰς Ἀθήνη On the relationship between Odysseus and Athena, see on 10.275.

10.246 ἐκ πυρὸς αἰθομένοιο Petegorsky points out that this particular image calls to mind "the background of Achilles' challenge to the Achaeans to avert the danger that threatens the ships by employing μῆτις. His words acquire a strong 'horizontal resonance' by pointing back to Achilles' challenge and forward to the Patrocleia [cf. *Iliad* 16.81]. And yet, his description of Odysseus also has a strong 'vertical resonance'; for it evokes an image of Odysseus that corresponds remarkably well to that which we find in the *Odyssey*" (1982:193). The types of resonance that Petegorsky reveals remind us of how oral poetry can have complex ways of creating meaning that are different from those in written texts.

10.247 ἄμφω νοστήσαιμεν, ἐπεὶ περίοιδε νοῆσαι Odysseus' primary heroic identity is concerned with *nostos* 'homecoming', which is the subject of the epic devoted to him. (See Nagy 1979:35 and 38–39.) Douglas Frame has shown that the words *nostos* and *noos* 'mind' share the verbal root *nes-, whose meaning has to do with "returning to life and light" (a meaning best understood, according to Frame, in the context of solar symbolism), and that the two concepts are combined on a conceptual and verbal level throughout the *Odyssey*. (Cf. e.g. the opening lines of the *Odyssey*, 1.3–5: πολλῶν δ' ἀνθρώπων ἴδεν ἄστεα καὶ <u>νόον</u> ἔγνω ... ἀρνύμενος ἥν τε ψυχὴν καὶ <u>νόστον</u> ἑταίρων ["Many are the cities of men and their *ways of thinking* he came to know, as he strove to win the life and *homecoming* of his companions."]) See especially Frame 2005a and 2005b; on the root *nes, see also Frame 2009 and Bonifazi 2009. We can see that the deep connection between *nostos* and *noos* is built into the traditional character of Odysseus and comes into focus whenever he is featured, be it in the *Iliad* or the *Odyssey*.

We have already seen some indications (on 10.211–212) that spying missions share some traditional language and thematic associations with journeys. Diomedes' choice of Odysseus as the master of the kind of journey called a *nostos* (due to his quality of *noos*) is another example of this commonality. See also below on 10.509.

10.248 πολύτλας δῖος Ὀδυσσεύς In this book Odysseus is also referred to as ὁ τλήμων Ὀδυσεὺς ("that enduring Odysseus," 10.231 and 10.498; cf. *Iliad* 5.670 and *Odyssey* 18.319). Although Odysseus is *polutlas* 'much enduring' five times in the *Iliad*, the epithet is by far more common in the *Odyssey*, where it is naturally associated with the many travails he endures in that epic (cf. *Odyssey* 1.4: πολλὰ δ' ὅ γ' ἐν πόντῳ πάθεν ἄλγεα ["many are the pains he suffered"]). It is significant therefore that this formula appears directly following the verse in which Odysseus' Odyssean association with *nostos* is conjured. But as we saw in our discussion of the etymologically related epithet τλήμων on 10.231, this formula may well have another aspect to it. When Achilles excoriates Agamemnon in *Iliad* 1 for his lack of participation in the hardships of war, he says:

οἰνοβαρές, κυνὸς ὄμματ᾽ ἔχων, κραδίην δ᾽ ἐλάφοιο,
οὔτέ ποτ᾽ ἐς πόλεμον ἅμα λαῷ θωρηχθῆναι
οὔτε λόχον δ᾽ ἰέναι σὺν ἀριστήεσσιν Ἀχαιῶν
<u>τέτληκας</u> θυμῷ· τὸ δέ τοι κὴρ εἴδεται εἶναι.

Iliad 1.225–228

"You drunkard, with a dog's eyes and a deer's heart,
   whenever it comes to arming yourself for war with the rest
     of the warriors
   or going on an ambush with the champions of the Achaeans,
   you don't have the heart to *endure* it. That looks like death
     to you."

The verb Achilles uses is τέτληκα. In Idomeneus' description of ambush warfare in *Iliad* 13 (discussed above, pp. 45–47), the verb τλάω is not used, but the need for endurance is likewise emphasized. Warriors on an ambush must endure fear, the discomfort of sitting/crouching as they wait for a long period of time to attack, and the cold of the night (as evidenced by the clothing chosen for ambush, clothing which Odysseus forgets to take both in *Iliad* 10 and in the story narrated in *Odyssey* 14). When Menelaos tells Telemakhos the story of the wooden horse in *Odyssey* 4, he praises Odysseus' endurance (ἔτλη) on that occasion (*Odyssey* 4.271–272): οἷον καὶ τόδ' ἔρεξε καὶ ἔτλη καρτερὸς ἀνὴρ / ἵππῳ ἔνι ξεστῷ ("What a thing he accomplished and endured, the mighty man, inside the wooden horse"). Odysseus' steadfast character and ability to endure the *lokhos* are contrasted in Menelaos' anecdote with that of the weaker-willed heroes, Diomedes, Menelaos himself, and Antiklos, all of whom Odysseus has to restrain from succumbing to Helen's trick. In *Odyssey* 9, Odysseus describes how in the cave of the Cyclops he hid beneath the ram and held on, awaiting dawn "with an enduring heart" (τετληότι θυμῷ, 9.435; for this same formula in other ambush contexts, see also *Odyssey* 4.447 and 4.459, Menelaos' ambush of Proteus, and *Odyssey* 24.163, the description by the shades of the suitors of how Odysseus ambushed them). This kind of waiting—during the dark of night, in a hiding position—is what a warrior undergoes in an ambush. When Athena tells Odysseus in *Odyssey* 13 that he will need to conceal his identity in order to take control of his home, family, and kingdom again, she tells him he will have to endure (σὺ δὲ τετλάμεναι καὶ ἀνάγκῃ, 13.307). He will have to take them by ambush, not outright force. (Cf. *Odyssey* 13.309–310: ἀλλὰ σιωπῇ / πάσχειν ἄλγεα πολλά, βίας ὑποδέγμενος ἀνδρῶν ["{You must} suffer many pains in silence, submitting to the *biē* of men."]) Odysseus' ability to withstand this particular kind of hardship is an important part of his epithet *polutlas*, and the endurance that Menelaos remembers as being so remarkable during the ambush of Troy is fundamentally connected to Odysseus' ability to withstand the many *algea* he suffers on his journey home. (On the connection between the *tla-* compounds that describe Odysseus and the endurance required for ambush, see also Edwards 1985:17, and on the second half of the *Odyssey* as an ambush, see again Edwards 1985:35–37.)

10.249–250 Τυδείδη μήτ' ἄρ με μάλ' αἴνεε μήτε τί νείκει· / εἰδόσι γάρ τοι ταῦτα μετ' Ἀργείοις ἀγορεύεις Gregory Nagy sees this response by Odysseus as a meta-commentary on the epic tradition and the question of who is the best of the Achaeans (see 10.236). Nagy writes: "It is as if he were saying: 'The Achaeans are aware of the tradition, so please do not exaggerate.' With the words of Odysseus himself, the epic tradition of the *Iliad* has pointedly taken Odysseus out of contention" (1979:34). But just as Ajax can be called best for battle so long as Achilles remains withdrawn (*Iliad* 2.768; Nagy 1979:27, 31), Odysseus here can contend for "best" at nighttime missions, since Achilles is not available now, either.

10.251–253 μάλα γὰρ νὺξ ἄνεται, ἐγγύθι δ' ἠώς, / ἄστρα δὲ δὴ προβέβηκε, παρῴχηκεν δὲ πλέω νὺξ / τῶν δύο μοιράων, τριτάτη δέ τι μοῖρα λέλειπται The amount of time that the events of *Iliad* 9 and *Iliad* 10 take up has been used, by Leaf and others, to argue that *Iliad* 10 does not belong to the *Iliad*. Of course, the events related in *Iliad* 11.1–18.242 all take place on one day, so narrative time seems quite flexible, expanding as the dramatic intensity increases. Thus this crucial night could dramatically include the "three-part" structure implied in these lines: the first part would include the embassy to Achilles, the second part when the Achaeans, other than Agamemnon, slept, and now this episode, comprising the remaining third part. In any case, these lines call attention to the urgency of the time, as well as suggesting the possibility of multiple episodes during the same night.

10.253 According the scholia in the Venetus A, Zenodotus "did not write" this line. For more on the Alexandrian editorial procedures, see on 10.240 above.

10.254 ὣς εἰπόνθ' This is the first dual verb used for Diomedes and Odysseus. As soon as Odysseus agrees to be Diomedes' partner, they are spoken of as a team, working together in every way. For more on the use of the dual verb forms, see on 10.53, 10.228, and 10.243.

10.254–272 The passage that begins here functions much like an arming scene. In a well-known article, James Armstrong (1958) shows how formulaic arming scenes are employed at climactic moments in the *Iliad* with great effect. He analyzes in detail the four major arming scenes of the *Iliad* (those of Paris in *Iliad* 3, Agamemnon in *Iliad* 11, Patroklos in *Iliad* 16, and Achilles in *Iliad* 19), arguing that formulaic language in these passages is manipulated for various poetic purposes, and that each scene resonates with what came before, so that there is a cumulative effect over the course of the poem.

In the night raid/*lohkos* tradition, the dressing and arming of heroes would no doubt have had a poetic purpose similar to the expanded arming scenes of conventional battle. These scenes contribute both to suspense, by increasing the audience's anticipation of the coming ambush or raid, and to characterization, as the details of each dressing or arming passage reveal important aspects of the hero's character as a fighter. But even more importantly, the passages serve to signal that the poet is moving into a different poetic register. The poet transitions by way of such scenes from one megatheme to another, and the alternative style of clothing is emblematic of not only this alternative mode of fighting but also an alternative poetics.

The armor described here is in many ways atypical. Most distinctive is what the heroes wear on their heads. Diomedes and Odysseus wear leather skull caps (κυνέην ... ταυρείην ... ἥ τε καταῖτυξ κέκληται—the word καταῖτυξ is used only here in extant Greek literature), and the history of Odysseus' cap is elaborately described: Odysseus' own maternal grandfather Autolykos stole it and gave it away as a gift to Amphidamas, who likewise gave it as a gift to Molos, who then gave it to the Cretan Meriones, who now gives it to Odysseus along with the other weapons Odysseus will carry, a bow and quiver and sword. Meriones must give Odysseus all of this gear because when Odysseus leaves his tent, unlike the other heroes who dress in skins and cloaks and take their weapons, he takes only his shield. (See above on 10.149.)

But both heroes, it should be noted, are given weapons and armor by the two leaders of the guards, Meriones and Thrasymedes, who came out into the night fully armed. Diomedes, we are told here, borrows a sword and shield from Thrasymedes, just as Odysseus uses Meriones' bow, quiver, sword, and helmet. Such borrowing may reflect the impromptu nature of the mission—a quality that will be seen again when it changes from a spying mission to an ambush/night raid. Or it may give the mission a communal aspect, which can also be seen in the rest of the leaders remaining in this same spot, beyond the ditch, until Diomedes and Odysseus return. They are all invested in the success of these two.

But while the clothing they wear and weapons they carry are unusual for extant Homeric epic, they are completely appropriate for a night raid, where, unlike the *polemos*, it is important not to be conspicuous. (See also Shewan 1911:55.) The history of the cap as a gift indicates that such an object has prestige as well as utility, and possession of it may indicate "the best," who would wear such equipment for these dangerous and important missions. That it was originally stolen by the thief extraordinaire Autolykos seems related to the stealth that it affords the wearer, and also makes it even more fitting both for Odysseus personally, who is very much like his grandfather, as we know from *Odyssey* 19.395–412, and for the night mission that requires stealth. Petegorsky (1982:200) also argues that the helmet connects all of these elements of Odysseus' identity: "This helmet functions as a kind of identity marker for Odysseus, and it is in effect the equivalent of the scar in *Odyssey* Nineteen, which was the result of a wound inflicted on the hero by the tusk of a boar."

10.257 ἀμφὶ δέ οἱ κυνέην κεφαλῆφιν ἔθηκε Nowhere else in surviving Homeric epic do we find heroes putting on leather caps, but we must also recognize that no other expanded descriptions of night raids of this nature survive. If more of the Epic Cycle narratives describing Diomedes' and Odysseus' nighttime exploits survived (for these, see on 10.243 above), such items of clothing might not seem so exotic. In the Nisus and Euryalus episode in the *Aeneid*, Euryalus makes the fatal mistake of putting on the helmet that he takes as spoils from a corpse, and the reflection of the moonlight off the helmet gives him away to the enemy (*Aeneid* 9.373–374: "alea Euryalum sublustri noctis in umbra / prodidit immemorem radiisque aduersa refulsit"). Whereas heroes strive for conspicuous distinction (*kudos*) on the battlefield, ambush warfare is characterized by hiding and concealment. Cf. the Venetus B scholia on 10.258, which note that the kind of leather helmet worn here is ἄφαλον and ἄλλοφον "for being inconspicuous" (διὰ τὸ λανθάνειν).

10.259 θαλερῶν αἰζηῶν 'flourishing, vigorous young men': Botanic imagery is used here to describe the warriors whose heads are protected by these helmets. The imagery of the hero as a plant that blossoms beautifully and dies quickly is an important theme in Greek lament traditions, as we see in Thetis' lament for Achilles in *Iliad* 18.54–60 and in other passages throughout the *Iliad*. It is also a metaphor that encapsulates what glory means in the *Iliad*. One of the primary metaphors for epic song in the *Iliad* is that of a flower that will never wilt:

410 μήτηρ γάρ τέ μέ φησι θεὰ Θέτις ἀργυρόπεζα
δυχθαδίας κῆρας φερέμεν θανάτοιο τέλος δέ.
εἰ μέν κ' αὖθι μένων Τρώων πόλιν ἀμφιμάχωμαι,
ὤλετο μέν μοι νόστος, ἀτὰρ κλέος ἄφθιτον ἔσται·
εἰ δέ κεν οἴκαδ' ἵκωμι φίλην ἐς πατρίδα γαῖαν,
415 ὤλετό μοι κλέος ἐσθλόν, ἐπὶ δηρὸν δέ μοι αἰὼν
ἔσσεται, οὐδέ κέ μ' ὦκα τέλος θανάτοιο κιχείη.

Iliad 9.410–416

410 My mother the goddess Thetis of the shining feet tells me
that there are two ways in which I may meet my end.
If I stay here and fight around the city of Troy,
my homecoming is lost, but my glory in song [*kleos*] will be
unwilting:
whereas if I reach home and my dear fatherland,
415 my *kleos* is lost, but my life will be long,
and the outcome of death will not soon take me.

Here Achilles reveals not only the crux of this choice of fates around which the *Iliad* itself is built, but also the driving principle of Greek epic song. The unwilting flower of epic poetry is contrasted with the necessarily mortal hero, whose death comes all too quickly. (See especially Nagy 1979:174–184 and Dué 2006a:64–69. Nagy shows that the root *phthi-* in the Greek word *aphthiton* 'unwilting' is inherently connected with vegetal imagery, and means 'wilt'.) The *Iliad* quotes within its narration of Achilles' *kleos* many songs of lamentation that highlight the mortality of the central hero, as well as underscoring the immortality of song. The traditional imagery of these quoted laments spills over into epic diction itself, with the result that similes, metaphors, and other traditional descriptions of heroes are infused with themes drawn from the natural world, as here.

With Diomedes, Meriones, Neoptolemos, and even Achilles as examples, we might also argue that ambush is associated with younger men in particular, and thus the cap that is good for ambush is worn by young men. In the "Tradition and Reception" essay above we noted Gernet's (1936) work on the Dolon myth, in which he argues that the episode is suggestive of initiation rituals in which young men must spend a period of time apart from society as well as other rites of initiation that take place at night. (See also Johnston 2002 on cattle raiding as a form of initiation; we have explored above in "The Poetics of Ambush" the thematic overlap between cattle raiding and ambush in Homeric epic.) The word *thaleros* used in this line to describe the young men may be important here. This word is used several times in Homer of husbands or young men and women on the verge of marriage. See e.g. the *Homeric Hymn to Demeter* 79, where Persephone is called a θαλερὴν ἄκοιτιν; *Iliad* 6.430, where *thaleros* is used of Hektor by Andromache and 8.190, used by Hektor of himself as the husband of Andromache; *Iliad* 4.474, where it is used of Simoesios, who dies before marriage—i.e. at the age when he should have been getting married; *Iliad* 3.26, where it is used of young hunters, who are likewise αἰζηοί; *Iliad* 8.156, where it is used of the Trojan husbands whom Diomedes has killed; *Odyssey* 6.66, where it is used of Nausikaa's impending marriage; and *Odyssey* 20.74, where it is used of the requested marriage of the daughters of Pandareus. In the *Theogony*, it is used of Gaia's first "husband" Ouranos, but there he is being described as the parent of Zeus. If we posit that ambush expeditions could serve as a rite of passage or form of initiation, it would explain why fear is said to be such an important factor: the success or failure of the mission would hinge on how the young men handled that fear. (See e.g. *Iliad* 13.277–278, where ambush is described as "the place where the merit of men most shines through, where the coward and the resolute man are revealed" and *Odyssey* 11.528–530. Both passages are discussed in "The Poetics of Ambush" above.)

10.260 βιὸν ἠδὲ φαρέτρην On the bow as a particularly appropriate weapon for night attacks, see the arguments of McLeod 1988. The Townley scholia at this line explain that Odysseus takes the bow so that he can shoot at those who are in the light (as the Trojans would be beside their campfires). McLeod adduces "half a dozen sources, spread over two millennia, testifying to a recurrent connection between the dark of night, the bow, and aiming at light" (McLeod 1988:123). The bow is of course also Odysseus' signature weapon in the *Odyssey*, and similar to the lineage of the boar's tusk helmet below (see 10.267), the bow that Odysseus leaves in Ithaka also has a particular story, being both an heirloom and guest-gift (*Odyssey* 21.13–41). Steven Farron succinctly describes the importance of the bow in that epic: "Odysseus boasts of his pre-eminence at military archery (*Odyssey* 8.215–222), establishes his right to Penelope with his skill at using the bow and it is his main weapon against the suitors" (Farron 2003: 182). It has been argued (by e.g. Lorimer 1950:296–297 and 483) on this basis that *Iliad* 10 must be composed later than the *Odyssey*. On the problems with this argument, see "Interpreting *Iliad* 10."

10.263–264 ἔκτοσθε δὲ λευκοὶ ὀδόντες / ἀργιόδοντος ὑὸς θαμέες ἔχον ἔνθα καὶ ἔνθα As Hainsworth notes (1993 *ad* 10.261–265), "There is no doubt that a piece of bronze-age equipment is being referred to." But how does this much-discussed example of Bronze Age material culture contribute to our understanding of the composition and poetics of the *Iliad*? Sherratt (1990:818) observes that the boar's tusk helmet "though still occasionally found in graves as late as the 12th and 11th centuries, disappears from representational art of a military nature after 1200 BC." (See also Lorimer 1950:212–219 and Stubbings

1962:516.) Is the boar's tusk helmet evidence that Homeric poetry was being composed in the Bronze Age? Many scholars have rejected such a proposition, and instead have viewed this helmet as an instance of an eighth-century poet deliberately "archaizing" (on this concept, see e.g. Dickinson 1986, Kirk 1960:190ff., and Morris 1986:89ff.). Hainsworth questions whether the verses could survive from the Bronze Age, "their language being in no respect exceptionally archaic"; rather, he asserts that "[t]he poet of this book wanted to introduce an interesting and exotic object." Those who see *Iliad* 10 as a particularly late composition are not inclined to accept that such an old object forms a natural part of this book, and instead prefer to see its inclusion as the work of an archaizing individual. But Sherratt (1990) has shown that, just as there are linguistic layers in the traditional language of Homeric poetry, so too are there archaeological layers that are not well explained by those who seek to isolate and dismiss individual Bronze Age relics as heirlooms or as products of deliberate archaizing. And just as the poetic diction evolved in such a way that we cannot easily separate out Aeolic language from Ionic (see above on 10.18), so too elements of disparate material cultures are integrated into the *Iliad* in such way that they can only be explained as the result of an evolving but also conservative process of oral composition, hundreds of years in the making. The arming scene of Odysseus and Diomedes in *Iliad* 10 is no different than countless other passages in the *Iliad* that include weapons from very different eras (see e.g. Sherratt 1990:810–811 on *Iliad* 19.369–391). Here, the boar's tusk helmet seems to serve a poetic function beyond that of simply being an exotic object, for which see on 10.267.

10.267 Ἀυτόλυκος was Odysseus' maternal grandfather. According to some traditions (Apollodorus 1.112, Pausanias 8.4.6, Ovid *Metamorphoses* 13.146), Autolykos is the son of Hermes (thus making Odysseus Hermes' great-grandson). In *Odyssey* 19.395–396, Autolykos is said be a favorite of Hermes and "preeminent among men in thieving and perjury" (ἀνθρώπους ἐκέκαστο / κλεπτοσύνῃ θ' ὅρκῳ τε), a gift given by Hermes himself. Odysseus is in turn a favorite of Autolykos (see *Odyssey* 19.393ff.). The relationship with Autolykos is one of many links that Odysseus has to the god Hermes, with whom he shares the epithet πολύτροπος ("of many turns," *Odyssey* 1.1; *Homeric Hymn to Hermes* 13). Hermes is the god described in the *Homeric Hymn to Hermes* 13–18 as "crafty of counsel, a robber, a driver of cattle, a leader of dreams, a spy at night, a thief at the gates ... Born at dawn, at mid-day he played the lyre, in the evening he stole the cattle of far-shooting Apollo." Athena's intelligence is central to the attested ambush episodes in Homeric epic (see on 10.275), but Hermes' thieving and crafty ways play a vital role as well. (See also on 10.41 above for the use of the formula νύκτα δι' ὀρφναίην in the *Homeric Hymn to Hermes* 578.) Here Autolykos is said to have stolen the boar's tusk helmet that Odysseus wears from a house that is *pukinos*. The house, in other words, is carefully and solidly built. Its many beams and planks are closely joined one upon the other, much as the boar's tusks are made to fit seamlessly around the helmet. The word *pukinos* unites the *mētis* associated with Odysseus, his maternal grandfather, and Hermes with the cunning required to break into a well-built house and the craft required to construct such a helmet. The invocation of the history of Autolykos' cunning thievery here thus places Odysseus' own cunning in a continuum that stretches back through several generations, much as Diomedes' role in the night raid of *Iliad* is placed in the context of his father Tydeus' ambush history in 10.285–286. See 10.5–9 for more on the meanings of *pukinos*, epsecially as it relates to ambush.

For a similar "lineage" of an object of prestige, see the history of Agamemnon's scepter at *Iliad* 2.101–108. The fact that the object was originally stolen does not seem to disqualify it from becoming a valued guest-gift.

10.273 βάν ῥ' ἰέναι See on 10.32.

10.273 πάντας ἀρίστους In *Iliad* 7, Hektor challenges whoever is the best of the Achaeans (Ἀχαιῶν ... ἄριστος, 7.50) to a duel, which at first only Menelaos accepts, followed (upon the reproach of Nestor) by Agamemnon, Diomedes, the two Ajaxes, Idomeneus, Meriones, Eurypylos, Thoas, and Odysseus. Here, many of the same heroes are being referred to as *aristos*, namely Agamemnon, the two Ajaxes (if Ajax the son of Oileus is indeed present, as he seems to be in our text; see above on 10.228), Idomeneus, and Meriones. For who is "best of the Achaeans" in epic, see above on 10.236.

10.274 ἐρῳδιὸν This bird is a night heron. The Venetus A scholia says that it is an auspicious sign for Diomedes and Odysseus as they depart for clandestine activities and appropriate to the marshy area that they are in (see also 10.466–468 on the tamarisk bush for the marshy place of the ambush of Dolon, as well as "The Poetics of Ambush" for the kind of location where ambushes are often set up). The scholia in the Townley (T) manuscript, according to the edition of Maass, likewise call the bird a good sign for ambushers (ἀγαθὸν λίαν τὸ σημεῖον τοῖς ἐνεδρεύουσιν) and appropriate both because of the marshy place and because it hunts at night and is rapacious (νυκτὸς ἀγρεύει καὶ ἁρπακτικόν ἐστιν). The night heron does exhibit ambush-like behavior in its hunting: it waits while standing still for its prey to come into range at night and also plunders the nests of other birds (see e.g. http://www.enature.com/fieldguides/detail.asp?recnum=BD0117 or http://www.sdakotabirds.com/species/black_crowned_night_heron_info.htm). But what we see in these scholia is part of a "system of associated commonplaces" (Black 1962:39 and above at 10.5–9) that the ancient audience would have had for this bird—namely, that the bird itself is an ambusher found in places used by warriors for ambushes—and those associations make it an appropriate omen. Such associations can be common without empirical evidence of the creature's actual behavior. The fact that the bird is heard but not seen is also appropriate to the poetics of the night, where hearing is the predominant sense.

See Thompson 1895:58–59 for ancient sources on the ἐρῳδιός: he notes that the heron is a symbol of Athena on coins. See also Pollard 1977:68–69 for this bird in general. Pollard notes a story from Aelian relating that Diomedes' men were transformed into herons (Pollard 1977:164), and Vergil alludes to the story that Diomedes' men were turned into some kind of bird at *Aeneid* 11.271–274. Other stories show evidence of a connection between herons and horses (Thompson 1895:59, Pollard 1977:167).

For another bird omen at night, compare the bird omen Zeus sends to Priam before he infiltrates the Achaean camp (*Iliad* 24.315–321).

10.275 Παλλὰς Ἀθηναίη Walter Burkert describes Athena this way: "More than any other Greek deity, Athena is always near her protégés—'Goddess of Nearness' is how Walter F. Otto described her [Otto 1929/1956]. Wherever difficulties disappear and the impossible becomes possible, Athena is at hand, but her presence does not detract from the achievement of the other" (Burkert 1985:141). Athena is present for Odysseus throughout the *Odyssey*, and indeed she guides his entire *nostos* from the opening scene among the gods in Olympia to the conclusion of the strife on Ithaka in the final lines of *Odyssey* 24. They rival one another in cunning intelligence (*mētis*) and, as Burkert notes, Odysseus and Athena's special relationship is exemplified by the way they reveal themselves to one another in *Odyssey* 13. Each knows the other by the false identity/lying tale that each offers to the other. Odysseus' story is that he killed a man in Crete (by ambush—λοχησάμενος, 13.268) and fled, ending up in Ithaka. But Athena knows exactly who he is:

ὣς φάτο, μείδησεν δὲ θεὰ γλαυκῶπις Ἀθήνη,
χειρί τέ μιν κατέρεξε· δέμας δ’ ἤϊκτο γυναικὶ
καλῇ τε μεγάλῃ τε καὶ ἀγλαὰ ἔργα ἰδυίῃ·
290 καί μιν φωνήσασ’ ἔπεα πτερόεντα προσηύδα·
κερδαλέος κ’ εἴη καὶ ἐπίκλοπος, ὅς σε παρέλθοι
ἐν πάντεσσι δόλοισι, καὶ εἰ θεὸς ἀντιάσειε.
σχέτλιε, ποικιλομῆτα, δόλων ἄατ’, οὐκ ἄρ’ ἔμελλες,
οὐδ’ ἐν σῇ περ ἐὼν γαίῃ, λήξειν ἀπατάων
295 μύθων τε κλοπίων, οἵ τοι πεδόθεν φίλοι εἰσίν.
ἀλλ’ ἄγε μηκέτι ταῦτα λεγώμεθα, <u>εἰδότες ἄμφω</u>
<u>κέρδε’, ἐπεὶ σὺ μέν ἐσσι βροτῶν ὄχ’ ἄριστος ἀπάντων</u>
<u>βουλῇ καὶ μύθοισιν, ἐγὼ δ’ ἐν πᾶσι θεοῖσι</u>
<u>μήτι τε κλέομαι καὶ κέρδεσιν·</u> οὐδὲ σύ γ’ ἔγνως
300 Παλλάδ’ Ἀθηναίην, κούρην Διός, ἥ τέ τοι αἰεὶ
ἐν πάντεσσι πόνοισι <u>παρίσταμαι</u> ἠδὲ φυλάσσω,
καὶ δέ σε Φαιήκεσσι φίλον πάντεσσιν ἔθηκα.
νῦν αὖ δεῦρ’ ἱκόμην, ἵνα τοι σὺν <u>μῆτιν</u> ὑφήνω
χρήματά τε κρύψω, ὅσα τοι Φαίηκες ἀγαυοὶ
305 ὤπασαν οἴκαδ’ ἰόντι <u>ἐμῇ βουλῇ τε νόῳ</u> τε ...

Odyssey 13.287–305

So he spoke, and the goddess owl-radiant Athena smiled,
and took him by the hand. In form she resembled a woman
who was beautiful and tall and skilled in splendid
  handiwork.
290 She spoke out and addressed to him winged words:
"He would have to be a wily thief, the man who could get
  past you
in every sort of deception, even if you had a god for an
  antagonist.
You are intractable, crafty in intricate ways, insatiate of
  deception, nor were you about,
even now that you are in your own country, to leave off
  from deceiving
295 and the beguiling words that are constantly dear to you.
But let's no longer talk about these things, *since we both know
  how to be
wily. You are the best of all mortals
in planning [boulē] and words, while I among all the gods
have glory for my craft [mētis] and wiles.* Yet you did not know that

300 I am Pallas Athena, the daughter of Zeus, who always
stands by you in all your labors and watches over you,
who made you dear to all the Phaeacians.
Now again I have come here, in order to weave *mētis* with
you
and hide all the goods that the noble Phaeacians
305 gave to you when you went home*wards by my planning*
[*boulē*] *and my thinking* ... "

Athena is the god that most resembles Odysseus; she embodies the
boulē, mētis, kerdea, doloi, and *noos* that Odysseus is legendary for in the
epic tradition (skills that are the hallmark of ambush warfare). So here
too in *Iliad* 10 Athena is near to Odysseus, and he prays that she stand
by him as she has done in the past (παρίστατοσαι, 10.279). Note the same
formula used in 10.279 and *Odyssey* 13.301: Athena there asserts that
she does indeed stand by him in his many labors.

On Odysseus' relationship with Athena in the *Iliad*, see also Haft
1990:42, who, in discussing the many parallels between *Iliad* 2 and 10,
notes that Athena makes an epiphany to Odysseus in that book. On
Diomedes' relationship with Athena, see below on 10.285.

10.278–279 ἤ τέ μοι αἰεὶ / ἐν πάντεσσι πόνοισι παρίστασαι This same
formulaic language is used at *Odyssey* 13.300–301, when Athena asserts
that she does indeed always stand by Odysseus in every kind of labor.
For a full discussion of that *Odyssey* passage, see on 10.275. For a similar
use of παρίστημι, see below on 10.291.

10.281 πάλιν ἐπὶ νῆας ἐϋκλεῖας ἐφικέσθαι See above on 10.211–212
and "The Poetics of Ambush" for more on the thematic similarities
between nighttime missions and journeys and for the importance of
the safe return. Cf. 10.247.

10.282 ῥέξαντας μέγα ἔργον, ὅ κεν Τρώεσσι μελήσει An interlinear
scholion on this line in the Venetus A indicates that Aristarchus
understood this "great deed" to mean murdering Hektor. See the
Rhesos section of the "Tradition and Reception" essay for more on the
theory that a mission to assassinate Hektor might have been told in
some versions. Just such an assassination attempt is the initial object
of Odysseus and Diomedes' mission in the tragedy *Rhesos* (575–576).
But we should note that, within the context of *Iliad* 10, the murder of
Rhesos and his men fulfills Odysseus' prayer (see below on 10.524).

10.283 βοὴν ἀγαθός The epithet βοὴν ἀγαθός has been used four times in *Iliad* 10 already, for both Menelaos (10.36, 10.60) and Diomedes (10.219, 10.241), as it is used elsewhere for these heroes in the Homeric epics. We take the opportunity to examine in detail the epithet βοὴν ἀγαθός here because an argument has been made (Machacek 1994) that this particular use of it, in this line, has a special meaning, one that should make us reconsider Parry's ideas about how epithets work in Homeric epic. Machacek's article as a whole is a larger reconsideration of Parry's work, from a stated position sympathetic to Parry (Machacek 1994:322). His basic argument pertaining to the use of this formula here is that "a great shout is a liability at this moment" (Machacek 1994:332)—as noise can indeed be in the night. Machacek argues further that this final use of the epithet in the book is contextually appropriate: once the Achaeans have departed on their mission, they will have to be quiet. Machacek makes several assumptions about the ancient audience's reception of this episode, including the assumption that they would notice the absence of the epithet after this point, having noticed its use in previous lines (Machacek 1994:331–333). Before we deal with this argument any further, however, let us examine closely what Parry has to say about this epithet and others like it.

The epithet βοὴν ἀγαθός is what Parry calls a fixed epithet. The four characteristics of fixed epithets, as Parry describes them, are as follows:

> (1) Fixed epithets are used in accordance with their metrical value and not in accordance with their signification;
> (2) they are traditional;
> (3) they are always ornamental;
> (4) they are often generic.
> And these four characteristics—a point which cannot be too much insisted on—are interdependent.

> MHV 165–166

We will elaborate on what each of these characteristics means for our understanding of this traditional epithet, keeping in mind Parry's point that they are all interdependent. We can see that βοὴν ἀγαθός is fixed because it is always used in the same position in the line: it follows the so-called weak or feminine caesura, where the previous word ends at the first short syllable of the third foot, and the first (short) syllable of βοὴν completes the third foot. This placement within the line is common for epithets, and Parry comments that βοὴν ἀγαθός fulfills the same purpose as other epithets that extend from the weak caesura to the bucolic diaresis (that is, where the word-end coincides with the end of the fourth foot), even though this epithet extends beyond the fourth foot (MHV 66). Because of its length, this epithet phrase is used most often with the same two names we see here in Book 10, Menelaos and Diomedes, which have the same metrical shape, ∪∪−×. (It is used with the name Diomedes in the *Iliad* at least twenty-one times; with Menelaos, at least fourteen times in the *Iliad* and at least eight times in the *Odyssey*.) But it has the flexibility to adorn other warriors' names as well: Ajax, Hektor, and Priam's son Polites are also given this epithet, which stays in its same position, while the rest of the line follows a different pattern, from small adjustments such as the inclusion of a τε before Polites' name to greater differences in the metrical patterns for Hektor and Ajax. Thus, as Parry argues about these kinds of "rigorously" fixed epithets as a category, they "clearly must have had, for the poets who used them, an existence independent of any particular type of noun-epithet formula" (MHV 64–65). More controversial is Parry's contention that the poet uses these epithets for metrical reasons rather than their signification. We will have more to say on this below.

The fixed epithet, as Parry says, is also traditional, having been used again and again over time once it was found to be useful for composing in performance. The principle of analogy applies here since the use of the epithet with more than one hero's name is profitable for the singer in performance. Parry describes the process as occurring over time, within the tradition, and argues that we cannot discover which hero had this epithet originally:

> To try to discover in which formula the use of a given epithet is oldest would be pointless. The significant fact is that the bards had no hesitation in applying to any hero an epithet which at some point in time had first been ascribed to one particular hero. It was used a first time for this one person; then it was used again for the same person, when the rhythm allowed it and made its use easy. Then the bards applied it to other persons whose names were of the same metrical value with that of the original owner.

MHV 87

There are five names in the *Iliad* that are given this epithet, but if we had more of the epic tradition, we might see it used even more widely. Conversely, if we had only the *Odyssey*, we would consider this epithet to belong solely to Menelaos. We must be mindful of the limitations of our data when it comes to the larger tradition.

This epithet is also ornamental, meaning that it is not being used in a context in which the warrior is actually shouting in battle. The non-ornamental epithet is one Parry terms "particularized," meaning that it is essential to the context, and to completing the thought of the sentence (see MHV 158–164 for more on particularized epithets). A typical example of an ornamental use of this epithet is found at *Odyssey* 4.307, which describes Menelaos as βοὴν ἀγαθός as he awakes, gets out of bed, and gets dressed at home in Sparta, not displaying any of his shouting prowess. Similarly, the uses here in *Iliad* 10 do not accompany any battlefield cries. There is one case in which the epithet is followed by a shout on the battlefield: in *Iliad* 17, when Ajax and Menelaos are protecting the corpse of Patroklos, Ajax asks Menelaos to call others to help them. Menelaos is called βοὴν ἀγαθός in both the lines that open and close Ajax's request (*Iliad* 17.237, 246). Menelaos then gives a loud, piercing shout to the Danaans (ἤϋσεν δὲ διαπρύσιον Δαναοῖσι γεγωνώς, *Iliad* 17.247). Here, then, we might think the epithet is particularized to the context, since Menelaos is demonstrating his battle-cry. One objection to that idea, however, might be that, with a different vocabulary and purpose—a cry for help—this kind of shout is not the same as the battle shout. But that distinction is not what would matter to Parry, for he says of ornamental epithets like βοὴν ἀγαθός: "After what we have learned of the ornamental meaning of the Homeric epithet, we must recognize the principle that an epithet used in a given noun-epithet formula cannot sometimes be ornamental, sometimes particularized: *it must always be one or the other*" (original emphasis, MHV 156).

Finally, this epithet is also generic. The fixed epithet, according to Parry is also often (though not always) a generic epithet; that is, it is used in noun-epithet formulas without specific characterization of the person it is applied to. Just as the ornamental epithet is contrasted with the particularized, in this case, the generic epithet is the opposite of the distinctive epithet in Parry's terminology. Distinctive epithets are those used for only one hero. In fact, Parry uses βοὴν ἀγαθός as an example of a generic epithet with a general meaning: "The expression βοὴν ἀγαθός will, if used of only one hero, say Diomedes, assign to that hero an unusual power of voice, just as ποδάρκης assigns to Achilles a singular swiftness; said of any hero whatever, the expression will mean no more than 'good at the war-cry as ordinary men are not'" (MHV 146). This idea of the generic meaning of an epithet, especially in combination with Parry's assertion that the fixed epithet is used for its metrical value rather than its signification in context, has elicited strong reactions from critics.

But let us notice first that Parry does not say here that this epithet has no meaning at all; he says only that it does not specify one hero in a way that it specifies no other hero. In other words, the heroes designated βοὴν ἀγαθός are, indeed, good at the battle shout. The fact that more than one hero is so designated suggests that such a skill would have been considered a good and useful one for a warrior, just as the formula itself is good and useful for the singer who is composing in performance. And let us also note that there are situations, such as Menelaos getting out of bed at home in Sparta, in which the epithet carries no immediate meaning for the immediate context. In these situations, especially, Parry's arguments were most illuminating when he first made them, and they freed the critic from spending any more time or energy trying to come up with a reason that the immediate context called for this particular epithet.

With those important insights in mind, we can turn to the more controversial idea that the poet chooses a fixed epithet such as this for metrical purposes. Parry expresses this idea in two ways: first, he argues that, if a generic epithet is applied to several heroes, it is chosen "not according to the character of the hero, but according to the metrical value of his name" (MHV 95). According to this argument, Menelaos and Diomedes both share this trait because their names have the same metrical value. Second, he argues that the metrical shape of the beginning of the line (in this case, that which ends at the weak caesura) determines which epithet is used in that particular line. In other words, heroes acquire certain epithets according to the metrical value of their name, and then which epithet is used in a particular line is determined by the other words in that line. But as we have already seen, this fixed epithet, even as it stays in the same metrical position, can be used for heroes whose names have different metrical values, such as Ajax or Hektor. And the poet is of course shaping the rest of line using the traditional, formulaic language he commands: the use of this language by a skilled singer is as natural as using spoken language is for anyone fluent in it, including the use and creation of formulas by analogy, as Lord has eloquently argued (Lord 1960/2000:30–36). Additionally, as scholars who have followed Parry and Lord have gone on to demonstrate more fully, thought precedes meter in Homeric diction. Meter and formulas do not imprison the poet (see e.g. Nagy 1996b:22–25 and Foley 2002:133–134).

There are additional factors that we need to consider as we use and evaluate Parry's work on epithets. One is that Parry himself did not live to complete his work on Homeric poetry, dying at the young age of thirty-three. Thus the emphasis, seen all too often in scholarly discussions, on his "failures" or the limitations of what he accomplished is, to be frank, unfair. More egregious, however, is treating Parry's work as though nothing has come after it, when its issues and questions have been thoroughly addressed and its insights expanded upon by generations of scholars. To properly evaluate Parry's work, these subsequent studies must also be acknowledged and accounted for.[2]

With that in mind, how should we understand this use of the epithet, or the four others in this Book, or those in the Homeric epics overall? As we have already noted, the epithet has a general meaning for a warrior with a particular skill. For the heroes who are given this epithet, it has a larger meaning within the epic tradition as a whole: although we may not see the heroes shouting at the times when they receive the epithet, within the tradition as a whole, it tells us something about what kind of a warrior the hero is. This larger meaning has already been noted by Parry (MHV 137–138) and Lord (1960/2000:65–67), and both the concept of a formula's traditional meaning and its significance for the poetics of the epics have been expanded upon by Nagy, Foley, and many others. (See the discussion above on the epithet ποιμένα λαῶν at 10.3.)

We can now return to the question of whether this particular use of the epithet has a contextual meaning in connection with the need for silence on an ambush. Machacek's argument implicitly understands this aspect of the poetics of ambush, the need for stealth and quiet. In fact, in the earlier episode of this night, Agamemnon asks his herald to summon the Achaeans for an assembly, but tells him not to shout (μηδὲ βοᾶν, *Iliad* 9.12), indicating that, even at that point in the night, and even within the encampment, only quiet speaking is appropriate. This need for quiet and stealth, however, prompts the question of whether the epithet should be used at all during night episodes if its meaning is felt to be tied so closely to the current circumstances, as Machacek suggests it is. His answer is that the singer uses it four times

---

[2] For a concise bibliography of scholarship since Parry that seeks to appreciate the creativity of a poet working within a traditional medium, see Martin 1989:151n16. This brief bibliography is of course already twenty years out of date. See "Interpreting *Iliad* 10" for a survey of more recent work. The journal *Oral Tradition* regularly publishes interdisciplinary scholarship that builds on the fieldwork and insights of Parry and Lord.

in *Iliad* 10 precisely so that the audience will notice its absence in the rest of the book, when Diomedes is actually on the mission. Machacek proposes that the audience members even "listened carefully to see if he [the singer] would slip up and so describe Diomedes" (Machacek 1994:332). Beyond being an odd conception of the relationship between the singer and audience—in which the audience's reception is focused on waiting for the singer to make a mistake, and a "literary" mistake at that—such a formulation also misunderstands the important point that the audience, as well as the singer, knows Diomedes to be well-known for his battle shout at all times, whether or not he is shouting (and in all instances where Diomedes gets this epithet in *Iliad* 10, he is not).

Instead, we have to recognize that this epithet is not particularly associated with the ambush theme, even though it is used several times in this particular ambush episode. On some deeply felt level, but perhaps not an immediate one, the audience would associate this epithet with Diomedes' (and Menelaos') prowess as a warrior in the *polemos*, where the battle shout is appropriate, and they would know from hearing many episodes from the Trojan War, and perhaps even the Theban epic tradition, that Diomedes is a warrior who excels at both *polemos* and *lokhos*. (See also our discussion of Diomedes in these terms in "The Poetics of Ambush.") In some ways, though, the uses of this epithet reaffirm Parry's own observations about how epithet formulas, in particular, can be used in situations in Homeric poetry where they would seem odd or even contradictory in poetry that was not oral and traditional. The singer was not forced by metrical considerations to use this formula, but it was useful for the composition of this Book, even though a battle shout happens nowhere in the episode itself and Diomedes, as well as Odysseus, avoids making excessive noise.

There is one other major methodological problem with Machacek's argument: it is predicated on this line containing the final instance of this epithet formula. When we consult modern editions of *Iliad* 10, this can easily appear to be the case. But when we consider the full range of evidence, including papyri and the scholia, and when we fully grasp what composition-in-performance means for the multiformity of the epic tradition (for more on these topics, see our essay "*Iliad* 10: A Multitextual Approach"), we see that such arguments about epithets in particular can be refuted on an empirical basis. On the papyrus that both Allen and West refer to as "p90" (Oxyrhynchus 6.949 from the second–third century CE), there is a possible use of this epithet again at

10.446: [τον δ ημειβετ επειτα βοην αγα]θος Διομηδης, which would put it squarely in the middle of the mission, after Diomedes and Odysseus have captured Dolon. And from the scholia to both the Venetus A and Townley manuscripts, we hear of a version of 10.349, known to the Homeric critic Aristophanes, that also uses this epithet: ὣς ἔφατ', οὐδ' ἀπίθησε βοὴν ἀγαθὸς Διομήδης. (See our textual commentary, on the the Venetus A text, p. 217, for more on this multiform.)

Since name-epithet formulas were so useful, flexible, and traditional—all qualities that Parry himself identifies—it is difficult to prove the argument that the absence of one in a particular passage is significant: even with our limited evidence we can see that this epithet could indeed be used again in this episode, and that doing so would not be considered a "mistake" that an audience would find out of place. Instead, a thorough understanding of the oral traditional poetics of these formulas requires us to take a larger view of their meaning, just as an understanding of the textual tradition requires us to take into account all the evidence we have and to recognize that a singer might have sung this same episode with the variation natural to composition-in-performance. These are some of the differences between Homeric epic and modern poetry that Parry enjoins us to acknowledge and to appreciate with a different aesthetics.

10.284 Διὸς τέκος Ἀτρυτώνη As an epithet of Athena, Ἀτρυτώνη is used within the epic tradition for direct address: in our texts, she is addressed this way either by Hera (*Iliad* 2.157, 5.714, 21.420) or by a mortal praying to her (Diomedes here and at *Iliad* 5.115; Penelope at *Odyssey* 4.762; Odysseus at *Odyssey* 6.324). The Venetus A manuscript at *Iliad* 2.157 has a gloss written directly above this epithet that says "inexhaustible" (ἀκαταπόνητε). In all of these cases the name is part of an extended formula Διὸς τέκος Ἀτρυτώνη, and in all other instances besides this αἰγιόχοιο precedes Διός (see 10.278 for a use of the formula αἰγιόχοιο Διὸς τέκος without Ἀτρυτώνη). Thus the formula is one we see regularly throughout the epics, and it is therefore an example of the traditional nature of the language of *Iliad* 10. But should we find the absence of αἰγιόχοιο in this line evidence of nontraditional usage? We would argue no, since what actually seems to alter the compositional needs of this line is the fact that this is the second in a two-fold prayer to Athena ("Hear now *also me*"), which is not the case in the other attested examples.

Wherever this formula is used, Athena is reported as having listened to the prayers of the mortals who address her as such (see

Iliad 5.121, *Iliad* 10.295, *Odyssey* 4.767, and *Odyssey* 6.328). When Hera addresses her with this epithet, Athena springs into action to do whatever Hera has asked after that initial address. Thus within the tradition it seems a particularly effective way to address the goddess in order to gain her attention. Formulas involving the gods are used especially in prayer contexts (Parry MHV 77–78, 181–182), and this one should be counted among them.

10.285 σπεῖό ... ἕσπεο Within the epic tradition this verb can have a marked meaning, signifying a god who accompanies a hero and gives him special protection or help. We see the same verb later indicating that Athena is indeed accompanying (ἕπουσαν, 10.516) Diomedes— Apollo is said to see her doing so. Athena has already signaled her presence through a bird sign (10.274–275), and will later speak to Diomedes (10.507–512), although she remains unseen throughout. In other cases, Athena "accompanies" mortals in disguise: at *Odyssey* 2.287 while disguised as Mentor she offers to accompany Telemakhos on his journey, and at *Odyssey* 6.32 appearing to Nausikaa in a dream in the guise of the daughter of Dymas she says she will accompany her. (Although she does not go with Nausikaa in this form, she is present at the washing place.)

Parallel to Athena accompanying Diomedes and Odysseus on this night mission, Iris tells Priam in a dream that Hermes will accompany him on his night mission to the Achaean camp to ransom Hektor's body (*Iliad* 24.182), and of course, Hermes does so in disguise (see above on 10.1ff. for more on how Priam's mission is similar to the ambush theme). Thus we find that this particular use of the verb for gods accompanying mortals has associations with dreams, disguise, and night missions. As we have noted in "The Poetics of Ambush," there is thematic overlap between such missions and journeys. Therefore, in addition to Athena saying she will accompany Telemakhos on his journey at *Odyssey* 2.287, we can also include among the examples of this theme Nestor's proclamation that the gods in general accompany Telemakhos on his journey: τοι νέῳ ὧδε θεοὶ πομπῆες ἕπονται (*Odyssey* 3.376). Athena has a special relationship with Odysseus (see the commentary on 10.275 for more on that relationship), and that intimacy extends to his son. Here, Diomedes asks for the same kind of consideration based on her relationship with his father. We know that Diomedes indeed has such a relationship with Athena from *Iliad* 5. See also 10.291.

Finally, we may compare this use of ἕπομαι for god and mortal pairs to its use for teams of warriors; it is used not only of the team of ambushers here in *Iliad* 10 (10.222, 10.227, 10.246), but also of warriors who team up in daytime battle, as at *Iliad* 11.472, 15.559, and 16.632. In each of those latter cases, the one warrior asks the other to join him in pushing the enemy back, and when the second follows/accompanies him, he is called "a man equal to a god," using the same formula: ὣς εἰπὼν ὃ μὲν ἦρχ', ὃ δ' ἅμ' ἕσπετο ἰσόθεος φώς ("So speaking he led the way and the other man, equal to a god, accompanied him").

10.285–290 Another rich epic tradition, one centered on the city of Thebes, is alluded to here, as it is at other places in the *Iliad*. The story of the Seven Against Thebes seems to have been a parallel epic tradition to that of the Trojan War, out of which the *Iliad* and *Odyssey* emerged: Hesiod refers to these two wars as those fought by the generation of Heroes (*Works & Days* 161–165). Yet, because the ancient Greek epics known as the *Thebaid* and *Epigonoi* are not extant, with only a few fragments surviving in other sources, the *Iliad* is one of our best and earliest sources for this tradition. The *Iliad* refers to this other tradition in some detail not only here, but also at *Iliad* 4.376–410, *Iliad* 5.800–808, *Iliad* 6.222–223, and *Iliad* 14.113–126. (See Gantz 1993:502–525 for other sources.) These *Iliad* passages refer to two different wars on Thebes. The first attack is instigated by the Theban Polyneikes (son of Oedipus) after his brother Eteokles denies him his share of the kingship of Thebes. Polyneikes then gathers a large military force with the help of his father-in-law Adrastos of Argos and Tydeus, Diomedes' father, who is also an exile from his native city Kalydon (see *Iliad* 14.115–120). The other leaders vary according to the source, but can include Kapaneus, Amphiaraos, Parthenopaios, Eteoklos, Hippomedon, Mekisteus, and Lykourgos. The Seven are defeated at Thebes, as is at least implied at *Iliad* 4.405–409, *Iliad* 6.222–223, and *Iliad* 14.114. The second war was one of revenge by the sons of the Seven, called the *epigonoi*, some time later, when the sons reached manhood (Diomedes tells Glaukos he never knew his father because he was so young when Tydeus died at Thebes, *Iliad* 6.222–223). The sons who fight at Thebes include Diomedes and his daytime fighting partner Sthenelos, son of Kapaneus. As Sthenelos indicates, they are successful in sacking Thebes (see *Iliad* 4.403–410). Thus these two are a link between the two epic traditions, since they fight both at Thebes and at Troy. In an oral performance tradition, the singer can allude to the subject matter of other epics in this kind of compressed way and expect an audience to understand the allusion (see further on 10.289–290 below).

10.288 μειλίχιον μῦθον The semantic range of μειλίχιος when used to describe words or speech is a broad one. Kind or gracious words are used to persuade or encourage. The adjective modifies both *muthos* (used three times) and even more often *epos* (used nineteen times) in our texts. It is also used as a substantive with the verb προσηύδα (used three times) to indicate this kind of speech. These persuasive words are used between friends. The one context in which this is patently not the case is informative because it uses its antonym to indicate how unsuccessful such persuasion can be between enemies. At *Iliad* 11.137 two Trojans, Peisandros and Hippolokhos, beg Agamemnon in battle to ransom them as prisoners of war rather than kill them. The narrator says they use gracious speech in their request, but hear an ungracious voice in response (ὣς τώ γε κλαίοντε προσαυδήτην βασιλῆα / μειλιχίοις ἐπέεσσιν· ἀμείλικτον δ᾽ ὄπ᾽ ἄκουσαν, *Iliad* 11.136–137). Agamemnon refuses their pleas and kills them (compare *Iliad* 21.98 for a similar refusal also termed an "ungracious voice in response").

As we will discuss further below (see 10.542), the semantic range of μειλίχιος also includes speech between friends in which the adjective is used with words of welcome (see also *Odyssey* 19.415 and 24.393). Similarly, Diomedes uses such words with Glaukos once he realizes that their grandfathers were guest-friends (*Iliad* 6.214).

This last example brings us to contexts where the words are used to address those who are, could be, or should be friends, but who either are or could be angry with or hostile to the speaker. For example, Helen speaks to Hektor this way when he comes to retrieve Paris, and her words are meant to show him her shame at her own conduct as well as that of Paris (*Iliad* 6.343; see Ebbott 1999 for more on the way Helen's shame is portrayed in the *Iliad*). When Odysseus and Nausikaa see each other, he wonders what would be the best way to approach her: to supplicate her by taking hold of her knees, or stand further off and use gracious words (ἐπέεσσιν ἀποσταδὰ μειλιχίοισι, *Odyssey* 6.143). He decides on this second option because if he clasps her knees (naked as he is), she might get angry (*Odyssey* 6.145–147), and so he speaks a gracious and cunning speech (μειλίχιον καὶ κερδαλέον φάτο μῦθον, *Odyssey* 6.148), which, of course, he hopes will persuade her to help him.

In addition to these cases of such words meant to assuage or forestall someone's anger, we have two final examples that are even closer to the case of Tydeus and therefore help us understand the traditional story behind his embassy to the Thebans. Odysseus speaks with such words to Ajax in the underworld, hoping to persuade his friend turned enemy to speak with him (τὸν μὲν ἐγὼν ἐπέεσσι προσηύδων μειλιχίοισιν, *Odyssey* 11.552). And Nestor proposes approaching Achilles with these kinds of words as well as with gifts to persuade him to return (δώροισίν τ' ἀγανοῖσιν ἔπεσσί τε μειλιχίοισι, *Iliad* 9.113). Once we see the wide range of contexts in which this kind of speech can be used, we understand better that Tydeus is sent as a messenger to the Thebans in order to persuade them, and that he comes as a friend to friends who may nevertheless be hostile to him (as indeed they turn out to be). Tydeus comes on behalf of Polyneikes, of course, who was supposed to share the kingship of Thebes with his brother Eteokles. When Tydeus' words of persuasion (presumably, urging him to follow this original arrangement) fail, he is later ambushed. The attack of the Seven against Thebes will be the next step. But we can infer that Tydeus' speech, if we had an example of it from an ancient epic about the Theban war, would have started from a friendly stance and would have been gracious toward Eteokles and the Thebans.

10.289–290 This allusion provides a good illustration of the workings of the *Iliad*'s performance context. Diomedes says only that Tydeus is able to "mastermind astounding deeds" with Athena's help on this occasion, without any further detail needed for his internal audience, since Athena would know what happened. A traditional audience of the *Iliad*, however, would also readily know the events to which Diomedes refers, and this compressed reference would evoke the entire episode for them, whereas we have to try to reconstruct it as best we can. As we have seen, this episode is also related to Diomedes by Agamemnon at *Iliad* 4.382–398 and Athena at *Iliad* 5.800–808 as they both try to spur him on to live up to his father's fighting prowess. As we saw above on 10.48, the phrase *mermera erga* refers to one man defeating many more, and Tydeus does this twice, in fact, when he is sent alone to Thebes as a messenger. In *Iliad* 4 and 5, we learn that Tydeus challenges the Thebans to athletic contests, and defeats them all easily, because Athena helps him (*Iliad* 4.389–390 ≈ 5.807–808). But in *Iliad* 4, Agamemnon continues the story by saying that the Thebans in retaliation send fifty men to ambush Tydeus (they go on a πυκινὸν λόχον, *Iliad* 4.391–393; see above at 10.5–9 for the implications of *pukinos* in an ambush context). Tydeus defeats them as well, slaying all of them except for Maion, whom he intentionally leaves alive in obedience to the portents of the gods (*Iliad* 4.396–398). The A scholia on *Iliad* 4.394 inform us that "some guess that Maion was a herald, and for that reason he alone was saved."

Nevertheless, Tydeus' status as *angelos* does not protect him from being attacked. In his much later (and Latin) epic *Thebaid*, Statius portrays Maion as a seer, and Tydeus makes him a herald by default, giving him the message to take back to Thebes to prepare for war (*Thebaid* 2.682–703).

We see here that, in addition to *mermera erga* indicating one man defeating many, it can apply to either daytime fighting in open battle (as in the case of Hektor above [10.48] and at *Iliad* 11.502, in the case of Achilles at *Iliad* 21.217, and in Zeus' phrase πολέμοιό τε μέρμερα ἔργα at *Iliad* 8.453) or nighttime/ambush fighting, as in this case and also below on 10.524. Here and on 10.48, these astounding deeds are associated with verbs like μήδομαι (10.52 as well as this line) and μητίομαι (10.48), so whether daytime battle or nighttime ambush, whether attacker or attacked, such success against greater numbers can be thought of as "devised" or "masterminded." Also, in this case, the fact that one ambusher is left alive is a significant detail. In the poetics of ambush, there is narrative tension surrounding the possibility of not knowing what happens to those who go on a spying mission, an ambush, or another nighttime expedition unless they return successfully. Maion's return, although apparently granted by the gods, is also necessary for Tydeus' victory to be known.

This allusion indicates that ambush was a theme in the Theban epic tradition as well. Like Bellerophon (*Iliad* 6.187–190), Tydeus is successful in defeating the ambushers even though he is vastly outnumbered. Another night episode within this tradition that shares features with *Iliad* 10 is Tydeus' arrival in Argos after his exile. The scholia to *Iliad* 4.376 from the Venetus A relate the story that both Tydeus and Polyneikes arrive at the house of Adrastos at night, each wearing an animal skin, like those of the heroes in *Iliad* 10. Tydeus wears a boar skin, and Polyneikes a lion skin. Adrastos had received an oracle that he should marry his daughters to a lion and a boar, and seeing these men on his doorstep he realizes that they should be his sons-in-law. As we have argued above, the wearing of animal skins puts the episode in a distinct register. The connection to the animals mentioned in the oracle plays off that register, by making the meaning of the skins symbolic in a more particular way. See also the commentary on Dolon's wolf skin at 10.334.

10.291 ὡς νῦν μοι ἐθέλουσα παρίστασο καί με φύλασσε As we saw with the verb ἕπομαι on 10.285, Athena in particular is a goddess who stands by and protects the heroes she favors. She asserts to Diomedes on the battlefield that she indeed does what he asks her to do in his prayer: σοὶ δ᾽ ἤτοι μὲν ἐγὼ παρά θ᾽ ἵσταμαι ἠδὲ φυλάσσω ("Indeed I stand by you and guard you," *Iliad* 5.809). In the *Odyssey*, she claims the same thing to Odysseus, using the same verbs: ἐν πάντεσσι πόνοισι παρίσταμαι ἠδὲ φυλάσσω (*Odyssey* 13.301). For the use of παρίσταμαι we can also compare the use of this same verb at *Odyssey* 3.222, when Nestor tells Telemakhos that Athena used to stand beside Odysseus openly: ὣς κείνῳ ἀναφανδὰ παρίστατο Παλλὰς Ἀθήνη. (See above on 10.275 and 10.278–279 for more on Odysseus' relationship with Athena.) Thus this line is yet another clear example of the traditional language in *Iliad* 10. Diomedes requests Athena's assistance here on the basis of that which she had given his father, and when Athena uses this combination of verbs at *Iliad* 5.809, it is also in the context of a comparison between Tydeus and Diomedes. Thus we see again (cf. 10.285) a patrilineal continuation of Athena's special protection of her favorite heroes.

10.292–294 These lines are the same as those found in our texts at *Odyssey* 3.382–384. In the *Odyssey*, it is Nestor making the promise of such a sacrifice, again to Athena. Nestor prays to Athena for good *kleos* for himself, his children, and his wife and promises her in return this same kind of unbroken one-year-old cow with gilded horns. The identical vow in both contexts suggests that an unbroken cow is especially appropriate for Athena, perhaps because of her own virgin status, and, of course, that the sacrifice is made in reciprocity for success. But also suggestive is the vow's close association in both cases with Athena's personal involvement with heroes, and specifically her accompaniment of them on a particular mission. Although it is not Telemakhos who makes the vow (the way Diomedes does here), Nestor mentions that she accompanies Telemakhos before he makes the vow in return for his own *kleos*.

10.296 It is a typical feature of Homeric poetry and its oral traditional nature to say again that they had both prayed even after the previous line, which closes Diomedes' prayer, indicates the same. The "fullness of expression" that may at times seem feeble or repetitive in poetry composed in writing is a natural component of oral composition-in-performance.

10.297 βάν ῥ᾽ ἴμεν See on 10.32.

10.297 ὥς τε λέοντε δύω There are other examples in our Homeric texts of a pair of lions together. Only in the case of Hektor and

Patroklos fighting do we find a simile of two lions fighting each other (*Iliad* 16.756–761). There are three examples, however, of lions hunting together as a team. At *Iliad* 5.539–560, Aeneas kills two twin brothers, Orsilokhos and Krethon, who are compared to two lions that prey on cattle and sheep until they are finally killed by the weapons of men. At *Iliad* 13.170–202, Teucer kills the Trojan Imbrios, and Hektor in return kills Amphimakhos. Ajax beats Hektor back, and the Achaeans drag both corpses out of battle. The Aiante, when they carry the corpse of Imbrios off the battlefield, are compared to two lions snatching a goat from the guard dogs and carrying it high in their jaws into the brush. These lion similes belong to a tradition of similes about lions attacking herds of domesticated animals, whether cattle, sheep, or goats, which are often protected by dogs and men. There are also two lions depicted on the shield of Achilles that attack a bull, drag it off, and gorge themselves on its blood while keeping dogs at bay (*Iliad* 18.579–586). A pair of lions working together, therefore, seems to be a traditional image, and as we can see from the similes in *Iliad* 5 and 13, this image is associated with special pairs of fighters. See above on 10.243 for Diomedes and Odysseus as one of these special pairs, especially in ambush situations, and also on 10.53 and 10.228 for the Aiante, when that dual form means Ajax and Teucer, as it seems to in *Iliad* 13. For more on lion similes in Homeric epic, see Scott 1974, Moulton 1977, Schnapp-Gourbeillon 1981, Lonsdale 1990, and Muellner 1990.

Also noteworthy in this simile, in terms of composition, is the lack of clear division between the lions and the warriors—both can be imagined going through the night, slaughter, corpses, war gear, and black blood. That is, at the end of 10.297 it seems like we could be going into an extended simile, but once we reach 10.298, and especially the mention of the war gear, we must reconsider the boundary of the simile. The simile then seems to be of the sort that is the ultimate compression: simply "like two lions" (compare other compressed lion similes at *Iliad* 5.299, 11.129, 12.293, 15.592, 17.542, and 24.572 and at *Odyssey* 9.292 and 23.48). Leonard Muellner (1990) has compellingly argued that these shorter similes are indeed compressed versions of the longer, more detailed lion similes, rather than the longer being (newer) extensions of these shorter types. Therefore, even this short phrase would evoke the imagery of two lions working together, as we see in greater detail in other similes. For similes involving lions that attack at night, see 10.485–488. See Scott 1974:90 for the combination, as on this line, of the formula βῆ/βᾶν δ'/ῥ' ἴμεν followed by a simile.

10.298 ἂμ φόνον, ἂν νέκυας, διά τ’ ἔντεα καὶ μέλαν αἷμα As we have already seen on 10.199, corpses and gore are a significant feature of the landscape on this night. The second half of this line (διά τ’ ἔντεα καὶ μέλαν αἷμα) appears again at 10.469 as Odysseus and Diomedes move toward the Thracians. The scholia cite this phrase in different ways, reflecting various practices of ancient textual criticism. Looking at just the scholia in the Townley manuscripts (in the edition of Maass), for example, we see that the phrase is cited as a parallel use of διά with an accusative, as on *Iliad* 15.1 and 22.190. In this way, 10.298 is treated no differently from any other line in showing "Homeric" usage. This same phrase, however, is objected to on *Iliad* 23.806, because it is "transferred from the Doloneia," an argument that reflects the Alexandrian dislike of repeated phrases, even though we know they are a natural and necessary element of oral composition-in-performance (see also 10.51–52).

10.299–300 οὐδὲ μὲν οὐδὲ Τρῶας ἀγήνορας εἴασεν Ἕκτωρ / εὕδειν, ἀλλ’ ἄμυδις κικλήσκετο πάντας ἀρίστους At the beginning of *Iliad* 10, where Agamemnon cannot sleep because of worry, he looks out at the Trojan encampment and wonders at both the sight of the many fires and the sounds of flutes and pipes and the clamor of men (see 10.11–13). From that description, we already know that the Trojans are not sleeping. But this passage can also be a compressed version of the theme of a leader who cannot sleep and so calls together a council to make a plan. We see such a theme at the beginning of *Iliad* 2, as well as in this book (see comments at 10.1ff.). In the process of oral composition-in-performance, the singer can compress or expand a theme, Lord's term for "the groups of ideas regularly used in telling a tale in the formulaic style of traditional song" (Lord 1960/2000:68; for the singer's ability to expand and compress themes, see Lord 1960/2000:78–80, 88–91). So here the singer, who has already sung a version of the theme for the scene at the Achaean camp, merely mentions sleeplessness and the calling together of the council without the development and expansion seen earlier. Even the enjambment of the verb εὕδειν on the second line of this compressed version is reminiscent of that at *Iliad* 2.2 and 10.2, indicating a compositional pattern.

10.300–301 The identity of the ἄριστοι (10.300) whom Hektor calls together is explained by the following line: the leaders and rulers of the Trojans. On both sides, the leaders are regularly called the ἄριστοι (compare the same sense of the word on 10.1, 10.117, 10.214, and 10.273, as well as below on 10.326). Within this group, however, there is a competition to be the best of all, and participation in these dangerous nighttime missions is part of that competition: see above on 10.236 for this heightened sense of the word ἄριστος and the role that the best men play in ambush.

10.302 πυκινὴν ἠρτύνετο βουλήν See above on 10.5–9 and 10.43–44 for more on the significance of πυκινός and planning in the ambush theme. This same phrase is used at *Iliad* 2.55, another episode that begins at night, when the Achaeans are similarly debating the very thing that Hektor wants to find out on this night: whether they should continue fighting or return home. There, the plan they decide upon also involves deception. In other contexts, too, the verb ἀρτύνω is used to set an ambush (*Odyssey* 14.469) or to devise false stories (*Odyssey* 11.366), so it, too, has thematic associations with cunning, deception, and ambush. Thus the whole phrase thematically encompasses the kind of plan that Hektor here proposes.

10.304 μισθός Disapproving interpretations of this term have added to the negative reception of the character of Dolon, from the scholia in the Venetus B and Townley manuscripts through to negative assumptions made in passing in more recent studies such as Schnapp-Goubeillon 1982:58, Holoka 1983:8, and Coffee 2009:62. (Hektor is criticized as well for offering a reward that he does not himself have, at that point, to give.) In Homeric diction, the term is used as remuneration for work, such as woodworking (*Iliad* 12.435) or shepherding (*Odyssey* 10.84), and can be used within a taunt (*Odyssey* 18.358, although so can 'guest-gift' [see *Odyssey* 9.370]). But *misthos* is also used for what Poseidon and Apollo expect in return for building the walls of Troy (*Iliad* 21.445, 21.450, 21.451, 21.457), so the labor itself need not be common. μισθός is also connected with another ambush episode: Menelaos says that the "pay" for the men who watched for Agamemnon's return on Aegisthus' behalf was two talents of gold (*Odyssey* 4.524–526). There, the task has a negative sense to it, but does the fact that pay is involved make this so? Focusing exclusively on the word *misthos* here ignores both that the reward is called a δῶρον in this same line (similar to Nestor calling his offer a δόσις, see 10.213) and that the spy will get κῦδος (10.307) for this mission as well. There may indeed be an implicit contrast in the poetry between the rewards offered on each side on this night, but condemnation of Dolon based on a notion of "work-for-pay" is too extreme, nor does it seem evident that *misthos* is indicative of the "unheroic" character of Dolon or of the Doloneia as a whole.

10.305 ἐριαύχενας ἵππους Parry notes that ἐρι- is the Aeolic prefix. The Ionic form, ἀρι-, has the same metrical value, and so we would expect such words to shift to the Ionic. But, Parry argues, exceptions to that general rule of the evolution of Homeric language, such as we have in this case, show that "not only the bards' habit of using epithets with the Aeolic prefix, but also their sense of the formula which contained such epithets, protected the prefix here from their tendency to keep only those elements of the λέξις ξενική which differed metrically from the corresponding Ionic forms." Parry also notes that ἐριαύχενας appears only within this formula (Parry, MHV 181n1). From this we can see how conservative the oral composition process can be, in addition to how formulaic phrases can be thought of, used, and preserved by the singers as a unit.

10.305–306 The recorded textual multiforms for 10.306 provide a good example of how oral composition operates within its tradition. In 10.305, Hektor offers as the great gift a chariot and two horses, and in the reading of the main text of the Venetus A, in 10.306, he further qualifies that he will give whichever horses are best at the swift ships of the Achaeans (οἵ κεν ἀριστεύωσι θοῆς ἐπὶ νηυσίν Ἀχαιῶν). The scholia in the A manuscript record three different readings by the three major Alexandrian Homeric scholars, which in turn all differ from this main text. First, it says that Aristarchus read οἵ κεν ἄριστοι ἔωσι θοῆς ἐπὶ νηυσίν Ἀχαιῶν. The meanings of that version and that of the main text of A are similar: Hektor indicates that the gift will be the best of the Achaean horses, but he does not make it any more specific. The difference between ἀριστεύωσι and ἄριστοι ἔωσι may be a performance variation, or it might have been introduced at some point in the textual tradition. Both Zenodotus and Aristophanes, however, knew versions of a line that did specify which horses: those of Achilles. Zenodotus read αὐτοὺς οἳ φορέουσι ἀμύμονα Πηλείωνα ("the ones which carry the faultless son of Peleus"), similar to line 10.323 below. Aristophanes read something slightly different: καλοὺς οἳ φορέουσι ἀμύμονα Πηλείωνα ("the fine ones which carry the faultless son of Peleus").

In these four readings, then, we see how from performance to performance certain words or phrases might be used in place of one another, ἀριστεύωσι or ἄριστοι ἔωσι, αὐτοὺς or καλοὺς. But the choice between simply stating "whichever are best" and specifying the horses of Achilles reveals a deeper layer. In either case, Dolon would likely name the horses of Achilles in his reply, as he does in our version (see 10.323), so it is not a question of someone else's horses being offered as a prize that is at issue here. Instead, if the singer sings "whichever are best at the ships of the Achaeans," a traditional audience will immediately think of Achilles' horses, knowing that they are indeed the best. We know this, too, because at the end of the catalog of ships, the narrator asks the Muse who was the best of the men, and who the best of the horses (*Iliad* 2.761–762). Eumelos' mares are at first mentioned as the best horses (*Iliad* 2.763–765) and Ajax, son of Telamon, as the best man, but then both are qualified by the statement that this was true only so long as Achilles stayed angry, since both he and his horses were by far the best (*Iliad* 2.768–770; there, too, we have a similar phrase to describe the horses: ἵπποι θ᾽ οἳ φορέεσκον ἀμύμονα Πηλείωνα). So the singer may be implicit or explicit about which horses Hektor is offering, and these textual variations record different possibilities for how the line was performed. As we will see in further detail below (see 10.332), in both the Iliadic tradition and in other versions of this story, Hektor has his own designs on capturing the horses of Achilles (for example, he pursues them after the death of Patroklos, who drove them into battle, see *Iliad* 17.483–496), and the performance variation of whether Hektor is explicit or not in naming Achilles' horses as the reward may be related to whether the singer has in mind that aspect of the tradition. In any case, these variations recorded in the scholia of the Venetus A reveal the multiplicity of the compositional possibilities here.

10.307 τλαίη See p. 75 and on 10.248 for the connection between this verb and ambush.

10.307 κῦδος ἄροιτο For this use of *arnumai* with *kudos* or *kleos*, compare *Iliad* 4.95 and 5.3 and *Odyssey* 1.240. Just as Nestor promises both κλέος and a δόσις for whoever will undertake the spying mission for the Achaeans (see above on 10.212–213), so also Hektor promises a δῶρον (304) and also κῦδος to the volunteer among the Trojans. As we argued above, these are clear indications that success on an ambush was considered prestigious for Homeric warriors.

10.312 καμάτῳ ἀδηκότες See on 10.98 for more on this phrase.

10.313 ὣς ἔφαθ᾽, οἱ δ᾽ ἄρα πάντες ἀκὴν ἐγένοντο σιωπῇ This is a whole line formula, which we find in nine other places in our texts: *Iliad* 3.95, 7.92, 7.398, 8.28, 9.29, 9.430, 9.693, 10.218, 23.676. At 10.218, the same verse is used for the Achaean reaction to Nestor's proposal for a spying mission. In general the formula is used after a challenge by one man to a group, whether his own comrades or the enemy, and this verse serves as a pause before another individual responds in one way or another to the challenge. It is another example of the traditional nature of the language of *Iliad* 10.

10.314–317 These four lines provide us a brief introduction to Dolon. We are given his father's name (314), and we learn that his father was a herald (315) and that Dolon was his only son, but that he had five sisters (317). Dolon is also described as wealthy (315), not good looking, and swift (316). We discuss in detail in the Dolon section of our essay "Tradition and Reception" how we understand Dolon's traditional status. Here, we will look at each of these elements individually, each in its own context. To understand these characteristics properly, we must investigate what each attribute would mean to a traditional audience by examining evidence from the tradition itself, leaving aside any of our own cultural assumptions.

10.314–315 Εὐμήδεος υἱὸς / κήρυκος θείοιο A patronymic is often read as a sign of traditionality: that is, a character with a patronymic has a lineage within traditional epic (for more about this initial line of introduction, see "Tradition and Reception" above). As we see here, and again when the patronymic is used on lines 412 and 426, it is also a useful formula for composition: combined with Dolon's name, it fills the line from the weak caesura to the end of the line, one of the most common metrical patterns for name-epithet formulas. The enjambment of his father's occupation on the next line is compositionally noteworthy: it is not necessary to complete the thought of the previous line (indeed, none of these details are strictly necessary—line 318 could follow 314 with no loss of sense). As Lord reminds us, "This absence of necessary enjambment is a characteristic of oral composition and is one of the easiest touchstones to apply in testing the orality of a poem. Milman Parry called it an 'adding style'; the term is apt" (Lord 1960/2000:54). Eumedes' role as herald must strongly suggest itself to the singer when his name is used in the patronymic formula. Scholiasts offer the possibility that Odysseus and Diomedes would perhaps know Dolon because he accompanied his father on official dispatches to the Greek camp (see below on 10.447). But there may also be implicit contrasts here: his father the herald visits the Achaean camp in an official capacity during the *daylight*. We can compare *Iliad* 7.370–415, when the Trojans decide *at dinner time* to send Idaios to the Achaeans *at dawn* the next day (see *Iliad* 7.370–372, 380–381). That is, it is made explicit that the herald will wait for daylight to go to the opposing camp, rather than immediately going in the dark. Dolon, as a spy at night, is a different kind of unofficial "visitor" to the enemy camp. Heralds are divinely protected in their duties, as the epithet θεῖος indicates, but spies are not, and Dolon cannot expect protection, or even mercy, when he encounters the Achaeans on his mission.

10.315 πολύχρυσος πολύχαλκος Dolon is also described as wealthy: "rich in gold, rich in bronze." These epithets are more commonly used of places in our texts, and Dolon is the only person to be called by them. Mycenae is called πολύχρυσος three times (*Iliad* 7.180, 11.46, *Odyssey* 3.305). Sidon is called πολύχαλκος (*Odyssey* 15.425), as is the *ouranos* (*Iliad* 5.504; *Odyssey* 3.2), perhaps because of an association between the sky and the homes of the gods, which have bronze floors (*Iliad* 1.426, 14.173, 21.438, 21.505, *Odyssey* 8.321). The combination of both adjectives πολύχρυσος and πολύχαλκος is used only of Troy in our texts (*Iliad* 18.289), when Hektor says that formerly all mortals used to speak of Priam's city as rich in gold, rich in bronze, but now the Trojans have had to sacrifice most of that wealth (*Iliad* 18.285–292). So the question emerges whether the combination of these adjectives evokes an association between Dolon and Priam's Troy and its eventual doom, despite its wealth. Such an association may be too far-reaching, since in our texts Troy is described with these adjectives only once, although it is a very wealthy city according to tradition. Certainly Dolon's wealth comes into play after his capture: when he promises Diomedes and Odysseus a great ransom (10.378–381) the traditional characteristic of his wealth indicates that he could indeed pay handsomely in exchange for his life.

10.316 ὃς δή τοι εἶδος μὲν ἔην κακός, ἀλλὰ ποδώκης These two characteristics are contrasted, one negative (ugly) and one positive (swift-footed). The phrase εἶδος ... κακός is analogous to the more frequently used constructions for being good-looking, such as εἶδος ἄριστος / -η (*Iliad* 2.715, 3.39 = 13.769, 3.124, 13.365, 13.378, 17.142, *Odyssey* 11.469 = 24.17) and εἶδος ἀγητός / -όν / -οί (*Iliad* 5.787 = 8.228, 22.370, 24.376, *Odyssey* 14.177). Compositionally, it is most like *Odyssey* 11.469 (= 24.17), which is also a relative clause with ἔην between the noun and adjective.

When we think of Homeric heroes who are explicitly labeled ugly, the first to come to mind is Thersites, who is described as "the ugliest man who came to Troy" (αἴσχιστος δὲ ἀνὴρ ὑπὸ Ἴλιον ἦλθε, *Iliad* 2.216). We know that αἴσχιστος refers to his looks in particular because the next three lines expand on this adjective with details of his physical appearance: he is bandy-legged and lame in one foot, his shoulders hunch over his chest, and his head is pointy, with sparse hair on top (*Iliad* 2.217–219). He is especially hateful to Achilles and Odysseus, two preeminent heroes of the epic tradition (*Iliad* 2.220). Of course, Odysseus has a bitter encounter with Thersites in *Iliad* 2, and we know from Proklos' summary of the *Aithiopis* that Achilles will eventually kill him in anger. Indeed, although we are told by the narrator that Thersites is a source of laughter (γελοΐϊον, *Iliad* 2.215), and in his lameness he might be thought similar to Hephaistos, whose bustling provokes laughter (*Iliad* 1.599–600), Thersites provokes anger from the Achaeans (see Kouklanakis 1999). Dolon's ugliness, by comparison, is not dwelled upon, and does not seem to provoke any particular strong reaction, whether ridicule, repulsion, or irritation (see, however, 10.400 for Odysseus' smile and 10.446 for Diomedes' glare as their reactions to Dolon upon his capture). Yet pairing Thersites and Dolon based on their looks might also suggest that, in the *Iliad*, Odysseus, whose own appearance is not unequivocally impressive (*Iliad* 3.209–224), seems to have the role of confronting ugly men (but in neither case is he their killer).

In contrast to his bad looks, Dolon does have the positive attribute of being swift-footed (ποδώκης). For a traditional audience, as well as for us, the epithet "swift-footed" brings to mind Achilles, of course. Achilles has two other "distinctive" (in Parry's terms) epithets that indicate his swiftness, ποδάρκης and πόδας ὠκύς (Parry, MHV 64, 145), but he is also called "swift-footed" with the adjective ποδώκης twenty-two times in the *Iliad* and twice in the *Odyssey*. In addition to Achilles and Dolon, the adjective is also used for horses four times (in one of these cases, it is applied to the horses' drivers in an apparent transference of the epithet). So, here, the epithet evokes both Achilles and horses just before Dolon asks for Achilles' horses as his reward for undertaking the spying mission (10.322–323). Achilles, we know, is the best looking of the Achaeans, as well as the best overall (his horses are the best as well, see *Iliad* 2.769–770), and the trait of swiftness that Dolon shares with him heightens the contrast of Dolon's ugliness. As we will see below (10.330), there seems to be a prohibition on the taking of Achilles' horses by his enemies within the Iliadic tradition, and Odysseus' reaction to Dolon's confession that he has been promised them also points to this contrast: Dolon is like Achilles in being fast, but he is no Achilles. Like Dolon, however, Achilles is also involved in ambushes at night (see e.g. *Iliad* 21.34–39 and "The Poetics of Ambush"). Achilles' swiftness has been understood as an important quality in battle, and it may also be so for ambush missions. If this is the case, Dolon's swiftness will likewise be important for the spying mission he volunteers to undertake. We will see Dolon run, but he is outsmarted and overtaken by Odysseus and Diomedes. In one of his Cretan lies, Odysseus claims to have ambushed and killed Orsilokhos, a son of Idomeneus, in Crete, and he says that Orsilokhos is swift-footed, faster than all other seafaring men in wide Crete (*Odyssey* 13.259–270). That story provides another example of the victim of an ambusher being swift. It may be that the strategy involved in ambush is traditionally associated with overcoming physical talents, such as being a fast runner.

10.317 αὐτὰρ ὃ μοῦνος ἔην μετὰ πέντε κασιγνήτῃσιν Dolon's status as an only son may be a detail that increases the audience's sympathy for his death. Although some modern scholars revile Dolon completely (on this line, see e.g. Holoka 1983:8–9 and Hainsworth 1993, who calls Dolon a "sissy"), an ancient audience might have reacted quite differently. For example, we might compare Ilioneus the son of Phorbas: he is a Trojan identified as an only son, and his brief life story, given at the moment of his death, seems intended to arouse sympathy based on that status (*Iliad* 14.489–492). Both Achilles and Odysseus are only sons (as is Odysseus' son Telemakhos, in the Odyssean tradition), and the epics offer intensely emotional scenes about the potential loss of the son. In *Iliad* 24.485–512, Priam appeals to Achilles to think of his father and how much he hopes to see his son return home, and Achilles weeps remembering both Patroklos and his father. In *Odyssey* 24.345–348, Laertes indeed sees his only son return home after twenty years and faints. We see the hope of and joy at the son's return also embodied in a simile comparing Eumaios' joy at greeting Telemakhos to a father greeting his only son (μοῦνος at *Odyssey* 16.19, just as here) coming home from a foreign land in the tenth year, having suffered greatly (*Odyssey* 16.17–19). Following this self-referential Odyssean simile, Eumaios kisses Telemakhos as though Telemakhos has escaped death. In fact, Telemakhos has just outsmarted the suitors in their ambush attempt, and so has escaped death (see also *Odyssey* 17.47, where Telemakhos says he has just escaped sheer destruction). Dolon will not return after he is ambushed, so his status as an only son should engender some sympathy for his father. Hainsworth (1993 *ad loc.*) objects to any notion of sympathy because Dolon's status as an only son is mentioned here, but not at his death. At the moment of his departure, however, we already know that Dolon will die (10.336–337), so any sympathy evoked here is not that far from the indication of his death.

The detail of Dolon's five sisters might add to the pathos in a different way, for brothers are possible avengers, and Dolon has none. (As an example of a brother as an avenger, compare *Iliad* 14.478–485, where Akamas stands over his fallen brother, claiming a *poinē* for him and saying that a man prays to leave someone behind him in his home to avenge his death in battle.) The death of a brother often causes anger and desire for revenge (e.g. *Iliad* 9.567, 11.248–258, 16.320) or is offered as a standard measure of a great loss (e.g. *Iliad* 9.632–636, 24.46–49). Once Dolon is dead, his sisters have a potential future fate as captive women: both Andromache and Briseis mention the loss of their brothers in war as a factor in their dire straits (*Iliad* 6.421–424 for Andromache; *Iliad* 19.293–294 for Briseis). Both of these factors, then, can be seen within the Homeric tradition to potentially evoke sympathy for Dolon's death.

Throughout the *Iliad* passages that introduce warriors just before they die and provide details of their biographies would likely have served a commemorative function, and, compressed though they are, often share themes and imagery with traditional female laments, such as those sung by Andromache, Briseis, and Achilles' mother Thetis in the *Iliad*. Many of these passages seem to be focalized through the eyes of a mother or widow. There are several examples of this phenomenon. In *Iliad* 11.221–228, we hear the story of Iphidamas, who leaves behind his bride to "go after the *kleos* of the Achaeans." In *Iliad* 4.473–489, we learn how Simoeisios comes to be named by his parents, and that he dies before he can repay their care in raising him. He is compared to a felled poplar, a use of plant imagery that is also common in lament. The death of Gorgythion at *Iliad* 8.302–308 is a particularly beautiful example of this kind of passage, for which we use the evocative translation of Samuel Butler:

> ὃ δ' ἀμύμονα Γοργυθίωνα
> υἱὸν ἐΰν Πριάμοιο κατὰ στῆθος βάλεν ἰῷ,
> τόν ῥ' ἐξ Αἰσύμηθεν ὀπυιομένη τέκε μήτηρ
> καλὴ Καστιάνειρα δέμας ἐϊκυῖα θεῇσι.
> μήκων δ' ὡς ἑτέρωσε κάρη βάλεν, ἥ τ' ἐνὶ κήπῳ
> καρπῷ βριθομένη νοτίῃσί τε εἰαρινῇσιν,
> ὣς ἑτέρωσ' ἤμυσε κάρη πήληκι βαρυνθέν.

The arrow hit Priam's brave son faultless Gorgythion in the chest. His mother, fair Kastianeira, lovely as a goddess, bore him after she had been married from Aisyme, and now he bowed his head as a garden poppy in full bloom when it is weighed down by showers in spring—even thus heavy bowed his head beneath the weight of his helmet.

translation based on that of Samuel Butler

We can easily imagine these words spoken in the first person by Kastianeira upon learning of the death of her son in battle. Indeed, epic poetry is infused with the imagery, themes, and language of lament, so much so that a number of scholars have speculated that women's lament traditions played a crucial role in the development of epic. Epic poetry narrates the glory of heroes, the *klea andrōn*, but it also laments their untimely deaths and the suffering they cause. That these lament-filled passages are more often than not sung for the death of the Trojans and their allies, and in this case the spy Dolon, is a testament to the remarkable parity of compassion that underlies the *Iliad*. Both sides are mourned equally. On the relationship between lament and epic, women's songs and men's songs, see Murnaghan 1999, Nagy 1999, Sultan 1999, and Dué 2002 and 2006a. On the mortality of the hero as a central theme of epic, see also Schein 1984, Greene 1999, and above on 10.259. On passages that lament the death of heroes in a highly compressed form, such as the one quoted from *Iliad* 8 here, see also Tsagalis 2004:179–187. Tsagalis argues that lament is "the form of speech that best represents the poem's perspective" (167). If he is right then it is illuminating to consider that Dolon may once have been understood to be as deserving of sympathy and lamentation as any of the warriors who fall in battle in the *Iliad*.

10.319 Ἕκτωρ ἔμ' ὀτρύνει κραδίη καὶ θυμὸς ἀγήνωρ The same formula is used when Diomedes volunteers, with Nestor's name in place of Hektor's. See the commentary on 10.244 for the connection between "heart and audacious spirit" (κραδίη καὶ θυμὸς ἀγήνωρ) and alternative warfare tactics like spying missions or ambush.

10.325–327 As we know from 10.56, 10.126–127, 10.180, and 10.198–199, the council first gathers at the watch station and then crosses the ditch to hold their deliberations. Dolon's supposition of where to find them, then, is wrong, but not entirely misguided. Earlier that morning, the Trojan herald Idaios found the Achaeans assembled near the stern of Agamemnon's ship (*Iliad* 7.382–383). Earlier on this night Agamemnon held a council of the leaders in his shelter (*Iliad* 9.89–90), and it was there that the embassy returned to deliver their news (*Iliad* 9.669). Another council had been held at night at Nestor's ship (*Iliad* 2.53–54). That such councils are usually held at the ships gives even greater meaning to the choice of a meeting place across the ditch (see on 10.194 and 10.199).

Another question that scholars have raised about his supposition, however, is whether Dolon is ignorant of the ditch and wall, since he does not mention them. In discussing another so-called problem connected to the wall—namely, whether or not it is present in *Iliad* 10, and if it is, how Agamemnon can see over it to the Trojan camp at the beginning of the Book—Shewan (1911:181) argues against such prosaic demands of the poetry. Fenik (1964:60) argues that presuming some version of the Doloneia in which there is no wall goes too far, and he notes that, in the *Rhesos* (213), Dolon is aware of the ditch and the wall but intends to be able to spy anyway. So when Dolon says that he will go through the Achaean encampment all the way to Agamemnon's ship, we can easily understand that he is including making his way across the ditch and wall. But, of course, he will never make it that far. Exactly how he will get over them becomes a moot point, especially given that this is a traditional story in which his fortunes are not only known but are even foretold as he leaves (see below on 10.336–337).

10.329 Ζεὺς αὐτὸς ἐρίγδουπος πόσις Ἥρης At 10.5 Zeus is named only as "the husband of Hera with her beautiful hair" (πόσις Ἥρης ἠϋκόμοιο); here, his name is combined with the epithet phrase "the loud-sounding husband of Hera." These two epithets reveal more about how oral traditional language operates within composition-in-performance. Zeus is called the husband of Hera with these two formulas, and Alexander is called "radiant Alexander, the husband of Helen, with her beautiful hair" (δῖος Ἀλέξανδρος Ἑλένης πόσις ἠϋκόμοιο, *Iliad* 3.329 = 7.355 = 8.82; see also *Iliad* 11.369 and 11.505, where δῖος is replaced by αὐτάρ and εἰ μή, respectively). In Homeric diction the word πόσις is used in other cases, such as that of Hektor as the husband of Andromache (*Iliad* 6.484, 8.190, 22.439) and of Odysseus as the husband of Penelope in the *Odyssey* (18.253, 19.126, 19.549), when the wife of a man is part of his epic identity and so is used in naming him within the tradition. In the case of Paris and Zeus, then, that key relationship has been fashioned into traditional epithets. Their epithets that include the adjective ἠϋκόμοιο have likely been formed by analogy. Parry notes that the formula found on this line is especially associated with prayer, whether expressing a wish or calling Zeus to witness oaths (MHV 181–182; for an oath, compare *Iliad* 7.411). See above on 10.305 for the prefix ἐρι-.

10.330 ἐποχήσεται This verb is likewise used (in its only other appearance in our texts) at *Iliad* 17.449, when Zeus will not allow Hektor to take Achilles' horses after he kills Patroklos, whom the horses mourn nearby. A telling cross-reference can be made, then, with this resonant verb: Hektor promises to Dolon that no one else will take Achilles' horses, and in Book 17 it is Hektor himself who is prohibited from doing so by Zeus. Within the larger tradition, this verb may be part of a traditional vocabulary about Achilles' horses and may therefore evoke for a traditional audience the embedded knowledge that Achilles will never lose his horses to his enemies. (See also below at 10.402–404.) At *Iliad* 17.75–78, Apollo actively dissuades Hektor from going after the horses. Disguised as Mentes, Apollo tells Hektor that he runs in pursuit of something unattainable (Ἕκτορ νῦν σὺ μὲν ὧδε θέεις ἀκίχητα διώκων). In both of these cases, it is a god who forbids the theft from happening, and Zeus recalls there how it was the gods who gave the horses to Peleus. That the horses were originally a wedding gift to Peleus from the gods may account for why Achilles' horses are not subject to the same vagaries of warfare as, say, Rhesos' horses are. Deep familiarity with this vocabulary would also shape the audience's reception of the request by Dolon and promise by Hektor.

10.331 ἀγλαϊεῖσθαι is a *hapax legomenon*: that is, this verb appears only here in our texts. Some critics who have argued that *Iliad* 10 is later and/or separate from the rest of the *Iliad* use the number of *hapax legomena* in this book as evidence of different composition and/or authorship. Yet an understanding of oral poetics and the techniques of oral composition-in-performance can account for such seeming anomalies in a different way. When we look at the entire "database" that the *Iliad* and *Odyssey* provide, we find, not this verb, of course, but the adjective ἀγλαός used in many contexts in which the heroes receive material goods as a result of their actions. Most often the phrase is ἀγλαὰ δῶρα (used twenty-one times in our texts). These gifts "shine" not just physically (as they do if they happen to be made of precious metal), but metonymically as the physical manifestation of the radiant glory the hero either has won or stands to win. (See on 10.212–213 above for the connection between gifts and glory in this epic tradition.) We also see phrases like ἀγλά' ἄποινα (*Iliad* 1.23 = 1.377, *Iliad* 1.111), ἀγλά' ἄεθλα

(*Iliad* 23.262), and even ἀγλαὸν εὖχος (*Iliad* 7.203) in contexts in which the hero has something to gain through his victory. These phrases may have been created by analogy with the phrase ἀγλαὰ δῶρα, especially because the idea of victory bringing both gifts and glory was so fundamental (see Parry MHV 68–76 for the principle of analogy in the composition of oral poetry). So if a singer has learned the idea encapsulated in the adjective, it would be natural to create a phrase using the verb instead. As Albert Lord has argued, the language of oral poetry operates just like spoken language, and learning and using the language of the poetry is no more mechanical and no less fluid than learning and using a spoken language (Lord 1960/2000:35–37). And in fact, a related, compound verb form, ἐπαγλαΐεσθαι, is used to describe Hektor exulting in Achilles' armor, which he puts on after he strips it from Patroklos' corpse (*Iliad* 18.133). So even if from our perspective it may seem that this verb is unusual within the texts we have, we cannot say that all those uses of the adjective were sung and resung before any singer thought to use the verb in the same kind of context. The fact that ἀγλαΐεῖσθαι is a *hapax* does not prove that it is untraditional. In fact, in making such determinations, we need to examine whether the idea, and not just the morphology, of the word or phrase is traditional if we are to understand it properly within the system of the poetic language.

10.332 ὣς φάτο καί ῥ᾽ ἐπίορκον ἐπώμοσε In the other instances of ἐπίορκον and related words in the *Iliad* it means a 'false oath': that is, one swears an oath and then violates it, or one is lying when he swears about some action in the past. At *Iliad* 3.276–280, Agamemnon calls on Zeus, Helios, the Earth, the rivers, and those in the underworld who punish swearers of false oaths (ἐπίορκον, *Iliad* 3.279) to guard the sanctity of the oaths that the Achaeans and Trojans are about to take in advance of the duel between Menelaos and Paris. In *Iliad* 19.187–188, Agamemnon responds to Odysseus' request that he swear to Achilles that he never slept with Briseis by saying that he is willing to swear to it and that he is not falsely swearing (οὐδ᾽ ἐπιορκήσω). When Briseis is then brought back to Achilles, Agamemnon does indeed take an oath to that effect, beginning it in much the same way as in *Iliad* 3 (*Iliad* 19.260 ≈ *Iliad* 3.279), but adding the stipulation that, if he is swearing falsely (ἐπίορκον, *Iliad* 19.264), he wishes that the gods may give him the many sufferings that they give to those who transgress their oaths. These contexts leave little doubt that the false oath is either intentionally broken or is an intentional lie.

Yet in this case readers, translators, and critics over the ages have been reluctant to think of Hektor as intentionally lying. Over a dozen manuscripts have ἐπεὶ ὅρκον, and some of these have it as a "correction," indicating perhaps a felt need to remove the characterization of Hektor's words as an intentionally false oath. The main scholia in the Venetus A similarly suggest that Hektor is not purposefully swearing a false oath, but that it is false because what he swears will happen is not fulfilled (οὐχ οἷον ἑκουσίως, ἀλλὰ διὰ τὸ ἀποτελεσθῆναι τοῦτο, ὅπερ ὤμοσεν). Cunliffe (1963) likewise makes an exception of this use in his lexicon, saying its use is "here of unintentional falsity, the fulfilment of the oath turning out to be impossible." As we have just seen on 10.300, fulfillment of the oath is indeed impossible, and because there is no sense that Hektor should be punished (an idea that does appear in the other contexts), perhaps we should interpret Hektor's oath as unintentionally false. In *Iliad* 17, Hektor goes after the horses himself, suggesting that he does not know that they cannot be captured by an enemy of Achilles.

But there are other possibilities for interpretation by a traditional audience. The Trojans are portrayed as oath breakers, as when Pandaros breaks the ceasefire in *Iliad* 4 (Idomeneus explicitly says the Trojans have broken their oaths at *Iliad* 4.269–270). Even for the duel between Paris and Menelaos itself, Agamemnon requires Priam to come to the battlefield to swear the oath because he does not trust his sons (*Iliad* 3.105–106). The earlier Trojan king Laomedon reneged on his deals both with Apollo and Poseidon for building the walls of Troy (see *Iliad* 21.439–460) and with Herakles, to whom he had promised to give his horses upon the rescue of his daughter Hesione (an episode alluded to at *Iliad* 5.640). So a traditional audience might have understood Hektor's promise within the general traditional framework of Trojan promises in return for work or missions that are subsequently broken. Another possibility is offered in the tragedy *Rhesos*, where Hektor makes plain that he has designs on getting Achilles' horses for himself, recounting their immortal origins (*Rhesos* 184–188). When he acquiesces to Dolon's request, he explicitly says that he will not be false (ἀλλ' οὔ σ' ἐπάρας ψεύσομαι, *Rhesos* 189). The *Rhesos* employs different, yet traditional, narrative possibilities for the story (Fenik 1964), and the possibility that Hektor really plans to get Achilles' horses for himself may underlie the mention of a false oath here in a compression of details that would have meaning nevertheless for a traditional audience.

10.333–335 These lines function as an arming scene, as 10.254–272 did for Diomedes and Odysseus. Lord (1960/2000:89–91) uses arming scenes from *Iliad* 3.328–338, 11.15–55, 16.130–154, and 19.369–391 as examples of a traditional theme in Greek oral epic, and demonstrates that this theme can be expanded or compressed as the singer sees fit. Lord notes that, in *Iliad* 3, the arming of Paris is given in some detail, while the parallel arming of Menelaos is compressed into a single line. (That compression is what we find in the manuscripts that survive, but we should note that there is an expanded description in a third-century BCE papyrus—Allen's papyrus 40, Hibeh 19—of the arming of Menelaos, comprising four lines, all in traditional language, but the individual pieces of armor are put on in a different order from what we find in the other surviving arming scenes.) When we compare the earlier arming scene with this one, we also see that the arming scene of Diomedes and Odysseus is described at greater length than that of Dolon here. In addition to that more expanded arming scene, the details of Dolon's equipment are also reminiscent of the night dressing scenes earlier in the episode (see 10.21–24, 10.29–31, and 10.177–178), since Dolon puts on his animal skin now to leave for his mission, while Agamemnon, Menelaos, and Diomedes had put on theirs when rising from bed. It does not seem that Diomedes wears his lion skin while on the mission, although he is twice compared to a lion (10.297 and 10.485). The cap Dolon wears is similar to that worn by Diomedes in that it is made of animal skin (κυνέην), but instead of being made from a bull's hide, it is made from a marten (κτιδέην). The details of his equipment will be revisited when Odysseus and Diomedes strip Dolon's corpse (see 10.458–459).

10.333 καμπύλα τόξα Odysseus, too, carries a bow on this night mission (which he will end up using only to whip the horses, see 10.260 and 10.500). McLeod (1988) argues that the bow is an effective weapon at night. See on 10.29, 10.260, and our essay "The Poetics of Ambush" for thematic associations between archery and ambush.

10.334 ῥινὸν πολιοῖο λύκοιο There is a substantial history of reading a ritual significance to Dolon's wolf skin, starting with Gernet (1936). Gernet (1936:190–191) argues that the tragedy *Rhesos* is needed to understand the meaning of the wolf skin. In that tragedy, Dolon makes the wolf skin explicitly a disguise for the purpose of deception. He implies that he will look like a wolf and says that he will walk like a wolf, too, to confuse anyone who tracks him (*Rhesos* 208–215; see Plate 5 for a similar visual image). Being or playing a wolf, according to Gernet, can be interpreted as a kind of liminal stage of an initiation ritual (1936:193–196). He also considers the symbolism of the wolf as an "outlaw figure" (1936:200). Gernet's ritual interpretation is followed, in later examinations of Dolon as a wolf, by Davidson 1979, Petegorsky 1982, and Wathelet 1989. See further on 10.465–466, where Odysseus hangs the wolf skin on the tamarisk bush.

Other arguments have proposed that the wolf skin marks Dolon as a type of figure usually featured in other kinds of narratives outside of epic. Davidson (1979:65) expands on the notion of the outlaw figure and argues that this story follows a mythical pattern in which Dolon is a trickster figure who is tricked upon, and she sees a connection between trickster imagery and lone wolf imagery. Malcolm Davies argues for a folktale background, proposing that Dolon is like the "ambivalent helper" figure in quest stories and that his wolf skin is suggestive of the metamorphosis or disguise such figures often take (Davies 2005:31–32).

Schnapp-Gourbeillon (1981:112–114) questions the interpretation of the wolf skin as initiatory, and she finds "serious difficulties" with Gernet's approach, for using another source to understand Dolon's wolf skin in the *Iliad*, singling out Dolon's animal skin alone as ritually significant, and ignoring Athena's possible ritual role. Instead, she argues that animal skins are worn for a particular type of nocturnal action, or by a specific type of persons, or both (Schnapp-Gourbeillon 1981:119–120). She argues that the symbolism of wearing the skins of particular animals is similar to what we see of the animal's symbolism in the similes. Dolon is above all "like a wolf" in that he is a minor predator: when Dolon, the wolf, meets Diomedes, the lion, he never has a chance (1981:120). One further question regarding an initiatory significance, which arises from the differences between the ways in which the wolf skin is presented here and in the tragedy *Rhesos*, is that here, the wolf skin, although worn on the mission, is not presented as a disguise for Dolon. Rather, it is connected to the ambush theme like the earlier night dressing scenes, as we have explored above (see 10.21–24, 10.29–31, and 10.177–178). Wathelet notes with an eye to the practical that the gray color of the wolf skin provides a kind of camouflage in the night (1989:220). There may also be some harbinger of failure in that Dolon goes as a "lone wolf": Homeric similes involving wolves always refer to them as plural, hunting in packs (see *Iliad* 4.471–472, 11.72–73, 13.101–106, 16.156–166, 16.352–356).

10.335 κρατὶ δ' ἐπὶ κτιδέην κυνέην Dolon's helmet, like those worn by Diomedes and Odysseus on this night, is made of animal hide rather than metal, as is appropriate to maneuvers in the dark. It provides stealth, whereas metal can reflect whatever light is available and give an ambusher away. (See on 10.257 and our essay "The Poetics of Ambush" for a full discussion.) The animal from whose hide Dolon's cap is made, the ἴκτις, is the marten, a member of the weasel family. It is tempting to make the connection that, by wearing this helmet, Dolon is being characterized as "weasely." (About this animal but not this passage, Aristotle notes that the ἴκτις has the "wickedness of character like the weasel," *History of Animals* 612b10.) Even with that ancient testimony, however, we need to be careful not to make assumptions about associations with this animal in Homeric epic. This helmet is the only mention of the marten in our Homeric texts, so we can only speculate about what the associations might have been. The significance may instead be that this omnivorous animal hunts at night (Schwanz 2000). Nicander's *Theriaca* 196–197, from the second century BCE, describes the ἴκτις as an animal that kills domestic birds in their sleep, making it very much like an ambusher at night. Also, Wathelet argues that the marten, like other members of the weasel family, is perhaps known for spying (Wathelet 1989:220). If these are indeed the associations an ancient audience would make, then not only are the physical qualities of the hide appropriate to the night, but also the marten's characteristics mark Dolon as a "creature of the night."

10.336 βῆ δ' ἰέναι See on 10.32.

10.336–337 οὐδ' ἄρ' ἔμελλεν / ἐλθὼν ἐκ νηῶν ἂψ Ἕκτορι μῦθον ἀποίσειν Based on his experience with living singers composing in performance, Albert Lord notes that planning and a sense of the song as a whole is usual in oral poetry. Although there is pressure to compose rapidly, "In all these instances one sees also that the singer always has the end of the theme in his mind. He knows where he is going. As in the adding of one line to another, so in the adding of one element in a theme to another, the singer can stop and fondly dwell upon any single item without losing a sense of the whole. The style allows comfortably for digression or for enrichment. Once embarked upon a theme, the singer can proceed at his own pace" (Lord 1960/2000:92). The traditional nature of the story means that Dolon's death is expected by the audience even as it is anticipated here. We also see this sort of planning in anticipation of a character's impending death in daytime battle.

We can compare, for just one example, the even longer-range planning evident in the death of Asios. Soon after Asios is introduced (*Iliad* 12.95–97) and begins his headstrong attack by chariot on the Achaean wall, the narrator similarly reports that Asios will not escape death or ever return to Troy because Idomeneus will kill him (*Iliad* 12.113–117; note the same introductory language, οὐδ' ἄρ' ἔμελλε, *Iliad* 12.113). Idomeneus does indeed kill him, but not until *Iliad* 13.383–393. This type of planning is not literary, but rather based in tradition: both the singer and the audience know that Idomeneus will kill Asios, so announcing it early confirms that the traditional story will be followed. By understanding this oral traditional feature, we can assume that Dolon's lack of return follows tradition as well.

Within the ambush theme, moreover, there is a particular emphasis on the need to return. A failure to return means not only that the mission is unsuccessful, but also that the family and comrades may not know what has happened to the spy or ambusher. We see this aspect of the theme in Nestor's words about the need to come back safely (10.212) and Diomedes' choice of Odysseus as his partner based on Odysseus' ability to return home (10.246–247). But we also see it in compressed versions of the theme, such as Glaukos' narration of the ambush of Bellerophon, in which the ambushers are said not to return home because Bellerophon killed them all (*Iliad* 6.189–190). In this case, just as Dolon begins his mission, we are alerted already that Dolon will not be successful. This anticipation of his failure and impending death adds to the pathos inherent in the description of his family (10.317). But it also adds to the success of the Achaeans on this night: they triumph in preventing Dolon from bringing information to Hektor as well as in killing Rhesos and his comrades and stealing the horses.

10.339 ἐφράσατο Odysseus does just what Diomedes had wanted from a partner (see above, 10.224–226): he observes first what Diomedes has not yet seen—the presence of another man out in the night. His powers of observation stand in contrast to Dolon's lack of attention, his ἀφραδίη (10.350), which shares the same root with this verb.

10.341–343 One aspect of these night missions that informs the poetics of the ambush theme is the lack of sure visual knowledge in the dark. Odysseus can see someone, but cannot yet be sure who he is or why he is there. We have already seen manifestations of this aspect of ambush, such as when Nestor tells the man he cannot see well enough to recognize that he should speak out and not sneak up on him (10.82–85). Odysseus displays his talent for ambush by anticipating that this man may be the enemy and by employing a strategy that gives them the advantage. See also the section on the sensory and spatial aspects of the night in "The Poetics of Ambush."

10.347 προτιειλεῖν is a *hapax legomenon*. See on 10.331 for how to understand such a linguistic phenomenon in our texts and in this book in particular.

10.349 ὡς ἄρα φωνήσαντε The dual verb form reflects the poetics of teamwork that we see beginning on 10.243. So, although Odysseus is the only one quoted, the two ambushers are still spoken of in the dual, which may also imply Diomedes' affirmative response. But see our note on this line in the textual commentary on the Venetus A for evidence of another possible way to perform this line.

10.349 πὰρ' ἒξ ὁδοῦ An ambusher may hide just off a road to attack someone traveling along it. In the Homeric epics we have another example of this strategy in one of Odysseus' Cretan lies in *Odyssey* 13; Odysseus describes a similar position for the ambush he narrates there: ἐγγὺς ὁδοῖο λοχησάμενος (*Odyssey* 13.268). We also see such a place for an ambush in Pindar's description of Herakles' ambush of the Molione (*Olympian* 10.26–34, ἐφ' ὁδῷ, 10.30). At this point we begin to see how easily a spying mission transitions into an ambush once the presence of the enemy is detected.

10.349 ἐν νεκύεσσι See on 10.199 and 10.298 for more on corpses as a feature of the landscape on this night.

10.351–352 ἀλλ' ὅτε δή ῥ' ἀπέην ὅσσόν τ' ἐπὶ οὖρα πέλονται / ἡμιόνων The distance of the mule's plow range seems to take us out of the realm of war and into a farming setting, but when we look at other instances in Homeric epic of this description of distance, it takes us rather into the world of athletics. During the funeral games for Patroklos, this same word οὖρα is used for the distance of a discus throw of a young man, and it serves as a point of comparison for the distance during which Antilokhos' horses were even with those of Menelaos (*Iliad* 23.431–433). And in the games on Phaeacia in the *Odyssey*, it is used to describe by how much Klytoneos won the footrace (*Odyssey* 8.123–125). Since we find many similarities of language between this section of *Iliad* 10 and *Iliad* 22 (see below on 10.363–368), we might also compare from that episode how Achilles' chase of Hektor is compared to both a footrace and a chariot race at a hero's funeral games, but with Hektor's life as a prize (*Iliad* 22.157–166). Here, too, begins a "footrace" that will end in Dolon's death.

10.352–353 According to the Townley scholia, Aristarchus understood this elaboration on the length of the furrow as redefining the length meant here. It is not the length of a standard furrow, but rather the difference in distance between that which a team of mules would plough and that which a team of oxen would—according to Aristarchus, mules are faster (presumably that is how we should understand προφερέστεραι). The fact that no reference to oxen appears in the comparison to the mules' furrow at *Odyssey* 8.123–125 may suggest that here it is indeed a difference in length. As we try to understand the comparison and envision what this distance represents, we should also consider the poetics of night missions: Odysseus' strategy is to let Dolon pass them by so that they can run up behind him and prevent his escape, but they also cannot lose sight of him. That factor may speak in favor of the shorter distance that Aristarchus proposes. See also Scott 1974:20–24 on Homeric similes describing measurement in general.

10.354–356 Odysseus' plan also works to their advantage in another way—because they are now behind Dolon, that is, because they are coming at him from the same direction he has just come, he assumes they must be Trojans. The fact that he stops momentarily allows them to catch the swift-footed Dolon. Another of the sensory aspects of the night that is part of these poetics is the primacy of the sense of hearing. Yet, what one hears requires correct interpretation. In the next two lines, Dolon will realize that he has fatally misinterpreted what he heard as his sight contradicts his supposition.

10.357 ἀλλ' ὅτε δή ῥ' ἄπεσαν δουρηνεκὲς ἢ καὶ ἔλασσον As at 10.351, here distance is expressed through comparison. Scott observes that in the Homeric epics, "Similes of distance are the most numerous type of approximate measure" (Scott 1974:21). Since Diomedes will indeed throw his spear at Dolon (10.372–374), this comparison also seems to anticipate how far they remain apart during the chase. The distance of a spear cast is used to picture other distances, such as the length of the pathway by which Apollo bridges the Achaean ditch (*Iliad* 15.358–360), the length of Achilles' leap away from the river Xanthos as it pursues him (*Iliad* 21.251), and how far the Trojans give way to the Achaean charge (*Iliad* 16.589–592: there, the spear cast may be either in battle or in athletic games, compare 10.351–352 above).

10.360–363   As Diomedes and Odysseus start to pursue Dolon, they are compared to hunting dogs chasing after prey. Scott (1974:72–73) has identified hunting as a traditional subject matter for Homeric similes. In several similes, dogs accompanying hunters may confront powerful animals such as lions or boars (e.g. *Iliad* 8.337–342, 11.292–295, 12.41–49). But other similes are closer to what we have here: dogs chasing after weaker, non-predatory animals such as fawns or hares. In two similes in the *Iliad* that have this structure, at *Iliad* 15.579–581 (Antilokhos pouncing on Melanippos) and *Iliad* 22.188–193 (Achilles pursuing Hektor), a fawn has been chased from its lair (ἐξ εὐνῆφι, *Iliad* 15.580; ἐξ εὐνῆς, *Iliad* 22.190). We have seen above (10.5–9) how the adjective *pukinos* connects the ideas of an animal's lair and ambush, and εὐνή means a 'lair' for a fawn, but a 'bed' for humans, further connecting the idea to night and sleeping. The animal in this simile has not explicitly been chased from its lair, but the association may be a traditional one for this kind of hunting simile, and it reverses the position of the ambusher and the ambushed, just as Dolon's position of spy has now been reversed to the one being spied.

We can also compare this simile to the one likening the watchmen to guard dogs at 10.180–189. Although both similes compare the men to dogs, we can see in the differences of detail how similes are attached to and elaborate themes in this oral tradition (see also 10.5–9 for our detailed discussion of Homeric similes). At 10.180–189 the theme is one of being on the defensive against a night attack. Here, the Achaeans are the ones on the attack, and so the simile shows dogs acting in a different manner. That dogs are featured as the vehicle in both instances shows the flexibility and multiformity of Homeric similes.

10.360   καρχαρόδοντε δύω κύνε εἰδότε The dual forms that the text of the Venetus A manuscript records for the hunting dogs in this simile seem to emphasize the coordinated attack by the dogs and, by association, by Diomedes and Odysseus. We often see dual forms used for these two in this book (see also on 10.243), and we find dual forms used in another simile elsewhere when the Aiante are compared to two lions in the dual as they fight together (*Iliad* 13.198–202). Some manuscripts, however, record the plural κύνες instead.

10.361   ἤ κεμάδ' ἠὲ λαγωὸν Providing alternative possibilities is a traditional feature of Homeric similes (Muellner 1990:62–64). κέμας is a *hapax legomenon*, but λαγωός appears in two other contexts, both related to this one in different ways. It appears in another simile, as

Hektor swoops at Achilles like an eagle at a lamb or a hare (*Iliad* 22.308–310, note here also the alternatives for the prey). We can compare also the hunting dog simile at *Iliad* 22.188–193 as Achilles pursues Hektor. As we will see further at 10.363–368, this scene shares language in common with *Iliad* 22; so also in these two similes, the object of the chase or attack in both places can be a hare. The other place we see a similar alternation of the object of a hunting dog's pursuit is in a description of an actual hunt rather than a simile: Odysseus' dog Argos is described as having hunted wild goats and deer and hares (*Odyssey* 17.295) when he was younger.

10.363 ὃ πτολίπορθος Ὀδυσσεύς This epithet, "sacker of cities," is one that Odysseus often receives in the *Odyssey*, but he also shares it with other heroes, like Achilles, and war gods, such as Ares and Enyo, within the tradition. Parry has shown that such epithets belong to the whole tradition and not any one line (MHV 137–138, 146, 171): that is, Odysseus is a sacker of cities within the whole tradition, not simply, or in this line, not yet at this particular point in the story. Similarly, Haft (1990) argues that this epithet, used frequently in the *Odyssey*, but only here and at *Iliad* 2.278 in the *Iliad*, implies that the audience would be familiar with Odysseus' later exploits, especially his role in sacking Troy through the ambush strategy of the Wooden Horse, and thus would understand the epithet to mean the sacker of Troy in partic-ular. In this last detail, she disagrees with Parry, who labels this epithet generic (MHV 146). Haft argues that the use of the definite article with the epithet makes its meaning more specific (see also above on 10.231). Haft also draws parallels and connections between the ambushes in *Iliad* 10 and the sack of Troy (Haft 1990:51–55).

10.363–368 This "chase scene" has language in common with the scene in which Achilles chases the fleeing Hektor in *Iliad* 22. The same formula is used for the departure of the one who will be chased (λαιψηρὰ δὲ γούνατ' ἐνώμα, *Iliad* 10.358 and 22.144). The move Odysseus and Diomedes employ here to isolate Dolon and cut him off from the warriors (λαοῦ ἀποτμήξαντε, 10.364) is like the move Andromache, who knows her military strategy, imagines that Achilles might use to cut Hektor off from the city and force him to the open plain (δείδω μὴ δή μοι θρασὺν Ἕκτορα δῖος Ἀχιλλεὺς / μοῦνον ἀποτμήξας πόλιος πεδίον δὲ δίηται, *Iliad* 22.455–456). When Dolon is approaching the guards' post, Athena puts *menos* into Diomedes so that he can capture Dolon before anyone else (10.365–368). Similarly, while Achilles is pursuing

Hektor, he signals to the other Achaeans not to shoot at Hektor and win his radiant glory (*Iliad* 22.205–207). In both cases the formula ὃ δὲ δεύτερος ἔλθη / ἔλθοι is used (*Iliad* 10.368, 22.207). These similarities indicate two things about the language in this section of *Iliad* 10: one, that this scene is expressed with traditional language, and, two, that there is *kudos* 'radiant glory' for capturing or killing a spy, just as there is for being one (see above, 10.307). Using such language gives the competitiveness to be "first" in this case traditional associations with a hot, yet focused, pursuit of a significant individual enemy.

10.369 δουρί This spear is the one Diomedes brings with him when he leaves his shelter at 10.178; it is not mentioned again in the arming scene at 10.255–295.

10.376 χλωρὸς ὑπαὶ δείους As a color for objects, χλωρός is somewhere on the yellow–green spectrum: in Homeric epic it is used to describe honey (*Iliad* 11.631; *Odyssey* 10.234) and also various kinds of plants or wood (*Odyssey* 9.320, 9.379, 16.47). But in these epics it is most often associated with fear, as it is here. This color describes fear (δέος) itself in several related formulas with the verb αἱρέω, all of which have as their basic meaning "green fear seized me/them/ everyone" (see *Iliad* 7.479, 8.77, 17.67; *Odyssey* 11.43, 11.633, 12.243, 22.42, 24.450, 24.533). John Miles Foley (1999:216–217) identifies "green fear" as a traditional phrase, one which reveals "psychological states and tangible objects woven into the fabric of the narrative tradition that are singularly meaningful and recognizable to bard and audience alike." He argues that a fear so described "is by traditional definition a superhuman, unconquerable force" (1999:217). According to Foley, then, this phrase is a single unit of utterance, with its own, irreducible meaning. At *Iliad* 15.4 we find a phrasing very similar to the one here, and it does show the supernatural element that Foley identifies: there Poseidon has turned the tide of the battle and the Trojans are pushed back across the Achaeans' ditch. They are described as χλωροὶ ὑπαὶ δείους πεφοβημένοι ("green with fear after they were put to flight"). The ὑπαί in these phrases (ὑπό also shows up at *Iliad* 8.77 and *Odyssey* 22.42 = 24.450) perhaps conveys the idea of this green color rising up to the skin's surface. In ambush situations in particular, the paleness or changing color of a man's skin is considered revealing. Idomeneus mentions that ambush especially exposes who is a coward and who is a brave man. The coward is exposed by his skin changing colors from his fear, as well as by an inability to sit still and a pounding heart. By contrast, the brave man's skin does not change color, and he does not feel too much fear (*Iliad* 13.276–286). Here, Dolon's fear is explicit (10.374), and the chattering of his teeth and paleness are manifestations of it. The suitors are similarly described at the moment they realize that the stranger is Odysseus: τοὺς δ' ἄρα πάντας ὑπὸ χλωρὸν δέος εἷλε (*Odyssey* 22.42). Thus, in two cases, at least, green fear is also associated with men who realize at that moment that they have been ambushed.

10.378–381 This offer of ransom for being taken alive rather than killed is another example of both the traditional language of *Iliad* 10 and the Doloneia's place within the Iliadic tradition. Donna Wilson has demonstrated that, although there are references to ransoming practices that occur before the direct action of the *Iliad*, within that direct action the taking of prisoners does not happen, and all appeals to ransom are rejected (2002:29–34). As she notes, "The *Iliad* develops the compensation theme temporally in such a way that all offers of *apoina* mentioned as taking place *before* Chryses' offer in Book 1 or *after* Priam's in Book 24 are successful or potentially successful. But all offers of *apoina* in the time *between* Chryses' and Priam's offers fail" (Wilson 2002:31, original emphasis). Thus the refusal to ransom Dolon (and killing him instead) fits into the overall treatment of this theme in the *Iliad*. See *Iliad* 21.34–44 for the example of Lykaon as a prisoner taken alive during a nighttime ambush (which temporally happens before Chryses' offer).

The offer that Dolon makes uses the traditional, formulaic language of such offers of *apoina* in the *Iliad*. We see the same language of 10.379–381 used at *Iliad* 6.48–50, when Adrestos supplicates Menelaos to ransom him, and also at *Iliad* 11.133–135, when two brothers, Peisandros and Hippolokhos, supplicate Agamemnon (with the necessary changes of singular and dual/plural pronouns in each of the three situations). In all three cases, just as Wilson has observed, the plea is rejected and the supplicant is killed instead (Dolon will attempt a supplicatory gesture just before he is killed, see 10.454–456).

10.382 πολύμητις Ὀδυσσεύς See above on 10.148 for this epithet of Odysseus.

10.384 ἀλλ' ἄγε μοι τόδε εἰπὲ καὶ ἀτρεκέως κατάλεξον This same formula appears below at 10.405 and also at *Iliad* 24.380, when the disguised Hermes says it to Priam as he goes to the Achaean camp. See above on 10.1ff. for the ways in which Priam's journey is thematically similar to a spying mission. Higbie (1995:86–87) identifies both of these passages as places where we might expect the first question to be a request for the addressee to identify himself by name, but this happens in neither case. (In fact, after Hermes asks Priam questions about what he is doing using this formula, Priam asks *Hermes* to identify *himself*, and Hermes tells a false story in reply.) In the *Odyssey*, the formula generally introduces a series of further questions (*Odyssey* 1.169, 1.224, 8.572, 15.383; the exception is *Odyssey* 11.140, which has only one question that follows). See Finkelberg 1987 for her argument that the verb καταλέγω "connotes both an ordered succession and truth" (Finkelberg 1987:138) and that Homeric epic uses it to represent its own genre.

10.386 νύκτα δι' ὀρφναίην This is the reading of the Venetus A, as well as p46, but p425 has instead the phrase νύκτα δι' ἀμβροσίην. See on 10.41 for the meanings of these two formulas. See the textual commentaries on p46 and p425 on this line for more information about the textual record.

10.394 θοὴν διὰ νύκτα μέλαιναν We find this phrase also at *Iliad* 10.468, 24.366, and 24.653. In *Iliad* 24, the formula is used during Priam's infiltration of the Achaean camp, and is associated particularly with the danger of his mission. Thus this formula as a whole seems to be connected with the ambush theme. (See "The Poetics of Ambush" and the commentary above on 10.1ff. on how Priam's mission to retrieve the body of Hektor shares in the ambush theme.) Night is also "swift" at *Iliad* 12.463 and 14.261 and *Odyssey* 12.284. Hainsworth (1993 *ad loc.*) has tentatively suggested that the phrase may have been composed by analogy with θοὴν ἐπὶ νῆα μέλαιναν (which also occurs in the dative with other prepositions). Certainly these examples suggest that the structure of the phrase is deeply ingrained in the traditional diction and that the adjectives "swift" and "black" go naturally together. But what about night is swift? And is "swift" even the correct definition of θοός? The scholia in the Venetus A, Venetus B, and Townley (T) manuscripts on these lines offer possible associations, such as how quickly the sky becomes black after the sun has set. The T scholia here also note several other possible meanings of θοός besides "swift," including "pointed" (see Chantraine 1968/1999 s.v. θοός), and discuss the angle of the earth in relation to the sun, which results in shadows with angles that are "sharp" and make night "cone-shaped." Another possible definition of θοή offered by the B and T scholia is "the placer": τὴν θετικήν—ἀποτίθησι γὰρ ἡμᾶς εἰς ἀνάπαυλαν ("the placer—for it places us into a state of repose"). This definition associates θοή with the verb τίθημι. The question was considered from a cosmological perspective by the ancient Homeric scholar and philosopher Crates of Mallos, who accepted "swift" (see Eustathius *ad* 10.394 and Mette 1952:55ff.) and related it to the speed of the sun and the night.

10.396–399 Repetition is normal and natural within the system of oral composition-in-performance in which the *Iliad* was composed, and these lines repeat Hektor's charge for the spying mission at 10.309–312. Each of the lines 10.397–399 is marked with an *obelos* in the Venetus A: see on 10.51–52 for the Alexandrian scholarly practice of athetesis. The scholia, however, tell us that there is some dispute about whether Aristarchus indeed meant for the *obeloi* to be placed here: one scholion says that they should be, if we can trust the work of the scholar Ammonios. The second scholion informs us both that, in the work of the scholar Nemesion, he states that no reason for the *obeloi* is found in the *hupomnēmata* of Aristarchus, and that the work of Ammonios says that Aristarchus did place those signs in the margin, but in the end took them out. All of this serves as a reminder that we have access to Aristarchus' work only as mediated by his successors.

The scholia also inform us that there are recorded differences in how this particular repetition operates: in the version in the main text of the Venetus A, Dolon has changed the person of the verb from Hektor's third person—find out whether *they* are making plans—to the second person—find out whether *you* are making plans—now that Dolon is speaking to those on whom he was intending to spy. (This change seems to be the reason why 10.398 also has the critical mark of a *diplē* next to it in the Venetus A, which indicates a comment about the language used.) We can compare 10.409–411, where Odysseus repeats the questions that Nestor had given as the charge for their mission. He retains the third-person plural verbs that refer to the Trojans (those lines are marked with *obeloi* and also with asterisks in the Venetus A, indicating that they are repetitions). The A main scholia indicate that it should still be the third person here, while the intermarginal scholia note that in other manuscripts these verbs are indeed in the third person. If we compare this type of repetition to messengers delivering their message, however, we do find that a pronoun change often happens. For example, when Zeus sends Dream to Agamemnon, he orders him using imperatives and the third-person pronoun for Agamemnon (e.g. "Tell him to arm the Achaeans, who have beautiful hair," *Iliad* 2.11), but when Dream speaks to Agamemnon, he uses indicative verbs and the second person ("He has told you to arm the Achaeans, who have beautiful hair," *Iliad* 2.28), keeping all other words the same. Similar changes naturally happen, as we can see also at *Iliad* 9.157, where Agamemnon is speaking about Achilles in the third person, and *Iliad* 9.299, where Odysseus is delivering the message to Achilles himself. The formulas have such flexibility.

This phenomenon seen within repeated passages and the disagreement over whether it is the second or third person in 10.398 suggests that this passage is in fact playing on the conventional repetition by messengers. Dolon, after all, was supposed to gather information about the Achaeans and report it back to Hektor. He is not a messenger, and therefore he was not supposed to repeat Hektor's words to anyone else. When Odysseus likewise repeats Nestor's questions (10.409–411), he is in the process of obtaining the answers he seeks, not confessing what he was sent to find out, as Dolon is. We noted above (10.314–315) that there is an implicit contrast between Dolon the spy and his father the herald, and here, when Dolon repeats what Hektor asked him to find out, he seems to be doing so more in the mode of the herald he was not supposed to be.

10.399 καμάτῳ ἀδηκότες See our discussion of this phrase on 10.98.

10.400 τὸν δ᾽ ἐπιμειδήσας προσέφη πολύμητις Ὀδυσσεύς The detail of a facial expression within this formulaic reply introduction raises important questions about how such formulas work. We can compare 10.382 and see the same line with only the change of ἐπιμειδήσας for ἀπαμειβόμενος: if the singer uses this facial expression in this context, we have the opportunity to ask what meaning it brings with it. (See Beck 2005 for speech and reply introductions in general. It is important to note that p425 records ἀπαμειβόμενος in this line: see our textual commentary on that papyrus.)

Smiles that are not spontaneous reactions of joy carry particular meanings within a culture and within a context, and our task in interpreting this line is to decode the meaning of Odysseus' smile. We might start by asking whether Dolon can see him smile in the dark or whether this smile is for the audience's "view" only. Another question is whether this verb here means 'smiling', or 'laughing' (as some have translated it). One potential problem with such translations is that our own cultural expectations as to what is appropriate to the situation may affect what we interpret as smiling and what as laughing, while the traditional audience may have had different expectations.

Halliwell (2008:520–529) has recently argued that ancient Greek has separate words for smiling (those with roots in μειδ[ι]ᾶν) and laughing (γελᾶν). He notes that there can be complications in classification of these verbs, but he nevertheless maintains a greater distinction between them than other scholars have, with an emphasis on the vocalization and therefore sound accompanying laughter. Following his distinctions, then, Odysseus' smile here is silent, and because it occurs in the dark, as we interpret its meaning in this context, we must wonder whether Dolon himself sees it.

To investigate what the smile means, we can look to other complete instances of this formulaic line, and also at other uses of the verb and its non-compound form μειδάω or μειδιάω, paying particular attention to Odysseus' other smiles. Why take such an approach? Since oral poetry is composed in performance within a system of specialized grammar and specialized vocabulary (Lord 1960/2000:35–36), accounting for all the examples of how that vocabulary is deployed demonstrates how it operates within the system. The *Iliad* and *Odyssey* constitute our surviving "database" of the traditional language of this poetry, so we examine what data we have, while being cognizant of the fact that what has survived is a limited "data set" from a larger tradition (see e.g. Parry MHV 4, 9; Lord 1960/2000:47).

When we examine the fifteen instances of μειδάω, the three instances of μειδιάω, and the four instances of ἐπιμειδάω in the two epics combined, we find that the gods smile eleven times and mortals eleven times. Odysseus smiles most often among mortals, although his status as the hero of the *Odyssey* may skew the frequency. As we might expect, many of these cases can be understood as smiles of affection between loved ones, whether mortal or immortal. But the complexity of the multiple possible cultural meanings of smiles can also be seen when Hera smiles twice, once at Aphrodite and once to herself (*Iliad* 14.222–223) after successfully obtaining the alluring *zōnē* from Aphrodite without revealing her true purpose for it. These smiles seem to indicate deception and self-satisfaction, respectively. In another example, Ajax combines a smile with a grim expression (*Iliad* 7.212) as he enters a duel with Hektor, presenting us with a menacing smile that reveals a desire for victory in battle. Halliwell (2008:55–58) describes this smile as one of "bloodlust" and cites Odysseus' smile here as the closest parallel to it. And, of course, Odysseus' famously described "sardonic smile" after he dodges the ox foot that Ktesippos throws at him (*Odyssey* 20.301–302) conveys a nexus of emotions including contempt and a desire for revenge.

These last two examples give us good comparisons for the context of this smile: instead of a smile between loved ones, we have also in this case a smile between or about enemies. When we look at the syntactical context of these verbs, we also see that they are used in speech introductions or reactions to speeches (five of the smiles happen in speech introductions; in thirteen cases, the smile comes in reaction to the words of another, either with no speech following or another line introducing the response; in four cases, the smile occurs in narrative between speeches). When we narrow our focus down to the compound form ἐπιμειδάω, which we have in this line, all four instances of this verb are part of the formula τὸν δ' ἐπιμειδήσας προσέφη + epithet + name (*Iliad* 4.356, *Iliad* 8.38, and *Odyssey* 22.371, the last of which matches exactly the line we have here). So smiling *at* someone within this specialized vocabulary is associated directly with speaking to that person.

As we noted, Odysseus is the mortal who smiles most often in these two epics: here in this line and then three times in the *Odyssey*. All other mortals who smile with these verbs (Agamemnon, Hektor, Achilles, Menelaos, Telemakhos, Ajax, and Antilokhos) do so only once in our "database." Odysseus is also most often the mortal smiled at (by Agamemnon, Telemakhos, Athena, and Kalypso) and is once the cause of the smile (Antilokhos). Again, this frequency may be a coincidence of having the *Odyssey*, Odysseus' story, as one of the two epics we have to examine. But it does also seem to be part of his characterization, especially that he smiles at foes: the sardonic smile toward the suitors and the smile at Medon (*Odyssey* 22.371), as well as his smile at Dolon here. In Levine's (1984) analysis of Odysseus' three smiles in the *Odyssey*, his argument is framed explicitly in terms of disproving "Parry's insistence on economy as a basic principle of composition"; instead his approach, he claims, will show how to "determine one among a series of different meanings which could be attached to traditional language" (1). In other words, Levine sets up an opposition between Parry's concept of thrift and the idea that a formula such as the one we see in this line can generate meaning in context. He concludes, "Since the psychology behind Odysseus' smiles changes in accordance with the development of the narrative, we see how Homeric formulaic language can be charged with thematic meaning" (Levine 1984:8–9). Levine is focused in that article especially on the smiles of Odysseus at *Odyssey* 20.301, 22.371, and 23.111, but his arguments have been influential about smiles in Homeric epic in general, giving us an opportunity to reexamine Parry's concept of thrift and how exactly formulaic language does generate meaning in context.

Taking Parry's idea of economy or thrift to mean that a formula does not respond to context is an all too common misunderstanding of it. Here is how Parry defines thrift: "The thrift of a system lies in the degree to which it is free of phrases which, having the same metrical value and expressing the same idea, could replace one another" (MHV, 276). We have already seen that ἐπιμειδήσας has the same metrical value as ἀπαμειβόμενος, so according to this definition, they do not express the same idea if they adhere to the principle of thrift. But the idea of thrift does not at all imply that the meaning of any one word is diminished, and that is what Levine seems to be arguing against. All Parry's argument about the thrift of system is saying is that the system would not include another metrically equivalent word or phrase to mean 'smiling', not that smiles cannot mean different things in different contexts. (As discussed above at 10.41, if such a metrically equivalent word or phrase for smiling did exist, we would expect it to carry with it a difference in "idea," such as tone, theme, or meaning).

Levine explicitly says he is following those critics who have demonstrated "Homer's relative freedom from the shackles of a traditional system" (1984:1). Yet Albert Lord has demonstrated in clear and straightforward terms that the singer is not shackled by the tradition, because he *is* the tradition. Formulas are the singer's craft and he uses them in service to the song: "Indeed, it is easy to see that he employs a set phrase because it is useful and answers his need, but it is not sacrosanct. What stability it has comes from its utility, not from a feeling on the part of the singer that it cannot or must not be changed. It, too, is capable of adjustment. In making his lines the singer is not bound by the formula. The formulaic technique was developed to serve him as a craftsman, not to enslave him" (Lord 1960/2000:53–54). And as John Foley has persuasively argued throughout his work (1991, 1995, 1999, 2002), in oral traditional poetry such formulas accrue *more* meaning through time, not less, and, importantly, a particular instance is not limited to one among a series of meanings. A traditional singer and a traditional audience bring to the interpretation of this smile their recollections of all other instances of Odysseus smiling and of similar smiling situations, as represented by the formula of this speech introduction, in their understanding of what kind of smile it is. Because Levine's arguments are based on false premises about thrift and how the formulaic, traditional language creates meaning, his distinctions about cases that exhibit "a greater sensitivity to plot movement and sophisticated composition" (Levine 1984:7) are deeply flawed. As Lord reminds us about oral traditional singing, "The complexity and artistry of the result are often surprising to anyone who feels that illiterate singers can produce only simple structures" (Lord 1960/2000:54).

With an acknowledgement of the possibility of such artistry and complexity, then, we can return to our attempt to discover the *traditional* meaning underlying this particular smile. So far we have seen that within the system of Homeric poetry this smile should be interpreted in terms of Odysseus' relationship (one of enmity) with and reaction to Dolon, and that it may be characteristic of Odysseus to smile in this way, but that we have to understand all of this from the standpoint of oral poetics. The closest parallel is the same speech introduction formula used in *Odyssey* 22.371, when Medon is asking Odysseus to spare his life and Odysseus smiles at him before reassuring him that he will do so. In an earlier article, Levine argues that reassurance is the meaning of this formulaic speech introduction: "The words τὸν/τὴν δ' ἐπιμειδήσας προσέφη always introduce speeches of reassurance. The essential meaning of this formula is 'He smiled reassuringly at him/her.' The facial expression so described is meant to have a calming effect" (Levine 1982:101). In the case of Medon, this seems to be so, as the speech that follows does indeed reassure him that he will live.

In the case of Odysseus' interrogation of Dolon, such an interpretation might make Odysseus the "good cop" to Diomedes' "bad cop" (see below on 10.446 for Diomedes' very different facial expression). Levine applies such a meaning to this case as well: "Odysseus smiles at a fearful Dolon (10.400) in order to calm his fears and have him continue his report" (Levine 1982:101). This interpretation assumes, of course, that Dolon can see Odysseus' smile. Such a characterization of the speech that follows the introductory formula, as a speech of reassurance, applies better to Odysseus' previous speech, when he does indeed begin by telling Dolon to take courage and put thoughts of death from his mind. That speech is introduced without the smile, however (10.382–383). Here, the beginning of the speech is Odysseus' reaction to the thought of Dolon driving Achilles' horses, and any reassuring Odysseus does is to assure Dolon that he has reached too far in thinking that he is worthy of such a prize.

Should we take this smile to be one of amusement or derision, then, or what else might this tell us about Odysseus' character? Levine compares *Odyssey* 22.371 with this line in asserting that both of these smiles express Odysseus' "security and confidence in his superior position" (1984:6) and notes in his earlier work that victory and amusement are not mutually exclusive, but that a smile can, in fact, indicate both (1982:102). The smile as a sign of confidence seems to come closer to the situation in this line than does a notion of reassuring Dolon. Lateiner argues that Odysseus' "smiles (especially the sardonic one [*Odyssey* 20.301–302]) characterize menacing resources and mark each context as a significant, if ambivalent, moment" (1995:42). If that is so, what, then, would be the significance of this moment? Does Odysseus' smile indicate that from Dolon's initial response Odysseus knows he will get the information he wants from him? One more possible characterization: Corrine Pache, while agreeing with Levine's argument that it is a speech of reassurance, focuses on Odysseus in the *Iliad* alone, and she notes that he is unlike other heroes in that he does not cry in this epic. That observation leads her to conclude that this smile "reveals gleeful indifference to the other man's fate" (Pache 2000:19) and that Odysseus' intentions when he smiles are "of the coldest and cruelest kind" (2000:20). In other words, if Odysseus can smile while Dolon begs for his life and blames Hektor for his predicament, does that indicate an emotional disengagement?

In a traditional song culture, these varying interpretations are not necessarily mutually exclusive. Let us remember that this smile carries with it associations from past performances for the audience. So Odysseus' smile could show his confidence that he has Dolon right where he wants him in terms of getting information out of him, his derision at the prospect of Dolon receiving the prize of Achilles' horses, and an overall characterization of one who smiles at his enemies before taking vengeance upon them. The traditional nature of this introductory line can imbue it with greater meaning, yet for a singer singing in performance, the immediate context, what Dolon just said and what Odysseus was about to say, may have called for a smile from Odysseus related to these many meanings. (See Lord 1960/2000:54 for the reminder that "lines cannot be isolated from what precedes them.") The meaning here combines this immediate context with that from the larger tradition. That combination and its resulting complexity of meaning does not contradict Parry's concept of thrift.

As we mentioned at the beginning of this discussion, however, p425 does not include the smile at all, but rather has the common formula including ἀπαμειβόμενος 'answering'. Thus in a performance, a singer may not include this detail, as revealing as we may find it. We may think that a *better* singer would include it, but there are so many factors involved, including the experience and training of the singer, the versions of this episode he has heard from others, and the pressures of rapid composition-in-performance, that we cannot make this judgment for certain. What is important to keep in mind is that these performance variations do exist, even in our textual record.

10.402–404 These lines are the same as those at *Iliad* 17.76–78. There, Apollo, in disguise as Mentes, leader of the Kikones, warns Hektor not to chase after Achilles' horses, which carried Patroklos into battle (see also *Iliad* 16.864–867, where we are reminded that the gods gave these horses as a gift to Peleus). For this traditional language expressing a prohibition against Achilles' enemies capturing these horses, see above on 10.330.

10.405 See above on 10.384 for this formula.

10.406 ποιμένα λαῶν See on 10.3 for more on the traditional epithet "shepherd of the warriors," there applied to Agamemnon.

10.406–407 D.M. Gaunt argues that these lines are the point at which the theme changes from a spying mission, or "reconnaissance-story," to "a direct attack" (1971:197). Gaunt postulates that there were at one time two traditional episodes, one that focused on reconnaissance and the other on an assassination of "Hector or some great hero" (1971:195). (See also on 10.282.) Gaunt argues that when oral poetry is composed and performed, "paratactic" thinking allows for this kind of shift, since both the singer and the audience are most focused on the immediate scene. We disagree with Gaunt's characterization of oral composition as primitive and his assertion "that sometimes the narrative leads the poet" (1971:195). Instead, we can see how these themes are linked in ways that Lord (1960/2000) and Petegorsky (1982) have explored, a phenomenon that reveals the complexity, rather than the simple-mindedness, of oral traditional epic. (Note that Hainsworth 1993 calls 10.433–441 the "turning-point of the Book.")

10.406–411 Odysseus asks Dolon what Nestor had wanted them to find out, and in oral traditional style, he asks using the same words Nestor himself used: compare 10.409–411 to 10.208–210. Thus we might notice that here Odysseus does fulfill the objectives of the spying mission, even as it is in the process of evolving into an ambush. Nestor, after all, had suggested that they might get this information by capturing one of the enemy (10.206). There is a consistency to the mission. But we should also note that Odysseus asks other questions first, about Hektor, armor, horses, and the arrangement of the night watches. Fenik (1964:19–20) argues that there was another version in which the night mission was to assassinate Hektor (which is seen briefly in the tragedy *Rhesos*). We might, however, understand Odysseus' question about Hektor as being related to the question of what the Trojans are planning to do, since it was Hektor's idea in the first place to camp on the plain during this night. But the questions about armor, horses, and night watches are directly relevant to what comes next: infiltrating the enemy camp and stealing horses. Dolon's immediate response covers Hektor and the night watches. That response prompts Odysseus' further questions about the allies, and then Dolon's answer includes horses and armor, specifically the spectacular horses and armor of Rhesos. In terms of the sequence of information gathered, Odysseus' questions here can be seen to prompt Dolon's revelation that Rhesos has arrived. But in a larger sense, these questions may also reflect the traditional theme of night raids, and their traditional outcomes: targeting a leader through ambush and getting horses and armor through plunder. Understood in a traditional framework, neither the questions themselves nor the actions they lead to seem disjointed or strange from the point of view of the original mission.

10.413 τοὶ γὰρ ἐγώ τοι ταῦτα μάλ' ἀτρεκέως καταλέξω In several sources the verb here is ἀγορεύσω (see textual commentary on the Venetus A for more detail). We see this whole-line formula elsewhere in the Homeric epics, with the multiforms of καταλέξω and ἀγορεύσω. In *Odyssey* 4.399, Eidothea uses this same formula to introduce her instructions to Menelaos on how to ambush Proteus. She is not a captive of Menelaos, and so the main use of this formula seems to be as an introduction to a detailed set of information, and ambush requires such details to be successful. The formula seems also to be associated with false identities in answering the question of who one is: compare *Odyssey* 1.179, where Athena claims to be Mentes, and *Odyssey* 14.192, where Odysseus uses the line to introduce his Cretan lie to Eumaios. The "trickiness" on display in those answers might also be a point of connection with the ambush theme. We should note, however, that here Dolon is not being obviously tricky, unless we understand that by mentioning that the allies are unguarded he is diverting Odysseus from going after the Trojans and Hektor himself. In any case, Hektor, we know, is awake and not an ambush target on this night.

10.415 βουλὰς βουλεύει For the importance of "plans" in night and ambush contexts, see pp. 69–73 and also on 10.1ff, 10.43–44, and 10.302.

At 10.302, Dolon's spying mission is the plan that Hektor proposes, but here Dolon implies that Hektor is still in the process of making plans. We might note that Dolon's use of the present tense also seems to imply that he expects Hektor to still be there, just as the Achaean leaders wait at the council meeting place for Diomedes and Odysseus to return (see below on 10.564).

10.415 θείου παρὰ σήματι Ἴλου From the geneaology of the Trojan royal family that Aeneas tells Achilles at *Iliad* 20.213–240, we learn that Ilos was the son of Tros, the father of Laomedon, and grandfather of Priam. His name is related to the name of Ilion. His grave mound acts as a landmark on the Trojan plain: both its prominence and the adjective θείου suggest that it was the site of a hero cult for Ilos (see Nagy 1979 on hero cult and the Homeric epics). This landmark also appears in two other episodes related to ambush. In *Iliad* 11, Paris hides behind the stele on the grave mound as he shoots an arrow at Diomedes (*Iliad* 11.369–383; at *Iliad* 11.372 Ilos is called Dardanos' son, perhaps meaning descendant, or perhaps reflecting a different geneaology: see Gantz 1993:557–558 for the question). This grave mound acts as a landmark again at *Iliad* 24.349, when Priam journeys to the Achaean camp to ransom Hektor's body. After they pass the grave mound, Priam and his herald stop to water the horses and mules at the river, and it is there that Hermes meets them (see "The Poetics of Ambush" for both of these episodes as related to the ambush theme, and also 10.1ff. for Priam's night journey). That Hermes meets them at this point suggests that Priam is then in a dangerous space and needs protection (as Thornton 1984:154 also observes). The grave mound is also used as a landmark during the daytime fighting: when Agamemnon routs the Trojans, they pass by this grave mound (*Iliad* 11.166) and then the fig tree as they move to the city. Thornton identifies the features of the Trojan landscape, in order from the walls of Troy to the ships of the Achaeans as: "the oak-tree of Zeus, the fig-tree, the tomb of Ilus, the ford of the Scamander, the "rise" or hillock on the plain, and the Achaean ditch or wall" (Thornton 1984:150; see also Hainsworth 1993:243 on *Iliad* 11.166 for this grave mound's place in the Trojan landscape). Thus we can see that the Trojans are rather close to the Achaeans on this night, and that the fearful thoughts Agamemnon has at the beginning of *Iliad* 10 are justified.

The spatial information Dolon gives here in terms of this landmark will recur in even greater detail in his subsequent answers. Spatial indications are important to ambushers moving through the darkness.

(See also Clay 2007 on spatial indications in descriptions of battle in Homeric poetry.)

10.416 νόσφιν ἀπὸ φλοίσβου Dolon describes the meeting place as being apart from the noise of the rest of the encampment. It seems likely that we should envision the Trojan meeting as closer to the Achaean camp than the Trojan camp, just as the meeting of the Achaean leaders is closer to the Trojans: they cross the ditch and move out onto the plain (10.194–195).

10.416 ἥρως This term often is used as the sixth foot in a line (over twenty times in the Homeric epics), and is used as a vocative (in any metrical position, but most often in the first or sixth foot) four times in the *Iliad* and four times in the *Odyssey*, either alone, as here (see also *Iliad* 20.104, *Odyssey* 4.423, 7.303, 10.516), or with the personal name of the hero (*Iliad* 11.819 and 11.838 with Eurypylos and *Odyssey* 4.312 with Telemakhos). So although Hainsworth (1993:194), commenting on this line, says that "the unqualified vocative in the sixth foot in mid-speech is otiose and rare," isolating this usage with that many qualifications may be overstating it. The equivalent nominative form is often found in the sixth foot, and there is even a fairly common formula that uses it in this position, αὐτὰρ ὅ γ' ἥρως (*Iliad* 5.308. 5.327, 8.268, 11.483, 13.164, 23.896), indicating that this word in the sixth foot was useful and good for composing-in-performance. The other vocative uses in this position that appear in our texts, it is true, are those in which ἥρως modifies a name, but since the vocative is used elsewhere, to find this particular use strange may be a case of already concluding that *Iliad* 10 as a whole is strange, and using this as one more piece of evidence for that conclusion. From a compositional point of view, a word often used in the sixth foot could easily be used in this way by analogy.

10.416–422 The lack of watches among the allies creates a situation ripe for ambush, and we can at least consider the possibility that Dolon gives this information, as well as the information about Rhesos and the Thracians in his next response, to divert the Achaeans away from the Trojans themselves. We have seen night watches arranged by the Trojans before this night: when the previous night fell, Priam set up a night watch around the city of Troy (*Iliad* 7.370–371; these same lines appear again at *Iliad* 18.298–299, when Hektor likewise sets up a night watch on the night following this one). The implication of those watches is that a night ambush may happen on any night (and, of course, we do hear about such episodes at Troy at *Odyssey* 4.244–258 and *Odyssey* 14.468–503). Because the Trojan army and its allies are spending this night out on the Trojan plain, however, more elaborate arrangements are made as night falls at the end of *Iliad* 8. The night watch in the city will on this night be manned by elders and boys, while the women light fires, all to prevent an attack on the city while the army is outside it (*Iliad* 8.517–522). Hektor also establishes a watch "on ourselves" (*Iliad* 8.529), and the fires he orders lit so that they can see if the Achaeans try to sail away (*Iliad* 8.507–511) number one thousand, with fifty men and their horses stationed at each (*Iliad* 8.562–565). The allies are not mentioned separately at this point, but Dolon's words here make it appear that they are not included in those groups around the watch fires. At the beginning of *Iliad* 10, we can recall, Agamemnon both saw these fires and heard music and men talking around them (*Iliad* 10.11–13). So there is a key contrast here between the awake and watchful Trojans and the sleeping allies—and also one between the kind of watch that the Achaeans arrange for the whole army (see *Iliad* 9.66–88) and the more diffuse watches of the Trojans.

This latter arrangement may show how unusual the situation is for the Trojans: camping out on the plain for the first time, they are grouped as if they had gone to their family homes within the city. This arrangement is also consistent with what we see of the Trojans elsewhere in the *Iliad*. Gould argues that Trojan society "is a model based on an almost complete equation between the city of Troy and the οἶκος 'household/family' of Priam, with the consequence that ties of obligation in Troy are seen as those that obtain within an extended family" (2001:343–344). The fact that the watch fires are here called "home-fires" (πυρὸς ἐσχάραι, 10.418) reinforces the idea that these are family groups, each responsible for its own watch.

10.423 See the textual commentary on p609 for its recorded multiform on this line.

10.424–431 Here, we see again the need for spatial information in a night ambush. Odysseus wants to know exactly the arrangements of the Trojan camp, and such knowledge will help not only his entrance but also his exit and successful return.

10.430 Θύμβρης Thymbrē is located on the Trojan plain, where the Thymbrios river meets the Skamander in "the inner recesses of the Trojan plain southeast of Troy" (Luce 1998:124, with reference to Strabo 13.1.35) and is the site of a sanctuary dedicated to Thymbraion Apollo. Thornton (1984:150) argues that most places in the topography of Troy "are consistently associated with a particular sort of situation or with a particular party or person in the poem." Thymbrē, mentioned only here in our *Iliad*, is associated with ambush in the larger epic tradition about the Trojan War. It is the site of Achilles' ambush of Troilos (according to the scholia in the Townley manscript on *Iliad* 24.257; see also Apollodorus, *Epitome* 3.32) and also the site where Achilles himself is killed in an ambush by Paris and Apollo (see above on 10.29). It is also known as the place where Laokoon's sons are killed (see Gantz 1993:648). Thus it is not surprising to find it mentioned here, and only in *Iliad* 10 within our *Iliad*, since it is so closely tied to the ambush theme.

10.432–434   See the textual commentary on p609 for its recorded plus verse in this passage.

10.433   εἰ γὰρ δὴ μέματον Τρώων καταδῦναι ὅμιλον We also find this use of καταδύω to mean 'go behind enemy lines' in an ambush theme at *Odyssey* 4.246: ἀνδρῶν δυσμενέων κατέδυ πόλιν εὐρυάγυιαν, and again at 4.249. (Athena's action at *Iliad* 4.86 seems to have a similar flavor, but Apollo also "sinks into" the crowd of Trojans below at 10.517, and the Trojans are not his enemy, so the verb seems to specify gods visiting mortals in those cases.) It is also used to mean 'enter' battle (*Iliad* 3.241 and 18.134).

10.435   The scholia on this line in the Venetus A, Venetus B, and Townley manuscripts provide information on the multiform, traditional story of Rhesos. See the section on Rhesos in our essay "Tradition and Reception" for the texts of these scholia and a full discussion. As we saw on 10.406–411, Odysseus' question about the horses and armor in general might have prompted this answer. Or Dolon may be directing them to the allies "furthest" from the rest in an attempt to deflect a more destructive attack. But in this version, in which Rhesos has not yet fought in battle at Troy and in which we have no oracle about his possible invincibility, it is through Dolon's "advice" here that Rhesos becomes a target. That Rhesos is the son of an Eioneus here, and not the river Strymon as he is elsewhere, also serves to make him a more "mortal" target, although one still important as a king of freshly arrived troops who has spectacular horses.

10.436–437   The horses of Rhesos are thematically significant in multiple ways. In one version of the story of Rhesos (see the Rhesos section of our essay "Tradition and Reception"), the so-called "oracle version," Rhesos' horses are intimately tied to the destiny of Rhesos and to that of Troy, since the oracle declares that, if Rhesos and his horses eat and drink at Troy, Rhesos will be invincible. The whiteness of the horses, as we see later in this episode (see commentary on 10.547), makes them highly visible even in the dark of night. (Schnapp-Goubeillon sees a ritual significance to their color, saying that a white horse is the sacrificial victim par excellence in horse cults, 1981:117.) Their size and swiftness, noted by Dolon here, also make them a valuable prize. The practical and symbolic importance of horses in general in the *Iliad* is evident in the singer's questions that follow the catalog of ships: the narrator asks who had the "best" horses as well as who was the best warrior (*Iliad* 2.761–770). That is, horses seem to be as much a part of the competition to be the best as is excellence in battle. (The answer given to these questions is that Achilles and his horses were the best, but only after it has been said that Eumelos' mares and Telamonian Ajax were the best so long as Achilles was absent.) The value of horses is also seen in Diomedes' acquisition of his enemies' horses in *Iliad* 5. When he gives instructions to Sthenelos to capture the horses of Aeneas at *Iliad* 5.263–273, the most prominent example, Diomedes says capturing them will win them good *kleos* (εἰ τούτω κε λάβοιμεν, ἀροίμεθά κε κλέος ἐσθλόν, *Iliad* 5.273), making their symbolic value glory itself.

The possibility of taking these horses, when added to the attractiveness of the target of the sleeping, unguarded Thracians, combines ambush with horse-rustling, a closely associated theme. We will consider below (at 10.513–514) whether the theme of horse-rustling affects the composition of this nighttime horse-stealing episode, as compared to the taking of horses in daytime battle. But just as we have seen that spying missions frequently become ambushes, so also can ambushes incorporate this type of night raid (see pp. 80–84 of "The Poetics of Ambush" for other examples).

Shewan 1911:179–180 has already dismissed the argument that the lack of reference to these horses subsequently in the *Iliad* is evidence that *Iliad* 10 is a late addition to the epic.

10.438–441 The elaborate chariot and gold armor of Rhesos also mark him as an important and desirable target. Agamemnon's armor includes gold (*Iliad* 11.25), as does the armor Hephaistos makes for Achilles (*Iliad* 18.475, 549, 612). Gold armor is memorably seen elsewhere in the exchange between Diomedes and Glaukos, in which Glaukos gives Diomedes his gold armor for Diomedes' bronze as a sign of their inherited guest-friendship (*Iliad* 6.232–236). Nestor also has an all-gold shield, which Hektor hopes to capture. He says that if he does take Nestor's shield, along with Diomedes' breastplate, then the Achaeans will depart that very night (*Iliad* 8.191–197)—in fact, the night on which this ambush episode occurs. So there may be an association between the taking of gold armor and the outcome of the war, and Rhesos' gold and silver chariot and gold armor may have a similar significance, relating it to versions of the Rhesos story in which his death prevents a possible Trojan victory (see "Tradition and Reception" for a full discussion of these other versions).

The phrase θαῦμα ἰδέσθαι is used elsewhere in the *Iliad* for armor (that which Achilles inherits from Peleus but which Hektor is wearing at that point, *Iliad* 18.83) and other golden objects (Hebe's chariot, *Iliad* 5.725, and Hephaistos' wheeled tripods, *Iliad* 18.377). Since Achilles' original armor was a wedding gift to Peleus from the gods, all these examples are also associated with the gods, as Rhesos' armor is in Dolon's words. In the *Odyssey*, θαῦμα ἰδέσθαι is associated with cloth or clothing (*Odyssey* 6.306, 8.366, 13.108) or buildings (*Odyssey* 7.45), but always those of divinities or the Phaeacians. From a compositional point of view, then, the following comment that his armor seems like that of the immortals is an expansion of this phrase.

10.446 ὑπόδρα ἰδών is another formulaic facial expression that is part of speech introductions (compare 10.400). This look is given at least twenty-six times in the two epics, twenty times within the formula τὸν/τὴν/τοὺς δ' ἄρ' ὑπόδρα ἰδών προσέφη + epithet + name (thirteen times in the *Iliad*, seven in the *Odyssey*, Holoka 1983:3n6; Beck 2005:34, 284). Holoka, quoting Stanford, asserts that "The actual facial expression signified by ὑπόδρα ἰδών is quite unmistakable: 'looking (out) from beneath (scil. beetling or knit) brows'," and also cites research on facial expressions for the "distinctiveness of this positioning of the brows as a universally recognized sign of anger" (1983:4n8). That anger, Holoka argues, is a reaction to what the previous speaker has just said. In sum, Holoka argues: "In both Homeric epics, to look darkly is to employ a nonverbal cue fraught with judgmental significance. The speaker, whatever his message, transmits by his facial demeanor that an infraction of propriety has occurred ... In all instances, the facial gesture ὑπόδρα ἰδών charges the speech it introduces with a decidedly minatory fervency and excitement: a threshold has been reached and such inflammable materials as wounded pride, righteous indignation, frustration, shame, and shock are nearing the combustion point"

(1983:16). Holoka is focusing especially on the cases (twelve times in the *Iliad*) in which this look is given by one comrade (often a superior) to another (often a subordinate), and he says that the situation with Dolon is a different case because it is between enemies (1983:8).

In fact, the most telling parallels for this fierce look of Diomedes at Dolon come from the *Odyssey*, where Odysseus gives this look to the suitors, either individually (*Odyssey* 22.60, 22.320) or as a group (*Odyssey* 22.34), as well as to Iros (*Odyssey* 18.14) and the disloyal slave Melantho (*Odyssey* 18.337, 19.70). (These last two are exceptional in that the look is given to a woman; other than Zeus looking at Hera this way, all those who receive the expression are male. But the formula is flexible in accommodating the gender change.) These looks given to the suitors show both contempt and suspicion, anger and fear, and we can see this same mix of emotions in the words of Diomedes that follow this instance. Both Diomedes here and Odysseus in *Odyssey* 22 follow up this look at an enemy with beheading him. In the *Odyssey*, Odysseus gives this look to Leiodes, the suitor who, as we hear upon his introduction as the first to try the bow (*Odyssey* 21.144–147), had found the reckless deeds of the suitors hateful and felt righteous indignation toward them. It is this man who supplicates Odysseus; Odysseus rejects his plea for mercy and beheads him (see also below on 10.456–457). Given to an enemy, then (and we can add that Achilles gives this look to Hektor three times at *Iliad* 20.428, 22.260, 22.344), this look carries with it a danger of sudden violence: the combustion point is not merely approached, it is quickly reached. So here also we see the flexibility of the formula within its context: the essential meaning of the expression is maintained, but the expectation of what will follow is shaped by whether the look is given to a comrade or to an enemy.

As we saw above on 10.400, these telling facial expressions are sometimes absent in other versions. Allen's (and subsequently, West's) papyrus 90 (Oxyrhynchus 6.949) has the possible multiform [τον δ ημειβετ επειτα βοην αγα]θος Διομηδης. See 10.283 for more on this multiform.

10.447 μὴ δή μοι φύξίν γε Δόλων ἐμβάλλεο θυμῷ The scholia in the Venetus A and B and Townley manuscripts on this line are all concerned with the fact that Diomedes calls Dolon by name, when Dolon has not told them his name. In the Venetus A, the line is marked with a *diplē*, indicating that Aristarchus made a comment about the language of the line. The lemma in this manuscript for the comment is actually the beginning of the line, demonstrating that a lemma can be simply an indication of the line being commented on, and not the specific words concerned. The scholion in the Venetus A explains that the line is marked "because Aristarchus is asking, how does he know the name? Thus some read 'δολῶν' [that is, "being tricky"], like νοῶν [that is, the participle would be formed the same way]." With this alternative reading, the line would read "Don't be tricky and put thoughts of escape in your heart." There is at least a sound-alike connection between Dolon's name and δόλος 'trick' (see also Higbie 1995:12). The scholion goes on to point out that Odysseus also later uses Dolon's name, in 10.478, implying that it cannot be the participle there, and so we have to accept that Diomedes and Odysseus know his name without knowing exactly how they know it. The scholion goes on to suggest that it is likely that they would know the names of some men, since it has been ten years, and perhaps especially Dolon's since he is the son of a herald who is wealthy (citing 10.315). The scholia in the other two manuscripts take a similar approach to the problem, noting Dolon's father's role as a herald and that Dolon is among the leaders of the Trojans who are called to the meeting earlier in the book, or suggesting simply that we should understand that they asked his name when they overpowered him. Higbie (1995:87) compares a similar case in the *Odyssey* in which the narrator has introduced Theoklymenos to the audience, and Telemakhos knows his name without a direct introduction within the narrative. This concern for how they know his name, although understandable from a literary point of view, does not apply to an oral traditional narrative composed in performance. As Hainsworth (1993:197 *ad* 10.447) affirms, "what his audience knows an epic poet may let his characters know too."

10.454–456 Diomedes kills Dolon before Dolon can touch him in a gesture of supplication. On supplication in Homeric epic, see Crotty 1994, Wilson 2002, and Naiden 2006. According to these analyses of the act of supplication, Dolon's supplication begins at 10.378–381 with his offer of ransom (*apoina*) if he can be taken alive (see also our comments at 10.378–381). At that point, Odysseus and Diomedes have grabbed Dolon's hands, so that he is unable to make this clasping gesture. (Such a scene is visualized by the Dokimasia painter on a kylix cup from c. 480 BCE [St. Petersburg, Hermitage B.1539], with Dolon pictured in his wolf skin.) According to Naiden's arguments, the person being supplicated always has the freedom to reject the request, as Diomedes does here (see Naiden 2006:181 for this particular example of supplication).

10.455–457 Beheading the enemy, as gruesome or repulsive as it may seem to a modern audience, does occur several times in the Homeric epics, either as the method of killing or as an act carried out after killing, and in most cases, it is the Achaeans who do it. In *Iliad* 13, the two Ajaxes take the corpse of the Trojan Imbrios, a husband of one of Priam's illegitimate daughters. They strip the corpse of his armor, and Ajax, son of Oileus, cuts off Imbrios' head and throws it so that it ends up at Hektor's feet (*Iliad* 13.201–205). Oilean Ajax, the rapist of Kassandra, is known to commit war atrocities during the sack of Troy, but this beheading happens during the course of regular, daytime battle. Achilles beheads Deukalion at *Iliad* 20.481–483 after pinning his arm with a spear (in other words, Deukalion cannot fight back at that moment). Although Achilles is acting beyond normal human boundaries at this point in his story, he is also depicted in two sixth-century vase paintings as beheading Troilos (see Gantz 1993:600), an incident much earlier in the war, and one that also involves ambush. Agamemnon beheads Köon over the body of his brother Iphidamas (τοῖο δ' ἐπ' Ἰφιδάμαντι κάρη ἀπέκοψε παραστάς, *Iliad* 11.261) without hesitation. Hektor plans to behead Patroklos' corpse after he strips it (*Iliad* 17.126). In a series of back-and-forth killings with vaunting afterwards, Penelos kills Ilioneus, a Trojan introduced as he dies as the beloved of Hermes and an only child of a wealthy man. Penelos' spear hits Ilioneus in the eyesocket, and then Penelos cuts off Ilioneus' head with his sword and holds it up, helmet still on and spear still in eyesocket, to show it to the Trojans (*Iliad* 14.493–507). All of these examples come from the battle that rages on the day following this night, when the fighting is most intense and the stakes at their highest for the Achaeans.

The closest parallel to the beheading of Dolon in terms of language and situation, however, occurs during Odysseus' ambush of the suitors. During the slaughter in Odysseus' home, Leiodes supplicates Odysseus, but Odysseus kills him anyway (*Odyssey* 22.310–329). In both cases, then, there is an attempted supplication, and a verbal response followed by a swift beheading. As Odysseus responds to Leiodes' arguments for why he should be spared, Odysseus gives him the same fierce look (*Odyssey* 22.320) that Diomedes gives Dolon here (see 10.446). In both cases the killer drives a sword through the victim's neck (αὐχένα μέσσον ἔλασσε, *Iliad* 10.455, *Odyssey* 22.328), and the graphic detail of the victim's head still talking as it mixes with the dust is included (*Iliad* 10.457 = *Odyssey* 22.329). We may certainly question how these actions inform the character of the killers and the action of the episode, but we must also recognize that beheading is "Homeric" in the sense that the *Iliad* and *Odyssey* represent it as happening in the intensity of battle and of ambush.

10.456 φασγάνῳ ἀΐξας This formula is used to describe a particular cutting motion with the sword. ἀΐσσω generally refers to any quick motion, but we can see from the few other uses of this phrase in the *Iliad* that it means to use the sword to cut rather than to stab. At *Iliad* 5.81, Eurypylos flashes his sword at Hypsenor and cuts off his arm. In *Iliad* 8, one of Nestor's horses has been struck with an arrow as Nestor is trying to retreat from the battlefield. Nestor uses his sword at *Iliad* 8.88 (there the present participle ἀΐσσων is used instead of the aorist participle) to cut the harness straps from that horse in his attempt to escape (compare the use of ἀΐξας alone for cutting a horse loose at *Iliad* 16.474). Thus we should imagine this motion to be quick, with the edge of the sword positioned to cut through whatever it is aimed at. The one use of the phrase in the *Odyssey* (at 22.98) occurs when Telemakhos is afraid that one of the suitors will attack him in this way if he stops to remove his spear from one of his victims during the battle with the suitors; it gives no other indications about what the motion is. As in all of the cases in the *Iliad*, however, the example from the *Odyssey* does show that this phrase is used in a line initial position, enjambed with the previous line. That consistent position gives us an important clue as to how a singer would use this phrase in performance.

10.456 ἀπὸ δ' ἄμφω κέρσε τένοντε Compare the same phrase at *Iliad* 14.466, where a spear thrown by Telamonian Ajax cuts through the top vertebra of Arkhelokhos, effectively beheading him.

10.458–459 If we compare these lines depicting the stripping of Dolon's weapons and "armor" (the wolf skin) to the arming scene at 10.333–335 where he put them on, we find that different epithets or adjectives and even names of the items are used here. Such differences suggest that compositionally the theme of stripping armor employs different combinations of formulas to repesent the same items described in arming scenes. The ambush-related items nevertheless remain prominent: the headgear made of animal hide, the animal skin, and the bow. Holoka (1983:9) calls this stripping of armor "a near parody of standard battlefield practice" particularly because of the "paltry panoply" of the wolf skin, spear, and bow. Yet it is precisely this panoply that will indicate that Diomedes and Odysseus have ambushed an ambusher.

10.459 δόρυ μακρόν As Sherratt 1990:811 points out, the single long thrusting spear (as opposed to lighter, smaller, paired throwing spears) is a weapon "most at home in the 13th century or considerably earlier." Achilles' Pelian ash spear is likewise of this earlier kind, and Hektor's spear, which is eleven cubits long (e.g. *Iliad* 6.319), may be as well. See above on 10.263–264 for more on the way that such artifacts can reveal archaeological layers in the text.

10.460–464 In the prayers to Athena at the outset of the mission, both Odysseus and Diomedes emphasize their personal relationships with Athena in asking for her help and protection (see commentary on 10.275 and 10.291). In this address to the goddess, that request is renewed, but their initial success in capturing and killing Dolon is associated with the goddess as well. Athena's prominent role not only here but also in the *Odyssey* reveals her to be a goddess of ambush. At *Odyssey* 20.44–51, she tells Odysseus that, with her on his side, they could take far more men than the suitors and drive away their livestock, a description that combines the ambush narrative pattern of one or two killing many with that of a cattle raid. Odysseus similarly states earlier that, with Athena on his side, he could fight three hundred suitors (*Odyssey* 13.389–391). Proklos' summary of the epic *Little Iliad* describes the building of the wooden horse as "according to Athena's plan of action" (κατ' Ἀθηνᾶς προαίρεσιν), indicating that she is the mastermind of that ultimate ambush at Troy. On the shield of Achilles (*Iliad* 18.516), Athena and Ares together lead an ambush from the city at war. And it is of course Athena who warns Telemakhos about his impending ambush by the suitors (*Odyssey* 15.28). Stagakis (1987–88:70) examines the language here in detail and concludes that this passage does "not indicate that the spoils were vowed or dedicated to Athena," but the technicalities of the religious nature of what is or is not happening here do not diminish the association between Athena and ambush.

10.465–466 Gernet (1936:192–196) and Davidson (1979:64) both connect the hanging of the wolf skin in a tree with initiation rituals in which the initiate must remove his clothes, hang them on a tree, and live "like a wolf" for his period of separation. We have seen other hints that ambushes and night raids are associated especially with young men, those at the right age for such an initiation (Odysseus would be an exception, of course): see commentary on 10.259. For more on the wolf skin, see commentary on 10.334.

10.466–468 We see here another example of details appropriate to nocturnal actions. Odysseus and Diomedes could leave these spoils behind without worrying that someone else will take them during the night; instead, the concern is that they may not be able to find them again in the darkness, hence the need to make a sign conspicuously or clearly (δέελον δ᾽ ἐπὶ σήματ᾽ ἔθηκε, 10.466). Odysseus creates such a sign by tying the branches of the tamarisk tree (a large, dense, shrub-like tree) to the reeds below. We will see later, of course, that this sign works, when Odysseus and Diomedes stop and pick these spoils up on their return (10.526–529). This sort of planning is necessary in the dark.

The tamarisk grows often near water, and the reeds mentioned here also suggest a wetland environment, perhaps the bank of a river. We see these characteristics of the plant in its other appearances in the *Iliad*: Achilles leans his spear against a tamarisk before he leaps into the Xanthos river to kill the Trojans he has forced into it (*Iliad* 21.18) and later, when Hephaistos sets the corpses in the river on fire, tamarisks are among the plants listed as burning along the river (*Iliad* 21.350). The denseness of the plant is seen at *Iliad* 6.39, when the horses of Adrestos become tangled in a tamarisk and his chariot is broken, setting the horses loose. We have seen that a woody or marshy area—that is, one filled with plants—is often chosen for an ambush (see "The Poetics of Ambush"), and the tamarisk itself may also have a particular association with ambush. In the *Homeric Hymn to Hermes*, the god, who is called "a robber, driver of cattle" (λῃστῆρ᾽, ἐλατῆρα βοῶν, *Homeric Hymn to Hermes* 14) and "a spy at night" (νυκτὸς ὀπωπητῆρα, *Homeric Hymn to Hermes* 15), among other epithets, is himself associated with the night and the ambush theme, as we also see in his role in guiding Priam during Priam's infiltration of the Achaean camp in *Iliad* 24 (see "The Poetics of Ambush" and above on 10.1ff. for fuller discussion). According to the hymn, on the evening of the day he is born, Hermes steals the cattle of Apollo (see "The Poetics of Ambush" also for how cattle rustling is part of the larger ambush theme). When Hermes is driving these cattle at night, he stops and makes himself sandals, weaving together tamarisk and myrtle branches (συμμίσγων μυρίκας καὶ μυρσινοειδέας ὄζους, *Homeric Hymn to Hermes* 81). Odysseus ties together tamarisk and reeds here in another kind of weaving of this plant, accompanying another night ambush. Schnapp-Gourbeillon (1981:115) suggests that this plant has religious associations (see also Wathelet 1989:221n35).

10.468 θοὴν διὰ νύκτα μέλαιναν See on 10.394 for this formula.

10.469 τὼ δὲ βάτην προτέρω For the use of the dual for a pair of ambushers working together, see on 10.254.

10.471–475 The sleeping arrangements of the Thracians seem quite orderly from this description, even though they are exhausted before falling asleep (see also the following note). One implication of this orderliness seems to be that the only arrangement not made was setting up a guard, and this lack results in their being vulnerable to ambush. Within the Achaean camp, the sleeping arrangements of Nestor (10.74–79) and Diomedes (10.150–156) are similarly detailed, suggesting that such descriptions are part of the night ambush theme. We see that the details of the scene are appropriate to each hero or group, similar to the way arming scenes are adapted for each hero.

10.471 οἱ δ᾽ εὗδον καμάτῳ ἀδηκότες See note on 10.98 for more on καμάτῳ ἀδηκότες. There, we saw that this formula is especially connected to night themes, and that the weariness can be from either fighting all day or traveling, as we saw in the example from *Odyssey* 12. Since we are dealing here with a version of the Rhesos myth in which he has not yet fought at Troy—Dolon has to tell Diomedes and Odysseus of his presence since he is "newly arrived" (10.434)—the formula seems to be used for their deep sleep after traveling that day to Troy. For more on the versions of the Rhesos myth in which he fought for one day at Troy, see the Rhesos section of our essay "Tradition and Reception."

10.482 τῷ δ᾽ ἔμπνευσε μένος γλαυκῶπις Ἀθήνη Athena breathes *menos* 'force' into Diomedes as he starts the slaughter. A similar expression is used for Apollo breathing *menos* into Hektor so that he may return to battle (ὣς εἰπὼν ἔμπνευσε μένος μέγα ποιμένι λαῶν, *Iliad* 15.262; Apollo does so at Zeus' suggestion, see *Iliad* 15.60), and he does the same for Aeneas later (*Iliad* 20.110). We also see a connection between *menos* and breathing at *Iliad* 3.8, where the Achaeans breathe *menos* as they enter battle. During Diomedes' *aristeia* in the *polemos*, Athena tells him that she has put *menos* into his chest, the kind of *menos* his father used to have (*Iliad* 5.124–126). Thus this "inspiration" happens between gods and their favorites, and we find in this episode in Book 10 a pattern of opposition between Athena and Apollo (we can compare their direct rivalry in *Iliad* 7). In the *Rhesos*, Athena uses speech instead to incite ambush, as she prompts Diomedes and Odysseus to attack Rhesos and the Thracians though they are ready to turn back to their own camp (*Rhesos* 594–625; see also Fantuzzi 2006b:163–170).

10.485–488 This compressed lion simile describing Diomedes' slaughter of the Thracians calls our attention to the lion similes elsewhere in the *Iliad* that happen explicitly at night. The shepherd-less flocks in this simile correspond well to the Thracians who sleep unguarded, and the absence of a shepherd suggests that, like Diomedes, the lion is attacking at night. To support this argument, we can compare the slightly longer simile at *Iliad* 15.323–326, where the attackers also find the herds or flocks unguarded:

> οἳ δ' ὥς τ' ἠὲ βοῶν ἀγέλην ἢ πῶϋ μέγ' οἰῶν
> θῆρε δύω κλονέωσι μελαίνης νυκτὸς ἀμολγῷ
> ἐλθόντ' ἐξαπίνης σημάντορος οὐ παρεόντος,
> ὣς ἐφόβηθεν Ἀχαιοὶ ἀνάλκιδες·

> They, like a herd of cattle or large flock of sheep
> that two wild beasts in the dead of dark night drive to
>   confusion
> when they come suddenly and no herdsman is present,
> just so the Achaeans, with no battle resolve, were routed.

In this simile, two wild beasts, which Lonsdale (1990:66, 131) identifies as lions, attack. Important details here include the time, the dead of night, and the lack of a shepherd, just as in 10.485. The sudden appearance of the lions (ἐλθόντ' ἐξαπίνης) is likewise similar to ambush language, in which the attacker appears out of the darkness or his hiding place to surprise his victims (compare 10.496–497 below for how the poetic language represents such a sudden appearance of an ambusher). Because this simile has so much in common with the one at 10.485–488, we can draw the inference that the simile of Diomedes' attack is also imagined to be happening in the dead of night, but that compression has left that detail implicit. We can compare also *Iliad* 12.299–308, where Sarpedon is compared to a lion trying to get inside the πυκινὸν δόμον (*Iliad* 12.301) of the sheep—that attack is also likely to be taking place at night, when the sheep are in their pen. See 10.5–9 for more on the relation of the adjective *pukinos* to the ambush theme. The lion attacks because he is hungry, but also because his audacious spirit bids him to: κέλεται δέ ἑ θυμὸς ἀγήνωρ, *Iliad* 12.300. Compare the "audacious spirit" that motivates both Diomedes (10.220) and Dolon (10.319) to undertake the spying missions.

We see lions attacking flocks explicitly at night in still other similes, such as at *Iliad* 11.172–178, where the Trojans are compared to cattle when a lion has panicked the whole herd. In that simile, similar to *Iliad* 15.324, the time, the dead of night, is indicated by the phrase ἐν νυκτὸς ἀμολγῷ (*Iliad* 11.173; see also Tsagalis 2008:153–187 for more on this phrase and what he sees as its Indo-European imagery, connected to cattle, the sun, and danger), and the fear and confusion of the herd animals is a central feature (ἐφόβησε, *Iliad* 11.173), while death comes to one in particular (*Iliad* 11.174–176). This fear and confusion is replayed on the battlefield as Agamemnon routs the Trojans, but the simile itself has the feeling of an ambush. Lonsdale (1990:118–122) has also argued that lion and cattle similes like this one adapt the epic theme of the cattle raid. See "The Poetics of Ambush" for the cattle raid as part of the ambush theme.

In two of the similes of lions attacking at night, similes that share much of the same formulaic language, the lion is unsuccessful because of the watchfulness of the men and dogs who guard them (*Iliad* 11.546–557 and *Iliad* 17.655–666). In these examples, we see that they must keep watch all night long (πάννυχοι ἐγρήσσοντες, *Iliad* 11.551 and *Iliad* 17.660), and it is only at dawn that the lion finally withdraws (*Iliad* 11.555 and *Iliad* 17.664). These lions, who go away empty-handed, provide a contrast to what we see depicted at 10.485–488, where the lack of a shepherd watching the herd enables the lion to successfully attack: in the simile world, a steadfast night watch can counteract ambush tactics. We can also hearken back to the watchdog simile at 10.180–189 and see that comparison as an indication both that the wakeful and watchful Achaean guard is indeed the kind needed on this dangerous night and that it is a mistake on the part of the Thracians to fall asleep without a guard to watch over them. Lion similes, so common in the narration of fighting in the *polemos*, also have affinities with the ambush theme, and a lion attacking at night should especially be seen in this light. That lion similes work for both themes can also be taken as another indication that the two types of warfare are not diametrically opposed, just as we have seen warriors such as Diomedes himself, but also Achilles, who excel at both. See also Schnapp-Gourbeillon 1981:104–131 for her extended discussion of Diomedes the lion in *Iliad* 10.

10.488 δυώδεκ'(α) Gernet (1936:200) argues that twelve victims is a number with ritual significance, and we can compare the sacrifices of twelve cows (*Iliad* 6.93 = 6.274 = 6.308) and twelve sheep (*Odyssey* 8.59), as well as the twelve Trojan youths Achilles sacrifices on Patroklos' pyre (*Iliad* 21.27–28, *Iliad* 23.175). Germain (1954:17–18) notes that in the the *Iliad* twelve is a number used for enemies killed and similarly relates that usage to its use as a number of sacrificial victims.

10.488 πολύμητις ’Οδυσσεύς See above on 10.148 for this epithet of Odysseus.

10.495 τρισκαιδέκατον The number thirteen seems to be almost a "round number" or to have a completing or capping aspect to it in Homeric diction. Just as the most important victim, Rhesos, is thirteenth, Alkinoos counts himself as the thirteenth *basileus* among the Phaeacians (*Odyssey* 8.390–391). Similarly, when Odysseus chooses men for the mission to investigate further the land of the Cyclopes, he chooses twelve, counting himself as thirteenth, although the number itself is not cited there (*Odyssey* 9.195–196). Thirteen also seems to round off or cap lengths of time, such as the thirteen months that Ares is held bound in chains by Otos and Ephialtes before Hermes rescues and frees him (*Iliad* 5.387). It is on the thirteenth day that Odysseus and his crew leave Crete after being trapped there by a north wind (*Odyssey* 19.202). When Odysseus recounts to Laertes the gardens his father had promised him as a young man (as part of proving his identity to him), the numbers are all what we would consider round (ten apple trees, forty fig trees, fifty vines), but also include thirteen pear trees (*Odyssey* 24.340). Perhaps the completing aspect is related to the lunar calendar, the year coming round in the thirteenth moon. Germain (1954:10) includes thirteen among numbers that are "presque fantomatiques."

10.497 This line was omitted by Zenodotus and Aristophanes, according to the A scholia, and athetized (but therefore included) by Aristarchus. Papyri such as p425 and the medieval manuscript tradition do include it. Objections have been made to the accusative τὴν νύκτ’, which would more often mean 'all night long' than 'on that night', as the sense seems to demand. Indeed, according to Allen, the tenth-century Laurentian manuscript (D) has τῇ νύκτ’, seemingly correcting the problem. But Fenik finds another parallel and concludes that the accusative can have the sense of "time when" (Fenik 1964:49). What has been less well understood is the equation this line makes between Diomedes and the bad dream standing at the head of Rhesos. We discuss this use of language in detail in our essay "The Poetics of Ambush" (pp. 68–69). In brief, the syntax has Homeric parallels in other ambush situations and seems to replicate the emergence of an ambusher in the dark. As Fenik (1964:51–52) has argued, with the parallel of the charioteer's nightmare in the tragedy *Rhesos*, a dream may have been part of the Rhesos tradition, and we may have a very compressed allusion to it in 10.496. That dream, alluded to, then becomes reality in the figure of Diomedes.

10.497 διὰ μῆτιν Ἀθήνης This phrase has been considered problematic by ancient and modern critics alike. A comment in the Venetus A scholia objects that the ambush of Rhesos is happening through the information given by Dolon rather than Athena's plan. Fenik (1964:52–54) argues that these words "suit perfectly well the non-Iliadic versions" of events, those suggested by the scholia on 10.435 (see our commentary on that line) and that seen in the tragedy *Rhesos*, in which Athena has a more direct role in instigating the attack on Rhesos. We have seen, however, both that *mētis* is thematically central to ambush (see commentary on 10.19 and "The Poetics of Ambush") and that Athena is associated with ambush tactics (see commentary on 10.460–464). Thus this phrase can be understood not literally but thematically. That is, the very fact that this is an ambush accounts for how Diomedes stands over Rhesos "through the scheme of Athena." It need not be explained by means of another version in which Athena directly sent the Achaeans against Rhesos, even though we know such versions existed at some point in the tradition.

10.498 ὁ τλήμων Ὀδυσεὺς For more on this epithet for Odysseus (and the whole phrase), see above on 10.231 and 10.248. Like πολύτλας, τλήμων is a distinctive epithet of Odysseus (see Parry MHV 92). As a traditional epithet, it describes Odysseus within the tradition as a whole. As a supreme ambusher both here and in other episodes, including his own epic, his endurance is a key characteristic.

10.500–501 Diomedes specifically chooses Odysseus as his ambush partner for his *noos*, his ability to perceive important things (see commentary on 10.224–226 and 10.247), and we have seen that Odysseus does just that earlier in the episode, when he is the first to notice Dolon (see commentary on 10.339). So why does he not notice the whip, which seems to be apparent (φαεινήν)? Is this detail an indication that Odysseus simply ignored the chariot altogether (see below on 10.503 and 10.513–514)? Does it reflect the hurried nature of the ambush attack: even a perceptive warrior like Odysseus may simply use what is nearest at hand? Or does the theme call for an employment of the bow he brought on the mission? (On the bow and the connection between archery and the ambush theme, see "The Poetics of Ambush.") It is difficult to know if any or all of these possible factors lie behind this detail because we have such limited evidence for the ambush theme, but it does create a vivid visual image of the "getaway" that begins here.

10.502 ῥοίζησεν The A scholia explain that this verb means to "make a nonverbal sound, which we call συρίζειν," a verb that means to whistle or hiss. Compare the related noun at *Odyssey* 9.315: πολλῇ δὲ ῥοίζῳ πρὸς ὄρος τρέπε πίονα μῆλα ("With much whistling (?), he [the Cyclops] was turning his fat flocks to the mountain"). At Hesiod *Theogony* 835, ῥοιζέω is used of the monstrous Typhoeus, and because this monster has snakes as part of his body, ῥοιζέω is generally assumed to mean 'hiss'. Both this verb and that to which the scholia compare it seem to include both meanings, and we can understand both as sounds the mouth makes by moving air through the teeth and/or lips. So whichever sound we imagine Odysseus making here, the key for the poetics of ambush is that it is a single, quiet, nonverbal sound, lest the other sleeping Thracians awaken before he and Diomedes make their getaway.

10.503 μερμήριξε A type scene in which two options are pondered appears numerous times in both the *Iliad* and the *Odyssey*, and this verb is a signal of that traditional scene (see also Arend 1933:106–115 for this type scene). Some of these type scenes involve ambush, as here: Odysseus ponders several times how to ambush and slaughter the suitors (*Odyssey* 16.237, 16.256, 16.261, 19.2 = 19.52, 20.10, 20.28, 20.38, 20.41), while Phemios ponders during that ambush whether to try to escape or to supplicate Odysseus (*Odyssey* 22.333). Aegisthus is also "pondering hideous things" (ἀεικέα μερμηρίζων, *Odyssey* 4.533) when he plans his ambush of Agamemnon. In addition, although these episodes are not strictly ambush themes, we find such "pondering" involved prior to plans to deceive, such as Zeus' sending the deceptive dream to Agamemnon (*Iliad* 2.3), Hera's seduction of Zeus (*Iliad* 14.159), Penelope's "trick" (*dolos*) against the suitors (*Odyssey* 2.93, *Odyssey* 24.128), and Odysseus' deception of his father about his identity (*Odyssey* 24.235).

10.503 κύντατον This superlative adjective is found only here in the Homeric epics, but we should note that thirty manuscripts, according to Allen, have the comparative κύντερον instead, as does p425. Other uses of the comparative in the *Iliad* and *Odyssey* describe situations of suffering loss and perhaps also attempting to avenge it: it is used of Hera when she wants to defy Zeus and help the Achaeans in the war (*Iliad* 8.483); of Clytemnestra, who kills her husband Agamemnon and avenges her daughter's death (*Odyssey* 11.427); of the insistence of a hungry belly, overriding all other concerns (*Odyssey* 7.216); and of the day that the Cyclops eats Odysseus' men (*Odyssey* 20.18). We can also compare its uses in the *Homeric Hymn to Demeter,* where the year during which Demeter is withdrawn is called κύντατον (*Homeric Hymn to Demeter* 306) and her grief is κύντερον (*Homeric Hymn to Demeter* 90). With this underlying notion of loss and grief connected to possible revenge as part of the traditional resonance of the word, in this line it may possibly allude to the version of the story of Rhesos in which he fights at Troy for one day and inflicts such huge damages on the Achaeans that Diomedes and Odysseus are sent to assassinate him at night (see "Tradition and Reception" for a full discussion of the variations of his story). Considering that version, Diomedes' actions and his thoughts about further actions could be understood as fueled by grief over the loss of his comrades and as amounting to vengeance for them. The "need" on this night for action is similarly motivated by the Achaean losses earlier that day.

10.504–505 Vermeule notes that these lines had at one time been taken as evidence of the "lateness" of the Doloneia, but that Spruytte's (1977) reconstruction of a Bronze Age chariot shows that it could indeed "be lifted by any healthy man, and conventional thinking on the *Doloneia* must be rethought, with hundreds of other conventions" (Vermeule 1986:83). See also Littauer and Crouwel 1983 on Bronze Age chariots. If Diomedes does choose to take the chariot, whether by the pole or by picking it up, he presumably does so in order to move it to where Odysseus has led the horses so they can tie the horses to the chariot for the getaway (see also below on 10.513–514). But such a supposition makes it seem as though Odysseus, at least, did not take the chariot when he took the horses from where they had been tied to it (facing it, it seems, rather than in a position to pull it, at 10.475, or else why untie them?).

10.507 ἕως ὃ ταῦθ' ὥρμαινε κατὰ φρένα, τόφρα δ' Ἀθήνη This line is formulaically similar to the first four feet of *Iliad* 1.193 and the last two feet of *Iliad* 1.194 (ἧος ὃ ταῦθ' ὥρμαινε κατὰ φρένα καὶ κατὰ θυμόν, / ἕλκετο δ' ἐκ κολεοῖο μέγα ξίφος, ἦλθε δ' Ἀθήνη) and thus may be considered a slightly more compressed version of Athena's appearance to a hero who is deciding on a course of action. This is a more specific form of the type scene of "pondering options" (see 10.503) and scenes in which a decision must be made between two options, of which there are several examples in the *Iliad* and *Odyssey*. We can compare also *Iliad* 5.671 (μερμήριξε δ' ἔπειτα κατὰ φρένα καὶ κατὰ θυμόν) where it is

Odysseus who is divided and then Athena directs his *thumos*. Stagakis (1986:237–239) argues that the situation here is parallel to that in *Iliad* 1, when Athena appears to a pondering Achilles and offers an option different from the two the hero had been contemplating. Just as Athena's suggestion to Achilles to insult Agamemnon with words (*Iliad* 1.211) is related to his previously considered option of checking his fury (*Iliad* 1.192), so also may Athena's command to remember their *nostos* here be related to the previously considered option of taking the chariot, if we understand that Diomedes does take the chariot for their getaway. For more on Athena's role in this ambush, see our commentary on 10.285, 10.482, and 10.497.

10.509 νόστου δὴ μνῆσαι We have seen (in "The Poetics of Ambush" and the commentary on 10.211–212 and 10.247) that the mission Diomedes and Odysseus undertake has thematic language in common with journeys, and with homecomings in particular. Thus the word *nostos* here has a thematic significance. In order for the spying mission, now turned ambush, to be fully successful, Diomedes and Odysseus will have to get back safely to the Achaean ships, which is what Athena reminds Diomedes of here. In the *polemos*, a warrior might be mindful of his battle lust (some form of μιμνήσκω + χάρμης, *Iliad* 4.222, 8.252, 13.721–722, 15.380, 15.477, 19.148) or his furious resolve to stand his ground (μιμνήσκω + θούριδος ἀλκῆς, *Iliad* 6.112, 8.174, 11.566, 15.487, 15.734, 16.270, 17.185). But in an ambush, the ambushers must be mindful of their return to their own comrades. Not surprisingly, being mindful of one's *nostos* is seen more often in the *Odyssey*. At *Odyssey* 3.141–142, Nestor recalls how Menelaos bid all the Achaeans to be mindful of their homecoming as they were about to leave Troy. In a different phrasing, Odysseus' men ask him to be mindful of his fatherland (μιμνήσκεο πατρίδος αἴης) specifically in the context of wanting to go home (ἱκέσθαι οἶκον, *Odyssey* 10.472–474). And in the closest parallel to this language, Athena goes to Sparta to remind Telemakhos of his *nostos* and to urge him to return home (νόστου ὑπομνήσουσα καὶ ὀτρυνέουσα νέεσθαι, see *Odyssey* 15.1–3).

10.513–514 One difficulty that has puzzled and divided commentators on *Iliad* 10 is the question of whether or not Odysseus and Diomedes do indeed take the chariot or whether they ride only the horses back to the Achaean camp. That ἵπποι is used in Homeric diction for both "horses" and "horses and chariot" adds to the confusion here. We have seen Odysseus untie the horses from the chariot rail and tie them together (10.498–499, see 10.475 for where the horses had been tied). We have also seen Diomedes contemplate taking the chariot (10.504–505). But did he take it? Leaf's comment on 10.513 in his first edition (1886) says that ἵππων must mean the horses and chariot, because of the plural and because horseback riding happens only in similes, never in narrative in Homeric epic. In his reasoning, the option of killing more Thracians that Diomedes had been pondering is forbidden by Athena's injunction to leave, and so, by default, the first option of taking the chariot has been followed. In his second edition (1900–1902), however, Leaf says that a general view of the passage leads to the conclusion that the heroes ride the horses themselves, and that this riding is "among the marks of lateness in this book." Shewan (1911:180) notes that there is no consensus on whether they ride or drive, but argues that riding would not prove *Iliad* 10 to be late. He says that he first thought they ride the horses, but is now convinced that they drive the chariot (1911:274). He goes on to consider the phrase ἵππων ἐπεβήσετο and other details of the episode as well as arguments for and against either the riding of the horses or the taking of the chariot (1911:274–278).

These questions and disputes continue in more recent examinations of the passage. Anderson (1975), writing about chariot use in the *Iliad*, argues that Diomedes and Odysseus are riding horseback even though the poet uses formulas (like the verb ἐπιβαίνω here) that elsewhere are used for chariot driving. Because chariot driving is more common in the epics, "[t]he poet therefore had no ready-made set of formulae to describe riding when the need arose" (Anderson 1975:182). Although Odysseus seems throughout the episode to control both horses, as a driver would, Anderson cites a ninth-century Assyrian visual image that represents a warrior and attendant mounted on horses, and the attendant "seems to control both horses" (1975:183). Thus Anderson argues that the language used in this episode can be understood as horseback riding, and that horseback riding of this sort would have been known in the Bronze and early Iron Ages (1975:184), but his point is that any conclusion about either chariot driving or horseback riding in Homeric epic cannot be based on this one particular representation. Examining these same formulas, however, Stagakis (1985 and 1986) argues that they do seize the chariot and that they therefore drive the horses back. Hainsworth (1993:202–203) argues, as Anderson does, that the formulas are regularly used for chariot driving, but because the chariot is never mentioned again, we must assume that they are riding: "That we must imagine the heroes' harnessing the horses to the chariot would imply an improbable ellipse after the detail of 498–502.

Therefore the heroes do not take the chariot; they were after all in a hurry, and yoking a team of horses was not a simple operation, see 24.268–77" (Hainsworth 1993:203).

The intense scrutiny to which these phrases have been subjected, as well as the changes in interpretation by individual scholars, demonstrates just how intractable the question of whether or not they take the chariot is. Although we cannot necessarily resolve the question by considering it within the theme of ambush, we can note that a cattle-rustling or horse-stealing theme, such as we see at *Iliad* 11.669–684, seems to involve taking the animals alone. Because the themes of ambush and horse-stealing are closely related, the latter may explain the emphasis on the horses alone (so too might the traditional importance of Rhesos' horses, see commentary on 10.436–437), even if the chariot is imagined to be taken. If they do ride, not drive, then that fact, as Shewan and Anderson have argued, would not be a sign of the "lateness" of composition. Rather, riding may instead be a signal of the horse-stealing theme, seen elsewhere in the *Iliad* only in Nestor's reminiscences.

10.515 οὐδ' ἀλαοσκοπιὴν εἶχ' This phrase is used not of a human guard or spy, but always of a god in our texts. In addition to Apollo here, it is used of Poseidon twice (*Iliad* 13.10 and 14.135), with different epithets completing the line, as he watches the battle so that he may help the Achaeans. In the *Odyssey* it is used of Ares, who (in the story sung by Demodokos) watches to see when Hephaistos leaves so that he can be with Aphrodite—but he then falls into Hephaistos' trap. We can also compare the use of this formula at Hesiod *Theogony* 466, where Kronos keeps a close watch on Rhea so that he can swallow their children as soon as they are born. These last two stories have affinities with the ambush theme, and we can note that, in the cases of both Ares and Kronos, they are the ones who eventually become the victims of an ambush. Those examples may help us to understand the use of the formula with Apollo here, since at first glance it seems odd that he is characterized as not keeping a negligent watch when the Thracians have just been slaughtered. We can also perhaps understand it better by comparing it to Poseidon's role in helping the Achaeans while they are losing badly: his watch comprises seeing what disaster is befalling them (and then helping them), not preventing it entirely.

10.516 ἕπουσαν See above on 10.285 for the use of this word to describe gods accompanying a hero on a mission.

10.518–522 The moment of initial discovery and reaction by Hippokoon is quite compressed. A contrast is provided by the tragedy *Rhesos*, in which Rhesos' charioteer delivers a messenger speech about the murder of Rhesos, and after his confrontation with Hektor, the divine mother of Rhesos appears to perform a lament for him. (See our essay "Tradition and Reception" for more on the portrayal of Rhesos and his death in the tragedy.) Here, Hippokoon is both the one to realize that Rhesos is dead and the one to perform a lament, although that lament is compressed into only one line (see also below on 10.522). The implication of this compression, however, is that an expanded version could be possible in performance (see also our commentary on 10.317 for more on the compression of lament in the *Iliad*). The particular version of the story that *Iliad* 10 presents de-emphasizes Rhesos and his traditional significance for the Trojan War. Petegorsky (1982) explores ways in which this de-emphasis is itself significant for the *Iliad*'s focus on Achilles and its portrayal of his return as necessary to save the Achaeans. This episode as presented here highlights instead the Achaean success in ambush, while only referring briefly to the loss and grief of their victims.

10.522 ὤμωξέν τ᾿ ἄρ᾿ ἔπειτα φίλον τ᾿ ὀνόμηνεν ἑταῖρον The scholia in the Venetus A indicate that Zenodotus' edition had this line following 10.519 and preceding 10.520. It is not clear from the comment whether that order represents his own editorial choice or whether he knew witnesses that recorded that arrangement. Fenik (1964:54–55) notes that this same formula is used at *Iliad* 23.178 and *Iliad* 24.591, both in cases of Achilles lamenting Patroklos. Fenik observes that, in those two cases, the formula acts as a speech introduction formula "followed by an actual address and lament" (Fenik 1964:55). He interprets what he considers the "clumsily abbreviated reference" here as an indication of an expanded version elsewhere. But the very "referential character" that Fenik ascribes to this line would mean that it would not need to be expanded to have meaning for a traditional audience. If the formula had a special resonance with the death of Patroklos or lamentation in general, its use here would add to the significance of what Diomedes and Odysseus have done. Thus we can consider this a simple compression, rather than a bungling of the traditional formula.

10.524 μέρμερα ἔργα For this phrase, see also 10.47–48 and 10.289–290. The awakened Trojans wonder at the astounding deeds. They are astounding because a night raid is unexpected, perhaps, but in Homeric diction this phrase is used for the slaughter of many by one man: see *Iliad* 8.453, 10.48, 11.502, 21.217. In 10.48, the emphasis is on *one* man devising astounding deeds; here the Trojans assume that more than one must have been involved, but we the audience know that it is just two. And as we saw at 10.289, this phrase is useful for both daytime battles and for ambush, as it is used here. The references at 10.48 and *Iliad* 11.502 refer to Hektor's deeds, and at *Iliad* 21.217 to Achilles', attesting to the "heroic" quality of the astounding deeds. At *Iliad* 11.502 and 21.217, the same verb is used as here, ῥέζω. Some commentators have questioned the value of Diomedes' and Odysseus' activities on the night raid, especially since the danger inherent in the presence of Rhesos is not emphasized in this version. For example, Fenik sums up his feelings about *Iliad* 10 this way: "A marked inferiority in technique here cannot possibly be interpreted away, even with the best of will. There is no good reason for the patrol, it performs no function whatever, it brings no change or development in the situation" (Fenik 1964:40). By understanding the traditional resonance of the phrase *mermera erga*, however, we can see that the Trojans react to what has happened as a disaster. This reaction may imply the same importance of Rhesos as we see in other versions of his traditional narrative (for more on those, see the Rhesos section in our essay "Tradition and Reception")— in one version, he is the one committing *mermera erga* and has to be stopped; in another, he would have been invincible and so would have committed *mermera erga* had he lived.

10.527–530 These lines use formulaic language that is employed elsewhere in the Homeric epics for chariot driving. See commentary on 10.513–514 for a discussion on the question of whether the heroes take Rhesos' chariot and are therefore driving, or whether they are riding the horses.

10.530 μάστιξεν δ' ἵππους In the intermarginal scholia in Venetus A, it is noted that "in others, 'Odysseus whipped'" (ἐν ἄλλῳ "μάστιξεν δ' Ὀδυσσεύς"), making it clear that Odysseus is the one driving or controlling the horses. Indeed, forty-three manuscripts, according to Allen, have the variation that the A scholia record, showing the flexibility of leaving either the subject or the object of this verb understood. Of the forty-three manuscripts Allen lists as having this variation, only eight also omit line 531 (see below), perhaps indicating different channels of transmission for these two variations.

10.531   The Venetus A manuscript, like many others—including some of the oldest, such as the Venetus B and the Townley manuscripts—does not include the line that is canonically called 10.531: νῆας ἔπι γλαφυράς· τῇ γὰρ φίλον ἔπλετο θυμῷ ("toward the hollow ships; for this way was dear to them in their hearts"). According to Allen, thirty of the one hundred eighteen manuscripts he collated do not include this line. At *Iliad* 11.519–520, we see the same pair of lines that some manuscripts record as 10.530–531: in that context, it is Nestor and Machaon who depart the fierce battle after Machaon is wounded by the arrow of Paris. The presence of this line in some witnesses to *Iliad* 10 should caution us about overinterpreting the formula in either context. It is tempting in *Iliad* 11 to see the horses' desire to go a certain way as relating to their desire to leave battle, or that heading toward the ships, toward home, is what makes the direction dear to their hearts. But in the context of *Iliad* 10, those same interpretations cannot apply to Rhesos' horses, which have just arrived at Troy and are now under the control of new drivers or masters. Instead, we can understand it in both places, in conjunction with the horses "flew not unwillingly" (τὼ δ' οὐκ ἀέκοντε πετέσθην), as a formula dealing with horses who are whipped and then respond by moving quickly in a particular direction.

10.532   Νέστωρ δὲ πρῶτος κτύπον ἄϊε   One aspect of the poetics of the night is the emphasis on senses other than sight, especially hearing. But as we see here, as well as in other examples, what one hears requires interpretation. (See the section on the sensory aspects of the night in "The Poetics of Ambush.") This same verb of perceiving by hearing is used in 10.160 and 10.189 of hearing the Trojans from a distance (compare *Iliad* 18.222 and *Iliad* 21.388).

10.534   This same line is also found at *Odyssey* 4.140, where Helen speaks it as she recognizes Telemakhos. Thus we may think of it as a formula used when a person interprets a sensory input, whether sight (Helen notes how much Telemakhos resembles Odysseus) or, as here, sound. Nestor hears the hoofbeats and goes on to interpret what he thinks that sound means.

10.535–537   Nestor says that he hears hoofbeats and hopes that that sound indicates a successful return for Odysseus and Diomedes, driving horses off from the Trojans (after all, they did not leave with horses). That a return with horses is interpreted as success for what was originally a spying mission is another indicator of the thematic association between horse stealing and night themes in general. See "The Poetics of Ambush" for more on how these themes are associated within the epic tradition.

10.539 ἄριστοι See commentary on 10.236. Nestor calls those who have gone on the spying mission the best men, a common designation in the ambush theme.

10.540 ἄρ(α) Egbert Bakker's work on this particle, as on many other aspects of Homeric diction, illuminates both what it means and how it is used in performance. Bakker explains that ἄρα is a marker "of visual evidence in the here and now of the speaker" and, more precisely, "the interpretation of such evidence" (Bakker 2005:97). Visual evidence had not yet been present during Nestor's speech; he instead only heard the hoofbeats and tried to interpret them—as we have seen, in the poetics of night action, hearing precedes seeing. Although this ἄρα is not in a direct speech of a character, the action happens during Nestor's speech: "He had not yet spoken every word when, look! they came." ἄρ(α) marks the point at which Diomedes and Odysseus become visible, and thus their success in returning to the camp is confirmed. The particle happens to be omitted in three manuscripts, according to Allen's edition, including the Townley.

10.542 δεξιῇ ἠσπάζοντο ἔπεσσί τε μειλιχίοισι From the three uses of the verb ἀσπάζομαι in the *Odyssey*, we can see that it is used in contexts of welcoming someone who has just arrived after a journey. Nestor and the Pylians greet Telemakhos upon his arrival in Pylos (*Odyssey* 3.39), Autolykos welcomes his grandson Odysseus after he arrives for a visit (*Odyssey* 19.415: the whole line is very similar, χερσίν τ' ἠσπάζοντο ἔπεσσί τε μειλιχίοισι), and the slave women welcome Odysseus home after Eurykleia has told them of his arrival (*Odyssey* 22.498). Thus its use here is one more indication that spying missions and ambushes share the traditional thematic language also used for journeys in these epics, and we can understand such "Odyssean" language as related to the theme, rather than any indication of "lateness."

See above on 10.288 for more on the meaning of μειλίχιος. On that line, it is used to describe a *muthos*, and here it is used with *epos*. Although we may translate both words as 'word', Richard Martin has demonstrated that there are important distinctions between the terms in Homeric diction: *epos* is the unmarked term for "utterance," while *muthos* is the marked term for a public speech-act, a "performance" of sorts that conveys authority and power (1989:22–30). When we compare the different contexts of the adjective μειλίχιος in these lines, then, we can observe that Tydeus' *muthos* was indeed a public, performative speech in which he was at least trying to exert his authority, whereas these words of welcome carry none of those connotations. Martin also notes that "a muthos focuses on what the speaker says and how he or she says it, but epos consistently applies to what the addressee hears" (1989:16). Thus words of welcome are appropriately *epea*, since they are particularly heard as such by the addressee.

10.543–544 These lines use the same formulas as *Iliad* 9.672–673, although there it is Agamemnon (instead of Nestor) asking Odysseus what Achilles' answer was to the embassy's request that he return to battle. As we discussed in our essay "Interpreting *Iliad* 10," a singer could have composed these two episodes paratactically (with both episodes occurring during the course of the same night), as they appear in our *Iliad*, or they may have been performance alternatives of each other. The contrast between them is that while the embassy fails, Nestor treats this return as a resounding success, regardless of the insistence of some modern critics that Diomedes and Odysseus have not fulfilled their mission (see 10.406–411 for our discussion of whether Odysseus gets the information that Nestor suggested for the spying mission). Petegorsky (1982:175–254) argues that the Doloneia responds directly to the embassy's failure, and especially to Achilles' challenge that the Achaeans find some better *mētis* (*Iliad* 9.423).

10.544–553 Nestor's greeting focuses on the horses with which Odysseus and Diomedes return. His statement that he has been active in battle but has never seen horses like these is particularly appropriate to the version of Rhesos' story presented here, in which Rhesos and his Thracians arrive that night but have not yet entered battle. (See our essay "Tradition and Reception" for a full discussion of the Rhesos tradition.) Odysseus' response describing the horses as "newly arrived" (νεήλυδες, 10.558), which is the same adjective that Dolon uses to describe the Thracians at 10.434, similarly reinforces this version of events. Petegorsky (1982:205–206) has interpreted Nestor's suggestion that the horses were given to them by a god (10.546, 551–553), along with Odysseus' rejoinder that a god could give much better horses (10.556–557), as an allusion to the horses of Achilles, which were indeed a gift from the gods. This allusion, according to Petegorsky, shows how the success of the night raid as evidenced by the capture of the horses is "oddly concessive to Achilles" (Petegorsky 1982:206).

10.547 ἀκτίνεσσιν ἐοικότες ἠελίοιο Nestor's statement that the white horses "look like the rays of the sun" implies that they are particularly visible in the darkness, and it also has a temporal correlation in that dawn is now near. But on a deeper level, the important concept of *nostos* in the ambush theme (that is, the importance of the return of the ambushers) is also connected to sun imagery (see Frame 1978/2005 and 2009 for the connection between *nostos* and the rising, or return, of the sun). The conversation between Odysseus, the hero who achieves *nostos* (see also on 10.247), and Nestor, whose name, according to Frame, reflects an earlier function of "he who brings back to life and light" (Frame 1978/2005:96–115), thus connects the horses, which look like the sun that will soon rise, and the safe return of Odysseus and Diomedes, marking the success of their night mission. We may compare the moment at which Odysseus reaches Ithaca in *Odyssey* 13.93–95: at that moment, twenty years in the making, the sun rises just as the ship draws near to land.

10.560 πὰρ δ' ἑτάρους δυοκαίδεκα πάντας ἀρίστους We have seen in several places that, in the theme of ambush, it is the best, the *aristoi*, who are chosen for such missions. The thematic association of the best seems to be so strong that it applies to the victims of the ambush here as well. It would seem to apply to Rhesos in particular on the deeper mythic level, in which Rhesos is a grave threat to the Achaeans.

10.561 τρισκαίδεκατον See above on 10.495 for more on the number thirteen within the tradition. There Rhesos is the thirteenth victim among the Thracians and the number caps the killing as last and most important. Dolon is sequentially their first victim, but in Odysseus' narrative of the events, he is mentioned last and so caps off this list of victims as thirteenth. In other words, the thirteenth victim is once again the one singled out for a special focus. The A scholia note the discrepancy and say that some critics before Aristarchus made the number here 'fourteenth'. Counting both Rhesos and Dolon as the thirteenth victim may also indicate something about the convergence of the Dolon story and the Rhesos tradition in this episode.

10.564 τάφροιο διήλασε μώνυχας ἵππους Crossing the ditch is once again a spatial indication that Odysseus and Diomedes have truly arrived back safely—and successfully, since Odysseus leads the horses of Rhesos with them. As we saw at 10.194, the summoned Achaean leaders move across the ditch to hold the council. This movement indicates that they are then on the offensive and thus presages the night's mission. Here, we notice that they all have remained there while Diomedes and Odysseus were on their mission. That solidarity among the whole group is made explicit in the next line as they cross back together, exulting in what Diomedes and Odysseus have accomplished. Compare 10.414–416, where Dolon assumes that Hektor is still at the place of the Trojan council while he is on his mission.

10.565 καγχαλόων See above on 10.400, where Odysseus smiles, for our discussion of how to understand facial expressions within their cultural context as well as their formulaic and episodic contexts. Those same caveats apply to Odysseus' laughter in this line, since laughter is another kind of nonverbal expression that has specific meaning within a culture. Some studies of laughter in Homer take their starting point from the suitors in the *Odyssey*, since their laughter is so memorable, but such an approach suggests the conclusion that laughter is negative in Homeric epic. Levine (1982) argues that laughter in the Homeric epics "generally implies a real or imagined physical or moral superiority over another person" (Levine 1982:97). As he strives to make that one idea fit every instance, the natural variety we would expect of different kinds of laughter in different situations is lost. He does not distinguish between the words καγχαλάω and γελάω or γελώς in his list of examples of laughter from the *Iliad* (Levine 1982:97). Colakis (1986) argues that laughter in the *Odyssey* "usually indicates some sort of weakness of character" (Colakis 1986:137). (The fact that Paris laughs on more than one occasion in the *Iliad* may contribute to this kind of interpretation.) Although she does not cite Levine 1982 on this argument, Colakis also asserts that smiles mean an actual superiority, a control of the situation, while those who laugh only think they are superior (Colakis 1986:139).

Such interpretations of laughter do not get us too far in this case: certainly Odysseus could be expressing his superior position after he reports the victory that he and Diomedes have achieved. But he could also be expressing relief at having made it back and/or showing social solidarity with the other Achaeans who here, as earlier, exult (χαίρω on this line and on 10.539). We need to be careful about how we interpret such culturally specific nonverbal communication, and not base our conclusions on the meanings of laughter in our own culture or on our personal feelings about the characters who laugh. For insightful approaches to and examinations of laughter in ancient Greek culture, including in the Homeric epics, see Halliwell 1991 and 2008. Halliwell recognizes the broad range of laughter in these epics, maintaining that "it would be misguided to claim a univocal significance for 'Homeric' laughter" (Halliwell 2008:97). Instead, he argues that "Homeric laughter spans a spectrum of feeling that includes both positive and negative emotions" (Halliwell 2008:53). So we must still pay close attetion to the uses of this particular verb in context in order to understand what its connotations for the ancient audience may have been.

When we do look at other uses of this same verb, we find that it is used in situations of ridicule (such as when Hektor imagines that the Achaeans are laughing at the idea of Paris as the Trojans' best fighter, *Iliad* 3.43) or perhaps excessive celebration in triumphing over an enemy (Eurykleia laughs this way in *Odyssey* 23.1 and is warned against such laughter by Penelope at *Odyssey* 23.59). Halliwell (2008:57n15) notes that the verb καγχαλάω is later associated with animal noises, inlcuding a horse's neigh, so here we might wonder whether it emphasizes the particular sound Odysseus makes while perhaps evoking the horses he is leading.

In terms of composition, though, the closest parallel comes from *Iliad* 6.514, which describes Paris returning to battle:

ὣς υἱὸς Πριάμοιο Πάρις κατὰ Περγάμου ἄκρης
τεύχεσι παμφαίνων ὥς τ' ἠλέκτωρ ἐβεβήκει
καγχαλόων, ταχέες δὲ πόδες φέρον·

Iliad 6.512–514

Just so the son of Priam, Paris, down from the height of Pergamon,
all shining in his armor like the sun, had gone,
laughing, and his swift feet were carrying him.

In this passage, too, we have the participle accompanying a verb of motion and enjambed as the first word of the following line. What is Paris feeling as he makes his way out of the city that makes him laugh? This passage follows the simile that compares Paris to a running horse that has broken free. (That simile is remarkable because it is repeated: compare *Iliad* 6.506–511 and *Iliad* 15.263–268, where it is used as a comparison for Hektor returning to battle.) The simile, as well as the laughter of Paris, conveys a sense of exhilaration as he moves. But the differences between the situations should caution us from making broad pronouncements about laughter and character.

The parallel between these two passages has to do with the verbs of motion and the direction of the person who laughs. Paris laughs as he moves from the safety of home, the fortified citadel of Troy, back to the plain where the battle is raging. Odysseus laughs as he moves across the ditch, from the dangers of the night to the safety offered by the ditch and the wall the Achaeans have built. They are moving in opposite directions, yet the movement itself seems to provoke the same reaction. Thus within the traditional diction this kind of laughter may accompany such a transition between safety and danger.

10.566–579 The end to the episode confirms what we have seen earlier: that the ambush theme is structurally similar to that of the journey, in that the return takes on a special importance. Now that Diomedes and Odysseus have been welcomed "home" to the camp, the end of their journey into the enemy camp and their successful return is marked by taking a bath and eating a meal, as we see so often in the *Odyssey*, an epic which is itself an extended version of a journey theme with many journeys and arrivals embedded within it.

10.572–575 First, the two rinse off in the sea and "cool off" (ἀνέψυχθεν); then, they take a bath in a bathtub. The latter is perhaps a hot bath, even though the language seen elsewhere in the epics about heating the water is not included here. See the next comment on 10.576 for more on bathing words.

10.576 ἀσαμίνθος appears only here in the *Iliad*, but ten times in the *Odyssey* (3.468 = 23.163, 4.48 = 17.87, 4.128, 8.450, 8.456, 10.361, 17.90, 24.370). Because it ends in –νθος, the word is generally taken to be a non-Greek word that has been adopted into the epic language (see Hainsworth 1993:210 *ad* 10.576 and Stanford's [1961] commentary on the *Odyssey ad* 8.450). Hainsworth also notes that the word is attested on a seal from Knossos, and Stanford points out that earthenware bathtubs have been found at Knossos and Tiryns.

This line is the same as those found at *Odyssey* 4.48 and 17.87. The word ἀσαμίνθος is part of a formula system for getting in and out of the bathtub: eleven of its twelve appearances are part of a phrase that starts a line with ἔς ῥ'/δ' ἀσαμίνθον/ἀσαμίνθους or ἔκ ῥ'/δ' ἀσαμίνθου/ ἀσαμίνθων and in most of these cases is followed by some form of βαίνω. So taking a bath in a bathtub is a frequent enough event in the epic tradition that this formula developed. The one exception to its line placement in the first two feet of the line is at *Odyssey* 4.128, which details the gifts that Helen and Menelaos received from Alkandre and Polybos in Egypt: Polybos gave Menelaos two silver bathtubs, among other things. Such a list of guest-gifts is, of course, a theme very different from narrating a hero getting in or out of a bath, and so it is not surprising that the formulas used are different in that case.

Getting in or out of the bath is more frequent in the *Odyssey* because it is associated with an arrival after a journey, which is a common occurrence in that epic. Telemakhos on his journey bathes at both Nestor's palace (*Odyssey* 3.468) and at Menelaos' (*Odyssey* 4.48, where it is both Telemakhos and Peisistratos bathing, and plurals are used as they are here). Odysseus gets in and out of the bath in the palace of Alkinoos and Arete (*Odyssey* 8.450–456) and tells of how he bathed at Circe's once he had an oath from her for his safety (*Odyssey* 10.361). The association seen in that case between baths and safety appears many more times and is part of the poetics of the bath. Telemakhos (*Odyssey* 17.87–90), Odysseus (*Odyssey* 23.163), and Laertes (*Odyssey* 24.370) all bathe in an ἀσαμίνθος once they return home. Telemakhos has arrived safely after the suitors' attempted ambush, and Odysseus bathes after his slaughter of the suitors: the baths, which involve an associated vulnerability of nakedness, signal safety after danger. Laertes is not so much in danger as in a prolonged state of suffering, and this kind of recovery has parallels elsewhere in the epic. Odysseus is of course known for his suffering on his journey, and he is given his distinctive epithet πολύτλας just before his bath in Phaeacia (*Odyssey* 8.446). In *Odyssey* 17, we have seen that Telemakhos' bath implies safety after the danger of the suitor's planned ambush, but his guest Theoklymenos bathes in that passage as well. Theoklymenos is an exile because he killed a man of his community (*Odyssey* 15.271–278), so Telemakhos taking him in is a measure of safety for him, and he is called here the "long-suffering guest" (ξεῖνον ταλαπείριον, *Odyssey* 17.84), a phrase used elsewhere of Odysseus himself (*Odyssey* 7.24; compare also Odysseus as a "long-suffering suppliant" ἱκέτην ταλαπείριον at *Odyssey* 6.193 and 14.511). Bathing in an ἀσαμίνθος, then, has associations with an arrival after a journey and with getting home safely after being in danger, and marks an end to suffering.

Bathing does indeed happen in other situations in the *Iliad*, but the word used in these other situations is λοετρόν (*Iliad* 14.6, 22.444–445, 23.44) or a related word (*Iliad* 18.346). We might expect the Trojans to bathe in their own homes, and we do see Andromache's preparations for a bath for Hektor that he will never take (*Iliad* 22.444–445). But the Achaeans have hot baths as well, as we see when Nestor tells the wounded Machaon that Hekamede will prepare a hot bath for him and wash away the blood (*Iliad* 14.6–7) and when Achilles refuses the hot bath that Agamemnon ordered be prepared for him (*Iliad* 23.39–44).

(Note that Achilles has also refused to eat since Patroklos' death: as the following lines here also make clear, there is a thematic connection between bathing and eating a meal.) The corpse of Patroklos is also washed when it is brought back from battle (*Iliad* 18.343–353). There, we see in detail the water heated in a bathwater tripod, using formulaic language seen also when a bath is prepared for Odysseus in Phaeacia (*Odyssey* 8.435–437 ≈ *Iliad* 18.346–348). Similar to the way that Diomedes and Odysseus rinse and cool off in the sea here, we also see the Achaeans ritually wash in the sea after the end of the plague (*Iliad* 1.313–314). The *Iliad* thus displays several examples of other language about washing or bathing, and the language used here is particularly associated with journeys and ambush.

In a recent article, Jonas Grethlein (2007) examines the poetics of the bath in the *Iliad*. He confines his examination to the baths in the *Iliad*, saying that others have treated the theme in the *Odyssey* as part of the "ritual of hospitality," which does not hold for the *Iliad* (2007:25). Grethlein argues for two types of baths in the *Iliad*: that of a warrior returning from battle (and he includes this bath in *Iliad* 10 in this category) and the washing of the corpse of a dead warrior (2007:28). Then he shows how these two types of bath create narrative tensions and connections, focusing especially on the bath that Andromache prepares for Hektor (2007:28–49). Grethlein also argues that both kinds of bath share a connection with a transition: the bathing of the corpse involves the transition from life to death, and the warrior's bath involves a transition from the danger of death in battle to a place of safety (2007:28–29). Our arguments about the bath here in *Iliad* 10, developed before Grethlein's article appeared, agree in many ways with his. But in his separation of the *Iliad* and *Odyssey*, he seems to have overlooked that the arrival after a journey, beyond being simply hospitality, often in the *Odyssey* includes a similar measure of safety after danger as that which he sees in the warrior's return from battle in the *Iliad*. And although he pays close attention to formulaic language in these types scenes, he does not mention the particular language used in this case, which differs from the other baths in the *Iliad* in particular ways.

We can now see what ἀσαμίνθους adds to this particular scene. This type of bathtub is formulaically associated with the safe arrival from a journey, and a night mission, whether spying or ambush, is thematically like a journey particularly in that it involves a return. We have seen (1) Nestor describe the spying mission as (ideally) a going out and coming back safe and sound (see 10.211–212), (2) Diomedes choose Odysseus as his partner for the mission because of his abilities to get home (10.247), and (3) Athena tell Diomedes to remember his homecoming while he lingers momentarily in the Thracian camp (10.509). As Albert Lord notes briefly regarding the bath Odysseus takes in *Odyssey* 23: "The bath belongs in the tale of the return—it surely has ritual significance" (1960:176). There is an idea of a *nostos* associated with this kind of mission, and the traditional association of a bath in a tub with a safe arrival after a journey appears in this expanded version of the spying/ambush theme.

10.577–578 τὼ δὲ <u>λοεσσαμένω</u> καὶ <u>ἀλειψαμένω</u> λίπ᾽ ἐλαίῳ / δείπνῳ <u>ἐφιζανέτην</u> Even at the end of the mission, dual forms are used for the actions of Diomedes and Odysseus. Such dual verbs and the teamwork they embody are such a deep-rooted part of the ambush theme that they continue to be used in these final actions of the night. See above on 10.243 and 10.254 for more on these dual forms.

10.578 δείπνῳ ἐφιζανέτην An older style of criticism was concerned about the so-called "unity" of *Iliad* 9, because the members of the embassy have multiple meals within one evening (see also Shewan 1911:186–187 for a review of scholarly objections that this is Odysseus' third meal on this night). At *Iliad* 9.65–73, Nestor advises Agamemnon to prepare and host the evening meal, and the guards for the night have their dinner at their station (*Iliad* 9.88) while the leaders eat at Agamemnon's tent (*Iliad* 9.89–92). It is after dinner that they discuss the embassy to Achilles. Three of the leaders who must have eaten with Agamemnon, Phoinix, Ajax, and Odysseus, go on the embassy. When Achilles welcomes them, he and Patroklos immediately prepare a meal (*Iliad* 9.205–220), and it seems that all of them eat and talk only after they have finished (*Iliad* 9.221–222). We should first of all note that these two lines indicating that they eat their fill are the same formulas as *Iliad* 9.91–92, which transition from the meal preparation scene to the conversation. So meal preparation and consumption is, from the standpoint of oral poetics, a theme that is closely associated with gatherings of leaders and, as is made explicit in the advice of Nestor to Agamemnon, with the hospitality offered by those leaders. Thus it makes sense that more than one supper is prepared for these men: there is much more to it than satiating their hunger.

Once we recognize that there are multiple associations with the poetic theme of a meal, then, how should we understand Diomedes and Odysseus eating once again here? According to the A scholia, Aristarchus marked the dual form of the verb here because the meal

should apply to all, not just these two, since they are having break-
fast in the early morning at this point. This objection seems to apply a
similar logic to that which we have already discussed, namely keeping
track of which meal the men should be eating. Instead, we can look for
other associations that meals have within this tradition, focusing, as
the dual verb form does, on the two warriors who have just returned
from a dangerous mission. As we saw with the baths at 10.576, the meal
here has associations with an arrival after a journey, and the return
after a spying mission or an ambush has much in common with the
theme of the journey. Indeed, there seems to be a traditional sequence
of bathing and then eating after such an arrival, and we see such a
thematic sequence in the examples from the *Odyssey*: after the arrivals
in *Odyssey* 3, 4, 8, 10, and 17, in which a bath in an ἀσαμίνθος takes
place, a meal follows the bath as part of the hospitality for a guest or
the arrival home. As Foley says about baths in the *Odyssey* in general,
its theme is securely linked to that of the feast (Foley 1999:185, 245).
Thus, the bath–meal sequence here is entirely traditional and should
be expected rather than suspected.

Bibliography

Note: In the notes and essays of this volume we have used the abbreviation MHV (= *The Making of Homeric Verse*) for Adam Parry's 1971 edition of the collected works of Milman Parry.

Ahlberg-Cornell, G. 1992. *Myth and Epos in Early Greek Art: Representation and Interpretation*. Jonsered.

Aitken, E. B., and J. K. B. Maclean, eds. 2001. *Flavius Philostratus: Heroikos*. Atlanta.

Alden, M. 2000. *Homer Beside Himself*. Oxford.

———. 2005. "Lions in Paradise: Lion Similes in the *Iliad* and the Lion Cubs of *Il.* 18.318–22." *Classical Quarterly* 55:335–342.

Allan, W. 2005. "Arms and the Man: Euphorbus, Hector, and the Death of Patroclus." *Classical Quarterly* 55:1–16.

Allen, T. W. 1924. *Homer: The Origins and the Transmission*. Oxford.

———, ed. 1931. *Homeri Ilias*. Oxford.

Anderson, J. K. 1975. "Greek Chariot-Borne and Mounted Infantry." *American Journal of Archaeology* 79:175–187.

Arend, W. 1933. *Die typischen Scenen bei Homer*. Berlin.

Armstrong, J. 1958. "The Arming Motif in the *Iliad*." *American Journal of Philology* 79:337–354.

Arnim, J. von, ed. 1903. *Stoicorum veterum fragmenta* II. Leipzig.

Austin, N. 1975. *Archery at the Dark of the Moon: Poetic Problems in Homer's Odyssey*. Berkeley.

Bader, F. 1980. "Rhapsodies homériques et irlandaises." *Recherches sur les religions de l'antiquité classique*, ed. R. Bloch, 9–83. Paris.

Bakker, E. 2005. *Pointing at the Past: From Formula to Performance in Homeric Poetics*. Cambridge, MA.

Bakker, E., and A. Kahane, eds. 1997. *Written Voices, Spoken Signs: Tradition, Performance, and the Epic Text*. Hellenic Studies 12. Washington, DC.

Barrett, J. 2002. *Staged Narrative: Poetics and the Messenger in Greek Tragedy.* Berkeley.

Basson, A., and W. Dominik, eds. 2003. *Literature, Art, History: Studies on Classical Antiquity and Tradition in Honor of W. J. Henderson.* Frankfurt am Main.

Beck, D. 2005. *Homeric Conversation.* Hellenic Studies 14. Washington, DC.

———. 2008. Review of R. Friedrich, *Formular Economy in Homer: The Poetics of the Breaches.* Stuttgart: Franz Steiner Verlag, 2007. *Bryn Mawr Classical Review* 2008.10.27. http://ccat.sas.upenn.edu/bmcr/2008/2008-10-27.html.

Beissinger, M., J. Tylus, and S. Wofford, eds. 1999. *Epic Traditions in the Contemporary World: The Poetics of Community.* Berkeley.

Benardete, S. 1968. "The *Aristeia* of Diomedes and the Plot of the *Iliad*." *Agōn* 2:10–38.

Bentley, R. 1713. *Remarks upon a Late Discourse of Free-thinking, in a Letter to F.H.D.D. by Phileleutherus Lipsiensis.* London.

Bernabé, A., ed. 1987. *Poetae Epici Graeci: Testimonia et Fragmenta I.* Leipzig.

Bird, G. 2009. "Critical Signs—Drawing Attention to 'Special' Lines of Homer's *Iliad* in the Manuscript Venetus A." In Dué 2009a:89–115.

Björck, G. 1957. "The Authenticity of Rhesus." *Eranos* 55:7–17.

Black, M. 1962. *Models and Metaphors: Studies in Language and Philosophy.* Ithaca, NY.

Blackwell, C. and C. Dué. 2009. "Homer and History in the Venetus A." In Dué 2009a:1–18.

Block, E. 1985. "Clothing Makes the Man: A Pattern in the *Odyssey*." *Transactions and Proceedings of the American Philological Association* 115:1–11.

Boardman, J., and C. F. Vafopoulou-Richardson. 1986. "Diomedes." *Lexicon Iconographicum Mythologiae Classicae* III, ed. P. Müller et al., 396–409.

Bond, R. 1996. "Homeric Echoes in Rhesus." *American Journal of Philology* 117:255–273.

Bonifazi, A. 2009. "Inquiring into *Nostos* and its Cognates." *American Journal of Philology* 130:481–510.

Boyd, T. 1995. "A Poet on the Achaean Wall." *Oral Tradition* 10:181–206.

Bradley, E. 1967. "Hector and the Simile of the Snowy Mountain." *Transactions and Proceedings of the American Philological Association* 98:37–41.

Bremer, J. M. 1976. "Why Messenger-Speeches?" In Bremer, Radt, and Ruijgh 1976:29–48.

Bremer, J. M., S. L. Radt, and C. J. Ruijgh, eds. 1976. *Miscellanea Tragica in honorem J.C. Kamerbeek*. Amsterdam.

Brooks, P. 1981. "Introduction." In Todorov 1981:vii–xix.

Bryce, T. R. 1990–1991. "Lycian Apollo and the Authorship of the *Rhesus*." *Classical Journal* 86:144–149.

Buchan, M. 2004. *The Limits of Heroism: Homer and the Ethics of Reading*. Ann Arbor.

Buck, C. 1955. *The Greek Dialects: Grammar, Selected Inscriptions, Glossary*. Chicago.

Burgess, J. 1995. "Achilles' Heel: The Death of Achilles in Ancient Myth." *Classical Antiquity* 14:217–243.

———. 1997. "Beyond Neo-analysis: Problems with the Vengeance Theory." *American Journal of Philology* 118:1–19.

———. 2001. *The Tradition of the Trojan War in Homer and the Epic Cycle*. Baltimore.

———. 2005. "The Death of Achilles by Rhapsodes." In Rabel 2005:119–134.

———. 2006. "Neoanalysis, Orality, and Intertextuality: An Examination of Homeric Motif Transference." *Oral Tradition* 21:148–189.

Burian, P., ed. 1985. *Directions in Euripidean Criticism*. Durham, NC.

Burkert, W. 1985. *Greek Religion*. Oxford.

Burnett, A. P. 1985. "*Rhesus*: Are Smiles Allowed?" In Burian 1985:13–51.

Cantieni, R. 1942. *Die Nestorerzählung im XI. Gesang der Ilias (V. 670–762)*. Zurich.

Carlisle, M., and O. Levaniouk, eds. 1999. *Nine Essays on Homer*. Lanham, MD.

Carter, J. B., and S. P. Morris, eds. 1995. *The Ages of Homer: A Tribute to Emily Townsend Vermeule*. Austin.

Casali, S. 2004. "Nisus and Euryalus: Exploiting the Contradictions in Virgil's Doloneia." *Harvard Studies in Classical Philology* 102:319–354.

Chantraine, P. 1937. "Remarques critiques et grammaticales sur le chant K de l'*Iliade*." *Mélanges offerts à A. M. Desrousseaux par ses amis et ses élèves, en l'honneur de sa cinquantième année d'enseignement supérieur (1887–1937)* 59–68. Paris.

———. 1968/1999. *Dictionnaire étymologique de la langue grecque: Histoire des mots*. New ed. with suppl. Paris.

———. 1988. *Grammaire Homérique. Tome I: Phonétique et Morphologie*. 6th ed. Paris.

———. 1997. *Grammaire Homérique. Tome II: Syntaxe*. 6th ed. Paris.

Clark, M. 1994. "Enjambment and Binding in Homeric Hexameter." *Phoenix* 48:95–114.

Clay, D. 1988. "The Archaeology of the Temple to Juno in Carthage (*Aen.* 1.446–93)." *Classical Philology* 83:195–205.

Clay, J. 2007. "Homer's Trojan Theater." *Transactions of the American Philological Association* 137:233–252.

Coffee, N. 2009. *The Commerce of War: Exchange and Social Order in Latin Epic.* Chicago.

Coffey, M. 1957. "The Function of the Homeric Simile." *American Journal of Philology* 78:113–132.

Colakis, M. 1986. "The Laughter of the Suitors in *Odyssey* 20." *Classical World* 79:137–141.

Cook, E. 2003. "Agamemnon's Test of the Army in *Iliad* Book 2 and the Function of Homeric *Akhos.*" *American Journal of Philology* 124:165–198.

———. 2009a. "On the 'Importance' of *Iliad* Book 8." *Classical Philology* 104:133–161.

———. 2009b. Review of Kelly 2007. *Classical Review* 59:14–16.

Crissy, K. 1997. "Herakles, Odysseus, and the Bow: *Odyssey* 21.11–41." *Classical Journal* 93:41–53.

Crotty, K. 1994. *The Poetics of Supplication: Homer's Iliad and Odyssey.* Ithaca, NY.

Cunliffe, R. 1963. *A Lexicon of the Homeric Dialect.* Norman, OK.

D'Agostino, B. 1987. "Achille et Troïlos: images, textes et assonances." In Detienne, Loraux, Mossé, and Vidal-Naquet 1987:145–154.

Danek, G. 1988. *Studien zur Dolonie.* Vienna.

———. 1998. *Epos und Zitat: Studien zu den Quellen der Odyssee.* Wiener Studien 22. Vienna.

———. 2002. "Traditional Referentiality and Homeric Intertextuality." In Montanari and Ascheri 2002:3–19.

Davidson, O. M. 1979. "Dolon and Rhesus in the *Iliad.*" *Quaderni Urbinati di Cultura Classica* 30:61–66.

Davies, M., ed. 1988. *Epicorum Graecorum Fragmenta.* Göttingen.

———. 1989. *The Epic Cycle.* Bristol.

———. 2005. "Dolon and Rhesus." *Prometheus* 31:29–34.

Davison, J. A. 1958. "Notes on the Panathenaea." *Journal of Hellenic Studies* 78:23–42.

De Jong, I. J. F. 1991. *Narrative in Drama: The Art of the Euripidean Messenger-Speech.* Leiden.

Descœudres, J.-P., ed. 1990. *Eumousia: Ceramic and Iconographic Studies in Honour of Alexander Cambitoglou.* Sydney.

Detienne, M., and J.-P. Vernant. 1974/1978. *Les ruses d'intelligence: la métis des Grecs.* Paris. Trans. as *Cunning Intelligence in Greek Culture and Society* (trans. by J. Lloyd, 1978). Chicago.

Detienne, M., N. Loraux, C. Mossé, and P. Vidal-Naquet, eds. 1987. *Poikilia: Études offertes à Jean-Pierre Vernant.* Paris.

Devereux, G. 1976. *Dreams in Greek Tragedy: An Ethno-Psycho-Analytical Study.* Berkeley.

Dickinson, O. 1986. "Homer, Poet of the Dark Age." *Greece and Rome* 33:20–37.

Diggle, J., ed. 1994. *Euripidis Fabulae III.* Oxford.

Dihle, A. 1970. *Homer-Probleme.* Opladen.

Dik, H. and F. Létoublon, eds. 1998. *Hommage à Milman Parry: Actes du Colloque Milman Parry.* Amsterdam.

Diller, H. 1948. "Προθέλυμνος." *Philologus* 97:361–363.

Duckworth, G. 1967. "The Significance of Nisus and Euryalus for *Aeneid* IX–XII." *American Journal of Philology* 88:129–150.

Dué, C. 2001a. "Achilles' Golden Amphora in Aeschines' *Against Timarchus* and the Afterlife of Oral Tradition." *Classical Philology* 96:33–47.

———. 2001b. "*Sunt Aliquid Manes*: Homer, Plato, and Alexandrian Allusion in Propertius 4.7." *Classical Journal* 96:401–413.

———. 2002. *Homeric Variations on a Lament by Briseis.* Lanham, MD.

———. 2005. "Homer's Post-Classical Legacy." In Foley 2005a:397–414.

———. 2006a. *The Captive Woman's Lament in Greek Tragedy.* Austin.

———. 2006b. "The Invention of Ossian." *Classics@* 3. http://chs. harvard.edu/publications.

———. 2009a, ed. *Recapturing a Homeric Legacy: Images and Insights from the Venetus A Manuscript of the Iliad.* Cambridge, MA.

———. 2009b. "*Epea Pteroenta*: How We Came to Have Our *Iliad*." In Dué 2009a:19–30.

———. Forthcoming (2010). "Agamemnon's Densely-packed Sorrow in *Iliad* 10: A Hypertextual Reading of a Homeric Simile." In *Homeric Hypertextuality*, ed. C. Tsagalis. Special issue, *Trends in Classics* 2.2.

Dué, C., and M. Ebbott. 2009. "Digital Criticism: Editorial Standards for the Homer Multitext." *Digital Humanities Quarterly* 3.1. http:// www.digitalhumanities.org/dhq/vol/003/1/000029.html.

Ebbott, M. 1999. "The Wrath of Helen: Self-Blame and Nemesis in the *Iliad*." In Carlisle and Levaniouk 1999:3–20.

———. 2003. *Imagining Illegitimacy in Classical Greek Literature.* Lanham, MD.

Edgeworth, R. 1985. "Ajax and Teucer in the *Iliad.*" *Rivista di filologia e di instruzione classica* 113:27–31.

Edgeworth, R., and C. Mayrhofer. 1987. "The Two Ajaxes and the Two Kṛṣṇas." *Rheinisches Museum* 103:186–188.

Edmunds, L. 1997. "Myth in Homer." In Powell and Morris 1997:415–441.

Edwards, A. T. 1981. *Odysseus Against Achilles: The Role of Allusion in the Homeric Epic.* PhD diss., Cornell University.

———. 1984. "P. Mich. 6972: An Eccentric Papyrus Text of *Iliad* K 421–34, 445–60." *Zeitschrift für Papyrologie und Epigraphik* 56:11–15.

———. 1985. *Achilles in the Odyssey.* Königstein.

Edwards, M. W. 1966. "Some Features of Homeric Craftsmanship." *Transactions of the American Philological Association* 97:115–179.

———. 1980. "Convention and Individuality in *Iliad* 1." *Harvard Studies in Classical Philology* 84:1–28.

———, ed. 1991. *The Iliad: A Commentary.* Vol. 5, *Books 17–20.* Cambridge.

———. 1997. "Homeric Style and 'Oral Poetics.'" In Powell and Morris 1997:261–283.

———. 2005. "Homer's *Iliad.*" In Foley 2005a:302–314.

Evans, S. 2003. Review of Dué 2002. *Bryn Mawr Classical Review* 2003.01.36. http://ccat.sas.upenn.edu/bmcr/2003/2003-01-36.html.

Fantuzzi, M. 2005. "Euripides (?), *Rhesus* 56–58 and Homer, *Iliad* 8.498–501: Other Possible Clues to Zenodotus' Reliability." *Classical Philology* 100:268–273.

———. 2006a. Review of F. Jouan, *Euripide: Tragédies, tome VIII, 2e partie: Rhésos.* Paris: Les Belles Lettres, 2004. *Bryn Mawr Classical Review* 2006.02.18. http://bmcr.brynmawr.edu/2006/2006-02-18.html.

———. 2006b. "The Myths of Dolon and Rhesus from Homer to the 'Homeric/Cyclic' Tragedy Rhesos." In Montanari and Rengakos 2006:135–176.

Farron, S. 2003. "Attitudes to Military Archery in the *Iliad.*" In Basson and Dominik 2003:169–184.

Fenik, B. 1964. *Iliad X and the Rhesus: The Myth.* Collection Latomus 73. Brussels.

———. 1968. *Typical Battle Scenes in the Iliad: Studies in the Narrative Techniques of Homeric Battle Description.* Wiesbaden.

Fick, A. 1883. *Die homerishe Odysse in der ursprünglichen Sprachform wiederhergestellt.* Göttingen.

———. 1886. *Die homerische Ilias.* Göttingen.

Finkelberg, M. 1987. "Homer's View of the Epic Narrative: Some Formulaic Evidence." *Classical Philology* 82:135–138.

————. 2003. "Neoanalysis and Oral Tradition in Homeric Studies." *Oral Tradition* 18:68–69.

Finnegan, R. 1977. *Oral Poetry: Its Nature, Significance and Social Context.* Cambridge.

————. 1988. *Literacy and Orality: Studies in the Technology of Communication.* Oxford.

Fletcher, K. F. B. 2006. "Vergil's Italian Diomedes." *American Journal of Philology* 127:219–259.

Foley, J. 1991. *Immanent Art: From Structure to Meaning in Traditional Oral Epic.* Bloomington, IN.

————. 1995. *The Singer of Tales in Performance.* Bloomington, IN.

————. 1997. "Oral Tradition and its Implications." In Powell and Morris 1997:146–173.

————. 1998. "Individual Poet and Epic Singer: The Legendary Singer." *Arethusa* 31:149–178.

————. 1999. *Homer's Traditional Art.* University Park, PA.

————. 2002. *How to Read an Oral Poem.* Urbana and Chicago, IL.

————, ed. 2005a. *A Companion to Ancient Epic.* Oxford.

————. 2005b. "Analogues: Modern Oral Epics." In Foley 2005a:196–212.

Fournet. J.-L. 1997. "Du nouveau dans la bibliotèque de Dioscure d'Aphrodité." *Akten des 21 Internationalen Papyrologenkongresses, Berlin 1995.* Archiv für Papyrusforschung Beiheft 3:297–304.

————. 1999. *Hellénisme dans l'Égypte du VIe siècle. La bibliothèque et l'oeuvre de Dioscore d'Aphrodité.* Cairo.

Fowler, D. 2000. "Epic in the Middle of the Wood: *Mise en Abyme* in the Nisus and Euryalus Episode." In Sharrock and Morales 2000:89–113.

Fowler, R., ed. 2004. *The Cambridge Companion to Homer.* Cambridge.

Frame, D. 1978/2005. *The Myth of the Return in Early Greek Epic.* New Haven. Online ed. 2005: Center for Hellenic Studies. http://chs.harvard.edu/publications.

————. 2005a. Acknowledgements and introduction to *The Myth of Return in Early Greek Epic.* Center for Hellenic Studies. http://chs.harvard.edu/publications.

————. 2005b. "The Return of Odysseus." Chap. 3 in *The Myth of Return in Early Greek Epic.* Center for Hellenic Studies. http://chs.harvard.edu/publications.

————. 2009. *Hippota Nestor.* Hellenic Studies 37. Washington, DC.

Fraenkel, E. 1965. Review of W. Ritchie, *The Authenticity of the Rhesus of Euripides (Cambridge 1964). Gnomon* 37:228–241.

Fränkel, F. 1921. *Die homerischen Gleichnisse.* Göttingen.

Frazer, J., ed. 1921. *The Library of Apollodorus.* Cambridge, MA.

Friedrich, R. 2002. "Oral Composition-by-theme and Homeric Narrative. The Exposition of the Epic Action in Avdo Medjedovic's *Wedding of Meho* and Homer's *Iliad*." In Montanari and Ascheri 2002:41–71.

Friis Johansen, K. 1967. *The Iliad in Early Greek Art.* Copenhagen.

Gantz, T. 1993. *Early Greek Myth.* Baltimore.

Gaunt, D. 1971. "The Change of Plan in the Doloneia." *Greece and Rome* 18:191–198.

George, D. 1994. "Euripides' *Heracles* 140–235: Staging and the Stage Iconography of Heracles' Bow." *Greek, Roman and Byzantine Studies* 35:145–157.

Germain, G. 1954. *Homère et la Mystique des Nombres.* Paris.

Gernet, L. 1936. "Dolon le loup." *Mélanges Franz Cumont. Annuaire de l'Institut de Philologie et d'Histoire Orientales et Slaves* 4:189–208.

Gladstone, W. 1858. *Studies in Homer and the Homeric Age.* Oxford.

Goatley, A. 1997. *The Language of Metaphors.* London.

Gould, J. 2001. *Myth, Ritual, Memory, and Exchange.* Oxford.

Gow, A. S. W., and A. F. Scholfield, eds. 1953. *Nicander: The Poems and Poetical Fragments.* Cambridge.

Goward, B. 1999. *Telling Tragedy: Narrative Technique in Aeschylus, Sophocles, and Euripides.* London.

Graf, F. 2002. "Myth in Ovid." In Hardie 2002:108–121.

Grafton, A., G. Most, and J. Zetzel, eds. 1795/1985. F. A. Wolf, *Prolegomena to Homer.* Princeton.

Grandsen, K. W. 1984. *Virgil's Iliad: An Essay on Epic Narrative.* Cambridge.

Graziosi, B. 2002. *Inventing Homer: The Early Reception of Epic.* Cambridge.

Graziosi, B. and J. Haubold. 2005. *Homer: The Resonance of Epic.* London.

Greene, T. M. 1999. "The Natural Tears of Epic." In Beissinger, Tylus, and Wofford 1999:189–202.

Greg, W. W. 1955. *The Shakespeare First Folio: Its Bibliographical and Textual History.* London.

Grethlein, J. 2007. "The Poetics of the Bath in the *Iliad*." *Harvard Studies in Classical Philology* 103:25–49.

Grube, G. M. A. 1961. *The Drama of Euripides.* Revised ed. London.

Haft, A. 1984. "Odysseus, Idomeneus and Meriones: The Cretan Lies of *Odyssey* 13–19." *Classical Journal* 79:289–306.

———. 1990. "The City-Sacker Odysseus in *Iliad* 2 and 10." *Transactions and Proceedings of the American Philological Association* 120:37–56.

Hainsworth, J. B. 1962. "The Homeric Formula and the Problem of its Transmission." *Bulletin of the Institute of Classical Studies* 9:57–68.

———. 1964. "Structure and Content in Epic Formulae: The Question of the Unique Expression." *Classical Quarterly* 14:155–164.

———. 1968. *The Flexibility of the Homeric Formula.* Oxford.

———. 1970. "The Criticism of an Oral Homer." *Journal of Hellenic Studies* 90:90–98.

———, ed. 1993. *The Iliad: A Commentary. Vol. 3, Books 9–12.* Cambridge.

Halliwell, S. 1991. "The Uses of Laughter in Greek Culture." *Classical Quarterly* 41:279–296.

———. 2008. *Greek Laughter: A Study of Cultural Psychology from Homer to Early Christianity.* Cambridge.

Hardie, P., ed. 1994. *Virgil: Aeneid Book IX.* Cambridge.

———, ed. 2002. *The Cambridge Companion to Ovid.* Cambridge.

Heiden, B. 2009. Review of L. Ferreri, *La questione omerica dal cinquecento al settecento.* Rome: Edizioni di storia e letteratura, 2007. *Bryn Mawr Classical Review* 2009.02.17. http://ccat.sas.upenn.edu/bmcr/2009/2009-02-17.html.

Henry, R. 1905. "The Place of the Doloneia in Epic Poetry." *Classical Review* 19:192–197.

Hermann, G. 1832. *De interpolationibus Homeri.* Leipzig.

———. 1840. *De iteratis Homeri.* Leipzig.

Heubeck, A., S. West, and J. Hainsworth, eds. 1988. *A Commentary on Homer's Odyssey. Vol. 1, Introduction and Books I–VIII.* Oxford.

Hexter, R., and D. Selden, eds. 1992. *Innovations of Antiquity.* New York.

Higbie, C. 1995. *Heroes' Names, Homeric Identities.* New York.

———. 1997. "The Bones of a Hero, The Ashes of a Politician: Athens, Salamis, and the Usable Past." *Classical Antiquity* 16:279–308.

Hoekstra, A. 1965. *Homeric Modifications of Formulaic Prototypes.* Amsterdam.

Holland, G. 1993. "The Name of Achilles: A Revised Etymology." *Glotta* 71:17–27.

Holmberg, I. 1997. "The Sign of ΜΗΤΙΣ." *Arethusa* 30:1–33.

Holoka, J. 1983. "Looking Darkly (ΥΠΟΔΡΑ ΙΔΩΝ): Reflections on Status and Decorum in Homer." *Transactions and Proceedings of the American Philological Association* 113:1–16.

Horrocks, G. 1987. "The Ionian Epic Tradition: Was there an Aeolic Phase in its Development?" In Killen, Melena, and Olivier 1987:269–294.

———. 1997. "Homer's Dialect." In Powell and Morris 1997:193–217.

Howald, E. 1924. "Meleager und Achill." *Rheinisches Museum* 73:402–425.

Janko, R. 1982. *Homer, Hesiod, and the Hymns: Diachronic Development in Epic Diction.* Cambridge.

———. 1986. "Hesychius Q 216 and Empedocles Fragment 21.6." *Classical Philology* 81:308–309.

———, ed. 1992. *The Iliad: A Commentary. Vol. 4, Books 13–16.* Cambridge.

Johnston, S. I. 2002. "Myth, Festival, and Poet: The Homeric Hymn to Hermes in Its Performative Context." *Classical Philology* 97:109–132.

Kahane, A. 1997. "Quantifying Epic." In Powell and Morris 1997:326–342.

Kelly, A. 2007. *A Referential Commentary and Lexicon to Homer, Iliad VIII.* Oxford.

Killen, J., J. Melena, and J.-P. Olivier, eds. 1987. *Studies in Mycenaean and Classical Greek Presented to John Chadwick.* Salamanca.

Kirk, G. 1960. "Objective Dating Criteria in Homer." *Museum Helveticum* 17:189–205.

———. 1962. *The Songs of Homer.* Cambridge.

———. 1976. *Homer and the Oral Tradition.* Cambridge.

———, General ed. 1985–1993. *The Iliad: A Commentary I–VI.* Cambridge.

———, ed. 1985. *The Iliad: A Commentary. Vol. 1, Books 1–4.* Cambridge.

———, ed. 1990. *The Iliad: A Commentary. Vol. 2, Books 5–8.* Cambridge.

Kitto, H. D. F. 1977. "The *Rhesus* and Related Matters." *Yale Classical Studies* 25:317–350.

Klingner, F. 1940. "Über die Dolonie." *Hermes* 75:337–368.

Knox, P. 1995. *Ovid, Heroides: Select Epistles.* Cambridge.

Kopff, E. C. 1981. "Virgil and the Cyclic Epics." *Aufstieg und Niedergang der Romischen Welt* II.31.2, ed. W. Haase, 919–947.

Kossatz-Deissmann, A. 1981. "Achilleus." *Lexicon Iconographicum Mythologiae Classicae* I, ed. H. C. Ackermann and J.-R. Gisler, 37–200.

Kouklanakis, A. 1999. "Thersites, Odysseus, and the Social Order." In Carlisle and Levaniouk 1999:35–53.

Kullmann, W. 1960. *Die Quellen der Ilias.* Hermes Einzelschriften 14. Wiesbaden.

Lachmann, K. 1847. *Betrachtungen über Homers Ilias.* Berlin.

Lang, M. 1995. "War Story into Wrath Story." In Carter and Morris 1995:149–162.

Lateiner, D. 1995. *Sardonic Smile: Nonverbal Behavior in Homeric Epic.* Ann Arbor.

Lattimore, R. 1958. *Rhesus* (trans. with introduction). *Euripides IV: Four Tragedies*, ed. D. Grene and R. Lattimore, 1–49. Chicago.

Leaf, W., ed. 1886. *The Iliad.* 2nd ed. 1900–1902. London.

———. 1892. *A Companion to the Iliad for English Readers.* London.

———. 1915. "Rhesos of Thrace." *Journal of Hellenic Studies* 35:1–11.

Lennox, P. 1977. "Virgil's Night-Episode Re-examined (*Aeneid* IX, 176–449)." *Hermes* 105:331–342.

Létoublon, F. "Le jour et la nuit: Formulaire épique et problèmes de narratologie homérique." In Dik and Létoublon 1998: 137–146.

Levine, D. 1982. "Homeric Laughter and the Unsmiling Suitors." *Classical Journal* 78:97–104.

———. 1984. "Odysseus' Smiles: *Odyssey* 20.301, 22.371, 23.111." *Transactions and Proceedings of the American Philological Association* 114:1–9.

Lissarrague, F. 1980. "Iconographie de Dolon le Loup." *Revue Archéologique*, no. 1:3–30.

———. 1990. *L'autre guerrier.* Paris.

Littauer, M. A., and J. H. Crouwel. 1983. "Chariots in Late Bronze Age Greece." *Antiquity* 57:187–192.

Lonsdale, S. 1990. *Creatures of Speech: Lion, Herding, and Hunting Similes in the Iliad.* Stuttgart.

Loranger, C. 1999. "'This Book Spills Off the Page in All Directions': What is the Text of *Naked Lunch?*" *Postmodern Culture* 10.1. http://www3.iath.virginia.edu/pmc/text-only/issue.999/10.1loranger.txt.

Lord, A. B. 1948. "Homer, Parry, and Huso." *American Journal of Archaeology* 52:34–44.

———. 1951. "Composition by Theme in Homer and Southslavic Epos." *Transactions and Proceedings of the American Philological Association* 82:71–80.

———. 1960/2000. *The Singer of Tales.* Cambridge, MA. 2nd ed. 2000 by S. Mitchell and G. Nagy. Cambridge, MA.

———. 1991. *Epic Singers and Oral Tradition.* Ithaca, NY and London.

———. 1995. *The Singer Resumes the Tale.* Ithaca, NY.

Lorimer, H. 1950. *Homer and the Monuments.* London.

Lowenstam, S. 1992. "The Uses of Vase-Depictions in Homeric Studies." *Transactions of the American Philological Association* 122:165–198.

———. 1993. "The Pictures on Juno's Temple in the *Aeneid*." *Classical World* 87:37–49.

———. 1997. "Talking Vases: The Relationship between the Homeric Poems and Archaic Representations of Epic Myth." *Transactions of the American Philological Association* 127:21–76.

———. 2008. *As Witnessed by Images: The Trojan War Tradition in Greek and Etruscan Art.* Baltimore.

Luce, J. V. 1998. *Celebrating Homer's Landscapes.* New Haven.

Lynn-George, M. 1988. *Epos: Word, Narrative and the Iliad.* London.

Maass, E., ed. 1887. *Scholia Graeca in Homeri Iliadem Townleyana.* 2 vols. Oxford.

Machacek, G. 1994. "The Occasional Contextual Appropriateness of Formulaic Diction in the Homeric Poems." *American Journal of Philology* 115:321–335.

Maclean, J., and E. Aitken. 2001. *Flavius Philostratus, Heroikos.* Atlanta.

Maehler, H., W. Müller, and G. Poethke. 1976. "Ilias-Handschriften aus der Berliner Papyrus-Sammlung." *Archiv für Papyrusforschung und verwandte Gebiete* 24/25:13–26.

Magrath, W. 1982. "Progression of the Lion Simile in the *Odyssey*." *Classical Journal* 77:205–212.

Marks, J. 2003. "Alternative Odysseys: The Case of Thoas and Odysseus." *Transactions and Proceedings of the American Philological Association* 133:209–226.

Maronitis, D. N. 2004. *Homeric Megathemes: War - Homilia - Homecoming.* Trans. D. Connolly. Lanham, MD.

Marshall, K., ed. 1993. Rediscovering the Muses: Women's Musical Traditions. Boston.

Martin, R. P. 1989. *The Language of Heroes: Speech and Performance in the Iliad.* Ithaca, NY.

———. 1993. "Telemachus and the Last Hero Song." *Colby Quarterly* 29:222–240.

———. 1997. "Similes and Performance." In Bakker and Kahane 1997:138–166.

———. 2000. "Wrapping Homer Up: Cohesion, Discourse, and Deviation in the *Iliad*." In Sharrock and Morales 2000:43–65.

Martini, E. 1902. *Parthenii Nicaeni quae supersunt.* Leipzig.

McLeod, W. 1988. "The Bow at Night: An Inappropriate Weapon?" *Phoenix* 42:121–125.

Mellink, M., ed. 1986. *Troy and the Trojan War: A Symposium Held at Bryn Mawr College, October 1984.* Bryn Mawr.

Messer, W. S. 1918. *The Dream in Homer and Greek Tragedy.* New York.

Mette, H. J. 1952. *Parateresis: Untersuchungen zur Sprachtheorie des Krates von Pergamon.* Halle.

Minchin, E. 2001. *Homer and the Resources of Memory.* Oxford.

Montanari, F. 1998. "Zenodotus, Aristarchus, and the Ekdosis of Homer." In Most 1998:1–21.

Montanari, F., and P. Ascheri, eds. 2002. *Omero tremila anni dopo.* Rome.

Montanari, F., and A. Rengakos, eds. 2006. *La Poésie Épique Greque: Métamorphoses d'un Genre Littéraire.* Geneva.

Morris, I. 1986. "The Use and Abuse of Homer." *Classical Antiquity* 5:81–138.

Morris, S. 1992. *Daidalos and the Origins of Greek Art*. Princeton.

Most, G., ed. 1998. *Editing Texts/Texte edieren*. Göttingen.

Moulton, C. 1977. *Similes in the Homeric Poems*. Göttingen.

Muellner, L. 1976. *The Meaning of Homeric EYXOMAI through Its Formulas*. Innsbruck.

————. 1990. "The Simile of the Cranes and Pygmies: A Study of Homeric Metaphor." *Harvard Studies in Classical Philology* 93:59–101.

Murnaghan, S. 1999. "The Poetics of Loss in Greek Epic." In Beissinger, Tylus, and Wofford 1999:203–220.

Murray, G. 1907. *Rise of the Greek Epic*. Oxford.

Mynors, R. A. B., ed. 1969. *P. Vergili Maronis Opera*. Oxford.

Nagler, M. 1967. "Towards a Generative View of the Oral Formula." *Transactions and Proceedings of the American Philological Association* 98:269–311.

————. 1974. *Spontaneity and Tradition: A Study in the Oral Art of Homer*. Berkeley.

Nagy, G. 1974. *Comparative Studies in Greek and Indic Meter*. Cambridge, MA.

————. 1979/1999. *Best of the Achaeans: Concepts of the Hero in Archaic Greek Poetry*. 2nd ed. Baltimore.

————. 1990a. *Pindar's Homer: The Lyric Possession of an Epic Past*. Baltimore.

————. 1990b. *Greek Mythology and Poetics*. Ithaca, NY.

————. 1992. "Mythological Exemplum in Homer." In Hexter and Selden 1992: 311–331.

————. 1996a. *Poetry as Performance: Homer and Beyond*. Cambridge.

————. 1996b. *Homeric Questions*. Austin.

————. 1997. "Ellipsis in Homer." In Bakker and Kahane 1997: 167–189.

————. 1999. "Epic as Genre." In Beissinger, Tylus, and Wofford 1999:21–32.

————. 2000. Review of M. L. West, ed., *Homeri Ilias. Recensuit / testimonia congessit. Volumen prius, rhapsodias I-XII continens*. Stuttgart and Leipzig: Bibliotheca Teubneriana, 1998. *Bryn Mawr Classical Review* 2000.09.12. http://ccat.sas.upenn.edu/bmcr/2000/2000-09-12.html.

————. 2002. *Plato's Rhapsody and Homer's Music: The Poetics of the Panathenaic Festival in Classical Athens*. Cambridge, MA.

————. 2003. *Homeric Responses*. Austin.

————. 2004. *Homer's Text and Language*. Champaign, IL.

————. 2009. *Homer the Classic*. Hellenic Studies 36. Washington, DC.

Naiden, F. 1999. "Homer's Leopard Simile." In Carlisle and Levaniouk 1999:177–203.

————. 2006. *Ancient Supplication*. Oxford.

Neils, J., ed. 1992a. *Goddess and Polis: The Panathenaic Festival in Ancient Athens.* Hanover, NH and Princeton.

———. 1992b. "The Panathenaia: An Introduction." In Neils 1992a:13–27.

Newton, R. 1998. "Cloak and Shield in *Odyssey* 14." *Classical Journal* 93:143–156.

———. 2005. "The Ciconians, Revisited." In Rabel 2005:135–146.

———. 2008. "Assembly and Hospitality in the *Cyclôpeia.*" *College Literature* 35:1–44.

———. 2009. "Geras and Guest Gifts in Homer." In K. Myrsiades, ed., *Reading Homer: Film and Text.* Madison, NJ.

Nickel, R. 2002. "Euphorbus and the Death of Achilles." *Phoenix* 56:215–233.

Notopoulos, J. A. 1957. "Homeric Similes in the Light of Oral Poetry." *Classical Journal* 52:323–328.

Orzulik, K. 1883. *Über das Verhältnis der Doloneia zu den übrigen Teilen der Ilias und der Odyssee.* Progr. Teschen.

Otto, W. 1929/1956. *Die Götter Griechenlands.* Bonn. 4th ed. Frankfurt.

Pache, C. 2000. "War Games: Odysseus at Troy." *Harvard Studies in Classical Philology* 100:15–23.

Paduano, G. 1973. "Funzioni Drammatiche nella Struttura del *Reso.*" *Maia* 25:3–29.

Page, D. 1959. *History and the Homeric Iliad.* Berkeley.

Palmer, L. 1962. "The Language of Homer." In Wace and Stubbings 1962:75–178.

———. 1963. *The Interpretation of Mycenaean Greek Texts.* Oxford.

Papaioannou, S. 2000. "Vergilian Diomedes Revisited: The Re-evaluation of the *Iliad.*" *Mnemosyne* 53:193–217.

Parry, A., ed. 1971. *The Making of Homeric Verse: The Collected Papers of Milman Parry.* Oxford. (= MHV)

Parry, M. 1928. *L'épithète traditionelle dans Homère: essai sur un problème de style homérique.* Paris. Trans. as "The Traditional Epithet in Homer" in A. Parry 1971:1–190.

———. 1930. "Studies in the Epic Technique of Oral Versemaking. I. Homer and Homeric Style." *Harvard Studies in Classical Philology* 41:73–147. Reprinted in A. Parry 1971:266–324.

———. 1932. "Studies in the Epic Technique of Oral Versemaking. II. The Homeric Language as the Language of Oral Poetry." *Harvard Studies in Classical Philology* 43:1–50. Reprinted in A. Parry 1971:325–64.

———. 1936. "On Typical Scenes in Homer." Review of Arend 1933. *Classical Philology* 31:357–60. Reprinted in A. Parry 1971:404–407.

Pavlock, B. 1985. "Epic and Tragedy in Vergil's Nisus and Euryalus Episode." *Transactions of the American Philological Association* 115:207–224.

Petegorsky, D. 1982. *Context and Evocation: Studies in Early Greek and Sanskrit Poetry.* PhD diss., University of California, Berkeley.

Poe, J. P. 2004. "Unconventional Procedures in *Rhesus.*" *Philologus* 148:21–33.

Poethke, G. 1985. "*Ilias* K 372–443 (P. Berol. 10570)." *Yale Classical Studies* 28:1–4.

Pollard, J. 1977. *Birds in Greek Myth and Life.* London.

Porter, W. H. 1929. *The Rhesus of Euripides.* 2nd ed. Cambridge.

Powell, B. 1977. *Composition by Theme in the Odyssey.* Beiträge zur klassischen Philologie 81. Meisenheim am Glan.

Powell, B., and I. Morris, eds. 1997. *A New Companion to Homer.* Leiden.

Pucci, P. 1987. *Odysseus Polutropos: Intertextual Readings in the Odyssey and the Iliad.* Ithaca, NY.

Putnam, M. 1998. "Dido's Murals and Virgilian Ekphrasis." *Harvard Studies in Classical Philology* 98:243–275.

Rabel, R. 1991. "The Theme of Need in *Iliad* 9–11." *Phoenix* 45:283–295.

———, ed. 2005. *Approaches to Homer: Ancient and Modern.* Swansea.

Reece, S. 1994. "The Cretan *Odyssey*: A Lie Truer than the Truth." *American Journal of Philology* 115:157–173.

Reinhardt, K. 1961. *Die Ilias und ihr Dichter.* Göttingen.

Renan, E. 1890. *L'avenir de la science: pensées de 1848.* Paris.

Rengakos, A. 1993. *Der Homertext und die hellenistischen Dichter.* Hermes Enzelschriften 64. Stuttgart.

Reynolds, L. D., and N. G. Wilson. 1991. *Scribes and Scholars: A Guide to the Transmission of Greek and Latin Literature.* Oxford.

Richardson, N. 1978. "Homer and Oral Poetry." *Classical Review* 28:1–2.

Ritchie, W. 1964. *The Authenticity of the Rhesus of Euripides.* Cambridge.

Robertson, M. 1990. "Troilos and Polyxene: Notes on a Changing Legend." In Descoeudres 1990:63–70.

Rolfe, J. C. 1893. "The Tragedy Rhesus." *Harvard Studies in Classical Philology* 4:61–98.

Russo, J. 1997. "The Formula." In Powell and Morris 1997:238–260.

Sauge, A. 2000. *L'Iliade, poème athénien de l'époque de Solon.* Berne.

———. 2007a. *Iliade: langue, récit, écriture.* Berne.

———. 2007b. "Προθέλυμνος." Collège de Saussure online research. http://icp.ge.ch/po/de-saussure/espace-pedagogique/espaces-des-disciplines/grec/recherche/prothelumnos.pdf: edition of 4/4/2007.

Scaife, R. 1995. "The *Kypria* and Its Early Reception." *Classical Antiquity* 14:164–192.

Schein, S. 1984. *The Mortal Hero: An Introduction to Homer's Iliad*. Berkeley.

Schnapp-Gourbeillon, A. 1981. *Lions, héroes, masques. Les représentations de l'animal chez Homère*. Paris.

———. 1982. "Le lion et le loup. Diomédie et Dolonie dans l'*Iliade*." *Quaderni di Storia*. 8:45–77.

Schoeck, G. 1961. *Ilias und Aithiopis*. Zurich.

Schwanz, L. 2000. "Martes martes." *Animal Diversity Web*. http://animaldiversity.ummz.umich.edu/site/accounts/information/Martes_martes.html (accessed October 02, 2009).

Scott, J. 1921. *The Unity of Homer*. Berkeley.

Scott, W. 1974. *The Oral Nature of the Homeric Simile*. Leiden.

———. 2005. "The Patterning of the Similes in Book 2 of the *Iliad*." In Rabel 2005:21–54.

Shapiro, H. A. 1992. "*Mousikoi Agones*: Music and Poetry at the Panathenaia." In Neils 1992:53–76.

Sharrock, A., and H. Morales, eds. 2000. *Intratextuality: Greek and Roman Textual Relations*. Oxford.

Sheppard, J. 1922. *The Pattern of the Iliad*. London.

Sherratt, E. 1990. "'Reading the Texts': Archaeology and the Homeric Question." *Antiquity* 64:807–824.

Shewan, A. 1911. *The Lay of Dolon: Homer Iliad X*. London.

Shipp, G. 1953/1972. *Studies in the Language of Homer*. 2nd ed. Cambridge.

Simonsuuri, K. 1979. *Homer's Original Genius: Eighteenth-Century Notions of the Early Greek Epic (1688-1798)*. Cambridge.

Singor, H. 1992. "The Achaean Wall and the Seven Gates of Thebes." *Hermes* 120:401–411.

Slatkin, L. 1991. *The Power of Thetis: Allusion and Interpretation in the Iliad*. Berkeley.

Smith, R. A. 2005. *The Primacy of Vision in Virgil's Aeneid*. Austin.

Snodgrass, A. 1998. *Homer and the Artists: Text and Picture in Early Greek Art*. Cambridge.

Spruytte, J. 1977. *Études experimentales sur l'attelage*. Paris.

Stagakis, G. 1985. "Homeric Warfare Practices." *Historia* 34:129–152.

———. 1986. "The ἵπποι of Rhesus." *Hellenika* 37:231–241.

———. 1987–88. "Athena and Dolon's Spoils." *Archaiognosia* 5:55–71.

Stanford, W., ed. 1961–1965. *The Odyssey of Homer*. Revised reprint of the 2nd ed. London.

Stanley, K. 1965. "Irony and Foreshadowing in *Aeneid*, I, 462." *American Journal of Philology* 86:267–277.

———. 1993. *The Shield of Homer: Narrative Structure in the Iliad.* Princeton.

Strauss, B. 2006. *The Trojan War: A New History.* New York.

Stubbings, F. 1962. "Arms and Armour." In Wace and Stubbings 1962:504–522.

Sultan, N. 1993. "Private Speech, Public Pain: The Power of Women's Laments in Ancient Greek Poetry and Tragedy." In Marshall 1993:92–110.

———. 1999. *Exile and the Poetics of Loss in Greek Tradition.* Lanham, MD.

Thiel, H. van. 1982. *Ilias und Iliaden.* Basel.

Thomas, R. F. 1983. "Virgil's Ecphrastic Centerpieces." *Harvard Studies in Classical Philology* 87:175–184.

Thompson, D. W. 1895. *A Glossary of Greek Birds.* Oxford.

Thornton, A. 1984. *Homer's Iliad: Its Composition and the Motif of Supplication.* Göttingen.

Todorov, T. 1981. *Introduction to Poetics.* Trans. R. Howard. Minneapolis.

———. 1990. *Genres in Discourse.* Trans. C. Porter. Cambridge.

True, M. 1997. "Rhesus." *Lexicon Iconigraphicum Mythologiae Classicae* VIII, ed. P. Müller et al., 1044–1046.

Tsagalis, C. 2004. *Epic Grief: Personal Laments in Homer's Iliad.* Berlin.

———. 2008. *The Oral Palimpsest: Exploring Intertextuality in the Homeric Epics.* Cambridge, MA.

Turner, F. 1997. "The Homeric Question." In Powell and Morris 1997:123–145.

Van Erp Taalman Kip, A. M. 2000. "The Gods of the *Iliad* and the Fate of Troy." *Mnemosyne* 58:385–402.

Vermeule, E. 1986. "'Priam's Castle Blazing': A Thousand Years of Trojan Memories." In Mellink 1986:77–92.

Villoison, J. B. G. de., ed. 1788. *Homeri Ilias ad veteris codicis Veneti fidem recensita.* Venice.

Wace, A., and F. Stubbings, eds. 1962. *A Companion to Homer.* London.

Walton, J. M. 2000. "Playing in the Dark: Masks and Euripides' *Rhesus.*" *Helios* 27:137–147.

Wathelet, P. 1989. "Rhésos ou la Quête de l'Immortalité." *Kernos* 2:213–231.

Webster, T. B. L. 1958. *From Mycenae to Homer.* London.

Wees, H. van. 1988. "Kings in Combat: Battles and Heroes in the *Iliad.*" *Classical Quarterly* n.s. 38:1–24.

West, M. L. 1969. "The Achaean Wall." *Classical Review* 19:256-260.

———.1973. "Greek Poetry 2000–700 B.C." *Classical Quarterly* 23:179–192.

———. 1988. "The Rise of the Greek Epic." *Journal of Hellenic Studies* 108:151–172.

————, ed. 1989. *Iambi et elegi Graeci ante Alexandrum cantati.* 2nd ed. Oxford.

————. 1997. "Homer's Meter." In Powell and Morris 1997:218–237.

————, ed. 1998–2000. *Homeri Ilias. Recensuit / testimonia congessit.* Stuttgart and Leipzig.

————. 2001a. *Studies in the Text and Transmission of the Iliad.* Munich.

————. 2001b. "West on Nagy and Nardelli on West." *Bryn Mawr Classical Review* 2001.09.06. http://ccat.sas.upenn.edu/bmcr/2001/2001-09-06.html.

————. 2004. "West on Rengakos (*BMCR* 2002.11.15) and Nagy (*Gnomon* 75, 2003, 481–501) on West: Response to 2002.11.15." *Bryn Mawr Classical Review* 2004.04.17. http://ccat.sas.upenn.edu/bmcr/2004/2004-04-17.html.

West, S. 1967. *The Ptolemaic Papyri of Homer.* Cologne and Opladen.

Whitman, C. 1958. *Homer and the Heroic Tradition.* Cambridge, MA.

Wilamowitz-Moellendorff, U. von. 1884. *Homerische Untersuchungen.* Berlin.

————. 1916. *Die Ilias und Homer.* Berlin.

Willcock, M. 1964. "Mythological Paradeigma in the *Iliad.*" *Classical Quarterly* 14:141–154.

————. 1977. "*Ad Hoc* Invention in the *Iliad.*" *Harvard Studies in Classical Philology* 81:41–53.

Williams, D. 1986. "Dolon." *Lexicon Iconographicum Mythologiae Classicae* III, ed. P. Müller et al., 660–664.

Williams, R. D. 1960. "The Pictures on Dido's Temple (*Aeneid* 1.450–93)." *Classical Quarterly* n.s. 10:145–151.

————. 1973. *The Aeneid of Virgil: Books 7–12.* Basingstoke and London.

Wilson, D. 2002. *Ransom, Revenge, and Heroic Identity in the Iliad.* Cambridge.

————. 2005. "Demodokos' *Iliad* and Homer's." In Rabel 2005:1–20.

Wolf, F. 1795. *Prolegomena ad Homerum: sive, De operum Homericorum prisca et genuina forma variisque mutationibus et probabili ratione emendandi.* Halle. Republished in Grafton, Most, and Zetzel 1985.

————, ed. 1804–1807. *Homērou epē: Homeri et Homeridarum opera et reliquiae.* Leipzig.

Zuntz, G. 1965. *An Inquiry into the Transmission of the Plays of Euripides.* Cambridge.

Image Credits

Index of Sources

Homeric and Related Sources

Iliad

Iliad 1: 232, 270, 283, 337
1.23: 325
1.47: 57
1.50: 263
1.60: 78n75
1.111: 325
1.161: 279
1.171: 278–279
1.174: 279
1.175: 72n67
1.192: 367
1.193–194: 366
1.211: 367
1.225–228: 35, 287, 288
1.227: 48n28, 283
1.241: 270
1.254: 270
1.313–314: 380
1.337: 268
1.377: 325
1.412: 279
1.426: 319
1.489: 268
1.503–510: 279
1.508: 72n67
1.529: 254
1.599–600: 320

Iliad 2: 3, 53n37, 231–233, 237, 243, 250, 256, 267, 299, 314, 320
2.1–5: 231–234
2.2: 314
2.3: 233, 365
2.5: 233
2.11: 339
2.19: 254
2.23–24: 232
2.24–25: 237
2.28: 340
2.42–46: 250
2.53–54: 324
2.55: 256, 315
2.101–108: 296
2.113: 78n75
2.157: 306
2.166: 217
2.197: 72n67
2.205: 72n67
2.215–220: 319–320
2.278: 335
2.288: 78n75
2.319: 72n67

2.324: 72n67
2.336: 212
2.390: 218
2.441: 217
2.563: 37
2.715: 319
2.761: 283
2.761–770: 317, 352
2.768: 290
2.768–769: 283
2.769–770: 317
2.810: 211
2.827: 60

Iliad 3
3.1–9: 247
3.8: 360
3.17: 251
3.23–26: 251
3.26: 293
3.39: 319
3.43: 377
3.95: 317
3.105–106: 327
3.124: 319
3.202: 72n67
3.204: 171
3.209–224: 320
3.222: 244

Iliad **3**, *cont.*
  3.241: 351
  3.276–280: 326
  3.313: 78n75
  3.328–338: 40, 54,
    54n38, 56n43,
    290, 328
  3.329: 324
  3.339: 54
  3.373: 214

Iliad **4**
  4.49: 72n67
  4.68: 217
  4.75: 72n67
  4.86: 351
  4.88: 59
  4.92–104: 59
  4.95: 317
  4.105: 218
  4.107: 59
  4.112–115: 59
  4.145: 214
  4.219: 214
  4.222: 367
  4.269–270: 327
  4.274: 245
  4.275–282: 245–246
  4.337: 212
  4.339: 72n67
  4.354–355: 43
  4.356: 342
  4.369: 212
  4.376–410: 308
  4.378: 261
  4.382–398: 310
  4.385–398: 70
  4.391–393: 310
  4.391–398: 244
  4.392: 242, 244
  4.392–393: 71
  4.397: 78
  4.404–410: 37
  4.411–421: 37–38

  4.429–438: 247
  4.435: 217
  4.449: 211
  4.471–472: 329
  4.473–489: 322
  4.474: 293
  4.489: 268

Iliad **5:** 138, 307
  5.1–8: 39
  5.3: 317
  5.9–12: 110
  5.12–26: 110
  5.22–24: 114
  5.24: 115
  5.81: 357
  5.115: 306
  5.119: 58
  5.121: 307
  5.242: 270
  5.263–273: 352
  5.299: 313
  5.308: 349
  5.327: 349
  5.387: 363
  5.432–442: 38
  5.504: 319
  5.539–560: 313
  5.640: 327
  5.670: 288
  5.671: 366
  5.714: 306
  5.716: 78n75
  5.719: 217
  5.725: 353
  5.733–747: 55–56
  5.749: 217
  5.751: 47n27
  5.767: 217
  5.787: 319
  5.800–808: 308, 310
  5.809: 312
  5.826: 270

Iliad **6**
  6.48–50: 337
  6.75: 214
  6.93: 362
  6.112: 367
  6.151: 247
  6.187: 71
  6.187–190: 70, 243,
    311
  6.188: 48n28, 283
  6.188–189: 71
  6.188–190: 78
  6.189–190: 331
  6.198: 72n67
  6.214: 309
  6.222–223: 308
  6.232–236: 353
  6.274: 362
  6.308: 362
  6.319: 358
  6.343: 309
  6.421–424: 76, 113,
    322
  6.430: 293
  6.484: 324
  6.506–511: 377
  6.512–514: 377–378
  6.518: 254
  6.521–523: 251

Iliad **7:** 360
  7.4–7: 265
  7.43: 217
  7.50: 296
  7.92: 317
  7.162–168: 281
  7.164: 281
  7.180: 319
  7.203: 326
  7.212: 341
  7.235–242: 59n48
  7.325: 262
  7.355: 324

7.370–371: 349
7.370–415: 318–319
7.382–383: 324
7.383: 221
7.398: 317
7.407–411: 275
7.411: 325
7.433: 274
7.478: 72n67
7.479: 336

***Iliad* 8**
8.28: 317
8.38: 342
8.59: 211
8.63: 211
8.77: 336
8.82: 324
8.88: 357
8.95: 274
8.112: 217
8.156: 293–294
8.170: 72n67
8.174: 367
8.190: 293, 324
8.191–197: 353
8.213–216: 275
8.228: 319
8.252: 367
8.253–265: 275
8.261–266: 281
8.266–272: 60
8.268: 349
8.273–277: 60
8.302–308: 322–323
8.337–342: 334
8.340–343: 275
8.381: 217
8.384–391: 55n41
8.393: 217
8.453: 311, 371
8.474: 215
8.483: 365

8.491: 275
8.499: 78n75
8.507–511: 248, 350
8.517–522: 350
8.529: 350
8.555ff.: 242
8.562–565: 248, 350

***Iliad* 9:** 6–7, 13, 103,
     142, 232, 242,
     256, 263, 290, 381
9.1–11: 231–233
9.9: 242, 270
9.11–12: 65
9.12: 304
9.14–16: 242
9.20: 78n75
9.29: 317
9.32–49: 270
9.37: 72n67
9.54: 270
9.65–73: 381
9.66–88: 350
9.74–76: 256
9.75: 233
9.80–88: 261
9.84: 262
9.88: 381
9.89–90: 324
9.89–92: 381
9.113: 310
9.157: 340
9.160: 284
9.205–220: 381
9.221–222: 381
9.224: 212
9.224a: 212
9.299: 340
9.323–327: 43
9.346: 270
9.346–355: 102–103
9.377: 72n67
9.392: 284

9.410–416: 279,
     292–293
9.421–426: 103
9.423: 249–250, 374
9.430: 317
9.433: 247
9.474–477: 65n56
9.567: 322
9.632–636: 322
9.669: 211, 324
9.672–673: 374
9.673: 270
9.693: 317
***Iliad* 10**
10.1: 314
10.1ff.: 231–235
10.1–4: 123
10.2: 234, 235, 314
10.3: 235–237
10.3–4: 99
10.5: 71
10.5–9: 237–246,
     248, 334
10.10: 208, 247
10.11–13: 63, 123,
     247–248, 350
10.11–16: 99
10.12: 248
10.17: 85, 233, 249,
     256
10.18: 249
10.19: 249–250
10.21: 250–251
10.21–24: 328, 329
10.23–24: 146, 274
10.25: 251
10.29: 251–252
10.29–31: 328, 329
10.30: 252
10.30–31: 252
10.32: 95, 253
10.35: 221
10.36: 254, 300

Iliad **10**, cont.
  10.36–72: 123
  10.37: 254
  10.37–41: 99
  10.41: 254–256
  10.43: 99, 263
  10.43–44: 256–257
  10.43–45: 70
  10.46: 208
  10.47: 257
  10.47–48: 259
  10.48: 311, 371
  10.49: 259
  10.51–52: 208,
    259–260
  10.52: 311
  10.53: 209, 260
  10.54: 209
  10.55: 95
  10.56: 249, 261, 323
  10.57–59: 261
  10.58–59: 261
  10.60: 262, 300
  10.62–63: 65
  10.65: 65, 209, 262
  10.67: 65, 263
  10.68–69: 268
  10.70: 267
  10.73: 253, 262
  10.74–79: 51, 360
  10.75: 262
  10.76: 262
  10.80–85: 128
  10.82–83: 255
  10.82–85: 332
  10.83: 190, 254–255,
    263
  10.84: 209, 263
  10.85: 65, 99, 263,
    263–264
  10.89: 267
  10.97–99: 63
  10.98: 209, 264
  10.100–101: 70, 272

  10.101: 265
  10.102: 265
  10.103: 266, 268
  10.103–107: 103
  10.104: 72n67
  10.104–107: 266
  10.109: 266
  10.110: 281
  10.110–113: 266–267
  10.116: 267
  10.117: 267, 314
  10.118: 99, 263
  10.121: 251, 267
  10.126–127: 323
  10.133: 267
  10.136: 253, 267
  10.137: 267–268
  10.139: 263, 268
  10.141: 209
  10.141–142: 268
  10.142: 99, 209, 254,
    263–264, 268–269
  10.144: 268–270
  10.145: 263, 270–271
  10.148: 271–272
  10.149: 272
  10.150–156: 51, 360
  10.151: 272
  10.152–154: 62, 252,
    273
  10.159: 211, 270, 273
  10.159a: 273–274
  10.160: 372
  10.164: 267
  10.168: 211
  10.169: 211
  10.172: 99, 263–264
  10.175–176: 267
  10.176: 95
  10.177: 251
  10.177–178: 63n54,
    146, 274, 328, 329
  10.178: 336
  10.179: 95, 253, 274

  10.180: 211, 323
  10.180–189: 63–64,
    123, 274, 334, 362
  10.183: 274
  10.185: 211
  10.189: 372
  10.191: 211
  10.194: 274
  10.194–195: 349
  10.198–199: 323
  10.199: 275
  10.202: 220
  10.203: 212
  10.205: 150n112,
    275
  10.206: 346
  10.206–210: 275–276
  10.208–210: 219, 346
  10.211–212:
    276–278, 380
  10.211–213: 103
  10.211–217: 77
  10.212: 145, 331
  10.212–213: 278–280
  10.213: 315
  10.214: 314
  10.218: 317
  10.219: 212, 280, 300
  10.219ff: 250
  10.220: 280, 287
  10.220–221: 81
  10.220–226: 71
  10.221: 212
  10.222: 280, 308
  10.222–226: 281
  10.224–226: 64,
    280–281
  10.227: 308
  10.227–231: 281
  10.228: 260, 281
  10.231: 150n112,
    282–283, 288
  10.234: 270, 283
  10.236: 283

10.237–240: 253, 283–284
10.240: 212, 284
10.241: 284, 300
10.241–247: 79
10.243: 250, 284–287
10.244: 150n112, 287
10.245: 267, 287
10.246: 287, 308
10.246–247: 331
10.247: 287–288, 381
10.248: 150n112, 288–289
10.249–250: 289–290
10.251–253: 290
10.253: 212, 284, 290
10.254: 284, 290
10.254–272: 146n103, 290–292, 328
10.254–273: 51–53
10.255–257: 53
10.257: 55, 292
10.257–259: 253
10.259: 292–294
10.260: 57, 294, 328
10.260–271: 146n103
10.261–265: 253
10.263–264: 294–295
10.273: 253, 296, 314
10.274: 296–297
10.274–275: 307
10.275: 297–299
10.276: 254
10.278: 306
10.278–279: 299
10.279: 267, 299
10.281: 214
10.282: 299
10.283: 300–306
10.284: 306
10.285: 307
10.285–286: 296

10.285–290: 308
10.288: 309–310
10.289–290: 310
10.291: 214, 311–312
10.292–294: 312
10.295: 307
10.296: 312
10.297: 146, 253, 312–313, 328
10.298: 275, 314
10.299–300: 314
10.299–301: 123
10.300: 327
10.300–301: 314–315
10.302: 243, 256, 257, 315, 348
10.304: 150n113, 315
10.305: 316
10.305–306: 316–317
10.306: 185, 214
10.307: 145, 150n112, 315, 317
10.311: 219
10.312: 264, 317
10.314–315: 110, 318–319, 340
10.314–317: 318
10.314–318: 106–116
10.315: 319, 355
10.316: 65, 319–321
10.317: 321–323, 331
10.318: 214–215
10.319: 150n112, 287, 323
10.322–323: 320
10.323: 215
10.325–327: 323–324
10.326: 314
10.329: 324–325
10.330: 325
10.331: 325
10.332: 215, 326–327
10.333: 57, 328
10.333–335: 54, 57,

328, 357
10.334: 63n54, 134n73, 328–329
10.335: 253, 330
10.336: 185, 209, 215, 253, 330
10.336–337: 78, 107, 322, 330–331
10.338: 215
10.339: 331
10.341: 185
10.341–343: 331–332
10.341–377: 109
10.343: 275
10.344–348: 64
10.344–350: 73
10.345: 75–76
10.347: 332
10.348: 76
10.349: 306, 332
10.349–350: 217
10.350: 331
10.351–352: 332–333
10.352: 263
10.352–353: 333
10.354: 76
10.354–356: 333
10.354–359: 64–65, 76
10.357: 333
10.358: 335
10.360: 334
10.360–363: 334
10.361: 334–335
10.362: 217
10.363: 335
10.363–368: 335–336
10.369: 336
10.369–375: 61
10.372: 185, 189, 218
10.372–374: 333
10.372–377: 150
10.373: 185, 189, 218
10.374: 337

Iliad **10**, cont.
10.376: 189, 218,
   336–337
10.377: 172
10.378–381: 109,
   319, 337, 355
10.380: 189–190
10.382: 272, 337, 340
10.382–383: 344
10.384: 186, 190,
   337–338
10.385: 190, 218
10.386: 185, 190,
   254, 338
10.387: 275
10.394: 338
10.396–399: 339–340
10.397–399: 185,
   190, 219
10.399: 190, 264, 340
10.400: 186, 340–346
10.401–404: 103
10.402–404: 346
10.405: 186, 190,
   337, 346
10.406: 215, 346
10.406–407: 346
10.406–411: 346–347
10.408: 66
10.409–411: 219,
   339–340
10.412: 318
10.413: 186, 190,
   219, 347
10.414–416: 376
10.415: 58n46,
   347–348, 348–349
10.416: 349
10.416–422: 349–350
10.420–422: 264
10.423: 171, 190, 350
10.424–425: 66
10.424–431: 350

10.425: 171
10.426: 171–172,
   190, 318
10.427: 172, 186,
   219, 220
10.428–431: 66
10.430: 350–351
10.431: 191
10.432–434: 172, 351
10.433: 81, 351
10.433–434: 186, 191
10.433–441: 99, 346
10.434: 66, 276, 360,
   374
10.435: 91, 95n5, 351
10.436–437: 351–352
10.438–441: 140n91,
   352–353
10.446: 305–306,
   344, 353–354
10.447: 354–355
10.448: 173
10.451: 173
10.454–456: 337, 355
10.455–456: 150
10.455–457: 147,
   356–357
10.456: 357
10.458–459: 357
10.458–468: 134
10.459: 358
10.460–464: 358
10.463: 220
10.465–466: 358
10.466–468: 65, 359
10.468: 338, 359
10.469: 275, 314, 360
10.471: 264, 360
10.471–475: 360
10.475: 368
10.477: 185
10.477–481: 101
10.478: 220, 355

10.479–481: 146
10.480–481: 66
10.482: 87, 360
10.482–484: 61
10.485: 328
10.485–486: 146
10.485–488: 134,
   361–362
10.488: 272, 362, 363
10.489: 61
10.492: 247
10.494–497: 67–69
10.495: 363
10.496: 134, 363
10.497: 67, 363, 364
10.498: 288, 364
10.498–499: 368
10.500: 61, 328
10.500–501: 364
10.502: 66, 186, 220,
   365
10.503: 186, 365
10.504–505: 366
10.507: 366
10.507–512: 87, 307
10.509: 79, 367, 381
10.513–514: 367–369
10.515: 369
10.516: 61, 307, 369
10.517: 351
10.518–522: 370
10.522: 370
10.524: 370–371
10.526–529: 359
10.527–530: 371
10.530: 371
10.530–531: 281
10.531: 220, 372
10.532: 372
10.534: 220, 372
10.535–537: 372–373
10.536–539: 78
10.539: 221, 373, 376

10.540: 373
10.540–542: 61
10.542: 78, 373–374
10.543–544: 374
10.544: 270
10.544–553: 374
10.545–546: 81
10.547: 375
10.555–557: 103
10.556–557: 374
10.558: 374
10.560: 375
10.561: 375
10.562: 173
10.564: 375–376
10.565: 376–378
10.565–566: 61
10.566–579: 378
10.570: 221
10.572–575: 378
10.576: 378–381, 382
10.577–578: 381
10.578: 381–382

Iliad 11
11.7–9: 267
11.15–55: 40, 54,
  54n38, 290, 328
11.25: 352
11.41: 55
11.46: 319
11.66: 273
11.72–73: 329
11.83: 273
11.129: 313
11.133–135: 337
11.136–137: 309
11.166: 348
11.172–178: 361–362
11.195: 217
11.221–228: 322
11.248–258: 322
11.253: 218

11.261: 356
11.292–295: 334
11.310–319: 286
11.369: 324
11.369–383: 348
11.371–372: 58
11.372: 58n46,
  75n70, 348
11.379: 58
11.430: 72n67, 270
11.450: 72n67
11.472: 308
11.483: 349
11.502: 311, 371
11.502–503: 259
11.505: 324
11.519–520: 372
11.546–557: 274, 362
11.566: 367
11.600: 221
11.629: 218
11.631: 336
11.668ff.: 237
11.669–684: 82–83,
  369
11.709–752: 281
11.819: 349
11.838: 349

Iliad 12: 275
12.41–49: 334
12.60: 214
12.73: 78n75
12.95–97: 331
12.113–117: 331
12.115: 78n75
12.176: 80n76
12.210: 214
12.278: 244
12.293: 313
12.299–308: 280, 361
12.364: 217
12.435: 315

12.460: 217
12.463: 338

Iliad 13: 74, 288–289
13.10: 369
13.101-106: 329
13.113: 215
13.164: 349
13.170–202: 313
13.198–202: 334
13.201–205: 356
13.266–294: 260
13.269–287: 45–47
13.274–291: 58
13.276: 48n28, 283
13.276–286: 337
13.277–278: 47, 294
13.333: 221
13.365: 319
13.378: 319
13.383–393: 331
13.557: 247
13.594: 218
13.650–652: 58
13.663–672: 111–112
13.666–668: 115
13.674–688: 114
13.706: 218
13.721–722: 367
13.725: 214
13.754–755: 238–239
13.769: 319

Iliad 14
14.6–7: 379
14.46: 78n75
14.78–79: 265
14.104: 270
14.113–126: 308
14.135: 369
14.159: 365
14.170: 254
14.173: 319

Iliad **14**, cont.
  14.222–223: 341
  14.261: 338
  14.277: 217
  14.466: 357
  14.470: 171
  14.478–485: 322
  14.489–492: 321
  14.493–507: 356
  14.520–522: 266

Iliad **15**
  15.1: 314
  15.4: 336
  15.60: 360
  15.78: 217
  15.168: 217
  15.262: 360
  15.263–268: 377
  15.295: 78n75
  15.305: 78n75
  15.323–326: 361–362
  15.348: 221
  15.358: 218
  15.358–360: 333
  15.380: 367
  15.477: 367
  15.487: 367
  15.559: 308
  15.579–581: 334
  15.592: 313
  15.734: 367

Iliad **16**
  16.81: 287
  16.130–154: 40, 54,
    54n38, 56n43,
    290, 328
  16.143: 214
  16.156–166: 329
  16.244: 261
  16.247: 278
  16.252: 78n75, 278
  16.270: 367

  16.281: 215
  16.320: 322
  16.323: 218
  16.352–356: 329
  16.431: 72n67
  16.458: 217
  16.469: 217
  16.474: 357
  16.589–592: 333
  16.599: 239
  16.632: 308
  16.670: 254
  16.680: 254
  16.702–711: 39
  16.756–761: 313
  16.784–793: 39
  16.862–867: 99
  16.864–867: 346

Iliad **17**
  17.67: 336
  17.75–76: 99
  17.75–78: 325
  17.76–78: 346
  17.126: 356
  17.142: 319
  17.185: 367
  17.237: 302
  17.246: 217, 302
  17.247: 302
  17.406: 78n75
  17.415: 78n75
  17.424: 211
  17.449: 325
  17.461: 211
  17.483–496: 317
  17.491: 217
  17.542: 313
  17.575–580: 113
  17.582–590: 114
  17.591: 115
  17.655–666: 362
  17.656: 217
  17.741: 211

Iliad **18**
  18.54–60: 292
  18.70: 239
  18.83: 353
  18.133: 326
  18.134: 351
  18.165: 214
  18.222: 372
  18.243–313: 276
  18.261: 215
  18.267: 215
  18.268: 254
  18.285–292: 319
  18.289: 319
  18.293: 72n67
  18.298–299: 349
  18.314–323: 240
  18.315: 239
  18.343–353: 380
  18.346: 379
  18.346–348: 380
  18.355: 239
  18.377: 353
  18.475: 352
  18.513–522: 70
  18.516: 70, 86, 358
  18.520: 73
  18.526: 71
  18.526–527: 76
  18.527: 75
  18.549: 352
  18.579–586: 313
  18.580: 217
  18.612: 352

Iliad **19**
  19.38: 254
  19.148: 367
  19.187–188: 326
  19.260: 326
  19.264: 326
  19.293–294: 322
  19.301: 239
  19.312: 239

19.313: 246
19.363: 273
19.364–424: 40, 54, 54n38, 290
19.369–391: 295, 328
19.373–379: 40
19.388: 55
19.390: 214

Iliad 20
20.27: 215
20.45: 215
20.104: 349
20.110: 360
20.187–190: 76–77n72, 84n81
20.212: 78n75
20.213–240: 348
20.260: 217, 218
20.359: 246
20.428: 354
20.481–483: 356
20.484: 253

Iliad 21
21.18: 359
21.25: 218
21.27–28: 362
21.34–39: 36, 68–69, 76, 250, 320–321
21.34–44: 337
21.37: 44
21.98: 309
21.205: 253
21.217: 311, 371
21.237: 217
21.251: 333
21.350: 359
21.355: 271
21.388: 372
21.420: 306
21.438: 319
21.439–460: 327
21.445: 315

21.450: 315
21.451: 315
21.457: 315
21.505: 319
21.561: 78n75

Iliad 22: 139, 332, 335
22.26–32: 39
22.144: 335
22.157–166: 333
22.188–193: 334, 335
22.190: 314
22.193: 215
22.205–207: 336
22.229: 254
22.239: 254
22.260: 354
22.344: 354
22.370: 319
22.439: 324
22.444–445: 379
22.455–456: 335

Iliad 23
23.35: 215
23.39–44: 379
23.94: 254
23.111: 263
23.115: 263
23.155: 214
23.175: 362
23.178: 370
23.211: 239
23.262: 326
23.290–292: 102
23.294: 268
23.431–433: 332
23.434: 267
23.529: 218
23.590: 281
23.617: 214
23.626: 211
23.638–642: 281
23.676: 317

23.700–737: 279
23.725: 72n67
23.793: 215
23.806: 314
23.821: 218
23.859–883: 58
23.895: 217
23.896: 349

Iliad 24: 78, 84, 86, 87, 125, 139, 233, 235, 242, 256, 279, 337, 359
24.24: 86
24.46–49: 322
24.120: 217
24.170: 263
24.182: 307
24.282: 235
24.287–288: 78
24.315–321: 297
24.330: 78n75
24.339: 217
24.349: 58n46, 348
24.362–363: 255–256
24.363: 254, 255
24.366: 338
24.376: 319
24.380: 337
24.483–484: 76
24.485–512: 321
24.566: 65
24.572: 313
24.589–595: 279
24.591: 370
24.653: 338
24.656: 186
24.673–689: 233–235
24.681: 65, 261
24.689: 95
24.716: 263
24.746: 239
24.779: 242

Odyssey

Odyssey 1
  1.1: 295
  1.3–5: 287–288
  1.4: 288
  1.65: 286
  1.96–101: 55n41
  1.128: 218
  1.169: 338
  1.179: 347
  1.205: 268
  1.206: 186
  1.214: 186
  1.224: 338
  1.234–243: 77–78,
    276–277
  1.240: 317
  1.296: 72

Odyssey 2
  2.93: 365
  2.287: 307
  2.368: 72

Odyssey 3
  3.2: 319
  3.39: 373
  3.101: 171
  3.122: 72n67
  3.141–142: 367
  3.222: 312
  3.305: 319
  3.325: 72
  3.376: 307
  3.382–384: 312
  3.468: 378, 379

Odyssey 4: 74, 76, 82
  4.48: 378, 379
  4.72: 273
  4.92: 72
  4.128: 378
  4.140: 220, 372

4.220–239: 80
4.240–243: 81
4.244–249: 81
4.244–258: 349
4.246: 351
4.249: 351
4.251: 81
4.252–256: 81
4.257–258: 81–82
4.265–289: 82
4.267–270: 257
4.271–272: 47, 289
4.272: 283
4.277: 47n26, 244
4.278: 48n28
4.280: 253
4.307: 302
4.312: 349
4.314: 171
4.331: 171
4.351–480: 72–74
4.372: 267
4.384–480: 97
4.388–390: 78
4.388–463: 253
4.399: 347
4.409: 283
4.423: 349
4.435–437: 73
4.437: 71
4.441–443: 75
4.445: 254
4.447: 75, 289
4.453: 71
4.454: 75
4.459: 289
4.462–463: 71
4.524–526: 315
4.530–531: 283
4.531–532: 71
4.533: 365
4.535: 76
4.536–537: 77
4.590: 218

4.642: 171
4.658: 280
4.663–672: 71
4.762: 306
4.767: 307
4.778: 71n64
4.842–847: 73

Odyssey 5
  5.26: 277
  5.29–42: 279
  5.43: 217
  5.93: 254
  5.144: 277
  5.168: 277
  5.199: 254
  5.237: 218

Odyssey 6
  6.32: 307
  6.66: 294
  6.143: 309
  6.145–147: 309
  6.148: 309
  6.193: 379
  6.306: 353
  6.324: 306
  6.328: 307

Odyssey 7
  7.24: 379
  7.45: 353
  7.216: 365
  7.303: 349

Odyssey 8
  8.59: 362
  8.123–125: 332, 333
  8.215: 218
  8.215–222: 57, 294
  8.276: 71
  8.282: 71
  8.317: 71
  8.321: 319

8.366: 353
8.390–391: 363
8.435–437: 380
8.446: 379
8.450: 378
8.450–456: 379
8.456: 378
8.494: 71
8.512: 48n28
8.512–513: 283
8.515: 47n26, 75, 244, 286
8.518: 43
8.572: 338

Odyssey 9
9.19: 72
9.79–81: 278
9.142–143: 87
9.143: 254
9.143–145: 84
9.195: 84
9.195–196: 363
9.213: 280
9.292: 313
9.315: 365
9.318: 85
9.320: 336
9.334: 85
9.359: 254
9.370: 315
9.379: 336
9.406–408: 85
9.420: 85
9.422: 85
9.424: 85
9.435: 85, 289
9.435–436: 85
9.439: 217
9.476: 85

Odyssey 10
10.163: 217
10.234: 336
10.361: 378, 379
10.413: 217
10.472–474: 367
10.516: 349

Odyssey 11: 74
11.43: 336
11.120: 72
11.140: 338
11.355–361: 279
11.366: 315
11.373: 246
11.391: 171
11.410: 76
11.427: 365
11.439: 72
11.469: 319
11.523–524: 283
11.523–532, 538–540: 47–48
11.525: 47n26, 74, 242
11.528–530: 294
11.552: 310
11.633: 336

Odyssey 12
12.243: 336
12.281: 264
12.284: 338
12.302: 214
12.395: 217

Odyssey 13
13.93–95: 375
13.108: 353
13.256–286: 70
13.259–270: 62–63, 321
13.259–272: 76
13.259–275: 260–261
13.268: 63, 70, 297, 332
13.268–270: 73
13.270: 65n56
13.287–305: 298–299
13.292–293: 72n67
13.293: 257
13.297–298: 257
13.300–301: 299
13.301: 299, 312
13.307: 289
13.309–310: 289
13.389–391: 358

Odyssey 14: 53, 70, 74, 74n69, 243, 272, 289
14.147: 254
14.177: 319
14.192: 347
14.217–218: 71, 283
14.217–219: 280
14.218: 48n28
14.219–221: 74
14.220: 75
14.243: 72n67
14.255: 278
14.268: 273
14.365–372: 78n74, 277
14.462–506: 56
14.468–503: 76, 250, 350
14.469: 315
14.470–471: 253
14.471: 70
14.473–476: 73–74
14.508: 261
14.511: 379
14.526: 56
14.528–531: 56n44

Odyssey 15
15.1–3: 367
15.28: 48n28, 71n64, 358

Odyssey 15, cont.
15.226–240: 83
15.266: 186
15.271–278: 379
15.383: 338
15.392: 246
15.425: 319

Odyssey 16
16.17–19: 321
16.47: 336
16.237: 365
16.256: 365
16.261: 365
16.298: 72n67
16.365–370: 76

Odyssey 17
17.47: 321
17.84: 379
17.87: 378
17.87–90: 379
17.90: 378
17.295: 335
17.437: 273

Odyssey 18
18.98: 217
18.253: 324
18.319: 288
18.337: 354
18.358: 315

Odyssey 19
19.2: 365
19.52: 365
19.70: 354
19.126: 324
19.202: 363
19.212: 72n67
19.395–396: 295
19.395–412: 53,
    291–292
19.415: 309, 373

19.439: 74n68, 244
19.453: 218
19.454: 217
19.509–522:
    241–242
19.516–517: 239
19.521: 244
19.549: 324
19.586: 218

Odyssey 20
20.10: 365
20.18: 366
20.28: 365
20.38: 365
20.41: 365
20.44–51: 358
20.44–53: 87
20.74: 294
20.102: 72n67
20.257–303: 114
20.287–291: 113–114
20.301: 342
20.301–302: 341

Odyssey 21
21.13–38: 83
21.13–41: 294
21.38–41: 57
21.92: 218
21.144–147: 354
21.281: 218
21.286: 218
21.326: 218
21.336: 218
21.415: 72n67

Odyssey 22: 70
22.2: 75
22.34: 354
22.42: 336, 337
22.60: 354
22.71: 218
22.98: 357

22.166: 171
22.230: 257
22.285–291: 115
22.310–329: 356
22.320: 354
22.333: 365
22.371: 342, 344
22.492: 217
22.498: 373

Odyssey 23
23.1: 377
23.48: 313
23.59: 377
23.111: 342
23.163: 378, 379

Odyssey 24: 115, 297
24.17: 319
24.70: 211
24.123: 186
24.128: 365
24.163: 289
24.235: 365
24.280: 171
24.340: 363
24.345–348: 321
24.370: 378, 379
24.393: 309
24.450: 336
24.515: 286
24.533: 336

Scholia to the *Iliad*

Venetus A manuscript
('A') scholia, keyed to
lines of the *Iliad*
    2.157: 306
    4.376: 311
    4.394: 310
    10.53: 260
    10.84: 263
    10.159: 273

10.274: 296
10.282: 299
10.306: 214, 316–317
10.394: 338–339
10.396–399: 339–340
10.435: 90–97, 364
10.447: 354–355
10.497: 67, 363, 364
10.502: 365
10.522: 370
10.530: 371
10.561: 375
10.578: 381–382
22.188: 45

Venetus B manuscript ('B') scholia, keyed to lines of the *Iliad*
10.258: 292
10.394: 338–339
10.435: 90, 91–96
10.447: 354–355

Townley manuscript ('T') scholia, keyed to lines of the *Iliad*
10.1: 5
10.10: 208
10.159: 273
10.274: 296–297
10.349: 217
10.352: 333
10.394: 338–339
10.435: 90, 91–96
10.447: 354–355
13.663: 112n34
16.196: 266
21.37: 43–44
24.257: 351

Epic Cycle

Epic Cycle: 28, 33, 34, 41, 49, 61, 72, 82, 87, 94, 112, 118, 144, 162, 285, 292
***Aithiopis*:** 137, 252, 320
***Cypria*:** 41–42, 44, 77n72, 83, 233, 256, 285–286
***Little Iliad*:** 42, 82, 96, 142n96, 279, 285–286, 358

Homeric Hymns

***Homeric Hymn to Apollo*:** 264
***Homeric Hymn to Demeter*:** 72n67, 293, 366
***Homeric Hymn to Hermes*:** 84, 86, 254, 295–296, 359

Other Sources

Aeschylus
  ***Agamemnon*:** 251
  ***Libation Bearers*:** 251
  ***Persians*:** 259
Apollodorus: 44n20, 70n62, 95n5, 98, 295, 351
Apollonius of Rhodes, ***Argonautica*:** 212
Aristotle, *History of Animals*: 330
Dares: 252
Dictys of Crete: 252
Diogenes Laertius: 273–274
Euripides
  ***Herakles*:** 61
  ***Rhesos*:** 121–135, 347

1–10: 123
16–17: 127
123–130: 127
128: 127
149–157: 124
158–159: 124
184–188: 327
189: 327
205: 124
205–215: 134n73
208–213: 134n73
208–215: 124, 328
213: 324
216: 125
219–223: 116n40
264–317: 130
284–316: 129, 130–131

319–326: 125
396–421: 125
422–443: 125–126
443–453: 126
491: 126
497–509: 126
509: 126n56
510–511: 126
512–517: 126–127
520–521: 129
521–522: 66n57
560: 127
565–571: 130n67
572–573: 66n57
573: 129
575–576: 299
577: 127
591–593: 134n73

Euripides, *Rhesos,* cont.
  594–625: 360
  644–645: 127
  687–688: 66n57
  687–689: 129
  756–803: 129,
    131–135
  906–949: 127
  938–940: 135n74
Eustathius, *Commen-*
  tarii ad Homeri
  Iliadem: 5n5, 93,
  274, 339
Hesiod
  Theogony: 72n67,
  365, 369
  Works & Days: 308
Hipponax: 104
Hyginus: 252
Nicander, *Theriaca:* 330
Ovid
  Ars Amatoria: 120,
  120n46
  Heroides: 120,
  120n46, 120n47
  Metamorphoses: 295
Parthenios, *Romances:*
  104
Pausanias: 41, 286, 295
Philostratos, *Heroikos:*
  104–105, 252
Pindar
  Nemean **10:** 83
  Olympian **10:** 70n62,
  74n68, 98, 332

Solon: 278
Sophocles, *Philoktetes:*
  285
Statius, *Thebaid:* 311
Thucydides: 65–66
Virgil, *Aeneid:* 135–151
  1.453–493: 136–142
  1.469–473: 93
  1.469–474: 137–139,
  141
  1.474: 140n88
  1.474–478: 140
  1.483–487: 136
  2.7: 138
  2.44: 138
  2.90: 138
  2.122: 138
  2.162–170: 144
  2.164: 138
  2.166: 144
  2.250–267: 144
  2.261: 138
  2.355–360: 143n99
  2.762: 138
  3.273: 138
  3.613–654: 138
  9.59–66: 143
  9.148–155: 143–144
  9.150–153: 144
  9.151: 144, 144n100
  9.186: 145
  9.189–190: 145
  9.195: 145
  9.195–196: 145
  9.236–237: 145

  9.236–245: 145
  9.237: 145
  9.242: 145
  9.252: 150n111
  9.303–307: 145
  9.306: 146
  9.307: 146n106
  9.316–323: 145
  9.321–323: 146
  9.332–333: 147
  9.339–341: 146
  9.355–356: 146
  9.359–364: 146n103
  9.365: 146, 146n106
  9.372–374: 146
  9.373: 146n106
  9.373–374: 292
  9.411–419: 147
  9.446–449: 145n101
  9.465–467: 147
  10.497–499: 140n91
  10.649–650: 150n113
  11.271–274: 297
  11.511–516, 522–531:
  147
  11.768–777: 140n91
  11.809–815: 143n99
  11.896–915: 147
  12.346–361: 148–150
  12.699ff: 239

General Index

Achilles, 6–7, 12, 13, 33, 35–36, 38–40, 43–45, 47–49, 54, 55, 59, 61, 68–71, 73, 76, 83, 86, 99, 100, 102–105, 107, 111–113, 118, 125–126, 136, 138, 140–141, 149, 156, 164, 215, 231, 233, 234, 235, 239–240, 242–243, 250, 252, 254, 256, 261, 263, 266, 268, 270, 275, 276, 278, 280, 281, 283, 287, 288, 290, 292–293, 302, 310, 311, 313, 316, 320–322, 325–327, 332–335, 340, 342, 344–346, 348, 351–354, 356, 358–359, 362, 367, 370, 371, 374, 379, 381
  death of, 252
  epithets of, 35, 215, 268, 320
  etymology of, 271
Adrastos, 308, 31
Aeneas, 38, 76, 83, 102, 110, 114, 123, 127, 136–150, 313, 348, 352, 360
Aeneid, night raids and ambush in, 142–147
Aeolic dialect, 14, 189–190, 249, 253, 295, 316
Agamemnon, 35, 37, 40, 43, 50, 54, 55, 62, 63, 65, 70–72, 76–77, 82, 85, 99, 123, 146, 221, 232, 234–237, 239, 242, 243–245, 247–248, 249–251, 253, 256, 259, 262–263, 265–268, 270, 272, 274, 278, 283, 287, 288, 290, 296, 304, 309, 310, 314, 315, 324, 326–328, 337, 339, 342, 346, 348, 350, 352, 356, 362, 365, 367, 374, 379, 381
  epithets of, 235
Aiante, 60, 209, 260, 281, 284, 313, 334
ainos, 261, 272
Aithiopis, 137, 252, 320
Ajax, son of Oileus, 260, 266, 281, 296, 356
Ajax, son of Telamon, 60, 126, 260, 267, 268, 270, 279, 281, 283, 290, 296, 302, 310, 313, 317, 341, 342, 352, 357, 381
akhos, 115, 239, 263, 270, 271
Aktorione-Molione, 70, 74, 98, 281, 332
ambush
  as traditional theme, 10, 13, 25, 32, 36, 50, 69, 70 and passim
  as warfare for the "best" men, 46, 48, 53, 70, 72, 84, 283, 373, 375
  endurance during, 32, 34–35, 45, 47, 70, 74–75, 81, 85, 143, 244, 250, 275, 282, 289, 364
  iconography of, 44, 59, 74, 117–119

ambush, *cont.*
  links to initiation, 53, 116, 262,
    292–294, 329, 358
  locations for, 32, 44, 63, 71,
    73–76, 98, 243–244, 252, 296,
    332, 348, 351, 359
  of Achilles, 252
  of Agamemnon, 71–72, 76–77,
    82, 283, 365
  of Andromache's brothers, 76,
    113
  of Bellerophon, 70–71, 77–78,
    243, 283, 331
  of Hektor, 45, 49, 299, 347
  of Helenos, 82, 97
  of Lykaon, 36, 44, 76
  of Orsilokhos: 62–63, 70, 73, 76,
    260–261, 297, 321
  of Proteus, 71–72, 74–76, 78, 82,
    85, 97, 253, 283, 289
  of Telemakhos, 71–73, 76–77,
    82, 280, 321, 358, 379
  of the Cyclops, 42, 84–85, 87,
    268, 280, 289
  of the suitors, 33, 42, 57, 61,
    69–70, 72, 73, 75, 77, 81, 87,
    268, 289, 294, 337, 342, 354,
    356, 365, 379
  of Troilos, 33, 44, 59, 118,
    140–141
  of Troy, 61, 70–71, 74–77, 82, 98,
    138, 244, 283, 289, 335, 358
  of Tydeus, 33, 70–71, 77–78, 244
  weapons and gear, 32, 50–52,
    54–62, 75, 83, 112, 147, 250,
    291, 292, 294, 328, 354, 357,
    364
analogy, 12, 13, 18, 26, 160, 301,
  303, 324, 326, 338, 349
Analyst scholarship, 3–10, 28, 117
Andromache, 76, 113, 292–293,
  322, 324, 335, 379–380
animal skins worn during
  ambush, 32, 50, 52, 54, 56,
    63, 73–74, 85, 116–118, 124,
    134, 146, 250–252, 267, 272,
    311, 328–329, 336, 337, 355,
    357–358
Antilokhos, 267, 332, 334, 342
Apollo, 3, 38, 39, 57, 84, 114, 129,
  261, 264, 295, 307, 315, 325,
  327, 333, 346, 350–351, 359,
  360, 369
archaeological evidence, 6, 294,
  358
archery, as an ambush tactic, 44,
  57–61, 118, 140, 252, 294, 328,
  364
Argos, 86, 308, 311, 335
Aristarchus, 47, 163, 185–186,
  190–191, 208–209, 211–212,
  214, 218–220, 247, 259–260,
  263, 273, 284, 299, 316, 333,
  339, 354, 363, 375, 381
Aristophanes, 160
Aristophanes of Byzantium, 67,
  208, 211, 212, 214, 217, 219,
  259, 284, 306, 316, 363
aristos, 46, 48, 52, 283, 296, 315,
  373
arming scene, 18, 40, 50, 51–62,
  69, 72, 145–146, 272, 290, 295,
  328, 336, 357, 360
Asios, 331
Athena, 39, 55, 59, 60, 67, 71, 73,
  79, 87, 92, 93, 95, 136, 138,
  140, 236, 257, 268, 270, 286,
  287, 289, 297–299, 306–307,
  310–312, 329, 335, 342, 347,
  351, 358, 360, 364, 366–368,
  381
  arming scene of, 55
  as a god associated with
    ambush, 70, 86, 295, 299, 310,
    358
  as a patron of Diomedes, 58
  as a patron of Odysseus, 358
  as instigator of Pandaros, 59

augment, 235, 257
Autolykos, 52–53, 291, 295–296, 373

baths, at the conclusion of ambush and journeys, 79, 378–382
beheading, 116, 354, 356–357
Bellerophon, 70–71, 77–78, 243, 283, 311, 331
Bentley, Richard, 5, 120
biē, 24, 34–35, 43, 49, 85, 243, 250, 286, 289
boar's tusk helmet, 53, 294, 296
boulē, 71, 85, 231, 233–234, 243, 249, 256–257, 262–263, 298–299, 314, 315
Briseis, 108–109, 112, 234, 270, 278, 322, 326
Bronze Age, 6, 33, 249, 294, 358, 366
Burroughs, William, 160

Calypso, 120, 270
cattle raid, as traditional theme, 18, 32, 50, 76, 80–84, 86, 293, 358, 362
Chrysippus, 247
Circe, 270, 379
cloak, as narrative signal, 53, 56, 261, 272
composition-in-performance, 11–12, 14, 16–18, 19, 29, 32, 69, 94–95, 108, 155–157, 160–161, 217, 236, 249, 305–306, 312, 314, 324–330, 339, 346
Cretan lies, 53, 70–76, 260, 272, 278, 280, 283, 321, 332, 347
Crete, 63, 83, 252, 260, 278, 297, 321, 363
Cyclops, 42, 76, 84–87, 254, 268, 280, 289, 365–366

Cypria, 41–42, 44, 76, 83, 136, 233, 256, 285–286

Demodokos, 43, 80, 286, 369
diachronic view of Homeric poetry, 19, 26–27, 159, 164–165
Diogenes Laertius, 273
Diomedes, epithets of, 235, 254, 270, 301, 303, 305
ditch and wall of the Achaeans, 261, 274, 275, 280, 291, 323–324, 333, 336, 348–349, 375, 378
Dolon
    epithets of, 34, 319, 320
    in vase paintings, 117-118
    lineage of, 106, 318
    links to folktale motifs, 117
    links to rituals of initiation, 116
    traditionality of, 106–119
dolos, 49, 71–73, 85, 121, 124, 127, 299, 355, 365
dual forms in *Iliad* 10, 10, 60, 71, 217, 260, 281, 284, 290, 313, 332, 334, 337, 360, 381–382

embassy to Achilles, 7, 49, 102, 266, 275, 284, 290, 324, 374, 381
ennukhios, 44
Epic Cycle, 28, 33–34, 41, 49, 61, 72, 82, 87, 91, 94, 112, 118, 144, 162, 285, 292
Epigonoi, 37, 112, 237, 308
Epipolae, Athenian attack on, 65
epithets, 17, 34–37, 42, 72, 75, 84, 85, 110, 156, 171, 190, 215, 217, 235–237, 253, 254, 262, 265, 268, 270, 271, 280, 282, 284, 288, 289, 295, 300–307, 316, 318, 319–321, 324, 335, 337, 342, 346, 353, 357, 359, 363, 364, 369, 379

epithets, *cont.*
  distinctive, 171, 236, 268, 271,
    364, 379
  fixed, 300–303
  generic, 236–237, 271, 300–303,
    335
  meaning of, 17, 236, 265, 270,
    303
  ornamental, 55, 215, 236,
    300–303
epos, 244, 309, 373
Eteokles, 308, 310
Eumaios, 56, 70, 243, 253, 254,
  272, 277, 321, 347
Eurypylos, 91, 97, 296, 349, 357
Eustathius, 5, 93, 274, 339
evolutionary model for Homeric
  poetry, 19–20, 163

facial expressions, formulas for,
  340, 344, 353, 354, 376
Fick, August, 4, 14, 249
fieldwork of Parry and Lord,
  11–12, 14–16, 18–19, 23, 26,
  99, 155–156, 304
flexibility of Homeric diction, 18,
  156, 217, 232, 249, 253, 270,
  301, 334, 340, 354, 371
fluidity. *See* multiformity
folk poetry, Homeric poems as,
  6, 11
formula, 11, 14, 15, 17, 18, 27,
  55, 73, 79, 83, 90–92, 99,
  110–111, 113, 133, 161, 162,
  171, 186, 190, 211, 212, 214,
  215, 217, 218, 233, 236–237,
  249, 253–256, 264–265, 270,
  280, 282–283, 287–289, 296,
  299, 300–306, 308, 313,
  316–318, 323, 324, 335–347,
  349, 353–354, 357, 359, 360,
  368–370, 372, 374, 379, 381
Gaia, 72, 394
genius, Homer as, 4, 10, 11, 14,

15–16, 20, 22, 25, 29, 54, 107,
  108, 161, 304
genre, 18, 19, 32, 104, 127–129,
  134, 338
gerēnios, 265–266

hapax legomena, 9, 173, 246, 274,
  325, 332, 334
Hektor, 45, 55, 58, 64, 77, 78, 86,
  99, 102–103, 105, 106, 107,
  113, 114, 115, 123–130, 135,
  136, 139, 140, 215, 219, 233,
  235, 238, 243, 248, 251, 254,
  256, 259, 261, 264, 266, 275,
  279, 281, 292, 293, 296, 299,
  301, 303, 307, 309, 311, 312,
  314–317, 319, 323–327, 331,
  332, 334, 335, 338, 339, 340,
  341, 342, 345, 346, 347, 349,
  353, 354, 356, 358, 360, 370,
  371, 376, 377, 379, 380
Helenos, 42, 82, 96, 97, 101, 285
Herakles, 61, 70, 74, 83, 98, 112,
  251, 327, 332
Hermann, Gottfried, 4–5
Hermes, as a god associated with
  ambush, 58, 84, 86, 116, 125,
  233–235, 254, 256, 295, 296,
  307, 337–338, 348, 356, 359,
  363
heroes and "heroic" behavior,
  8, 19, 24, 29, 33–36, 40–43,
  46–50, 55, 58, 61, 69, 72, 81,
  85, 100, 104, 116, 236–237,
  243, 250–251, 266, 268,
  279–280, 285–286, 291, 293,
  304, 315, 325, 326–327, 333,
  341, 355, 356, 360, 366–371,
  375, 378
heron, as a bird associated with
  ambush, 296–297
Hesiod, 161, 308, 365, 369
Hipponax, 104
Homer Multitext, 91, 153–165

Homeric poems
  authorship of, 4, 6, 10, 12, 15,
    18, 20–27, 28, 49, 86, 89–91,
    95, 101–102, 105, 120–121,
    122, 127, 139, 142, 154, 155,
    160, 161, 173, 275, 282, 325
  literary criticism of, 6, 8, 10,
    18, 21–22, 238
Homeric Question, 4, 165
horse-rustling, as a traditional
    theme, 352, 369, 373
horses, 7, 53, 61, 66, 82–83,
    90–93, 97, 99–105, 110, 116,
    120, 126, 130–135, 137, 139,
    141, 149–150, 239, 248, 254,
    256, 272, 275, 280, 282, 297,
    316, 320, 325, 327, 328, 331,
    332, 344–348, 350–352, 357,
    359, 366, 367–369, 371, 372,
    374–375, 377
  as "best" (*aristos*), 317, 320, 352
  of Achilles, 99, 103, 149, 150,
    316–317, 325–327, 344–346,
    352, 374
  of Aeneas, 102, 352
  of Ajax, 317, 352
  of Iphitos, 83
  of Laomedon, 327
  of Rhesos, 7, 66, 82, 90–93, 97,
    99, 100–102, 104, 116, 120,
    126, 130, 133–135, 137, 139,
    280, 331, 347, 351, 366–367,
    372, 374–375

Idomeneus, 45–46, 70, 260–262,
    283, 288, 296, 321, 327, 331, 336
immanent art, 17, 236
invented characters, alleged, 90,
    107–109, 115, 149
  Briseis, 108
  Dolon, 107–109
  Euphorbos, 108
  Patroklos, 108
  Rhesos, 90

Ionic dialect, 14, 189–190, 249,
    253, 295, 316

journey, as traditional theme
    connected to ambush, 50, 66,
    76–79, 81, 256, 264, 276–278,
    288–289, 307, 337, 348, 373,
    378–382

Kalypso, 342
kernel theory, 4–9
kleos, 24, 37, 54, 77, 103, 145,
    277–280, 293, 312, 317, 322,
    352

Lachmann, Karl, 5
Laertes, 379
lament, 85, 115, 127, 149, 232,
    239–240, 242, 244, 292,
    322–323, 370
"late-arriving ally," theme of, 92,
    96–97, 104, 125
lays, 5, 19
Leaf, Walter, 3, 6–8, 13, 50, 90,
    134, 237, 266, 290, 368
Linear B, 248
lions, 251, 362
  in similes, 143, 217, 240, 251,
    280, 312, 313, 334, 361–362
literacy, 12, 15–16, 25, 108, 239,
    246
Little Iliad, 42, 82, 96, 142, 279,
    285, 358
lokhos, 28, 32, 34–36, 41, 43,
    46–49, 69, 84, 96, 127, 242,
    244, 272, 285, 289, 305 and
    passim
Lord, Albert, 9–29, 32, 36,
    54–55, 69, 80, 82, 94, 97,
    108, 155–156, 161–163, 233,
    236, 246, 255, 270, 303–304,
    314, 318, 326, 328, 330, 341,
    343–346, 381

Lykaon, 36, 44, 68–69, 76, 84, 116, 337

Maion, 70, 310–311
marten, significance of for ambush, 330
Memnon, 91, 97, 136
Menelaos, 36, 47, 50, 54, 59, 65, 70–72, 74–76, 78, 82, 95, 97, 99, 113–114, 123, 235, 251–252, 254, 257, 260, 263, 267–268, 270, 272, 283, 289, 296, 300–303, 305, 315, 326–328, 332, 337, 342, 347, 367, 378–379
Meriones, 45–46, 48, 52–53, 57–58, 146, 260, 261, 291, 293, 296
mermera erga, 77, 126, 259, 310–311, 371
messenger
    as narrator in the *Rhesos*, 129–130
mētis, 24, 34–35, 42, 49, 61, 64, 67, 72, 85–86, 102–104, 243, 250, 252, 256–257, 266–267, 271–272, 281, 286–287, 296–299, 364, 374
misthos, 150, 278, 315, 317
multiformity, 12–13, 17, 19, 32, 54, 93, 106, 113, 139, 153–165, 171–173, 186, 190, 208, 214, 217, 233, 273, 306, 316, 334, 347, 350, 351, 354
multitextual approach, 153–165, 273
muthos, 107, 309, 373

Nausikaa, 294, 307, 309
need, theme of, 40, 99, 104, 263, 268, 274, 366
Neoptolemos, 42, 47, 48, 96, 97, 101, 150, 278, 285, 293
Nestor, 50, 62–65, 77, 82, 98, 103,

114, 120, 128, 219, 235, 237, 249, 256, 262–263, 265–268, 270, 272, 274, 276–277, 280–281, 296, 307, 310, 312, 315, 317, 323, 324, 331, 339, 340, 346, 353, 357, 360, 367, 369, 372–375, 379–381
night
    as the time for ambush, 10, 32, 34, 35, 36, 55, 76
    formulas for, 83–84, 87, 185, 209, 254–256, 263–264, 268, 296, 338
    sensory and spatial aspects of, 62–69, 128, 247–248, 263, 274
night raids, 10, 13, 18, 32, 34, 36, 49, 54, 55, 58, 82, 84, 86, 127, 250, 272, 274, 281, 291, 352
night watch. *See* watch fires
nightmare of the charioteer in the *Rhesos*, 131–134, 363
Niobe, 242
Nisus and Euryalus, 136, 141–147, 292
noos, 79, 81, 267, 281, 287–288, 299, 364
nostoi ("returns"), 12, 60–61, 83
nostos, 77, 79, 81, 103, 267, 278, 280–281, 283, 287–288, 297, 367, 375, 381

"Odyssean" language in *Iliad* 10, 9–10, 24, 50, 79, 86, 102–103, 215, 265, 278–279, 288, 321, 373
Odysseus
    epithets of, 75, 85, 171, 235, 268, 270–271, 282, 288–289, 295, 335, 337, 363–364, 379
    smiles of, 113–114, 340–345
oral poetry, 4, 6, 8, 11–29, 31–32, 35, 49, 54, 80, 89, 91, 94–95, 99, 102, 106–109, 112, 118, 144, 153–156, 159, 161,

164–165, 172, 215, 219–220,
236, 246, 249, 255, 272,
276, 287, 295, 305–306, 308,
312, 314, 316, 318, 324–326,
328, 330–331, 334, 339, 341,
343–344, 346, 355, 381
planning in, 12, 94, 330, 331
Ouranos, 72, 294
Ovid, 119–120, 160

Palamedes, 41, 42, 286
Palladion, 33–34, 42, 44, 61, 82,
97, 126, 140, 142, 144–145,
279, 285
Pandaros, 58–61, 327
Panhellenic poetry, Homeric
epics as, 105–106, 112, 163
papyri, 153, 158–159, 161, 162,
163, 165, 169–191, 208, 209,
212, 218, 305, 328, 340, 354
Paris, 40, 54–55, 58–59, 61, 75,
111, 114, 127, 166, 251, 252,
254, 261, 265, 290, 309, 324,
326–328, 348, 351, 372, 376,
377
Parry, Adam, 4
Parry, Milman, 4, 9–29, 32,
155–156, 161–162, 215,
235–236, 249, 255–256, 271,
282, 300–306, 316, 318, 320,
324, 335, 342–343, 345
Parthenios, 104
Patroklos, 39, 40, 54–55, 99, 102,
108, 113, 114, 139, 239–240,
254, 261–262, 268, 278–279,
290, 302, 313, 317, 321,
325–326, 332, 346, 356, 362,
370, 380, 381
Peisistratos, 5–6, 163
Penelope, 120, 236, 239, 242–243,
294, 306, 324, 365, 377
Penthesilea, 91, 97, 104, 136
Philoktetes, 57, 96, 101, 285
plus verses, 172, 217, 351

poikilos, 252, 272
polemos, 34–41, 45–47, 54, 57–61,
70, 77–78, 87, 96, 98, 103, 117,
126, 243, 265, 285, 290–291,
305, 360, 362, 367
Polyneikes, 308, 310, 311
Polyphemos. *See* Cyclops.
Polyxena, 33, 41, 42, 44, 224, 252,
285
Poseidon, 315, 327, 336, 369
Priam, 6, 36, 42, 58, 65, 68, 76, 78,
84, 86, 125, 136, 150, 233–235,
242, 256, 285, 297, 301, 307,
319, 321, 323, 327, 337–338,
348–350, 356, 359
principle of economy, 14, 236,
254–256, 270, 342–345
Proklos, 42, 44, 76, 82, 83, 96, 279,
285, 320, 358
Proteus, 71–76, 78, 82, 85, 97, 253,
283, 289, 347
pseudo-archaisms, 7, 9, 295
pukinos, 48, 52, 71–74, 133,
234–235, 237–245, 252, 256,
280, 296, 310, 315, 334, 361

quantitative approach. *See* statistical analysis of Homeric
poetry.

resonance, 17, 18, 54, 109, 232,
244, 246, 251, 287, 366, 370,
371
return, importance of for spying
missions, ambush, and journeys, 70, 77–78, 125, 147, 235,
264, 276–277, 287, 291, 299,
311, 331, 367
rhapsodes, 4, 9, 284
Rhesos
armor and chariot of, 104, 116,
352–353, 366, 367–369, 371
as "late-arriving ally," 97, 25,
361

Rhesos, *cont.*
  invincibility of, 90, 96, 100, 126,
    139, 351, 352, 371
  lineage of, 95–96, 351
  traditionality of, 90–106
Rutulians, 146

sack of Troy, 33, 41–42, 47, 61,
    70–71, 74–75, 77, 138, 141,
    244, 268, 285, 289
Schliemann, Heinrich, 6
scholia, 5, 7, 19, 43, 45, 47, 57,
    67–68, 90–98, 100, 106, 107,
    125, 154, 158, 185, 186, 190,
    191, 208–212, 214–215, 217,
    219, 220, 245–247, 259, 260,
    263, 266, 273, 284, 290,
    292, 294, 296, 305, 310–311,
    314–317, 327, 333, 338–339,
    351, 354, 363–365, 370–371,
    375, 381
Seven Against Thebes, 37, 308,
    310
Shakespeare, 159–164
Shewan, Alexander, 3, 4, 7, 8–11,
    23, 104, 324, 352, 368, 369, 381
Shield of Achilles, 70, 76, 358
similes, 57, 60, 63, 85, 134, 143,
    146–147, 217, 232, 237,
    238–246, 248, 251, 265, 273,
    274, 280, 313, 321, 334, 361,
    362, 377
  as conveyors of a heightened
    emotional state, 232
  birds in, 43, 239, 241
  compression of, 236, 238, 246,
    313, 361
  dogs in, 63, 274, 280, 313,
    334–335
  lions in, 63, 134, 143, 240, 251,
    280, 313, 334, 361–362
  wolves in, 63, 143, 147, 329
Skamander river, 90, 92–93, 101,
    217, 350

sleeplessness, 63, 99, 232,
    233–235, 241–242, 244, 247,
    251, 262, 270, 314
smiling, in Homeric poetry,
    113–114, 340–345
song culture, 12, 122, 345
South Slavic epic tradition,
    11–19, 55, 155
spoils, 65, 134, 146, 251, 292, 358,
    359
spying missions
  as a traditional theme, 32–33,
    54, 62, 77, 79–83, 96, 99, 114,
    124–125, 145, 173, 235, 262,
    275–278, 280, 288, 332, 338,
    373, 382
statistical analysis of Homeric
    poetry, 161–162, 165
Sthenelos, 37, 270, 308, 352
supplication, 87, 136, 140, 150,
    355–356

tamarisk, as a tree associated
    with ambush, 359
Telemakhos, 70–73, 76–77, 80,
    82, 83, 114, 120, 257, 268,
    276–277, 280, 289, 307, 312,
    321, 342, 349, 355, 357, 358,
    367, 372–373, 379
Teucer, 60, 260, 281, 313
textual criticism of Homeric
    poetry, 153–165, 314
thaleros, 292-3
Thebaid, 305, 308, 311
Thebes, 37, 112, 237, 261, 308,
    310
theme, 10–13, 18, 25–26, 28,
    32–33, 34, 37, 49–50, 54–56,
    69–70, 77–87, 99, 101, 114,
    121, 136, 233, 265, 293, 314,
    322–323, 328, 334, 346–347,
    360, 362, 365, 369, 373
therapōn, 261
Thersites, 319–320

Thymbrē, 350
Townley manuscript, 5, 43,
    90–92, 95, 112, 208, 266, 294,
    296, 306, 314, 315, 333, 338,
    351, 354, 372, 373
traditional audience, 27, 32, 68,
    99–101, 214, 236, 244, 246,
    253, 272, 310, 317–318, 320,
    325, 327, 340, 343, 370
traditional referentiality, 27, 236,
    244, 251
Troilos, 33, 44, 59, 84, 118, 136,
    138–141, 225, 351, 356
Trojan War, 6, 12, 33, 94, 96, 98,
    124, 135–136, 143–144, 147,
    305, 308, 351, 370
Turnus, 127, 141, 143–150
Tydeus, 33, 37–39, 51, 67, 70–71,
    77–78, 137, 148, 244, 270, 296,
    308–312, 374

Unitarian scholarship, 3, 4, 6, 7,
    10, 24

variations. *See* multiformity.
vase paintings, ambush depicted
    in, 44, 59, 74, 106, 117–119,
    356
Venetus A, 5, 45, 67, 90–93,
    95–96, 153, 154, 166, 171–173,
    185–186, 193–221, 259–260,
    268, 284, 290, 296, 299, 306,
    311, 316, 317, 327, 332, 334,
    338–339, 347, 351, 354, 364,
    370–372
    scholia, 208–221
Venetus B, 5, 90–92, 95, 166, 220,
    292, 315, 338, 351, 354, 372

wall of the Achaeans. *See* ditch
    and wall of the Achaeans.
watch fires, 62–63, 248, 314, 350
Wilamowitz-Moellendorff, Ulrich
    von, 4

Wolf, Friedrich August, 4–5
wolves
    in similes, 143, 147, 329
    in the nightmare of the chari-
        oteer, 133–134
    symbolism of in initiation
        rituals, 116, 328–329, 358
wooden horse, 33, 47, 61, 70–71,
    74–77, 82, 98, 139, 141, 144,
    244, 257, 283, 289, 335, 358

Zenodotus, 67, 208, 212, 214, 220,
    247, 284, 290, 316, 363, 370
Zeus, 42, 51, 55, 62, 72, 78, 86, 116,
    231, 232, 233, 237, 245, 248,
    254, 256, 267–268, 278, 286,
    294, 297, 299, 311, 324–326,
    339, 348, 354, 360, 365

ἀγλαΐεῖσθαι, 325
ἀναστεναχίζω, 239
ἄριστος. See *aristos*
ἀρτύνω, 315
ἀσαμίνθος, 378–379, 382
ἀσκηθής 'unscathed,' 276-278
ἄχος. See *akhos*

βῆ δ' ἴμεν, 253
βοὴν ἀγαθὸς, 38, 79, 217, 254,
    262, 280, 284, 306
βουλή. See *boulē*

Γερήνιος ἱππότα Νέστωρ. *See*
    gerēnios

δόλος. See *dolos*
δόσις. See *misthos*

ἕπομαι, 86, 280, 307, 311
ἔχω, 132, 232, 251

ἠθεῖε, 254

θαῦμα ἰδέσθαι, 353

καμάτω ἀδηκότες, 264
κλέος. See kleos
κραδίη καὶ θυμὸς ἀγήνωρ, 79,
  280, 287, 323

μειλίχιος, 309, 373
μέρμερα ἔργα. See mermera erga
μῆτις. See mētis
μοῦνος, 106, 321

νύκτα δι' ἀμβροσίην, 254–255,
  268, 338
νύκτα δι' ὀρφναίην, 84, 133,
  254–256

ποδάρκης, 302, 320
ποδώκης, 34, 319–320
ποιμένα λαῶν, 235, 262, 271, 304,
  346

πολύμητις, 243, 268, 271–272,
  337, 340, 363
πολυμήχανος, 268
πολύτλας, 75, 171, 282, 288, 364,
  379
πολύχρυσος, 319
πόνος, 267
πυκινὸν λόχον, 47, 242, 244, 310
πυκινὸν ἄχος, 239
πυκινός. See pukinos

στενάχω, 239

τιμή, 279
τλήμων, 75, 282, 288, 364

φοβοῦμαι, 247

χρεώ. See need, theme of

CPSIA information can be obtained
at www.ICGtesting.com
Printed in the USA
FSHW012059260120
66327FS

9 780674 035591